E. M. Forster: A Life

P. N. FURBANK

E. M. Forster
A Life

Harcourt Brace Jovanovich

New York and London

Printed in the United States of America

Requests for permission to make copies of any part of this work
should be mailed to: Permissions, Harcourt Brace Jovanovich, Inc.,
757 Third Avenue, New York, N.Y. 10017.

Library of Congress Cataloging in Publication Data

Furbank, Philip Nicholas.
E. M. Forster: a life.

Includes index.
1. Forster, Edward Morgan, 1879–1970—Biography.
2. Authors, English—20th century—Biography.
PR6011.O58Z655   1978   823'.9'12   78–54671
ISBN 0–15–128759–7

First American edition 1978

BCDE

For E. M. F.

Contents

Note on Unpublished Sources   xv

Acknowledgements   xvii

Family Trees   xxii

VOLUME ONE

1   A Birth and a Death   1

2   Childhood   14

3   School   33

4   Cambridge   49

5   Italy   81

6   A Choice of Landscapes   97

7   Elizabeth's German Garden   124

8   *Where Angels Fear to Tread*   135

9   Pessimism in Literature and Optimism in Life   147

Contents

10   'An Advance to a Narrower Outlook'   160

11   The Year of *Howards End*   188

12   'A Sense of Unused Strength'   198

13   Adrift in India   220

14   *Maurice*   255

VOLUME TWO

1   Facing Facts   1

2   Alexandria   21

3   Sins of Empire   52

4   The Maharaja's Secretary   68

5   *A Passage to India*   105

6   A Section House in Hammersmith   131

7   'Saving Civilization'   170

8   Trees   197

9   The Last Parade   205

10   A Visit to Ferney   230

11   The Reluctant Lion   259

12 Writing Again   277

13 E. M. Forster Described   291

14 Last Years   309

    Notes   327

    Appendix: *The Maharaja of Dewas*   337

    Index   341

List of Illustrations

VOLUME ONE

BETWEEN PAGES 166 AND 167

Marianne Thornton

Louisa Whichelo

Maimie Aylward

Laura Forster

E. M. Forster with his mother

E. M. Forster, aged 10 or 11

E. M. Forster, aged 12 or 13

The Whichelo sisters

'Rooksnest', Stevenage

Tonbridge School

E. M. Forster as an undergraduate

King's College in the 1890s

H. O. Meredith

R. B. Smith

R. C. Trevelyan

List of Illustrations

Malcolm Darling

E. M. Forster in Italian cloak

'Harnham', Monument Green, Weybridge

E. M. Forster with Steinweg

E. M. Forster and Masood

Masood and friends

E. M. Forster and Forrest Reid

Edward Carpenter

H.H. Sir Tukoji Rao III, Maharaja of Dewas State, Senior

E. M. Forster, aged 36

Map of E. M. Forster's Indian itinerary, 1912–13   page 221

VOLUME TWO

BETWEEN PAGES 192 AND 193

Florence Barger

E. M. Forster on the beach at Alexandria, circa *1916*

Constantine Cavafy

Mohammed el Adl

Siegfried Sassoon

Goldsworthy Lowes Dickinson

E. M. Forster, in Mahratta turban

The Royal Palace at Chhatarpur

*Card-players in the Palace courtyard at Dewas.
   From left: 3 The Maharaja, 5 E. M. Forster*

E. M. Forster, by Jessica Dismorr, 19 February 1926

Edward Hilton Young, later Lord Kennet, with son, 1929

J. R. Ackerley, in his flat at 6 Hammersmith Terrace

W. J. H. ('Sebastian') Sprott

At Garsington, 1926. From the left: unidentified, Mark Gertler, E. M. Forster, Julian Morrell

Gerald Heard

Tom Wichelo and L. E. O. Charlton

Harry Daley and 'prisoner'

R. J. Buckingham

R. J. Buckingham in Section House

Boat-race Day party at 6 Hammersmith Terrace. Front row: 2 Anwar Masood (?), 3 Tom Wichelo, 4 Mrs Ackerley, 5 L. E. O. Charlton, 6 Akbar Masood, 8 J. R. Ackerley, 9 E. M. Forster

May Buckingham, early 1930s

Garden at West Hackhurst

Lily Forster in her '80s

BETWEEN PAGES 256 AND 257

E. M. Forster and Christopher Isherwood, at Ostende, June 1937 (?)

E. M. Forster and R. J. Buckingham, 1930s

Ronald Kidd

John Simpson ('John Hampson')

At Dover, circa *1937*
   R. J. Buckingham, E. M. Forster and J. R. Ackerley
   J. R. Ackerley and William Plomer
   E. M. Forster and J. R. Ackerley

E. M. Forster at International Congress of Writers, Paris, 1935

At the Abinger Pageant, 1938: Lady Allen, E. M. Forster, R. Vaughan Williams, bandmaster

List of Illustrations

E. M. Forster, late 1930s (?)

E. K. ('Francis') Bennett

Unveiling plaque to Forrest Reid at 13 Ormington Crescent, Belfast, 10 October 1952. From left: H. O. Meredith, Lennox Robinson, Eric Ashby, Lord Mayor, E. M. Forster, S. Knox Cunningham

E. M. Forster, Benjamin Britten and William Burrell, in Burrell's boat

E. M. Forster and Eric Crozier, at Crag House, Aldeburgh, 1949

W. J. H. Sprott and J. R. Ackerley, 1950s

May Buckingham, E. M. Forster, J. R. Ackerley and Robin Buckingham, at 129 Wendell Road, Shepherd's Bush, early 1950s

E. M. Forster and Charles Mauron, at St Rémy, 1950s

E. M. Forster and William Roerick, late 1960s

E. M. Forster in his rooms at King's, 1950s

Drawing-room at West Hackhurst, date unknown

Note on Unpublished Sources

Of the unpublished material drawn on in this biography, the greater part is in the possession of King's College, Cambridge (who own the copyright of all Forster's writings). Sources which have been used and which are not in the college's possession are listed below.

Letters from E. M. Forster (The present owner, when not the recipient, is indicated, where known, in brackets.)

To:

J. R. ACKERLEY (University of TEXAS); EDWARD ARNOLD (Edward Arnold Ltd); FLORENCE BARGER (Mrs Mollie Barger); THE B.B.C.; BENJAMIN BRITTEN; R. J. BUCKINGHAM and Mrs MAY BUCKINGHAM (Mrs May Buckingham); ROBIN BUCKINGHAM (Mrs Sylvia Buckingham); PETER BURRA (Mrs Nell Moody); PAUL CADMUS; CLIVE CAREY (Hugh Carey); ERIC CROZIER; LADY FAITH and SIR MICHAEL CULME-SEYMOUR; HARRY DALEY (David Daley); SIR MALCOLM DARLING (Mrs April van Biervliet); NORMAN DOUGLAS (Yale University); ERIC FLETCHER; JARED FRENCH; P. N. FURBANK; KENNETH HARRISON; THE INTERNATIONAL P.E.N. (University of Texas); CHRISTOPHER ISHERWOOD; LORD KENNET (Cambridge University Library); JAMES KIRKUP; JOHN LEHMANN; SYED ROSS MASOOD (Mrs Sultana Masood); CHARLES MAURON (Mme Alice Mauron); JOHN MEAD (Mrs Shelagh Mead); JOHN MORRIS; LADY OTTOLINE MORRELL (University of Texas); Mrs FRANCES PARTRIDGE; WILLIAM PLOMER (Durham University); SIR ALEC RANDALL; FORREST REID (Stephen Gilbert); FRANK SARGESON; SIEGFRIED SASSOON (George Sassoon); PROFESSOR NORMAN SCARFE and PAUL FINCHAM; SIDGWICK & JACKSON (Bodleian Library, Oxford); STEPHEN SPENDER (University of California, Berkeley); LYTTON

STRACHEY (Strachey Trust); WILLIAM TAYLOR; E. V. THOMSON; PROFESSOR GEORGE THOMSON; R. C. TREVELYAN (Trinity College, Cambridge); THEODOR UPPMAN; HUGH WALPOLE (University of Texas); SYDNEY WATERLOW (John Waterlow); LEONARD and VIRGINIA WOOLF (University of Sussex and New York Public Library); PROFESSOR ANDREW WRIGHT.

Also letters written by E. M. Forster as President of the National Council for Civil Liberties (University of Hull).

Memories of E. M. Forster by Lady Faith Culme-Seymour.

Talking About Morgan: taped conversations of Robert and May Buckingham with Eric Crozier, recorded by Eric Crozier in 1971 (Mrs May Buckingham).

Taped Interview of E. M. Forster with Quentin Bell, on the subject of Virginia Woolf (Quentin Bell).

Whichelo Family Scrapbook (Philip Whichelo).

Brief manuscript notes by William Plomer (P. N. Furbank).

Acknowledgements

VOLUME ONE

This book was made possible by the kindness of the Provost and Fellows of King's College, Cambridge, in putting the Forster papers in King's at my disposal. My warmest thanks are due to them for this and also for electing me in 1970 to a temporary fellowship.

I should also like to thank the Leverhulme Trustees for their generosity in giving me a Research Award in 1968.

Among the many people who have helped me with this first volume of my biography, and to whom I would like to acknowledge my indebtedness and gratitude, are the following: Mr H. S. Airey, Syed Ali Akbar, Mrs Barbara Buchanan, Mrs Mollie Barger, Professor Quentin and Mrs Olivier Bell, Mr Andrew Best, April Darling, Mr John Blackwell, Mrs Amélie Boyd, Mr John Boyd, Professor Richard Braithwaite, Mr Bentley Bridgewater, Mrs Mary Brownlow, Mrs May Buckingham, Mrs Corwin Butterworth, Mr Hugh Carey, Mr Glen Cavaliero, Mr R. Hedley Charlton, Mr David Chipp, Professor M. L. Clarke, Mrs R. Cooper, Major Sardar Deolekr, Canon Victor De Waal, Mr W. J. Evans (Warden of the Working Men's College), Ms Pamela Eyres (at the National Gallery), Mr Anthony Forster, Mr Roger Fulford, Mr Arthur Gardner, Mr David Garnett, Mr Stephen Gilbert, Mr A. W. Gillett, Mr Jan B. Gillett, Mr Duncan Grant, The Reference Librarian at Guildford Central Library, Miss S. J. Hardy (of Kent County Library), Sir Rupert Hart-Davis, the officials of the Hertfordshire County Library, Mr Robin Hodgkin, Mr G. P. Hoole, the officials of the India Office Library, Mr David

Acknowledgements

Isitt, Chief Justice Saeed Jung, Lord Kennet, Mrs M. Keppel-Compton, Sir Geoffrey and Lady Keynes, Mrs Avril Lansdell (Curator of the Weybridge Museum), Mr Paul Levy, Miss Eveline Luxford, Dr J. F. A. Mason, Mrs Sultana Masood, Miss Rosamund Matthews, Mr G. E. Mawson (of the Central Library, Weybridge), Mr Ralph Meredith, Mr Sajjad Mirza, Mr A. M. Morley, Mrs Mary Moorman, Sir Joseph Napier, the New York Public Library and Mrs Lola Szladits (Curator of the Berg Collection), Mr Nigel Nicolson, Mr Meyrick Owen, Sir Dennis Proctor, Mrs Frances Partridge, Mrs Philpot, Miss Marjorie Rackstraw, Mrs Mabel Roach, Mrs Lilian Roome, Mr Peter Scott, Mrs M. Ursula Sharp, Professor H. K. Sherwani, Sidgwick & Jackson Ltd, Professor Amrik Singh, Mr K. Natwar-Singh, Mrs M. S. Smith, Mrs R. B. Smith, Mr Michael J. Taylor (Deputy Librarian of Goldsmith's College), Mr W. S. Taylor, Sir Charles Tennyson, the Humanities Research Center at the University of Texas, Mr E. V. Thompson, Mr Julian Trevelyan, Dr Thomas Trevelyan, Miss M. Warren, Mr John Waterlow, Mrs J. E. Wedmore, Mrs J. L. West (of Hilden Oaks School, Tonbridge), Mr and Mrs Patrick Wilkinson, Professor Andrew Wright, Miss May Wyld.

I should like to express particular thanks to the following, who read this volume in draft and made suggestions and criticisms: Andrew Best, Piers Brandon, Gour Das, David Farrer, Mary Flannery, David Hutter, Mary Lago, Graham Martin, Derwent May, John Sibbald, Oliver Stallybrass. I am also indebted to Mrs Penelope Bulloch, the archivist at King's, for her assistance, and to Elizabeth Ellem and Hilary Purves, who undertook research for me. And I feel a special obligation to Forster's cousin Philip Whichelo for his constant help and support.

I am grateful to the following for their help in finding and for permission to reproduce illustrations: Eric E. F. Smith, Philip Whichelo, King's College Library, Mrs R. B. Smith, Julian Trevelyan and April Darling.

Finally, my thanks are due to Harcourt Brace Jovanovich, Inc. for permission to reprint the passages from letters on pp. 240–44, first published in *The Hill of Devi*, copyright 1953 by E. M. Forster.

VOLUME TWO

Among the many who have helped me with this second volume of my biography, and to whom I give my warmest thanks, are the following: Dr Donald Adamson, Mr Ahmed Ali, Mr Hashim Ali, Syed Ali Akbar, Mr Walter Allen, Lord Amulree, Mr Mulk Raj Anand, Miss Felicity Ashbee, Miss Constance Babington-Smith, Mrs Mollie Barger, Michael Barrie, Professor and Mrs Quentin Bell, Mr Neville Braybrooke, Mr Gerald Brenan, Mrs Barbara Buchanan, Mrs Sylvia Buckingham, Mrs Penelope Bulloch, Mrs R. H. Bulmer, Mr William Burrell, Mr Paul Cadmus, Mr Herbert Cahoon, Mr Sandy Campbell, Mr Hugh Carey, His Ex-Highness Shahaji Chhatrapati, Mr David Chipp, Mrs Daphne Clay, Mr Thomas Coley, Mr Eric Crozier, Lady Faith Culme-Seymour, Mr David Daley, April Darling, Dr G. K. Das, Mr Ronald Ewart, Dame Frances Farrer, Mr Howard Ferguson, Mr Paul Fincham, Mr Brian Finney, Mr Eric Fletcher, Mrs Aida Foster, Mr Jared French, Mr Phillip Fry, Lady Furness, Dame Helen Gardner, Mr David Garnett, Mr Edwin Gilcher, Mr Jan B. Gillett, Mr Robert Goodyear, Mr Duncan Grant, Mrs James Hanley, Mr Kenneth Harrison, Mrs Elizabeth Hart, Sir Rupert Hart-Davis, Professor Francis Haskell, Mr Carlos van Hasselt, Mr Francis Hennessy, Mr Michael Holroyd, Miss Imogen Holst, Professor Samuel Hynes, the officials of the India Office Library, Mr Christopher Isherwood, Chief Justic Saeed Jung, Mrs Yvonne Kapp, Mr Francis King, Mr James Kirkup, Mr Eardley Knollys, Mr Paul Levy, Professor James McConkey, Professor F. P. W. McDowell, Mr Peter Mansfield, Mr George Martin, Scheherazade Masood, Mrs Lucy Masterman, Mme Alice Mauron, Mr Sajjad Mirza, Professor Donald Mitchell, Mrs Helen P. Moody, Mr Raisley Moorsom, Mr John Morris, Mr Raymond Mortimer, Ms Elizabeth Neame, Mr Nigel Nicolson, Mr David Norton, Mr David Painting, Sir Edward Playfair, Mrs Frances Partridge, Mr J. Peters, Mr J. B. Priestley, Sir Alec Randall, Mr Oliffe Richmond, Sir Alec Robertson, Ms Lucy Robertson, Mr William Roerick, Mr David Rose, Mr Norman Routledge, Mr Robert Rowe, Mr G. H. W. Rylands, Mr Frank Sargeson, Professor George Savidis, Mrs Sylvia Scaffardi, Professor Norman Scarfe,

Acknowledgements

Professor V. A. Shahane, Mr Desmond Shawe-Taylor, Professor H. K. Sherwani, Mr Richard Shone, Messrs Sidgwick & Jackson, Mr Dennis Silk, Mr K. Natwar-Singh, Mr George Spater, Mr Stephen Spender, Miss Velda Sprott, Mr Oliver Stallybrass, Mrs Taqui Stephens, Mr Sewell Stokes, Dr Brian Taylor, the Hon. Stephen Tennant, the Humanities Research Center at the University of Texas, Professor George Thomson, Lady Thornton, Mr Julian Trevelyan, Mrs Diana Trilling, Mr Theodor Uppman, Mr P. Beaumont Wadsworth, Mr Gordon Waterfield, Mrs Nancy West, Mr George Weys, Mr Philip Whichelo, Mr and Mrs Patrick Wilkinson, Professor Angus Wilson, Mr Donald Windham, Mr William Winterbotham, Mr A. Wood-Corfield, Professor Andrew Wright.

I should like to express particular thanks to the following, who read this volume in draft and made suggestions and criticisms: Andrew Best, Piers Brendon, David Farrer, Mary Flannery, Graham Martin, Derwent May; also to Mr F. T. Dunn, who compiled the index to both volumes. And I owe a special debt to May Buckingham and the late Bob Buckingham for their endless help and sympathy.

I am grateful to the following for their help in finding and for permission to reproduce illustrations: Gerald Duckworth & Co. Ltd, for the photograph of Constantine Cavafy; Christopher Isherwood, for the photograph of himself with Forster; Julian Morrell, for the group at Garsington; William Roerick, for the photograph of himself with Forster; Mrs Sylvia Scaffardi, for the photograph of Ronald Kidd; Miss Velda Sprott, for the photographs of her brother; Quentin Stevenson, for the drawing of Forster by Jessica Dismorr; Mrs Nancy West, for the group photograph at Hammersmith Terrace and the photograph of her brother Joe Ackerley with William Plomer.

Finally, in regard to the biography as a whole, I should like to thank the following for kindly giving permission to quote from copyright sources: Harcourt Brace Jovanovich, Inc. for letters in *The Hill of Devi;* Quentin Bell and Nigel Nicolson for letters from Virginia Woolf; Quentin Bell for extracts from Virginia Woolf's unpublished diaries, the use of which was originally granted by the late Leonard Woolf; Mrs April van Biervliet for letters from Sir Malcolm Darling; the B.B.C. for a letter from Lord Reith; the Trustees of the British Museum and the Governors and Guardians of the National Gallery of Ireland and Royal Academy of Dramatic Art for a letter from G. B. Shaw (copyright © Shaw Text 1978); Faber & Faber Ltd for the poem 'To E. M. Forster' from *The English Auden* edited by Edward Mendelson; Ann E. Hardham for letters from Elizabeth von Arnim; the India Office Library for unpublished crown-copyright material in the India Office Records transcribed by permission of the Controller of Her Majesty's Stationery Office; the T. E. Lawrence Letters Trust for letters from T. E. Lawrence; Dr Thomas Trevelyan for a letter from the late G. M. Trevelyan; Mrs Margaret Meredith for letters from H. O. Meredith to Bertrand Russell; Mrs Eva Reichmann for a letter from Max Beerbohm; George Sassoon for letters from Siegfried Sassoon; the Strachey Trust for two letters from Lytton Strachey; The Viking Press for letters from D. H. Lawrence and Frieda Lawrence, from *The Collected Letters of D. H. Lawrence,* copyright © 1962 by Angelo Ravagli & C. Montague Weekley, Executors of the Estate of Frieda Lawrence Ravagli.

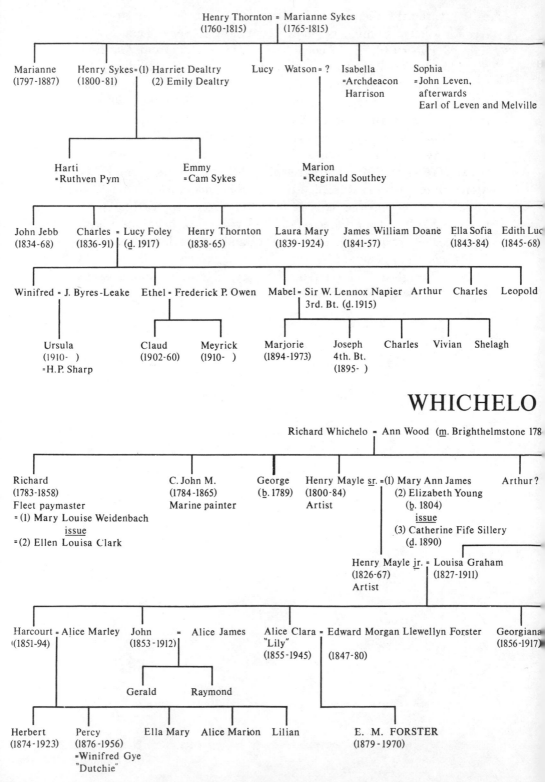

THORNTONS

Henry Thornton = Marianne Sykes
(1760-1815)   (1765-1815)

Marianne   Henry Sykes=(1) Harriet Dealtry   Lucy   Watson = ?   Isabella   Sophia
(1797-1887)   (1800-81)   (2) Emily Dealtry   =Archdeacon   =John Leven,
                                                                         Harrison   afterwards
                                                                                           Earl of Leven and Melville

                         Harti   Emmy   Marion
                         =Ruthven Pym   =Cam Sykes   =Reginald Southey

John Jebb   Charles = Lucy Foley   Henry Thornton   Laura Mary   James William Doane   Ella Sofia   Edith Luc
(1834-68)   (1836-91) (d. 1917)   (1838-65)   (1839-1924)   (1841-57)   (1843-84)   (1845-68)

Winifred = J. Byres-Leake   Ethel = Frederick P. Owen   Mabel = Sir W. Lennox Napier   Arthur   Charles   Leopold
                                                                3rd. Bt. (d.1915)

        Ursula   Claud   Meyrick   Marjorie   Joseph   Charles   Vivian   Shelagh
        (1910-)   (1902-60)   (1910-)   (1894-1973)   4th. Bt.
        =H.P. Sharp   (1895-)

WHICHELO

Richard Whichelo = Ann Wood (m. Brighthelmstone 178

Richard   C. John M.   George   Henry Mayle sr. =(1) Mary Ann James   Arthur?
(1783-1858)   (1784-1865)   (b. 1789)   (1800-84)   (2) Elizabeth Young
Fleet paymaster   Marine painter   Artist   (b. 1804)
= (1) Mary Louise Weidenbach   issue
        issue   (3) Catherine Fife Sillery
= (2) Ellen Louisa Clark   (d. 1890)

                                                        Henry Mayle jr. = Louisa Graham
                                                        (1826-67)   (1827-1911)
                                                        Artist

Harcourt = Alice Marley   John   = Alice James   Alice Clara = Edward Morgan Llewellyn Forster   Georgiana
(1851-94)   (1853-1912)   "Lily"   (1856-1917)
                                                      (1855-1945)   (1847-80)

                              Gerald   Raymond

Herbert   Percy   Ella Mary   Alice Marion Lilian   E. M. FORSTER
(1874-1923) (1876-1956)   (1879-1970)
             =Winifred Gye
             "Dutchie"

and FORSTERS

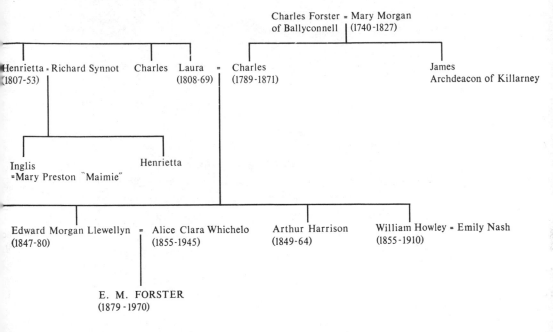

Charles Forster = Mary Morgan
of Ballyconnell (1740-1827)

Henrietta = Richard Synnot (1807-53) — Charles — Laura (1808-69) = Charles (1789-1871) — James Archdeacon of Killarney

Inglis
=Mary Preston "Maimie"   Henrietta

Edward Morgan Llewellyn (1847-80) = Alice Clara Whichelo (1855-1945) — Arthur Harrison (1849-64) — William Howley = Emily Nash (1855-1910)

E. M. FORSTER
(1879-1970)

FAMILY

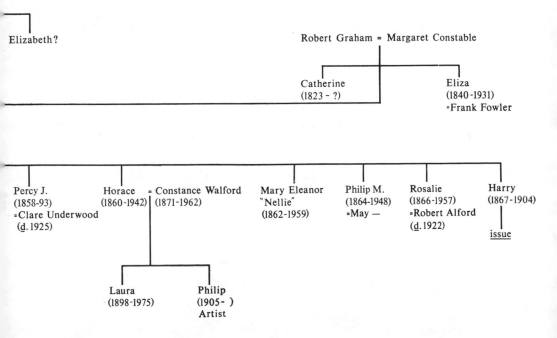

Elizabeth?

Robert Graham = Margaret Constable

Catherine (1823 - ?)   Eliza (1840-1931) =Frank Fowler

Percy J. (1858-93) =Clare Underwood (d. 1925) — Horace (1860-1942) = Constance Walford (1871-1962) — Mary Eleanor "Nellie" (1862-1959) — Philip M. (1864-1948) =May — — Rosalie (1866-1957) =Robert Alford (d. 1922) — Harry (1867-1904) issue

Laura (1898-1975)   Philip (1905-) Artist

The notes for this book are divided into two categories. Those which appear on the page in question are indicated by numerals. The longer notes that appear at the end of the book are indicated by asterisks, and begin on p. 327 of Volume Two.

Volume One

The Growth of the Novelist
1879-1914

But when I die and they write my life
they can say everything.

E.M.F. to T. E. Lawrence
3 May 1928

1 A Birth and a Death

E. M. Forster's last book of substance was a biography of his great-aunt, Marianne Thornton. She was a relative on his father's side; and by the time that he wrote the book he had come to love her memory and to be curious about her influence, and that of his father's family generally, upon his career. This represented a shift of allegiance. He once wrote[1] that a 'curious duel' is fought over every baby. It proved so in his own case; and all through his early years he felt himself to belong, not to the wealthy Thorntons and Forsters, but to his mother's family, the socially obscure and penniless Whichelos. It is with them that I shall begin my narrative.

His maternal grandfather was a drawing-master named Henry Mayle Whichelo. H. M. Whichelo was born in Lambeth in 1826, and for the length of his brief career was employed in the Stockwell and Stepney grammar schools, where his father had taught before him. He came from a family of artists. His father, stepbrother and an uncle all made their careers in painting or drawing; indeed his uncle, John Whichelo, was a water-colour painter of some celebrity, receiving in 1812 the title of 'Marine Painter to the Prince Regent'. Other Whichelos were in the navy. Richard Whichelo, John's elder brother, was Fleet paymaster aboard the *Victory*; and no doubt it was through this connection that John Whichelo painted the well-known last portrait of Nelson.

The curious name 'Whichelo' is generally thought to be a corruption of 'Richelieu', and some of the Whichelos used the Richelieu crest and motto, though a cousin of Forster's made not very con-

---

[1] *Where Angels Fear to Tread*, Chapter 1.

vincing efforts to derive the family name from Uccello, on the strength of their talent for painting.

Forster never knew his grandfather the drawing-master, for he died when Forster's mother was twelve. From all Forster could gather, he was 'unselfish, considerate, sensitive, handsome, cheerful, and alive to scenic and architectural beauty'. All he left to remember him by was a few topographical sketches, some verse-letters to family friends and a pamphlet published in 1849 entitled *Hints to Amateurs: or Rules for the Use of the Black Lead Pencil*. Certainly no money.

His wife, Forster's grandmother Louisa, survived him for forty or more years, and her Forster knew well and loved dearly. Her maiden name was Graham, and she came of Cumberland stock – being, as she frequently repeated, related to a general: Lt-General Sir Gerald Graham, vc. Not that she ever liked him. She was 'a terrible snob', said Forster, 'though not a very deep one', and she liked to hint at a childhood spent among ancestral acres, though in fact her father ran an artist's colourman's business in Soho, and her elder sister Kate was for a time in service.

She was a sensible, breezy, witty woman, with a great zest for life, and Forster eventually used her as his model for Mrs Honeychurch in *A Room With a View*. When her husband died, at the age of forty-one, she was left more or less penniless, with ten children to support. She took lodgers, habitually undercharging them, and lived in a running battle with servants, alternately scolding and spoiling them, and by hook or by crook the family survived, though always under the shadow of the bailiffs' men. They were a good-looking family, with vivid, clear-cut, Italianate features. There was something foreign and out-of-the-ordinary, a carnival air, about the Whichelos, or so people said. 'They had no enthusiasm for work,' wrote Forster himself; 'they were devoid of public spirit, and they were averse to piety and quick to detect the falsity which sometimes accompanies it . . . But there were good looks about them and good taste and good spirits.'

Forster's mother, Alice Clara ('Lily') was born in 1855, being the third child and the eldest girl in the family. She was an intelligent and self-reliant girl and soon earned herself the reputation of the 'solidest' of the family, so that much of the mothering of her younger brothers and sisters fell on her. Her mother leaned on her. She called Lily 'the ready beast', meaning that she always had an answer for everything. And Lily knew her role, as one can perceive from an inscription on the flyleaf of her diary for 1872:

Alice C. Whichelo
Present to herself 1872 January 16th
Herein are recorded the acts and adventures of a great heroine named above, age 17, manners 71 years of age, from her infancy always very old for her age.

The Whichelos had no friends with influence – apart from the legendary general, who showed no disposition to exercise his – so it was plain the children must go out and earn their living as soon as they were able. It was assumed that the boys would take jobs as clerks or the like, and the girls find places as governesses. However, in 1867, the year in which her father died, there was an unexpected development in Lily's life: she acquired a rich benefactress. It was an event with important consequences not only for her but for her whole family.

For three generations, one of the leading families in Clapham had been the Thorntons, of Battersea Rise House. They were a merchant and banking family, who had moved from Yorkshire to Clapham in 1735, when the then head of the family became a director of the Bank of England. In the first place they had settled on the south side of the Common, spreading there into several houses; then in 1792 they had bought and enlarged a Queen Anne house, known to the family as 'Battersea Rise', on the west side. The Thorntons were rich, pious and philanthropic and were influential in Evangelical circles (William Cowper and his friend and mentor the Rev. John Newton were among their protégés); and in due course, through their connection with William Wilberforce, a relative of theirs, they became leading figures in the anti-slave-trade movement and the Clapham Sect.

The Thornton most intimately linked with Wilberforce was Henry (1760–1815). He was a remarkable man, not only an energetic reformer and philanthropist, but a pioneering theoretical economist, whose pamphlet on Paper Credit[1] has a permanent reputation. He gave house-room to Wilberforce for four years before his own marriage, and, as a consequence, most of the other leaders of the anti-slavery movement – Granville Sharp, Zachary Macaulay, James Stephen,

---

[1] *The Nature and Effects of the Paper Credit of Great Britain* (1802).

3

Charles Grant and John Shore – came to settle in Clapham, using the Oval Library[1] at 'Battersea Rise' as their headquarters. It was in this way that the Clapham Sect was born. The reformers and their families lived a communal existence, treating one another's houses and gardens as their own; and the village of Clapham became the centre of the whole Evangelical movement: the source of innumerable Bible Societies and Missionary Societies, and a place of resort for politicians, publicists, missionaries, converts, Quaker prison-reformers and founders of every sort of charity.

Henry Thornton left a family of nine, and the eldest of these, Marianne, who was born in 1797, was still living, unmarried, in Clapham in the 1860s. By now she was the acknowledged head of the family, though as the result of a family quarrel she had been exiled from 'Battersea Rise', and lived in a house (variously known as 'East Side' or 'The Cockpond') on the east side of the Common, sharing it with her niece Henrietta Synnot. Marianne was a downright, rather autocratic woman, distinctly pre-Victorian in her attitudes. She used to say she was the last survivor of the Clapham Sect, her brothers and sisters having all become high church and Tory; but if so, she was not noticeably marked by the Sect's pietism.

Now it so happened that she and the Whichelos employed the same doctor, a kindly old man named Tayloe; and, wishing to be of service to Mrs Whichelo, who had just been widowed, Dr Tayloe took Lily, then twelve years old, to visit Miss Thornton and Miss Synnot. He may have meant no more than to give her an outing. But at all events the ladies took a great fancy to Lily, who was pretty and had charming manners, and they decided to take her up. Soon she became a regular visitor at 'East Side'. Indeed for a time she quite wearied her mother with praises of her new friends. 'I'm sick of Miss Synnot already,' her mother exclaimed; though, very sensibly, she encouraged the friendship. And as time went on, it came to be understood that Marianne would take charge of Lily's future. If ever she consulted Lily's mother about her, the latter's answer was, 'Lily is your child, Miss Thornton, now – never ask me about her. I only feel thankful that it is so.'

Lily was shown about to various Thornton relations – to begin

---

[1] It was designed by William Pitt the Younger.

with, distinctly in the role of poor dependant. When Marianne took her down to Weymouth in 1869, to stay with her own niece and nephew-in-law, Emmy and Major Sykes, the kindly Dr Tayloe offered to pay for new clothes for Lily, but Marianne, who prided herself on her worldly cunning, insisted on her wearing her shabby old dress: 'Waifs and strays,' she said, were never liked unless they showed their lowly estate. Gradually, however, Lily was taken into the family on more equal terms; and in a year or two she was visiting on her own account among the Thornton circle.

As for her education, Henrietta Synnot, whose friendship for Lily grew steadily warmer, at first took charge of it herself; then, when Lily was seventeen, she found a place for her and her sister Georgie at a school in Hackney. School came as a disagreeable shock to the girls; they loathed it and only survived Hackney for three weeks. Then, however, another school was found for Lily, a superior establishment in Brighton, conducted by a Mme Collinet. Its tone proved the most superior thing about it, but Lily settled down better there, picked up a little French and some other mild accomplishments, and acquired social assurance.

On the completion of Lily's schooldays, it was no problem for Marianne, with her wide circle, to procure her a post as a governess. First a place was found for her in the family of James Knowles, the friend of Tennyson and editor of *The Nineteenth Century*; then in that of Marianne's niece and nephew-in-law the Southeys; and finally in the household of Effie Wedgwood,[1] an old friend of Marianne's, now married to T. H. Farrer[2] of Abinger Hall in Surrey. Mr Farrer, who was Permanent Secretary to the Board of Trade, had two young sons by a previous marriage, who would be Lily's particular care.

She found life distinctly agreeable at Abinger Hall. Being a governess had done nothing to crush her spirit; she was very much her own woman, lively, composed, and charmingly good-looking – rather self-contained in company, but with a free, slashing style of comedy in her letters. One to Marion Southey catches her note:

> Mr and Mrs Wedgwood are staying here at Abinger Hall, he really hardly looks human, he is so screwed up and wizen looking, more like one of his own spirits than anything else. He is as spirit mad

[1] Katherine Euphemia Wedgwood (1839–1931).
[2] He was raised to the peerage in 1893.

as ever and has now another spiritual grandchild who is also black named 'Cissy'. If you remember he had one named Pokey without a head – Oh! the nonsense of it is too dreadful!! The spirits sometimes take his spectacles off and put them on someone else which makes Mr W. rather nervous and he calls out to the spirits to 'take great care of them'. I can't think who the grandchildren can be because he has had none. Mrs Alfred Wedgwood is nearly a black but she has had no children, so it seems odd whom these children can profess to be . . .

Marianne once accused Lily of 'finding depreciation a luxury'. None the less, she loved her sharp tongue; and Lily became a general favourite in Farrer circles, making particular friends with Mrs Farrer's stepdaughter Ida.

Not long after her arrival at Abinger, she met another of Marianne's nephews, Edward Forster,[1] and before very long these two fell in love. The affair progressed rapidly, and before the end of the year they had announced their engagement. Mrs Farrer reported the occasion to Eddie's elder sister Laura, from the Farrers' house in town (7 November 1876):

> Fancy our surprise just after our arrival as we were sitting in the drawing room having just said 'we *needn't* say not at home, no one will come', to see the door open and Lily and Eddy appear. I was as innocent as usual and thought no evil and Eddy had to tell me plainly 'Lily and I are engaged' before I took in the situation. She was half wild with excitement – fell upon Ida's neck kissing and ejaculating and looking quite lovely. The two girls soon fled and left me and Eddy by the fire and we had *such* a nice talk together. He was not wild like L. but as befitted his seven more years all aglow with happiness, and having looked 'things' steadily in the face I should say.

Edward was to become Forster's father, and to explain his origins I shall have to go back a little in time. He was the son of Marianne's sister Laura (1808–69), who had married a penniless Irish clergyman named Charles Forster. The Forster family derived from Northumberland but had been settled in Ireland for several generations, and Charles's own father had married a Welshwoman of the name of May Morgan. (It was from her that Edward, and Edward's son E. M. Forster, took their Christian name 'Morgan'.) As a young man,

---

[1] Edward Morgan Llewellyn Forster (1847–80).

Charles Forster had been curate to John Jebb, Rector of Abingdon, near Limerick; and when Jebb became Bishop of Limerick, Charles became his chaplain, henceforth living with him as a son. Eventually the Bishop retired to England, bringing Charles with him, and it was through this Jebb connection that Charles gained the *entrée* to, and eventually married into, the wealthy Thornton clan. In a worldly sense it was all he ever did gain from the Bishop, for he was given no stipend, and the Bishop, on dying, bequeathed him only some books[1] and a pair of shoe-buckles that he, Charles, had previously given the Bishop. However, he bore no grudge and never ceased to hymn the praises of the 'Blessed Bishop' – till his children grew sick of the name.

In due course Charles Forster became Rector of Stisted, in Essex, and produced ten children. It was a comfortable living, carrying with it a handsome, if insanitary, rectory, and – until a mournful succession of deaths from consumption in the family – the children enjoyed a cheerful country upbringing, indulged by their mother, and left largely to their own devices by their father – preoccupied as he was with the geography of the Holy Land and the growing menace of Mohammedanism.[2]

Edward was born in 1847, the youngest but two of the family, and he went to Charterhouse, like his brothers, and then to Trinity College, Cambridge. His father expected him to enter the church or the law, the only occupations suitable for one of gentlemanly but pious upbringing; however, Edward made up his mind to be an architect. There was some opposition, but he got his way, and enrolled as a pupil of Sir Arthur Blomfield. By the time of his engagement to Lily he had qualified and was in practice on his own account and had begun to receive little commissions through his family connections.

Marianne – or 'Monie' as I shall now call her, that being her name within the family – was enchanted with this romance between Eddie and her *protégée*. Others in the family were less delighted. Edward's eldest sister, Laura, who, now that their parents were dead, felt

---

[1] Among them was an original copy of Blake's *Songs of Innocence*, acquired from Blake's widow, to whom he had been of service. The volume eventually came into possession of E. M. Forster.

[2] He wrote a number of books, including *A Historical Geography of Arabia* (1844) and *Mohammedanism Unveiled* (1829).

herself responsible for the family dignity, thought Lily 'wanting on the intellectual side' and wished Eddie could have 'kept up at higher level'. However, Mrs Farrer told her Lily had 'stuff and character in her – witness her dealings with her own people'. As for Lily's mother, she was in raptures over Eddie. 'He is a man in 10,000,' she told Lily. 'How my dear mother would have liked him! Strange is it not that you should marry someone so like your own father?'

Edward and Lily got married in early 1877 and took a house at 6 Melcombe Place, Dorset Square, near Marylebone Station; by December Lily was expecting a child. She and Edward were a lively couple; Monie adored them and was always angling for visits from them. Edward was good-looking, impractical, impatient of interference and with a nice vein of sarcasm. He would tease Monie for her benighted taste and make her buy 'high art' curtains – which, she said, looked like the results of too much country washing. As for Lily, she was the ideal unpaid companion. No one wrote her such letters as Lily, or was as clever at retrieving her stick and spectacles. Monie transferred to them the hopes once centred on an earlier married nephew, Inglis Synnot, who had died young and childless, and she began already to frame plans for their child.

Eventually Edward's sister Laura, also, was reconciled to the match; and having just received a legacy, she commissioned Edward to design a house for her, taking a lease of some land from the Farrers for the purpose. This house in Abinger, a red-brick mansion known as 'Laura Lodge' (later renamed 'West Hackhurst') was his first large commission, and, as events turned out, it was to be his only one.

During these early days of the marriage, Thornton patronage was at work on all sides. Monie took up Lily's brothers and sisters, regularly inviting them to stay in Clapham or at her country house at Milton Bryan in Bedfordshire; Edward came to the rescue when an execution was threatened on the Whichelo furniture; and Ruthven Pym, one of Monie's nephews, found a job for Lily's brother Horace in Coutts's Bank. Lily was grateful, but all the same she found disadvantages in having married into so nepotistic a clan. Monie expected to follow her and her 'dear Eddie's' doings in daily detail. She was always sending Lily on errands or writing her humorous, interfering letters. 'My dear Lily what a good thing it is that you are not an old maid,' ran a needling letter about food (June 1878):

I am one, & therefore dare not bring such railing accusations as
you do against all men who know good cooking from bad. Why
should not a man care about having good cooking as much as a
girl does about a pretty ball dress? Both are artistic, a greasy
tough vulgar looking dinner is as much to be eschewed as a
frightful or shabby dress. It isn't *you* but Effie Farrer who can't
endure a man to know or care or even mention whether his food is
good or bad & you have caught her tone about it . . .

There was another particularly exasperating one (December 1877) in
which she exhorted Lily to be less 'ostrich-like' in regard to her
pregnancy:

> . . . my dear, it beats me all to shivers (as the Americans say) to
> know how to order your bassinette (it shall be such a beauty)
> when you won't tell me when you will want it . . . My dear child,
> do shake the sand off your head and start and run with the rest of
> the flock of birds on the beaten high road, where nobody will
> notice you or talk about you . . .
>
> I have known you a goodish bit of time dear Lily, and one of
> your attractions to me was your never setting yourself up, as if
> you thought you were wiser or better or prettier than the rest of
> the world. Governesses are generally supposed to carry a flag and
> to strike out some new and superior path, but during your brief
> taste of the profession you never did. Why should you unfurl one
> now, that of being more 'proper & particular' than all the rest of
> the creation . . .

This, as Forster remarked later, though not exactly a patronizing
letter, 'left the victim no outlet' and made her feel hunted and
cornered. Another approaching trouble was that the once-ardent
friendship of Lily's patroness Henrietta Synnot had begun to turn
sour.

Lily and Eddie's first baby died at birth, but on 1 January 1879
Lily was safely delivered of another. It was a boy, and they registered
his name as 'Henry Morgan Forster'; the name 'Henry' pleased
Monie, who said that if he turned out at all like the last Henry
Forster[1] he would prove a 'burning and shining light'. The birth was
an event full of significance for her, and she told Lily, 'I feel so full of
things I want to say and hear about this olive branch, or rather bud.
It is "the hopes & fears of future years" that seem suddenly to
connect me – a decrepit old root – with a fresh generation.'

---

[1] Henry Thornton Forster (1838–65), an elder brother of Edward.

Another who took a particular interest in the baby was Inglis Synnot's widow, Maimie; and on the strength of this she and Lily began what was to be a lifelong friendship. Maimie was the daughter of an Indian Army surgeon, James Blair Preston: she was a dear, innocent, pious, sentimental creature, always swathed in the deepest mourning, and gifted chiefly at painting flowers on greeting-cards and embroidering handbags with brilliants. She had had no home of her own during her marriage, and as a childless hanger-on of the Thornton circle she did not carry much weight. Later she revealed more character: she acquired a retinue of charitable dependants ('Maimie's beggars'), and once marched into a public house and dragged out a drunken man of her acquaintance. When friends said, 'But Maimie, how could you do it?' she replied simply, 'But I had to!'

Two months after the baby's birth he was taken to 'East Side' to be christened at Holy Trinity church on the Common. On the way to church, the verger asked Edward what the child's name was to be, and absent-mindedly he gave his own, 'Edward Morgan', instead, which the verger wrote down. When the clergyman asked the same question, Lily's mother, who was holding the child at the font, merely pointed to the paper in the verger's hand. And so, to her horror, Lily heard the child christened 'Edward'; he had been registered one way and baptized another. There was much anxious discussion, but in the end it was decided that 'Edward' he must remain. At the reception afterwards, Henrietta Synnot, who was a godmother, gave the child a bible, and this too was not a good omen: for when Henrietta disliked people she gave them a hymn-book, and when she detested them she gave them a prayer-book, so what a bible meant didn't bear thinking of. Monie interpreted the disaster over the name in her own way. She had never liked the name 'Morgan', it not being a Thornton name, and maintained to her death he had been called it by mistake.

Not long after Morgan's birth, his father's health began to break down; he developed a chronic cough and was constantly catching colds. Aunt Monie seems to have recognized the symptoms as consumption, the family disease, and she insisted on proper medical attention. However Lily, who came from a robust family, was too inexperienced to take alarm. Moreover, as family friends were quick to point out, she had no notion how to nurse an invalid. Henrietta Litchfield (the celebrated 'Aunt Etta' of Gwen Raverat's *Period*

Piece) sighed to her friend and neighbour Laura Forster on the subject:

> It must be a gt relief to know that Ed. was safe at his journies end and plenty of care will be taken of him at Milton won't it? I wish Lily was not quite so like Lady Stephen[1] for the safety of husband and children. I think it is a fearful loss to have no instinct abt nursing – sometimes children develop it in a way that grown up life doesn't, and I'm glad to hear she was frightened about a non-existent cold of the baby: tho' that mightn't seem a v. hopeful beginning of insight into illness. – I wonder children live.

Soon there could be no more doubt about Edward's condition: he was in an advanced state of consumption. The doctors, not very hopefully, recommended sea-air, and Lily went off with him to Bournemouth. They took a furnished house there, and Maimie Synnot came down to help nurse him and support Lily in her trouble. But by 30 October 1880 Edward was dead. The blow was a shattering one for Lily. It left her grieving and bewildered, and conscious that Edward's family secretly half-blamed her for the tragedy. She felt herself a lonely and unwanted widow. Her only hope for the future, it seemed to her, now lay with her baby.

She had one main support at this time, and that was Maimie Synnot. Maimie helped Lily extricate herself from her Bournemouth house, and for a time they shared lodgings in Bournemouth; and whenever they were parted Lily poured out her misery to her in long lamenting letters. 'Good night, I wish the night wd. never turn into day and that I cd. go on sleeping for ever, it wd. be so nice,' she ended one 'very dull grumbly letter'. Lily had been visiting her family, and they had got on her nerves, and so had the baby Morgan. Even her friendship with Ida Farrer seemed to have cooled, and she felt lonely and useless. There were many such letters. Only Maimie gave her the love she needed, and they would have set up house together permanently were it not that – as they agreed – the childless Maimie would have idolized the baby too passionately. The infant Forster, like Helen's baby in *Howards End*, was the lifeline for two shipwrecked women and their hopes haloed his head, and coloured his own sense of himself, all through his childhood.

As, too, with Lilian's baby in *Where Angels Fear to Tread*, a 'duel'

---

[1] The wife of Sir James Fitzjames Stephen.

soon developed over the possession of him. Monie, having lost two adored nephews, concentrated her affection on the infant Morgan and wanted him and Lily wholly under her management. 'Her thirst for youth had become cannibalistic,' Forster wrote; she was perpetually badgering Lily to bring Morgan to 'East Side' and then would make scenes when she wanted to leave. 'I am so happy dearest Lily that you were so happy and well here – but why didn't you stay longer?' she wrote. 'You know what a comfort *you* are to me – to say nothing of baby – who seems a sort of "Dieu donné" child to make up both to you and to me.' Lily, though she was still fond of Monie, grew fretful under these persecutions and exclaimed once, 'Well well – I hope in the next world there will be a compartment labelled "Thornton" and that it won't be anywhere near me.' On another occasion she became so exasperated, when Monie simply *would* not let her leave Clapham, that she dramatized the scene for Maimie's benefit.

> *Monie* Oh I hope you are not going to take that dear child away
>   from me, not only on my account but his.
> *Lily* (obstinately) I must go on Tuesday.
> *M.* Why must? London is very bad for that child.
> *L.* (aside) Dr Southey thinks it better than Clapham. (aloud)
>   I don't think a fortnight can do him any harm.
> *M.* Yes it can. I thought you *promised* you would not go near
>   London.
> *L.* No. If I thought it bad for baby, there would have been no
>   object in my leaving Bournemouth at all.
> *M.* The North East winds are so bad.
> *L.* No worse than Clapham.
> *M.* Yes they are. People go abroad to avoid them.
> *L.* If the North East winds are confined to London then they
>   could avoid them by going to some other part of England.
>   They go abroad because they can't avoid them. – But it does
>   not much matter as Baby does not go out in North East
>   winds, and he may just as well be in the house at Melcombe
>   Place as anywhere else.
> *M.* By no means. Your rooms are so small.
> *L.* I am afraid I shall never have such large ones again.
> *M.* I am sure I hope you will.
> *L.* (mildly) The sitting rooms are 12 ft. high and 20 ft. square.
> *M.* Well that is something.
> (*L.* relapses into moody silence and knows nothing is any good
>   but just sitting and enduring. Monie said she would like the

baby for her birthday so again I have feebly given in, and let us hope it will be the death of me, for flesh and blood certainly ought not to be able to hold out against such worry.)

There was a further trouble in that Henrietta Synnot, Marianne's niece and companion, had become definitely hostile to Lily and the baby. No one ever discovered why exactly, though of course Monie's financial plans for Morgan may have had to do with it. It was, anyway, part of Henrietta's restless character to take people up and then drop them, and she had an ungovernable temper. Lily had a temper of her own, and when Henrietta once again, in her meaning way, gave Morgan a bible, she was speechless with rage. After a while the two women were no longer on speaking terms, and, when Lily was at 'East Side', the message 'Miss Synnot desires me to say, ma'am, that she is coming down', meant that Lily and baby must clear out of the drawing-room. In the end, Henrietta went too far. She complained about Lily to Monie, who up to now had pretended to notice nothing, and, hearing this, Lily's fury boiled over, and she fired off such a letter to Henrietta as should, she said, make her hair stand on end. After this, for a time, Henrietta was more placable.

2 Childhood

Through most of the year 1882 Lily wandered disconsolately from one friend's house to another, intermittently searching for a home of her own. Monie would have liked Lily and the baby to live with herself, but Lily, who was able to support herself financially, was set upon independence. 'She is the most self contained woman I ever met with,' Monie told Edward's sister Laura, 'but to be sure she's been brought up to independence.'[1] Sometimes Lily would leave the baby with Monie, who was overjoyed to have sole charge of the 'Important One', as he was called. His reunions with his mother were passionate occasions, as appears from Monie's rueful account of one to Laura:

> When his mother came for him to get him ready, tho' full of his gooseberries & a touch of my egg, the moment he saw her he ran to her in a sort of extacy as tho' they had been separated for years, & half stifling her with kisses as she carried him off. I wouldn't let her bring him back to say good bye, not on his account but mine, & when the carriage had rolled away it seemed as if all the light of the house had gone also.

He was a demonstrative child, prone to violent passions of love or fury, and Lily was accused of spoiling him, though Monie denied the charge to Laura:

---

[1] I have not been able to discover how much she inherited from her husband. Under the terms of his will she received their furniture and possessions, a sum of £550, and the income on his residuary estate, the capital being held in trust for Morgan. Against the entry in the Probate register there is a note: 'Personal estate under £8,000. Resworn June 1881 under £7,000.'

I cannot but think you would agree with Enty,[1] Emmy[2] and me that she really does not spoil him, if by that is meant letting him have what he cries for after forbidding him. Weenie[3] was much more likely to do that. There is a sort of firmness which Emmy said amounted to sternness in the way in which she let him scream & go into a violent passion when refused anything on which he had set his mind. – And it was piteous to behold him trying to get over her & make her kiss him, which she professed she never would the days he beat & kicked Morris & scratched her face when taken out of bed forcibly to be washed & dressed. Tho' he tried so hard, I never saw her give way about this.

Monie was a far-seeing woman, and there was prescience in her diagnosis of the infant Forster:

One thing I don't believe any body makes allowance enough for, & that is his intense enjoyment of this world & all it contains & his proportionate misery when anything is withheld from him. He seems to have the attachment of grown up people for each other, for inanimate objects, . . .

With his 'memory for old toys and love for sticks and stones', she told Laura, she feared he would grow an idolater; for him 'any pleasure I am sure is double what it is to other people'.

At last, some time in the autumn, Lily reported success in her house-hunting. 'I do believe I have at last found a house,' she told Maimie.

Last Tuesday I went to Stevenage. . . . I was told by the station people that the 'Rooksnest'[4] was 2½ miles from the station & not 1½ as the agents said but for once in their lives the agents spoke the truth. . . . It is a very old gabled house, & yet it is perfectly new. It has been rejuvenated, the inside scooped out – everything as pretty & nice as possible – good sanitary arrangements. The rent is £55 with 4 acres of land . . . I should not have *chosen* to live in such a lonely place if I could have helped it but I can't find anything else & here is winter upon me again.

Her mother 'raved' about 'Rooksnest', and Aunt Monie, though perturbed that the house was not on gravel, gave her approval also. She

---

[1] Henrietta Synnot.
[2] Marianne's niece, Emmy Sykes.
[3] 'Weenie' was Maimie Synnot's nickname at 'East Side'.
[4] 'Rooksnest' was originally the name not of the house itself but of a hamlet including both it and the neighbouring farm.

wrote that Ruthven Pym, her nephew-in-law, knew Lily's new landlord, Colonel Wilkinson, and that she was so glad he was 'respectable',
as they were to live so near. Lily longed to retort that she didn't see
why Mr Pym's knowing him made him respectable. 'What a pity one
can't take a little fling sometimes in speech,' she told Maimie. 'I
always feel happier when I do – no perhaps I don't afterwards.'

She and Morgan moved in during the March of the following year
(1883). (Forster remembered asking the names of the stations on
their way to Stevenage and of pronouncing 'Welwyn' as it is spelt and
not as 'Wellin' in the approved fashion.) His mother, in the first
instance, took the house for three years only, and once or twice in
early days she decided it was too lonely and they must leave. But
before long they had fallen in love with the place. And indeed it was,
and is, a charming house, with its rosy brickwork, its ancient vine,
and its steep-pitched roof, pierced by dormer windows, sweeping
down at the rear, in an odd way, almost to the ground. Forster
evoked the house and his love for it in *Howards End*[1] and wrote later,
'The house is my childhood and safety. The three attics preserve me.
Only a little of my passion and irrationality was used up in *Howards
End*.' Already at the age of fifteen, by which time he was a depressed
schoolboy at Tonbridge, he was looking back nostalgically to
'Rooksnest' and made a sentimental inventory of its rooms. 'Inside
the house was peculiar,' it ran:

> You entered through the porch into a tiny ante-room & then into
> the hall, the pride of the house. It was the kitchen when the house
> was a farm & sad to say once had an open fire-place with a great
> chimney but before we came the landlord, Colonel Wilkinson,
> closed it up, put a wretched little grate instead & made the
> chimney corner into the cupboard I have marked. Five doors
> opened out of the hall, the dining room, the drawing room, the
> door to the lobby leading to the kitchen, the door leading to the
> porch & the door to the staircase which was thus quite shut in &
> could not be found by new people, who wondered how ever we got
> up. Though the big fireplace was blocked up the big chimney still
> remained & once the sweep brought a little boy who went up it to
> mother's great alarm, but came down safe. There were signs of a
> trap door in the ceiling. At the end of the chimney cupboard was
> a little door which mother once got open & found an old basin
> which we still have. The ceiling had a beam across as had most of

---

[1] The house had at some period belonged to a family called Howard.

the rooms. The dining room & drawing room were nice rooms but had nothing peculiar about them. On going through the lobby door you came to a door on the left which opened on to a flight of stairs leading to the cellar, which was under the drawing room. Then from the lobby opened three doors to the pantry, larder & kitchen. The pantry was a little room but the larder was big & had a yellow brick floor & nice large shelves on which the eatables were put. It was always very cool. In one corner were large red vessels one of which held the bread & the others, at first, our drinking water. The kitchen was rather warm & paved with squares of red & blue stone. From it opened a cupboard under the stairs. It had a porch with two doors which were useful when parleying with a tramp. All the windows at the back had bars whether they were upstairs or down & all in the front had shutters so we were pretty safe from tramps or burglars. Upstairs there was the landing which had a window over the back porch & in front three large rooms, the big spare room, the nursery, & mother's room over the dining room, hall & drawing room respectively. Mother's was large & cold but she liked it. The nursery was delightful. It had a large cupboard shaped like an L in which my toys were & had also the large wardrobe which took up one side of the room. The big spare room was nice but I did not often go in. Then opposite was the little spare room over the scullery, a later addition which was very nice in winter because of the kitchen chimney. In the passage between it & the big spare room was a trap door to the rafters where was a cistern which was filled every day, till we had a regular water supply from the scullery pump. Here was a little window which commanded a view of the back garden. The only other room on this landing was the store-cupboard by mother's bedroom over the larder. Hence always came a mingled odour of apples, mice & jam. Above were three attics, a bedroom on each side & a box-room in the middle. This was a curious part of the house for at the entrance of each room was a beam of wood perhaps 18 inches high by 12 wide on the top of which the door swung. New maids were always much aggrieved at having to stride to bed over these logs. In the attic over the spare room was an L shaped passage leading nowhere round the chimney stack. When I arrived I am told I ran to the top of the house & then down this passage. The mice had eaten away all the rafters & I nearly came down quicker than I had come up.

The house was surrounded by a paddock and apple-trees, and in the front was a pond, which Lily had drained and which became known as the 'Dell'ole'. But the greatest feature of the garden was a magnificent wych-elm, which sheltered the house to the west.

It was of great height & had a very thick stem, but the curious part in it was this. About four feet from the ground were three or four fangs stuck deep into the rugged bark. As far as I can make out these were votive offerings of people who had their toothache cured by chewing pieces of the bark, but whether they were their teeth I don't know & certainly it does not seem likely that they should sacrifice one sound tooth as the price of having one aching one cured.

All along the far side of the front garden ran a meadow, which Lily rented to some neighbouring farmers, the Franklyns. It was an oddly-shaped field, with hedges full of bryony and dogroses, and a tall oak-tree carrying a swing. It was fenced with wire only, for the sake of the view beyond, so whatever animals were in the meadow, there would be a sample straying in the 'Rooksnest' garden also. In the Forsters' time they had hens, guinea-fowl, cows, sheep and pigs, as well as the keeper's puppies.

The Forsters became very friendly with the Franklyns, and Forster, who spoke of them later as 'that honoured family', liked to think that by the end of his life he had known five generations. At that period they consisted of Mr Franklyn himself and his wife, two very fat daughters, a son Tom and a grandson named Frankie. They were Baptists and rather 'near', inclined to skim the milk, but on the other hand they never refused a beggar: Mrs Franklyn would say, 'Well I've done my part, and if they go to the public house I can't help it.' The farm buildings were always in a state of dirt and chaos; nevertheless Mr Franklyn was a shrewd and successful farmer. Every year he would come to 'Rooksnest' to pay the rent for the meadow, always a very lengthy business, and on the last of his visits, his parting words were 'Well, well, it's been a dear *maidy.*' 'Still,' retorted Lily, 'you wouldn't give it up when I wanted it for the pony.' 'That he wouldn't,' chimed in Mrs Franklyn; 'and glad enough he's been to have it too.' All the same the cunning old man got it cheaper from the incoming tenant. As a child, Forster spent half his days at the farm. He would hasten nervously across the farmyard, which was always full of enormous and ferocious-looking pigs, and would play for hours in the great barns, scampering about and hunting for eggs in the mysterious twilight. In one of the barns lived a machine, with great wheels, for cutting oil-cake and hay. Young Frankie Franklyn used to spread himself out on the wheels and whirl round like Ixion, while Morgan looked on admiringly, wishing he dared do likewise.

It was generally understood in the family that Morgan was 'delicate', so for the first year or two his mother took him off to Bournemouth for the winter. As a result of her grim lesson from fate, she was morbidly anxious about Morgan's health and coddled him obsessively. All through his childhood he was never allowed out if there were the slightest threat of rain, and in the mildest wind he had to be swathed in warm coats and mufflers. He imbibed the anxiety himself, and right up to middle age he thought of himself as extremely frail and likely at any time to develop consumption. In fact, as he came to realize late in life, he had an extremely sound constitution.

He was a pretty child, at the age of three or four, with large expressive eyes. At Monie's insistence, he wore his hair in curls to his shoulders and dressed in Little Lord Fauntleroy suits with lace collars; he was, he said, one of the very last children to be tormented in this manner.[1] Being so much the curled darling of admiring females, he was extremely precocious. 'We have rather a life of it if we do anything baby doesn't like,' wrote Lily to Aunt Monie, when he was three. 'He calls us "monstrous crows and rats", and when his grandmother asked him "not to do it" he said "I shall, Mrs piece of suet". I can't think what made him think of it. I suppose, the rhyme.' At the age of four, with the aid of the picture-books at 'East Side', he discovered he could read, and he took himself very seriously in consequence. 'Tiresome to be interrupted in my reading when the light is so good,' he would say severely to Aunt Monie's nurse. 'Can't you tell the people I am busy reading, Havell?' His favourite book in early years was *The Swiss Family Robinson*; he loved it because the boys in it were happy, whereas Robinson Crusoe was always worrying over savages. Very soon, when he was still only five, he began composing stories on his own account, 'long stories about things that have never happened except inside my head,' he called them. They had sensational titles like 'Dancing Bell', 'Chattering Hassocks', 'Scream', 'Scuffles in the Wardrobe', 'The Earring in the Keyhole'

---

[1] Once, when staying with Maimie Synnot's sisters in the Isle of Wight, he was told to offer the coachman a sandwich, for which the coachman said 'Thank you, miss.' He reported this, and, on the Preston sisters' advice, he went back to the man and said: 'I'm a little boy.' 'Yes, miss,' said the coachman.

and 'The Adventures of Pussy Senior'. In 'Chattering Hassocks', fifty lions and fifty unicorns sat on hassocks and the lions made speeches in favour of tolerance and liberty of opinion; Monie declared it was better than *Alice*.

His dolls, especially one called Sailor Dollar, figured in interminable narratives at this time. He bullied and mothered Sailor Dollar unmercifully, and the saga of their daily adventures, as retailed in detail by Lily for Aunt Monie's benefit, gives a good picture of the forces at work in this fatherless, husbandless and brotherless household.

Morgan was in great distress yesterday – he had poked Sailor Dollar's eye out – boy-like he tried to see whether 'it would go into his head'; it did and then there was a yell of agony and we rushed up to see whether he had fallen off the sofa where he was resting. He is more resigned now as Sailor Dollar is supposed to have lost his eye in battle and the hole is convenient to put his food into. M. said this morning 'I quite forgot to give Sailor Dollar a goody last night, but he shall have it now and when he has eaten it I will put it back in the box.' He has been much interested this morning in reading an Etiquette book called *Don't* . . .

I am afraid Sailor Dollar's end is drawing nigh – he was supposed to be ill and sick this afternoon, but M. threw him over the staircase – by way of a cure I conclude – he did not discover until some time afterwards that the other eye had gone and his face was cracked in every direction, and then – dear me the heart-rending sobs which rent the air – he sat cuddling S.D. in a disconsolate heap on the floor, hoping he would not 'break to bits if tenderly cared'. I was hard-hearted because he has such a stupid habit of throwing things for no reason in the world – he had just flung my prayer book and hymn book across the room and when we were with Laura he all but knocked down some valuable vases by throwing a sofa cushion at them . . . S.D. is put to bed in the nursery, well covered, and has a cup of water and box of biscuits by his side. M. says he would much rather be a coward than brave because people hurt you when you are brave . . .

I do wish you could have seen his excitement yesterday when your box was opened and when the wool was taken off the face. He flew with it to show the maids and it has never been out of his hands since except when he was in bed and then it was on sofa near with poor haggard Sailor Dollar. He chose the new name immediately and modestly remarked 'I don't think it is a bad name, do you?' Sailor Duncan had a good dinner of potatoes, water and suet pudding; wanted it after his 'miserable journey'.

After dinner the introductions took place. 'This is Sailor Dollar, don't laugh at him, he was handsome once but he has met with an accident' . . . After tea we played our usual game at Bézique. M. had S. Duncan stuck under his arm, which a good deal interfered with his play. At last he said so gravely 'I am having such a miserable time with this doll. Do you think he would much mind not learning the game?' . . .

I washed my hair yesterday afternoon. S.D. and Morgan would look on. I left my hair down and told M. I was 15 and not his mother at all. 'I know you are, you look just like her, do up your hair and you will be 30.' At last he got quite nervous about it and said 'Now do come out of joking – let me look at you. I am sure you are my mama.'

As this last passage hints, a love-affair sprang up between Morgan and his mother at this time. He wanted it to last for ever and became fearful at any threat of alteration. 'Morgan was much excited & commissioned Emma to buy me a present,' Lily wrote to her mother on her thirtieth birthday, when he was now six.

– a vase of course, it is his *one* idea for a birthday present . . . He was very nervous lest I shd get up in the morning much changed. 'I really don't think you can differ much in one night, my darling. We may as well call you 30 now, but you will always be pretty to me, whatever you look like.'

Even franker was the following dialogue, reported by Lily to Monie:

Morgan. When I grow up, my darling, I shall call upon you every day.
Lily. You can live with me if you like.
M. That will be best, and I will only sit with you and pay visits with you when you go with me.
L. What shall I do when you marry?
M. I shall only marry to you.
L. You can't.
M. Why not? People can marry twice, so I don't see it will make any difference to you.
L. Boys can't marry their mothers.
M. What a bother. Well, I shall take care then never to go to any wedding in case I should be married and I don't want it.

This love-affair made Forster's childhood a radiantly happy one, and it went on, in a sense, for the rest of both their lives. Indeed it dominated Forster's existence and caused him much frustration in later years. All the same, it was not the sort of mother–son affair which leads to tragedy. Lily was an extremely possessive mother, but not an emotionally smothering one: there was a coolness and briskness – something of the sister as well as of the mother, one might say – in her feelings for Morgan, and this kept a certain balance in their relationship.

Having discovered reading, Morgan developed a passion for instructing others, and at the age of six he took the maids' education in hand. 'Morgan invited the maids to tea with him yesterday, and he said he must give them some amusement,' Lily wrote to Aunt Monie.

> So he armed himself with astronomical diagrams and said they had better do a little learning. He explained all & they giggled like a pair of noodles. He then proposed Hide & Seek . . . He then took them both into the hall and instructed them in moves at chess. He flew all over the hall carpet saying 'now I go like a knight, now like a castle' etc. He is chalking a map of South America and implored me to help him before I went out yesterday, 'for I know Emma won't think it matters a bit whether I put Patagonia in the place of Ecuador.'

Later Lily overheard him give Emma an examination.

> *Emma.* You know a good deal about stars, don't you, Master Morgan?
> *Morgan* (humbly). No, not very much. Do you?
> *E.* Oh no.
> *M. What* do you know about? ('What indeed!!!', comments Lily.)
> *A long pause.*
> *E.* Oh only what you have taught me.
> *M.* Botany?
> *E.* Yes, about the Great Bear and Little Bear.
> *M.* (scornfully) That's not Botany, that's Astronomy. Botany is about flowers and *Cology* about shells. I don't know very much of both those.
> *E.* Oh I think you know a great deal, Master Morgan.
> *M.* (very self-satisfied tone) Oh, do you?

Though he tormented and patronized Emma, just as he did Sailor Dollar, the two became boon companions, giggling together and wildly dancing the polka till the windows rattled. Eventually, though, his rudeness and cleverness were too much for her. They had a quarrel while picking primroses; he hit her, and with great simplicity she hit him back and tore his coat, so she had to be dismissed. He felt sorry and ashamed, knowing it to have been his own fault.

Lily and he were often at Aunt Monie's house, 'East Side', still, though now more from duty than from choice. Morgan found the place dull after 'Rooksnest', though he was popular below stairs. He complained, 'The room gets lighter and darker, but the sun never throws his rays in as he does at home.' Aunt Monie would invite him to her bedroom to share her breakfast egg, a ritual he soon began to dread. He got angry, too, and was rude, when Monie insisted on talking about him to others in his presence, saying silly things, such as how he slept in the big bed and his mother in the small, and then telling him his shoelace was undone. 'Did you ever hear such conversation before visitors?' he fumed. 'I realised without being told,' he wrote later, 'that I was in the power of a failing old woman, who wanted to be kind but she was old and each visit she was older. How old was she? Born in the reign of George the Fourth, my mother thought. "More likely Edward the Fourth" cried I.'[1] Henrietta Synnot sometimes appeared on the scene, a sombre and silent figure, in a gown of plum-coloured silk, buttoned all the way down to the ground. As he realized later, she was present only because she had positively declared she would not be.

He sometimes came up against male cousins at 'East Side', and then his curls and his favoured status as 'The Important One' got him into trouble. A cousin, known as Blowdy Wags, once blew a whistle in his ear and he screamed and cried for hours. 'This horrid boy got me altogether on the hop, pointed his finger at me whenever we met, and was the first to demonstrate to me that I was a coward,' related Forster subsequently. His mother was very angry with Blowdy, but cross with Morgan also for being a cry-baby. 'I think you find Morgan more fascinating than Blowdy because the former is half a girl,' she wrote to Aunt Monie. '*I* wish he was more manly and that he did not cry quite so easily.' He sensed how the land lay, and when one day his mother said she believed that Jack, the lively third son, was his favourite in *The Swiss Family Robinson*, he was careful not to correct her, though in fact he preferred the priggish Ernest. Aunt Monie herself, having acquired her ideas before the Victorian

---

[1] *Marianne Thornton*, p. 269. Monie was born in 1797.

cult of manliness, was always indulgent towards Morgan's mollycoddle characteristics. A year or two later, by which time he was seven, he became a terrible liar, whereupon she was again all for gentle measures.

> I have not an idea what I should do if I had a child who indulged in that stile of talk, but I do think it ought to be stopped somehow, and I see no way of doing it except as Harty[1] said 'Scold him when he's good and not when he's naughty', but when in one of his loving affectionate moods if you were to talk to him as if he were about 20, and show him the evil consequences of saying what is not true for one thing and what will make mothers who have good children afraid of letting them play with a boy who says such shocking and such untrue things. You know I'm never for punishment which leads only to eye service as men pleasers [?], but I do quite think that if you could convince that precocious little head of his that it really grieved you, he would reform – but if not, with school looming in the distance, I suppose he must look forward to the time when you will be his refuge from the torments his fellows will bestow upon what they call cheek.

But Monie was by now very old – old enough, after all, for one of her early memories to be of seeing George III open Parliament[2] – and in 1887 she died. In her will she left £2,000 to Lily and £8,000 in trust for Morgan. The interest on the £8,000 was to be used for his maintenance and education and the capital paid over to him on his twenty-fifth birthday. This £8,000, he was to say later, represented his 'financial salvation', enabling him to travel and to write. As for Lily's legacy, she told Maimie she feared it might be a 'stumbling-block' to her.

> Even now everybody takes it as a thing of course that I should pay, pay, pay & I do feel a good deal annoyed sometimes when I hear and see them doing & buying things that I should never dream of. I think perhaps I am not naturally extravagant & I don't know many others in my family who take after me.

The 'pay, pay, pay' was no empty complaint on her part. She was always exceedingly generous to her relations, and often had to stint

---

[1] Mrs Ruthven Pym, née Harti Thornton; one of Monie's nieces.

[2] This was in 1804, the occasion when the unfortunate king began his speech, 'My Lords and Peacocks.' Forster prints a remarkable letter to himself about it from Aunt Monie in *Marianne Thornton*, pp. 282–3.

herself in consequence. It was a habit Forster was to learn from her.

Monie's legacy included more than money. Through her influence, Forster's childhood became a far more genteel and sheltered one than his mother's had been, or that of his Whichelo cousins. For one thing, Lily, by temperament and training, was exceedingly 'proper', whereas the Whichelos were distinctly free-and-easy. As time went on, she disapproved strongly of some of their friends, and there were family secrets she would never reveal to Forster even in his adult years. Further, she was quietly contending for social position. In Stevenage she was quick to resent slights from the 'County', and she positively refused to see her landlord when he called on her at the back door. On another occasion she was furious when he seemed to be bracketing her socially with the Franklyns.

Lily did not, in fact, become much involved in local society in Stevenage. The fiction was that it was the fault of their pony, whose limit in any direction was half a mile, after which he would back into the hedge or get himself crossways in the shafts. Among those friends that she had were the Rector, Mr Jowitt, and his wife, the parents of the future Lord Chancellor. Mr Jowitt was a genial, out-of-doors style of parson, who rode to hounds. When he preached on the text of Jacob and Esau – as he frequently did, not possessing a large stock of sermons – it became all too clear he thought God had made a great mistake in preferring Jacob to Esau, who was a huntsman and a perfectly spendid fellow. There were also some friends named Poston, who lived in a big house called 'Highfield'. Mr Poston was a retired business man, and the family lived in expensive style, with a billiard-room and their own coachman; Forster later defined them as 'country residents rather edging in to be society'. There were three Poston daughters and a son named Charlie. Lily was fond of Mrs Poston, and they used to go 'district-visiting' together; and when Forster was a little older he was often at 'Highfield' for tennis-parties and the like. Eventually, as we shall see, the family became in some respects a model for the Wilcoxes in *Howards End*.

For the most part, though, the Forsters depended for company on their own relations, and I must give an account of these. I will begin with the Whichelo aunts: Georgie,[1] Nellie[2] and Rosie.[3] Georgie was

---

[1] Georgiana Louisa Whichelo (1856–1917).
[2] Mary Eleanor Whichelo (1862–1959).
[3] Rosalie Whichelo (1866–1957).

the eldest. She was gay and slapdash, always covered in bows, and a little hysterical. Everything was larger than life for Georgie; once, after the dentist had given her gas, she convinced herself, and him too, that she was dead. She had a knack of succeeding at things without trying and would perform extraordinary feats at croquet, casually swiping at the ball on the run. She and Nellie were bosom friends and both had posts at the Royal School of Needlework in London. Nellie was 'artistic' and romantically handsome; she was a cool and 'deep' one, always with troops of male friends, but fundamentally independent and self-sufficient. She was quite distinguished in her profession and held the post of Chief Designer at the Royal School for fifty years, designing the embroidery on the royal robes for three coronations. Nellie and Georgie, then or a little later, rented a cottage in Whitstable together and used to go down there for rather rackety weekends; Lily and Morgan were sometimes asked down but were not told all that went on. It catches the flavour of Nellie and Georgie that, at the time of Edward VII's approaching coronation, Forster's uncle Horace, while spending a weekend at their cottage, found the royal robes stuffed under the bed. He put them on and strutted about in them, hoping he would not be caught and sent to the Tower.

It was Rosie who was Forster's favourite, however, as she was his mother's. Rosie was simple and affectionate, with a queer abrupt way of speaking, one of her favourite phrases being a brusque 'I don't agree with that!' She was chronically tactless and perpetually relating, choking with laughter, her latest dreadful *gaffe*. At the age of seventeen she had gone to France as a governess; this had left her in some confusion about her nationality, so that ever afterwards she spoke with a foreign accent. When Forster was a child she used to wear extraordinary bustles, on which he used to ride. He was always 'Morgie' to her. It was a name his mother allowed no one else to use, and indeed she wasn't altogether pleased at Rosie's using it.

Sometimes, too, one or other of the uncles would come to stay: either Horace,[1] who was a clerk in Coutts's bank, or John,[2] who had become an actor, or Phil,[3] who was in Sandeman's wine firm. Horace was a man's man, a great rifle-shooter, conscientious and rather

---

[1] Horace Winder Whichelo (1860–1942).
[2] John Graham Whichelo (1853–1912).
[3] Philip Mayle Whichelo (1864–1948).

dominating; Forster always disliked him, though Lily was fond of him; later he became a 'heavy' father and was well known in croquet-circles, giving his name to the 'Whichelo Wired Ball Tester'. Uncle Phil was more easygoing, a large, burly, bushy-moustached man, famous for his clumsiness and absent-mindedness. He was more 'ordinary' than the rest of the Whichelos and was felt to be slightly *déclassé*. It was rumoured he had married a maidservant, having got her into trouble; at all events there was a mystery about his wife and she was never produced. Harry,[1] the youngest, often came down too. He was a handsome and adventurous young man – though, according to Lily, exceedingly idle. He loved the open air and would tell Morgan tales about explorers and bucking broncos. Morgan greatly hero-worshipped Harry at the age of eight or nine and wrapped up in many layers of paper a Swiss coin Harry gave him when he left to join the Bechuanaland police.

Another frequent guest was Maimie. By now Maimie had re-married; and the story of this second marriage is worth a digression, as it exhibits the darker side of the Thornton clan-system and, I think, contributed to the plot of *Where Angels Fear to Tread*. Maimie had gone to Salisbury to keep house for her young half-brother Willie Preston who had recently been ordained, and while there she received a proposal of marriage from her music-teacher, an elderly gentleman of the name of Aylward. Much as she cherished Inglis's memory, she was inclined to accept, partly to rescue the old man from a bullying daughter. However, as soon as the news reached Monie's ears, a most appalling storm broke over Maimie's head. For Mr Aylward dropped his aitches, and he was in trade – he kept a music shop in the town. True, he had twice been mayor of Salisbury – and was, indeed, if the Thorntons and Forsters had realized it, quite a distinguished old man, well-known in musical circles and a friend of Parry and Joachim. It was no good; in the family's eyes he could only be a fortune-hunter, and Maimie must be deranged in her mind to entertain any such scheme. Monie daily despatched letters in every direction, while Morgan's Aunt Laura begged that Mr Aylward's name should not be mentioned in her presence; and as a result poor Maimie's mind did for a time become deranged, upon which Aunt Monie put the matter in the hands of lawyers and proposed to buy

---

[1] Harry Whichelo (1867–1904).

Mr Aylward off. At this point Lily, who loyally took the line that it was no one's affair but Maimie's, boldly went to see Mr Aylward. She found him perfectly honourable and quite bewildered by the whole clamour. ('My dear lady,' he told her later, 'they all thought I wanted to marry Mary[1] because of her money, but my dear lady she *has* no money.') It was plain Aunt Monie's activities could only produce scandal, and Lily induced her to call them off; in a little while Maimie recovered, and, having recovered, with great firmness of purpose she married her elderly suitor. It turned out a very happy marriage – though, as everyone had predicted, the County refused to call. The Bishop refused likewise, though he was an old friend of the Prestons, with the result that Willie gave up his curacy and left Salisbury. However, Maimie did not repine and busied herself taking care of her 'beggars'. Morgan, after his first introduction to her husband, told Maimie he was a 'nasty fat waddling old thing', which she received with peals of laughter. He never became fond of Mr Aylward but was always deeply attached to Maimie and spent some of his happiest days at their house.

Maimie had two half-sisters, Kate and Maggie Preston, who lived at Brightstone in the Isle of Wight. They were, if anything, even more pious, early-Victorian and unworldly than Maimie herself. Maggie was reckoned artistic and played the violin, very badly. Kate, the elder, was just a little simple in the head: she taught Sunday school and went to church service every day and otherwise did little but trim the lamps and write letters. The sisters were intensely genteel and once wrote to Lily complaining how the crickets kept them awake all night with their 'coarse voices'. Lily and Morgan, now and for many years, regularly went to stay with them. They formed part of that 'haze of elderly ladies' within which, as Forster said later, he had spent his childhood.

At 'Rooksnest' the most constant guest of all was Morgan's grandmother, Louisa Whichelo. She and Morgan adored each other. She was so shrewd, downright and gay and – as Forster put it later – was someone who knew how to live: no one, he said, aimed more at being commonplace or succeeded less. With her high lace cap, plump rosy cheeks, and snowy locks, she was an impressive figure. Forster used to collect her sayings: 'Lor' bless me dear, why notice anything?

---

[1] i.e. Maimie.

What *does* it all matter?' 'My sons are all quiet. They have need to be – they are married.' 'She looked at me as if I was Ananias and Sapphira rolled into one.' 'E— *said* she'd wash my laces for me. But what's the good of *saidd*ing?'

Guessing what lay in store for Morgan in a fatherless household, she formed an alliance with him against all old cats of women, with their gossip and sewing-parties. She always declared she detested women, and when he reminded her she was one herself, she replied, 'I'm not a woman, so I must be a mule.' Later, as a schoolboy, he wrote her a poem on this theme, which she relished greatly.

> *The Opinions of Mistress Louisa Whichelo,*
> *the Chastiser of her Sex*
> 'Here come the women! Out they walk
>   In groups of two and three
> To chatter forth their silly talk
>   O'er filthy cups of tea.
>
> 'They gulp the bread and butter down
>   With shovellings and pecks,
> They drop the jam upon their gown,
>   I hate the female sex.
>
> 'I hate their spaldering [?] wet feet;
>   Why will they trail and roam?
> If they must eat – well let them eat,
>   But let them eat at home.
>
> 'The proper place for womenkind
>   Is *not* to walk outside;
> But see the house is clean and mind
>   The men are well supplied.'
>
> So spake Louisa, free and fair,
>   Yet bowed not to her rule,
> For Heaven's providential care
>   Had classed her as a mule.

When Morgan was about eight, his mother engaged a tutor for him, an officious, snobbish Irishman named Hervey, a master at a private school in the village. Morgan's grandmother considered him 'a most uninteresting man' and thought Lily too much inclined to tell him all her business. To begin with, though, Morgan worshipped him. Some time after Mr Hervey's arrival, it was decided that

Morgan needed company of his own age, and it was arranged that his cousin Percy, son of Lily's brother Harcourt,[1] should come to live at 'Rooksnest' and share Mr Hervey's lessons. Percy was two years or so older than Morgan. For a while they too got on very well; then, or so Morgan thought, Percy grew tired of him, considering him too much of a baby, and began to tease and rebuff him, being abetted in this by Mr Hervey.

Morgan had a solace, however, and this was the garden-boys. His mother engaged a succession of these boys and gave them Wednesday afternoon off so that they could play with Morgan, this afternoon soon spreading over the rest of the week. Forster remembered their names all his life: William Taylor, Wray, Ansell, Bible, Field and Chalkley. William Taylor first appeared on the scene as the fishmonger's roundsman, when he used to give Morgan rides in his van (he and Forster renewed their friendship sixty years later). As for Wray, all that is recorded of him is Morgan's grandmother's crushing verdict: 'Wray is a silently impudent boy *I think* and awfully idle – but, as I said before, respectable and not swarming with vermin, which is the rule with country people I believe and thought no disgrace.' Morgan's greatest affection was for Ansell, his first and never-forgotten friend: 'a snub-nosed, pallid, even-tempered youth'. The two used to spend hours larking among the Franklyns' straw-stacks or swinging on the tree in the meadow and enjoyed lying in each other's arms, screaming and tickling. One year there was a stack close to the hedge, and Ansell built a straw penthouse between, with a tiny entrance for them to crawl through, and they kept house in it and stored apples there. Morgan insisted on improving Ansell's mind, as he did with everyone's, and managed to impart to him a good deal of *The Swiss Family Robinson*, though arithmetic was too much for Ansell. When asked how many chickens his mother had, he could only wave his arms – so that 'Ansell and the chickens' became a family saying. The two sided against Frankie Franklyn and the farm boys. They considered them too rough, though sometimes they allowed Frankie to play with them. It usually ended with their teasing him, till Frankie stumped off in a fury threatening to tell his father they were spoiling the ricks.

---

[1] Henry Harcourt Robert Whichelo (1851–94), the eldest of the Whichelos. He became a tea-taster but lost touch with his family and was believed by them to have 'gone to the bad'.

The Ansell period was an idyllic one for Morgan, and instinctively he clung to his happiness and was unwilling to grow up. He hated the end of *The Swiss Family Robinson,* in which the children are supposed to be ten years older, and he used to pretend to himself that Ernest and the others were magicked back into boys. He had a 'return-to-the-womb' daydream at this period, when he was about ten; he imagined that he had got inside a horse – it was a real horse, named Royalty, belonging to Major Sykes in Weymouth – and that it was wonderfully warm and exciting there.

Mr Hervey, who disapproved of his childish rompings with Ansell, began a campaign to make a regular, manly English boy of him, telling his mother it was high time Morgan learned cricket or some other sensible sport. Morgan resisted with great resourcefulness, and not much came of it. All the same, it was a foretaste of what lay ahead; the hour of school and schoolmasters was approaching, and soon he would look back on his afternoons with Ansell as a lost paradise.

*   *   *

There is one more piece of family history to be related. Lily had a brother Percy,[1] not so far mentioned in this narrative; and an interesting story attaches to him, one of some consequence for the whole family. One day, in the 1870s, the young Percy and his brother Harry were on a train, dressed in their white cricketing things, when they caught the eye of an elderly dundreary-whiskered military gentleman, General Guy Phillips, who got into conversation with them. Finding them friendly, the General pursued their acquaintance, and before long he was inviting them for weekends on his Thames houseboat. He took a particular fancy to Percy, who was a handsome and dashing young fellow, and eventually he more or less adopted him. It was a somewhat different adoption from Lily's by Marianne, and, looking back on it, Forster thought 'the implication was obvious.'

The General died in the late 1880s, and left Percy his whole fortune, which was considerable, including part of a *palazzo* in Venice. Percy now blossomed out as a man-about-town. He joined the Pelican Club, rubbed shoulders with Edward VII, and broke the bank at Monte Carlo. He had always been open-handed, so for the moment the Whichelos were all in funds, and his sisters and their mother moved into a spacious new house in Barons Court. One of the General's legacies was the houseboat, the *Doris*. It was a palatial

---

[1] Percy James Whichelo (1858–93).

affair, moored near Datchet, and for the next year or two the Whichelos, with troops of friends, collected there for uproarious weekends and holidays. Percy ('Pucky Ruby') would be there as host, dispensing champagne and punting and flirting in a fascinating manner. With him would be his favourite brother John, the gentle Adonis – 'queerer of all pitches' and 'collarer of wheezes' – whom all the girls were in love with; and at the weekends came Phil, with his ocarina and bad puns, and Harry, the cigar-smoking 'Pygmy'. Nellie did the housekeeping and looked after everyone's comfort. She spent the day ferrying visitors, drawing claret and icing champagne – helped spasmodically by Georgie, who drank more of the champagne than was good for her. There was fishing and boating and bathing; and occasionally discarded sweethearts of Percy's would come slowly rowing by the *Doris* for a sight of him, when he would be afflicted with blindness. At night the dining-room floor was littered with sleeping young men, while sounds of moonlight kissing drifted down from the foredeck; and when Horace arrived by the first train, roaring for eggs and bacon, he would be met by haggard faces and complaints of heads 'as large as houses' or with 'angry birds in them'.*

This was the Whichelos' moment of glory – regarded a little askance by Lily, who was caustic about Percy's grandeur and passion for first-class travel. The glory did not endure. Percy ran rapidly through the General's fortune and before long was deep in debt. His situation had grown very black, when one of his female cronies, an older woman with a 'past', offered to pay his debts, in return for marriage. He had always sworn he would kill himself rather than make a loveless marriage, but in desperation he agreed. The pair went for a gambling honeymoon at Dinard, and within a fortnight Percy was dead. No one ever knew the full story of his death; or at least, if Lily knew it, she never told Morgan.†

As a consequence of his ruin, Nellie, Georgie and their mother had to give up their grand house. However, to Lily's disapproval, they became great friends with Percy's widow 'Fair',[1] who subsequently married a doctor named Bert Kynsey, and bought a cottage near theirs in Whitstable. 'Fair', a gay, generous, voluble woman with hennaed hair, survived for many years and, with her cartwheel hats and her purple motorcar upholstered in mauve, was a glamorous figure to the Whichelo nephews. She died in poverty in the 1920s.

[1] Her real name was Clare Underwood.

3 School

Morgan became eleven in January 1890, and it was evidently high time for him to be at school. His mother investigated several prep schools and eventually settled upon one called Kent House, in Eastbourne. This was a small school – about thirty boys in all – and very much for the sons of gentry; it had been founded three years before and had just moved into new buildings overlooking the seafront. The headmaster, Mr C. P. Hutchinson, was a kindly, pious, ineffectual man, and being told that Morgan was delicate he promised to keep a special watch over him. Morgan's first encounter with him seemed of good omen: Mr Hutchinson, he wrote home, had had to hunt about 'for ever so long' to find a cane – to serve as a handle for Morgan's butterfly net. The other masters were also fussy but kind, and the music-master told him he had been very well taught. Having gone for a walk on the downs, Morgan decided that Eastbourne was 'a lovely place, beaten only by Bournemouth'. After his first week there was a reaction, and he wrote home dispiritedly:

> . . . I have been to the baths once and did not like or dislike them. When I got in a little way I could not get my breath. After a few seconds I did. Then they made me dip my head, which I did not like, and then a gentleman, not a swimming-master, belonging to the baths, took me by one hand, and led me along the baths. I think I will tell you I am not happy. What with the moving, and other things it makes me feel bad. I was not well yesterday (Sunday), so I had to finish my letter to-day. Please send another bible. Take care of kitty.

A visit from his mother soon cheered him, and in his next Sunday letter he told his 'bonne mère que je toute aime' that he was happier than ever and that Mr Bailey, who had chosen him to play in a trio at the end-of-term concert, said he was the only one who knew his part. Another Sunday, they had 'such a nice sermon'. It was about Society and how it led people astray; Mr Hervey ought to have heard it, he remarked disrespectfully.

As the term dragged on he began to grow desperately homesick, and his letters became more and more doleful. Here is one he wrote near the end of term – and a remarkably articulate, in some ways adult, letter it is.

> . . . We come home on Sat. 20th, am I to go London Bridge or Victoria from here? I should think Victoria, write and tell me . . . I have now heard that we go at all times of the day, according to the distance we have to go; do let me come by an early one, although I have not far to go. I shall only get tired and worrying by not coming sooner and seeing you . . . mind you meet me at Victoria, for I shall be in a terrible state of mind if I get there and find you not on the platform . . . Again I say take care you meet me. My cold is much better, nearly well, so is my cough. Write me a nice long letter, it is so nice to have them. You must think me rather odd to write about meeting me, but I feel so very nervous somehow. I don't know why it is, but perhaps it is excitement, but lately I have always been taking the dark side of things. I have never been like it before, but it is not at all nice. It is very much like despondency; I am afraid I shall miss the train in the morning, afraid you will not meet me, afraid I shall lose my tickets; these are instances of the kind of state of mind I am in; it is not so bad in the daytime as at night, then I cry a lot. I also have a kind of foreboding that something dreadful will happen before the holiday. I have not told you that in a grumbly mood, but because I think you could write a nice long comforting letter, you can always comfort me when I am at home, so why could you not comfort me with a letter? The worst of school is that you have nothing and nobody to love, if I only had somebody. . . .

The truth was, he had discovered during that first term what it was to be unpopular. The other boys, for some reason, cold-shouldered him; they called him 'Mousie' or jeered 'green-eye' or 'sucks' at him. He did everything he could think of to win acceptance. One day at the baths, he made a special bid for their admiration, by jumping in at the deep end, though he couldn't swim. When he came to the surface, the boys fished him out, chorusing excitedly 'Sir, sir,' and the headmaster hurried up angrily with a towel. Morgan felt himself a hero for once and greatly enjoyed the experience, repeating self-importantly, 'I did it by my own wish, sir; I jumped by my own wish. I fully trust them.' Next Thursday he offered to jump again. Why not sink down for hundreds of feet, he asked himself, if it makes you of consequence afterwards. But this time the boys were not interested; by taking their dare, he had lost his last claim on their interest. Ever afterwards he had a vivid remembrance of the baths, with their clammy, sour smell and the queer mingled moan, or roar, from them that seemed to follow one out into the street. The whole scene, in retrospect, became for him a parable on the theme of 'only connect'.

> The Baths were connected with the sea, and their contents were changed – at high tide said some of the boys, others said at low – but they were not connected in our minds. We had no idea that they were the vestibule of a physical glory. They led nowhere – in my case not even to popularity.[1]

In his class there was a boy called Henson whom nobody liked much, and Morgan announced to his mother that he was going to be kind to him. 'We are going for a walk this afternoon, so it will be a good time to begin.' In a week or two he reported that Henson was 'much happier' for his attentions, and now the other boys were nicer to him too. Henson turned out to be dreadfully ignorant of religion, a complete heathen in fact, and as Morgan in his daydreams was already an experienced missionary, he decided to take Henson's faith in hand. On Good Friday they both had colds and could not go to church, so he thought it a good moment to begin.

> I asked him if he knew why they went to church. He did not. Then I explained why, and told him about Easter and Ascension Day. I was so shocked. He did not know anything about Christ. He did not understand. He would say that Jesus could not have lived before if he had been born on earth at Xmas.[2]

Soon after this he lost interest in Henson, having fallen for a boy named Waldron, one of the seniors and said to be awfully strong. He showed off in front of Waldron and was snubbed for his pains, which mortified him bitterly, and a few days later he rushed up to Waldron and mumbled an apology, dashing off again before he could reply. A few weeks later, when his hero was playing with some friends in the library, Morgan crawled between his legs and Waldron nipped him

---

[1] Unpublished fragment, 'Swimming in the Sea'.
[2] Undated letter to his mother.

between them, exclaiming, 'How are the mighty fallen, Forster!' Morgan, who couldn't move, or at least pretended he couldn't, experienced great joy.

When Waldron left, Morgan tried transferring his affections to a boy who resembled him, but the boy was too young really, and his head was too large. Before long, however, he had attached himself to the headmaster's nephew. The headmaster had been as good as his word in looking after Morgan and had given him the run of his house, so that Morgan and the nephew used to play there most afternoons. The nephew, who was called Haworth, was a big, fair, good-tempered boy, and the two got on amicably, except when Morgan grew too importunate for Haworth's friendship. For years afterwards he continued to think about Haworth, picturing both him and Waldron not as prep-school boys but as clean-shaven young men.

All these passions, of course, were the commonest kind of prep-school experience; but later that year, when Morgan and Lily were in Bournemouth, he experienced a more significant moment of augury. He was looking out of the sitting-room window at the deserted road and thought, 'It all depends upon whether a man or a woman first passes.' From the right there came a man with a brown moustache, and he felt much relieved.

He had had no acquaintance with 'smut' till he came to Kent House, so he was rather mystified when he heard it in the dormitories. Not that so very much was talked, but he learned that there were queer things in the Bible; and an older, but virtuous, boy told him how he had seen a woman wringing out her bathing-drawers, and what a wonderful sight it had been, only Forster wouldn't understand – as indeed he didn't. He also learned the word 'cock' from the other boys. One of them said, 'Have you seen Forster's cock? A beastly little brown thing,' which depressed him. His own word for his penis up till now had been his 'dirty', and the fact is revealing. When, as a young child, he had discovered masturbation and announced the fact to his mother, she told him it was 'dirty'. She did not say it in an alarmist way, but he sensed her anxiety, and henceforth 'help me to get rid of the dirty trick' figured in his prayers. He also began to think of his penis as unique and as some kind of punishment – though, inconsistently, he used to look for the 'dirties' in Smith's *Classical Dictionary* and was annoyed when, in Kingsley's *Heroes*, they were covered up with drapery. He told his mother about this too, and she reproved him but did not take the books away.

Lily's whole attitude to sex was that it was a dreadful subject and to be thought of as little as possible. She made no attempt at any stage to tell Morgan the 'facts of life'. During his first term at Kent House he formulated his own theory of them, which was that 'lying together' meant that a man placed his stomach against a woman's and it was a crisis when he warmed her; and on his return for the holidays, he told his mother he knew what 'committing adultery' meant. She looked worried, and replied, 'So you understand now how dreadful it would be to mention it, especially if a gentleman was there.' For some years this remained more or less the total of his knowledge of the facts of life. Indeed he said later that it was not till he was thirty, by which time he had published three novels, that he altogether understood how copulation took place.

Thus it was with extreme incomprehension that, during his second term at Kent House, he figured in a sexual drama. It is an interesting story and has some significance, I think, for his later development. One afternoon, in midwinter, he was sent for a walk on the downs, and on reaching the summit he came on a middle-aged man, in a deerstalker hat and knickerbockers, urinating in full view. When the man had finished, he spoke to Morgan and made him come and sit on his mackintosh, near some gorse-bushes, and after a moment or two of conversation he undid his own flies and told Morgan to play with his penis. Morgan obeyed, being more puzzled than alarmed – though he was startled by the sight of the inflamed tip of the penis and was further astonished when he saw some white drops trickling out. This having taken place, the man quickly lost interest; he asked Morgan where he lived, and offered him a shilling, and when Morgan refused it, he let him go without more ado. As Morgan returned down the hill, he began to feel upset, and thought how, if he had accepted the shilling, he would have hurled it into the snow. Next day he wrote obscurely to his mother about the incident.

His letter, naturally, caused consternation. Lily rushed off to consult Mrs Jowitt and then wrote to Morgan, saying he must report the affair, and enclosing a note to Mr Hutchinson. She promised to come down herself at the weekend; though, as she said, 'it was such a dreadful thing that she could not speak to Mr H. about it unless she were positively forced to.'

Mr Hutchinson, when Morgan duly went to see him, was solemn and most fearfully embarrassed. He seemed to imply, too, that Morgan was somehow to blame and spoke darkly about 'mortal sin'. However, by now, Morgan was in, as he later describes it, a 'hard and important' mood and was enjoying the limelight. 'You know your bowels, sir?' he asked. Mr Hutchinson said he did. 'Well, this man's bowels were diseased'; and he went on to give details. This floored poor Mr Hutchinson. Nevertheless, as they walked down to the police station he made a further attempt to draw a moral from the occasion, remarking mysteriously, 'We know from the Bible about certain things . . . There is the story of Adam and Eve . . . Boys may do great harm to themselves . . . etc.' He asked Morgan if he would be able to recognize the man. All for vengeance, Morgan said yes, he was sure he would; at which the headmaster murmured about the danger of accusing the innocent. 'But we shall know him, sir, by his disease,' said Morgan. Mr Hutchinson was silent.

Morgan made an entry in his diary ≪Nothing≫, to remind himself that there had been something, and for a time he kept an eye out for men in deerstalker caps, but the stranger was never caught, and the excitement died down. When his mother finally came down later that term, she told him again what a fearful thing it had been for her to have to write to Mr Hutchinson on such a subject. She also asked him if he had cured himself of his 'dirty trick'. He said, with honesty, that he hadn't, but this seemed to distress her, so he decided he would never be so frank again. 'So ended my last chance of a confidant,' he reflected later. This first sex-encounter had taught him nothing he could understand, and it soon sank out of his daily thoughts; but as a pattern of panic and cross-purposes it evidently left a lasting impression on him. One senses that he returned to the incident, and his own reactions during it, when writing *A Passage to India*, and that it became a model for Adela's vengeful and confused behaviour after she imagines herself molested by Aziz.

The rest of his time at Kent House, so far as one can tell, passed uneventfully. He became more successful in acquiring friends (among them William Beveridge, the future author of the Beveridge Report), and in his Christmas exams for 1892 he came out top of his form in classics, French and scripture. He left in the following spring, and it was planned that he should go to Uppingham in the autumn. Meanwhile he was sent to fill up the summer term as a weekly

boarder at Mr Seager's local school, 'The Grange' – the one at which
his old tutor, Mr Hervey, had been a master.

'The Grange' was a school of some reputation, run on Arnoldian
principles, but Morgan's stay there was brief and disastrous. Almost
at once, he was writing to report trouble, though for the moment in a
vein of school-story valour.

> Dear Mother,
>   I got your letter and my hat to day. I am getting on very well
> but I actually have very certain prospects of a fight! Two of the
> boys in my dormitory last night kept on taking my pillow, and
> wetting my clothes; so I bore it for a long time and then when they
> began hitting me and hurting my face, I thought 'no more of this'
> and I slapped their faces. So they say they will take it out on me
> this evening. Let them do it!, but I shan't go at them with my
> fists closed till they do the same to me. And I believe the reason of
> this is that I did not bring back any grub on Sunday. I don't feel
> at all worried about it, but I am threatened with all the school
> setting on to me to morrow. I rather hope they do, and I don't
> intend to stand still and be bullied; and perhaps I shall get on
> better afterwards . . .

He could not sustain the bravado, and within a few days he was in
great straits. Indeed, he sounded so desperate, his mother promised
to come to his rescue; and by the time her letter arrived he had
reached the point of hysteria, scrawling on the flap of his reply: 'Do,
do come at 3.30. I must talk to you. I am in a dreadful muddle, yet I
can't tell you by letter. Don't mention this to Mr Seager. Do come I
will explain.' She found him in tears and distraught and could get
very little out of him: only that, as well as bullying him, the boys
talked wicked smut. One of the things they said was 'too dreadful to
be repeated'[1] – a remark she passed on to the headmaster. The boys
had tried to make him say this shocking thing too, and when he
refused, one of them had told him, 'When we get you to Uppingham
we will make you say it.' His mother reassured him as best she could
and once again went to the Jowitts for advice. But meanwhile she
received an even more despairing appeal.

> Why have you not come, what are you going to do? Do write and
> tell me or come and see me directly. I will write to morrow if I do

---

[1] The obscenity which had upset him so much was the rhyme:
        Little Robin Redbreast sat upon a pole [or po];
        He wagged his tail and whitewashed the pole.

not hear or see you before. I did not understand what you were
going to do when you went. Do write and see me. If you tell about
the boys *do do* take me away or I shall be worse off than I am now.
I was so muddled and excited that I did not know what you meant
to do. I heard something about going home and locking up the
house and walking down. Didn't you do it or wouldn't they let
you see me? O what is going to happen? I felt I could not say
anything when you came, I feel utterly wretched, I would like to
come away. Every one is against me except Squire and Sworder.
Oh what am I to do? . . .

There was nothing for it but to withdraw him from the school, and
he returned to 'Rooksnest' in floods of tears. His beloved Maimie was
there, and between them the two women soon comforted him; but
he could tell from his mother's manner that she was ashamed of him
as a cry-baby. It had been impressed on him when he went to 'The
Grange' that it was a school for the sons of gentlemen, and all
through his troubles there the refrain ran through his mind: 'If they
were not the sons of gentlemen they would not be so unkind. If only
I was at the Grammar School!'

Lily was now faced with a problem, or rather with two problems
combined. For it was plain that Morgan was not robust enough for
Uppingham. And it so happened that they would also soon have to
turn out of 'Rooksnest', since their landlord – partly owing to Lily's
indecision – was refusing to renew their lease. Her mother, who
loved the place, received this news mournfully: 'Never shall we see
such a sweet place. They say here "Rubbish". "Be kind enough to
find one", *I* say.' She sent Lily strict injunctions not to be soft with
the landlord: 'Recollect . . . not one blind or roller *to be left* unless they
are *bought*. I will tear them to pieces before they shall reap the
benefit of anything I have done.'

After consulting with various friends, Lily at length arrived at a
plan. This was that they should move to Tonbridge, where Morgan
might go to Tonbridge School as a dayboy. There was special
financial advantage in this, in that, under an ancient statute, the
school provided education at low fees to boys living within ten miles
of Tonbridge church. With the rise of Tonbridge as a public school,
other parents – retired army people and the like – had had the same
notion, and the streets round the school were lined with their villas.
Morgan was found lodgings in Tonbridge while Lily searched for a
house, and some time during his first term they moved into

'Dryhurst', in Dry Hill Park Road. It was not a very attractive house, but it had a fine long sloping garden, abutting on a church which Morgan's grandmother named 'the Back Kitchen'.

The choice of Tonbridge School was a sensible but ill-fated one, and Forster's first two years or so there were wretched, probably the most unhappy in his life. He was reticent about the details always, and no doubt he tried to forget them; though he revenged himself for his sufferings – not that this is the best description of his motive – in his scathing portrait of Sawston School in *The Longest Journey*. The picture sticks closely to the facts of Tonbridge. Originally a small and ancient grammar school, founded in the sixteenth century and run by the Skinners' Company, Tonbridge, like many foundations of the same kind, had turned itself into a public school in the mid-nineteenth century, changing from what was mainly a day-school for children of local tradesmen into a boarding-school for the sons of business and professional people. It had its first period of expansion in the 1850s and 60s and had entered upon a second very rapid one a year or two before Forster's arrival, with the coming of a new headmaster. This new head, the Rev. 'Joey' Wood, DD, was a great 'thruster', expert at wooing socially-desirable parents. He was a splendid showman, with the sort of beaky-nosed, beetling-eyebrowed countenance that petrifies small boys, though in fact he was kindly enough. He would ride about Tonbridge on a white horse and was said to keep a mistress in the town, which gave rise to much gossip. During his eight years at Tonbridge the school boomed and new buildings went up right and left: an assembly hall with an organ, a tower with a carriage-way beneath, a rackets court and a swimming bath. Much attention was also paid to *esprit de corps*: a Volunteer Rifle Corps was formed; the boys' old academical caps were replaced by caps with house-colours; and the dayboys were organized into two 'houses', so as to bring them into line with the boarders. The school even acquired a new anthem, written by the wife of one of the staff. The chorus, in Kiplingesque tones, ran:

> Here shall Tonbridge flourish, here shall
>   manhood be,
> Serving God and country, ruling land and
>   sea . . .

'Joey' Wood was fond of remarking in his sermons on the truths contained in the school anthem, particularly the lines:

> Choose we for life's battle harp or sword or
> pen;
> Perish every laggard, let us all be men.

He would say, according to Forster, that first we must choose a profession, and secondly, having chosen, we must *stick*.

> The sword is the noblest choice, because it might lead to the death of a fellow-creature; still, those boys (he always called them 'bies') who felt unequal to murder had other opportunities reserved to them. Only, 'bies' must stick. They must stick even if it was a case of harps. How depressed I used to feel! The pen was perhaps the best of the three evils presented, but I always imagined it as a quill, to whose squeaks I should be chained eternally. One was clearly going to be a prisoner throughout life's battles – unless, indeed, one had the courage to become a laggard or that equally contemptible creature the 'bi' who didn't know his own mind.[1]

The school at the time of Forster's arrival was a hard, jostling, athletics-ridden place. There was not much violent bullying in the school but a good deal of kicking and calling of names in corridors; by convention senior boys were allowed to kick the 'novi' or new boys, and a local 'novus' learned to 'dodge like hell'. The staff encouraged inter-house rivalry, and boys who strayed into the wrong house would get manhandled and ducked in cold baths, whilst the boarders united in despising the dayboys. The social inferiority of dayboys extended to their parents, the staff tending to treat them with condescension.

It is not plain how much Forster was physically bullied at the school. He must have been so to some extent, for one of his school-mates, when questioned about him in the 1950s, said 'Forster? The writer? Yes, I remember him. A little cissy. We took it out of him, I can tell you.' All that Forster himself would ever say, dismissively, was that he was frightened of the other boys and they pelted him with chestnuts. (In fact he escaped some of the rough-and-tumble of the school, for he was excused games on health grounds and allowed to go bicycling instead – an enlightened gesture at that time for a public school.) Whatever the truth about his miseries, no doubt what wounded him most was the general atmosphere of unkindness.

---

[1] 'Literature or Life? Henry W. Nevinson; the Boy who never Stuck', *New Leader*, 2 October 1925.

His feelings were those he voiced later through Rickie Elliot: 'Physical pain doesn't hurt – at least not what I call hurt – if a man hits you by accident or in play. But just a little tap, when you know it comes from hatred, is too terrible.' His experience left him with a horror of gangs; and he said afterwards that when he was bullied, as he had been at school, he recovered his balance best by mentally resolving the gang back into individuals.

He joined the classics side, and this still meant, at that period, a weekly diet of nineteen hours of classics, with not all that much else besides – at most a modicum of French and mathematics and a very little history and geography. During his early days at school, depression made him stupid and torpid, and indeed, throughout his time there, only one master ever captured his imagination. This was Isaac Smedley,[1] the original of 'Mr Jackson' in *The Longest Journey*. Smedley was hopeless at keeping order, and moreover was a militant agnostic, neither of which traits went down well with the school or with parents; but boys who bothered to attend to him found him a brilliant teacher. He insisted that the classics were literature, to be enjoyed in the same way as English literature – which he loved and could quote from endlessly. Also he made one realize, said Forster, that Plato and Virgil were men who had actually lived and were writing for other living men.

Forster in his middle teens was no longer the vivid, imperious spoilt darling of his childhood. He had become muted and subfusc, timid and buttoned-up in manner, with a queer pedantic trick of speech. Physically he was unathletic, with sloping shoulders and a habit of casting his eyes down – the very model of what a healthy English schoolboy was not supposed to be. In his interests he was old for his age. He read very widely, was becoming an excellent pianist and was knowledgeable about church-architecture. In his demure way, too, he was by now a sharp-eyed observer, with an adult sureness in judging character.

He was very much a 'home' boy, out of his element at school. His schoolmates, on the principle of contraries, called him 'Morgan the Freebooter' and regarded him as rather a 'muff'. When one of them, a boy named A. M. Morley, asked him what his initials were, he

---

[1] Smedley went shortly afterwards to Westminster School, where many legends survive of his erudite vagueness and old-fashioned ways. He died in 1934.

answered 'E.M. – Emm – sounds rather girlish, doesn't it?' Morley, in later years, was very much surprised, as other of his boyhood friends were, to find his books so vigorous.

His demureness was his cover to the world, and safe from the eyes of his schoolmates he could still be excitable and skittery. Indeed, at home, he was forever falling about and breaking things. Once when Uncle Horace and his future wife were visiting, Morgan was sent to fetch the tea-things and managed to drop so many *en route* that the whole place was in confusion. Uncle Horace really considered him almost an imbecile, and none of Forster's uncles ever believed he would get anywhere in the world. The awkwardness and helplessness were, one may guess, a clue to his heart, and secretly he was tempted, like his Rickie Elliot, to make 'impossible' gestures; he was dying, like the hero of an unfinished story of his,* to abandon all shame and roll on the floor *demanding* to be loved. His mother, seeing him so vulnerable, coddled him all the more and centred her life upon him, and for both of them it became an all-embracing relationship. From time to time, unknown to Morgan, she received proposals of marriage, one of them from a housemaster at the school, but she rejected them with violence.

Incited by Ruskin, Morgan persuaded his mother, in the April of 1895, to come with him on a tour of Normandy churches; it was the first of many such occasions on which they would be fellow-tourists. He planned the tour scientifically, and Lily accompanied him with cheerfulness up church-towers and through innumerable Gothic aisles and cloisters, only becoming restive when, as tended to happen, he took charge of the map and got them lost. He kept a detailed travel-journal, and there are hints in it already of his future manner – as in what he wrote about the Bayeux tapestry, which he found, not moth-eaten and indecipherable as he had imagined, but deliciously funny.

> . . . No. 17 is perhaps the best. Harold, of gigantic size, is engaged in fishing Normans out of a quicksand. He has one on his back like a satchel & is pulling out another. Horses, coloured blue and red, are sinking in all directions. Mont St Michel is represented as ⌒.
> Water ≋ . A town 👁 with men at the top & the town arms displayed, looking like the bottom of a filter. 26. Funeral of King Edward at Westminster. A large procession is endeavouring to get

into a church the size of a match box. In the picture after the
funeral he dies, which seems out of place. 31. Harold on his throne.
He appears to be sitting on pins. 32. The comet. The people are
greatly terrified. The comet is close on them, so no wonder. 53.
Battle of Hastings. Arms & legs are falling in all directions. Heads,
sliced off from their bodies, strew the ground. 57. Death of Harold.
He falls from his horse like a long yellow serpent. There are 58
pictures in all, & Matilda has been so kind as to write the title of
each on the top, but as they are in Latin, & in very odd shaped
letters, they were not much help.

Lily and he also enjoyed the game of nicknaming and dissecting their
fellow-travellers, a pastime that would always be a great standby for
them. They were severe on some 'awful' Englishmen and 'awfully
showing off English girls' at their hotel at Mont St Michel and
entertained themselves with the fortunes of a nice old French lady,
with a bland smile and insatiable appetite. She was suffering from
cathedral-madness and kept praising the arches, 'such beautiful
arches'! But of this disease, Morgan noted, 'I also have a touch.'

If his Whichelo relations were pessimistic about his future, his
Aunt Laura Forster[1] was beginning to form schemes and ambitions
for him. Every summer and New Year, he and Lily would go and
stay with Laura in Surrey. She lived with a paid companion, Agnes
Hill, but to safeguard the proprieties, now that Morgan had entered
his teens, Miss Hill was sent on holiday during his visits. It was his
Aunt Laura who provided the County element in Forster's early
experience, and I must digress for a little to describe her.

Having seen most of her brothers and sisters into their early
graves, she had, in 1878, settled in that house at Abinger which her
brother Eddie, Morgan's father, had built for her. Here for twenty
years, until invalidism overtook her, she lived a busy County
existence, visiting extensively, founding a local branch of the
Liberal Unionists, setting up a Mission Room, and establishing
classes in leather-work for the youth of the village. She was a tall,
Roman-nosed, autocratic woman, with a fighting quality which made
her welcome physical danger. In the village she carried much
weight, and the village children would touch their hats or curtsy as
her carriage passed. She had a passion for 'exerting her influence', and
she counted various famous literary figures, men like Leslie Stephen

[1] My account is based on an unpublished memoir, 'West Hackhurst: a
Country Ramble', begun by Forster in 1943.

and George Meredith and Sir G. O. Trevelyan, among her acquaintance – though, in Forster's view, she made out she knew them better than she did. She was a good organizer, and eventually the leatherwork classes turned into a local industry, supplying cigar-cases, blotters, chair-seats and the like all over Surrey.

The Mission Room turned out less successfully – and indeed, in a sense, it was to prove her downfall. The parish church of Abinger lay some two miles away from Abinger Hatch, where she lived, so in 1895 she persuaded Lord Farrer to build a Mission Room to serve her part of the parish. The Rector grudgingly agreed, and promised to supply a curate, while she herself took charge of the choir. All went well for a year or two; but then the Rector, who had bided his time, announced he could no longer afford a curate and the services must cease. Letters flew, there were scenes; and finally, one fatal day, Laura offered to run the Mission Room herself, engaging curates week by week. To this the Rector agreed, cunningly reserving the right to approve the curates. Sundays henceforth became a nightmare to Laura. The Rector could never be found to approve the curates, and the curates themselves would prove crazed or get lost on the way. Sometimes the services had to be taken by a layman, and on one or two occasions Forster officiated himself. (He could remember giving the Absolution, and reading a lesson with the word 'piss' in it.) Laura's battle with the Rector lasted several years, and soon afterwards, probably in part as a result, she took to her bed. It was a tactical withdrawal of the Florence Nightingale type, and she remained in bed, vigorously conducting her affairs from there, for the rest of her life.

The true centre of her interest, even before this, had been her house, round which she had woven all sorts of sentimental tradition. There had been a tulip-tree[1] at Battersea Rise, so a tulip-tree must be planted at West Hackhurst; her uncle the Archdeacon[2] had loved jasmine, so she must take some indoors on his birthday anniversary. All the upstairs rooms (following the pattern of her friend Hope Wedgwood's[3] much larger house in the Potteries) were labelled

---

[1] It is mentioned many times in *Marianne Thornton*. The young Marianne told her brothers and sisters that Napoleon intended to cut it down.

[2] James Forster, her father's brother.

[3] Hope Elizabeth Wedgwood (1844–19?), who married a cousin, Godfrey Wedgwood, the head of the Wedgwood firm.

with the names of places she had loved: 'Stisted', 'Battersea Rise', 'Penn', 'Chelsea', 'Clapham', etc. It infuriated Lily, who would ask why she couldn't say 'Aunt Laura's bedroom', 'big spare-room' etc. and have done with it. Lily was always rather critical of Laura and maintained a reserve with her, remembering that Laura had opposed her marriage. As for Forster, he liked and respected his aunt, though he spotted her weaknesses, and though, too, he felt he never stood up for himself in her house. Even when he inherited West Hackhurst, in the 1920s, he felt an eternal nephew there.

By the time he had reached the sixth form at Tonbridge, Aunt Laura was giving much thought to his career. She took it for granted that he must go to Cambridge, as his Forster uncles had done; and she made enquiries from her friends the Darwins as to the best college. The choice fell on King's; and at Christmas 1896 he sat the scholarship examination at King's, and, though he failed to win an award,[1] he secured a place at the College. As regards a career, it was vaguely understood that he might become a schoolmaster. He told his aunt he would like this, 'if he could teach big enough boys not to worry him'.

By now the miseries of his early days at Tonbridge belonged to the past, and he had begun, in a quiet way, to make himself felt in the school. He possessed a wider range of ideas than most boys; and in his last year or so he acquired a little coterie, among whom he enjoyed a reputation as a talker. Three of his friends, Howard MacMunn,[2] Sydney Worters and Francis Fulford,[3] were destined, like him, for Cambridge. He was most intimate with Fulford, a very earnest boy whom his friends all backed to become a bishop.

He began, also, to have some academic success. In his last year at school he won prizes both for a Latin poem (a patriotic effusion entitled 'Trafalgar') and for an English essay, on 'The influence of climate and physical conditions upon national character', and he had

---

[1] In November 1897 he was, after all, awarded an Exhibition of £40 for two years, presumably on the strength of his performance in the 'Previous examination' (or 'Little-go').

[2] See p. 157 and footnote.

[3] Francis Woodbury Fulford (1879–1941). His father was Dean of Clare College, and Forster stayed at their house in Cambridge before he joined the university. Francis Fulford became a country clergyman and in 1911 published a monograph on Kierkegaard.

to read extracts to the assembled school on 'Skinners' Day'.[1] The English essay, an excellent pastiche of Ruskin, shows him profiting from his Normandy tour:

> ... In the north the builder heaved from the mountain side masses of rock, and with them he made his church, huge, rough, irregular like one of his own cliffs, with great dark entrances like the caverns that yawned in the face of the hills. And he would not do without ornament, but hastily struck out from rough blocks fantastic forms and grotesque shapes, such as we may see today in the churches of Rouen and the houses of Lisieux, not the creation of a diseased mind, like the gods of India, but the creations of a new and vigorous life ...

From the conventional point of view he had 'made good' at Tonbridge. None the less, he was always to bear a grudge against his schooldays.[2] Writing many years afterwards, in a review of some 'old-school' memoirs,[3] he said:

> If the impossible ever happens and I am asked to help break up a school what I shall say is this: 'Ladies and gentlemen, boys and bies. School was the unhappiest time of my life, and the worst trick it ever played me was to pretend that it was the world in miniature. For it hindered me from discovering how lovely and delightful and kind the world can be, and how much of it is intelligible. From this platform of middle age, this throne of experience, this altar of wisdom, this scaffold of character, this beacon of hope, this threshold of decay, my last words to you are: There's a better time coming.'

---

[1] Day of the annual visitation of the school governors, the Court of the Skinners' Company.

[2] Characteristically, on the only group-photograph of the school he preserved, he has ringed the head of one of the masters, with an accusing legend: 'Mr Watson, who doubted my word in the 1880s.' This referred to some dispute about the possession of a book.

[3] 'Breaking Up', *Spectator*, 28 July 1933.

4 Cambridge

Forster entered a Cambridge very different from what it is now – still, perhaps not too hard to reconstruct. Nowhere outside England has there been an institution like Victorian Oxford and Cambridge – that Cockaigne or 'great good place' for the sons of the professional middle classes. For good or evil it gave a special stamp to their careers, prolonging boyhood and opening fresh vistas – of friendship, of intellectual self-fulfilment, of social climbing – at an age when for most of their contemporaries the choices had been made. It was common for young men to fall in love with Oxford and Cambridge, and some did so tragically, living ever afterwards a 'scholar-gypsy' existence.

Forster fell in love with Cambridge himself, though not in any tragic sense; but then, he was already, in some ways, a very wise young man when he arrived there. It was not an awestruck provincial who entered the gateway of King's, and he would not have been over-impressed by the picture-book setting. (For one thing – shall we say – he would not have mistaken the gateway for medieval.) None the less, Cambridge transformed him, and he always acknowledged the debt. He 'found himself' there, or at least began this process; and his Cambridge acquaintance widened, and cushioned, his existence ever afterwards. Though his feelings towards Cambridge fluctuated later, the place always had a precise significance for him; it was the place where things were valued for what they were in themselves, not for what use you could make of them. Too much has been made of the influence of G. E. Moore on him, for he never read Moore; but the epigraph to Moore's *Principia Ethica*, 'Everything is what it is, and not another thing,'[1] hits off his own idea of the Cambridge 'truth'.

[1] A quotation from Bishop Butler.

And apart from the Cambridge truth, there was, I think, a Cambridge prejudice which he acquired – namely, that it was scholars and civil servants, not business men, who ran Britain. The effects of the Cambridge reforms of the nineteenth century had been to strengthen rather than weaken this assumption. The underlying aim of the reformers had been to increase the prestige of the professions; they were casting professional men for the role of the new gentlemen of England, the successors to the landed aristocracy; and the complement of this was a low view of 'business'. Forster was never a eulogist of the professional classes, indeed he habitually regarded doctors and schoolmasters and clergymen with suspicion, as likely to be bullies or bores, but he imbibed the Cambridge attitude to business. It was one he would re-examine, in an effort of self-criticism, in *Howards End*.

Aunt Laura had busied herself, and he came with the entrée to various Cambridge households: the Frank Darwins,[1] the Horace Darwins,[2] some old family friends called Grant,[3] and Leslie Stephen's Quaker sister Caroline. During his first term or two he saw a good deal of the Darwins, either at Newnham Grange or one of the other Darwin households off the Huntingdon Road. He was not quite sure how comfortable he felt among them: during a walk, he heard one of the Darwin girls whisper loudly to her mother: 'What do you think of him?' All through life he was to be put out by Darwin self-assurance[4] – though Aunt Laura would say that the Darwins did not pretend to manners; 'It is their kindheartedness that gets them through life.'

In general he lived a quiet, what he called a 'puddling', existence during his first year in Cambridge. He worked, but not with much confidence, went for bicycle rides, attended Chapel, and drank coffee and played mild card-games with friends after Hall. He was in lodgings and partly for this reason did not have a wide circle of

---

[1] Francis Darwin (1848–1925), son of Charles Darwin. He wrote a *Life and Letters* of his father.

[2] Horace Darwin (1851–1928), son of Charles Darwin, and founder of the Cambridge Scientific Instrument Company. He married Lily's erstwhile friend Ida Farrer.

[3] Descendants of Charles Grant (1746–1823), director of the East India Company and friend of Henry Thornton.

[4] I myself remember him, in 1953, coming back from a party, vexed at having spent so much effort at ingratiating himself with Gwen Raverat (daughter of George Darwin), and being brought up short by 'a great blank face'. It was not exactly snubbing, he said.

friends. Altogether, though not positively lonely, he felt rather out of
things – 'stupefied' he called it later. He would gaze out of the window
at the other undergraduates, wondering if he looked like them or if
his clothes were right. He told his mother he was looking for more
friends, but it was uphill work. 'One never seems to get to know the
nice people, though there are plenty of them.'

Meanwhile, he kept up with school and its gossip and contributed
to the school magazine, *The Tonbridgian*. During the Easter vacation
he went with his mother and aunts to see Albert Chevalier at the
music-hall, and he sent *The Tonbridgian* an account of it, in fourth-
form Latin. (A month or two before, *Punch* had published a dog-
Latin review of the Beerbohm Tree *Julius Caesar*, by 'Binkins Minor',
and Forster's effort took the form of an answer to Binkins.) '*Spero hoc
non erit vulgare*' [I hope this isn't going to be vulgar] it reports his
mother as saying, when they reached 'Knocked 'em in the Old Kent
Road'. '*Sed ut omnes diximus, Cur in terra venisti si tam elegans et
superior es?*' [But as we all said, 'Why on earth did you come if you
are so particular?'] To his gratification, this effort was reprinted next
month in *The Public School Magazine*.

At King's itself his closest acquaintance was a medical student
called Mollison, later to become a famous surgeon.[1] 'A very intelligent
but perhaps not very profound man,' he said of Mollison later. They
were very friendly for a time; but by the end of the year – he already
had much deliberateness in managing relationships – Forster was
planning to 'slide away' from so much intimacy. 'It will be difficult',
he told his mother:

> for I think that in a certain way and under certain circumstances
> he likes me, or he would not so often come to see me. I never go to
> see him unless he asks me, & as this plan suits him I don't think
> there is much hope of another.

In the main, though, he stuck to the company of his schoolfriends
MacMunn and Worters, neither of whom was at King's. During his
second term, Worters insisted on his learning golf. 'Seems a queer
game,' Forster noted in his diary.

---

[1] William Mayhew Mollison (1878–1967), described in the *British Medical
Journal*, at his death, as 'the last and perhaps the greatest of the old school of
otolaryngologists which brought so great a lustre to English medicine in the
years between the two world wars'.

> 28 *Jan.* 1898. Played golf for the first time, with Worters. Did 9 holes in 133. Think however I shall like it . . . 1 *Feb.* In aft. to golf with Hobson, played far worse than ever before. My cleek is a little bent [beast?] . . . 3 *Feb.* My score was worse than ever before: 148, but about 40 were bosses wh. I hadn't counted before . . . Like golf very much.

One way and another – though indeed this was the style of the period – he seems to have spent an enormous amount of time upon games. There would be picquet or bagatelle with Mollison; evenings at the Fulfords playing Clumps, Up Jenkins or 'a game of passing a penny down, like the Greek torch race'; and, at Darwin tea parties, puff-billiards and a 'good game with penny and tennis ball', also a 'good one with circular board and bellows'. He made one attempt to row, and – he recalled later[1] – since no one made any remark on his performance, he thought to himself: 'This is going well. Very good.' He was never allowed into a boat again and discovered that neither the coach nor the crew had thought it worth while to instruct him, so much did they consider his rowing 'beyond human aid'.

His schoolmate Worters eventually proved a nuisance, dropping in uninvited at all hours. 'All this struggling for friends is very unbecoming,' Forster remarked to his mother; 'but I suppose all go through it. I often think of your precept, "don't rush into everybody's arms, but be very pleasant to all".'

Both MacMunn and Worters were very churchy young men, and Forster, though he no longer dreamed of converting the natives of New Guinea, thought of himself as a Christian and attended Chapel regularly. He was bad at getting up and so couldn't manage morning service, but luckily King's, a notoriously unzealous college, had recently abolished compulsory Chapel. Those who failed to attend had to sign a book in the porter's lodge before 8 a.m., so every morning a sleepy mob of undergraduates, Forster among them, converged on the lodge in pyjamas and dressing-gowns. It was a system which 'proved the undoing of many an earnest child',[2] said Forster later.

He had, according to his own description, come up to Cambridge 'immature, uninteresting, and unphilosophic, but earnestly disposed', and in a little while he began to warm to the atmosphere. In many ways King's was the ideal place for him. The College had only

---

[1] In conversation with Peter Scott, in 1969.
[2] Presidential address to the Cambridge Humanists, Summer 1959.

recently re-entered the general stream of university life. Once the
leading college in Cambridge, it had slept for three centuries,
becoming not much more than a grace-and-favour annexe to Eton.
Only Etonians could be scholars of King's, and, as long as they did
not marry, scholars could proceed automatically to life-fellowships;
thus a scholarship to King's was frequently a passport to lifelong
idleness. Change had come only in the 1850s, just before the great
wave of university reforms. The College, then, of its own volition,
gave up the privilege of claiming degrees without examination, and a
few years later it threw open its gates to non-Etonians. The results
were striking, and by the 1880s the College was once again a thriving
institution, indeed one of the most attractive of the Cambridge
colleges. It was academically forward-looking – being, for instance,
the first college to treat history on a level with classics in its teaching
– and it put into practice the cardinal principle of the reformers, that
dons should be teachers, not mere recluse scholars or port-drinking
dignitaries. It was helped in this by the best feature of its enclosed
Etonian days, its sense of close-knit community. King's undergraduates saw more of their dons than those of most other colleges
and were on more familiar terms with them.[1] As a result, it was a
very cosy place; it throve on legends about its donnish eccentrics, of
whom it possessed a choice collection; and indeed, though not a
Philistine college, it was not intellectually very strenuous. (Santayana,
who spent a year at King's High Table in the 1890s, thought 'the
birds were not worthy of the cage'.) An anecdote[2] about M. R. James,
who was Dean in Forster's time, catches the tone of, at least, its
more *bien-pensant* and Etonian element. James was extremely
hospitable and kept open house for undergraduates, providing
whisky, tobacco and cards, and encouraging good conversation; but
at one of his 'evenings' two young men were heard discussing some
philosophic problem. He was greatly put out and, rapping the table
with his pipe, called out anxiously: 'No thinking, gentlemen, please!'
    One of the architects of the new King's was the famous Oscar
Browning, for twenty years the most energetic, most preposterously
snobbish, most ignorant, and in some ways most far-seeing, don in

---

[1] A Fellow of Clare once said to A. H. Cooke, who was Tutor in Forster's
time, 'You know, your men don't cap me; they only say "Good morning".'
'You do better than I do,' replied Cooke. 'I only get " 'Morning, Cookee!" '
[2] Related by Nathaniel Wedd, in his unpublished Memoirs.

either of the older universities. He was certainly the best-known one. The thing about the 'O.B.', as he was called, was that he was always *there*, taking an interest – calling out of the window to any passer-by to share his lobster, or accompany him in a duet, or be told of the very particular attention lately paid him by the Queen of Roumania. He was not a scholar or thinker; his strength was that, in his sanguine way, he diffused a vision of glory. He saw in King's the material of a new Athens, a new Florence; and any undergraduate – who could tell? – might be born to be its Pericles or its Michelangelo. If not, he could still be of use to swell the 'O.B.'s' court, to play the violin to him or dry his back at his daily levée. And, being in his way an extremely kind man, Browning would not forget him and if need be would take great pains to be of service to him.

During his first year Forster was given lunch by Browning, receiving an account of all the royal weddings and funerals Browning had ever attended, after which they played Schubert duets. From then on, from time to time, when they met in the court, Browning would put his plump hand through Forster's arm and bear him off. Once Forster, who was contemplating buying a set of Jane Austen with some college prize-money, was on his way to the University Library, to inspect their editions, when Browning waylaid him. He must come and see *his* editions, Browning cried, when he heard his errand; they were *far* more beautiful. Having displayed them – there was nothing in the least remarkable about them – he asked suddenly 'Are you fond of chickens?' 'I felt rather dazed,' Forster told his mother, 'but said I was, and he then said "Come a little stroll with me and see mine; I have such beauties".'

> On the way he drew me out. 'Did I like Sophocles?' 'No.' 'A great mistake!' 'Pindar?' 'Yes, very much.' 'For his part he never could stand him.' And so on till we reached a small house in the back yard of which were six disconsolate hens. When I had sufficiently admired we gathered up the eggs they had laid and started back. Progress was slow, for we met heaps of his acquaintances, among them Frank Darwin. 'Dear me, do you know him,' said O.B., 'how is that?' I explained, and his interest in me rose visibly.

Forster was taking classics, and for the purposes of his studies he came under J. E. Nixon and Nathaniel Wedd. Nixon, at least within King's, was quite as legendary a figure as Browning himself. A little old man, in a reddish beard and queer spectacles, he moved about in a fury of self-generated activity. Once, in a meeting, having spoken for a motion that stood in his name, he claimed the right of reply and argued exhaustively against it, and when it was put to the vote, being the sole voter, he voted against it. He lacked one hand and one eye, and Forster and his friends used to speculate as to how much else unscrewed when he went to bed. The legend was that, in the early days of the railways, two King's dons had been involved in a dreadful accident, and Nixon had been made up from what was left. 'I threw up my hands in amazement,' he was fond of saying, which made Forster want to giggle.

Forster grew fond of Nixon, but the don who had serious influence on him was Wedd. Wedd was a younger man: small, thick-set and ferrety, a warm-hearted, pugnacious, hypochondriacal character, militantly egalitarian, and with a passion for bad language. Forster knew him in his Fabian period, when he was regarded as a dangerous radical. Later he became a fanatical Tory, but, as friends said, 'never respectable'. At all periods he was a virulent anti-clerical, accustomed to spit when he saw the procession into Chapel and inclined to blaspheme, with cheerful irascibility, against 'the High Church doctrines about the Presence and all the bloody swinish bunkum that the prize idiots of the two Universities use to cloak their erotic tendencies.'[1] Forster and he took to each other, and in due course they became very friendly; indeed it was to Wedd more than anyone, Forster said, that he owed his own 'awakening'. Their friendship developed during Forster's second year at Cambridge, and I shall return to it.

Neither Wedd nor Forster himself was sanguine about his chances in the 'Mays' examination. Wedd told him he had been very badly taught at Tonbridge; he was appalled at the hours Forster had spent there on 'repetition', i.e. learning by heart, which was 'Joey' Wood's speciality. A 'dank despair' seized Forster, he told his mother, as the 'Mays' approached – though the despair could not have weighed heavily, for he was spending most of his time in miscellaneous reading. His reading-list for his second and third terms includes *Paradise Lost*, *A Doll's House*, Howells' *The Rise of Silas Lapham*, *Omar Khayyam*, some Kipling, and a good deal of Robert Browning and Christina Rossetti. He also found time to attend Lord Acton's

---

[1] Letter to E. F. Bulmer, 13 September 1898.

lectures on the French Revolution and Professor Waldstein's on Flemish painting. And at Waldstein's instigation he bought a season ticket for some lectures on the Venetian painters by Waldstein's 'most able and brilliant' young protégé, Roger Fry. He paid the fee grudgingly, but the lectures proved magnificent; Fry marshalled schools and influences in a way that made all seem clear and satisfying. When, with others, he went round to Fry's rooms afterwards, to be shown photographs, his timid remarks seemed to bore Fry; but he remembered the lectures for the rest of his life.

During the same Easter term he made a laconic entry in his diary, with echoes for readers of *The Longest Journey*. 'May 1898. Went for a short ride up the Madingley Road. Walked into old chalk pit full of young trees.'[1]

He ended this rather quiet and colourless first year at King's with a full-scale quarrel. Usually he was no good at quarrels, being inclined to take them too much to heart, but it so happened just then that he was spoiling for one, and he reported events to his mother in triumph (19 May 1898).

> It was like this. Worters came in with his dog, & Mrs L. – who had already shown herself in a bad temper – told him it was not to come in. However he murmured his way past her & came in; when he was well in the room she said in a most insolent voice 'well for this once you may bring him in'. I was furious, & we looked at the Univ. regulation which runs as follows: – 'A landlady cannot be required to allow a dog to be *kept* in the house'. Not a word about prohibiting it from coming in for a visit in the day time. But 'it wasn't so much the things she did as the saucy way she did them', so I attacked her this evening, beginning with the dog, & showing her the regulations. With much hauteur she said 'Mr Forster I am not a baby; I know what I'm about; I'm not accustomed to be spoken to by anyone like this, much less by a *youth* (!!), and it's not the first time you've insulted me. I think you forget who you are speaking to.' Here I struck in, in the illogical fashion that I knew would strike home to 'the class': – 'I think you forgot who *you* were speaking to this morning; you behaved most impertinently to Mr Worters.' This was the last straw of 'insolence', and she could only bubble, with a dust-sheet face, and say 'I shall tell Mr Cooke; I shall certainly go & tell Mr Cooke', whereupon I chanted 'go', 'go', 'go', and the duologue only ended with the visit. The arguments were not very recherché on either side, and of

---

[1] Evidently the source for the 'secluded dell' near Madingley beloved of Rickie Elliot. (See *The Longest Journey*, Part 1, Chapter 2.)

course I had lots of things I meant to say & didn't, but I think that for a 'youth' I did pretty well. Like other poor speakers we used much gesture: she was drawn up to her 'full height' so much that I thought she would topple backwards, and whenever I spoke I extended a grubby denunciatory finger. At the end of the engagement she retreated down the staircase, talking to herself in 'German' as Mr Poston says.

* * *

His mother and he had decided to leave Tonbridge that summer and, if possible, to find a house in the country again. They spent much of the vacation house-hunting, though with no great success. In the end they did no more than move to a semi-detached villa (10 Earl's Road) in Tunbridge Wells, no very distant step either in miles or in social atmosphere. It was at Tunbridge Wells, more even than at Tonbridge, that he would form his vision of oppressive English suburban life, with 'its semi-detached houses and snobby schools, its book teas and bazaars', the vision embodied in 'Sawston' in *Where Angels Fear to Tread*. Looking back on Tunbridge Wells in 1912, he thought of it as a 'Filthy, self-righteous place'.

* * *

He returned to Cambridge in a sanguine mood. He now had rooms in College,[1] which meant that he would be more in the swim. And, in general, he felt now that he had the hang of the place. Here was a society, so he put it to himself, where the only reason people need come together was that they should make the best of one another. It was a far cry from school, and he could safely forget school. Suddenly he found it quite easy to make friends, and before long he was on chatting terms with half King's.

He did not, for this reason, drop his schoolfriends. Indeed another, Fulford, came up to Jesus College this year. He was more pious than ever, and the mild gaieties of Forster's existence seemed quite rowdy to him. 'There is no reason,' he told Forster, clasping his hands, 'why we should not always wear our caps and gowns at all seasons that the University appoints, not merely at those hours when the proctors are on their rounds.' His piety was too much for the worldly Mollison. He told Mollison that the Master of Jesus was very glad that he (Fulford) was reading for orders, for there was great need of clever men in the church: 'High church men are apt to be either foolishly

---

[1] W.7, Bodley's building.

ritualistic or else too full of worldly ambition.' 'And which are you going to be?' snapped Mollison. Forster was fond of Fulford, finding him 'affected but amiable', but he too found him rather trying. Fulford once, in a 'yapping' voice, told him that he didn't like King's: 'They cultivate the aesthetic at the expense of the physical.' Forster was jubilant when, in the Lent Races, Jesus was bumped twice and went three places below King's on the river.

Forster felt he wished to be in no 'set', whether aesthetic or hearty; he decided that sets were a bad thing and caused unnecessary enmities. His own *mot* was that there were only two sets in King's, the exclusive and the excluded. He belonged vaguely to the excluded himself – those who wore untidy clothes and turned-down collars, and who spent their time in coffee-drinking and argument rather than at champagne breakfasts and race-meetings. But if this was so, it was from inclination and not on principle. For a time, for instance, he took quite a fond interest in the King's boat, and on three successive days in the Lent Races ran all the way with the first boat. 'I feel quite proud of myself,' he told his mother, 'for very few managed to keep up. I ought to have been an athlete.'

In his attitude to 'sets' he was encouraged by Wedd. He now became intimate with Wedd, calling on him uninvited, and frequently spending the evening with him, drinking Wedd's weak wine-and-water. Wedd was strongly against all coteries and all exclusiveness. In his younger days there had been a self-styled 'Best Set' in King's, who had kept a list of those whom one could and whom one couldn't know, and he had led an active campaign against them. On the other hand he equally disliked aesthetic coteries; and indeed he distrusted aestheticism in general; he would say that Wagner was the 'one big thing' the moderns had done in the way of art, for his music was essentially popular, as all good art had always been.

> It is only the stuffy hot house parasites of [*sic*] essentially inartistic people like making that cant about art being for the few . . . As a reward for the extreme unpleasantness of the discipline you have undergone you find compensation in despising the rest of the world and breaking all laws of decency and morality.[1]

If one is looking for Wedd's influence on Forster this may provide a clue; Forster, as his readers know, was very much concerned in all his early novels with the perils of the 'aesthetic' attitude, and his

---

[1] Letter to J. T. Sheppard, 14 September 1902.

views may owe something to Wedd. It was Wedd, too, who first
turned his thoughts towards Italy. Wedd's rooms were hung with
photos of Italian paintings and architecture, and Italy was much
discussed between them.

From time to time, following a College custom, Forster would also
walk in on Walter Headlam,[1] the Greek scholar, the one scholar of
international reputation at King's. Headlam had long given up
lecturing, more from absent-mindedness than any other reason, and
if no one disturbed him he would stay in his rooms for days on end,
voyaging about his library, while meals cooled or got overlaid in the
snowdrift of books. One day, when Forster had 'clawed' him out for a
walk, Headlam, more *distrait* than usual, alarmed him by having a
giddy fit and nearly falling in a ditch. On another occasion he led
the way straight across a field of young corn. 'Dear, clever people are
very strange,' Forster wrote to Lily, imitating his aunts' accents.

Little by little, too, he was being drawn into the orbit of Goldsworthy Lowes Dickinson. Dickinson was an important figure in
King's at this time. He was carrying on the work begun by Oscar
Browning and was building up in the College a school of political
science – a 'school for statesmen', where the fundamentals of political
philosophy could be discussed in Socratic manner. He was a man of
great zeal and good-will, standing for most of the Liberal virtues:
reason, decency and a very Cambridge brand of Hellenism. His books,
The Greek View of Life (1896), *A Modern Symposium* (1905) and so on,
are largely forgotten now, there being something fatally sedentary in
his thought – as if, burning as social and political problems were,
there was all the time in the world, the endless summer night of his
Modern Symposium, in which to solve them. He was, however, a
vigorous and impressive talker, with a *forte* for interpreting different
countries and schools of thought to one another. His own circle was
mildly 'advanced', with a fondness for blasphemous or slightly
louche jokes; God was referred to within it not as 'He' but as 'It'. The
advancedness was not very drastic, but it meant one could not
belong both to his circle and that of the Dean, M. R. James.[2]

Forster had come supplied with an introduction to Dickinson
through Aunt Laura, and Dickinson had invited him to lunch during

---

[1] Walter George Headlam (1866–1908).

[2] Or so it was later said by Percy Lubbock, who was a member of Monty
James's circle.

his first year, but the encounter had misfired. They had both been shy and had sat consuming 'Winchester cutlets' in gloomy silence, and Forster left feeling 'unprepossessing and unprepossessed'. However, there was a more auspicious sequel to their meeting. Forster had asked Dickinson to lend him a play, which enjoyed a great reputation among freshmen just then, and when he brought it back Dickinson asked what he thought of it. Forster replied, nervously, he was afraid he didn't think it very good, at which Dickinson's face lit up. 'No, of course it's no good,' he said. 'This lighting up of the face', said Forster later,[1] 'was a thing to watch for. It meant that he had seen something which must vaguely be called "Life", and it brought life to anyone who saw it.' In due course Forster became a member of his Discussion Society. Dickinson was at his best in such a setting. He would stand benevolently at the fireplace, as a contemporary described it, 'rubbing himself and saying clearly for each of us what in our muddled way we could not say clearly for ourselves.' Forster found the tone congenial, and by slow degrees he progressed towards a friendship with Dickinson, one that would count for much in his life.

The most significant development in his second year, however, was a friendship with a fellow-undergraduate, H. O. Meredith. Hugh Meredith had come up to Cambridge the same year as Forster, and before Forster knew him he had already heard of his brilliance and intellectual arrogance. Meredith was one of the eight children of an Irish legal shorthand writer, living in Wimbledon. The father was a talented and thwarted man, largely self-educated, and the family, though badly off, was socially ambitious, so Hugh was sent to a good prep school; by a strange chance it was Mr Seager's, the very school in Stevenage where Forster had suffered his débâcle – Forster could remember him as a dwarfish little boy there. He had gone on to Shrewsbury, where he had won every sort of prize for work and athletics. All the same, his had been a troubled boyhood: he quarrelled bitterly with his father and tended to conceive of himself as a friendless outsider. Some time in his middle teens, he had announced that he had become an atheist, and this had led to a violent flurry in the family, various clerical friends being called in, in vain, to shepherd him back to orthodoxy.

---

[1] E. M. Forster, *Goldsworthy Lowes Dickinson* (1934), Chapter 10.

Cambridge had come as a revelation to him. After the briefest acquaintance with it, he had decided that here, for him, was the good life. He was reading classics, like Forster, but liked best to spend his time in endless abstract debate, peregrinating from one set of college rooms to another. Forster, who had chosen rooms on the same staircase, expected to find him unapproachable, but at their very first encounter on the stairs Meredith met him with outstretched hand, evidently determined they should be friends. He was tall, good-looking and athletic, altogether rather noble in his appearance, and intellectually impressive in his quiet-voiced manner. Forster was attracted at once, feeling flattered to be thus singled out, and before long they were in and out of each other's rooms all day.

For a time Meredith had much influence on Forster. He was restless, high-spirited, and loved to *épater* the narrow-minded. He was an intellectual romantic, always with some new key to the universe: Forster has recorded a significant glimpse of him, chanting, as he bore Lowes Dickinson's new book, *The Meaning of Good*, down King's Parade, 'You shall never take away from me my Meaning of Good.' Under all the high spirits, however, ran a vein of cynicism, a shrugging conviction that nothing in the world was much good. Forster blamed him later for infecting all his friends with his pessimism. At heart, Meredith believed the good life could only be lived at Cambridge and the bulk of humanity were fated to misery and banality; they were the foredoomed victims of priestcraft and plutocracy. He wrote poems, vaguely in the John Davidson or modern ballad manner, expressing these sentiments.[1] Forster, in his Cambridge period, thought H.O.M. the cleverest by far of all his contemporaries, and he was not the only one who thought so. Oscar Browning was more percipient, telling Meredith once, 'You are very brilliant, but you will never do anything,' a remark Meredith used to brood over.

---

[1] Here, for instance, is the last stanza of 'The Ages of Man' in his collection *Week-day Poems* (1911):

> I haven't what would buy a meal
>   To feed a starving louse,
> And I must beg, or I must steal,
>   Or moulder in the House.
> Will any kindly clergyman
>   Explain the reason, why
> God sent me here to mar His plan
>   Of earth and sea and sky?

Meredith had strong crusading tendencies, and he soon found work to hand in demolishing Forster's Christian beliefs – which he said were simply 'foolish'. Despite his churchy friends, Forster was very ready to be parted from his faith, which did not go very deep. At home he attended family prayers, and sometimes he went to church with his mother, who attended when it happened to suit her. Otherwise, religion hardly figured in his life, and his mother, so he noticed, seemed 'offended' when the subject came up. As for Cambridge, scepticism, as he realized, was now in the ascendant there, at least in the higher intellectual circles. It was the era of Frazer[1] and G. E. Moore, who took the line, not of militant atheism, but of a calm ignoring of Christianity's claims to special revelation. Forster only received their influence at second-hand, but now, with Meredith's help, it started him thinking for himself about religion. He began with the Trinity. It began to look very odd to him.

> I tried to defend it in accordance with my inherited tenets, but it kept falling apart like an unmanageable toy, and I decided to scrap it, and to retain the main edifice. I did not realise that it was a question of all or none, and that the removal of the Trinity had jeopardised the stability of the Incarnation. I began to think about that. The idea of a god becoming a man to help men is overwhelming to anyone possessed of a heart. Even at that age I was aware that this world needs help. But I never had much sense of sin and when I realised that the main aim of the Incarnation was not to stop war or pain or poverty, but to free us from sin I became less interested and ended by scrapping it too.[2]

His collapse was hastened by the fact that, when he thought about it, he disliked the personality of Christ: Christ was lacking in humour, and he surrounded himself with disciples; also he seemed to welcome pain; all of which seemed faults to Forster. Within a short while, under Meredith's ministrations, he had lost his faith completely. It occurred with very little fuss; and when in due course he reported the fact to his mother, she took the news calmly. It so happened that his father had similarly mislaid his faith for a period and then retrieved it, and she assumed that this would be the case with

---

[1] Agnostic undergraduates at this time, under the influence of *The Golden Bough*, used to tease the orthodox by referring to College Chapel as 'Eleusis' and evangelicals as 'The Bacchanals', etc. (See Shane Leslie's novel, *The Cantab* (1926).)

[2] Presidential address to the Cambridge Humanists, Summer 1959.

Morgan. Meanwhile, it was agreed, he need no longer be present at family prayers.

Meredith introduced Forster to his friends, most of whom were doctrinaire agnostics and disciples of Moore. It was in this way that Forster got to know George Barger,[1] 'queer Barger', a handsome slow-voiced, unsentimental science student, half-Dutch by origin; also A. R. Ainsworth,[2] a voluble, untidy, disputatious classics scholar and philosopher. Through Meredith, in fact, he was receiving his introduction to intellectual circles in Cambridge. Wisely, he made no attempt to reciprocate and to introduce Meredith to his own friends; he knew too well that he would have had no time for them. Indeed, Meredith's arrogance had caused some resentment in the College, a fact which distressed Forster but didn't surprise him. The subject was frequently discussed, as can be seen from a letter of Forster's to George Barger.

July 27th [1899]

Acton House,
Felton R.S.O.

Dear Barger,

I will say without preamble that I do absolutely understand and that if I do not treat the subject at very great length it is because you have very much expressed my thoughts on it.

In one way my position is more complicated than yours, for I have much sympathy with the people who do not understand him [i.e. Meredith]. If he had not shown some liking for me I should have been as them, and when they accuse him of being conceited – of which I suppose the definition is that he has not any regard for their opinion – I know not what to reply. I did think that I saw what I should call an improvement in him – a tendency to suffer fools more gladly, to not only understand but also to sympathise with the opinions of the 'rest of King's', and Wedd said something to me of the same purport, though in other words, but from your experience in this Long [Vacation] I fear that at all events the rest of King's does not see this – beastly *profanum vulgus*, probably never will. . . . The reason that I take so much interest in M's relation to the outer world is that I like him so much that I cannot but wish he was in sympathy with it, and liked by it too. This is coupled with the knowledge that he is immeasurably superior to it and that it is (in a way) unworthy of his notice . . .

---

[1] George Barger (1878–1939). He became Professor of Chemistry at Edinburgh University. As we shall see, his wife Florence was to become one of Forster's close friends.

[2] See pp. 77 and 262.

So much, then, for his second year at Cambridge, which had been a very fruitful one, opening his eyes to all sorts of new possibilities and marking the beginning of several of his lifelong friendships.

As an occupation for the summer vacation, he decided to compete for the College essay-prize, selecting the subject 'The novelists of the 18th Century and their influence on those of the 19th'. (One must remember that there was no English 'tripos' at this time, so there was nothing odd in a classics student attempting this subject.)

* * *

Meanwhile, in July, as in one or two previous summers, he was sent to stay at his Uncle Willie's in Northumberland. This was the 'Acton House' of his letter to Barger, and here I must fit in this further piece of family background. It had a certain importance to him, for it was his introduction to the 'hunting, shooting, and fishing' side of English life. William[1] was the youngest of his Forster uncles: an intelligent, handsome, amusing man, driven slightly crazed by idleness; Forster drew on him in portraying Mrs Failing in *The Longest Journey*. Willie had wanted, originally, to be a soldier, and when his father forbade this, he had resolved to do nothing at all. To this end, or for some more obscure reason, he had married an heiress, Emily Nash, a woman much older than himself and plain and foolish into the bargain. In the 1880s they had taken a house at a village called Felton, in Northumberland, and here Willie had settled down, in Forster's words, to 'shooting and dominating people'. The house, a handsome, bare, classical block, was to serve as a model for 'Cadover' in *The Longest Journey*.

The marriage had turned out disastrously, as might have been expected. Willie, though a model of courtesy to the world in general, treated Emily abominably, and before long he had imported a rival into the household. This was Leo Chipman, known also as 'Canada', the schoolgirl daughter of a Canadian friend of Willie's. She was said to be his ward, or something of the sort – a theory received with scorn by Aunt Monie, who would enquire maliciously how Willie and his 'Australia' were, or when 'Nova Zembla' was coming to town. 'Canada', according to Forster, was '*très petite*, intelligent, hard, and a first-class horsewoman', and Aunt Emily accepted her presence meekly, as she accepted everything 'the Uncle' did.

---

[1] William Howley Forster (1855–1910). My account of him is based on an unpublished memoir by Forster, appended to his Diary for 1903–1909.

Mealtimes at Acton House could be torture. Uncle Willie made Emily keep a notebook by her plate, so she could note down complaints, and a meal rarely passed without some use for it. There was the row about the bull-trout, for instance. 'Is this salmon or is it bull-trout?' Willie asked ominously. 'It is what Leo got in the net,' answers Emily, clearing her throat. *Willie:* 'Would you kindly answer my question please? Everyone is waiting to be served.' *Emily:* 'I would only point out that . . .' *Willie:* 'I ask you to point out nothing, only to say whether this is salmon or bull-trout.' Emily rises, peeps at the dish, and quavers 'Salmon.' 'Bull-trout,' says Leo Chipman gruffly, not having intervened till now. *Willie:* 'Exactly. Take it away. It makes me sick and makes Morgan sick. No explanations please.' Forster would be miserable during such scenes. But, sorry as he might feel for Aunt Emily, it was no good trying to comfort her or take her part, for she would at once take advantage of his sympathy and try to worm some confidence out of him. She was, as he put it, a terrible 'sneak', always reporting scandal to Willie, so as to give herself importance. Poor Emily: Forster modelled Charlotte in *A Room With a View* on her, and, he would say gleefully, 'None of them saw it!'

Willie's hobbies, apart from sport, were scandal and the cherishing of grievances. On each visit of Forster's, soon after his arrival his uncle would take him aside and, fixing him with plausible blue eyes, pour out the saga of his grievances – an interminable tissue of lies upon which Forster would comment diplomatically: 'You and Miss Chipman seem to be the only ones who have behaved decently.' Willie's complaints were mostly against young men. With regard to girls, his reactions were unpredictable; he would play the witty host at one of his parties for the daughters of his County neighbours, and then, in the midst of things, suddenly bolt from the room as if about to vomit. Next morning at breakfast he would exclaim: 'I say aren't they awful, they *are* stupid. Oh lor!'

In all this he preserved a certain style and was never ridiculous. Forster and he, surprisingly, got on very well. His line with Forster was that he needed to be made a man of. 'Lily appears to treat Morgan as if still a child, pays his bills and won't even trust him to choose a pair of breeches,' he wrote to his sister Laura (August 1900).

> He loathes Tunbridge Wells and tea parties, which latter are all
> reserved for him he says. He is the only man present invariably

and if there were any they wd. be quite as bad as the women. My experience of that class is that they spend their time swapping lies and making mischief. The boy wants country air and pursuits with genial pals. His descriptions of the teas are very nice, being always in Jane Austin [*sic*] fashion.

Forster had no objection to country air, or to 'pursuits with genial pals' – if there should be any. At Acton House this meant outdoor sports; everyone was mad about sport at Acton House, even Aunt Emily, and Forster took his share, with some curiosity as to his own reactions. He was self-conscious with a gun, 'always in a fluster because I couldn't fit it into my normal activities,' but he found he enjoyed the excitement of otter-hunting. The ethics of blood-sports did not worry him greatly. He was only puzzled by the subtleties of Leo Chipman, for whom animals might suffer to any extent, so long as things were done by rule, but who was cut to the quick by any irregularity.

He would go to Acton for several more summers, until, in the end, he suffered the fate of all the other nephews and managed to offend Willie in some way he never understood, so that invitations ceased.

*   *   *

Forster's own account of his Cambridge days was that,[1] in his first year at Cambridge he wasn't sure of his clothes, in his second year he was too sure of himself – but in his third year he was 'just right'. Certainly, by his third year he felt in his element in Cambridge, liking and liked by people and feeling new powers expanding in his soul, though as yet he couldn't give a name to them. Other people found him hard to place and tended to think of him as someone else's friend. He went his own way. A little later Lytton Strachey coined the name 'the taupe' [i.e. mole] for him, and this was apt; he was drab-coloured and unobtrusive and came up in odd places and unexpected circles. There was something flitting and discontinuous about him; one minute you were talking with him intimately, the next he had withdrawn or simply disappeared. He was freakish and demure, yet at times could be earnestly direct, as if vast issues hung upon simple truth-telling. And all the time there was something hapless or silly-simple about him; friends likened him to Henry VI.

Was he naive or sophisticated? That somehow seemed a puzzle

---

[1] Reply to Lord Cohen, who had proposed the health of the College, at the Founder's Day Feast at King's. 6 December 1952.

about him. He seemed almost too fond of little *contretemps* and whimsicalities. The sort of thing that amused him was, having run out of soap, to dangle a string out of his window, for a friend to attach a new cake to it. Yet there was a queer sureness about him, a super-quick sensing of immediate situations, and – in flashes – an extraordinary sweep of human understanding. His remarks expanded in the mind.

Was he conventional or unconventional? That seemed to be another uncertainty. He puzzled over it himself. And was he mature or immature? He could afford to laugh at Uncle Willie's attempts to 'make a man of him', having already a clearer grasp of human reality than any vouchsafed to Uncle Willie. None the less, he was so used to playing the bright little girl to his mother that the habit was hard to break. He performed the role very charmingly, as in the following letter (24 October 1899):

> You will want to hear an account of the dinner party. I wore all my best things, including those you put ready, and looked very nice indeed – probably I was remarked on, though I did not hear it. We were ten in all . . . I was the only child, so I felt proud. I think I must have been to match Miss Omanney. We were all very hungry and ate a great deal. I lifted my elbow and did not bite my bread . . .[1]

What he found harder was to act the adult with her; and when, as sometimes occurred, he attempted to lecture her, his tone grew insecure and preachy. Here is one such attempt:

> I was so grieved, dear, at the depression in which I found and left you – all the more grieved because I felt that I could do so little to alleviate it. I was conscious that, whether I tried to show my sympathy with you or to change the current of your thoughts, I was equally unsuccessful, and at the end I felt unable to say or do anything at all. The reason that I am referring to this now is that I may beg and entreat you to make an effort to become more cheerful and happy. You may say that it is all very well for me, with all the enthusiasm and high spirits that are natural at my age, and with the prospect of a pleasant holiday before me, to preach contentment; but that it is a very different thing for you at your age, with the prospect of a lonely summer and the trials of packing

---

[1] He would sign his letters 'Poppy' (her pet name for him), 'Popsnake', 'Clever Clogs', 'Machiavelli Clogs', 'Gran's own grandson', 'Fred' or 'Occasionally peevish child'.

up to attain it. You may say too that there are grave reasons for your depressions: – the solitude in which you have lived generally, and during the last four years in particular: the discovery that in many of my interests you have not and are not likely to have a share.

I know that all this is true, but none the less I am writing. I feel that nothing in the world can now save you from permanent sadness and melancholy except your own effort. This effort I beg and implore you to make; and pray for happiness too, if you believe in the efficacy of prayer.

I am always your very loving and distressed Morgan.

It was the eve of the Boer War when he returned to Cambridge, and there was great excitement there, undergraduate opinion being, on the whole, hostile to the Boers. A kind of rehearsal of attitudes had taken place the previous year, when Kitchener, fresh from Omdurman, had paid a visit to Cambridge, provoking an extraordinary outburst of jingoism. On this occasion bands of rioting undergraduates had pillaged the town, to feed a vast bonfire in the 'Sirdar's' honour, and had been commended for it by the magazine *Granta*: 'There is nothing that a healthy youth admires so much as strength, whether strength of body or strength of character.' The jingo mood still prevailed, and at a Union debate the vote went by 101 to 84 in favour of the motion 'The present war must result in the annexation of the Transvaal and the Orange Free State.' Forster's friends, like Meredith, were bitter against the war, and he found his own sympathies turning against his country. 'The Ladysmith disaster is very serious,' he wrote to his mother.

I am afraid the Boers will cut the railway behind the town. What a dreadful war it is; and not certain after all that we are justified in it – at least not to me. Hasn't the Standard's attitude been disgusting: always sneering at the Boers and gloating over their future destruction: it was rather flat for it when its correspondent was so well treated after all its stories of Boer brutality.

When the news of the relief of Ladysmith arrived, a party of undergraduates in Hall called out for three cheers for the Queen, and the whole company stood on the forms singing. 'It was such jack's work,' Forster told his mother, 'and the poor dons were so terrified – thought it was a mutiny – but at last detected the noise of the National Anthem and stood up & joined, which was very kind of them. O.B. and Nixon, who are Pro Boer, were however very angry.'

His diary entries for three days in November 1899 give a taste of the idyllic, sociable, intelligently-idle undergraduate existence he was living during these war-months. It was a life he thought of afterwards, without nostalgia, as something only Cambridge could provide.

> 5 *November (Sunday)*. Spencer,[1] Mounsey,[2] & Gardner[3] to breakfast. Lunched with Meredith & met Swain.[4] Wilderness in the afternoon.
> 20 *November*. Monty[5] asked me to leave cards earlier. Ainsworth came in & ate bacon: then he & Meredith argued about beauty. Enter MacMunn with whom I walked up Huntingdon Road into Madd. Rd & Coton ft path. Tea with Miss Stephen:[6] talked of Tenn. & Browning. Coffee with Lubbock:[7] beautiful rooms & books: admirer of R.L.S.; saw the flat-backed Tennyson & didn't much like it.
> 21 *November*. Sat with Mathews[8] after lunch: then with Haward[9] same walk as yesterday. Tea with Mollison. After Hall coffee with Hasluck[10] & wrote letters at Union: Mrs Leader has asked me to dance but cannot go. Sent signature to S.P.A.B.[11] Debate going on: 'Trinity is too big'. Worked: Meredith came in & discussed beauty again.

Aunt Laura kept him supplied with wine from her cellar and liked to picture him holding distinguished dinner-parties. She hoped he would get to know G. M. Trevelyan, in whom she took a particular interest, and eventually the opportunity arrived. Forster went to hear a paper given by Trevelyan to Dickinson's Political Society, and

---

[1] B. A. Spencer (186?–1942). King's undergraduate; later Lecturer at the Royal College of Art.
[2] Possibly J. E. Mounsey.
[3] Arthur Gardner (1878–1972). He became a member of the Stock Exchange and published books on medieval sculpture.
[4] Edmund Gill Swain, the College Chaplain.
[5] M. R. James. See p. 53.
[6] See p. 50.
[7] Percy Lubbock (1879–1965); the future author of *The Craft of Fiction*.
[8] Charles Myles Mathews. He became a lawyer, and enjoyed a minor reputation as a writer of light verse. He married H. O. Meredith's sister Edith.
[9] Lawrence Haward (1878–1957); later music critic on *The Times* and curator of the Manchester Art Galleries.
[10] F. W. Hasluck. He became Fellow of King's and a member of the British School in Athens.
[11] Society for the Preservation of Ancient Buildings.

after it Trevelyan invited him to lunch. Trevelyan was already a fellow of Trinity and a vociferous champion of the new Liberalism, and over lunch he thundered kindly and helpfully, eating nothing whatever himself – the Trevelyans were very austere. Forster found his mind wandering. On his own plate, in the middle of a very small helping of lukewarm mince, mashed potatoes and brussels sprouts, was one sprout which was quite raw, and he kept wondering, as the inspiring torrent poured over him, 'What a very curious thing. How could it have got in? And how impossible to interest my host in the subject.' He was invited again, and this time, sitting on the floor on a hassock, was Lytton Strachey. Trevelyan introduced the two rather severely. It was Forster's first experience of the Strachey voice, and that extraordinary sound, issuing bizarrely from the carpet among the pipe-smoke and earnest masculine talk, abashed him, and he did not follow the acquaintance up.

In the midst of these pleasures he was working, with reasonable assiduity, and was reading in a multifarious way. Here is his reading-list for 1899: Homer, Pindar, Aeschylus, Sophocles, Euripides, Aristophanes, Thucydides, Plato, Aristotle, Plautus, Cicero, Lucretius, Lucan, Verrall's *Euripides the Rationalist*; Warde Fowler's *Caesar*; Mayor's *Outline of Ancient Philosophy*; Arnold's *On Translating Homer*; *The Tempest*; *Every Man in His Humour*; *The School for Scandal*; Maeterlinck's *Pelléas et Mélisande*; Pinero's *The Benefit of the Doubt*; Ibsen's *Pillars of Society* and *John Gabriel Borkman*; plays by Bernard Shaw; Browning's *Balaustion's Adventure*, *Asolando* and *Strafford*; Swinburne's *Atalanta in Calydon* and *Rosamund*; William Watson's *The Year of Shame*; *A Shropshire Lad*; *Tom Jones*; *Roderick Random*; *A Sentimental Journey*; *The Vicar of Wakefield*; *Evelina*; *Guy Mannering*; *Northanger Abbey*, *Mansfield Park* and *Persuasion*; *Adam Bede*; Meredith's *The Egoist*, *Evan Harrington*, *The Ordeal of Richard Feverel* and *A Reading of Earth*; Conan Doyle's *The Tragedy of the Korosko*; *Elizabeth and her German Garden*; Whiteing's *No. 5 John Street*; Saintsbury's *Corrected Impressions*; and F. Adam's *Essays in Modernity*. As this shows, he had been studying the English novelists systematically, in connection with his entry for the College essay prize. He won the prize, or rather a half-share of it – and also, to his great surprise, £4 from his College for Latin verse. The essay, though conventional in its judgements, contains some characteristic flashes, as for instance this feeling passage on Smollett:

It is a ghastly life he introduces us to, full of misery and sin, and his young men starting out in the world are as miserable and sinful as any. There is with them no 'everlasting wonder song of youth'; they find the world strange at first and are duped: soon they learn to dupe others, and are at home. The books are devilish – no other word will do, yet at the end we feel more sad than disgusted, and saddest of all is the thought that Smollett wished them to be as they are, and would not write them otherwise if he could.

His mother would come for long stays in Cambridge, all the time that he was there; and from time to time he would dutifully invite other relations. When he heard this October that his great-aunt and uncle the Fowlers were staying with his mother, he wrote saying how much he hoped he would see them in Cambridge. He marked the paragraph 'To be read aloud,' adding, for Lily's eye, 'There, am I not an apt pupil of Ma's deceit: but Ma is good as well as deceitful and I am not.' The invitation was snapped up, and he looked forward to the visit with some foreboding, for Aunt Eliza (Louisa Whichelo's sister) was an extremely talkative woman – rather a show-off Forster considered, though his mother was fond of her and the family in general thought her very amusing. She was full of swingeing opinions ('that mad one-armed fool' she used to call the Kaiser); for someone with so much to say, Forster would complain unkindly, she was remarkably ill-informed. The Fowlers lived in Plymouth, where 'stupid Uncle Frank' was in the railways; 'and very slow they must have been,' said Forster. Uncle Frank was as silent as Eliza was loquacious, and 'Fine run down from Newton Abbot' was the usual limit of his contribution to conversation.

Forster was a good host, and, so he told his mother, 'Loud were the exclamations of approval' when he took them over the Chapel. Aunt Eliza repeated 'It is so sumptuous, so rich: the glass is so rich – like woven silk, so . . .' and she waved her hands. 'Fine building, remarkably fine building,' kept on remarking Uncle Frank. Mollison and another friend, David Collingham,[1] were produced at lunch, and Aunt Eliza conversed with great energy, chanting a hundred times: 'I know you will all be very sorry to leave this place, that you will.' Growing excited, she promised to send them both some Devonshire cream. When they had gone she began to feel dull and wondered if

---

[1] David Horace Collingham (1879–1955). He became a doctor.

she had been too free and forward – but perhaps, she said, they would make allowances for country people.

Forster wondered at the extraordinary way in which time stood still on such family visits: long distances were traversed in a twinkling, even by the elderly, and meals seemed to pass no time at all. He wrote a little article, called 'A Long Day', on the subject. 'Of all days a long day is the longest,' it ran; 'a day that is when friends or relatives arrive by the first train in the morning and stop till the last train at night . . . A long day does not bow to the rules of nature. The sun stays in his path, neither does the evening come.'

'A Long Day' appeared, together with another article, 'The Stall-holder', in the first number of *Basileona*, a King's college magazine launched in June 1900. In subsequent numbers he published several more pieces. One, called 'The Pack of Anchises', was about looking back, like Aeneas at the end of his wanderings, to count the beliefs one had mislaid in three years at Cambridge. Why did one feel so much lighter and sadder? Because one's foolish old father Anchises (i.e. enthusiasm), who insisted on carrying a whole packful of assorted Penates (i.e. beliefs) away from burning Troy, had dropped the gods *en route*? Or because one had mislaid Anchises himself? Another item, 'A Tragic Interior', was a skit on Aeschylus' *Agamemnon*, provoked by a performance in Greek at the New Theatre in the Michaelmas term.[1] In Forster's version, Agamemnon, a cheeseparing and bourgeois monarch painfully henpecked by Clytemnestra, has to go through the motions of being murdered merely to satisfy the chorus, who have been prophesying it every day for years – and after this the poor man has to slink about the palace pretending to be a ghost. Forster's joke in all these *jeux d'esprit*[2] was to judge Cambridge or Argos by the standards of Tunbridge Wells.

He got an upper second class in his tripos (H.O.M. got a first) and the College had enough faith in him to renew his Exhibition, so both he and Meredith decided to stay on for a fourth year to read history. He would have liked to work under Dickinson, but to his chagrin Oscar Browning insisted on Forster's coming to himself. 'You're not coming to me at all, you must come to me,' he vociferated, in his

---

[1] The triennial Greek play was a great event in the Cambridge calendar.
[2] He wrote two more, 'On Bicycling' and 'On Grinds', for the *Cambridge Review*.

not very lucid manner. Going to the 'O.B.' was by now unrewarding; it meant reading weekly essays to him while he slept with his face under a red handkerchief.

Meredith, being a Scholar, would continue to have rooms in college by right, and he suggested that Forster should share with him, if the college would agree. Forster was delighted, but his mother, perhaps scenting a rival, took the line that their friends would clash and persuaded him to refuse. He wrote to her a few days later (16 February 1900) in a crestfallen tone, to report that Meredith had been 'very dull' since his refusal and was either hurt 'or more probably worried at the opinion I have shown I have of him, as I think now that he does like me better than any one else up here – or at least as well.' Lily replied briskly:

> I am very sorry that M. is hurt but I don't see how your decision proves you have a bad opinion of him. You only took half my advice; I said give the reason, which is in itself a compliment. Of course he likes you or he would not have suggested the plan & you might have said how much you appreciated his offer & as I said before that you valued his friendship too much to do anything which might strain it. If he is hurt, it is because he may think you would be willing to run the risk of giving up your other friends as he is, but you see he has always been considered a *one man* friend.

His decent but undistinguished tripos result did not worry him. It was much what he had expected, and what Wedd had expected too; Wedd had never considered him cut out for an academic career. They discussed various other professions, and one evening Wedd said, in his 'dreary' voice, that he didn't see why he shouldn't write. Forster took the suggestion to heart. By this time, his little articles had earned him a certain reputation in Cambridge; the *Cambridge Review* having singled 'A Tragic Interior' out as being the best of the flood of burlesques released by the Greek play. Now, some time late in 1900 or early in 1901, he embarked on a novel.[1] It features a boy named Edgar, living in a town much like Tonbridge, as the paying guest of an unsympathetic aunt and uncle. Life at the local public school of 'Sawstone' has proved too rough for the timid Edgar, so he has had to be removed; and for the moment he is in a sort of limbo, reading

---

[1] It remained without a title, so for convenience I shall refer to it by its opening sentence: 'They are Nottingham Lace!'

poetry and daydreaming his time away in his bedroom. The great cross in his life is mealtimes, for his uncle, an accomplished bully, chooses these as the moment to tell him to 'pull himself together and face life like a man'. What his uncle especially relishes is playing off Edgar's hearty schoolboy cousins against him, to remind him what a feeble creature he is. Edgar is too cowed, and also too conventional-minded, to picture any exit from this petty hell, till a young schoolmaster, Trent, with something 'lower-middle-class' and 'blowy' about him, moves into the house across the street and conceives the plan of rescuing Edgar. The plot is, you might say, a first sketch for the rescue of Lucy by the Emersons in *A Room With a View*; and in many ways the handling is already 'Forsterian'. The expert sense of suburban class-values is there; and so, in outline, is that masterly analysis of a pushing minor public school later perfected in *The Longest Journey*. Already, too, he demonstrates his supersensitive ear for tone of voice – for the imperceptible tones that betray bad faith and self-deception. There is a brilliant scene in which the uncle, who has had to go to Ireland on a business trip, sits down to answer an insubordinate letter from Edgar.

> He would give anything not to write. His personality, like himself, did not travel well. If he could talk to his nephew face to face he would soon get the upper hand. A few remarks like 'don't stoop, my boy, you're as round as an old woman' inserted into the conversation would make his opponent nervous & compliant. But to write 'don't stoop' by letter was impossible.
>
> He could write in many ways. First, a sound reproof, for impertinence. He longed to do this, but had no handle for it. Secondly acknowledgement that he did disapprove the friendship [i.e. with Trent] and permission to Edgar to show his letter to Trent. This he also wished to do, and it would have been the wisest course. But he was not himself; he was on alien shores and feeling unwell. He dared not do it. The third course was not to compromise himself, and to write a jovial breezy letter, laughing at his nephew & wife for the way they fretted over trifles. This he prepared to do, and sat down after breakfast with an aching head to write. It is impossible to be breezy to order & the letter was not a success. It betrayed irritation, and also betrayed hostility against Trent, together with timidity to avow it. However, he sent it, and spent the rest of the morning regretting he had done so.

What is not there in the fragment is much in the way of shaping or narrative power. Not only does he not know what will happen to his characters, he is not yet attuned to the idea that things *can* happen. 'This wasn't writing,' Forster said, looking back on it. 'The apparatus was working, not inaccurately, but feebly and dreamily, because I wasn't sure it was there.'

*   *   *

In his fourth year at King's Forster was elected to the 'Apostles'. This was the most exclusive intellectual coterie in Cambridge, so his election, which was sponsored by H. O. Meredith, was a step of some importance to him. His election did not actually take place till the Lent term (9 February 1901),[1] but it was usual for a prospective recruit (known in the Society as an 'embryo') to be looked over for some months, or even years, beforehand, so one must picture the whole of his last year in Cambridge as 'apostolic'.

The original, and still the official, name of the Apostles was 'The Cambridge Conversazione Society', generally shortened to 'The Society'. It had come into being in 1820, its titular founder being a St John's man named Henry Tomlinson, subsequently Bishop of Gibraltar. The purpose of the Society, according to one of its most devoted members, Henry Sidgwick, was 'the pursuit of truth with absolute devotion and unreserve by a group of intimate friends'. Ideally the friends, or 'brethren', would be in one another's company day in and day out; but every Saturday evening in term a formal meeting was held, at which one of the brothers would read a paper from 'the hearthrug' and 'whales' (anchovies on toast) would be eaten. Members were divided into the active brethren, who in the main would be undergraduates, and those who had 'taken wings' and become 'angels'. It was, however, quite usual for 'angels' to attend meetings, and many continued to do so throughout their lives.

The list of nineteenth-century Apostles was extremely illustrious – R. C. Trench, F. D. Maurice, John Sterling, Charles Merivale, James Spedding, Monckton Milnes, Clerk Maxwell, Tennyson and Arthur Hallam were all members – but according to the tenets of the Society worldly success counted for nothing. In its own jargon, borrowed from Kant and the German metaphysicians, 'reality' existed solely within the Society, the rest of mankind being merely

---

[1] His first paper, delivered on 5 May 1901, was entitled 'Are crocodiles the best of animals?' It has disappeared, and it is not known what it was about.

'phenomena' living in 'the world of appearances'. The Society had its rituals, and on solemn occasions the Secretary would read out an elaborate traditional curse, first pronounced against an early defector from the Society. The proceedings, and indeed the very existence of the Society, were kept secret, so that 'embryos' should not realize they were being inspected.

The Society had recently entered a particularly brilliant era, through the influence of G. E. Moore. The turn of the century was the golden age of Cambridge philosophy, and Moore (Moore rather than Russell at this early period) was by common consent its chief luminary, the prophet chosen to liberate philosophy from two thousand years of mystification. His integrity and purity of purpose, his conviction that one could find the truth, if one honestly desired it, by the ordinary powers of the mind, and express it in the most ordinary language, gave him a peculiar dominance over his Cambridge friends. Leonard Woolf has described the glorious, and sometimes gloriously comic, spectacle of Moore in action at Apostles' meetings – the astonishment and ferocity with which, his eyes goggling and tongue protruding, he would cry 'I *simply* don't understand *what* he means!' All the active brethren at the time of Forster's election, Ralph Hawtrey,[1] A. R. Ainsworth, G. H. Hardy[2] and H. O. Meredith himself, were under Moore's influence, and the words most commonly on their lips were 'What *exactly* do you mean . . .' Another favoured phrase was 'states of mind'; for it was a cardinal tenet of Moore's theory of ethics that the only things in the world possessing intrinsic value were good states of mind – of which the most important were 'the pleasures of human intercourse' and 'the enjoyment of beautiful objects'. Hawtrey retained a kind of vision of A. R. Ainsworth, coming into a group of Apostles at Sunday breakfast, and saying they all seemed to him to be in 'a thoroughly bad state of mind'. Keynes, looking back in 1905 to the brilliant past, alludes to the same shibboleth:

Hobby[3] broke out this afternoon against the Society; his latest

---

[1] Ralph George Hawtrey (1879–1975). He became a distinguished Treasury official.
[2] Godfrey Harold Hardy (1877–1947), later well known as a mathematician.
[3] A. L. Hobhouse, a Trinity undergraduate with whom Keynes was very friendly at this time.

instance was poor Greenwood[1] who persecutes him with a weekly letter, describing his 'states of mind' and what time he gets up in the morning at full and maudlin length.

Certainly there is a good deal of wreckage about. Still it was a glorious civilisation in its day.[2]

The opening scene of *The Longest Journey*[3] is evidently a picture of Saturday evening at the Society, and Ansell, whom we first see flicking matches on to Rickie's carpet, is – in externals at least – a portrait of A. R. Ainsworth,* a disciple of Moore who later married Moore's sister. (He was never a close friend of Forster's, and I suspect that, when it comes to Ansell's role as Rickie's conscience, there is more of H. O. Meredith in the portrait.) Forster loved the Society; that is to say, he loved all the friendship side of it, its mixture of intimacy and uncompromising intellectuality. For the rest of his life his Cambridge was essentially the 'Apostolic' one, and it was through this connection, more than any other, that he later was drawn into 'Bloomsbury'. He was not, however, a Moore-ite. In fact he always believed himself incapable of abstract thought; and so far as the actual discussions were concerned, he usually found them extremely tedious. Indeed he often didn't listen very closely – which helps to explain, what might appear puzzling, how it is that the problem which Ansell and his friends are discussing in that opening scene – about the cow in the field, and whether it is there when no one is looking – seems to belong more to the age of Berkeley than to that of Russell and Moore. The truth was, he had an idiosyncratic attitude to argument – to argument in general. 'Arguments, to me,' he said later, 'are only fascinating when they are of the nature of gestures, and illustrate the people who produce them.' He shocked Dickinson, in 1906 or thereabouts, by remarking, half-seriously, that for the first time, the previous weekend, he had actually had enjoyment at an Apostolic meeting. ('What a confession!' exclaimed Dickinson. 'What *have* you had? Instruction? Edification? Fatigue? Bewilderment?') By that time, through the influence of Strachey

---

[1] L. H. G. Greenwood (1880–1965). He was a New Zealander, and became a Fellow and Director of Studies in classics at Emmanuel College. His *Aspects of Euripidean Tragedy*, published in 1953, is written in an exact reproduction of Moore's prose-style.

[2] Letter to Lytton Strachey, 7 December 1905.

[3] The novel is dedicated 'Fratribus' – i.e. 'To the Brethren'.

and Keynes, the brethren had taken to discussing more everyday human subjects – a change Forster thought greatly for the better.

One human subject the Society already sometimes discussed at this earlier period, and this was sex. Homosexuality, in particular, was talked about in a spirit of free and rational enquiry. The freedom, however, was only at the level of ideas. In so far as the brethren actually had physical love-affairs with one another, they kept the fact to themselves; it was not till a few years later, after a long-drawn-out battle between Strachey and G. M. Trevelyan, that it became the done thing for the brethren to have homosexual 'affairs'.[1] In Forster's time, indeed, the Apostolic tone was exceedingly austere, pleasure being regarded as a very dubious ingredient in any 'state of mind'.

Forster, by now, I think we can assume, knew perfectly well that he was homosexual by temperament. With his intensely prim up-bringing, however, and having come to manhood during the after-math of the Wilde scandal, the thought of actual physical relations with friends seemed to him remote and impossible. Indeed, he didn't know much about them, or to what extent they went on in his circle. He had heard Lytton Strachey's reputation and vaguely knew that Keynes lived a 'fast' life in London; but otherwise – this was his later way of putting it – he thought of homosexuality as something which had come from Eton and would in due course go back there.

It would seem likely that, partly as a result of the traumatic experience at his prep school, the onset of puberty had brought with it very strong sexual inhibitions – so much so, that for much of his youth and early manhood, physical sex played very little part in his conscious thoughts; he did not have much in the way of erotic fantasies, or, if he did, they were infantile ones. It is true, he re-discovered masturbation when he was 15 or 16, and it was henceforth always to play a large part in his life; but, for the moment, it was something he did not relate to the rest of his existence. In these Cambridge days, where his own sex-life was concerned, he may be pictured as living rather happily in a void where things did not need to be labelled.[2] The discussion of sex in the Society would have

---

[1] They then became so much the done thing that, at least in Lytton Strachey's view, to have them was a kind of gesture on behalf of mankind's future. (See Michael Holroyd, *Lytton Strachey*, Vol. 1 (1967), p. 185.)

[2] This fits with a remark he made about his early writings; see *post*, p. 114.

dented his ignorance and helped to satisfy his intellect, but this would have been a purely mental liberation. Not that that was a small matter, of course: he always regarded it as one of his great debts to the Apostles.

One of the 'angels' present most regularly at the Society was Lowes Dickinson, and during this fourth Cambridge year of Forster's their friendship developed. Dickinson was a man of great personal charm. In appearance he was shortish, stocky and dowdily-dressed: altogether rather dun-coloured, with the air of someone hugging himself against the cold. In repose his face was wistful, sparkling up in conversation into a monkey-like and charming animation. His favourite tone was a mock-despairing one: 'Oh *why* will collar-studs. . . ?' etc. The tone was expressive, for he fought a lifelong losing battle with the natural life and with material objects. ('But I *disapprove* of nature!' he once remarked.) His handwriting was almost pathologically bad, and he was said to be the only man who could make a Corona type upside-down. Forster caught his tone of voice in his *Goldsworthy Lowes Dickinson*:

> The last time I saw him (outside a hospital) was in my garden which was overdone with pink sweet-williams. He murmured: 'I don't like pink. I did speak to God about it; however some people do, and anyhow it can't be helped'.

For Forster, Dickinson was proof that one could be middle-aged and successful without growing any kind of carapace; could remain responsive, gentle, serious-minded and yet gay. In subsequent years he made it a kind of touchstone for his friends, whether they appreciated Dickinson. Their friendship was slow in maturing, though. As late as 1910–11 Forster was noting in his diary: 'likes me more than he did, I think and hope' . . . 'approaching to real friendship,' etc.

Forster was due to go down from Cambridge in June, and he faced the prospect with cheerfulness. He would have been happy to stay in Cambridge, but was as happy to go; in any event, belonging as he did to the Apostles, the severance would not be total. It remained for him to choose a career, and here uncertainty descended. There had been the idea that he should become a schoolmaster, and, to seem to be taking some action, he asked the 'O.B.' what he thought. Browning was not encouraging. He told Forster that, with his not very good degree,[1] he would need a further certificate from a training college. He ran such a training college in Cambridge himself, and, with no great enthusiasm, he suggested that Forster might enrol. Meanwhile Aunt Laura was 'pulling strings' with great zeal. Her suggestions were the Education Office, where she had a cousin, or the South Kensington Museum; or perhaps a clerkship in the House of Commons. One point she was clear upon, he must not think of the British Museum, so notorious for its bad ventilation.

He said farewell to Cambridge. The summer wore on, and still nothing was settled. And in the end, he decided to travel. It was a common solution for young men with a small private income and no fixed purpose in life; and Aunt Monie, he thought, would have approved of this bold use of her inheritance. Also, it suited his half-admitted scheme of becoming a writer. His mother would come too, of course; that went without saying. And, indeed, Lily took up the plan with eagerness and was not at all unwilling to give up their house and put their furniture in store. As for where they should go, the most obvious choice was Italy, recommended so warmly both by Wedd and by Dickinson. Forster might study the art there, and perhaps Italian history, thus equipping himself to become an extra-mural lecturer. Another friend, E. J. Dent,[2] spent all his own vacations in Italy, researching in music history, and was equally encouraging, loading them with instructions about museums, hotels, *pensions* and tips. Having completed a round of family farewells, they set out on 3 October 1901, on a journey that would last a year and take them not only the length of Italy but to Sicily and Austria.

---

[1] In his History tripos he got, once more, a second class.
[2] Edward Joseph Dent (1876–1957), the well-known musicologist and translator of Mozart's operas.

5 Italy

Their expedition began as badly as possible. At Calais the through-train to Basle had been taken off. In Paris there was a violent altercation over tickets and they got parted from their luggage. Nor could they find any food for the journey. And the porters grumbled bitterly at the smallness of Forster's tips, which made him reduce them still further. Then, at last, as they thought they were reaching Switzerland, 'there came guttural noises & eagles bespattered everywhere, and we were in Germany, & had to descend with all our luggage & battle with helmeted officials who looked as blank at our French as at our English.'[1] Lily developed a sick headache, which lasted three days, during which she could neither eat nor drink. At last, however, as they neared Lake Maggiore, 'simply battered about by the dazzling scenery', Italy began to declare itself: 'Bullocks drew carts, boys of 16 lovingly cuddled babies, the chalets changed their shape, and wood was stored in their upper stories.' They had planned to press on to Milan, where Forster could begin to frequent the picture-galleries, but having taken the steamer up the lake to Cadenabbia, they decided to spend a night there, and this stretched on for ten.

Lily was secretly dreading the museums and churches, and more-over she thought Forster needed mountain air. Indeed, he thought so too; he felt travel-weary and had a cold and a sore on his lip. Recording their steamer-trip he reflected on the psychology of tired travellers:

> I missed nothing – neither the campaniles, nor the crooked bridges over dry torrent beds, nor the uniformity of blue sky, nor

---

[1] Diary, 4 October 1901.

> the purple shadows of the mountains over the lake. But I knew that I must wait for many days before they meant any thing to me or gave me any pleasure. We – that is I – are never too tired or unhappy to record, and while we are young a little time purges away our frailties and leaves us with the pure gold. But I would rather have the pure gold at once.[1]

The hotel seemed entirely inhabited by elderly English ladies. The ladies went on expeditions too long for them and returned home querulous and vociferous; altogether, Forster sighed, he might have been back in Tunbridge Wells. His thoughts were those of his own Lucy Honeychurch: 'It was for this that she had given up her home, made elaborate preparations, crossed the channel in a gale, had endless railway journeys and four customs examinations – that she might sit with a party of English ladies who seemed even duller than ladies in England.'[2] However, soon he and his mother settled down with zest to their old sport of dissecting their fellow-travellers. There was a 'terrible' American lady there, Lily wrote to her mother. She was equally voluble in English, French and German and never ceased wishing people godspeed or welcome, or holding their knitting, or turning over their music, or admiring their clothes. Forster called her 'Under Three Flags'. He guessed that this American would have liked to make overtures to them too but couldn't pluck up the courage; indeed, another American lady had told them people thought them very English and haughty. Every day, Lily and he made expeditions up the lake, but to Forster the scenery seemed 'curiously drowsy and unreal'. He felt a little let down by Italy. 'The truth is,' he reflected, 'I have got it up so well that nothing comes as a surprise.'

On 20 October they went on to Milan, and though it poured unceasingly he slopped his way to the Cathedral and came to the conclusion, though he knew he was not supposed to like it, that it was 'the ideal great building'. Baedeker in hand, and Dent's instructions in mind, he also made a start on the galleries, filling his diary with notes. In one of the earliest he took his stand, as he would increasingly through the tour, on the paramountcy of human value in art:

> The Spozalizio has as much or as little effect on me as the Ansidei Madonna. It seems so dull. More than all, I liked a Madonna of

---

[1] Diary, 10 October 1901.
[2] Early draft of *A Room With a View*.

Mantegna, surrounded by a circle of cherubims, who are warbling
– not singing, but with their tongues out and their mouths open,
like birds. In wonderful contrast to them is the face of the infant
Christ, who possesses a human mind and soul . . .[1]

On the 23rd the sun broke through at last. 'Shouts of joy seemed to
arise from the street,' and they took a train to Pavia to visit the
Certosa: 'Another dream building,' thought Forster, 'but not such
a one as the Cathedral in the dark. It is more of the style of the
pleasure dome in Xanadu. To me the secularisation and the 1 fr.
turnstile at the entrance were all as they should be.'

This trip, like every day's trip, was picked over in remorseless
details by the other guests at dinner. There were three spinster ladies
who, having carefully looked the Forsters over, had formed a
defensive alliance with them; and the whole group, the Forsters
included, became very down on three young girls in the hotel. Lily,
particularly, took against them exceedingly. 'They were very much
excited with a handsome boatman and went out daily on the lake,'
she told her mother.

> I especially disliked the fair haired [illegible] and M. used to say
> 'How angry you are with that girl, mother.' A gossipy lady says
> how surprised she is to hear the friend is a nurse. 'She is so unlike
> my idea of one.' (She had just thrown an apple at her friend in the
> drawing room to be noticed!) I touched M's foot and we thought
> we should laugh, for she was the worst type of nurse and we were
> not a bit surprised.

A day or two later they went on to Florence, and when Forster
wrote to Dent from there, they were on the point of moving to the
Pensione Simi, a *pensione* with a view of the Arno and a Cockney
landlady – much like the one where we first encounter Lucy and her
cousin Charlotte.

> Albergo Bonciani,
>   Firenze
>   Via Panzani   Oct. 30th
> Dear Dent,
>   Your very welcome letter came this morning. We go to morrow
> to the Pension Simi, 2 Lungarno delle Grazie.
>   We have been here three days, and very comfortable, but my
> mother hankers after an Arno view and a South aspect, so we are
> not stopping . . .

---

[1] Diary, 20 October 1901.

> Everything about the Pension Simi seems nice except the lady who keeps it, who scatters H s like morsels and calls me 'the young gentleman'. But perhaps this is fastidious . . .
>
> I have done little sight seeing as yet, and my mother none, as we are both rather knocked up, I don't know why. This afternoon I have been to the Uffizi and two rooms of Tuscan pictures.
>
> Yesterday I went to St Lorenzo. I had got ready all the appropriate sentiments for the New Sacristy, and they answered very well. More spontaneous perhaps were my feelings at seeing the cloisterful of starved and maimed cats . . .
>
> We went to the Certosa at Milan, for which I have to thank you, also to Monza. I went twice on to the Cathedral roof, the second time on Sunday, which is not so nice, as the people on the spire spit on you as you come up. I was also much struck by there being a forth[1] on the roof, I don't know whether I am more impressed by the number of the forths in Italy or by their fig leaf character. Talking of fig leaves, how flagrantly indecent are the statues in the Uffizi with their little brown paper bathing drawers. I almost feel that the permanent plaster article of the Catholic reaction is preferable. It did know its own mind . . .

'We go to churches, pictures and museums daily,' Lily reported stoically to her mother (3 November 1901). 'Sometimes I strike and insist upon going into the country.' She was worried about his health. And oh, she lamented, he was so dreadfully impractical. He had taken her a long walk on a perfectly freezing, windy day to call on some cousins of the Grants, and then in the end he couldn't remember their house-number: 'I said nothing, but like the parrot thought a good deal.' In Milan he lost his gloves and his guidebook and his Italian dictionary; indeed he left his dictionary in every shop. In Cadenabbia he lost his purse, which turned up later in his bed. 'Since then,' she told her mother, 'I never give him more than 3 or 4 francs daily.' Now, as she was writing, he was fidgeting about, looking for his pen. He lost it repeatedly, several times a day. 'I never saw anybody so incapable.'

Dent had given Forster an introduction to the art-scholar R. H. Cust, who had a flat in the Via dei Bardi and kept open house every Sunday at teatime to his circle of young art-historians. Cust, author of *The Pavement Artists of Siena*, is evidently the original of the 'Mr Reynolds' in an early version of *A Room With a View*, who 'delighted to fill his rooms with viewy young men and hear them talk on art'.

---

[1] 'Forth' or more correctly 'fourth' was undergraduate slang for a lavatory.

Forster enjoyed going to Cust's because, as he said, it was a *man's* tea-party, and 'because there was something both refreshing and luxurious in such a combination'. But he thought the 'viewy young men' awful. He drew on them in the first version of his novel to illustrate futile aestheticism, the quality later more subtly personified in Cecil Vyse. In the novel, the sole passion which animates the young men is attributions:

> 'It is inconceivable,' concluded Mr Rankin, 'how Alesio Baldovinetti can have been so long neglected. This alone' – he pointed to the Botticelli – Rafaellino – Baldovinetti – Lippi – Goudstinker Madonna, which hung behind them on the wall – 'would be sufficient to make his reputation enduring'.
> They stopped to listen to the discussion raging over the St John opposite, painted by Leonardo – Caravaggio – Granacci – Goudstinker. Mr Mildmay led it, an envious young man who never minded who painted a picture so long as it wasn't Granacci. His archaeology lacked the nobility of Mr Rankin's, whose Robin Hood method of robbing the rich to feed the poor was not without a certain charm.

Forster was introduced by Cust to a 'wonderful' priest, said to be able to teach one Italian quicker than anyone, and he began to take lessons with him. The priest was excessively grubby, so that Mrs Forster feared for the chair-covers, and he understood neither English nor French. However, it was not hard to follow his conversation, concerned as it invariably was with the magnificent wine, oil, views, eggs and antiquities of the Casentino, where he kept a *pensione*. The burden of all his lessons was that this was the very spot for the Forsters.

In all they spent some five weeks in Florence. In a conventional tourist way Forster was beginning to enjoy himself, and he formed a plan to go on to Greece later in the year. As to writing, he told Wedd (1 December 1901) that he had done none since the summer.

> What with sight seeing, and reading up, and trying to learn Italian, I find my time crammed . . .
> . . . the orthodox Baedeker-bestarred Italy – which is all I have yet seen – delights me so much that I can well afford to leave the Italian Italy for another time . . .
> I was let off the sermon this morning on condition we substituted for it Fra Angelico's frescoes in San Marco. But, as I remember your saying, he is almost too good, and when I got outside the

85

church I refused, and went to see the Fry-belicked Spring[1] in the Academy. The flowers are now astonishingly bright.

They went on to Cortona, where the hotel was so cold they had to run up and down in their bedrooms to keep warm. Lily bought a cloak and made Forster buy one likewise. His was a very full one, worn with the end thrown over one shoulder like a Roman toga. 'M. loves his cloak,' she told her mother, 'and is walking up and down with it on.' Forster added a P.S.:

> She is drunk as well as sleepy – with the 'wine of the country'. We went to the Etruscan Museum this afternoon, and the custodian was drunk too I think. He rolled with laughter at his own antiquities, and when he showed us a picture which represented an attempt to poison a saint, he was so convulsed that he could not speak.
>
> Well, I like the place, in spite of frozen feet. The views are magnificent and so are the Etruscan walls. As the city was founded by Noah acc. to one account, we cannot expect it to be up to date.

From there they proceeded to Assisi and then to Perugia, which would have been nicer, Forster wrote to Dickinson (15 December 1901), if Symonds had not written an Essay on it, or at all events if Miss Symonds had not 'trod so amply in her father's steps'.

> The pall of tragedy has been affixed to the unfortunate city, and the elderly ladies of the hotel make midnight excursions in the well lighted streets in search of blood and adventure, and come back breathing desolation & woe. The exalted level is sustained by an old lady who is understood to be waiting for an inspiration to write a book, and by an old lady who had really written one, which was squashed by the landslip at Amalfi. A welcome addition was a commercial traveller, who spent last evening in proving to me how vile and worthless I was, and I was too frightened to contradict him, though I had just finished a very nice little bit of prose on Italy in the Autumn . . .

There are foreshadowings of *A Room With a View* in this, and in his mother's letter of the same day they multiply, and we meet what are evidently the originals – in some sense at least – of Lucy Honeychurch, Charlotte and Miss Lavish.

---

[1] Roger Fry used to lick the dirt off Botticelli's 'Primavera' when the custodian wasn't looking.

Grand Hotel Brufani
15th December   Perugia

We left Cortona last Monday and only just in time . . . I think we should have been frozen and starved, the food was so awful M. looked quite wan . . .

This Hotel is kept by a youngish Englishman, with a very capable common wife and he and she have the most distressingly free and easy manners, wishing to appear at ease. I begin to be like Miss Walker.[1] I far prefer Italians, who shake hands when you leave and thank you for your visit, as if you were guests . . .

There were 12 ladies when we arrived, mostly middle aged and gushing. One solitary man at a side table who fled and was seen no more. Most of the ladies left and now there are only 4, who as M. says 'after looking us well over, have become very gracious and wish we were staying on'. Three travel together, one a girl, who looked in a furious temper one day, ill I think as she did not appear the day before. Her friends tried to mollify her but it was no use. The next day she looked less fierce and her red haired middle aged maiden friend was very cunning, lent across the table to M. and said 'did I gather you were a Kingsman? My friend was at Girton'. The girl blushed with joy and beamed on M. and thoroughly enjoyed her evening, talking Cambridge. She had been to lectures at King's and knew many men he knew and he had met Girton girls at tea in a don's rooms. So they had a gay time talking and also bemoaning leaving Cambridge and both saying being abroad did not make up to them. Afterwards the friend told me that [illegible] had had to leave Girton on account of bad health and never stayed for the final exam and was heartbroken.

There is a Miss Spender[2] here, who writes books and we see several copies of her book 'Romance of Perugia' for sale in the hall. If her books are like her conversation, I should think they were wearisome. So gushing about nothing. 'Oh, I had such an adventure. I went out in the evening and saw a dark dark hall and a man going across with a Roman lamp, and *that* is what I call an adventure' – and the gushing red haired maiden says 'Oh Miss Spender how delightful, I wish I had been with you, you are so brave'. Miss Spender is devoted to the officers and has got herself a long bluey grey cloak just like theirs and an officer gave her 2 stars which of course she cannot put on the collar. She smokes and tells what she calls 'most amusing stories' but we are not struck.

---

[1] Unidentified.

[2] Emily Spender (1841–1922). She was a great-aunt of the poet Stephen Spender and wrote romantic novels. *Soldier for a Day* (1901) deals with a Perugian girl who, during the wars of the *Risorgimento*, dresses in the uniform of her wounded twin brother and fights for the liberation of her native city.

> Now we have 2 more, one a German I think who is sighing and plunging close to me, bored I think, and the other a fat very common Englishman who arrived last night and looked so dull as if he longed to talk to us but all the ladies looked so forbidding. I daren't speak to him so made M. after we [illegible] went to bed. He told M. he was a commercial traveller and had been all over the world. He said there were not many travellers about and M. said no, they had all gone to Rome [home?] for the winter he thought. The man laughed very much as he meant Commercial Travellers. He asked M. whether he knew Latin and hearing he did, said 'Well what good has it ever been to you?' So M. said humbly he thought it had helped him to learn Italian . . .
>
> [Later] I have done for myself – been agreeable to the C. Traveller – he is American, an awful man, but very pleased with my attentions, wh. is all the more alarming.

With Christmas approaching, they went on to Rome. They looked 'terribly plain', Mrs Forster told her mother, with their spots, and their shabby clothes which had been old when they arrived in Italy and had been beaten to rags by Italian laundresses. For accommodation they chose the Pensione Hayden, which, like all the *pensioni* they had visited, was crammed with English old ladies. Miss Hayden was a tyrant and insisted the door of the drawing-room was to be kept open and forbade the guests to write there. The 'gentle worms' of old ladies were always feebly plotting rebellion, but Lily dare not join their conspiracies; for Miss Hayden had been so rude to her once, on their first arrival, that if it happened again, she would, she knew, lose her temper hopelessly. The sole males, apart from Forster, were an aesthetic American, who made himself scarce, and a fat Italian who was learning English for amorous purposes. 'Can one say "your face has pierced my heart"?' he inquired of Forster. He suffered from lumbago and explained to the company at dinner that 'My heart is sad because my flank is sore.' Forster told his mother he had never seen 'such stacks of females', and, when arranging picture-postcards of sculptures in his room, made her laugh by putting all the male ones together. 'No partnership with females,' he declared, echoing his grandmother.

Fate threw him even further into the hands of females. First of all, he slipped down the stairs and sprained his ankle and the *pensione* ladies were fertile in remedies: 'Let him bathe it continually with *cold* water and bandage it *tightly*'; 'Let him sponge it with *hot* water

and on *no account* tie it up'; 'If he will rub it with this liniment . . .';
'He must leave it *quite alone,* or he will be laid up for weeks.' Then,
early in February, as they were going up the steps of St Peter's to
see the candles blessed, he tumbled and broke his arm. Now he was
completely at the kind ladies' mercy. 'He is most patient and everyone marvels at the calm way in which he bears the inconvenience,'
Mrs Forster told her mother.

> Everybody has been kind. 2 young ladies brought M. a 'Marie
> tozzi' for his tea – a bun – another brought him ivy from Cicero's
> villa and an old coy spinster, who seems to have taken a fancy to
> Mr Spencer,[1] gave him a branch of mimosa for his bedroom.
>
> I dress him entirely and he makes me laugh. He says he thought
> I was a good washer, but that he is 'simply muddled' [?] He
> always uses heaps of soap and never rinses properly. He looks
> splendid now I do him. It is a long business – but now I get
> quicker and he always has a beaten up egg in the middle.
>
> . . . Poor M., added to his other misfortunes, is bitten all over
> with fleas, his bad arm especially. M. said this morning:
>> Morgy's so clean
>> He feels in a dream.
> Very true, I keep him 'beautifully'.

Teaching himself to use his left hand, he wrote to Dickinson
philosophically:

> I last wrote under weeping sky and perhaps a little disconsolately.
> But though I do love Italy she has had no such awakening power
> on me as she has on you. I believe it is the weather. When the sun
> is in she is uninteresting and even ugly – perhaps all ought to be –
> and unless the sun is out continuously her beauty never develops.
> The light is stronger now and I feel that the next month may have
> much in store.

In his own notebook, in the same wobbling script, he reflected, in
brilliant and Samuel Butleresque style, on writing with the left hand.

> The attempt to write with the left hand raises new hopes in the
> human heart. For how many years have our thoughts been
> transmitted by the nerves & muscles of the right hand. How much
> of their essence may not have been absorbed in the passage. Now
> when new organs are brought into play new thoughts or new parts
> of thoughts may find their way on to the page, how many old ones
> be absent and fail to reach it. A physiological outcry may be raised
> at this. But at all events the thought that it may occur is new.

---

[1] Probably B. A. Spencer; see p. 69.

> Hitherto it has failed to pass the nerves & muscles of the right arm. The attempt may result in the revelation of a Mr Hyde – perhaps even of the perfect individual who Dr Jekyll tried so unsuccessfully to evolve. More interesting than either, the thoughts that have so long struggled for expression may at last find it.
>
> Interesting again is that return to babyhood. Till lately, the epileptic characters of old copy books seemed but the result of insolence & depravity. Now it seems that mental and physical labour went to form them.

His accident compelled him to give up Greece, but he took the disappointment patiently, for he had the prospect of Sicily to console him. And at last Italy had begun to wake up, and he with it. 'My love of Scotch cold and chilliness has had gradually to thaw off me before I can like the South,' he wrote to Dickinson. 'I do believe at last I shall like it very much.' During his stay in Rome he wrote what he called some 'sentimental articles', in which his theme is Southern warmth and love of life, as against the ghosts and glooms, the self-denial and self-consciousness, of the Gothic north. 'When the body is feeble the soul is feeble,' he wrote in 'Museo Kirchneriano' (later rewritten as 'Macolnia Shops'). 'Cherish the body and you will cherish the soul. That was the belief of the Greeks: the belief in wearing away the body by penance in order that the quivering soul might be exposed had not yet entered the world.' With praise of the body went praise of friendship. In 'Via Nomentana', describing an evening walk in the Campagna, he idealizes that friendship which 'flashed forth for a moment in David and Jonathan but first shone as a heaven in ancient Greece, proclaiming to barbarians that human affection need not be confined to the home circle or extended to the harem.' As he crossed a railway bridge, says the narrator, he saw below, in the waste ground beside the line, 'two – whom the Romans called 'juvenes', the Greeks ἐφῆβοι, but for whom we have no word in English because in England they do not exist.'

> They were walking together in the blue dusk, and all I saw was that their age was about twenty and their shirts not the same colour. They had their arms round one another's necks, as English youths have, and were not mawkish, and when they unlocked, and sparred and charged into one another, as Hooligans do, they were not Hooligans . . .
>
> They turned behind the embankment and I have not seen them again, nor shall I know them if I do. Perhaps they parted in bitterness round the corner over a half lira loan, but to me they

are Orestes and Pylades, always young, always beautiful, always
together, always giving the truest blessing – the blessing of those
who know not that they give.

Caricaturing himself as the prim tourist, he concludes: 'I was
fortunate enough to catch the tram at once, and have not suffered
from the evening air.' In March, by which time they were in Naples,
he had two ardent dreams of friendship. 'It is not what happens in
dreams but the strength of our feelings that is so wonderful,' he
commented.

He found Naples the loveliest place he had so far encountered in
Italy, and it was here that, in a cheerful mood, he abandoned 'They
are Nottingham Lace!', which he had brought with him from England
and had been tinkering at without conviction. 'I've tried to invent
realism, if you see what I mean,' was his explanation to Dickinson.
'Instead of copying incidents & characters that I have come across,
I have tried to imagine others equally commonplace, being under the
impression that this was art, and by mixing the two methods have
produced nothing.' He thought now that, if he could, he would
venture upon 'imagination pure and simple'. Meanwhile he had a plan
for a new novel, 'which may be a little more practicable than the
last'. This was his 'Lucy' novel, later to grow into *A Room With a
View*. An early note on it reads:

> *Who?* Lucy Beringer. Miss Bartlett, her cousin.
> H.O.M.
> Miss Lavish
> Miss Dorothy & Miss Margaret Alan.
> *Where?* Florence, Pension Bertolini.
> *Doing What?*

In Sicily he wrote two more of his 'sentimental articles' – one of
them, about Syracuse, opening with a defence of sentiment: 'Those
who cannot reconstruct the past with the knowledge of the archaeologist or recreate it with the genius of the poet, must perforce call in
the aid of sentiment and dream inaccurately of its greatness.' It was
Syracuse that impressed him most in Sicily. Just outside their hotel
window lay the stone-quarries where the Athenian prisoners-of-war
met their grim end. 'And last night – just think,' he wrote to Dent
(23 April 1902), 'we had a total eclipse of the moon, with rows of old
gentlemen on the verandah quoting Thucydides & moralising on

the spread of knowledge since the time of Nicias. Other nights we have had the tarantella, with the cook in light brown dittoes and spats dancing with the waiter and the facchini with one another.'

They were back in Naples by May. He was a little sated with sight-seeing, but his feeling for ancient history had been quickened. With a Virgil in his pocket, he went for a walk in a high wind to places which the poet mentions, sitting down at each and reading the appropriate lines. 'Morgan has seemed better lately,' Lily told her mother (19 May 1902), 'but now he has a cold and is very quiet; but I think he is always much quieter than he used to be, before he went to Cambridge.' His quietness concealed more than she guessed. For, at Ravello, the spirit of place had presented him with an inspiration, his 'Story of a Panic'. It was the first fruits of what he had promised himself, the trying-out of 'imagination pure and simple', and forty years later the occasion was still vivid to him:

> I think it was in the May of 1902 that I took a walk near Ravello. I sat down in a valley, a few miles above the town, and suddenly the first chapter of the story rushed into my mind as if it had waited for me there. I received it as an entity and wrote it out as soon as I returned to the hotel. But it seemed unfinished and a few days later I added some more until it was three times as long.[1]

Despite its crudities, it remains one of his most memorable stories, expressing his feeling of standing in the sunlight at last and possessing his own soul. It is, in a way, a story about the act of creation. Eustace, liberated by Pan, is able, like some demiurge, to recreate the stars, sun and moon out of his own consciousness; this could be thought to symbolize Forster's realization that as an artist he could depend on his own resources and need not laboriously 'invent realism'. The story also shows him reflecting on his own upbringing. After his encounter with Pan, Eustace behaves 'like a real boy' for the first time, and this is Forster's way of saying: 'Let me develop in my *own* way, and I will be as healthy as you like.'

He had, in fact, received a revelation. Something had shifted in his soul, and energies he had only half-glimpsed in himself were now in his possession. For all the tameness of his outward existence, he was able, imaginatively, to respond to the 'greatness' of life. When his friends read his first books, what surprised them was their vigour

---

[1] Introduction to *Collected Short Stories* (1947).

and largeness. They had expected a book by him to be as they pictured Forster himself: charming, old-maidish, a little ineffectual; and up to now he had had no reason to think them wrong. Of course he knew he had gifts: a nice fanciful wit, an eye for human behaviour, also the capacity to generalize from experience. But it was not plain they were of importance. So far he had not felt 'important'. Now he did so, having trusted the imagination. Italy, which he had been slow to love, had at last done a great thing for him. It had told him that one could live in the imagination; and he knew now for certain that he was a writer.

But of course, he had to have a 'career' too, or at least some work to do; at least he supposed so. He discussed the problem with his mother, who thought him more troubled about it than he actually was. 'Morgan is most anxious to get some real work to do,' she told her mother (15 June 1902). 'I think he feels disappointed as most of his friends have already started work. I don't know what he will do, I am sure; he loves Cambridge and if the climate suited him better it would be worth while his doing something there.' He thought, himself, that he would have liked to be a don, if only his degree had been good enough. '. . . when all humorous remarks have been made, it is a very great thing to be a don,' he wrote (11 May 1902) to Dent, who had just been elected to a fellowship at King's. 'I can't think of any body who is in a better position for making new friends & keeping old ones.' (It was a characteristic reason.) He took his problem seriously enough to write to G. M. Trevelyan for advice – a commodity Trevelyan specialized in – and in his letter he described the kind of novel he was engaged on. He received a damping answer:

Trinity College   May 9, 1902
Dear Forster,
    Thank you very much for your letter. I understand what you say and appreciate much of it. But I think that without being a 'great man', you can experience many more healthy and strong states of feeling than boredom with Pension life, e.g. friendship and love of nature to which you own, and love to which you look forward. I add – work. But perhaps you know that already. Experience of all sorts, of the world in a healthy interesting way, of friends, of much else, comes fast at the time of life to which you are just approaching, if you seek it. If you seclude yourself in uncongenial and unhealthy conditions, of course it doesn't.
    I think you ought to get *study or employment*, to get your teeth

into, other than the shallower side of intricate psychology – I mean not for the sake of what is worth producing (tho' incidentally I think the intricate psychology for its own sake worthless), as for the effect that work on something else will have on you. One has to make oneself first; the work will then find itself out and follow. Your intricate psychology will (insensibly, indefinably) become interesting and healthy (not necessarily passionately), if you yourself have lived. There are so many sides of *life*, of which however Pension life is not one.

Understand, I am not urging you to take up this or that form of art (that you must settle for yourself) as to come home and get interested in something, and to know more people, and all the rest will then be added unto you.

England, with all its faults, working England is a better place than invalids and tennis players in Italian hotels.

Would you care to do some teaching at the W.M. College, next October. For a bye employment that is 'healthy' enough!! . . .

Pardon this jaw, which however your kind letter seemed to invite.

Yrs fraternally, [etc.]

Forster, though he resented unsolicited advice, listened to advice carefully when he had asked for it, and he acted on at least one of Trevelyan's suggestions; he wrote offering his services to the Working Men's College.

During the next six weeks, the Forsters travelled at a brisk pace, heading northward once more. They were venturing a little, after all, into the 'Italian Italy' recommended by Dent, and Forster considered writing a book on some Italian town. 'I have often thought of your suggestion of a *M*ediæval town – but I can't even make an *M*,' he wrote to Dent from Pisa. 'San Gimignano,[1] Volterra, Pisa and Lucca, are all undone, I believe, & the first two are particularly charming. But how to reach the ear of your powerful namesakes?'[2] In Pisa, Lily heartlessly told Forster that it would be just his luck if the Leaning Tower fell on him, he was 'so lamentably unfortunate'. To her mother she confided that she had just lent him her knife to cut a corn, and he had cut his toe instead and been quite ill with loss of blood. Then, on a subsequent expedition, he left it too late to get omnibus tickets. 'So let's take the train,' he said; but when they got

---

[1] Which became the model for 'Monteriano' in *Where Angels Fear to Tread*.
[2] He meant J. M. Dent & Co., who published a series called *Mediæval Towns*.

94

to the station the train had gone. At this, they got into another bus, but then

> M. begins clapping himself all over with a wild eye, which always makes my heart sink. He had forgotten his Baedeker, just bought for 11/–, so out he got and back he ran for it, by that time *you may imagine* I was fractious & M. was quite surprised.

At last the heat grew intolerable, so they fled to the mountains, settling at the Hotel Stella d'Oro at Cortina d'Ampezzo, in the Austrian Tyrol. The place suited them both, so they decided on a long stay, sending off to the Army and Navy Stores for books. Forster now began steadily 'committing noble thoughts to the green paper'. The ladies at the hotel provided him with 'intricate psychology' in abundance. There was such a tiresome girl there, Lily complained to her mother, who would sit on their balcony all day long painting wildflowers and bored Morgan at mealtimes. They called her 'The Pink Ass'. She was travelling with an older companion, who, Lily felt sure, had matchmaking designs on Morgan. When Forster went off to Innsbruck for a few days, to join Dent, the Pink Ass's companion, to Lily's fury, asked him to make all sorts of purchases there: paints, a sketch-book, plates for a camera etc. 'We know that they are for the stupid girl, as Miss S. does not paint. M. felt quite peevish, as he cannot speak German & so must take Mr Dent shopping.' Lily kept him in touch with developments while he was away:

> Pink Ass is still painting and is very fractious. She is very furious with one of the stuffy ladies who is mighty clever & has 'been finding fault with England and people'. Pink Ass thinks the nation perfect of course. I am afraid I am in disgrace too as I have agreed to some of our shortcomings & P.A. says 'if foreigners hear us talking of our faults they will begin to think we have some'. The whist party was most hilarious last night. Painted lady wants to get up a concert to help build the new church. The object was an afterthought! She sings and longs to distinguish herself. P.A. is to do the programme. I rather hope it will collapse, as one would have to be agreeable and helpful.[1]

Most of these details, in some disguise or other, found their way into early drafts of the 'Lucy' novel, which had begun to flow easily now.

---

[1] Undated letter.

The Forsters stayed six weeks in Cortina, and considered from time to time whether they might return to Italy; but in the end they set off home instead.

'It was a very timid outing,' Forster said later about this first Italian trip. And indeed neither he nor his mother had made any Italian friends, nor had they once entered an Italian home; at most they had struck up acquaintance with an occasional Italian hotel-guest or kindly museum-attendant or stationmaster. All the same, Italy had warmed Forster and given him a vision, and ever afterwards he would think of it gratefully as 'The beautiful country where they say "yes",' and the place 'where things happen'.[1]

---

[1] Extract from an early draft of 'Lucy':
    'If you look out of a window in London,' said P. dreamily, 'you hear all the people saying no to each other. "Naow – naow". And here it is all *si*: "Si, si. Il bel paese. Là dove il 'si' suona. The beautiful country where they say 'yes'." '
    'Where people respond, you mean?'
    'Yes. Where things happen.'

6 A Choice of Landscapes

It was still the idea, as regards Forster's future, that he might find a job in Cambridge – perhaps some unpaid post in the University Library. Aunt Laura had promised to 'exert her influence'; though Forster said he doubted if it would be perceptible at that distance. He had also applied for some university extension lecturing. And, pursuing Trevelyan's advice, he signed on at the Working Men's College (then in Great Ormond Street, in Bloomsbury) and began taking a weekly class in Latin there. He told Dent he was afraid he enjoyed it more than the students did. Meanwhile – their plans being so vague – he and his mother established themselves at the Kingsley Hotel in Bloomsbury; and for three weeks or so he shuttled between his grandmother and his aunts 'exchanging unprofitable embraces'.[1]

H.O.M. was in London, living in lodgings in Guilford Street nearby. He had now turned to economics as a subject, and had been given a two-year studentship at the recently-founded London School of Economics. He had also followed Forster's example and signed on for a class at the Working Men's College, where indeed several others of their Cambridge friends taught from time to time).[2] And in addition he was helping with the classical teaching at King's. He felt his 'real' life went on in Cambridge still, and he was there as much as he was able, rarely missing an Apostles' meeting.

For Forster, H.O.M. meant more than all his other friends. He regarded him as an emancipator; and in 'They are Nottingham Lace!', and again in his 'Lucy' novel, he took him as his model for the

---

[1] Forster's Whichelo aunts and their mother lived in Werter Road, Putney.
[2] For instance G. M. Trevelyan and Hilton Young. The list of Cambridge dons who taught there is very long. See pp. 174–5.

Deliverer, coming to rescue the hero or heroine from muddle and self-deception. Now, some time during this winter it seems, they became closer than before – indeed, in some sense or other, they became lovers. It seems to have been an affair very much on the lines of that of Maurice and Clive in *Maurice* – that is to say, it was not a physical relationship, or at least went no further than kisses and embraces. This was by mutual agreement, according to Forster – though one is sceptical of such 'mutual agreements'. It is not clear who took the initiative; most likely Meredith, for it was he who, so far, had taken the lead in their friendship. Forster said it was an 'experiment' for H.O.M., who had already had affairs with girls.[1] But if H.O.M. was the initiator, it was Forster for whom the affair counted most. For him it was immense and epoch-making; it was, he felt, as if all the 'greatness' of the world had been opened up to him. He counted this as the second grand 'discovery' of his youth – his emancipation from Christianity being the first – and for the moment it seemed to him as though all the rest of his existence would not be too long to work out the consequences.

This much about the affair he told me himself, and the rest has to be left to surmise, since the facts are now lost for ever. Perhaps there is not all that much to tell, as it was mainly a matter of inward devotion on Forster's part. The devotion lasted a number of years, giving way after that to a tolerant affection and then a gradual sense of disillusionment.

Partly through Meredith's influence, Forster found himself taking up his Cambridge life where he had left it off. All this winter he was in Cambridge regularly. In Dent's diary for 4 December 1902 there is a glimpse of him at a breakfast party, in misogynistic mood. The party had been fixed for 8.30 a.m., and the first to arrive was to call the host.

> I came towards 9, and found Greenwood only. Forster appeared about 9.15 and we waited for Haward. 'Just think,' said Forster, 'if we were a party of ladies, all late like this, how angry we'd be, and *we* don't mind it a bit.' G. went to call H. and roused him with difficulty by dripping hot water on his nose.

---

[1] He evidently took a cheerful attitude towards homosexuality. From Paris, that autumn, he wrote to Lytton Strachey, addressing him 'Mon cher bougre! (a form of salutation much used in his correspondence by G. Flaubert),' and concluding his letter: 'Goodbye then and a grasp of your hand to split your arm to the shoulder – as wishes the healthy Flaubert. I see you WRITHE under it!!'

Unexpectedly, Forster found himself in the thick of religious controversy. King's, as we know, had a reputation for religious indifference. It was almost the only college in Cambridge which did not run some kind of mission or settlement in London. However, during the autumn a group of low-church Kingsmen decided to remedy this, and they called a meeting in the College Hall, on Sunday 25 January 1903, to propose that King's should help run a church club in Southwark. To their surprise, there was considerable opposition, both from the agnostics and from the high-church party. The meeting was adjourned till the following Sunday; and at this point the militant agnostics in King's, led by George Barger and Maynard Keynes, saw the chance for a full-scale confrontation with the Christians. All the following week they canvassed busily, alerting London supporters like H.O.M. and Forster, and they let it be known that at the coming meeting they would propose the forming of a committee to devise a scheme of social work on purely secular lines. Meanwhile the low-church party found themselves in a dilemma. The clergyman whose club they were planning to adopt came up to Cambridge and proved to be a rigid high-churchman, not at all inclined to have his club run for him on 'undenominational' lines. Thrown into confusion, they were easily routed at the meeting on 1 February. The meeting went on till midnight, and after it Forster and his friends spent a cheerful hour or two drawing up a paper nominating (for some reason) the College Chaplain to the new committee and adding vocational descriptions to the list of signatories. (Forster's were 'Editor of *Home Chat*, and Society Entertainer'.)

All next week excitement ran high, and groups and countergroups could be seen assembling and dispersing in the courts. An Etonian in the high-church faction had remarked magnanimously that the opinions of 'Nonconformists and such' had the right to be heard, and the agnostics seized on this with glee, naming themselves the 'Such' party – 'Come along, aren't you going to join the suches? Be a such,' etc. Forster wrote a verse satire on the controversy in which, after the various religious bodies have said what they meant to do for the underpriviledged, 'Such' is asked to explain his own policy. He answers:

> My policy is simple, just and true;
> I'm willing to help you sir, you, and you.

99

This is received with enthusiasm, till he goes on to disclose that he means to infiltrate all parties and destroy them from inside:

> Till children, sniggering back from Sunday school,
> Know twenty ways of proving you a fool;
> Till hooligans have Hegel for their teacher
> And every navvy own his pocket Nietzsche.

Finally the hooligans in person, exasperated equally by belief and by unbelief, irrupt from the body of the Hall and wreck the proceedings. Forster intended them to typify the human heart.

Meanwhile, events had taken an unexpected turn. After his discomfiture at the Sunday meeting, the low-church leader, Alister Grant, had rushed off on his bicycle to Ely in a high state of religious fever, and, shutting himself up in a hotel room, had composed a flaming pamphlet, declaring that recent events in King's made him believe in a personal devil. He urged the College to meet again next Sunday to reverse their fatal decision; if they failed to, he threatened to publish his pamphlet. He distributed copies in King's and sent one to H.O.M. in London, who replied that, in what Grant had written, he saw 'in spite of all its extraordinary power and beauty, every element which has made Christianity an obstacle to the improvement of men'. He told Grant, 'You degrade the soul in men, for you encourage them to despair of themselves.' He ended by offering to pay ten shillings towards Grant's expenses in printing the pamphlet. George Barger, who was sitting with H.O.M. as he wrote, sent Grant an answer by the same post. Grant, he said, had been at pains to answer 'the Agnostics' claim to be regarded by Christians as on an equal footing with a Sect of the Church of Christ', to which his answer was:

> We did *not* ask to be recognised as a Sect, we don't want to be a Sect; *there is nothing about which we want to be organised.*

He concluded, with the same teasing generosity, by offering Grant ten shillings towards his printing costs.

Forster, who went back and forth between Cambridge and London bearing news, showed a wider humanity than his friends and was saddened by the whole business. He thought nothing could stop Grant now, and it was a case for a doctor. 'I can't see anything to do except cry,' he wrote to J. T. Sheppard[1] (8 February 1903). 'If only he cared for music or books or scenery or anything of the sort, he might

---

[1] John Tresidder Sheppard (1881–1968), a King's undergraduate, subsequently Provost of the College.

still be saved.' Grant could not be stopped. He speedily issued another, much longer, pamphlet, explaining that 'his spiritual senses were at present in such a high state of activity, that he felt impelled to deliver his message', and within it he printed H.O.M. and Barger's letters, which had been meant to be private, with his own lengthy replies. There followed a 'tremendous' discussion with Grant in Guilford Street and a flurry of telegrams, and it ended with Grant, in bitterness, returning their ten-shillingses. Soon afterwards he received a vision and went off to New Zealand to work among the Maoris, while he prepared himself to proclaim his revelation to humanity.

*   *   *

By Easter, nothing had yet come of Forster's efforts to find employment, so he resolved to go on the Greek cruise of which he had been cheated the previous year. His mother was game for more travel, so he took her and her friend Mrs Mawe[1] to Florence and settled them there in the Pensione Simi, before joining the boat for Greece. He took with him, on a scrap of paper, a quotation from Pindar's Eighth Pythian Ode which had become a charm or maxim for him:

> Man's life is a day. What is he, what is he not?
> Man is the dream of a shadow. But when the god-given
>   brightness comes
> A bright light is among men, and an age that is gentle
>   comes to birth.[2]

The cruise, which was an annual affair conducted by Professor E. A. Gardner,[3] uncle of Forster's college friend Arthur Gardner, was intended for serious classical students; and Forster soon became conscious of the 'competent observers' on board ship with him, so quick to spot that the blocks of stone they tripped over at Cnidus were 'masonry of the best period'. His erstwhile tutor Wedd was on the cruise with him; and during its course he made friends with an

---

[1] Cecilia Mawe, a friend from Tonbridge days. She was an enormously tall woman, who published waltzes under her maiden name of Cecilia Friend. Her husband had been struck by lightning in Australia.

[2] In his old age he kept a leaf from a notebook bearing the same quotation tucked into his barometer.

[3] E. A. Gardner (1862–1939). Director of the British School of Archaeology in Athens and subsequently Yates Professor of Archaeology at University College, London.

Oxford undergraduate named R. B. Smith. Smith was very public-school and true-blue and was destined for the Indian Civil Service. He was 'stickier' than most of his other friends, Forster would say, and regarded Forster as a sloppy-minded Liberal. They first got into conversation on a quayside near Pylos. It was a characteristic con-versation, about ancient Greece: Smith said that a great warlike spirit and a great artistic spirit were likely to arise at the same time – witness the Greeks and the Elizabethans. This theory did not appeal to Forster, it being not at all his idea of the ancient Greeks. However, the two got on extremely well and would go off on their own on day-long expeditions on donkeys. Forster would entertain Smith with imitations of the other passengers. Among their favourites were a pair of cultured middle-aged ladies, who punctuated the lectures every few minutes with a cry of '*Dates* please!' Once, during the trip, the news came through that the boat was to dock an hour earlier than expected. Smith always recalled the sight of Forster with his hands uplifted in glee as the *comme-il-faut* passengers tumbled out of their cabins half-dressed and furious.

Forster found, as he had done in Italy, that he came over-prepared to many of the famous sights, and they made no impression. Marathon was no more than a view, and 'Aegina by moonlight did not come off.' As for Troy, its ghosts were too military for his taste:

> *10/4/03. Troy.* Undulating plain. Simois choked with white ranunculus. Great stone bridges. Troy no great height, but joined on to hills behind. Remains confusing but well explained. Helen is the only one I'm interested in – and possibly Patroclus, whose tomb one sees. Hellespont terribly shallow: how could Thetis have risen from it? Several storks. How rotten is the translation of Lang, Leaf & Myers. Surely Pope better.

It was not till he reached Cnidus, and was floundering about it in the dark and pouring rain, that Greece took possession of him. The famous Demeter of Cnidus, in her exile in the British Museum, was already a private cult with him. She was for him the benevolent mother-deity, giver of 'corn and tears', and – I would surmise – she represented for him the reconciliation of male and female in his own nature. In his essay 'Cnidus'[1] he describes her as receiving 'prayers of idolatry from suffering men as well as suffering women, for she has transcended

---

[1] First published in the *Independent Review*, March 1904, and reprinted in *Abinger Harvest*.

sex'. He liked to keep his devotion to himself, and in *The Longest Journey*, where she figures,[1] he refers to her as one of the 'monuments of our more reticent beliefs'. But now, in the presence of her ransacked shrine, his 'sentimental imagination' came into its own. In the words of his essay, it 'took wings because there was nothing to bid it rise, flying impertinently against all archaeology and sense, uttering bird-like cries of "Greek! Greek!" as it flew.'

Later, near Olympia, the whole of a short story – so he put it – 'hung ready for him in a hollow tree'. This was 'The Road from Colonus', a story as central and important for him as 'The Story of a Panic'. It was a story of the chance of salvation lost, as 'The Story of a Panic' was a story of the chance of salvation taken – the chance, that is to say, of swimming with the tide of one's own being, getting in touch with the manifold 'greatness', the depths and splendours, of life.

The actual pattern of the plot, evidently suggested by Forster's own recent travel experiences, was an important invention for him too. The jaded traveller Mr Lucas, for whom the world has lost its colours (or he wonders if it ever had them), and who asks himself why he bothered to come abroad at all, for it all seems just like England – but who, unknown to himself, is nearing a confrontation with the powers of death and life – this became a favourite opening *motif* in Forster's stories. It reappears in the jaded Lucy, with her viewless room at the Pension Bertolini, and again with the jaded Mrs Moore and Adela at the opening of *A Passage to India*. Forster had relatively few fictional patterns and was content to use those he knew again and again.

On his return to Florence, he and his mother saw something of Dent. Dent would come and eat with them at the Pensione Simi and rather ruffled Mrs Forster by talking loudly and disparagingly about other guests. His remarks 'wanted a little interpretation,' Forster said, 'but the people who heard them would know what they were about'. For his part, Dent thought Mrs Forster had a very sharp edge to her tongue. He had been reading Mrs Piozzi's Travels in Italy and found her 'curiously like Mrs Forster in caricature'. The three of them went to *Lucia di Lammermoor*, in which Tetrazzini,

---

[1] The one item of decoration in Stephen Wonham's attic was a picture of the Cnidian Demeter, banished from the heartless Mrs Failing's drawing-room.

then not well known outside Italy, sang the lead, to an enraptured and very noisy audience – a scene later commemorated in *Where Angels Fear to Tread*. In June they retreated to their favourite Cortina, from which Forster wrote to Sheppard, once more lamenting his encirclement by women.

> I do very much long for the presence of some male who is neither decrepit, mountain-mad, or clerical. At the present moment I am the only man – unless one counts an American boy who left the table last night because he thought the cooking bad. It is such a depressing thing to look down the table and honestly believe that you are the cleverest person seated at it, which is what I do day after day: I know you won't misinterpret this.[1]

They returned to England early in August, and again put up at the Kingsley Hotel, the plan being that they should now search for a house or flat. Meanwhile, as soon as the university term started, Forster was often in Cambridge again; and it was at this time, it would appear, that he began to formulate those ideas of Cambridge and its role in the world at large on which *The Longest Journey* turns. Dent gives another glimpse of Forster in his diary. Forster had come up to Cambridge for a week to attend the Greek play, and Dent, who had lent him his rooms as a 'playground', came in one evening to find Forster in high indignation. A friend had taken him to coffee at Stephen Gaselee's, and he had met there a man called N. F. Barwell,[2] who had told obscene stories about another Kingsman with 'a great pose of elegance and ironic sympathy'. It was a perfectly disgusting performance, Forster said; 'Not because of the subject matter, but because of the mind that arranged it.'

Barwell, who just then was cutting a would-be Wildean figure about Cambridge, belonged to the 'advanced', the Stracheyan, set at Trinity. There was, at this time, a considerable difference between this set and the tea-drinking agnostics of King's, and evidently Forster and his friends discussed the difference, for Sheppard read a paper to the Apostles this week on the subject 'King's or Trinity?' Sheppard at this period had just been taken in hand by Strachey, who would scold him for consorting with intellectual inferiors; but it was no good, he couldn't help being a tolerant Kingsman, he couldn't

---

[1] Undated letter.
[2] He became a barrister and was for some time leader-writer on the *Pall Mall Gazette*.

help actually *liking* everyone. The tone of his Apostles' paper was blithe, but it seems that Forster himself took the subject more to heart and seriously wondered how to reconcile the 'King's' and the 'Trinity' virtues. This was characteristic, as was his damning judgement on flauntingly 'amoral' attitudes – his confidence in judgement upon bad behaviour having in it, always, something of his mother.

'Are we really divided into two different classes? Or is the whole theory of King's and Trinity mere fantasy?', asked Sheppard, in his paper.

That is not all fantasy . . . I am inclined to believe, in the first place because I myself, in general and when by myself a person of normal and commonsense judgements but weakheaded and impressionable, am apt to judge and to feel about things and persons very differently when I am in the company, for instance, of Woolf and Keynes respectively; secondly because Keynes is often enraged; thirdly because of the evident grief with which our brother Forster speaks of the cleavage and tells how serious the cleavage appears to him to be.

At the outset, it is of course understood that King's and Trinity are only convenient names, not inappropriate since on the whole there is a tendency for Trinity men to be found at Trinity and Kingsmen at King's . . . But of course there are Kingsmen at Trinity, Trinity men at King's. Ainsworth was Trinitarian; Trevelyan, I am told, is King's; McTaggart[1] I suspect has certain Kingsward tendencies. He likes bad novels and he is as moral as you can wish.

At first sight, then, Trinity appears to King's to be stern, arrogant, intolerant, generally rather unamiable, sometimes well nigh intolerable . . . She seems to think that there are two classes separated by a clear line of distinction, the clever and the not clever . . . whereas really there are as many classes as there are human beings, and we ought never perhaps to use the word 'clever' at all except when we say 'more clever' or 'less clever'. (I speak as a Kingsman.) King's has an unconquerable faith in the value and interest of human beings . . . We care for what we call 'character'. I think we care for it more than intellect; at any rate a bad clever man (which is I think quite a possibility) is so repulsive to us that we cannot enjoy the intellectual appreciation of him. We are what Strachey calls 'moral'; we have our moral tests. We should have been disgusted, I think, by the scene which Strachey today described to me as the supremacy of intellect, the triumph of the spirit of Trinity: a room full of all manner of drink,

---

[1] J. M. E. McTaggart (1866–1925), the neo-Hegelian philosopher.

Mr Lamb[1] seated in a state of drunken collapse; Adrian[2] embracing Lamb, pouring upon the floor claret which he could no longer drink, [and] kissing Barwell's hands; Mr Barwell himself, flushed & oozing with wine, crying to Strachey, 'Come, let us talk metaphysics together: my dear fellow, here is a paragraph of Moore which puzzles me.' Strachey & Turner,[3] I suppose, in complete aesthetic appreciation of this degradation of humanity, intellectually satisfied! I cannot describe the horror of the scene as Strachey described it: the more he piled horror upon horror, the greater I saw was his appreciation. 'But think of the state of mind,' he said,[4] 'at any rate of Adrian.' A spark of intelligence remained, unquenched by debauchery, & that fragment of an intellect raised him at once above the stupid crowd, the moral crowd, the people whom King's approve.

Well, even if the emotions of liking influence to some extent our judgements . . . I believe that on the whole our refusal to sacrifice everything to intellectual qualities, our faith & sympathy for the so-called 'stupid' man, even our morality . . . help us to appreciate better on the whole . . . 'Some of this is true,' Trinity answers. 'We are not so absurd as to deny that these people you like are human beings, or that human beings have as a rule good qualities. But we object to your liking these people, talking to them, recognising their existence, caring for their good opinion, wishing them to like you.' That protest is based, I think, upon the belief that a certain amount of capacity for liking people is dealt out to a man at birth, & that every grain of liking given to one person means a grain less for somebody else. A sovereign spent on French millinery is in fact a sovereign lost to British tradesmen. Fortunately I do not believe this is always the case . . . there is of course always the question of the use of time & opportunity . . . But what I do not believe is that to like many people means to like no one much, that to like one person much means to be indifferent to everyone else, except one's enemies. Rather I am inclined to believe that the Christian has some reason for thinking that a great love of God tends to give a greater capacity for loving men; & that King's, although she is sometimes led out of the way by her own special dangers, is at any rate partly right:

> I never was attached to that great sect
> Whose doctrine is, that each one should select

---

[1] Walter Lamb (1882–1961), elder brother of Henry Lamb the painter.
[2] Adrian Stephen (1883–1948), younger brother of Virginia Woolf and Vanessa Bell.
[3] Saxon Sydney-Turner (1880–1962).
[4] See p. 76.

Out of the world a mistress or a friend,
And all the rest, though fair and wise, commend
To cold oblivion, though it is in the code
Of modern morals, and the beaten road
Which those poor slaves with weary footsteps tread,
Who travel to their home among the dead
By the broad highway of the world, and so
With one chained friend, perhaps a jealous foe,
The dreariest and the longest journey go.[1]

Perhaps it was Forster who put it in Sheppard's mind to quote those lines from Shelley. At all events, what the Apostles debated that evening became a central antithesis in *The Longest Journey*, which takes its title from Shelley's lines. Ansell, in the novel, who refuses even to admit the existence of a person like Agnes Pembroke, evidently represents a 'Trinity' standpoint, and Rickie, who 'maintained that one can like many more people than one supposes', represents a King's one. (Though his weakness, which causes tragedy for him, is not that he likes too many people, but that he refuses to hate any.)

*   *   *

A promising prospect of publication had opened up for Forster in the autumn of this year, for a group of his Cambridge friends, led by G. M. Trevelyan, had decided to launch a new monthly, the *Independent Review*, and wanted him to contribute. The editor was to be Edward Jenks, a peppery-tempered jurist, formerly a fellow of King's; and the editorial committee was to consist of Trevelyan, Wedd, Dickinson, C. F. G. Masterman,[2] and Francis Hirst.[3] Wedd later, in an unpublished memoir, gave a description of the founding of the *Independent*:

> At the conclusion of the Boer War, when Chamberlain had started the 'raging tearing propaganda' for Protection, and the Tory party seemed likely to be stampeded into a policy of aggressive imperialism, when the Liberal party was suffering under the suspicion of anti-patriotic feeling during the war, and followed so thoroughly its leaders' advice to clean its slate, that it had nothing

---

[1] Shelley, *Epipsychidion*, lines 156–61. 'world' in the third line is from an early version of Shelley's poem and was later amended to 'crowd'.
[2] C. F. G. Masterman (1873–1928); author of *From the Abyss* (1902), *The Condition of England* (1909), and other influential works on the 'condition-of-England' question.
[3] Francis W. Hirst (1873–1953); subsequently editor of *The Economist*.

> but a blank to put before the electorate, a magazine was founded
> to advocate sanity in imperialism and in foreign affairs, and a
> policy of constructive reform at home, and to offer a free platform
> for the unfettered discussion of religious, philosophical, scientific,
> and literary matters.

Lytton Strachey, though Trevelyan assured him repeatedly that
'there was a majority of Apostles on the editorial committee', took
a flippant view of the enterprise and wanted to call it *The Phenomenal
Review*.[1]

The first number appeared in October 1903, with a cover-design by
Roger Fry. Its political programme, as set forth in its editorial,
included the taxation of land-values, measures against the drink-
trade, the right of trade unions to picket, women's rights and home
rule for Ireland. Through Masterman's influence the paper was also
to give much attention to the 'condition-of-England' question; and
another main concern would be religion – Dickinson's main contribution was a series of articles on religion, and in early numbers
Trevelyan and Bertrand Russell both published agnostic credos.
For the four years of its life (in 1907 it was reconstituted as *The Albany
Review*) the *Independent* was a periodical of some importance and
influence, and it attracted many of the most famous names in
Liberal journalism; its speciality, however, was solid articles by
experts – university historians and economists and the like. They
were those whom G. K. Chesterton, in his *Autobiography*, described
as 'Liberal specialists of the more frigid Cambridge type'. (They
irritated Chesterton, who said he found anarchists and atheists
better company.)

Forster, like many of his friends, thought the *Independent* the
herald of a new age. 'We were being offered something which we
wanted,' he said in his biography of Dickinson.

> Those who were Liberals felt that the heavy, stocky body of their
> party was about to grow wings and leave the ground. Those who
> were not Liberals were equally filled with hope: they saw avenues
> opening into literature, philosophy, human relationships, and the
> road of the future passing through not insurmountable dangers to
> a possible Utopia. Can you imagine decency touched with poetry?
> It was thus that the 'Independent' appeared to us – a light rather
> than a fire, but a light that penetrated the emotions.

He made his own real début as a writer in the *Independent*'s pages,

---

[1] See p. 76.

publishing his essay 'Macolnia Shops' in the second number and later a number of other articles and stories. He was, indeed, its main contributor in the line of 'creative' writing, apart from Hilaire Belloc, whose *Mr Burden* appeared in it as a serial. (Some readers thought 'E. M. Forster' a pseudonym of Belloc's, causing Jenks to announce mysteriously that 'in answer to anonymous inquiries it may be stated that all Mr Forster's contributions to this Review are signed by his own name.') Despite Forster's tribute to 'decency touched with poetry', his own nimble prose reads oddly beside so much worthy but leather-and-horsehair-style writing.

*   *   *

By the spring of 1904 the Forsters had found a flat, at 11 Drayton Court, in South Kensington. Never having lived in a flat, they were not much enjoying the experience, and in his diary Forster described with gloom the 'horrible' prospect from their dining-room window.

> First low houses – livery stables, calisthenic establishment, Baptist Chapel, all with cowls, which revolved & beckon to each other however still the air. Further away high houses – backs of a row of flats I think – above which appears a horrible spire, absolutely senseless and smooth save for one or two jutting windows on its slope: terminated in a coarse knob. All day the air has thickened & cleared from nowhere: the houses & spires go in & out of focus as if it were a magic lantern.

His grandmother came to stay frequently and kept a close watch out of the window on their neighbours and tradesmen, taking particular interest in the coal. Once she so belligerently accused the coalman of delivering short measure that Lily only just prevented his calling a policeman. Forster was working away intermittently at his reconstructed 'Lucy' novel and the story 'The Eternal Moment', and had also, sometime about this period, begun an entirely new novel, which was to become *Where Angels Fear to Tread*. The plot originated in a scrap of *pensione* gossip, overheard by him some time during the previous two years, about an English tourist who had a *mésalliance* with an Italian. Echoes of Maimie Aylward's second marriage were probably also in his mind.[1]

---

[1] Another conceivable source might be an incident in the Trevelyan family. In 1890 an aunt of the Trevelyan brothers, Florence Trevelyan, being then middle-aged, married a Sicilian doctor named Salvatore Cacciola and settled in Taormina – to the great disapproval of her family apart from G. M. Trevelyan, who used to pay her friendly visits in Sicily. It seems very possible that G. M. Trevelyan should have mentioned the story to Forster.

In addition to all this he had been commissioned by Dickinson, who was general editor of 'Dent's Classics', to edit Virgil's *Aeneid* for the series. Also, profiting from his Italian tour, he had begun to do some extension lecturing for the Cambridge Local Lectures Board. The headings of his earliest course read: *The Birth of Florentine Civilisation*, *The Times of Dante*, *Florence in the Trecento*, *The Medici*, *The Renaissance at Florence* and *The Fall of the Republic*; and, with modifications, it was a course he continued to give up and down the country for some years.[1] One of his present lectures took him to Lowestoft, and afterwards it was reported to him that the local sponsors had thought him 'an extremely nice young man, but perhaps not very intelligent' – which became a family joke.

In his personal life he was, just now, in a mood of resignation. What he had achieved with H.O.M. was, of course, a good deal; but he longed for more, he longed for physical fulfilment, and it seemed certain he would never attain it. Every time he looked at the Greek sculptures in the British Museum, they appeared more beautiful, but more discouraging in what they seemed to be saying to him:

> It's simple to say they are gods – down to the bulls going to sacrifice in the Parthenon frieze. But I don't believe gods would make one so unhappy. Up to Demeter & Persephone on the pediment they are human, and our perpetual rebuke.
> It's so unwise, this desire to be simple & beautiful & strong. But our only hope lies through all these complications – not by affecting simplicity. So I'll call the Parthenon not a rebuke but a comment – which makes me feel worse.
> That wonderful boy with the broken arm – who I suppose is to be called sugary because he's neo-Attic – stands all the afternoon warm in thick yellowy sunshine. He simply radiates light: I never saw anything like it. Right across the Assyrian transept he throbs like something under the sea. He couldn't have done it in Greece.

Greece had become his private 'stronghold for sentiment', and when he came across the string of beads he had bought at Rhodes[2] and found that one bead was missing, he was astonished how much

---

[1] In 1909 he was giving a series of University of London extension lectures on *The Renaissance at Rome* (*1350–1550*).

[2] They were cheap wooden beads. He kept them for forty years and then (which is somehow characteristic) he exchanged them for a string of amber beads belonging to his friend Bob Buckingham, and at his death this was hanging from one of his bookcases in King's College.

he minded; it was as if he had never been there. He had, he realized, come back from Greece more sentimental than ever. Though, it was true, the place had given him a red nose, thus ruining his appearance, such as it had been, for ever; he wondered what she had meant to express by this. Was it, 'They used to be that colour all over'? No, more probably, 'Don't go talking about your affinity with the antique.' Whichever it was, he felt that he approved of the irony; and, red nose or no, at least he had 'slept the sleep of the drunk at Troy, and in the Castalian Spring'. But after Greece, what now? he asked himself.

> I'd better eat my soul for I certainly shan't have it. I'm going to be a minority[1] if not a solitary, and I'd best make copy out of my position. There is nothing contemptible or cynical in this. I too have sweet waters though I shall never drink them. So I can understand the drought of others, though they will not understand my abstinence.

In April, he went for his annual visit to his Uncle Willie's, in Northumberland. There, as always, the chief occupation would be shooting and fishing; and with his present preoccupation with pagan simplicity he reflected that 'only the sportsman who is killing something leads the true life of the open air.' Not that, even now, he joined much in these pursuits himself. Indeed, his hearty young Napier cousins[2] thought him slow company and a very 'old' young man. They made him apple-pie beds, and were overcome with glee when, upon raiding his luggage, they found his mother had equipped him with a secret store of cake and biscuits. For his part, he thought them very silly, and spent most of his days in solitary walks and bicycle rides. It was an exquisite April, and in the woods round Acton House the chestnut buds and fresh spring foliage were almost overpowering. He asked himself, in a dreamy way, why people were so sure that plants were not conscious of procreation, for it might be 'the side by which we might understand them'.

At dinner-times Uncle Willie would lay down the law in his best man-of-the-world vein. He admonished the company one evening.

---

[1] 'A minority' and 'minority' were his regular terms for homosexuals and homosexuality.

[2] Joseph and Marjorie Napier. They were the children of Mabel Edith Geraldine Forster, daughter of Forster's paternal uncle Charles, who married Sir Lennox Napier.

'Always do as your host does. If the house is religious, wear your trousers out and pray like blazes.' It set Forster reflecting on the difference between believers and non-believers:

> Religious people are vigorous because they identify a certain set of opinions with divine will, and stick to them alone. They are just as human as the non-religious, but more consistent. The non-religious man is distracted by the variety of human voices, one speaking truth at one moment, one at another. It seems impossible to him that anything so powerful and sympathetic as a human voice can be wrong.

All this summer ideas for short stories flowed for him, and in June, while staying with Aunt Laura, he wrote a good deal of 'The Eternal Moment'. His most helpful critic, just now, was his friend R. C. Trevelyan, elder brother of G. M. Trevelyan. They had known each other vaguely since Forster's Cambridge days, and recently Trevelyan and his wife had become near neighbours of Aunt Laura,[1] with the result that Forster and he saw each other often. At Cambridge Bob Trevelyan had decided, in the face of opposition from his public-spirited father and brother, that his role in life was to be a poet. He was never a very good poet, nor a very successful one, and he had to publish his numerous books at his own expense; but he lived his chosen part wholeheartedly, striding about the country with a knapsack, his hair flying, or writing poems in a furrow. He was tall, benign-looking and untidy, with a wide mouth and steel-rimmed glasses. He referred everything in life to books and was ready to hold forth to anyone at hand, strangers if necessary, about the merits of Dostoevsky or the topography of the *Odyssey*. He would also read verse aloud for hours, usually with the preface 'This is not one of his best poems.' (Bertrand Russell once floored him by asking to have a poet read to him but saying 'don't read me a poem which is not one of his best'.) For a writer he was unhandy with words: 'intellectually clumsy' was his son Julian's description. He would run despairingly through lists of very ordinary epithets: 'She was . . . charming . . . pretty . . . attractive,' his arms flying as he searched unavailingly for the word. He was much liked and had innumerable friends, in Bloomsbury and outside it; though he suspected, what was true, that the Stephen sisters laughed about him

---

[1] They lived in Westcott, near Dorking, moving in 1905 to a house called 'The Shiffolds', which they had had built for them, in Holmbury St Mary.

in corners. As was customary with the Trevelyans, he chose a wife with great deliberation, marrying in 1900 a rich Dutch lady, Elizabeth des Amorie van der Hoeven. Bessie was kindly, solid, and devoted to music. She was close about money, and a little austere generally: when Bob was left a large legacy, late in life, and couldn't think what to do with it, a friend told him he should build a pleasure-pavilion in his garden, furnishing it with bare-limbed Circassian maidens. 'Just the very thing,' cried Bob; then his face fell. 'No . . . Bessie wouldn't like it.'

Soon after his return to London, Forster sent 'The Eternal Moment' to Trevelyan, who admired it but objected to a certain facetiousness in the style. This came home to Forster, who replied: 'I wish you had told me where are the facetiae; they are a most certain fault, & my taste doesn't guide me. Someone told me, many years ago, that I was amusing, and I have never quite recovered from the effects.'

On the following day, to his fury, he received a letter from Jenks, the editor of the *Independent*, criticizing his punctuation in 'The Story of a Panic'. 'Absurdly angry and ashamed of so being,' he noted. 'Probably shan't sleep.' He tried to take his mind off the subject by recalling one or two of the 'divine moments' of his two years' travel, but Jenks would not be silenced. 'Damn that letter. I think of it still. Shall read a little "Wings of the Dove".' 'Beast' Jenks had his way, and when the story came out in August, Forster found that he had altered the punctuation according to his fancy.

'The Story of a Panic' created a mild stir, and various people were complimentary to Forster about it. True, the *Church Times* thought it very surprising that such an effusion should have found its way into the *Independent Review*: 'It is a long time since we read anything quite so hopelessly foolish.' But his friends told him that abuse from the *Church Times* was an honour. What annoyed him more was that Charles Sayle,[1] a rather squeaky Cambridge aesthete and bibliographer, professed to be scandalized by the story. 'Oh dear,' Sayle exclaimed to Maynard Keynes, 'oh dear, oh dear, is this young King's?'; and he explained to Keynes what the story was really about. Having . . . how should he put it . . . having had an un-

---

[1] Charles Sayle (1864–1924), for many years Assistant Librarian at the University Library. He was reputed to have exclaimed to his hostess at a dinner-party, 'I am so much enjoying your delicious salt.'

natural act performed upon him by a waiter at the hotel, Eustace commits bestiality with a goat, then when he has told the waiter how nice it all has been, they try it on with each other again. 'While alive to the power of the writing, to its colour, its beauty, its Hellenic grace,' fluted Sayle, 'I am still amazed . . . I am horrified . . . and *longing* to meet the author.' Keynes went about Cambridge spreading the story, and it soon reached the ears of Forster himself, who was furious. He had had no thought of sex for his characters – sex simply hadn't been in his mind at all. So he said to himself; but years later he came to realize that, 'in a stupid and unprofitable way', Sayle had been right and that this had been the reason for his own indignation. The story had excited him as he wrote it, and the passages which excited him most were the ones where 'something was up'. It was the same with the scene in *Where Angels Fear to Tread*, in which Gino tortures Philip by twisting his broken arm. It had stirred him to write it, though at the time he neither knew nor wondered why. But then, he asked himself, why should he have done? It had been his right as a young author to write about beauty and lust without knowing which was which or giving either a name.

He had begun an extensive diary the previous year and one of its prime functions was regular self-appraisal; thus on 12 July he drew up a balance-sheet of his progress as a man and writer.

> My faculty for noticing things certainly gets better: I see that covered carts have a square hole cut in the tarpaulin to look out by: that enormous gas lamps hang from public houses: that Carlo Gatti & Stevenson's men are Italian: that conductors say 'two pence' not 'tuppence'. But I don't know whether I read people better. I am going now on the supposition that they live hand to mouth – don't mind being silly as long as they aren't checkmated that move. This attitude takes me a good way – but possibly not the right way. How far this is for 'copy', how far right, how far wrong, I don't know. Certainly not entirely the last. But I fear che penso e parlo troppo di me stesso, e faccio poco guadagno agli altri.[1] Lubbock's 'Morality'[2] hits me. But it's no good checking self consciousness – it shouldn't be the same as selfishness if it's watched well.

---

[1] (Italian) 'that I think and talk about myself too much and am not much help to other people'.

[2] Unidentified. Presumably a reference to one of the writings of Sir John Lubbock (1834–1913), the popular educator.

His mother and he were still house-hunting, and meanwhile he continued his work on the *Aeneid*. He also had another occupation at this time, which was to help Julia ('Snow') Wedgwood, an old family friend, in revising her book *The Moral Ideal*. 'Snow', then in her seventies, was a daughter of Aunt Monie's great friend Fanny Mackintosh and of Hensleigh Wedgwood, a brother-in-law of Charles Darwin.[1] Following in the steps of her grandfather, the celebrated Sir James Mackintosh,[2] she had become a writer on ethics and philosophy, contributing heavyweight articles to the *Spectator* and the *Contemporary Review*. These had brought her into contact with Robert Browning, and for a year or two after his wife's death they had kept up a brisk exchange on philosophical topics; 'Very high talk it would have been,' said Forster. Then, for some unexplained reason, she broke off the friendship. Browning took the rupture magnanimously, and when, in 1888, she brought out her *magnum opus*, *The Moral Ideal*, she dedicated it, in discreet reparation, to 'An Old Friend'. The book was a systematic study of ethical systems through the ages and was described by some critics (this was before Wilde's *mot* about Meredith and Browning)[3] as a prose version of Browning's philosophy. According to Richard Curle, who edited her letters, she was altogether a rather formidable old lady, 'whose manner was severe and whose mind was fixed on higher things'. Forster disagreed; he thought her polite and cordial, extremely modest about her work, and decidedly gay, with a passion for rapid movement: 'Faster, coachman, faster,' she would cry. He felt it an honour to go to her house (she lived in Lansdowne Road, near Ladbroke Grove), and he was treated with respect there, though regarded as a little immature. She paid him something for his help, though friends told him later not nearly enough, and she always agreed with what he did on her behalf, though she sometimes forgot what it had been.

Despite some sense of success, and a variety of occupations, he at times felt a drabness in his existence, and his thoughts would run nostalgically on Italy and Greece. When he went to hear the band in the park one Sunday evening, and the wind, though it was only

---

[1] She was a sister of Lily's erstwhile employer 'Effie' Farrer and of Hope Wedgwood; see pp. 5 and 46.

[2] Author of *Vindiciae Gallicae* (1791) and *Dissertation on the Progress of Ethical Philosophy* (1830).

[3] 'Meredith is a prose Browning; and so is Browning.' (*The Critic as Artist.*)

July, showered down dead leaves on the spectators – all as colourless as himself, in their bowlers or straw boaters – he thought, with a pang, of music in Italy. And at the *Venice by Night* exhibition[1] at the Empress Hall, he was quite overcome by Italian affections:

> . . . . absurdly moving and touched in me loves for Italy hitherto unimagined. Floated between pasteboard walls in water 18 inches deep, by a canvas panorama of the Piazetta and Doge's palace. But the gondola was real and so was the gondolier, who allowed me to move myself by the sound of my own voice speaking Italian. He was young, incompetent, & a little drunk. For a moment the place was real, just as a poem is real.

For all this he was just at this time developing a growing passion for the English landscape. That sense of his for the 'bone-structure' of England, its pattern of rock-formations and hill- and river-systems, is a product of these years. Like all Cambridge-bred liberals of his period he was an inveterate country-walker.* At this period, solitary journeys and walking-tours were a necessity to him, and his diaries record a long succession. He made one, this August, to Dartmoor, which rose to a high point of joy: having walked all day, traversing Cas Tor and finding a wild bees' nest, he could find no bed at the village of his destination, so he walked cheerfully on, and the wonderful day grew to a more wonderful evening:

> At 7.10 the sunset, seen from a druid altar. E dopo, altre cose, che no si può narrarle.[2] Among them 2 cattle against an orange sky, joined by a third. Two Bridges also full: a harmonium, drunken man in the moonlight.

Early in September he was back in the west country again, this time staying in Salisbury with Maimie Aylward; and on 9 September, during a solitary walk to Figsbury Rings, he had a more momentous encounter with the spirit of place, of much importance to his future novel *The Longest Journey*. Figsbury Rings are Iron Age earthworks lying between Salisbury and Porton, consisting of a double embankment, with crops between, and, in the centre, a single small tree. Forster met a lame shepherd boy there and got into conversation with him. The boy was friendly, did not call him 'sir', and offered

---

[1] This was the great popular attraction of the Italian Exhibition which opened on 11 May 1904.

[2] (Italian) 'And after that, other things, impossible to describe.'

him a smoke of his pipe; and when Forster offered him sixpence as they were parting, he refused it. This apparently trivial incident took on peculiar significance for Forster. He decided that the boy was one of the most remarkable human beings he had ever met. 'What strikes me even more than his offering me his pipe to smoke is his enormous wisdom,' he wrote in his diary;

> his head – whether he knows it or not – is out of the water: if only he isn't bowled over by the beastly money! I was: but I was simply bound to think myself unsympathetic, whether I offered that 6d or not and I got a comfort in the rebuff, by seeing that he is better than ever. Vorrei cercarlo ancora – ma come si può vivere quando si domanda sempre 'cosa fa?', 'dove va?'[1] This 'incident' assures my opinion that the English *can* be the greatest men in the world: he was miles greater than an Italian: one can't dare to call his simplicity naif. The aesthetic die away attitude seems contemptible in a world which has such people.

He went back to the Rings two days later to look for him again, but discovered he had gone to Wilton. Four days afterwards he made another attempt, and this time he met the boy's father, and received the same impression of a human being with his 'head out of the water'.

> He has shepherded for five years of Sundays, cannot read writing and has never been further than Andover. He is neatly dressed, and altogether less wonderful than the boy, though he also is free of saying 'sir'. I say I will look them up next year; he shows no enthusiasm, but I don't see why he should mind. The incident is now rounded off agreeably, and though the outline has softened I think that is only for a time.

This, in terms of actuality, was almost the end of the story, though many years later, revisiting Figsbury, he saw the younger shepherd again.

> I recognised him because he would have been, and was, a mid aged mangy farm labourer, with a club foot. I felt no pleasure, no sadness, nothing at all except a passing fancy that everyone and everything I encountered was equally unreal. I did not speak to him nor hand over his share in the royalties of The Longest Journey. He didn't see me, couldn't have spoken if he had, and stumped past.

---

[1] I should like to go and look for him again – but what is one to do when everyone keeps asking 'What are you doing?', 'Where are you going?'

In its deeper meaning, however, the incident had a different and much more significant after-history. During the previous July he had hit on an idea for a new novel, about a man who discovers he has an illegitimate brother. This is how it ran:

A 'Plot' *17/7/04*

1. Renée and Mr Aldridge – a practical, unsuccessful man – paid a visit to Humphrey ——, in his second year. They are old friends: but R. for the first time 'realises' him – that he [is] clever in the first place, & that something might be 'made' of him. She disapproved of his effeminacy, & of his friends – notably the brainy uncouth undergraduate, soaked with idea of mutability, Ford, and of a don who wished to run him also.
2. H. found happiness at Cambridge after a querulous childhood, and obscure life at school. Spirits and intelligence both improved. Literary powers developed. After the departure of the visitors, he, Ford, & three or four more swore eternal friendship one evening by the rifle butts.
3. During the year of cramming for the C.S., R's interest in H. increased. He got H.C.,[1] F. taking I.C.S.[2] in order that he might have it.
4. Soon after F's departure for India, R. & H. got engaged.
5. Uncle Basil and his household at Ponte Molino.
6. R. & H. came there for their honeymoon. Pasquale; whom Uncle B., for the sake of seeing what would happen, reveals to H. as his brother. H. wished to accept him. R. naturally objects, and their discussion begins.
7. R. gradually detached H. from his friends. Her behaviour at her father's death revealed him their dissimilarity, and the Italian brother was a constant source of discord.
8. Ford, broken down, returned to England, having stayed in Italy on the way. The first meeting with R. & H. giving up H.C. to reside in Cambridge.
9. Struggle between Ford & R. began.
10. Death of Uncle Basil, releasing Pasquale.
11. Ford & H. took holiday.
12. Ford met Pasquale: who knew he was H's brother but kept silence.
13. The fire: death of P. & H.
14. Epilogue: H's book successful.

As we can see, it was to have been another Anglo-Italian story, neatly plotted and rounded like *Where Angels Fear to Tread* and

---

[1] Home Civil (Service).
[2] Indian Civil Service.

'Lucy'. Then this incident on Figsbury Rings supervened, com-
bining in one symbol so many elements with meaning for him: the
ideal English landscape, heroic human quality in a working-class
guise, and an inherited handicap (as it might be, homosexuality)
courageously overcome. It released a charge of emotion in him that
swamped his first design, and the novel became the queer, ardent,
fumbling affair that we know as *The Longest Journey*. It spoiled it as
a work of art, he said himself, but gave it its quality. Talking to the
Bloomsbury 'Memoir Club', many years later, he drew a lesson from
this story, as an example of the two-way relation between books and
life.

> The original experience – of the kind called human, but really
> fatuous and shallow – is of no importance and may take any form.
> Soon it goes, and the continual births and deaths of such are part
> of the disillusionment and livingness of this our mortal state. We
> do constantly invest strangers and strange objects with a glamour
> they cannot return. But now and then, before the experience dies
> it turns a key and bequeaths us with something which philosophic-
> ally may be also a glamour but which actually is tough. From this
> a book may spring. From the book, with the violence and per-
> sistency that only art possesses, a stream of emotion may beat
> back against and into the world.
>
> *   *   *

On his return from Wiltshire, he and his mother moved into a new
house in Weybridge. It was a commonplace, three-storeyed suburban
villa, of the bay-windowed 1880s type, named 'Glendore', a name
which the Forsters found 'trying' and changed to 'Harnham'.[1] It
stood on Monument Green; the front windows looked out over a main
road to houses much like itself, but at the back there was a moderate-
sized garden and an outlook onto fields and trees. The impression it
left on visitors was of a gloomy panelled hall and too much knobbly
furniture. Forster never loved the house, but he and his mother were
to live there for twenty years.

His mother settled down with relief, having by now had enough of
museums and *pensioni* and ill-behaved landladies. Their cook from
Tunbridge Wells days, Ruth Goldsmith, came to join the household,
and Lily engaged a Dorset woman, Agnes Dowland, as a parlour
maid. When Agnes arrived on the doorstep, Lily exclaimed 'Oh dear,'

---

[1] Perhaps after Harnham Hill, near Salisbury.

Agnes looked so very odd – tall, long-toothed, stooping and bobbing and smiling in a strange manner. She took her on with misgivings; and in fact, though Agnes stayed for forty years, the two always got on badly. Lily was a methodical housekeeper, a stickler for propriety and method. The tea-things had to be set out just so; the silver polished in such-and-such a manner and no other; and when the maids kicked the furniture or raised their voice, they had to be 'talked to'. Indeed, she was inclined to be a tyrant towards her maids. She would remark: 'The maids say "No one notices: no one will mind." But I've noticed, and I do mind!'

Forster for his part, now as later, avoided falling into any routine. When at home, he would get up late, would work much of the day in his tiny study at the top of the house, would take walks, and, most days, would spend as much as two or three hours at the piano, but none of this according to a set pattern: it would depend on his mood or on whether they had guests in the house. As in the past, he and his mother did not move much in local society, depending for company mainly on his friends and on visits from cousins and aunts. For most of their neighbours, Forster was no more than the very pale young man in the cloth cap, who seemed tied to his mother's apron-strings.

He now had four projects in hand: his edition of the *Aeneid*, his 'Lucy'[1] and 'Gino'[2] novels, and the new novel which had begun to grow in his mind in Wiltshire.[3] After a little work on 'Lucy' he found himself in difficulties. 'I wish you would quickly inhabit your new house,' he wrote to Bob Trevelyan (14 November 1904).

> I want it for some people of mine; they are living there at present in the greatest discomfort, not knowing which way the front door opens or what the view is like, and till I go there to tell them they will never get straight. If you would also provide one of them with something to do and something to die of I should also be grateful.

He began to feel dispirited. His mother, and his grandmother who was staying with them, were in an ill-humour and nothing seemed to get done in the house without uproar and bother. Things, he began to think, looked bad all round.

---

[1] Ultimately to become *A Room With a View*.
[2] *Where Angels Fear to Tread*.
[3] *The Longest Journey*.

Independent going smash,[1] no one else takes my things, Virgil
hangs fire, so does University Extension. I'm that ass that if Fair[2]
was to praise my writing, I think I'd be pleased. I worry too about
myself. I write so slowly, and I think not so well. It is impossible
to work at Cambridge: here I'm dull and fairly bright.

Is it impossible to live with old people without deteriorating?

This complaint that his writing was going off reads oddly in such
a productive year, but it was a fear which kept returning throughout
his writing career and was to become much more acute in the next
decade. For the moment he put his novel aside and embarked on a
ghost-story, to be called 'The Purple Envelope'. The plot concerned
an old man who commits a crime, from high-minded motives, and
then, for complex reasons, feels compelled to reveal it, and is finally
shot in the head by an unknown assassin, in mistake for a wild duck.
It was an ill-fated story, which never found a publisher, and he came
to the conclusion that he was 'too refined to write a ghost story'.

On New Year's Eve, according to his custom, he made another
survey of his situation in life. It was a significant occasion, since he
had always regarded twenty-five as the end of youth, and he performed his self-scrutiny with especial thoroughness.

My life is now straightening into something rather sad & dull to be
sure, & I want to set it & me down, as I see us now. Nothing more
great will come out of me. I've made my two discoveries – the
religious about 4 years ago, the other in the winter of 1902 – and
the reconstruction is practically over. If I'm wrecked now it will
be on little things – idleness, irritability, & still more, shyness.
Self-consciousness will do for me if I'm not careful – drive me into
books, or the piano. The truth is I'm living a very difficult life: I
never come into contact with any one's work, & that makes things
difficult. I may sit year after year in my pretty sitting room,
watching things grow more unreal, because I'm afraid of being
remarked . . . It begins to look that I'm not good enough to do
without regular work . . . A few people like my work, but most of
them like me. As to lecturing, I go to Guildford, & possibly to
Cornwall next term. But I'm not good at it . . . I still want, in
all moods, the greatest happiness but perhaps it is well it should
be denied me . . . Unimportant as my youth has been, it's been less
unimportant than I expected & than other people think. And
ardently as I desire beauty & strength & a truer outlook, I don't
despise myself, or think life not worth while.

[1] It survived till 1907.
[2] See p. 32.

He followed up this profit-and-loss account with eight good resolutions.

> (1) Get up earlier, out of bed by 9.0 (2) Smoke in public: it gives a reason for you & you can observe unchallenged (3) try to plan out work, at least by the week (4) more exercise: keep the brutes quiet (5) don't ever shrink from self analysis, but don't keep on at it too long (6) get a less superficial idea of women (7) don't be so afraid of going into strange places or company, & be a fool more frequently (8) keep accounts.

Looking back on these resolutions three years later, he decided that he still approved of them, and in fact had actually kept some of them.

His lectures in the New Year were at Guildford, for which he used West Hackhurst as his headquarters, and on one of his visits to this part of Surrey he made a new friend, Sydney Waterlow. Waterlow, who appears on the fringes of Forster's life for many years, was then in the Foreign Office, though next year he was to resign, for a time, to try his hand at literature. He was almost the same age as Forster, and they had met at Cambridge and possessed various friends in common. Physically large and magnificent, with a stupendous cavalry moustache (he had it already when he was at Eton), Sydney was nicknamed 'Monarch' and was very grand in his manner; the whole family, Forster complained later, held itself higher than it needed. He was an impressive talker, but Forster's friendship with him was an edgy business and often got itself in a muddle. But indeed Sydney's life was haunted by muddle. Once in later years at the Athenaeum he was delivering a blistering diatribe against the policy of Austen Chamberlain, then his chief at the Foreign Office, when the old gentleman in the chair opposite lowered his *Times* and revealed the irate features of Chamberlain. At another time, he was simultaneously involved in a suit for the annulment of his marriage, on the grounds of his impotence, and in a threatened breach-of-promise case by a woman he had got pregnant. Under his imposing exterior, in fact, he was a very troubled character, longing to be accepted by Bloomsbury[1] and gnawing his knuckles at the consciousness that he was not. His aunt, the Countess Russell ('Elizabeth' of *Elizabeth and her German Garden*), described him in later life as

---

[1] This reference to Bloomsbury, of course, refers to a slightly later period.

'very sweet and dear and intelligent and highly peculiar . . . A most delightful *mind*. A most peculiar heart.'

Hearing Sydney's report of his new friend, his aunt 'Elizabeth', who lived in Pomerania and was always looking for tutors for her daughters, conveyed an invitation to Forster to come and join her household. The idea attracted him, though he replied making all sorts of difficulties: he couldn't come permanently, he couldn't teach mathematics, indeed he couldn't teach anything but English and a little Italian. As it proved, this was just the way to strengthen 'Elizabeth's' determination. She pressed, and eventually he accepted. His duties were to begin in April.

Meanwhile, he had completed his 'Gino' novel, and had sent it off, on a speculation, to Blackwoods. He sent a copy at the same time to H.O.M., who was much impressed and told him it was a 'great' work. 'I do not think it will ever seem so to me,' Forster remarked to himself soberly: 'it is not more than careful and praiseworthy.' By March he had heard from Blackwoods that they would publish it, though not on very generous terms. They told him he must change the title, as the present one would decrease the 'already very doubtful' chances of a sale; and, having no ideas himself, he consulted Dent, whose novel in so many ways it was. Dent supplied a whole list of suggestions, and from these he selected *Where Angels Fear to Tread* and *From a Sense of Duty*. Blackwoods, to his mother's disgust, chose the former. 'I quite agree it isn't "me",' he wrote to her, 'and it was perhaps unwise to accept it . . . Should I ever write another book it will be called 'The Longest Journey', and the one after that 'Windy Corner'. Those I think are quite nice names. It's been a trouble with this one all along that I never knew what I wanted to call it.'

By the time he wrote this he was already in Germany, as a retainer in 'Elizabeth's' feudal establishment.

7 Elizabeth's German Garden

'Elizabeth', whose *Elizabeth and her German Garden* (1898) became a sacred text for the English gardening cult, was the daughter of a self-made businessman who had made his fortune in Australia, and at the age of twenty-two she had married the Count von Arnim, a widowed Prussian landowner. They had set up house in Berlin, where for six years she lived the grand and – to her – stuffy life of German high society and bore a succession of daughters. Then, in 1896, she happened to discover that among her husband's properties was a *Schloss* at Nassenheide in Pomerania – a rambling countrified seventeenth-century mansion, standing amid some 8,000 acres of its own farmland and pine-forest. It had been standing empty for twenty-five years, and she promptly decided that they must live there. Her husband was persuaded without too much difficulty, for he had an interest in scientific farming, and they moved within the year.

To begin with, she found the change blissful. She could read Thoreau all alone among the pines and birches, or, when the fancy took her, romp among the crocuses with her baby daughters or whirl them off on a picnic. She wrote sentimental novels; and she set to work to construct a garden, among the wilderness of bird-cherries and birches. It was to be an English garden, a natural one, putting to shame the lumpish Germans and their parade-ground bedding-style.

Things did not continue quite so idyllically, for 'Elizabeth' and her husband quarrelled a good deal. She liked to make sudden dashes to England whenever she felt homesick, and he objected to this. More serious, he was set upon having a son, whereas further child-bearing did not appeal to her at all. The truth was, in many ways she was a tartar.[1] She was high-spirited and gay, and all the fun began when she was about the place. Her children worshipped her; but then, she meant them to worship her, at the expense of their father, 'The Man of Wrath' as she nicknamed him. And then, for a great part of the time, she was simply invisible, to her children as to everyone else – either typing in her summerhouse or studying seed-catalogues, or away with her family in England. Moreover, she had a ferocious tongue and took the keenest delight in teasing and bullying; if you were a dependant, you could expect to be mauled daily. At mealtimes she might be gay, and then the meal passed hilariously; more often, she would be in a mood to torment someone, and would goad him or her into tears or rudeness or embarrassed collapse; and on other days she would sit through the meal in implacable silence, withering all attempts at conversation. Hugh Walpole, who went as tutor to her children shortly after Forster, has left a scarifying account of her technique of harassment. She would wait till there was a full dinner-table of important guests and then say, in 'a cold, clear tone', something like: 'Oh Mr Walpole, I've had such an interesting letter from your father. *Do* you wear flannel next your skin?'

Forster came as one of a long succession of tutors, none of whom had lasted more than six months. Having tried without success an ineffectual German tutor, a sadistic German governess, and two timid English ladies, one of whom lasted only two days, 'Elizabeth' had hit on the plan of inviting young Englishmen just down from the university, preferably from one of the smarter colleges, offering them hospitality and the chance to improve their German in exchange for an hour or two of teaching daily. Her system of engaging them was capricious. She once engaged a new tutor by letter, then took against him for some reason and told him not to write again till he heard from her, since her movements would be uncertain. The next thing he heard was a message saying that, since she had received no word from him, she must conclude he was not interested in the post.

Forster set out for Nassenheide in late March, bringing a quantity of new clothes and, as he had been requested, a packet of orris-root for 'Elizabeth'. On the way he spent a few hours in Berlin, which repelled him. He thought it 'a terrible city, dirty, ugly, mean, full of

---

[1] I would guess that Mrs Failing, in *The Longest Journey*, is drawn in part from 'Elizabeth'. The resemblance is very close; though Forster always said she was based on his Uncle Willie.

unhappy soldiers', though the National gallery was full of astonishing plunder. 'I don't make out the Germans,' he wrote in his diary.

> They terrify me. I swear anything they're the coming nation, if only because they've prigged so many Italian pictures. The country is unthinkably large and contented and patriotic – I mean that is its spirit as you go in the train. It's got no charm, like Italy, where you think all the time of the glorious limb sliding southward between warming seas . . .

His arrival at Nassenheide was disconcerting. The train dropped him out, with all his luggage, in the middle of a farmyard, in the pitch dark; there was no one to meet him, and he hadn't the faintest idea where the *Schloss* lay. Fortunately, the guard was helpful and found him a farm-labourer willing to act as guide. Splashing across the fields, the two finally arrived at the house, which was in darkness, and Forster rang. The bell pealed, a hound bayed, and by this time he was beginning to giggle. He rang again, and at last a dishevelled boy opened the door, and he was grudgingly admitted, to a vast vaulted hall hung with the heads of small animals. After a further wait, the German tutor, who had been in bed, came down to greet him, telling him that he had not been expected till tomorrow and that the departing tutor was in the bed which should have been his. Eventually a sleepy maid made up a bed for him in the state wing; the cold was appalling, and he lay awake all night shivering and listening to the ghostly clanking of a pump.

'Elizabeth', when he met her after breakfast next day, was very cool about his misfortunes. Such things lowered people in her esteem. (She told him afterwards, she nearly sent him back to England on the spot, and that he had been wearing a particularly ugly tie.) 'How d'ye do, Mr Forster,' was her greeting. 'We confused you with one of the housemaids . . . Can you teach the children, do you think? They are very difficult . . . Ah yes, Mr Forster, very difficult, they'll laugh at you, you know. You'll have to be stern or it'll end as it did with Mr Stokoe.'[1] He gave her her packet of orris-root, and was dismissed. Later in the day he wrote to his mother that he found 'Elizabeth' 'pleasant but rather disappointing, having indifferent false teeth and a society drawl.' As for the famous garden, he claimed he

---

[1] See p. 166.

couldn't find it; the house appeared to be surrounded solely by paddocks and shrubberies.

His duties as a tutor, such as they were, were confined to the three eldest children: Evi, who was fourteen, Liebet, who was twelve, and Beatrix (Trix), who was eleven. Liebet, however, was away in Italy with her father and the governess, Fräulein Backe. The remaining two were subdued and were tearful over the departure of the previous tutor; 'Mr Gibb, he climbed trees,' they told him. They gave him no trouble during the first lesson; nor did he ever find 'Elizabeth's' warnings necessary, and he easily crushed their feeble efforts at naughtiness. He taught them spelling, by a method of his own devising, and made them write English compositions. Once the subject he prescribed was, 'If there were a war between England and Germany, which would you want to win?' Trix's essay ran simply 'If there was a war between England and Germany, I shouldn't care which won: I should run away as fast as I could.' She showed up the essay with a wail: 'I know I shall get no marks because I have spoken the truth!'

Outside lesson-time his stock seemed to go up and down. One day the children chattered to him and invited him to join their games, the next he was put in his place and reminded not to think himself one of the family. The intermittent haughtiness continued all the time he was there and no doubt they learned it from their mother. Indeed, as the household at Nassenheide had increased, 'Elizabeth's' dream of Rousseauistic freedom had given place to a crushing formality. 'Everyone in any kind of position of authority had to be waited on,' wrote the pseudonymous 'Leslie de Charms' ('Elizabeth's' daughter Liebet) in her biography of her mother. 'Trays for breakfast and tea . . . briquettes for stoves, water, lamps, shoes to polish and return, were endlessly carried to wherever, in whatever remote corner of the building, each of them was lodged. The place was in a constant ferment of respectful activity, of subservient bustle.' Forster and his fellow tutors and governesses ate with the family at luncheon and dinner, but at these rather freezing occasions they were not expected to initiate conversation; and when the servants brought round coffee after dinner, none was offered to them.

Forster did not resent his position; and certainly sometimes he found himself all too much in the thick of family life. One Sunday morning, for instance, the girls offered him a piece of bread to eat.

It was obviously, to his eyes, a cake of soap, but he duly bit it, noting the marks of the previous tutors' teeth. They were in ecstasies. 'All you tutors fall in,' they cried, and they tried it next on Mademoiselle, but she said she was too old a hand for such tricks and took up her zither. 'Elizabeth' was typing in the next room, so they went to inquire if the noise disturbed her. 'Non. Cela me soulage,' the reply came back. But then the pendant on Mademoiselle's bracelet caught in the strings of her zither, and neither Evi nor Forster could release her; and meanwhile Trix had twisted the baby's leg into the back of the chair, and the kitten, who had been given some pink medicine, began to stagger alarmingly . . . There was also, as he wrote to his mother (21 April 1905), a good deal of jollity in the evenings:

> I skirling about with E. in the Highland fling or leading the Cake Walk, to the intense joy of the company, while Mlle, whose head turns, turns the hurdy gurdy. Then musical chairs & then Oranges & Lemons – or – to give it its shocking Nassenheide name – 'Tummy-aches or Castor-Oil'. You have to choose which you will have. I was the only one who chose Tummy-aches, which was Elizabeth, and naturally we could not pull over the others, who were headed by Fräulein Backe, purple with excitement, and clad in white satin from head to foot. My muscles are quite enfeebled.

Altogether, Forster found he was enjoying himself and had rapidly made himself at home, a thing he was adept at doing. He made excellent friends with Herr Steinweg, the other tutor, and with the governesses. Steinweg and he went for long walks together and gave each other conversation-lessons in the other's language. Steinweg, a large and genial divinity student, was always cheerful and considerate. He was an art-lover, in a sentimental way, quoted poetry in the twilight and possessed a collection of photographs of old masters, which he displayed turn by turn in a special frame. He was autocratic and made a great fuss to the servants if the stoves didn't burn or there was jam on the teapot lid. 'Elizabeth' (who happened to be annoyed with him or Forster at the time) commented in a 'digging' tone: 'Herr Steinweg's bossing you, Mr Forster, you know. You won't be able to call your soul your own.' However, Forster was very content to be bossed, and there was scarcely ever a hitch between them. The only time Steinweg was at all put out was when Forster revealed that he thought telephone wires were hollow.

This seemed to Steinweg inconceivable ignorance, and he was cold and silent for a time.

The French governess, a queer-looking, round-shouldered, elderly spinster with a nutcracker face, was equally well-disposed. Forster, like everyone in the family, became very fond of her. She would sit in the schoolroom as a chaperone, her desk always littered with her own handiwork – strange objects such as a filigree rabbit or a pig constructed from shavings. She had read fewer books and acquired less information than Forster would have thought possible. 'C'est grand dommage que je n'étais pas poussée dans ma jeunesse,' she would say. 'J'aurai devenue quelquechose – comme Mme de Sévigné peut-être.' Forster always enjoyed her literary opinions: 'Je trouve que Loti est très léger – très décolleté,' she used to say. 'Zola aussi est très ordinaire dans ses expressions.'

As Easter approached, Liebet and Fräulein Backe returned from Italy, followed by the Count. The arrival of 'The Man of Wrath' made everyone nervous. He was so intensely musical, Forster was told, that no one else would dare play the piano while he was there, though nowadays he never performed himself. However, Forster decided, on meeting him, that he should like him too. Indeed, he assessed him as a more deserving character than 'Elizabeth'; though it was true he made tragic scenes about the food, reducing poor 'Teppi', the governess-housekeeper, to tears. Also, the ends of dinners were always agony for Forster, for the Count had a habit of sucking up water out of his finger-bowl and, after an awful moment, spewing it out again. This made Forster either wince or giggle, and, whichever he did, 'Elizabeth' spotted it.

Easter was a great festivity at Nassenheide. Forster went off to Stettin to buy marzipan eggs, and on Easter morning the whole household went out into the garden to search for Easter eggs. Having found forty or fifty or so of the smaller sort, they came upon the Easter Hare himself, with a whole basketful of giant eggs in his lap. The hare ('Teppi' in a washleather mask, mobcap and dung-coloured shawl) made a long rhymed oration, gave each child its eggs, and then hopped vigorously up and down the gravel paths. 'Teppi' was devoted to 'Elizabeth' and was put upon by everyone. She was tall and frog-faced and would have liked to 'live in art'. She would sing, when allowed to, which wasn't often as her voice was appalling, and she loved discussing opera. She nursed an affection for the local

Inspector of Forests and would speak lyrically of the beauty of his woodland existence.

It was not long before 'Elizabeth', who had thought her new English tutor so mousy and undistinguished, was forced to revise her opinion. Forster mentioned some acquaintances of hers in Dresden, and she remarked, 'They don't like me.' 'Yes, so I saw,' replied Forster; at which she gave a start; it was not at all the sort of answer she had been expecting. It set her wondering. A copy of the April number of the *Independent Review* had arrived, containing Forster's essay on 'Cardan', and she asked if she could borrow it. 'I'm a very severe critic,' she warned him. She brought it back in a chastened mood. 'You're simply to go on and win,' she said. 'I've no more to say.' And upon this she immediately veered to a new tack: Forster was a dark horse, a genius in disguise, he had an eye which took in everything and the talent to achieve anything he wanted. Forster found himself half accepting this new version of himself. How much of a dark horse was he, he wondered? He noted in his diary for 16 April 1905:

> Have got it into my head that Gr. [the Gräfin] thinks I write
> better than she does, & is distressed at it. Any how, contact with
> her makes me more self conscious, writhing round 'Am I modest
> or no?' I think I do think little of myself, but then I think a good
> deal about it.

In accordance with her new view of him, 'Elizabeth' suggested they should write something in collaboration. He was aghast and was greatly relieved when he managed to wriggle out of it.

Henceforth the two got on swimmingly. They played tennis together, and his peculiar action made her laugh so much that he sometimes even won. He read *Emma* aloud to her, and she lent him *Erewhon*. The Count looked on benevolently when they discussed literature, though he silenced them when they talked 'shop' (about advances and royalties, etc.), saying that if that sort of conversation were permitted, he had far more interesting information to impart about artificial fertilizer. Forster wrote to his mother what a delightful character 'Elizabeth' was and how much less frightened he was of her than he had expected.

His comments in his diary were less eulogistic. He didn't like the note in her voice when, one evening after dinner, she talked about church-going: 'I can't understand this conscientiousness,' she said.

'Sydney Waterlow and his wife won't go to church or Communion – they're shocked at me. I don't see why I shouldn't go if it does my soul good. You aren't obliged to look at things as the parson does. After all, our beliefs all lead to the same thing in the end. But perhaps you don't believe anything? In which case the conversation ceases.' He wondered why this was so jarring. 'Is she wrong for this reason – that her visit is no act of faith, but a kind of insult to the intellect – an insult, not a denial, which last may be the good thing? If she is not wrong she has put it very untakingly. It sounded shocking.' And gradually, as the three months passed, he arrived at a settled judgement on her and ceased to be concerned about her opinion of himself. 'The Gräfin's dicta,' he wrote in his diary for 25 July, 'are always suggestive & always worthless: her attitude to literary and spiritual questions is that of ours to food, which depends not on the food but on the state of the stomach. I hope that I shall never again be depressed when she thinks me rot – and more difficult – elated when she praises me.'

In July, the proofs of *Where Angels Fear to Tread* arrived and she issued a running report on her reactions. She hated the opening chapters; they were clever, she said, but *most* unattractive. 'Pfui, Mr Forster': they made her want to take a bath. Then she read Chapter 4, and found it beautiful, and took back all she had said. Then she reached Chapter 6 and promptly returned more firmly to her first opinion: it was a horrible book, 'full of underdone meat and spittle'.

While he was correcting his proofs, she was at work on *The Princess Priscilla's Fortnight*, spending her days in her summerhouse, over the door of which hung the notice *Procul Este Profani*. He was not invited to read her novel, and indeed he was only once admitted to the summerhouse. On this occasion, to show how her typewriter worked, she 'quickly and deftly' typed an exalted quotation from Swinburne: 'I have looked deep into the hand of God,' or something of the sort. It gave him a vision of her, he said much later;

> . . . a hard tight indestructible little spiritual existence seemed to bob up and down: hard, yet if ever I cracked it I should expect to find a spot of chocolate cream at the core . . . To be really liked, to really be liked, is probably her deepest inspiration, and when she brushes aside one's cleverness and exclaims 'But haven't you a heart?' it perhaps isn't tactics entirely. May this explain her extraordinary power? It does seem odd that one should be so

anxious to please such a person, for she isn't distinguished and she's always ungrateful. Yet one *is* anxious, and she will have menials, unpaid and paid, to wait upon her until she dies. To want to be loved does pay.[1]

Soon after Easter, 'Elizabeth' left for her annual holiday in England, carrying letters, and a chocolate hare for Maimie Aylward, to post there for Forster. Meanwhile spring arrived at Nassenheide, and the place gradually took on an extraordinary beauty. Pansies and tulips sprang up in the grass, and in the meadows kingcups, cowslips and small yellow anemones; the wild white *Faulbaum* blossomed along the ditches, and everywhere there strayed pale green birches. 'You cannot imagine the radiance that descended upon that flat iron-coloured land in May,' he wrote, recollecting this time. He sat in a birch-glade, reading his German grammar, with a pinewood one side of him, and on the other cornfields stretching away, mile after mile, as large as a county.

In this idyllic situation, once he had finished his work on the *Aeneid*, he lapsed into radiant idleness. Though so uneventful, it was one of the high points of happiness in his life, and he welcomed it as such. An extraordinary current of optimism was running through him, and he took his stand on optimism, as against the *fin-de-siècle* attitude to life. Re-reading his diary entry for 27 February, 'A taste for cheap tragic effects in life seems to be the penalty paid by those who have no taste for tragedy in Art,' he thought of its converse: 'Those who like tragedy in art are somewhat brutalized to it in life.'

> As to art, the prevalence of sad endings is a sign both of con-scientiousness & incompetence: the first ∵ artists now realise that marriage, the old full stop, is not an end at all, the second, because it would be finer to end happily, & they cannot. It doesn't mean that they are pessimistic in life, but that they are too clumsy to be optimistic in art.

He had been reading *Marius the Epicurean* and had disliked its hushed, defunctive tones, noting 'There is an absence of vulgarity which is something like fatal.' Pater, he felt, was only excited by death: 'any death is wonderful: dead or wounded flesh gives Pater the thrill he can never get from its healthiness' (2 May 1905).

---

[1] The words come from a paper read to the Memoir Club, most probably in the 1930s. The rather 'hard' tone is not that of his youth and is one that he adopted especially for Bloomsbury.

By comparison, Keats's letters, which he had also been reading, seemed more and more admirable. 'Keats, in his letters, shows a perfect attitude towards his art: absolutely serious but genial. And his enormous elevation above other men only makes him wish they would quarrel less.' – 'My dear fellow,' he addressed him, 'you are now (1818) 23, and it's the first of many times I shall sit at the feet of my juniors.' He thought Keats must have been nearly the best person in the world:

> He has seized upon the supreme fact of human nature, the very small amount of good in it, and the supreme importance of that little. He is contented with his stuffy set, as he would have been contented with anyone whom he knew long enough.

It was what he would have liked to aim at in his own life; but even at 'Elizabeth's', in this heavenly independence, the question kept recurring to him: 'He who loses his own soul for men's sake shall he find it?'

> To be enthusiastic & sentimental over the picturesque poor is no difficulty. One doesn't face the question till it comes to the vulgar and genteel. To know and help them are we to lose our souls – or how much of them?

This was to be a central question for him. The kind of life he had chosen for himself, full of aunts and tea-parties and little jokes and chocolate hares, was a thoroughly dowdy and tame and suburban one, beset on all sides by the 'vulgar and genteel'. He had chosen it because it was the most real existence offered to him; or rather he had not chosen it, it had chosen him. But could one live it and not in the end surrender to its values? It would not be easy. And whether it was worth attempting at all seemed to him to depend on whether you had faith in human life in general. He felt just now that he had.

> The conditions are appalling: poverty, matrimony, much of family life all work against love and clear vision: and to these are added the rules of the game – death and decay. Yet people contrive to get into touch – I believe because they are radically good.

Steinweg his fellow-tutor was a graduate of Greifswald, an ancient university on the Baltic coast, and to Forster's gratification he offered to take him to the annual reunion of his *Gesellschaft*. It was a curious experience, largely occupied with endless drinking-bouts, at which the professors were mobbed and fêted by singing, duel-scarred students. At his second evening's bout there was great embarrassment, as it had to be explained to him that one of the planned entertainments was an anti-British extravaganza. 'Had we known that you were coming,' his hosts chorused, 'this would *never* have happened. But the dresses are all bought, and the play rehearsed, so could you pardon our incivility?' He said he could, and the play proceeded. In strode an Englishman, carrying a Baedeker, and dressed in typical English costume – a white pot-hat with a blue veil, a long white umpire's coat, check trousers and red socks. He sang a song, every line of which ended in 'Aow yes,' and after this his German companions fell on him and beat him, for no reason that Forster could understand, and then they made friends with him, for reasons equally unclear. The singing was first-rate.

It had been agreed that his stay at Nassenheide should finish at the end of July, and he made plans to tour Rügen and various towns along the Baltic on his way home. He left Nassenheide in glory. 'Elizabeth' told him he had been a most successful tutor; Steinweg gave him a copy of Goethe's *Faust*; and as they saw him off on the train, the children produced gifts, all stuck over with flowers and ribbons. Evi's and Liebet's were poems and Trix, who hadn't been able to think of one, gave him gooseberries instead.

8 *Where Angels Fear to Tread*

On 5 October 1905 *Where Angels Fear to Tread* was published, a fact which he did not trouble to mention in his diary. It received an excellent press, almost all the reviewers recognizing a new and personal voice in the book. The *Bookseller* spoke of 'a brilliance and a unique charm' in the writing, and the *Bookman*, even warmer, said, perceptively, 'This is a book which one begins with pleased interest and gradually finds to be astonishing. Its amusing facility becomes amusing cleverness, and then, almost without realizing the development, we find that the cleverness is of a larger style than we thought, and the main issues of life are confronting us where we looked for trivialities.' Best of all was a long signed review from C. F. G. Masterman,[1] then the influential literary editor of the *Daily News*. It was headed 'A Remarkable Novel' and began: 'Not often has the reviewer to welcome a new writer and a new novel so directly conveying the impression of power and an easy mastery of material.' Even the true-blue *Spectator* admired the book and reported the practical lessons which it taught, such as 'the futility of ill-considered rebellion against convention', to be 'unimpeachable in their strong if indirect confirmation of orthodox views'. It was only a pity, the *Spectator* thought, that the novel was so painful, and it hoped that 'so original and searching a talent may yet give us a story in which the fallibility of goodness and the callousness of respectability are less uncompromisingly insisted upon'.

His friends, too, were mostly very enthusiastic. Hugh Meredith went so far as to tell him he was the only living writer to stand beside Turgenev.

---

[1] See p. 107, footnote.

> Of course you have an immense amount to learn yet, especially in
> the management of your subordinate scenes and your treatment
> of the characters which you dislike. But it will be worth going
> through with it even if no-one will publish or buy your books
> (which I don't for a moment believe) because you really under-
> stand tragedy. The death of the baby and the last conversation
> between Miss Abbott and Herriton are magnificent. I don't
> believe anyone else would have dared to write 'baby' instead of
> 'child'.[1]

'Snow' Wedgwood had him for tea and a serious talk about his work,
and she found him 'a most pleasing object of criticism', attending
most cheerfully to all her objections. She told him that what was
wrong with his story was that he hadn't made up his mind whether
it was to be tragedy or comedy. 'It seemed quite a new idea to him,'
she wrote, innocently, to his Aunt Laura. She even managed to say
to him, what was more awkward for her, that he should have been
more explicit about Gino's infidelities. 'Impropriety should be worth
while,' she advised him. She begged him to fall in love before writing
another novel, upon which he confided to her that he *was* in love –
with Hamlet! A more despondent note was struck by Aunt Laura's
friend Henrietta Litchfield. 'His novel is really not good,' she
lamented; 'and it's too unpleasant for the girls to read. I very much
hope he will turn to something else, though I am sure I don't know
what.' It was, she said, the same case as that of her nephew Vaughan
Williams, 'a foolish young man', who *would* go on working at music
when 'he was so hopelessly bad at it'.[2] As for Forster's family circle,
they took the reviewers' word as to his brilliance; though Aunt
Rosalie asked why he laughed at 'the nice Germans', and his mother
thought it 'a pity [he . . . said] a bad word'. His grandmother was
sure the book would have a *run*.

A week or two after the novel's appearance, he was on his travels
again, going to stay with his Uncle Willie. It was salmon-fishing
season, and he decided for once to join in the sport and was allowed
to play two fish. 'Fun pulling,' he noted, 'but none of the thrill I've
heard of.' He refused to fish again himself, deciding that collecting
the tackle would be a nuisance, and that anyway he might spoil the
fun for the rest of the party; moreover he didn't fancy wading. But

---

[1] Undated letter.
[2] See Gwen Raverat, *Period Piece* (1952), Chapter 14.

the scene, as the rest fished in the black stream beneath the dam, struck him as most glorious.

> The colours of the trees were not vivid – gentle browns, yellows & reds – and standing above the dam they rose in calculated beauty on either side of the stream, sunlit, whilst I was in shadow. It seemed intended – a spectacle made by a pleasure giving god, rather than a process of nature.

He decided that one couldn't write down Nature: 'we can write down Man, ∴ we employ similes from Nature, which the imagination revivifies. But to describe their source is hopeless.' In a way it was reassuring to him, that there should exist something so external, not subject to one's moods. Recently, in the interests of Victor Woolley's[1] psychical researches, he had tried putting himself into a trance, by repeating a name. He had had no success, and this suggested to him that he was growing more 'material' – 'the beautiful veil has become thicker'. He was not very sorry.

He greeted the year 1906 with a poem, presumably one of his own.

> We were not good enough for Heaven
>   Nor bad enough for Hell:
> And therefore unto us was given
>   Unseen on earth to dwell:
>
> To listen by the moonlit thatch,
>   By window-blinds to lurk,
> To watch men on their knees and watch
>   Men go about their work.
>
> We watch in hope to be forgiven:
>   But still we cannot tell
> Whose deeds are good enough for Heaven,
>   Whose bad enough for Hell.

It is not a very good poem, but it is significant for what it says about the novelist's ghostly and *voyeuriste* role in life. Already in Philip Herriton he had taken for his protagonist a Laodicean, one who was too half-hearted either for salvation or damnation and who treated life only as a spectacle. And in the hero of his current novel, Rickie Elliot, he was creating another of the half-hearted, one whose epitaph would be that he was 'one of the thousands whose dust

returns to the dust, accomplishing nothing in the interval'. It was a
fate he still feared for himself, as we have seen: 'culture', timidity and
self-consciousness might undo him. The poem is significant in
another way too. He had come to realize that, for a novelist, there
was one special weakness in his chosen way of life: he watched 'Men
go about their work,' but, never having had a job himself, he was in
no position to write about this working side of their life. As he said
a year or two later to his friend Malcolm Darling[1] (12 December
1908), 'It is the great defect of my position that I only see people in
their leisure moments.' This was an important truth about himself.
He had, and continued throughout life to have, very little power of
imagining what people did in their working hours, or indeed very
little interest in it. And this disability, though it was one that he
managed to turn to advantage in his fiction, tended to produce
difficulties, and comedies, in his own life and friendships.

He had to go down to Cornwall and Devon, this January, to give
his extension lectures, and his mother came with him. They put up
in Penzance. 'Lo the Esplanade!' he wrote to his friend E. V.
Thompson, 'and on it people walking whose NOSES plough the

shining horizons of the sea.' Thompson, a nephew of William de
Morgan, the pre-Raphaelite potter and author of *Joseph Vance*, had
been up with Forster at King's, and they had a jokey and facetious
relationship, based on the fiction of Thompson's extreme Pods-
nappery and Philistinism. His letters to Thompson from Cornwall
were in the approved style of undergraduate waggishness. He
requested Thompson in one of them (3 March 1906) to admit to 'a
certain ursino-ductility of soul'.

> I should be glad of a letter of apology, acknowledging this quality,
> for which I have a profound respect. It has made England what
> she is. If you write denying it, you prove that you possess it. If

---

[1] Malcolm Lyall Darling (1880–1969). See *post*, p. 171.

you don't write at all, the proof is even more conclusive, but
England will be what she is no longer.

Enough. I pant for facts. Let us have crude Life (as my long
haired friends say). For example:

No really nace person would stop here on account of the 4th.[1]
In itself 'tis a jolly young thing, with as pretty an action as any
4th in Europe.

But.

You can only reach it by going through the kitchen.

This in itself is not a great drawback for there do be (again I
summon literature) there do be a little courtyard, most chastely
intervening.

But.

The landlady is always in the kitchen, entertaining her lady-
friends.

'Ah!' I say, making as if I have lost my way and then again I
say 'ah!' making as if I have found it. 'Ah!' I say when I return,
thereby giving them to understand that I took the wrong road
after all, but I never say 'Ah!' a fourth time, or they would guess
where I have been.

I forget if you're going to find this vulgar.

To Thompson he also confided his observations on the Cornish
character.

It isn't nonsense to gas about the Celts. These are the first I've
struck, and they're absolutely unlike ourselves -- at least unlike
three quarters of me: one quarter of me being Irish, & I'm not
used to rely on it. They're above all civil: in the town their civility
becomes servile: in the country it is generally delightful, though
there's sometimes a false step, because they don't even persuade
themselves they're sincere. Italians, I think, do. These people are,
at the back of their minds, watching the stranger. 'What does he
want *this* time?' They're the beaten race all over, only they
combine defeat with good looks & physical courage.

Visiting Gurnard's Head, with such reflections in mind, he was,
for the third time in his life, 'met' by a fully-formed story. The
story, 'The Rock'[2] was about a man who, having been rescued
by Cornish fishermen when his boat is wrecked on a rock on their
coast, asks himself what he can give them in repayment, and
eventually concludes that the only appropriate gift is his whole life –
that is to say, he must give away all his possessions and go to live on

---

[1] See footnote to p. 84.
[2] It is printed in *The Life to Come and Other Stories* (1972).

the charity of his rescuers. He felt such conviction of his own inspiration that, as a thank-offering, he put a sovereign in the Royal Lifeboat Institution's collecting-box, being sure he would make the money over and again. The story turned out a complete flop and was turned down firmly by every editor, and he had to conclude that his inspiration had been 'genuine but worthless, like so much inspiration'.[1]

*   *   *

All this time, as regards his sentimental life, his feelings were still centred on Hugh Meredith. Meredith had taken a lectureship at Manchester University, and Forster often went up to stay with him there. Already, something was not going quite right with his life and career. During 1903, just after the development of his relations with Forster, he had had a nervous breakdown. The cause, or symptom, was his getting engaged to a Cambridge friend, Caroline Graveson.[2] On the strength of his engagement he had conceived the idea of starting a co-educational school and had written instantly to Bertrand Russell (21 April 1903), asking for his support. The letter was in characteristically assertive tones:

> My qualifications for this enterprise are the following:
>   1. I am going to marry an apostolic woman who is at present mistress of method at Liverpool University.
>   2. I shall probably persuade Mathews[3] to join.
>   3. I know exactly what I want . . .

Soon after writing this, he suffered a severe attack of depression, attributed to overwork, and had to take a long rest-cure under doctor's orders; and by July he was writing to Russell full of self-doubt and self-denigration and announcing the collapse of all his plans:

> Some months ago I wrote to tell you that I was going to marry Miss Graveson and for that and also on general grounds I want you to know that at the present time I feel more like letting drop my connexions with her and everyone else who is both better and worse than I am. I feel something like a horror of living with people who depend upon me and whose light goes out when mine

---

[1] Introduction to his *Collected Short Stories* (1947).

[2] Caroline C. Graveson (1874–1958). She later became Vice-President of Goldsmiths' College.

[3] Myles Mathews. See p. 69, footnote.

does. The fact that I give them pain irritates me so much that my irritation is directed not only against myself but against them too. This is silly of course; if I *am* silly (as apparently I am) it seems to me to follow that the less I have to do with people the better it will be both for them and for myself.

The trouble seems to be here as in every other department of my life that my feelings are not persistent or as Theodore[1] puts it that I have 'a bad will'. I am really I think the economic man without the directing desire for wealth.

Things had never really gone well for Meredith since. In Manchester he felt an exile, and Cambridge and the Society seemed to him to belong to another existence, 'I think I am dead really now,' he wrote to Keynes in April 1906. 'Or perhaps I should say I realise now what was plain to others two years ago. I come to life temporarily when I meet Forster.' Forster, as was his habit in friendship, made vigorous efforts to rouse Meredith out of his apathy. They would go for long walks, endlessly discussing Meredith's problems, or sometimes walking in total silence while he brooded.

Meredith got engaged again in 1906, to Christabel Iles,[2] another of his friends from Cambridge – a 'progressive' and left-wing educationalist, then lecturing in Liverpool. Forster went up to see him in June, a month before the wedding, and came home reflecting cheerlessly on his own future. It seemed as if his incomplete friendship with Meredith would always be the pattern for him, and anything more was a dream: physically he was fated to frustration, and he must clutch such compensation as he could. On the evening of his return (22 June 1906) he noted in his diary: 'I am cut off from [illegible]: but in recompense will it remain beautiful for ever? unattainable =Is unchangeable? From the window I see attainers: they look not happy.' He seems to have dallied with thoughts of suicide, for a fortnight later he noted: 'Reasons against suicide: i. selfish ii. nature ceaselessly beautiful.'

In August he made a sentimental pilgrimage to Stevenage. First he went to the Jowitts, and then, on a borrowed bicycle, he rode over to the Franklyns, where, for the first time, he was given tea in the

---

[1] Probably Theodore Llewellyn Davies, a Trinity friend of theirs.

[2] Christabel Iles (1876–1945). She was Mistress of Method at Homerton College 1909–12 and Lecturer in Educational Psychology at the Froebel Institute, Roehampton, 1928–38.

parlour reserved for intimate friends. After tea Frankie took him over the farm and into the 'dear meadow', and they found the swing-hooks in the oak-tree, on which they used to play, now almost covered over with bark. Stealing some lavender from his own old garden, he then rode on to the Postons at 'Highfield'. Here he had his first meeting with Mr Poston's new wife; and the sight of this charming, cultivated woman marooned in 'Highfield' philistia seems to have supplied the germ of *Howards End*. 'They were all on the lawn,' he told his mother.

> Mr P. looked very well indeed, but his voice is awful – a loud whisper. It will never get any worse I believe, and is annoying to others rather than to him. Like all such, he talks incessantly. The wife is so charming – pretty, pleasant, clever, and the Jowitts say so good & kind as well. She seems terribly incongruous there. The rooms are full of Fra Angelicos, etc., and P.C.[1] shows them off just as he used to show off his fields, though in this case he cannot always recollect the names. He has adopted culture, and it does not sit well on him. 'Here is the emperor Augustus.' I said 'And there's a Donatello.' He replied 'Oh that's only plaster.' They had got 'a gentleman and lady, very literary'[2] stopping with them. We talked about Elizabeth. P.C. enquired after you & sent his love, Slow[3] 'his duty', the wife some civil message. I said to P.C. rather maliciously that Aunt Rosalie was going to marry Mr A.[4] He at once began 'Ah *my* case was very different. Had May[5] not married I should *never* etc. etc. I cannot think that such an unusually charming person can love him deeply.

*   *   *

One of Lily's friends in Weybridge, their new home, was a Mrs Morison, the wife of Theodore Morison, a distinguished Anglo-Indian official. Morison was now a member of the India Council,[6] but before his return to England he had for some years been a professor at, and subsequently Principal of, the Muslim Anglo-Oriental College at Aligarh. The College had played an important role in the revival

---

[1] i.e. Mr Poston.
[2] Possibly 'Elizabeth' of the *German Garden*.
[3] The coachman.
[4] Aunt Rosie, in 1906, married Robert Alford, a middle-aged widower in the carriage-trade, whom she had known from childhood.
[5] One of the Poston daughters.
[6] A council of advisers to the Secretary of State for India. There were 15 members, mainly retired Indian officials.

(known as 'The Awakening') of the Muslim community in India.
After the Mutiny, Muslim fortunes in Indian had reached a low ebb,
and when, in 1875, with British assistance, the Muslim Anglo-
Oriental College had been founded, it was part of a general effort to
modernize Muslim education and restore the self-respect of the
Muslim community. Its founder was the celebrated reformer Sir
Syed Ahmed Khan,[1] described by his biographer as 'the foremost
Mohammedan in India', and the place can best be described as a sort
of Muslim Eton; it was – at least in its early days – very loyal and
British, with a famous cricket team and a residential system on the
English collegiate model. Morison had become a close friend of Sir
Syed, and, as a result of trouble in Syed's family, he had taken Sir
Syed's grandson, Syed Ross Masood, into his own household and
adopted him as his ward.* He always referred to Masood as 'my son',
and the boy had come to feel closer to him than to his real father.

Masood had just finished his schooling at the College and was now
in Weybridge, waiting to go up to Oxford. The Morisons were looking
round for a tutor for him, to coach him in Latin. Lily suggested that
the post might suit Morgan; and so it was arranged. When Maimie
Aylward heard he was going to have a black man for a pupil, she
said, 'Oh dear, I do hope he won't steal the spoons.'

Masood's arrival in his life was a major event for Forster. Masood,
by everyone's account, was a striking and vivid figure. He was large
and magnificent-looking, well over six feet tall, with a sonorous and
beautiful voice; one could not fail to notice his voice, for he never
stopped talking. He was volatile, expansive and masterful, always
very full of himself, one moment on the crest of the wave, the next
groaning in well-acted despair and loudly demanding comfort. He
was always rather grand and princely in his manner; he loved
swaggering with silver-topped canes and could flip a sixpence into a
beggar's hand from ten feet away. He was extravagant with money, a
lover of practical jokes, and very gregarious, so that in later years he
never went anywhere without a little court in attendance. Like his
grandfather, he was a blazing Muslim patriot, full of nostalgia for the
splendours of the Mogul past. 'Ah that I had lived 250 years ago,' he
would sigh, 'when the oriental despotisms were in their prime.' He

---

[1] Sir Syed Ahmed Khan (1817–98). See G. F. I. Graham, *The Life and Work
of Syed Ahmed Khan* (1885).

loved the verse of Ghālib, the elegist of the Mogul empire, and of Hālī,[1] the poet of the 'Awakening', and was already nursing grandiose schemes for reviving Urdu culture.

When Forster first knew him, experience had already taught him to expect slights from the British, and he was fully prepared to return them. He handled the British splendidly, according to Forster.

> If they patronised him, he let them have it back, very politely, and I have often been amused at the way in which Englishmen and Englishwomen who had begun by giving themselves airs were obliged to drop them, and yield to his masterful personality and his charm. There is a story that he was once involved in a 'railway-carriage' incident. He was stretched full-length in an empty compartment when a British officer bounced in and said 'Come on! get out of this.' Masood looked up quietly and said, 'D'you want your head knocked off,' whereupon the officer exclaimed, 'I say, I'm awfully sorry. I didn't know you were that sort of person,' and they became excellent friends.

Masood had a whole repertoire of stories of this kind; they were one of his staple topics. There was the occasion, for instance, when some undergraduates broke into his room, saying they objected to his 'unmanly' use of scent. 'We'll see who's unmanly', was his reply; and he challenged one of them to a wrestling-match and wiped the floor with him. He used to say that he had made one close English friend at Oxford and 'was able to give him some help'. Years later, when he was back in India, he heard that his friend had arrived in the neighbourhood, so he went to call on him, wearing native costume. The friend received him very coolly, keeping his hands behind his back and asking him what he wanted; to which Masood's rejoinder was: 'I only now realise that you have the soul of a tailor!' None of this caused him to hate the British. He rather enjoyed his skirmishes with them, and adopted a tone of despairing good humour towards them. 'As for your damned countrymen,' he once told Forster, 'I pity the poor fellows from the bottom of my heart, and give them all the help I can' – a remark Forster thought very funny.

Not very much Latin got taught at their meetings, for Masood

---

[1] Altaf Husain Hālī (1837–1914). Urdu poet who began writing in the traditional Persian style but became a patriotic and natìonalistic poet through contact with Masood's grandfather, Sir Sayed Ahmed Khan, and with the 'Aligarh movement'.

easily got bored. 'Never mind, never mind, let's leave that,' he would say impatiently. (When they were more intimate, if Forster became difficult, Masood would pick him up bodily and tickle him.) The two rapidly became friends. Masood's ruling passion was friendship, and Forster's earliest diary entry about him refers to that theme.

> *Dec. 24.* Masood gives up duties for friends – which is civilisation. Though as he remarks 'Hence the confusion in Oriental states. To them personal relations come first.'

The principle, of course, was precisely Forster's own, but, as he was to find, Masood held it with quite un-English recklessness. To all his close friends he habitually wrote in strains of the most exalted affection; they were his 'dearest', his 'darling', and the flame of their love must burn for ever. He insisted that nothing must ever come in the way of friendship, of *his* friendship in particular, and he loved to play the despot to his friends, his favourite phrase being 'I will never speak to you again if you don't . . .' No sooner did a friendship spring up between him and Forster, than he began to complain of Forster's horrid English formality. Once when Forster came to visit him in Oxford, he made such a fuss on the subject that Forster protested it made a thank-you letter impossible.

> What am I to write about? All the usual topics are barred. I mayn't say 'thank you for my { pleasant / beastly } visit, nor for the { beautiful / stupid } book that you { kindly / unkindly } gave me when I was { lucky / unlucky } enough to be in your { delightful / god forsaken } room. For if I do you will fly into a passion that I'm being formal. Well, make up a polite message for yourself. I'm hanged if I will bother myself.

Even when they knew each other well, Forster could be taken by surprise by him. Once, after a holiday in Paris,[1] he had to return home earlier than Masood, and at their parting in the station gave him a cool and sensible English goodbye. Masood remonstrated passionately at this coldness. 'But after all,' said Forster, 'we'll be seeing each other in three days.' 'But we're *friends*!' Masood wailed.

---

[1] See p. 180.

Masood, Forster was to say later, woke him up out of his suburban and academic life and showed him new horizons and a new civilization. The princely manner and good looks, the vividness and demonstrativeness, charmed and excited him; and gradually, as we shall see, he fell in love with Masood. It was his first affair of the heart since Meredith, and though it too was never fulfilled physically, it liberated him in other ways. It released him, or so he thought, from that negativity and defeatism with which Meredith had managed to infect all his friends.

9 Pessimism in Literature and Optimism in Life

Forster was very faithful in conducting his class at the Working Men's College. It is an interesting fact about him that in later years the term 'educational' became for him a term of abuse, yet, one way and another, in earlier years, he spent a great deal of his time and energy on adult education. In fact, it left its mark on his literary personality. As a critic and essayist he had a way of simplifying issues and putting them in words of one syllable, which was often effective and charming but on occasion could sound like 'talking down'; and it was through these adult-education activities that he came by this habit.

I shall say more later about his connection with the Working Men's College. Meanwhile, I am concerned with a speech he gave on 1 December 1906, to the College's debating society. The subject for debate was: 'Is the Pessimism in Modern Literature to be Deplored?', and in his opening speech he argued that pessimism in literature was *not* to be deplored. This was not because there was no happiness in daily life, but because in books, as opposed to life, what mattered most was the *end*. 'We do not judge a man by the words that he gasps on his death-bed. But we do judge a book by the words that are written on the last page.'

Thus, the question was, how should a novelist or playwright *end* his story? The optimist would tell him, 'with a marriage'. But the world of today knew that a marriage was not an end, but rather a beginning. So the writer turned to the pessimist, and the pessimist's answer – a more persuasive one – was, 'with a separation'. It was a matter of aims:

> In life we seek what is gracious and noble, even if it is transitory;
> in books we seek what is permanent, even when it is sad. I uphold
> optimism in life. I do not at present uphold optimism in literature.

The simple and aspiring tone of his speech, as I have suggested,
owed something to his audience, but the issue was a serious one for
him just then, the period of the writing of *The Longest Journey*. For,
emboldened by the success of *Where Angels Fear to Tread*, he was
taking greater risks in his new novel. He was writing from the heart
and getting on paper all the passion and magic and sentiment that
he found there. And this forced him to certain realizations. For he
knew that, as a novelist, he wanted to express what was 'gracious
and noble' and offer hope and salvation to humanity; but, for one
writing under the shadow of Flaubert and the *fin-de-siècle*, this was
an unfashionable aim. It compelled him, he felt, to define his position.

And the truth he was forced to face, he decided, was that he was a
sentimentalist. He had flirted already with the word, in calling those
early writings of his 'sentimental articles', and now, more squarely,
he took his stand on it. 'I must say something, not to you but to
"you", about sentimentality,' he wrote to Dickinson about this time.[1]

> All I write is, to me, sentimental. A book which doesn't leave
> people either happier or better than it found them, which doesn't
> add some permanent treasure to the world, isn't worth doing. (A
> book *about* good and happy people may be still better but hasn't
> attracted me yet so much.) This is my 'theory', and I maintain
> it's sentimental – at all events it isn't Flaubert's. How can he fag
> himself to write 'Un coeur simple', a life of this outline?

> And d'Annunzio can do the same. As to seeing life as I write it –
> certainly I don't do that. The traps are far fewer; perhaps
> negligeable.

The letter sums up his outlook at the time of writing *The Longest
Journey* – the most ostensibly tragic and the most truly optimistic of
his novels.

---

[1] 12 May 1907.

The Longest Journey was always his favourite among his novels. It was the one he had written most easily and with most rapture. He knew, even at the time, that it had terrible faults, and as the years went by they exasperated even more. Some perversity (it was this more than inexperience, he thought) had made him stray off into the fantastic in the late chapters, 'with no gain to the poetic'.* None the less, he thought, and continued to think, that he had been 'more considerable' in this book than elsewhere, and 'more in advance of his time'. It was the one book of his, he felt, that had given more back to the world than it had taken from it. 'Stephen Wonham – that theoretic figure –' he said later, with much insight, 'is in a sense so dead because he is created from without, in a sense so alive because the material out of which he was constructed is living.'

> Although so vague and stagey, he is the only character who exists
> for me outside his book . . . There was reciprocation – such as I
> discern in Matthew Arnold's poem of 'The Scholar Gipsy'. I
> received, I created, I restored, and for many years the Wiltshire
> landscape remained haunted by my fictional ghosts.[1]

The Longest Journey came out on 16 April 1907, and, like its predecessor, it received an enthusiastic press, the theme of the reviewers being that here was an author who drew from his own resources; 'Into his own well has his own cup dipped,' the *Westminster Gazette* put it, 'and the well is a deep one.' C. F. G. Masterman reviewed it at length in the *Daily News*, saying it was 'difficult, elusive, exasperating, with something of the cleverness of the young in it, and something of the cruelty.' It was not a great novel, he said, but it had many of the ingredients of greatness. *The Times* likened Forster to some 'sharp wholesome insect', fastening on the life of the suburbs and 'the ideals of those who dwell in red brick villas and the form rooms of public schools'. Almost all the reviewers took exception to the sudden deaths in the novel, the *Morning Post* calculating that, even ignoring the two children, they accounted for 44 per cent of the characters. The *Spectator*, too, was facetious – perhaps being less convinced this time of the author's 'unimpeachable confirmation of orthodox views'. It remarked that, if 'culture' led to so many blighted lives, 'we should seriously consider whether a Pass degree

---

[1] Unpublished note, partly reproduced in his Introduction to the World's Classics edition of *The Longest Journey*.

and a severe course on the river would not be the most salubrious curriculum for our sons'. There were also some reviewers, more numerous this time, who found the book simply baffling. The *Graphic* called it 'a museum of psychological freaks such as has rarely, if ever, been brought together before', and *Outlook* found it 'frankly the most impossible book we have read for many years'. *John Bull*'s brief notice sounded a note of warning: 'A rather slow book, and the reader is tempted to skip the pages. Should not be read on the S.E. and C. Railways.'

The verdict of Bloomsbury was on the whole unfavourable. Bob Trevelyan, always one for plain speaking on such occasions, put the matter very clearly. 'Desmond MacCarthy has been talking about your novel, Forster. He says there are two things in it which are very bad. They are not the only things in it that are bad, oh no, not by any means, but these two things are so bad that it is only common friendliness to let you know.'[1] MacCarthy thought that, at least, Forster had 'hit off those miserable muffs the Cambridge Apostles pretty well'.[2] Keynes was less decided. He told Lytton Strachey he was reading Forster's book with 'very great interest and a good deal of bewilderment as well as admiration'.

> What odd cranky disagreeable people he fills his mind with, and what a lot he gets out of them. I think he caricatures the Society rather cruelly, though he doesn't seem to be meaning it.

As for Strachey, he thought the book dreadful on the whole, and was mainly interested in who was who in it. He wrote to Duncan Grant (30 April 1907):

> I don't think you know Forster – a queer King's brother, and a great friend of Hom's. He's just written his second novel, and there's a rather amusing account of Cambridge in it, and Cambridge people. One of the very minor characters is asked to breakfast by one of his friends, and replies by putting his hand on his stomach, to show that he's breakfasted already. MacCarthy thinks that this is me. Do you? But the rest of the book is dreary fandango. After the hero (who's Forster himself), the principal figure is Hom.[3] By the way, Hom = Meredith. But he won't go into a book.

---

[1] One of the offending things was the incident, in the last chapter, of Stephen's daughter licking the polish off his boots.

[2] He was an Apostle himself.

[3] Not altogether a bad guess, perhaps. See p. 77.

The one Cambridge friend who approved of the novel was Bertrand Russell, and he wrote to Forster warmly. Forster, who was surprised, replied:

> I am glad that the book does, though I don't think I shall ever 'bite so much off' again. Hardly anyone had gone into what seemed an obvious and symmetrical field, so I determined to try. You are gentle, too, to the corpses. They, and other things, displease me a good deal.

The novel's most out-and-out admirer was 'Elizabeth'. She was hugely impressed and wrote to him (5 May 1907) in the very highest terms.

> It's a wonderful book, & I thank you herewith solemnly for the day you gave me with it. That, of course, is a little thing, but it's not at all a little thing to have written that book. I thought the Times review good till I'd read the book, then, strange to say, I discovered it fitted excellently to the 'Angels' but not in the least to this one. How can they talk of your tapping the people neatly with your pen on the head at the end? It all crumbles away – it was something like that – I don't quite remember. Never was any thing deeper, truer, more serious. No irresponsible pen-tapping – and, what the timid Angels hadn't, it has lovable people in it. Rickie is an absolute dear   & then there is Ansell, & the young animal – but don't ever marry an Agnes, will you, for if you did your future is certain. There it is in your book prophetically set forth. Well, I can't tell you how truly beautiful I think it, & if I could it would only make you shrug your shoulders, for what does it matter what the foolish & the illiterate think? But I think you must be very happy. You've got very near to the 'words of eternal life'.

Even this very handsome letter failed to shake Forster's resolve never to be influenced by 'Elizabeth', whether praising him or blaming him. And within a few months, as usual, the pendulum had swung again. He wrote to her to recommend a friend's school for her daughters and got sharply rapped for his pains.

> I do not know why people think I want to send my innocents to their schools. Lately I have been deluged with letters about it. If they ever went to anything it would be a High School, but what so uncertain in this world as their ever going? And so dim in the future? But at least it moved you to write which is so much to the good. How clever you all are over there! From the frost bound calm of Nassenheide you all look like a seething mass of wriggling

& struggling & aspiring brains – everybody busy from morning to night practising being clever. If I was to give you the context of these fragments it would take too long, so I'll wish you a merry Christmas instead.[1]

Forster, at some later date, inscribed the letter, 'Sample of an unpleasing woman.'

He was not much affected either by the praise or by the criticism the book received. Once a book had been written, he always re-bounded into confidence and felt he could trust his own opinion. What did affect him, on this occasion, was that friends of his had been upset by the book – 'vexed', as he called it. He did not for that reason regret writing it, for the book had been necessary to him and had said the things he most wanted to say. But it made him resolve that, for the future, he would not write so freely and 'sentimentally' again.

Shortly before publication day he had gone to Wales for a walking-tour with the Merediths and George Barger and his wife,[2] after which he continued, on his own, through Shropshire. And in Shropshire, A. E. Housman was much on his mind. He had loved *A Shropshire Lad* since Cambridge days. Most probably it had been H.O.M. who introduced him to it, though his copy had been given him by Mollison (and he had never liked it, Mollison seeming to him too worldly for such poetry). Very many young Englishmen, especially homosexual ones, must have been tramping the countryside just now, with Housman's volume in their pocket, and Forster's experience, in a way, sums theirs up. His diary runs:

> *April* 11. In the Angel, Ludlow. Wet walk from Wellington over Wrekin, wh. was foul with orange peel & bottles. No view but plumes of trains pushing through mist . . . Much Wenlock I hadn't time to see, since I lingered over cider at the 'Rock House' [kept] by A. Sankey. Two cats & two beer pots, a collie and a man: the latter suddenly mirthful when my chair was tottery. To go over the watershed a mystery to them. Train after a tunnel got out on Wenlock Edge. 'Hughley steeple'[3] below, & to right the Wrekin

---

[1] Letter dated 18 December 1907.

[2] Forster's Cambridge friend George Barger had in 1904 married a cousin, Florence Emily Thomas, an educationalist from Liverpool University. As we shall see, she was to become one of Forster's most intimate friends.

[3] An allusion to poem LXI of *A Shropshire Lad*: 'The vane on Hughley steeple.'

as an inflation. So did I see it yesterday from Uricon . . . Feel
very happy . . .
Shrewsbury (9th–11th) – the more said the better. Unspoilt and
alive: a city with vigour still adjusted to its beautiful frame.
Poetry – or luck – in every inch of it. Gloriously piled on a curve
of the Severn, wh. two fine bridges traverse – the English and the
Welsh, and against which laps the Quarry, with magnificent
avenue of limes . . . want to write to A. E. Housman.

He did write to Housman, telling him of his great admiration for *A
Shropshire Lad* and how this had grown with the years. He gave
Housman no address he could reasonably reply to, and felt no special
curiosity to know him. But next month, staying with a Professor
Phillimore[1] in Hampshire, he finally put certain vague surmises of his
own into words. He ventured to say, he thought the poems concealed
a personal experience, and when Phillimore agreed, he became certain
that the author had fallen in love with a man. In this way, he said
later, the poems accompanied his own development from sub-
conscious to conscious.

> The football, the cherries and poplars, the red coats and beer and
> darnel, the simplicity controlled by a scholarship whose strength
> I took years to realise, the home sickness and bed-sickness, the
> yearning for masculine death – all mingled with my own late
> adolescence and turned inward upon me. To meet the poet was
> not a possibility, but year after year I met the poems, and as one
> grew stale from familiarity another would come forward and stop
> with me until the earlier had time to recover. The book – as are
> both the books now – was inexhaustible, and the warmth of the
> writer's heart seemed unalloyed.[2]

In after years he looked back wryly to this walking-tour, and to how
he had 'lashed himself' into a liking for Shropshire, 'but never looked
out for the lads'.[3]

All that spring he had been working at his eternal 'Lucy' novel, for
which he had a contract with a new publisher, Edward Arnold. As

---

[1] John Swinnerton Phillimore (1878–1926), Professor of Humanity at
Glasgow University.

[2] As we shall see, he had to revise this opinion when he came to know
Housman.

[3] He told William Plomer that there were 'breaths' of Housman in *Howards
End*, in the part set in Oniton, which was Housman's 'Clun'. The last came at
the end of Chapter 29: 'Day and night the river flows down into England, day
after day the sun retreats into the Welsh mountains, and the tower chimes,
"See the Conquering Hero" ', etc.

before, the novel gave him misgivings. It was 'clean and bright', but after *The Longest Journey* it seemed thin to him. He confided his doubts to Bob Trevelyan (11 June 1907): 'I have been looking at the "Lucy" novel. I don't know. It's bright and merry and I like the story. Yet I wouldn't and couldn't finish it in the same style. I'm rather depressed. The question is akin to morality.' On the day of writing to Trevelyan, he observed an incident which seemed an allegory of self-reliance and obscurely comforted him:

> . . . a young giant manning a barge alone round the curve of Halliford – punting first, then rowing with one tree of an oar, then with two – standing on the high end of the deck and hanging over a gap as he pushed – a broken back if the blade slipped out of the water or the handle up the pin – at times sprinting down the barge to give a touch to the rudder: and sprinting back: tireless until the curve was passed when he sank underneath the rudder's handle, and I left him drifting in glory down the straight stream. Apparently an ordinary bargee – but his heroism is more than muscular.

By 16 June he was writing to Trevelyan more blithely:

> A slumber may your spirit seal:
>   Indulge no human fears;
> Miss Bartlett does not seem to feel
>   The touch of earthly years.
>
> No motion has she now, no force,
>   She neither hears nor sees;
> But, ere a dozen moons, her course
>   Will rack your hours of ease.

*   *   *

'Elizabeth' reappeared in his life this summer, with an invitation to join a caravan-tour in Kent – and, with some nervousness, he accepted. Caravanning, a fashionable Edwardian pastime, was the sort of elaborate 'simple-life' activity that 'Elizabeth' adored; in addition, she was hoping to find copy for a novel. She was bringing Liebet, Trix, and of course Teppi, from Germany with her, and she appointed the rest of the party – which included her niece Margery Waterlow and several ex-tutors from Nassenheide – to make rendezvous in a muddy field near Crouch, where two vans, harnessed to enormous carthorses, awaited them. Forster was to join them ten days later.

By the time he did so, the convoy had moved some twenty-five miles towards Canterbury, it having rained almost unceasingly. Margery collected him at Ashford in her pony-cart, and as they wandered vaguely through the lanes in search of the caravan he noted 'a sense of flux'. At last they got on the trail, and found the main party camped for the night on the Great Chart. Gaunt, one of the ex-tutors, cooked them all a stew; and afterwards 'Elizabeth' and Forster strolled out to visit a church by moonlight.

He was a little apprehensive, not feeling sure if he would fit in, and not having much experience of hearty young people, or at least of being thrown on their company all day. However 'Elizabeth' was all solicitude. She made him promise to go home if he fell ill or wasn't happy; and Gaunt, the most practical of the party, made up a bed for him in a farm-shed. He slept very soundly, with his head on a pile of baskets, and by next day felt sure he would enjoy himself. Everyone was extremely nice to him, overlooking his incompetence at such things as putting up tents. To his surprise, also, he got on very well with the practical-minded Gaunt. Sometimes they pushed the van together, while 'Elizabeth' tossed biscuits and fruit to them out of the window. Gaunt, he reflected somewhat schoolboyishly, kept him up to the mark, and checked him from 'being a worm'; also, it was cosy chatting to him, as they lay in their beds in barns and sheds. He could picture things warming to a friendship between them.

One morning 'Elizabeth' had an inspiration; they would go and visit Alfred Austin, the Poet Laureate, at his nearby home of Swinford Manor. The laureate, who had little notion who 'Elizabeth' was, received them with amazement, but he told them grandly 'Walk where you will', and they explored 'The Garden that I Love'[1] – which Forster condemned as too lush. His diary continues:

> Dismissed, we found a mill, where a miller with no roof to his mouth most kindly gave us bread, butter, jam, cheeses, tea. Clean dreamy water, with peat.
> *August 22nd.* Tried my shoes, but had to change to the brown boots while the van was resting. Most of the day seemed round Eastwell Pk. and up a weary hill . . . Chilham was touristy and they tried to charge us 4d. for a loaf. So the Gr.[2] – who tips 10/- a

---

[1] Title of a popular book of his, published in 1894.
[2] 'the Gräfin' (i.e. 'Elizabeth').

> night – led her flock into the rival shop . . . Camped a mile beyond
> by the river Stour. Tired and rather low. Tents to be put up, and
> there sat the Gr. reading Jane Austen. Found death in the pot.
> Smoked G's cigarettes round the embers. It was inclined to rain.
> *August 23rd*. It did rain.

The caravan-party staggered as far as Aylesford, and there they
gave up. 'Elizabeth', who had hoped to find material for another
country idyll like her *Adventures of Elizabeth in Rügen*, found that all
she could recall of the holiday was damp and discomfort. However,
she took an ingenious way round her difficulty; drawing on her invention, she composed a novel, *The Caravanners*, taking as her narrator a
'typical' Prussian officer, constitutionally incapable of appreciating
the good and the beautiful. As her biographer puts it, 'She could in
this way omit raptures she had not felt and study instead the effects
of discomforts and inconveniences on the one fictional member of
the party who was without grace.'

As for Forster, he was already, a week or two later, looking back
on the tour sentimentally, as 'the happiest spell since Greece'. He
remembered a final sunlit walk with Gaunt and a companion, and
their hymning 'Allah ist gross' on the Knaps in the morning; also
'Elizabeth', at Aylesford, dancing the Highland Fling with the
parson in his cassock; and Billie the horse, a symbol of it all – 'Nature
and Dignity'. London 'hummed to him strangely' when he returned
to it, he thought, for he had 'heard a new song'. It ran:

> Ten shadows flecked the sunlit road,
>   Ten shadows passed, yet we remain
> Still marching to the Dorian Mode
>   Still summoning the gods to reign.
> Gods of the country! still in Kent
>   The music of that pipe rings plain
> Through places where ten shadows went;
>   The shadows passed; but we remain.

     *   *   *

Steadily, all these six years, he had continued sorting out the
consequences of his 'two great discoveries'. As to the religious one,
the problem was no longer urgent for him. Christian belief was not
now an issue for him – not, anyway, a personal one; and the spirit of
the times, or at least the spirit of Cambridge, was on his side in this
respect. The church did not trouble him personally now, save when

it came to its views on sex – and there he did still feel challenged. He became quite excited this year over the Deceased Wife's Sister bill and wondered to himself why he was so 'hot about it'.[1]

The history of this bill is a curious one. Till the nineteenth century, a marriage to one's deceased wife's sister, though condemned by the church, was valid unless legal action was taken to make it void. Then in 1835 – ironically as the result of a private bill to legalize such marriages – they were rendered absolutely void. During the following years, bill after bill was brought in to redress the situation, and in 1906 marriages of the kind were actually made legal in the Colonies; but the bishops, and churchmen generally, still set their face firmly against them as regards Britain. Admittedly the Mosaic law, rather confusingly, positively enjoined a widow, if she had no issue, to marry her husband's brother; still the church, if not the Bible, had always been staunch on the matter. Of the new bill, the Earl of Shaftesbury said, in the Lords, that it 'struck a blow at the sanctity of home life – at the peace and purity of the English home', and the Bishop of Hereford thought it 'slammed the door in the face of the maiden aunt'.

All through 1907 the newspapers were full of the bill, which had become a sort of household joke; and when MacMunn, now a curate in Sunderland,[2] came down to Weybridge to stay in September, he was in a state of high excitement, chanting 'The Church is not going to lower her standards for the world, since she has decided ('date unknown', Forster silently commented) that "the twain shall be one flesh" means that the Wife's Sister becomes the Man's Sister'. Forster felt he could afford to laugh at this 'Gilbertian nonsense', because 'Science and the desire for truth have drawn its sting by these days'. All the same, he wondered 'Why the attempt to reach "God" has made men so horrible? . . . I think because they have mistaken their obstacle, which is not the animal but the mechanical.' Another of MacMunn's remarks was that the spiritual forces were dulled by puberty. 'One's hope is,' he said, 'to get hold of a lad before he's 15, and perhaps get him back after six years or so. If one had

---

[1] It was the marriage of Marianne Thornton's brother Henry to his deceased wife's sister which caused the great rift in the Thornton family and Marianne's exile from 'Battersea Rise'; see *Marianne Thornton, passim*.

[2] He became Vicar of St Columba, Southwick, Sunderland, and an honorary Canon of Durham.

developed the spiritual, he should pull through.' Forster felt he couldn't laugh at this, even if God could.

The Deceased Wife's Sister bill was finally passed in August 1907, and Forster wrote a little extravaganza to celebrate the occasion, entitled *The Deceased Wife's Husband*. His protagonist is the Rev. Paul Goodybrick, who, hitherto a happy widower, has responded to his country's command and, relinquishing his chaplaincy at Port Said, has hurried home to marry his deceased wife's detestable sister, Clara. Musing in Leicester Square on his fatal step, he falls into conversation with a stranger, a retired solicitor of the name of Flather, and relates the story to him. He has made an ill choice of confidant, for Flather is an ardent churchman – so much so that he has recently done time in Dartmoor for absconding with the securities of Agnostic widows – and he receives the confession with indignation. The two nearly fall to blows, when Clara herself appears; and in the ensuing vicissitudes, Goodybrick and Flather discover that they are related, through their first wife's bigamy. The fatal news overcomes them, and they rush off in different directions to commit suicide. Clara soliloquizes:

> . . . what am I to do now? Let me think. Which of these two gentlemen was my husband? Paul. Why had Paul to marry me? Because I was Lavinia's sister. Then surely, if Paul had a brother I shall have to marry him (*Roguishly*) We women are not so illogical as you think.

Waiting to hear no more, a policeman, who has been watching proceedings from behind the statue of Shakespeare, rushes from his concealment and handcuffs Clara. He has seen something of life's darker side, he says, but never in his gloomiest experience has he contemplated quite so vile a case. England may permit murder, she may permit suicide, but there is one evil she will never permit – that the laws for women should be the same as for men.

Forster showed this effusion (it is quite endearing, I think, though he was no Bernard Shaw) to R. B. Smith, who remarked that it 'expressed one of his moods with vigour but didn't exactly hit off his own'. Forster sighed: 'I wish he cared for fooling – but – furthermore – that he had not this dryness. It is impossible to proceed further. φιλεῖ με γοῦν. 'Αεὶ τοῦτο, etc.'[1]

---

[1] 'He does at least like me, and this will continue. Yet there remains a certain hubris; but my own will increase likewise.'

Calmly and unanxiously, in true Victorian fashion, he once more studied self-improvement in his New Year's Eve review for 1907. It had been a happy year, justifying 'optimism in life'.

το ἔνδον [Inward events], not eventful. An advance to a narrower outlook, or to be less unkind to myself – a tendency to look for the white squares in the pattern. Shall scarcely write another 'Longest Journey', for it vexed people and I can with sincerity please them . . .

τα ἔξω [Outward events], many and pleasant . . . my prospects very good – may I be equal to them . . . Financially poor, but have invested £85 in B.A.G.S. – £25 to follow in March. Payments for L.J. not till March. Then also £31 for Epsom lectures, and in October £100 down for novel. So next year should not be so bad and I ought not to be in arrears with payments to mother. Railway fares the chief cause . . . In Books most have been good. Conrad, Dante, Beddoes, H. N. Dickinson[1] . . . Sleepy – most of this seems rot – may be glad later on of it.

> Jeune homme sans mélancholie,
> Blond comme un soleil d'Italie,
> Garde bien ta belle folie.
>
> C'est la sagesse! Aimez le vin,
> La beauté, le printemps divin,
> Cela suffit. Le reste est vain.
>
> Souris, même au destin sevère!
> Et quand revient la primevère
> Jettes-en les fleurs dans ton verre.
>
> Au corps sous la tombe enfermé
> Que reste-t-il? D'avoir aimé
> Pendant deux ou trois mois de Mai.
>
> 'Cherchez les effets et les causes'
> Nous disent les reveurs moroses.
> Des mots! des mots! cueillez les roses . . .[2]

---

[1] A further book-list in the margin of his diary reads: 'Sturge Moore, A. E. Housman, Symonds, Pater, Shakespeare, Beddoes, Walt Whitman, E. Carpenter, Samuel Butler, Fitzgerald, Marlowe.'

[2] 'A Adolphe Gaiffe', by Theodore Banville.
(Young man, without melancholy, blond as the sun in Italy, cherish your fine folly. It is wisdom! Love wine, beauty, Spring the divine season. It is enough. The rest is all vanity. Smile, even when fate lours. And when the time of primroses comes again, put primrose petals in your glass. What remains to the body when it is in the tomb? To have loved for two or three months of May. 'Seek after effects and causes' say glum philosophers. Mere words! Mere words! Go, gather roses.)

10 'An Advance to a Narrower Outlook'

Time had brought the answer to the question which had once puzzled him, was he 'conventional' or not? He knew by now – it could no longer be adolescent illusion – that he was different from other people; they sensed it as much as he did. Such a continuous and passionate inner life as he led set him a little aside from ordinary daily existence. The knowledge left him neither pleased nor sorry; but, since he prized 'connection' and balance, his instinct was to reduce the difference. And looking back on his life of the previous year, he saw that, in fact, this was the direction he had tended in. Through his friendship with Gaunt and Malcolm Darling and the stiff and *bien-pensant* Rupert Smith, he had grown more attracted by conformist values – by 'social conventions, economic trend, efficiency', etc., as he vaguely summarized them. Or at least – foreshadowing Margaret Schlegel in *Howards End* – he saw better how they might be right for others. Maybe, he thought, he had been wrong to laugh at conventional values, in the Cambridge way, as much as he had done; there was something second-rate in the idea that the artist must be a rebel. G. M. Trevelyan urged him to break away from Weybridge and its tea-parties and come to live the literary life in London, but he thought it conventional advice and wrong for his case. Likewise, it had annoyed him when Dent, in discussing his 'Lucy' novel, had urged him to 'show up' *pension* life. 'Showing up' things, polemical satire, was a false tack for him, he felt. And yet, and yet, he could not but feel, what horrors one encountered in a suburban way of life like his! They were his 'copy' as a novelist; yet could one live one's life among them, and not be damaged?

The problem was much in his mind this New Year, staying with his Aunt Laura at West Hackhurst. It was in just this pretty, cosy, class-conscious Surrey, that he had set his new novel.[1] He knew the life so well. But, not for the first time, he felt imprisoned among its genteel comedies and atrocities. They had been especially abundant in the last few months. There had been the local curate, who had lectured on the joys of mountaineering, and the importance of 'a really nice guide', and how some mountains were 'gentlemen' but others were not. Also a woman neighbour who told – as a good joke – how her brother, when the Doctor shook hands with him, had wiped his hands on his trousers afterwards; 'and the Doctor saw him!' Or there was Kate Preston, Maimie's sister, and her recent letter to his grandmother: 'My neighbours earn their living, but this when combined with *blood* and good breeding makes them very good society I assure you.' It was 'monstrous' to like such people, even dear harmless snobbish Kate, Forster told himself. 'Continual disgust or we become like them. Sympathy too has its dangers. Follow either passionate love or truth – the latter purifies invisibly.' He prescribed more exercise, to take his mind off such things, and he went for nocturnal walks in the frozen countryside, teaching himself the constellations.

> Up downs with Cinders[2] before bed. Moon & no wind. The landscape uninspiring and remote. Orion a ghost, but the sight of him gives a physical joy, as if a man of the kind I care for was in heaven. The Plough was balancing on its handle in the north, and looked foolish . . . In Antiquity only the naif is attractive – hence the XX cent. will be unpopular in the future. Because we are self conscious we shall be accused of staleness.

He had another reason, too, to meditate on the twentieth century; for on the 13th of the same January, a man flew a heavier-than-air machine over a three-quarter mile circuit in one and a half minutes.[3] 'It's coming quickly,' he commented:

> and if I live to be old I shall see the sky as pestilential as the roads. It really *is* a new civilisation. I have been born at the end of the age of peace and can't expect to feel anything but despair. Science,

---

[1] 'Summer Street', where the Emersons come to live, was modelled on Holmbury St Mary.

[2] A dog.

[3] On 13 January 1908 Henri Farman won a contest, in France, for the flying of a heavier-than-air machine over a kilometre circuit.

161

instead of freeing man – the Greeks nearly freed him by right
feeling – is enslaving him to machines. Nationality will go, but the
brotherhood of man will not come . . . God what a prospect! The
little houses that I am used to will be swept away, the fields will
stink of petrol, and the airships will shatter the stars. Man may
get a new and perhaps a greater soul for the new condition. But
such a soul as mine will be crushed out.

But suppose 'the thing at the back of things' agreed with him?
Suppose that it intended the vanishing quietness to return, how
would this come about, he wondered?

(i) There must be a miracle. We must realise that the Kingdom of
God is within us . . . Passion is necessary – only Wells' comet[1] is
enough. For (ii) the alternative is that the machine should destroy
life, stop itself, and life begin again – perhaps no trees, perhaps
not even water.

His gloomy reflections on the Farman flight bore fruit later in the
year in his story 'The Machine Stops', described by him as 'a reaction
against one of the earlier heavens of H. G. Wells'. It pictures humanity
as it might be after the final triumph of the machine: hairless,
toothless, muscleless, living in air-conditioned underground cells, and
exchanging, by a sort of television, the 'last sloshy stirrings' of a
spirit that had once grasped the stars. In the story, the rebel hero
Kuno escapes for a day to the surface of the earth, and his last
glimpse of hope and freedom, before recapture by the Machine, is the
constellation of Orion. Seeing it, he feels – the words recall those
earlier in Forster's diary – as if 'a man of my own sort lived in the
sky'. The thought grew to be a favourite with Forster and became
his formula for religion. 'London is religion's opportunity,' he was to
write in *Howards End*, 'not the decorous religion of theologians, but
anthropomorphic, crude. Yes, the continuous flow would be tolerable
if a man of our own sort – not anyone pompous or tearful – were
caring for us up in the sky.'

Indeed, he was beginning once more to flirt with religion – a
purely humanistic religion, personal, fraternal and sentimental.
When this year he and his mother were on one of their visits to
Maimie's sisters, in the Isle of Wight, the many pious lithographs in

---

[1] In H. G. Wells's *In the Days of the Comet* (1906) humanity is regenerated
by the near approach of a comet, which causes a beneficient change in the
atmosphere.

his bedroom, depicting Jesus as an 'evangelical shop-walker', set him speculating on the Incarnation. Potentially, he felt, it was a wonderful conception.

> Suppose I could think of Christ not as an evangelical shop walker, but as the young carpenter who would smoke a pipe with me in his off time and be most frightfully kind. 'A man shall be a hiding place in a tempest' would suddenly mean something, and I would do all that was likely to please the fellow, and would ask other people's advice.

*   *   *

On the 16th of this January he went down to Rye to stay with Sydney Waterlow – hearing, with some excitement, that he was to meet Henry James. Sydney was now married to Alice Pollock (daughter of Sir Frederick Pollock the jurist) and had settled in Rye, where he had quickly struck up a friendship with James, who indeed had known Alice from childhood. He and James would go for afternoon walks, ending up for tea at one or other's house or at their friend 'Alice Dew's' (Mrs Dew-Smith); and meanwhile Sydney would play Boswell to James, who enjoyed the role of sage. When Forster arrived, the Waterlows were full of Henry James, and a visit to Lamb House was arranged for Sunday. Forster was pleasantly thrilled. It would be his first meeting with a first-rate literary celebrity; and moreover, whatever one might think of James as a writer (and neither then nor later could he make up his mind), James had a peculiar claim to respect on Forster's generation. With all his perversities, he was the 'Master', the man who had stood up most firmly for the novelist's art. Forster wrote to his mother with the news:

> I have been preceded by my short story in the Albany,[1] which the W's like, but H.J. will know better. I hear he likes people to be handsome and well dressed, so I shall fail all round. He is much distressed at the dirt of the Bells (she was a Miss (L) Stephen), saying 'Virginia[2] looked as if she had rolled in a duck pond and her monstrous little husband filled me with an almost uncontrollable antipathy.' He sounds rather a dear, however – has given his housekeeper a set of the best false teeth procurable, at his London dentist.

---

[1] The Celestial Omnibus', published in the January number of the *Albany Review*.
[2] Evidently a mistake for 'Vanessa'.

The meeting, when it took place, was not disappointing exactly, but, as one might have foretold, not the beginning of a friendship. It began a little disconcertingly. The Master, 'rather fat but fine, and effectively bald', laid his hand kindly on Forster's shoulder and told him, 'Your name's Moore.'[1] Further confusion followed between 'Weybridge' and 'Wakefield', for Forster had spoken rather stammeringly in explaining himself; but James finally seized on the right name in triumph, surrounding it with inverted commas. He said he could so easily imagine himself living in 'Weybridge'. It was almost the same remark as he had made at dinner, twenty years ago, to Aunt Laura: 'Ah,' he had said then, 'I *wish* I had an aunt in Clapham' – a statement condemned by Lily as 'very affected'. The beautiful Mrs von Glehn, one of James's Emmett cousins, poured out tea, and James was very urgent that everyone should eat and drink enough. After a little while there swept in the Alfred Lytteltons,[2] whereupon the conversation turned to Queen Victoria. James said he had been impressed by her letters: 'She is more of a man than I expected.' 'But she underlines her words so,' said Mrs Lyttelton. 'Well,' said James, 'she was an underlined man.' He spoke of a certain well-known actress, whom he described as 'not merely vulnerable, but positively divesting herself of armour and baring her breast.' Then someone turned the conversation to Mary Baker Eddy. James remarked 'She succeeded by saying to herself, "Hitherto things have been done gratis, for the poor; I will provide for the rich and charge accordingly." ' He went on to describe the long-wished-for occasion when he heard Tennyson read his own poems. 'It was all there . . . *everything* . . . except the appropriate response.'

Forster, in a sense, had enjoyed the appropriate response. 'It is a funny sensation, going to see a really first class person,' he wrote to Dent. 'I felt all that the ordinary healthy man feels in the presence of a lord.' However, he decided, James could never mean much to him personally. There was something stuffy and precious in the Lamb House atmosphere; it was not his own road. As he returned to the twilit street, he glimpsed a young labourer in the shadows, smoking

---

[1] G. E. Moore was a friend of Waterlow's and used to come and stay with him in Rye.

[2] Alfred Lyttelton (1857–1913) and his wife Edith. He was Secretary of State for the Colonies 1903–5, a member of the 'Souls' and a celebrated cricketer.

as he leaned against the street-wall. *There*, Forster told himself, was the reality he was after. And he purged himself of the precious Lamb House atmosphere by means of a poem:

> I saw you or I thought of you
>   I know not which, but in the dark
> Piercing the known and the untrue
>   It gleamed – a cigarette's faint spark.
> It gleamed – and when I left the room
>   Where culture unto culture knelt
> Something just darker than the gloom
>   Waited – it might be you I felt.
> It was not you; you pace no night
>   No youthful flesh weighs down your youth.
> You are eternal, infinite,
>   You are the unknown, and the truth.
> Yet each must seek reality:
>   For those within the room, high talk,
> Subtle experience – for me
>   The spark, the darkness, on the walk.

*   *   *

Something of the same motives as inspired his distrust of James made him discontented, just now, with his own work. 'The thing comes out in October,' he told Wedd (25 June 1908) about *A Room With a View*, 'and will probably gratify the home circle, but not those whose opinion I value most.' He felt he wanted to take on a broader subject. And some time during the summer the scheme for a new novel, the future *Howards End*, began to shape itself. The little scene on the Postons' lawn (see p. 142) had been one seed. Another, perhaps, was provided by Uncle Philip Whichelo, who came to Weybridge bringing 'squalid stories of flat-life'. It seemed to Forster a special English kind of hell they conjured up: 'No-one can know anyone nor run the tennis tournament, without quarrelling and forming a committee.' On 28 June 1908 he jotted down a first sketch:

Idea for another novel shaping, and may do well to write it down. In a prelude Helen goes to stop with the Wilcoxes, gets engaged to the son & breaks it off immediately, for her instinct sees the spiritual cleavage between the families. Mrs Wilcox dies, and some years later Margaret gets engaged to the widower, a man impeccable publicly. They are accosted by a prostitute. M. because she understands and is great, marries him. The wrong thing to do. He, because he is little, cannot bear to be understood, & goes to the bad. He is frank, kind, & attractive. But he dreads ideas.

By August he had got a certain amount written but complained that it was coming out 'a deal too cultured, and from hand to mouth'.

A subtle change had come over his personal life. For the first time, people were actually running after him, and he found himself in danger of disappointing and jilting them. He had a habit, then as later, of working very hard at friendships; he listened so attentively; he invested so much concern in the other's affairs and wrote so many letters. It had nothing flirtatious about it, for in matters of affection he always intended permanency, but people could be misled and believe they counted for more in his life than they did. R. B. Smith, for instance, got the impression at this time, quite wrongly, that he was practically Forster's only close friend – and he was probably not the only one who did so. Forster was beginning to realize the danger: 'Once no one cared for me,' he reflected, 'and I forget that this is no longer the case, and that superficially I am more attractive than I was. To rebuff is terrible.' He had to rebuff a friend called S—,[1] who had been writing him depressed letters over the last few months, complaining of loneliness. He found the letters undignified and neurotic. 'It isn't decent to say that nobody wants you,' he commented.

One of those who seemed eager for his friendship was Gaunt, his companion of the caravan-tour, and the Forsters had him to stay during the summer, but the visit turned out badly. Gaunt seemed bored – perhaps Weybridge was too tame for him – and Forster had to realize how much their friendship had depended on its setting. Roughing it with Gaunt in the open air, and finding him so good-humoured and thoughtful for others, he had romanticized him and seen him as making a case for the Kiplingesque virtues. Not for the first time, he philosophized, he would have to abandon an illusion:

> How small is *our* country where things have an objective value:
> – e.g. my Cambridge friends. How immense the countries around,
> into which we are impelled by curiosity or passion. It is too sad,
> or I could write down a list of people & places whom I have
> transfigured, and know at the bottom of my heart not to be what
> I pretend. One's comfort is that the transfigured is the real
> perhaps, and that indifference is blind, not love.

---

[1] Probably F. W. Stokoe, one of the succession of Nassenheide tutors. He was a poet, and became a lecturer in French at Cambridge. Forster remained a good friend to him and, in 1912, tried to persuade Arnold's to publish his volume of fairy stories.

Marianne Thornton
(E. M. Forster's paternal great-aunt)

Louisa Whichelo
(E. M. Forster's maternal grandmother)

Maimie Aylward
with her husband

Laura Forster
(E. M. Forster's paternal aunt)

E. M. Forster,
aged 5, with his mother

E. M. Forster,
aged 10 or 11

E. M. Forster,
aged 12 or 13

The Whichelo sisters,
from left Rosie, Lily (E. M. Forster's moth
Nellie, Georgie

'Rooksnest', Stevenage:
E. M. Forster's home 1883–93

Tonbridge School

E. M. Forster
as an undergraduate

King's College in the 1890s
(before the removal of the railings)

H. O. Meredith

R. B. Smith

R. C. Trevelyan

Malcolm Darling

'Harnham', Monument Green, Weybridge:
E. M. Forster's home 1904–25

E. M. Forster in Italian cloak

E. M. Forster with Steinweg and others at Nassenheide

*E. M. Forster
and Masood
at Tesserete, 1911*

*asood and friends, 1912. Standing left to right: Mohiuddin, H. K. Sherwani, Abu Saeed
irza, unidentified; seated: M. A. Raschid, Masood, E. M. Forster.*

E. M. Forster and Forrest Reid

Edward Carpenter

H. H. Sir Tukoji Rao III,
Maharaja of Dewas State, Senior.

E. M. Forster, aged 36

No such hitches occurred in his friendship with Masood, which, in its own way, flourished. He went from time to time to see Masood at New College in Oxford. Masood was enjoying himself in a dashing manner, doing extremely little work, but making a mark as a tennis-player and, as Forster pictured it, converting Oxford into 'an oriental radiance pierced by minarets and traversed by trains of revellers holding wine-cups'. His circle was largely an English one, and included various dons. He never showed his face at the university India Society and taunted his old friend Sherwani,[1] who had become president, for his passion for speech-making to earnest Indians. What time he could spare from his social life he spent reading the French Symbolist poets.

He was fond of addressing letters to Forster in the *Arabian Nights* style:

> . . . let it be known to thee that thy slave's house was this day brightened by the arrival of an epistle from thee – the source of all his happiness. May Allah always guard thee in thine under-takings for Verily he is the guide of all. And let it be known to thee that thy humble servant is overwhelmed by the kindness thou hast shown him in asking his very unworthy self to waste thy precious time. May Allah repay thy kindness!
>
> And let it be known to thee that thy obedient servant is overjoyed at the prospect of once again beholding the face of his master etc.

After one of Forster's visits to Oxford, Masood wrote (22 November 1908) protesting the most romantic affection:

> My very dear Forster,
> Centuries may pass, years may turn into 2000 centuries and you never hear from me & you are not to think that the great affection, the real love & the sincerest admiration that I feel for you has in any way diminished. Your coming to Oxford & your giving me the opportunity of seeing something of you & of having you all to myself for some time & the patience with which your good nature has suffered you to be bored by me, have all made me very very grateful to you indeed. Life is unfortunately too short to allow one or to give one the chance of making friends of persons like you; & the day the sympathy that I know you have & that you feel for

---

[1] M. K. Sherwani (*b.* 1891). He became a distinguished historian and was one of the first lecturers at the Osmania University in Hyderabad, founded in 1919.

me diminishes ever so little will be a day which should be mourned by me during all my lifetime.

Hence melancholy. I have had enough of thee!

Be it known to the worthy and highly esteemed Forster that the humble & like-unto-the-dust-beneath-thy-feet Scribe of this papyrus intends reaching the town which is known by the Name of Weybridge on Tuesday the 8th of December . . . etc.

The letter nearly turned Forster's head, till he remembered Masood's nationality. 'He's not that sort – no one whom I like seems to be.'

*   *   *

'Snow' Wedgwood's *The Moral Ideal* came out in the summer, though not making much impression on reviewers, and in gratitude for his help 'Snow' gave him £50 towards a foreign holiday. This for Forster spelled Italy, and he set out there in September, hoping to meet Woolley, a Cambridge friend, later on in the holiday. Italy seemed to him more glorious than ever, and his enthusiasm came back in a flood. He wrote rapturously to his mother from Baveno (14 September 1908):

> I have been perhaps *the* most beautiful walk it is possible to think of – quite incredible – the scenery so magnificent I could hardly believe myself alive . . . There was not only an enormous torrent in a gorge, & snow mountains in the far distance, but all the nearer hills were covered with chestnuts, acacias, and heather in flower, and the sun, which was brilliant but not too strong, spread a kind of purple bloom over them. Also little villages, spread one above another in every direction, all with graceful campaniles.
>
> At Costogno, which was my goal, I was met by the dearest brown dog, who took me into the church, walked round the high altar, and then led me out . . .
>
> Really I'm quite uneasy about the Italians – they have not a fault! No beggars, no [illegible] and every one so pleasant. No mosquitoes either, and no dust, and though the sky is cloudless, there is always a refreshing wind.

As for Victor Woolley, when he joined him in Venice, he proved a 'magnificent' companion. He was then a fellow of King's and a university demonstrator in physiology: a tall, moustached man with a rather dry manner, 'contentious in a pleasant way'. He collected books on sexology and psychical research and was thought of by his friends as a kind of wizard analyst. In Italy he became very stiff and British, constantly suspecting the natives of plotting to overcharge and pillage him. 'The long and short of it,' he would say, 'is that they're unreliable.' However, Forster found he could 'poke him out' of his stiffness, and they got on very amicably.

At Mantua they came upon Dent, who was sitting at a café table with two Italian officers. They joined the party, and Forster made efforts at conversation, in Italian, which went as follows:

> *Forster:* Lei è stato in Inghilterra? [Have you ever been to England?]
>
> *Lieutenant:* Mai. Ma l'anno prossimo vengo – scusa! ecco una donna bellissima che passa . . . [Never. But I am coming next year – excuse me! there's the most beautiful woman just going by . . .]
>
> *Major:* Una donna francese, credo. [She's French, I think.]
>
> *Lieutenant:* Francese – Italiana – Tedesca – a me lo stesso. [French – Italian – German – it's all the same to me.]
>
> *Woolley:* What's he saying?
>
> *Dent:* He has seen a beautiful lady.
>
> *Woolley:* Oh, I see.
>
> *Lieutenant* (to Forster): Ma scusa tanto! Cosa diceva? [I do beg your pardon. What were you saying?]
>
> *Forster:* Lei non è stato in Inghil . . . [You have never been to Eng . . .]
>
> *Lieutenant* (grasping him affectionately by the wrist): Ecco un'altra! Non mi piace tanto. E un' po borghese. [There's another! But I don't like her so much. Too middle-class.]
>
> *Woolley* (to Dent): Had not your Italian friend better change places with me? Then he will be able to see the passers-by without turning round in his seat. It is a pity I should have such a good position when I do not value it.

Dent passed the suggestion on; there were cries, protests and clankings of spurs, and everyone rose to their feet; then they all sat down again in the same places.

Saying goodbye to Woolley in Venice, Forster proceeded to Ravenna, where he spent the evening with a chauffeur named Aristides. They had sat at the same table in the hotel, while the chauffeur's English employers had dined at another, and having made friends over dinner they went on to a café. And after this – 'Lor's what are things coming to!' Forster wrote to Lily – he let Aristides treat him to the cinema.

> He was so dignified and nice, &, for an Italian, quiet, though he struck at me wildly with his fist when the lady in the cinematograph sat down on the top of the chimney, which had just been

smeared with glue for the reception of a cowl. Of course she stuck, and other people stuck to her, & finally the fire engine had to play upon them and they all fell off the roof into tubs or on to other people's heads.

Next day they met again and went to visit the tomb of Dante, where Forster improved the occasion with a lecture. Aristides said what a privilege it was to hear so accomplished a person – though, for his part, reading made his head go 'zzzzzzzzzzzzz'. Forster was to draw on this encounter with Aristides in *Arctic Summer*, the abortive successor to *Howards End*.

A Room With a View was published soon after his return, on 14 October 1908, and once again the press was flattering, if not especially perceptive. 'The characters are as clear and salient as a portrait by Sargent,' said the *Daily Mail*; and the *Spectator* was reassured to find less of the 'freakish and somewhat cynical humour' which had disfigured his earlier work. Only *Outlook* was seriously rude, saying:

> The heroine is one of those uncomfortable girls who cannot make up their minds. She is kissed on all possible occasions, and without provocation, by the uncouth George Emerson, and these osculatory overtures as often unsettle her intentions. We do not share the disquiet of her family when at last she decides to marry George; indeed we are grateful to the young man for taking her off our hands.

Among his own circle, Dent took against the novel. He was irritated by Cecil Vyse, a character with some traits of his own, and his letter brought Forster to the novel's defence (19 October 1908):

> No, I don't expect that you will do with the book very well: it does, sincerely or insincerely, commend an attitude that you will think insincere. Only I do wonder that you find it difficult to read – pretty straightforward isn't it, surely.
> I feel myself that it comes off as far as it goes – which is a damned little way – and that the character of Lucy, on which everything depends is all right: she and Mr Beebe have interested me a good deal. Cecil (described not entirely from Lucy's point of view) is certainly incomplete. But his 3 proposals don't strike me as unnatural. She may only be a peg to hang his artistic sensations on, but she is a peg he can't reach easily, and this at once increases her value. Of course when his amour propre is wounded it is a different thing – off he goes at the end of the book, & becomes a misogynist. But until that happens, I maintain he will be at-

tracted, and think that he is caring more about her than about himself. You say 'if he is too young to realise that he can know no one intimately, he does not seem worth bringing in'. Why?

Another of his friends wrote praising the novel to the skies. This was Malcolm Darling, the King's friend a year younger than himself, now in the Indian Civil Service. Darling was a zealous, high-minded, tender-hearted man for whom Forster developed a strong liking and respect. He was rather conventional in outlook in these early days; also distinctly unworldly – when two of his fellow-Etonians had been expelled, and left in the same taxi, he could not make out why their friends should have pelted them with rice. Later he broadened considerably, partly through his friendship with Forster, to whom he became devoted. Forster always thought of him, admiringly, as someone in touch with the realities of work and active life, and his praise of *A Room With a View* was a reassurance. 'I can't tell you how much pleasure your letter has given me,' he told Darling (12 December 1908):

> and apart from the pleasure, the pride, for it *is* gratifying when those who know the world and men at work can find a book by me not sloppy nor unconnected with life . . . But the pleasure is the more important – far more important. I am so glad that you see I'm not a cynical beast. Not that you've suggested I was! but information to the contrary is extraordinarily difficult for me to convey. I can't write down 'I care about love, beauty, liberty, affection, and truth', though I should like to.

It had, once again, been a happy and fruitful year, and on New Year's Eve, with half-an-hour left to him of his twenties, he made a cheerful review of it in his diary:

> ’Εν τοις ένδον [Inward events] the greatest by far is S.R.M. [Masood] . . . He and Italy – that is really all . . . I am reacting in the direction of L.J. [*The Longest Journey*]. In society I take more than I did to young women, but my fear of elderly men increases . . . Public affairs interest me more, especially when they touch Italy, Germany and India . . .
> Balkan incident[1] – bust up preparing?

After a promising start, the sale of *A Room With a View* tailed off disappointingly. However, Arnold's were eager for a new book from Forster. It began to be plain to him, though, that his new novel would be a long one, longer and more ambitious than anything he

---

[1] The annexation of Bosnia and Herzegovina by Austro-Hungary.

had so far attempted. It was to be his 'condition-of-England' novel, in the spirit of Wells and Galsworthy – not that he so much admired them, but, so he thought, perhaps he could do better. The novel would be less confessional than *The Longest Journey* but would have an altogether wider canvas than his Italian comedies. He saw no prospect of finishing it in time for the autumn list, so instead he offered Arnold's a collection of short stories. This they turned down, on the time-honoured grounds that there was no market for short stories.

All the ensuing year of 1909, casual experience flowed in to feed his novel. A dinner-table conversation, noted in his diary on 10 February 1909, set him thinking about money, rather in the vein of Margaret Schlegel.

> Dined with the Scotts.[1] He, who runs a mining paper, was depressing about America and the future generally. The former governed by $\frac{1}{2}$ dozen men, & Roosevelt probably had a hand in the late crisis, which the financiers brought on for their own benefit. 'Here and there you find individuals with private means and they do very well and the world leaves them alone, for it is doing very well.' He was prone to think 'real life' meant knowledge of finance; but he made me see how wide an abyss opens under our upper class merriment & culture. 'Money is power, and nothing else is, as far as I can see.' He spoke as if America may any minute sweep the pleasing erections of our civilisation away.

For the Schlegel sisters his model was, in some respects, Dickinson's three sisters, who lived in the family home at 1 All Souls' Place (off Langham Place). The sisters were all tall, dark-haired and bony, with forcible voices and an interest in 'slumming'. May, the eldest, was ugly, intelligent and something of an intellectual manqué. Francis Birrell, who knew her in later years, described her as scoring through a page of some book by Russell or Moore, writing in the margin, 'Some confusion of thought here' – though she was quite incapable of following it. None the less she was well-read and a good linguist, and was studying Greek when she was over eighty. She was the social hostess, while Janet, who was saintly and Martha-like, and Hester, who was commonsensical and practical (and later got married), ran a little school together. Their conversion into the Schlegel sisters was, Forster said later, a matter of seeing them with a

---

[1] Unidentified.

sideways glance and then refocusing them. 'May was, perhaps, more
definitely Margaret than anyone else was anything else in the two
worlds, though Janet has entered in too.'[1] (One mustn't put too
much weight on this 'model'; for, of course, in many important ways,
Margaret was Forster himself; her views are certainly his.)

The sisters lived just round the corner from the Queen's Hall and
regularly attended there for concerts. The Dickinson influence grows
strong here, for the Queen's Hall concert scene in *Howards End*, with
its discussion of different ways of listening to music, seems to hark
back to a dialogue by Lowes Dickinson, 'Noise that You Pay For',
published in the *Independent Review* in 1904. In Dickinson's dialogue,
a poet, returning in exalted mood from hearing Beethoven's Fifth
Symphony at the Queen's Hall, is denounced by a musician and a
painter – closely resembling Dent and Fry – for using music as a
substitute for living. In his defence, he expounds an allegorical
interpretation of the Symphony, vaguely recalling Helen Schlegel's.

> It was, to begin with, just the beat of Fate, and against that, like
> the sea against the cliffs, the passionate cry of Man. But, presently,
> that abstraction filled itself out, changed its form, became a world-
> drama. As though upon a wind of passion, the figures of history
> and romance – Clytemnestra with the axe, Dido on the shore,
> Caesar, Alexander, Napoleon, all who have ever fought and failed,
> all who have loved and despaired – with set lips, with outstretched
> hands, with cries of defiance or appeal, came driving down on the
> pitiless theme, till they seemed to fuse and blend with it, and, in a
> tragic reconciliation, to be themselves the Fate against which
> they strove . . . etc.

It seems clear, too, that, in *Howards End*, Forster was drawing on
his experiences at the Working Men's College. Culture put to the
wrong end was, as we know, a major preoccupation in all his early
novels. He had identified various versions; the use of culture as an
escape, as with Philip Herriton; the use of it to bolster one's superiority,
as with Cecil Vyse; the use of it as a conspicuous possession, as with
Mr Bons in 'The Celestial Omnibus'. All these were abuses, in his
view, cutting culture off from what gave it its value, the furthering
of humanness generally. Now, in his new novel, he was explaining
another misuse: the culture-snobbery of the under-educated. That
scene, a very touching scene, in which Leonard wrestles with Ruskin's

[1] Letter to G. L. Dickinson, 17 March 1931.

Stones of Venice, hoping 'to come to Culture suddenly, much as the Revivalist hopes to come to Jesus', was a vision bred in Forster by the Working Men's College. He taught at the College devotedly for twenty years or more; and not only that, he made personal friendships with students; he often wrote for the College journal, and he was active in all the College's social activities. Nevertheless – as one can sense from occasional references – he had his reservations about the College and was not sure it worked entirely for good. He shared some of Margaret Schlegel's doubts about Leonard and his fellows: 'She knew the type very well – the vague aspirations, the mental dishonesty, the familiarity with the outsides of books . . .'

But a word or two about the College. It was in many ways a remarkable institution, very important during its first fifty years or so – that is, from the 1850s onwards – though by the time Forster joined it, it had been overtaken by newer types of adult education (in particular the Workers' Educational Association). It had been founded by F. D. Maurice in 1854, in the period – just after the defeat of Chartism and the year of revolutions – when there was a concerted effort by intellectuals, and the 'clerisy' generally, to heal the class-war by means of 'culture'. ('We came forward to help the working man that we might help ourselves,' said Maurice.) Many very distinguished men served the College and lectured at it: Ruskin, who conducted an art-class there, Rossetti whom he co-opted, Frederic Harrison, Grove the musicologist, F. J. Furnivall, A. V. Dicey, Sidney Webb and so on. The College, unlike the earlier Mechanics' Institutes, set out to provide a full liberal education, with a social life modelled on Oxford and Cambridge – teachers and students meeting in fellowship and equality. It set much store by attracting manual workers as students, and at the time Forster arrived 43 per cent were still officially so described, though according to G. P. Gooch, who taught history there, manual workers were 'very rare birds'. In the main, the students were skilled craftsmen or clerks and the like.

The College had figured in Forster's background in various ways. Dickinson's father, the portrait-painter Cato Lowes Dickinson, was one of the founder members,[1] and the Dickinson sisters used to

---

[1] These were F. D. Maurice, Tom Hughes, J. M. F. Ludlow, J. Llewellyn Davies, F. J. Furnivall, J. Westlake, Cato Lowes Dickinson and R. B. Litchfield.

organize theatricals there. Another founder-member was R. B. Litchfield, husband of Aunt Laura's friend Henrietta Litchfield. He served as College Secretary for many years, and through him Aunt Laura came to take an interest in the College. (Forster used to invite the College Field Club down to her house 'West Hackhurst' for tea.) Further, as we have seen, many of Forster's Cambridge friends lectured at the College or gave regular classes there; and Cambridge undergraduates and dons were very active on the occasion of the College's annual visit to Cambridge. This visit was a tradition begun in the 1880s: every year a party of Working Men's College students came up to Cambridge and were parcelled out among undergraduates and dons for lunch and conversation and a night in college rooms. Forster himself never assisted on these occasions, but they may, all the same, be a clue to that passage in *Howards End* (slightly embarrassing, one feels now) about the 'decent-mannered undergraduate' who chatted to Leonard Bast in the train and gave him 'perhaps the keenest happiness of his life' by inviting him to coffee in his college rooms.

One of the friends whom Forster made among the students was a printer named Alexander Hepburn. He got into conversation with Hepburn at the College Supper of 1908, and over the next few years they frequently went for walks and meals together in London. (At one time, Forster made efforts to secure him a job with his own publishers.) Hepburn was a Scot and an agnostic, who claimed that his faith had been unsettled by *The Golden Bough*. He was one of the star performers at the College Debating Society, and the keeper of the minutes declared that he would go down to posterity as 'a wag of remarkable skill and dexterity'. Forster's private comment on him, after their first meeting, was 'W.Ms. differ from us by their full-scale badinage' – a remark that faintly evokes Leonard Bast.[1] The issue of humour tended to figure in their friendship, for on 5 February 1907 Forster opened a discussion in the Debating Society on the motion 'That the sense of humour should be cultivated with caution'. He

---

[1] Cf. *Howards End*, Chapter 16

As a lady's lap-dog Leonard did not excel. He was not an Italian, still less a Frenchman, in whose blood there runs the very spirit of persiflage and of gracious repartee. His wit was the Cockney's; it opened no doors into imagination . . .

argued that 'it was pernicious that the sense of humour should be made to direct our lives; it was not capable of performing such a task. The tendency was for the sense of humour to be cultivated in fields where it had never been sown before, and he believed the crop would be disastrous.'[1] Hepburn opened for the opposition and 'gave his capacious wit full scope', defeating the motion by 18 votes to 12.

Two or three years later, Forster got to know another of his students, E. K. Bennett, then a clerk in Crosse and Blackwell's pickle factory. Bennett stayed on at the College as a teacher, and, partly through Forster's influence, the College sent him up to Cambridge, on a scholarship endowed by G. M. Trevelyan. As a result, he became, in due course, a fellow of Caius and an expert on the German *Novelle*. In later years he became one of Forster's closest friends.

*   *   *

The critical success of *A Room With a View* floated Forster a little into the literary life. He was not eager for it, and did not venture far, but every now and then some host or celebrity pursued his acquaintance. At a literary dinner at Frascati's he made the acquaintance of Henry Newbolt and William Watson; and Clement Shorter, editor of countless journals (*Punch* called him 'The Wee Cham of Literature') expressed great joy at meeting him; he told Forster there was a great career in front of him. However, as it turned out, he couldn't remember which of Forster's books he had read, so the conversation languished. On the following day, Forster lunched with Lady Ottoline Morrell in Bedford Square and decided that she was 'really very nice' and that Dickinson was right in 'confining her affectations to manner'. Another who sought his acquaintance was Sir Edward Grey, the Foreign Secretary, and in July his friends the Francis Aclands[2] took him to dine with Grey. The great man was affable and charming, but, Forster guessed, would have been less so had he known more about him.

---

[1] This was a serious view of his. He was always suspicious of the vaunted British sense of humour and had a trick of deflating tiresome or joyless humour by remorselessly spelling it out. On one occasion, too, he broke out against some H. M. Bateman cartoon, such as 'The man who smoked before the royal toast', asking, angrily, how anyone could like such a 'horrible' thing.

[2] Francis Dyke Acland (1874–1939), a Liberal politician of some distinction.

On one of his Cambridge visits, too, he got to know Rupert Brooke. Brooke drew him the Cambridge face which, he said, looked like ⟨○⟩, whereas the Oxford face looked like ⟨●⟩. Once or twice, thereafter, Forster spent a weekend with Brooke in Grantchester, and through Brooke he got to know Edward Marsh, with whom he struck up an immediate friendship. 'My one fashionable friend' was his description of Marsh, a year or two later. 'A sensitive and sensible fellow too: he got up the Georgian Book of Verse – though perhaps this contradicts what I am trying to convey about him.'[1] Marsh was eager to launch him into London literary circles and from time to time would give him the key to his rooms in Gray's Inn, as a London *pied-à-terre*. He also pressed the latest books on Forster, lending him Masefield's *The Tragedy of Nan*, which Forster thought 'wonderful, unquestionably great', and Frank Harris's *The Man Shakespeare*, which infuriated him. He exploded to Marsh (18 November 1909):

> How *can* he say that Lear is the first attempt in all literature to paint madness? Or after his sneers at conventional morality, smugly absolve Shakespeare from the 'imputations' of the sonnets? Such lapses are unpardonable in a critic who boasts of his scientific equipment they reduce him to the level of me, and I tell you what, he's not really half as nice.

He laboured all the summer at *Howards End*, and then, in September, he went to stay with Maimie Aylward, to do some preparation for his next term's lectures. In this favourite scenery the mood of *The Longest Journey* returned powerfully, provoking him to write a poem, on the theme of possessing Wiltshire.

Between The Butts and Figsbury

The tints are here, to copy down,
　　Pale green, pale salmon, ochre pale,
Lifted above the creamy earth,
　　Faint coronals of beech trees sail.

The air is here to breathe, the flowers,
　　Fanned by its passion, rise and fall,
Knapweed and campion, feverfew,
　　They garland me, I see them all.

---

[1] Letter to Forrest Reid, 17 April 1914.

> And yet, when darkness comes, when sheets,
>   And all the prison of a room,
> Blots out the tints, shuts out the air,
>   Withers the flowers with breath of tomb.
>
> A richer treasure will be mine,
>   For all the glory will have past
> Into my blood and ticking brain
>   And Wiltshire will be mine at last.

One of the books he was reading in connection with his lectures was Pastor's *History of the Popes*, and prompted by this – and perhaps by the fact that Herbert Trench had asked him for a play for his Repertory Theatre – he suddenly took it in mind to write an historical drama, about St Bridget of Sweden. For a few days he wrote away with great enthusiasm, despatching postcards to Bob Trevelyan for further books on St Bridget, after which inspiration petered out.

The play, such of it as he wrote, concerns the famous embassy of St Bridget to the court of Naples in 1371, to persuade the Queen Giovanna to bring the Pope back from Avignon. It was a promising subject, this encounter between the world-renouncing northern visionary and the profligate, art-loving queen, typifying the coming Renaissance; and Forster's handling of the opening scenes – the saint arriving with her bickering family in the scandalous southern court – is quite in the style of his Italian comedies. In the unfinished second act something odder develops. A little girl comes in, dripping wet, through an open window in the queen's apartments, lies down on the sofa, and dies. A guard explains to a lady-in-waiting: she is Virgil's daughter. The palace, he says, was once the castle of Virgil, who built it on an egg and any day may crawl up, under the water, and break the shell. Mystery descends on the play at this point. Looking back on it in his New Year's Eve summary, he called it his one burst of inspiration during the year; but what it meant to him is not clear. There may be a clue in a diary entry of 16 October 1909:

> Would be content if the unseen power was an eternal memory.
> – This year I have been intellectually slack, and dallied with superstition. Have amused myself by finding apologies for the Papacy. The execution of Ferrer may remind me what this leads to.[1]

---

[1] Francesco Ferrer (1859–1909), Spanish revolutionary, executed for his part in anti-Catholic riots in Barcelona.

Twice during the year he was brought into contact with sudden death. In August he heard that Gaunt, who had gone to India, had died of malaria there. Gaunt's sisters sent him an unfinished letter from Gaunt, probably the last he ever wrote. 'Worlds into which the literary imagination cannot penetrate,' he commented wonderingly in his diary (30 August 1909):

> I feel that I cannot feel. This sense of dreaminess may prove our tiny scope in the universe. Where the dead are gone, we cannot expect to know, but the fact of their departure might strike us more. It is only when they have thrilled our blood that the sense of loss is sharpened.

The sisters wrote again in October, and Gaunt's image came back to him poignantly. 'May have put too much into him, but I cannot forget his eyes rolling happily over bedclothes. First and last I can't have seen him 14 days.'

The other death, though not a personal loss, was a mystery which impressed and disturbed him. On 8 July he had dined at a London restaurant with Darling, who was on leave, and with Darling's friend Ernest Merz, a King's contemporary, now living a bachelor existence in London. Forster had never met Merz before and found him very agreeable, and after the meal the two strolled a little, parting at 9.40 p.m. Next morning Merz was found hanged in his rooms in Albany. Darling, who had been very close to Merz, was shattered and bewildered by the news, which nothing had prepared him for; then he began to wonder, with horror, whether homosexuality were somehow at the root of it. Forster had jumped to this conclusion at once, though, out of regard for Darling's conventionality, he didn't say so outright. 'The more I think of it, the more distressed I get,' he wrote to Darling, guardedly. 'My own theory – one must have one – is that he was either insulted disgustingly or saw something disgusting. You mustn't be annoyed at me for writing so freely. The man whom I saw has never made a mess of things, I know that.' The tragedy provoked him to bitterness against society, a mood which returned a few months later.

> *Nov. 29th.* Was going to reflect sadly on life, but 'what's the use of my abuse?' A wrong view of S's. sonnets in a book Marsh lent me, and an attempted blackmail in this morning's paper are the main cause. How barbaric the world! If a tiny fraction of its energy would go to the understanding of man, we should have the millenium. This bullying stupidity.

It was a stirring time from the public point of view, this year of the Lloyd George budget and suffragette agitation, and Forster took at least a temperate interest in events. 'One says "Yah socialist" to everything these days,' he wrote to Darling (10 December 1909):

> if you think the omnibus fare is 1d and it turns out to be 2d, you say 'Yah socialist' to the conductor! You, being really a socialist, yah, would have a hot time: all respectable people sympathise with the Lords in their attempt to overturn the poor and the constitution! – You will see that I am a keen if inexpert politician: the issue does seem clearly marked for once in a way.

Towards women's suffrage he took a more cautious line – to the discontent of his friend Florence Barger, who was full of fire-breathing militancy. 'Lay the blame where one will,' he wrote to Darling in October, during the wave of window-breaking and the first hunger-strikes, 'the Suffragettes are becoming a real danger . . . It is difficult for an outsider to settle at what point physical force becomes justifiable.' He supported women's rights, in a general way, but rather out of abstract justice than because he thought the vote would do women much good. When he went to hear Christabel Pankhurst he found her 'very able, very clever and very unpleasant', but couldn't but agree with most that she said. Or so he told himself. Later in life, when he had become more misogynistic, he analysed his feelings differently.

> Twenty years ago I thought 'It's unpleasant to me, but it won't go further' and spoke with false enthusiasm of women's rights. She shall have all she wants. I can still get away from her, I thought. I grudged her nothing except my company.[1]

The 'biggest' thing of the year for him personally was still to come. Masood, who was going to Paris, suggested casually that Forster should come too, an invitation he promptly snapped up. The trip marked a definite step forward in their friendship, if not exactly in their intimacy – for Masood was bafflingly vague in his responses. Still, he was expansive and gay; they attended all the latest plays and bought Latin Quarter hats; and Forster returned in a glow of love and dazzlement and incomprehension. He found Masood an enigma; but was he so in himself, he wondered, or was it simply his being an oriental? Masood, he was sure, forgot him the instant he was

---

[1] Entry in a Commonplace Book, which he began to keep in 1925.

out of his sight, and this he could bear; but was he even aware of him when they were together? There seemed such light-years between them: on one side beauty and tradition; on the other a 'bourgeois cuteness' wanting to know where it stood (but perhaps, in the long run, just as fickle?). At all events, they were close enough for plain speaking, and he planned to speak out about his love; it would be for Masood's good as well as his own. 'So beautiful a mind will right itself,' he reflected, paternally. It was New Year's Eve as he put down these thoughts, his mind half on love and half, as always, on self-improvement. There were half-a-dozen words more to be said, and they turned into a prayer

> 'Oh love, every time thou goest out of my sight, I die a new death.' How can I keep quiet when I read such things? My brain watches me, but it's literary. Let me keep clear from criticism and scheming. Let me think of you and not write. I love you, Syed Masood; love.

*   *   *

There was a local Literary Society in Weybridge, which Forster and Lily sometimes attended, and early in 1910 he read a paper to the Society on Matthew Arnold. In preparing it, he lighted on a passage in Arnold's letters which came home to him with great force.

> I have ripened and am ripening so slowly that I should be glad of as much time as possible, yet I can feel, I rejoice to say, an inward spring which seems more and more to gather strength, and to promise to resist outward shocks, if they must come, however rough. But of this inward spring one must not talk, for it does not like being talked about, and threatens to depart if one will not leave it in mystery.

The words, he felt, confirmed his own deepest purposes. He was living much the same life as five years before, demanding no excitement, doing nothing to push himself publicly, and circulating unobtrusively in his own suburban and Cambridge circle. Yet, at the same time, he had given up none of his demand for 'greatness' in life, or 'in all moods, the greatest happiness'. He wrote as he could, pressing on through minor setbacks, but never seriously forcing himself, and not much ashamed of idleness. He knew he would go to India sometime – a point agreed upon with Masood – and he was preparing himself by reading and in imagination. He was in no hurry to form plans, though; nor would he 'speak out' to Masood for another whole year. Fundamentally, despite frustrations, he was happy and felt his life moving in the direction that he wanted.

Not that he was not troubled by physical longings and regrets. 'A vision of a khaki greatcoat has tormented me,' he recorded on 29 January 1910; 'of eyes so indifferent to mine; of manhood's hidden column: and though I have so much to be thankful for I cannot be grateful.' He was disturbed by a picture in a book on the Adriatic, in the London Library, showing two handsome youths with their arms round each other, and he went back to look at it again, deciding this time that the artist had deliberately meant to trouble him. One day, too, having coffee with E. V. Thompson at the Bath Club, he suddenly realized they were immediately over the swimming pool; just under his feet was the attendant, in nothing but a towel.

> The warm air heavy with tobacco smoke, and only half alive under electric light; and the oblong of blue green water; and the sleek members drying between their toes in luxurious cubicles and finally hurrying off suitcase in hand to get into taxis! and E.V.T. so remote from it all, yet appreciating it – ! Sensuous. Shouldn't have imagined it in England.[1]

On another occasion, lunching with Thompson at the Savile, he happened to say something about a 'charming boy', at which one of the members lowered his paper for an instant to stare at him. And after this, when he went to have a haircut, the barber hinted that he would like the loan of £10. The sequence of events plunged him into real gloom, and he wrote a 'free', i.e. confessional, letter to Meredith – who kept him on thorns for several days by not replying.

'Only half alive' – the feeling could not but come over him, every now and then, that the world went drab and dead without passion and sensuality, or at least without the thought of them. Also, there was the strangeness of the physical life existing so close at hand, an inch away from nodding clubmen and Weybridge gentilities. A Housmanesque poem of his, written at this period, catches this mood of his, a characteristically Edwardian one.

---

[1] Diary, 4 February 1910.

> . . . A thousand putties [*sic*] twinkled,
> A thousand boot soles beat,
> And half a thousand brown caps
> Went bobbing up the street.
>
> ' 'Tis death,' I murmured sadly,
> 'Death's universal grey,'
> But as I sighed, one soldier
> Lifted his face my way.
>
> From eyes I felt the fire flash,
> Through lips the hot breath drive;
> Battalion by battalion,
> That regiment came alive.

For all this, his attitude to sex was clear for the present. 'However gross my desires, I find I shall never satisfy them for the fear of annoying others. I am glad to come across this much good in me. It serves instead of purity.' A year later he would remark, with false security, that he was less troubled by lustful thoughts than for the last fifteen years. He added, characteristically, that it mustn't make him haughty, or, on the other hand, jump to the conclusion that everyone was as he had been: 'Two of the errors that make old men so unpleasant to the young.'

His greatest comfort was Masood and the thought that the ground gained with him in Paris had not been lost. He passed a 'joyful but inconclusive evening' with him on 13 January 1910. 'I figured innumerable crises, but we only care for each other more than before, each in his own way.' They talked about India and the day when they would see it together, and every now and then Masood flew into a passion against Anglo-Indian prejudice. He got 'flustered' over the new-style missionary, who put on native dress and said Siva was another name for Jesus; but then, Forster told himself, 'he generally *is* flustered about something'.

Later in the year, with the unpunctuality that life sometimes displays, Hugh Meredith made love to him, kissing and embracing him passionately on the sitting-room sofa at 'Harnham'. After so long a delay, the event was not, after all, of much significance to Forster. But, going to the opera next day with Masood, he noticed that he was not 'awake' to him. 'It is possible to love 2 people,' he noted in his diary, 'but not on successive days. That I have been attractive excites me most.'

183

India more and more occupied his mind – the place where he would complete his understanding of Masood and find a new opening for imagination. He was doing much reading about the country,[1] and wrote to Darling promising to be 'most helpful to him on the subject' – also asking for copies of seditious Indian newspapers. His mind wandered to parallels between western and eastern geography. 'Has it ever occurred to you,' he wrote to Darling (15 April 1910) from the Italian Alps, 'that the south coasts of Europe and Asia are analogous – three peninsulas, with the chief mountain chain knotted up at the head of the middle one. I am accordingly now in the Himalayas, while Dickinson is in Ceylon.'

Darling had been tutor to the young prince of Dewas State Senior, in Central India, and was a frequent visitor there since his pupil's accession as Raja. He wrote Forster a long account of Dewas and its *Alice in Wonderland* constitution, according to which there were two separate royal families, Dewas Senior (to which his pupil belonged) and Dewas Junior, each with its own territories, inextricably jumbled up among the other's. There were two royally-sponsored tennis-clubs, 200 yards apart, and a school with two headmasters appointed by the different monarchs, each claiming to be in sole charge.

The friendship between Darling and his pupil was intense. The Raja termed Darling his 'dearest and noblest brother', his one sure friend in the world, and spoke of the 'mission' taught him by Darling to 'achieve the Union of East and West'. The friendship extended also to Darling's mother, who used to visit Dewas and, in Hindu style, had become the Raja's 'mother'.[2] Darling had got married in 1909, and he and his wife Josie had spent Christmas with the Raja. Never was host so charming as his Highness, he told Forster:

> The Raja is indescribable: the oddest mixture of Prince and imp, a born diplomatist, the soul of honour and the best of friends. His thin spare frame is far too weak for the keen-edged emotions that are always passing through him. I have never met anyone who had a greater capacity for pleasure and pain. 'The most Christian person I have ever met,' said Josie the first time

---

[1] For instance Sir Alfred Lyall's *Asiatic Studies* (1882) and *British Dominion in India* (1893) and Ramsay MacDonald's *The Awakening of India* (1910).

[2] He felt much devotion towards her, and when she died in 1912 he wanted his name inscribed on her tomb as one of her children.

she came to Dewas. No one certainly could have a more loveable spirit and be so quick and humorous and gay and an admirable listener.

Malcolm had read the Raja one of Forster's short stories, an idea which took Forster's fancy greatly. 'That he, sitting in the heart of poetry, should tolerate it seems so odd.'

*   *   *

Edward Arnold had been shown a draft of thirty chapters of *Howards End* during March and had greeted it with great enthusiasm. He had, however, not liked the part about Helen's seduction and asked Forster to consider altering it, to which Forster replied that he knew it was faulty, but it was too late for change – the offending part was intrinsic to the plot.

His own running comments on the novel were, as usual, rueful: he was 'grinding out my novel into a contrast between money and death'; he was 'tired and discontented at the slightness of my work'. Nevertheless, he seems to have guessed he was set for a major success and was preparing his mind for fame and worrying about its effect on his character. He told himself to take more care of his health, remarking wryly, 'In my position it's a duty to be handsome and cheerful.' He reflected that he had been happier on his solitary walks and journeys, when he had been a nobody. 'Now I get self conscious and feel I have a position to keep up. God help me.'

The spectacle of success and literary professionalism filled him with dismay. There was Hugh Walpole, for instance, and what an object-lesson *he* presented! Walpole had entered his life a year or two before, as he did that of many distinguished people, by means of a fan-letter. He sincerely admired Forster, and said he could 'put the rest of us in his pocket'; and Forster, for his part, had written to Walpole encouragingly about *The Wooden Horse*. Privately, though, he thought him second-rate. 'He contains nothing that I value,' he complained to Marsh (22 August 1910) *à propos* of *Maradick at Forty*. 'They can't even get married, but the clergyman's fireplace has tiles of the "right blue". – I am afraid he does not know how bad it is essentially, and until he does, will scarcely do better.' Above all, he saw Walpole as a portent:

> *Oct. 15th.* Walpole's room – row of novels all along the floor, row of selections on the table, pile of hopelessnesses under the table. All these arrived last week, and he will review them for the Pearson

press, at the rate of one or more a day. He has also written a novel, is writing another, and if cut would reveal diminishing eggs, like a fertile hen. He is also secretary to an old gentleman,[1] in the mornings, and he is also in literary society. But primarily he is a 'product'. No other age can have produced such a mannikin of letters. He is the impact of commerce, or rather advertisement, upon belles lettres.

The lives of several of Forster's friends were in confusion during the year, and he was in demand as a confidant. Dickinson was in love with a young man, Oscar Eckhard,[2] and had been reduced to despair and collapse by Oscar's treatment: Oscar had invited him out to Germany and then, after a few days, had sent him packing with a wounding letter. Forster had some sympathy with Oscar, till he learned that the letter was not written on the spur of the moment but after several drafts; also that Oscar, who had made it his excuse that he was in love with a girl, was treating the girl in just the same way. 'But where is the physical urge?' he asked himself. 'Imagine myself if I was loved as I can love.'

Meredith, also, was in difficulties. Christabel, his wife, had borne twins in 1908, but, being a Fabian and a feminist, she had refused to give up her career at her Teachers' Training College in Cambridge. By now it was being said by their friends, for instance the Bargers and Waterlows, that she was a disastrous mother. The twins, though two years old now, neither played nor talked, and, so the friends said, it was all the fault of Christabel's self-centredness. Then, to exacerbate matters, Meredith was appointed to a chair in Belfast and Christabel refused to join him. Forster offered to intervene, but Hugh – rather absurdly, Forster thought – insisted it would be wrong to force her in any way. Eventually Sydney Waterlow, egged on by his wife and Florence Barger, sent Christabel a letter of remonstrance, but she bounced back with vigour, declaring that the babies were *perfectly* normal, and, if anything, she was *more* sentimental than the average mother. The volatile Sydney swung round, at this, but Forster remained unconvinced. He felt sorry for everyone – complaining, however, 'As usual, the women have precipitated the trouble & make no attempt to understand each other.'

---

[1] Walpole, through Edmund Gosse's arranging, was doing private secretarial work for Lord Stanmore (1829–1912) in the House of Lords.

[2] The affair is described in Dickinson's posthumously published *Autobiography* (1973).

He himself had been in difficulties with Sydney. He had refused an invitation to Rye, pleading pressure of work, but not long after, meeting Sydney again, he let slip that he was going to Cambridge to stay with Dickinson. The blow evidently registered – for, indeed, Sydney was morbidly sensitive – and Forster spent sleepless nights over it:

> The pain was physical. Small red hot irons seemed stamped over my body when I thought of it, and a clean stab thro' me, and I shall fall in the opinion of all our friends. *That* I mind. And all that touches affection. That I have not been straight worries me very little.[1]

Then, in September, a further trouble overtook him. He had given his mother the proofs of *Howards End* to read, and for some days afterwards she showed by her manner that she had been deeply shocked by the book – presumably by the business of Helen's seduction. Being intensely responsive to her feelings, he felt it as a serious matter; and to make things worse, he knew that the part which offended her was bad even on artistic grounds. With his mother so cold to him, and worrying now about Maimie and Aunt Laura's reaction, he began to wonder how he would get through the next few weeks. As usual with him, his spirits soon revived, and he reflected – concerned as always with self-improvement – 'The almost ceaseless worries of the last month have left me more interested in life. I feel older & more competent.'

---

[1] Diary, 12 February 1910.

11 The Year of *Howards End*

Howards End was published on 18 October 1910, and the press, almost unanimously, treated the occasion as marking Forster's 'arrival'. The book hit the note of the time. Even *Punch* said that anything could be forgiven an author who introduced us to the great Wilcox family. 'For the Wilcoxes *are* England; they contain more of the essence of England even than Sunday afternoon, or Lords, or Sir WILLIAM BULL.' For the first time, the word 'great' was bandied about: Archibald Marshall, in the *Daily Mail*, hailed it as 'The Season's Great Novel', and the *Daily Telegraph* went so far as to begin: 'There is no doubt about it whatever, Mr. E. M. Forster is one of the great novelists.' Frank Harris's *Saturday Review* said that, to express his genius in using everyday speech to betray 'cunning shadowings' of personality, the term 'Forsterian' was now a necessity. There was another development, too. Hitherto, reviewers had all been confident, as reviewers often are, that his true talent all lay in one single direction – though, to be sure, they had different views as to what this was: some thought social satire, some thought character-creation, some visionary profundity. Now one or two reviewers acknowledged, what seems plainer to us now, that his genius lay in a peculiar amalgam of talents and aims. R. A. Scott-James, by now an entire convert to Forster, saw this, and in his review in the *Daily Mail*, laid all his emphasis on coherence and 'connectedness'.

> 'Only connect . . .' is Mr Forster's motto. It is because he has taken this motto not only for his book but for his method of work that he has achieved the most significant novel of the year . . . to write a novel near to nature on the one hand, and true to the larger vision on the other, requires tremendous labour of thought

making perception and wisdom fruitful; the fitting of the perception of little things with the perception of universal things;
consistency, totality, *connection.* Mr Forster has written a
connected novel.

Forster's method, he said, was a sort of bridge between that of
Conrad and that of Galsworthy: Conrad began with an incident from
life and moved out from it towards a meaning, while Galsworthy
started with a generalization and searched round for facts to
illustrate it.

> But who could say of *Howards End* that the one method or the
> other had been adopted? The novel rises like a piece of architecture
> full-grown before us. It is all bricks and timber, but it is mystery,
> idealism, a far-reaching symbol.

One of the book's few enemies was Edmund Gosse. He had been sent
it by Edward Marsh and wrote to Marsh (27 December 1910) that he
could 'hardly remember such a disappointment'.

> I try to analyse why, when *Where Angels Fear to Tread* was so
> very promising, and when *A Room With a View* seemed to advance
> that promise, *Howards End* makes one fear that no good thing
> will come of these anticipations. I think it is due to the author's
> having listened to the people who (may have) said that he should
> give more 'story', and that he should be coarse in morals, and that
> he should coruscate in style. But these three things are not native
> to him, and so the man who gave us before such delicate and
> faithful studies of character, and who wrote so simply, now
> produces a book (which has many details of merit, but) which,
> taken as a whole, is sensational and dirty and affected.
> I should like to know what you think of the new craze for
> introducing into fiction the high-bred maiden who has a baby?
> It is the craze of the moment; it is beginning to attract the wonder
> of the Continent. I have read *three* new English novels this autumn
> of which it is the *motif.* The French, who allow themselves every
> other aberration, have at least preserved their horror of this one,
> which never occurs in their novels. I think it is a mark of feminisa-
> tion; the only French instance I recollect occurs in a novel by
> Marcelle Tinayre, which was very severely condemned by French
> opinion. I do not know how an Englishman can calmly write of such
> a disgusting thing, with such *sang-froid.* If you will look at Chapter
> 40 of *Howards End*, and will put it side by side with an incident in
> real life, *forcibly, without literature or cant,* you will feel the goose-
> flesh rise upon you.
> I hope you will not be vexed with me for speaking so plainly,

because I know that you have influence with the author of this unhappy book, and are genuinely interested in him. I cannot help hoping that you may be induced to say something which will redeem him from the slough of affectation and false sentiment into which he has fallen.

If I were asked to point to a passage which combined all that prose fiction should not be – lurid sentimentality, preposterous morals, turgid and sickly style – I do not think I could point to anything worse than the closing chapters of *Howards End* . . .

In giving permission, twenty years later, for the letter to be printed in the *Life and Letters of Sir Edmund Gosse*, by E. Charteris (where the full text is to be found) Forster reproached Marsh for his failure to use his 'influence' on him.

As for Forster's fears for his family circle, they proved groundless. Maimie found the book 'so thoughtful and clever' and told Lily that 'somehow' she was not shocked as Lily had thought she might be. 'Snow' Wedgwood was full of praise, too – though, as she told Laura Forster, she was astonished by the difference between the man, as she knew him, and the author. 'In all of them [his novels] there is a touch of cruelty which surprises me, & which somewhat takes off from my pleasure in his originality and vividness.' Even Bob Trevelyan had to admit he liked the novel. 'That is to say,' he explained, 'the parts I disliked I disliked less than Bessie disliked what she disliked.' Forster's own comment on the book, some forty years later, is of some interest.

> *Howards End* my best novel and approaching a good novel. Very elaborate and all pervading plot that is seldom tiresome or forced, range of characters, social sense, wit, wisdom, colour. Have only just discovered why I don't care for it: not a single character in it for whom I care . . . Perhaps the house in *H.E.*, for which I did once care, took the place of people and now that I no longer care for it, their barrenness has become evident. I feel pride in the achievement, but cannot love it, and occasionally the swish of the skirts and the non-sexual embraces irritate . . .[1]

Howards End marked a turning-point in his career, as it did in his life. For the moment he was a celebrity: friends flattered him, newspapers interviewed him, and letters and invitations poured in. As a result, his fears of the effects of fame redoubled. 'I don't like

[1] Commonplace Book, May 1958.

popularity. It seems so mad,' he wrote to Dickinson (21 November 1910). 'There isn't any reason why it should be this book and not another, or another of mine. I go about saying I like the money, because one is simply bound to be pleased about something on such an occasion. But I don't even like that very much . . . No, it is *all* insanity.' Privately, he addressed himself, in Evangelical fashion, with prayer and exhortation:

> *Dec. 8th.* Prayer. Not to imagine people are noticing me, especially when I am with one whom I love. How often I have met Masood the last two months, how little I have enjoyed it. I long to be out of London with him, but that is self indulgence. Let me not be distracted by the world. It is so difficult – I am not vain of my over-praised book, but I wish I was obscure again. Soon it shall be, let me re-enter it with sweetness. If I come an unholy smash let me never forget that one man and possibly two have loved me. In old age I shall look back enviously to this year which gave me so much, but it is the material for happiness rather than happiness. I knew I shouldn't and I don't enjoy fame. Never forget nature and to look at her freshly. Don't advance *one step more* into literary society than I have. . . . Henceforward more work and meditation, more concentration on those whom I love.

His fears were not only of an ethical nature; they were also, to a certain extent, superstitious. He showed symptoms, I think, of the psychology which Freud describes in his paper 'Those Wrecked by Success'.[1] Already, within a week or two, he was speculating – admittedly, fairly light-heartedly – on what would happen if he had a breakdown.

> Suppose I went smash. It would not disorganise or shock society, though I feel it would. A good remedy is to look at the carpet while people are praising you or being silly and to meditate on New Zealand, which lies through it, & on the boot soles of the Greenwood family.[2] It is an easier cure for self consciousness than Tennyson's star nebulae.[3] It is direct aid from the earth.

[1] In 'Some Character-types met with in Psycho-analytic Work'; Vol. 14 of *The Complete Psychological Works.*

[2] See p. 77.

[3] See Hallam Tennyson, *Alfred Lord Tennyson: a Memoir* (1897), Vol. 1, p. 20: 'There is a story current in the family that Frederick, when an Eton school-boy, was shy of going to a neighbouring dinner-party to which he had been invited. "Fred," said his younger brother (Alfred), "think of Herschel's great star-patches, and you will soon get over all that." '

He also began to worry in a new fashion about his mother. She was unhappy these days and turned everything to her own disadvantage. He felt that his success bored her; and the busier his own life became, the more she was bound to feel the emptiness of her own. Now that her mother, who was such a prop to her, was old and likely to die at any time, he feared to think what might lie in store for her.

Simultaneously he began to fear sterility as a writer, and this fear would dog him for the rest of his career. 'Must do something. What?', he addressed himself in his diary (15 December 1910). 'For a solid hour & half have done nothing, and so it was this morning. Shall I force myself to begin a book & trust to inspiration dropping in some time? Or shall I be learned and study Valla?[1] The latter, I think, if anyone would encourage me. My brain, though active with inferiors, is slack with superiors or alone.' He sketched out a scheme, or rather a 'desire', for a new novel, one in which he might get away from a conventional marriage plot.

> To deal with country life & possibly Paris. Plenty of young men & children in it, & adventure. If possible pity and thought. But no love making – at least of the orthodox kind, & perhaps not even of the unorthodox. It would be tempting to make an intelligent man feel towards an intelligent man of lower class what I feel, but I see the situation too clearly to use it as in Mon Frère Yves,[2] where the author is either deceiving the public or himself. My motive should be democratic *affection*, and I am not sure whether that has any strength. Am sketching a family – father a Tory candidate, a barrister, moderate, sensible, & generally kind, lets his children go loose, but expects them to enter their class without difficulty later. Eldest son – Nevil – at Oxford; second Jocelyn, the hero; two girls, 14 & 13, and perhaps another boy. A step mother, quiet and beautiful, who accentuates the father's faults. And an old boot boy now at the Swindon works, & his two brothers, one a choir boy in the Cathedral.

The year 1910 saw, among other things, his more definite entry into 'Bloomsbury'. During two 'swirling' days in London early in December he delivered a paper to the Friday Club, on 'The Feminine Note in Literature'. The Club, which was a successor to Vanessa Bell's informal Friday evenings, had been founded six months before, and at the previous meeting – a week after the suffragettes' 'Black

[1] Lorenzo Valla (*c.* 1407–57), the Italian humanist.
[2] A novel by Pierre Loti.

Friday'[1] – they had discussed the 'Subjection of Women' in the forty
years since Mill. Forster, in his paper, took his stand against Mill,
who had denied there was such a thing as a 'feminine note'. True,
he admitted, none of the usual definitions of the 'note' would do. For
one thing, they were contradictory: eighteenth-century women
writers were said, and rightly, to excel in raciness, charm, self-
revelation and fun ('often a little cruel'), whereas nineteenth-century
ones were good at just the opposite: 'grave, carefully ordered works,
full of brain and character-drawing, full of emotion, and full – almost
too full – of moral purpose'. All the same, he would hazard the
suggestion, women writers had, at least, a common weakness. They
were good at satirizing their own sex, but failed when they began to
idealize it, when 'unconsciously the note of personal arrogance
creeps in'. And the 'feminine note'? Yes, he thought after all there
was one: it was *preoccupation with relative worthiness*. The characters
in a woman's novel try not so much to be good, to measure up to
some impersonal standard, as to be worthy of one of the other
characters. It was a large gathering at the Friday Club, including
Roger Fry, Charles and Dora Sanger,[2] Hawtrey and Virginia
Stephen,[3] and his paper proved a hit. Virginia told him afterwards it
was the best paper the Club had heard so far.

In his present unsettled condition, troubled by praise and its
attendant anxieties, he felt more and more tempted to 'speak out' to
Masood. Their friendship seemed to be thriving; they were planning
a visit to Turkey together; and Masood confided in Forster about
his affairs with women. In November he had written to Forster
about their journey in terms of the most exalted friendship:

> My dear Forster,
>   What a dear fellow you are, & your letter shows me that you
> love me as much as I love you . . . Whatever happens, don't let us
> give up Constantinople. I shall go alone with you, but we must
> make an honest effort to make it come off. Dearest boy if you knew

---

[1] On Friday 18 November 1910, three hundred suffragettes marched on the
House of Commons, while Asquith was making a speech on the Women's
Rights question, and after a prolonged and violent scuffle a hundred and
seventeen women and two men were arrested.
[2] C. P. Sanger (1871–1930), a great friend of Bertrand Russell's, was a
lawyer and an authority on statistical economics. He and his wife Dora
belonged to the inner circles of Bloomsbury.
[3] As she then was.

how much I loved you & how I long to be alone with you in that romantic part of the world you would never dream of changing our original plans. England is all right but it does not possess a romantic or even a pathetic atmosphere. You know what I mean. Let us get away from the conventional world [?] & let us wander aimlessly if we can, like two pieces of wood on the ocean & perhaps we will understand life better . . . I only wish that you & I could live together for ever & though that is a selfish wish yet I feel sorry that it will never come to anything. Did you see the eclipse, how beautiful it was! And now I have nothing more to tell you except the old fact that I love you more than almost any other man friend of mine & so kiss you au revoir.

Ever your dearest boy
Syed Ross Masood.

In another letter, on 20 December, Masood praised Forster's rare power of fathoming the Indian soul.

You know my great wish is to get *you* to write a book on India, for I feel convinced from what I know of you that it will be a great book. I do not wish to flatter you in any way but the fact is that you are about the only Englishman in whom I have come across true sentiment & that, too, real sentiment even from the oriental point of view. So you know what it is that makes me love you so much, it is the fact that in you I see an oriental with an oriental view of life *on most things* & as the Frenchmen has said 'Cultivez Cultivez' etc., I say Go on Go on improving your imagination & with it your power of physically feeling the difficulties of another. This is what we call *Tarass*, the word I told you at the Saville. A true and well bred oriental always feels the atmosphere around him when he enters an assembly or a drawing room even though no one has spoken. Our senses both intellectual & physical are to use a Western simile like a marconigram always ready *to receive* & quivering to receive some impression. Of course the fault of this is that it makes our suffering acute but then it does the same to our pleasure. So now you understand why I felt so extraordinarily sad when I said goodbye to you at the Gare du Nord last winter, which you called mashing [?] emotion.

Nine days after this they met at the Oxford and Cambridge Musical Club in Leicester Square. Masood returned to the theme of Forster's insight into oriental things, and at this Forster could bear it no longer and burst out with his feelings. Masood took it easily, murmuring 'I know'. On getting back to Weybridge, Forster wrote him a letter, and then he and his mother, both in low spirits, went off to

West Hackhurst, where there was no reply awaiting him. He had brought his diary, to make a New Year's Eve review of his remarkable year, but he found he had no heart for it. 'Non respondit,' he wrote anxiously, 'and though I do believe it is all right, my breast burns suddenly & I have felt ill. He has sent me such a horrid ugly birthday present – tray with candlestick, match box and sealing wax rest, colourless message inside: probably posted before my letter reached.' He thanked Masood politely for his 'useful and original birthday present', but told him: 'My real need is a letter. If you will use your imagination, you will see that I am not having much of a time.'

Next day, the post having arrived, still with no letter, he began to wonder how to support life. The evening, especially, listening to Aunt Laura laying down the law, seemed never-ending; and at eleven he 'had a rotten bath by a rotten fire' and went miserably to bed. The following day there was a letter, but a rather vague and unconcerned one, to which he replied: 'Oh you devil! Why didn't you write at once? I was in an awful stew all Saturday and Sunday. You may say that this was not sensible of me, but when all that one is and can feel is concerned, how can one be sensible?' By now he was really in low water and began to fancy he was seriously ill. A friend had suggested he might be tubercular, so he made arrangements to see a specialist. Masood came to stay the night and was all concern about his health but otherwise was 'affected and scratchy' and no more comfort than his letter.

Amidst all these chagrins, the news came that his grandmother Louisa, who was staying down at Aunt Eliza's at Plymouth, had fallen dangerously ill. Lily hurried down there with Aunt Rosie, intending to bring her mother back to Weybridge, but a day or two later she wired Forster to say there was no hope. When Forster himself reached Plymouth, his grandmother was in a coma. She lingered for two or three days; and as he walked out at evening on the Hoe, the ghostly moonlit scene, and the faint cries of distant gulls, seemed to him an emblem of her state, 'so unapt to die and leave the land'. During the night of 15 January her death-agony began. He heard his mother in the next room, sobbing tragically 'Mother, mother,' and, 'I could have made her so happy,' and for a few moments in the dark he became hysterical too. Death came to his grandmother in the early morning, and they buried her the same day – Aunt Eliza being particularly 'vociferous and skipping' on the occasion. It was, Forster thought, the end to a happy and dignified career. 'She knew how to live, and to the end took it out of those who did not.' The day after the funeral he went for a glorious walk on Dartmoor, feeling glad to be alive.

On his return to London, however, the specialist told him his 'opsonic index' was dangerously low and that he was beating up for an illness. He thought he might have to go into a sanatorium, and when he told his mother the news she wept. To add to their worries, his Whichelo cousins Ray and Gerry had got themselves into serious trouble over money. 'Swaggering fools,' he burst out in his diary. 'Have told them so. No room for pity left in me.' It had been a month of disasters, and for the first time he looked at the future pessimistically. Here they were, without occupation for the coming year: he at the flood of his fame but, so he feared, without further prospects; and his mother sunk in morbid regrets.

Still, at least he had his love for Masood, and for all its frustrations, this gave his life some meaning. 'How it stays me up even when I do not think of it,' he reflected. In fact, for him, the shocks of the last few weeks cancelled one another, and he soon recovered balance. 'It is a degrading moment,' he philosophized, thinking of Masood, 'when we admit people can't help their behaviour.' He was ready to accept it in Masood's case: Masood was, and perhaps would always be, 'sensitive but not responsive'. One phase of his love for Masood was over, but there might be other phases. And, in fact, in April he had an evening with Masood so happy it seemed to mark a step in his own development. Masood had thawed out a 'frost' still lingering in him.

Meanwhile, he commanded himself to plan his work, to put in a solid hour's reading before dinner, to study the East and astronomy. By March he had completed the story 'The Point of It' (though he thought it inferior), and he had various ideas for essays: the use of history, poetry and criticism; the 'middle classes and literature'; perhaps a whole series. A new novel, too, was germinating in his mind. Indefatigably moralistic, he reminded himself how lucky he was: he had health, money, and friends. 'Most of my troubles come from within or because the ill luck of others worries me. Good luck has done me good hitherto but the future is doubtful. My faults are idleness, and inability to admit that I am wrong, unless I love the accuser very much. I might be envious, but the inevitable decline of my literary reputation will test that.'

The real sufferer from the past January was his mother. His forebodings proved all too correct: she plunged into a pit of misery, recrimination and bad temper. Like him, she kept a diary, and she filled hers with interminable complaints: how her existence was useless; how she could have done so much more to make her mother happy. Forster had a bad time with her all the remainder of the year; month after month he recorded, 'Mother so sad and teasing'; 'Mother prostrated with lumbago and morbidity.' For the rest of her life, January was always a bad month with her, reviving the bitterness of the present year. In Forster's view, the death of his grandmother had wrecked his mother's life and permanently altered her character; and their life together was never the same after it.

12 'A Sense of Unused Strength'

Forster was now, after *Howards End*, a figure in the public eye, with a literary position to maintain, and he greeted the fact with misgivings. In some ways, he felt more and more, a professional career as a novelist did not suit his temperament. For one thing, writing, for him, had up to now gone hand-in-hand with self-cultivation. Before attempting a new work, he always felt he needed to reappraise his own life, to have had a fresh vision of existence. It was not that he did not enjoy writing. On the contrary, he liked nothing so much; it was for him a different and superior kind of living. But a book had to come from his whole being; he did not know how to force himself to write, and indeed he thought it wrong to try. Added to this, there were his personal problems: sexual frustration, his mother's morbidity, the temptations of idleness. They needed not prove fatal, or so he hoped; all the same they seemed to cramp his will.

To work, nevertheless, was the necessity. But to work in what spirit, or supported by what desires? As usual, he broadened the question and made it a general issue of human conduct. Some of his friends, like Dickinson and George Trevelyan, Russell and the Sangers, worked very zealously at public causes, such as education, Fabianism, women's suffrage and international understanding. To work in their fashion, and to make this the goal of one's middle age, was a dignified and attractive ambition, but it had its dubious aspect too. It might make life better for humanity, but might it not also make it greyer? This antithesis preoccupied him and began to offer the subject for a novel. In *Howards End* he had weighed death against money; in his new novel – the one, never completed, which

198

he was to name 'Arctic Summer' – he would oppose battle to work. He would contrast the civilized and socially useful man, who longs for an 'arctic summer', a long cool spell in which to carry through worthwhile work, with the chivalrous man, the knight-errant, who wants not to work but to fight for his faith. It was a promising theme, and he addressed himself to it hopefully – suffering more seriously now, however, from fears of 'going smash'.

Meanwhile, at last, he had persuaded a publisher, Sidgwick & Jackson, to accept a volume of short stories. He had submitted ten stories, but Frank Sidgwick had decided on a selection of six only, all in Forster's fantastic vein – there being just then a vogue for mythological fantasy. Sidgwick also wanted illustrations: as like as possible, he said, to those in Laurence Housman's *All Fellows*. Forster was dismayed at this proposal. 'All Fellows is an awful work of Housman's,' he complained to Bob Trevelyan; '. . . "minor redemptions" – you never tasted such bilge'. As a concession, he agreed to pictorial endpapers, and he enquired from Bob whether Roger Fry might undertake them. Or rather, he asked Bob to find out tactfully if Fry liked his stories; he knew Fry was hard up, but would not want to procure him money by 'contemptuous' work. Fry turned out enthusiastic and, after much procrastination, produced a woodcut design to illustrate the title-story, depicting a rainbow, sunset, and Valhallan crags overtopping the terraces of Surbiton. In the foreground of Fry's cover-design stand two billboards bearing the legends 'Practical Culture' and 'Imperial Culture' – presumably Fry's own contribution to the story's indictment of culture-snobbery.

It was an exquisite spring when the volume, *The Celestial Omnibus*, came out. 'O lovely Spring!', Forster apostrophized it happily. 'Immense passenger – not settling down like the other seasons.' He was in high spirits; and amid cloudless weather, in the Fellows' Garden at King's, he began a new play, entitled *The Heart of Bosnia*. He soon got into difficulties; and on 16 June, having sat for an hour unable to write a word, he analysed the causes of his sterility:

> 1. Inattention to health – curable. 2. Weariness of the only subject that I both can and may treat – the love of men for women & vice versa. Passion & money are the two main springs of action (not of existence) and I can only write of the first & of that imperfectly. Growing interest in religion does not help me. 3. Depressing & enervating surroundings. My life's work, if I have any, is to live with a person who thinks nothing worth while.

199

By Coronation Day (22 June), marked at Weybridge by 'rather tepid' celebrations, his despondency had lasted for ten days. 'Wish my damned spirits would rise,' he sighed. As for the Coronation, it seemed to him 'all upholstery and froth': the beauty and mystery of monarchy had been 'Harmsworthed out of existence.' A week or two later, in the mounting heat wave, he paid a round of visits in London and went to see Shaw's *Fanny's First Play*. 'Slipshod and bungling,' was how it struck him, but it left him serious; and afterwards, in a queer mood of suspense, he wandered down the Embankment past the tramps and out-of-work men. 'Heat, the dimmed moon & the clock tower; sigh of the trees. Sleepers in a sort of alcove, and up a flight of steps on the Westminster end. Beauty, heavy with sadness and terror.'[1]

Some time about this period, as relief from his emotional, and perhaps his literary, frustrations, he embarked on a new activity, which was to write erotic short stories. The stories were deliberately facetious and frivolous, and he did not regard them as literature; he produced them, he said later, 'not to express myself but to excite myself'. He was not ashamed of them, or so he persuaded himself; all the same, he wrote them with trepidation, fearing he might injure his future as a novelist. For the moment he showed them to no one.

Through this or other means he at last overcame his inertia and completed his play – and a very strange play it was! The action takes place in the British Consulate in Bosnia.[2] The previous evening the consul, Mr Stevens, and his wife have given a ball, and their daughter Fanny, who has made a conquest of two of her Bosnian dancing-partners, thinks it might be amusing to flirt with them. Her father warns her not to trifle with them: neither she nor he, he says, understands 'that unknown quantity – the heart of Bosnia'. But Fanny is bored, so when one of her admirers calls she grants him a *tête-à-tête*. Nikolai is all fire and passion; he lays his naked knife on the table, swearing to guard the house against all foes. Fanny plays with the knife and cuts herself, whereupon he plunges her bleeding hand under his shirt and kisses her. Pretending outrage, she orders him

---

[1] Diary, 7 July 1911.

[2] Bosnia had been much in the news in recent years, first with its annexation by Austro-Hungary in 1908, and again in June 1910 when, at Sarajevo, during the opening of the new Diet, a Serbian anarchist made an attempt to assassinate the Governor.

out of the house . . . Her morning's flirtation is proceeding briskly when there enters her other suitor, Mirko, who, it turns out, is Nikolai's bosom friend. Left alone, the youths embrace passionately, each informing the other that he is in love. They promise to exchange their souls' secrets that night, on the mountain; and meanwhile they dance and frolic, till there dawns on them the fatal *anagnorisis* that it is Fanny they are both in love with. Their horseplay now turns into a duel to the death. Re-enter Fanny, who seizes the opportunity, as an educated Englishwoman, to teach them a lesson.

> *Fanny*. Bosnians have a bad reputation for quarrelling, and I mean to be firm. It does not please me, behaviour like yours. (*They are silent*.) You are young – or I should punish you more severely. But I regard you as boys and you are chivalrous – I do recognise that, though it is a perverted form. You need educating. I know that you used to be friends, and it is my pleasure that you become friends again, and do not allow your feelings for me to stand between you . . . It is best to be frank. I have no intention of marrying a Bosnian. I mean no disrespect, but my ways and yours are different, as you ought to have seen. I have been pleasant to you both, and, if I choose, I shall be pleasant again, but you have made yourselves ridiculous, by quarrelling about me. I simply laugh. Have you anything to say?

She confiscates their knives and returns into the inner room, leaving Mirko and Nikolai staring at each other in despair. All is over for them, they realize, and, kissing each other once more – this time with the kiss of blood – they follow the only course left, which is to murder her. The servants look on impassively; they tell the distracted Stevens parents, when they arrive too late on the scene: 'We are sorry for you, who did not know our customs, but we can do nothing.' 'Call for the mayor,' cries Mrs Stevens. 'Telegraph for troops – this is neutral ground – we have a case for war – the British Consulate!' 'My dear,' replies her husband, 'we have a case, but she is dead.'

Poor *Heart of Bosnia*! Dickinson, who was shown a copy, did not like it, nor did anyone else so far as one can discover. And indeed, though in a quaint way it looks forward to *A Passage to India*, there is not much to be said in its favour. Whereas, as you might say, Forster put his imagination into his stories, he put only his daydreams into his plays. One deeply cherished and lifelong daydream of his was to have a loving brother with whom he could share his secrets; it was a poignant dream, but in his play he found it impossible to clothe it in social realities.

*   *   *

Masood was by now in London and reading for the bar, having come down from Oxford with a bad second class in History – which, he said, was more than he deserved. He had set up in lodging at 12 Edith Road, at the far end of Chelsea, and had taken up the banjo: 'Why should I pay for theatres and operas,' he would ask, 'when I can make my own entertainment?' He filled no. 12 with Indian cronies, such as Sherwani, Raschid[1] and the brothers Ahmed and Abu Saeed Mirza,[2] commanding them – 'or else I shall never speak to you again', his usual threat – to take rooms there whenever in London. They formed a little court around him; and his English friends, apart from Forster and a man named B. H. Coode, tended to drop away. The Indians regarded Forster as much older than themselves, a very learned man who had taught Masood Latin. The fact that he was a novelist was rather vague to them, and he never referred to it himself. Occasionally he would take one or other to lunch or the opera, and, taking their tone from Masood, they developed a high regard for this strangely sympathetic Englishman. 'We thought him like an angel,' Abu Saeed said later.[3]

The time was fast approaching when Masood would have to return to India, and it grew plain to Forster that his declaration, which had cost him so much to make, had left little impression on Masood. Indeed, nothing impressed him for long. He flashed about ebulliently from one craze to another, vastly enjoying the drama of his life, and regarding the world, Forster surmised, 'as a roomfull of secondary persons with himself feeling intensely in the centre'. Forster therefore determined to speak again, and this time, if possible, to extract some definite response. They went off in August for a holiday in Italy, and soon after their arrival – they were staying at Tesserete in the Italian lakes – he renewed his declaration. It had no visible result: Masood was surprised and sorry and put the matter away at once. Forster

---

[1] M. A. Raschid. Many years later Masood, *en secondes noces*, married Raschid's daughter Amtul.
[2] Sons of Moulvi Mohammed Aziz Mirza, sometime Home Secretary to the Nizam of Hyderabad. Ahmed, the eldest, attended King's College, London. Abu Saeed, later Nawab Saeed Jung, was studying law at Lincoln's Inn.
[3] In conversation with the present author, in 1970.

was not too downcast, however, deciding: 'I have seen the worst of
him, but all is well. I bear his going better now, for we shall never be
nearer, & do seem firm at last.' And in fact the first week of their
holiday passed for Forster in 'incoherent joy'. He never forgot
certain details: the two of them kneeling in the train-corridor to
look at the stars; their buying crayons and messing about with them
'damnably' on the summit of Monte Generoso; also his own rage
when Masood, instead of attending to his law-books, would insist on
learning Italian, to equip him to seduce the waitress. Eventually
Masood grew bored with Tesserete, and with Forster too (or so
Forster thought). Still, he clung to the conviction that Masood liked
him better than he did any other man. In 1960 he came across his
letters to his mother and Aunt Laura from Tesserete and tore them
up, noting:

> I recall no scenery but faintly some scenes, for we were at the
> stage – so familiar to me – where the other person has ceased to be
> interested. It was a honeymoon slightly off colour, and perhaps
> that's why the letters are so dull. With difficulty do I recall an
> expedition up the mountains where Signor Ithen[1] bit ants in two
> to refresh himself with formic acid, while his daughters shrieked
> 'Papa!' And Masood having an uglier waitress, or visitor: for I
> think he had her, but thought me too much of a muff to be told.
> – There's a photograph of us somewhere, I starry eyed with a huge
> moustache looking very odd indeed. – But why, having already
> published 3 [sic] novels, did I write such wet letters?[2]

Masood was returning earlier, and Forster, having seen him off at
Milan, went back to the Lakes, joining Dickinson and his sisters at
Orta. It was radiant weather, and they sailed, bathed and – paying
tribute to Samuel Butler[3] – visited the Sacro Monte at Varallo.
Forster remembered a long walk with Dickinson and his remarking
that only in such upland country would humanity survive in the
event of a great war. 'Much did I bathe, much eat, and lived in a
dream,' Forster wrote lyrically to Josie Darling, 'till I fell suddenly
into England on Basle station – hundreds of tourists struggling for
half that number of seats on the midnight train, and shouting that all

---

[1] Their landlord in Tesserete.
[2] Commonplace Book, p. 236.
[3] Butler's *Ex Voto* (1888) was devoted to the Sacro Monte and its painted
wooden sculptures.

would be well if the others would behave like Gentlemen.' Slightly revised, these words became the first paragraph of 'Arctic Summer'.

Weybridge was bitterly cold and uninviting when he returned, but for the moment, to his relief, his mother seemed in a better humour. Soon, though, the clouds thickened again: he went to Aunt Laura's for two days; the maids were away, so his mother was alone; and on his return he found her plunged in gloom and ill-temper. Her mood lasted all October, and on the last day of the month (afterwards he realized it was the anniversary of his father's death) she grew unbearably trying. Left alone that evening, he had a 'Satanic' fit of rage against her and her fault-finding and pictured himself sweeping the mantelpiece of its china and rushing out to cut his throat. The vision left him 'all red and trembling', and he wrote it down next day, to laugh himself out of it. 'More exercise than cure,' he told himself soberly: 'Arctic Summer slowly moving in my mind.' He saw that if he was to survive he would have to change his life and gain more freedom from his mother. It filled him with compunction, and his New Year's Eve review was a sad and discouraged one.

> Literature, very bad. One good story – The Point of It[1] – one bad unpublished play – The Heart of Bosnia. That is all. I seem through at last, & others begin to suspect it. Idleness, depressing conditions, need for a fresh view of all life before I begin writing each time, paralyse me. Just possible I may finish Arctic Summer, but see nothing beyond. Like writing erotic short stories, some of which may be good. Lecturing. Successful course on Florence at Harrow in the autumn. Taught a diminishing class Latin at the W.M.C. till the end of July. Celestial Omnibus published.
>
> Terrible year on the whole. Have cheered mother a little, I think, but pleasure of home life has gone. Sorrow has altered her, and I have had to alter too, or leave. Ageing, though strong physically: often feel a perfect devil. Am influenced very little now by her, for I cannot respect her as I used. (Hate writing this, for am in tender mood: she has been sweet and herself again the last ten days, & enjoyed London. So perhaps she is on the mend. But all through the year, & in Nov. Dec. especially, have felt as I write.) Am only happy away from home. If only she would come away more. . . .
>
> Dickinson. Approaching to real friendship. S. P. Waterlow. Wish I *did* like him more, but he has never given me anything I seem to want. Florence – my only woman friend: though there

---

[1] Published in the *English Review*, November 1911.

are others, like Miss Mona Wilson,[1] whom I might make . . .
H.O.M. Have seen too little. He remains the ground work of my
life, but more unconsciously . . .
Foreign affairs. Tripoli.[2] Persia.[3] What a year. Brookfield as
censor.[4]
Prayer for courage. I can sympathise no more until I get braver.

*   *   *

Roger Fry, just at this time, was engaged on a series of portraits of
his friends, intending them for a forthcoming exhibition, and he
asked if Forster would sit for him. Forster was fond of Fry and agreed
happily, and in November he had his first sitting at Fry's house near
Guildford. His mother said she only prayed Mr Fry would give him a
clean face, but Fry said, 'Quite impossible.'

Fry was now forty-five and appeared older than his years. His
wife suffered bouts of insanity, and this tragedy in his married life
had marked him, though it had also strengthened him. He looked, in
the words of Virginia Woolf,[5] 'worn and seasoned, ascetic yet tough
. . . brown and animated'. Voluble, didactic, tirelessly inveighing in
his cracked voice, or in print, against the Philistinism of what he
called 'Bird's Custard Island', he had a zeal and a large-mindedness
that Forster found intensely attractive. He liked, too, Fry's way of
arriving at the truth, whatever it was, by a patent route of his own.
'How often on a lonely spot, known only to God and myself,' Forster
wrote to him later (3 November 1922), 'have I suddenly seen you
rising over the opposite brow of the hill, quite at your ease, and
suggesting that you had as much right to come as anyone and that it
was of course the only spot to come to. And I was flattered yet disconcerted, pleased to meet Mr Fry, unrecalcitrant to anything he
said, yet surprised that one who didn't like Housman's *Last Poems*,
Flecker's *Hassan*, or Mrs Darling's *Love in a Mist*,[6] should be thus

---

[1] Mona Wilson (1872–1954) contributed articles on social conditions to the
Independent Review and was the first woman Health Insurance Commissioner
(1911–19).
[2] In September 1911 Italy invaded Tripoli.
[3] During 1911 in Persia there was an abortive invasion by the ex-Shah and
a diplomatic incident between Persia and Russia.
[4] In November the playwright Charles Brookfield (1857–1913) was appointed
as Joint Examiner of Plays, greatly to the indignation of the newer school of
dramatists.
[5] See her *Roger Fry* (1940), p. 149.
[6] A novel by Malcolm Darling's wife Josie.

fronting his forehead to the morn.' He felt not merely admiration but a strong affection for Fry. (It meant a lot to him in later years to know that their portraits hung side by side in the Hall at King's; and once, when the College was rehanging its pictures, he said anxiously he hoped they wouldn't think of parting them.) As for Fry's art-theories, Forster, brought up on Ruskin, found them baffling, while Fry thought his frankly impossible. He would make Forster come to exhibitions with him, forcing him to give him his opinion on paintings, and then, when Forster nervously did so, throwing up his hands in the wildest astonishment, crying, 'But Morgan, can you *really* think that?' However, Forster now began to feel, as they talked, that he was grasping Fry's idea. It was 'to clear art of reminiscence. Romanticism the enemy. To paint the position of things in space.' Not that Fry was at his best, so he felt, when he succeeded in his aim: the canvas of Fry's he would have liked most to possess was one full of 'subject', a painting of green snakes. None the less, Fry's confidence was wonderfully invigorating. Miss March Phillips,[1] whose lectures on art-history Forster had been attending, came to tea with them, and afterwards he asked Fry's opinion of her: had she any real understanding of art? Fry snorted: 'Of course she doesn't understand. It wouldn't even occur to her to understand.'

The portrait itself proved too much for Forster. 'Roger Fry is painting me,' he wrote to Florence Barger (24 December 1911):

> It is too like me at present, but he is confident he will be able to alter that. Post-Impressionism is at present confined to my lower lip which is rendered thus . . . and to my chin, on which soup has apparently dribbled. For the rest you have a bright healthy young man, without one hand it is true, and very queer legs, perhaps the result of an aeroplane accident, as he seems to have fallen from an immense height on to a sofa.

His mother and aunts, when they saw the portrait at Fry's show[2] in January, thought it most peculiar – though not *quite* so dreadful as the one of McTaggart, which had blue worms crawling over it. However, he bought it (for £17/10/0), and it hung for some time in the drawing-room at Weybridge. It remained there till one day a

[1] Lisle March Phillips, author of *The Works of Man: The consideration of art as an expression of human life and character* (1911); *Form and Colour* (1915), etc.
[2] At the Alpine Club Gallery. The exhibition marked his conversion to a 'Post-Impressionist' style.

local clergyman, having studied it for some minutes, remarked anxiously to Lily, 'I hope your son isn't *queer?*' After this, a home was found for it with Florence Barger, who had always professed a fondness for it.

Fry had some influence on Forster's new novel. The novel begins, as so often with Forster, with the feelings of a jaded traveller; in this case Martin Whitly, Forster's idea of the cultivated and socially-useful Englishman. Whitly, who is on holiday in Italy with his wife and mother-in-law, tells himself that the hope of the future, and of his own approaching middle age, lies in Form.

> Youth demands colour and blue sky, but Martin, turned thirty, longed for Form. Perhaps it is a cold desire, but it can save a man from cynicism; it is a worker's religion, and Italy is one of its shrines . . . Martin had entered her [Italy] often before, but never with such sensations; he saw a quality that he would have despised ten years ago. She, like himself, had abandoned sentiment; she existed apart from associations by virtue of mass and line; her austere beauty was an image of the millenium towards which all good citizens are co-operating.

There are audible echoes of Fry and 'significant form' here; and, as we shall see, the novel turned, in a sense, on Martin's unlearning of Fry's doctrines.

The few chapters[1] which Forster completed are in his best style. They show the strength of that method of his, of finding some new and fruitful antithesis by which to set his convictions in play against one another, sharpening and redefining themselves. Here, his antithesis is battle and work. The story has two main characters: Martin Whitly, the representative of work, a civil servant in his thirties, civilized, intellectual and progressive; and Clesant March, the 'knight errant', a rather stiff and stupid but romantically-minded young army officer. They first meet when March saves the life of the older man, who is being swept off the platform in Basle station. There follows a comedy of incompatibilities. Martin, out of gratitude, tries to take Clesant up, but the young man's stiffness and crudity make friendship impossible; so the two go their ways, with some rancour on Clesant's part. To all appearances the incident is

---

[1] The MS in fact presents several conflicting versions, of which I have merely selected one. See 'E. M. Forster's "Arctic Summer" ' by Elizabeth Ellem (*Times Literary Supplement,* 21 September 1973).

finished; however, something has been set in motion in Whitly's soul. His admirable adjustment to life – 'He knew himself to be clever and kind and moral and energetic, and to be surrounded by friends who were like him' – has been disturbed. Visiting a castle near Milan, where there is a fresco of the battle of Lepanto, he notices, with strange emotion, that one of the warriors in the painting resembles Clesant March. He notes in his journal: 'Very moving: warriors about to fight for their country and faith,' and is amazed at what he has written, 'so little resemblance did it bear to his usual art-criticism'. The vision, for this is what it is, stays with him, and gradually it develops into a *malaise*. Not long after, from another quarter, he receives a more shattering blow to his composure. One evening, being left to his own devices, he decides, on a whim, to take the chauffeur to the cinema, and during the performance a fire breaks out; there is a rush to the exits; and, before he has realized it, he is safely outside in the street, having left the chauffeur, who is lame, to fend for himself. With shame and horror he realizes that he is a physical coward.

Attention now turns to Lieutenant March, whose boyish demand for moral absolutes and habit of rushing headlong at dangers, are shown in action again, this time disastrously. March's young brother has been 'sent down' from his Cambridge college for a sexual mis-demeanour, and Clesant, assuming quite wrongly that he is innocent, rushes baldheaded to his defence. The fruit of his efforts is that he drives his brother to suicide.

The fragments end here, and the larger shape of the novel is not easy to guess at. Enough exists, however, to give some idea of the themes and how they would have been interwoven. Among other things, Forster is returning to the 'woman question'. In 'The Feminine Note in Literature' he had put the case against chivalry and sexual 'chauvinism'. Now, subtly and characteristically, he is exploring the opposite point of view. 'I do hate that pseudo-chivalry so – Venetia [his wife] does so hate it. It's all against true intercourse with women, and all progress.' So muses Martin Whitly, after one of his disputes with Clesant March, who entertains extravagant notions of man's duty to women. Whitly's is the approved liberal-intellectual line; and when he is confessing his cowardice to Venetia, a simple-minded Newnham Fabian,[1] he reflects on his luck that he

---

[1] Forster probably took some hints for Venetia's character from Hugh Meredith's wife Christabel.

married a woman like her; she would forget the incident, whereas a 'womanly woman', though she might pity him, would never forget it as long as she lived. All the same, Venetia's mother, a much cleverer woman and a shameless reactionary, guesses what is wrong with Whitly: he lives too much among women. 'What could a man do that we don't do?' asks Venetia.

> 'He could be a man, my dear.'
> 'Well, as you know, I don't agree at all, and no more does Martin. He hates what we call "smoking-room civilisation". He's as anxious as I am that Hugo shouldn't be taught all the rubbish about "little girls do this" and "little boys do that". If he likes people – that's all he cares about.'
> 'No doubt that's the correct attitude, but I has my feelings. He'd be happier if there was another man.'
> 'Well, there's the chauffeur. Or did you mean a gentleman?' she added with a touch of scorn.
> 'Heaven help me, but I did mean a gentleman.'
> 'Oh.'
> 'Be it how it may, I'm afraid he's not enjoying motoring as much as we are. Don't you think he isn't as merry as usual?'
> 'Everyone has these ups and downs,' said Venetia. 'Sometimes I'm not merry.'
> Lady Borlase gave a clap of laughter.
> 'What is it mother?'
> 'Dearest Nettie, nothing.'
> 'I believe you're laughing at me. Did I say anything odd?'
> It was at moments like this that Lady Borlase saw the unalterable candour of her soul.

This masterly dialogue suggests what was lost in 'Arctic Summer'. Many years later,[1] Forster gave his own account of why he fumbled with it and failed to complete it.

> I had got my antithesis all right. . . . But I had not settled what is going to happen and this is why the novel remains a fragment. The novelist should I think always settle when he starts what is going to happen, what his major event is to be. He may alter this event as he approaches it, indeed he probably will, indeed he probably had better, or the novel becomes tied up and tight. But the sense of a solid mass ahead, a mountain round or over or through which . . . the story must somehow go is most valuable and for the novels I've tried to write essential.

[1] Interview with P. N. Furbank and F. J. H. Haskell: *Paris Review*, Spring 1955, pp. 30–1.

A further trouble seems to have been that, at this time, he was in a mood of reaction against *Howards End* and the whole style of patient, synoptic comment on social issues which it represented. 'I must keep myself from trying to look round civilization,' he wrote in 1913, when he had more or less abandoned 'Arctic Summer'. 'I haven't the experience or the power, & the influence of Galsworthy, Wells etc. is certainly bad for me. "Arctic Summer" would have involved the look round.' He was speaking after his first visit to India, and this experience, too, had helped to put him out of humour with the Galsworthyesque novel. He was attracted now by something more visionary.

*   *   *   *

It was during this period of difficulty with 'Arctic Summer' that Forster happened to read *The Bracknells*, by the Belfast novelist Forrest Reid. This story of a dream-haunted, affection-starved adolescent, beset by visions of evil, and of a young Oxford tutor's thwarted efforts to rescue him from his uncomprehending family, made a great impression on Forster, and he wrote Reid a fan-letter:

31 January 1912

Dear Sir,

I have read The Bracknells and wish to thank you for it. Most books give no less than can be got from people, but yours gives more, for it has a quality that can only be described as 'helpful'. I do not use the word in the vulgar sense; Denis[1] is no more likely to be prosperous after death than before it, but it does help one to distinguish between the superficial and the real, and to some minds there is something exhilarating in this. You show so very clearly that intelligence and even sympathy are superficial – good enough things in their way – they do what they can and would gladly do more; but the real thing is 'being there', and the worst of it is no two human beings can be in the same place. The book has moved me a good deal; it is what a friend ought to be but isn't; I suppose I am saying in a very roundabout and clumsy way that it is art.

The only point where I do not follow you spiritually, is in your introduction of visions of evil, but perhaps I am trying to define too much; at all events Denis escapes into a confusion that is not of this world.

The other qualities of your work – realism, character drawing,

---

[1] The hero of the novel.

construction etc. – seem to me admirable, but I have dwelt upon
the one that interested me most. I hope that you will excuse me
for having written to you.

As it turned out, Reid knew and admired Forster's work, especially
the short stories, and he responded warmly.

6 South Parade,

6 February 1912   Belfast.

My dear Sir,
     It is very kind of you to write as you do, & I need hardly say
that your letter has given me great pleasure, for the parts of my
book that you care for are just those I like best myself, while they
are also just those that leave most people either bored or indifferent. This encourages me to believe that you are the same
E. M. Forster who wrote The Celestial Omnibus. I remember very
well reading it last summer, lying on my back in a punt under the
trees, & how the beauty of everything around me melted into &
became part of the delicate beauty of your stories. If I have been
able, then, to give you some pleasure in return, that is sufficient
to make me think my work has not been wasted. I liked your
short stories better than your novels – than the three later ones,
for I have not yet read your first book. But in the novels too, &
particularly perhaps in The Longest Journey, there is the same
spirit if not quite so clearly revealed. That is to say the visible
world is not everything, there are deeper & more hidden things
touched on, & above all there is a sense of beauty, both of material
beauty & of spiritual beauty, without which, I confess, no book is
of much interest to me.
     You say that you cannot follow me in my introduction of visions
of evil. I do not understand why. I do not know whether you think
they are only wrong from the point of view of art, or whether you
mean that they are essentially wrong – that Denis wouldn't have
had them. With this latter opinion I cannot agree; but possibly I
misunderstand you. In any case I am very glad to have your
letter.

By the time this letter reached Forster, he was in Belfast himself,
on a visit to Meredith, so he wrote again suggesting they should meet.
'If we do meet,' he said, 'we might talk about "visions of evil",
are they clouds across the moon, or spots on it? That was my difficulty.
For my own part I don't believe there are any spots on the moon,
though I used to when I was Denis's age.' He proposed the Carlton
restaurant as a rendezvous: Reid would recognize him by his
'lightish cloth cap, purple and white scarf, and great coat'.
Reid was four years older than Forster. He was the child of an

impoverished upper-middle class Ulster family and had published a novel while still in his teens, being then an apprentice in a firm of Belfast tea-importers. In his middle twenties he was left some money and decided to send himself to Cambridge. His second novel, *The Garden God*, came out soon after his arrival there. Like most of his writing[1] it was an idyll of schoolboy friendship and featured a languorous bathing-scene, in which the schoolboy hero persuades his friend to pose naked for him among the rocks. With great innocence, he not only sent a copy to Henry James, who had taken an interest in his first novel, but dedicated it to him. James was appalled and wrote an exceedingly frosty letter; and when Reid lent a copy to one of his professors, Israel Gollancz, Gollancz positively fled him in the street. Reid professed to being mystified – saying that, perhaps, the answer would be plainer to him had he enjoyed an English public-school education.

In appearance, Reid was stocky and ungraceful, with a squarish, kindly, prosaic face; he talked in a slow, downright manner, and wore rumpled, old-fashioned suits with baggy pockets. As well as being a writer, he was a champion croquet-player and made regular visits to England to play in tournaments – though, according to Forster's later account, when one saw him in London after such a tour, he could give no account of where he had been.

Their first meeting took place, after all, not in a restaurant but at Reid's home. It was a success. Forster was introduced to Pan the bulldog, Nyx the Irish terrier and Puss the cat; and after lunch they rowed on the river Lagan, the background for so many summer idylls in Reid's novels. Reid, just then, happened to be arranging his old master prints, but instinct warned him not to mention this; he guessed, quite rightly, that Forster would disapprove of collectors. Forster took to Reid. 'A nice and very ugly man,' he reported to his mother, and Meredith pronounced Reid 'one of Morgie's finds.' Reid was equally pleased with Forster, and they began an extensive correspondence. Reid dedicated his next novel, *Following Darkness*, to Forster, who (being then in India) made propaganda for it up and down the country. Thereupon Forster told Reid, with an impudence characteristic of him, that he would like it if Reid would dedicate his following book to him, too. Reid did not do so.

---

[1] Forster later said to him, 'The only thing in daily life that seems to you beautiful *in itself* is school, friendship.'

Forster, who had just bid farewell to Masood, had come to Belfast in a disconsolate but diagnostic mood. As they steamed up Belfast Lough at daybreak, passing 'shattered cathedrals of iron' in the shipyards, the place struck him as full of harshness and mystery. 'That chilly Presbyterian spire! The soul of Ulster, observing but not welcoming the stranger, stands near the water's edge amid dark hedges and white fields,' he noted in his journal. Meredith took him to tea with a pillar of the Ulster Reform Club,[1] and he was given a taste of Orange Lodge politics. 'Belfast,' his host intoned, 'will listen to anyone except a Judas or a turncoat.' (He told Josie Darling, in a letter, that here he glanced nervously at his own coat, which had been turned so often he had forgotten which side was which.) 'We are not acting in accordance with principle,' his host went on majestically, 'and we do not pretend that we are.' His wife chimed in: 'It just shows the uselessness of principles,' and she repeated the remark to the baby.

> Behind them a hymn book stood open on a grand piano. It was an interesting scene: they were hypnotised by the passions of local life: they believed that Belfast was a city apart from morality and law, whose loyalty permitted her to shed blood. Truly rebellion is the sin of witchcraft, and as I listened to their civil educated voices and drank their tea, I thought of the savagery in each of us and of the dishonest brain that so easily finds arguments to justify its use.

It was a moment of high drama in Ulster when Forster arrived, with talk of secession and civil war. The great topic of the hour was the Churchill visit. Winston Churchill was coming to address the Ulster Liberal Association, bringing new Home Rule proposals. A mass-meeting had been arranged on the local football ground, and excitement was intense: Protestant employers were said to be arming their workers with clubs, revolvers and pocketsful of rivets, and the city authorities had called in 4,000 troops. Forster had written to Edward Marsh, who would be in attendance on Churchill as his private secretary, inviting him to visit Meredith and himself – adding that they would provide bandages. His mother had made him promise not to go to the Football Field, but on the morning of the meeting he went to the Central Hotel, where Churchill was staying. Having sent up his name, he joined the crowd in the lounge; and after some time

---

[1] The Club was 'unalterably opposed to Home Rule in any shape'.

there was loud booing from the street as Churchill showed himself at a window. The lift-gates then opened, and everyone rushed forward, expecting the great man; it was, however, Eddie Marsh, who, very slim and nonchalant, approached Forster with the words 'Have you read Wupert's new poem?' Churchill himself appeared soon afterwards, looking 'very pale like some underground vegetable', and, jostled by a booing throng, he brushed against Forster, who valiantly raised his cap. Then, amid a scuffle and a deafening din, he bundled into a car; and as he passed the Ulster club, Carson and Londonderry appeared at the window, whereat the crowd burst into 'Rule Britannia'. As for the meeting itself, it passed off calmly, only the suffragettes making any disturbance. Everyone then began explaining why Churchill Day had been a failure. 'To the outsider,' thought Forster, 'it looks uncommonly like a success.'

On his return from Ireland, pondering what he had learned there about the psychology of wars of religion, Forster set to work on a new play. It was a prophetic morality-play, depicting the rise and decline of civilizations. The action concerns a mountain-people who proceed from a golden age, when they 'worship the gods of gentleness', to an age of bustling militaristic dictatorship, and then to a time, many millennia later, when the lust for violence and possession has once more died out in men's breasts and they are ready for the reign of reason and humanism. As the last Act opens, the Emperor has summoned his people to the birthplace of their race to witness him lay down his authority at the feet of the Spirit of Man. The crowd, drably dressed in browns and greys, looks on ironically, having outgrown such childish pantomimes; the sea looks less blue and the mountain less red. One by one the kings of the earth approach and lay down their crowns before the statue of Man, first declaring what gifts they have brought Him in their time. Then the Emperor doffs his crown and robes, and clothes the statue in them, in the name of the old Queen, to whose kingdom they are returning. The statue fades, and in its place stands the Queen herself. 'Receive us back into your kingdom,' says the Emperor to her, expecting a grateful welcome.

> *Queen.* I cannot. I ruled over men.
> *Emperor.* These are men.
> *Queen.* They are not the men I knew. Mine were joyous and brave and loved sunlight. What have you done to my sky?
> *Emperor.* But we are the race of the Harvel and Vala. We have laboured to rejoin you.

Queen. In labouring you have blunted the instrument. You have
robbed death of its sting and love of its victory . . .

Forster wrote to Masood about the play (8 March 1912), saying he
didn't think it bad, though he doubted if it would ever grace the
stage. He had just been composing the procession of Kings, and,
Masood would be pleased to hear, when it came to the turn of the
King of Albion to announce what he had done for humanity, he could
think of nothing for him to say! He never got as far as having the
play typed, and it was soon stowed away in a drawer, to join *St
Bridget* and *The Heart of Bosnia.*

*   *   *

Everything seemed to suggest it was time for him to go to India.
Masood was there, homesick for 'ce charmant pays qui s'appelle
l'Europe',* and continually urging him to come. He badly needed
some change in his way of life. And with his royalties from *Howards
End* he could well afford the journey. Also, it turned out that, if he
went this autumn, he would have the company of Dickinson and
Bob Trevelyan. Dickinson, who had been awarded an Alfred Kahn
Travelling Fellowship, was planning an extended tour of the Orient,
and had persuaded Bob to come with him. (Another Cambridge
friend, Gordon Luce, would also be with them on the sea-journey,
en route for Burma.) The moment seemed a perfect one for Forster's
visit, and his only problem was his mother. It was hopeless to think of
taking her in her present state; but he feared to leave her alone for so
long a period. On the other hand, so far as he could foresee, it might
well be no safer next year than this. He pondered the problem all
through March, eventually deciding to go and risk the consequences.

The three set about collecting advice and introductions. They had
numerous friends in India; for it was a tradition for Kingsmen to
enter the Indian Civil Service, and there was also a standing arrangement by which, through the Senior Tutor W. H. Macaulay, Kingsmen were recruited for the Bombay-Burmah Trading Company, of
which his brother was managing director. Sir Theodore Morison
proved helpful, and wrote to many friends on Forster's behalf, including his old pupil the Maharaja of Chhatarpur. Aunt Laura
consulted her friends Sir Wilmot and Lady Herringham,[1] who were

---

[1] Sir Wilmot Parker Herringham (1855–1936) and his wife Christina. Sir
Wilmot was Consulting Physician at St Bartholomew's Hospital.

leading figures in the India Society; and, meeting the painter Sir William Rothenstein at the Herringhams', Forster was given by him a letter to a fakir in Benares. Dickinson received invitations from several princes.

Forster deliberately left his plans somewhat vague. He meant to spend all the time he could with Masood and, if it could be arranged, to join Darling for Christmas in Dewas. Otherwise he would let chance guide him. He wanted every experience India might offer, including that of solitude, so did not mean to tie himself too closely to Dickinson and Trevelyan.

Meanwhile he pursued his Indian education. He read Kalidasa's *Sakuntala*, which entranced him, taking him into 'a world of the sweetest and most absurd creatures.' He also re-read the *Bhagavad Gita* and thought he now had got hold of it: 'It's division of states into Harmony Motion Inertia. (Purity Passion Darkness.)' 'Can also think about Karma,' he noted. He studied Lady Herringham's copies of the Ajanta frescoes,[1] 'Full of animals and people smiling,' and he went to the zoo to inspect the India fauna. 'Having no idea which of them are common, and which rare, I expect to see them all as soon as I land at Bombay,' he wrote to Darling.

> There is a dear little monkey that I would particularly like you to provide. I do not know its name, but it takes straws from your hand through the bars of the cage so prettily, and plays with a bow that it has filched from a lady's bonnet. No doubt you will recognise it. It would also be pleasant to be met by some of the smaller bears.

A further preparation he decided on was to improve his riding, thinking this might be useful in India. The news reached the ears of Leonard Woolf, whom he had recently got to know, and Woolf volunteered to give him lessons on Putney Common.

Woolf had returned to England the previous year, after seven years in the Ceylon civil service, and, having fallen in love with Virginia Stephen, and moreover having decided that he disapproved of imperialism, he had resigned from the service and was planning to

---

[1] Sometime before the first world war Lady Herringham became insane, haunted by India and believing that the Indians bore her a grudge for intruding into the caves. Forster would certainly have known of this, so it seems possible that it was the germ of Mrs Moore's breakdown, after visiting the Marabar caves, in *A Passage to India*.

live by journalism. He and Forster already knew each other slightly,*
and got on well on their rides. Woolf was encouraging as a riding-
master, and they found they had much to talk about. Woolf, in
his rigid Cambridge-rationalist way, railed irritably at there being
no future life. It was maddening, he complained: there was so much
to do, yet life might end at any moment. Indeed, he said, it had
nearly ended for him already; and he told a story which impressed
Forster. He had been out riding with a man he disliked, and their
horses had bolted, making for a gap in the hedge only wide enough
for one man. It was clearly a problem in ethics; one of them had to
die, and it was up to him to choose which. 'I'm more worth keeping
alive than he,' had been Woolf's conclusion, and, quite calmly, he
had prepared to murder his companion by charging at him.[1] As it
turned out, the other man, in panic, had fallen off his horse, so no
murder was committed. And thereupon – the most characteristic
touch, thought Forster – Woolf had proceeded to tell the man exactly
what his reasoning had been. He wished, he told Forster, that the
incident could happen again, this time with someone worth sacrificing
himself to.

Forster saw the makings of a friendship between himself and
Woolf. 'If he likes me and is capable of affection, I foresee a great
deal. But both unknown so far.' Woolf quickly cast himself in
Forster's eyes, as he did in his own, in the role of the manly man –
someone you could ask practical questions of. 'Where d'you get your
boots?' Forster would ask him, when he knew him better; or 'Are
Waterman's pens the best?' Woolf, in turn, though he grew fond of
Forster, would always say he was 'a perfect old woman'. He and
Virginia used to tell how Forster, sometime during the 1920s, came
to dinner with them in Richmond, having spent the earlier part of the
day painting a garden seat. All through the evening, in the midst of
other conversation, his thoughts would return to the seat: was it wise
to have left it out all night? Would that 'stupid' garden boy. . . ? etc.

It had been a timely decision for Forster, to go to India. All the
summer, things had gone unhappily between him and his mother.
Misery made her unkind and irritable. One day they were talking of
Masood, whom Forster was missing bitterly, and she remarked un-
feelingly that, even if Masood came back to England, things could

---

[1] A good instance of the influence of G. E. Moore's ethical theories.

never be the same for the two of them. The remark gave Forster a
pang. The fact of its being said seemed, in a way, worse than the
thing itself, and he heard himself answering with stupid cheerfulness.
His mother, he felt, 'froze the depths' in him. On another occasion,
she said, casually, that one could not imagine the end of the world,
and he found himself answering that it was lucky: if human beings
could do so, they would never attempt anything. 'What a meagre
answer,' he rebuked himself in his diary; 'when I have and hope to
keep the power of thinking of death as beautiful . . . I shan't ever see
life as a draggled mess of old people, surely?'

Another trouble was, she made him feel small. One day, when they
were lunching at West Hackhurst, Aunt Laura asked if he liked the
cheese. It was very nasty, but he had not the nerve to say so, and
pretended he hadn't tasted it, leaving frankness to his mother.
Afterwards, Lily told him he was just like his father, unable to put
his foot down at the right time. It was the first time he had heard her
speak against his father, or so openly against himself, and he felt
ashamed. He wondered whether, after all, he were going to be a
failure in life.

> Can I do anything? To screw up the will power by discipline is not
> possible, but could I become spiritually more solid? It's an extra
> difficulty with mother too, now that I know she does not think
> highly of me. Whatever I do she is thinking 'Oh that's weak.'
> Just as I was going ahead with my novel a little.[1]

Not long afterwards he cracked one of her vases and was afraid to
tell her. He asked himself why. Was it thoughtfulness for her, in her
present condition? Or was he merely a schoolboy afraid of a scolding?
Physically he felt well and powerful, but it seemed he got idler and
more ineffective every day.

> Take today 6 July 1912. Breakfast 10.30. Read papers & errands
> for mother till 11.30. Read over old work till lunch. Slept in
> garden till 3.0 or later. Learnt a few Urdu phrases, & read a few
> chapters of an easy book on Buddha. After tea rowed mother on
> the river very slowly till dinner. Then played piano slackly and
> talked. Now it is 9.45. – It is serious, even frightening, and joined
> with a shamed sense of unused strength. I don't feel to have
> deserved India.

---

[1] Diary, 15 May 1912.

As October approached, letters of arrangement flew between the four fellow-travellers. They would be joining the boat (the *City of Birmingham*) in relays. Trevelyan and Luce would embark in England; Dickinson, who was going first to Cairo with his friend J. M. Furness, would come on board at Port Said. As for Forster, to soften the parting for his mother, he had persuaded her to come as far as Italy with him. He would thus embark at Naples, leaving her and her friend Mrs Mawe to enjoy a holiday in Rome at his expense. Meanwhile the travellers pooled information, about cummerbunds, celluloid underclothing, pith-helmets and deck-chairs, and Forster, who didn't take journeys lightly, went on a round of farewell visits.

During one of these visits, to George and Florence Barger, who were now living at Lewisham, Forster made a discovery. Florence was ready, indeed eager, for close friendship, even to the extent of discussing his homosexuality. There was much to draw the two together. Forster, though he complained of being hemmed in by women, needed their sympathy deeply, and all the more so now that he felt estranged from his mother. Florence, for her part, was lonely. George, though she idolized him, was remote and sardonic. He teased her rather cruelly about her crusades and enthusiasms, and – as she realized later, if not already – he wasn't always faithful to her. Moreover, he was wrapped up in his work. The friendship of Forster – who took so much trouble over friendship – was a great enlargement to her life, as well as being another 'cause' to take up, and before long she was more or less in love with him. He felt similarly grateful for her friendship and determined to be worthy of it, writing in his diary for 9 September 1912:

> She loves me and I her, and reverence her without feeling ashamed of my uselessness . . . Very great happiness, and must try not to impose on her and tout for sympathy.

1 3 Adrift in India

Forster's first visit to India was a carefree affair, and the dark colours of *A Passage to India* were the product of later experience. For one thing, of course, when he first came to India, the political scene was relatively calm. There had been violent disturbances a few years before, as a result of Curzon's policy in partitioning Bengal. But the partitioning had been rescinded; the extremist leader, Tilak, was now in jail; and the moderates had been appeased by the Indian Councils Act of 1909, which gave Indians a voice in the higher provincial administration. Congress at this time was still a moderate group, meeting once a year to pass mild resolutions, to which nobody paid much attention. And the new King-emperor, George V, visiting India in the winter of 1911–12, had announced at his durbar the transfer of the capital from Calcutta to Delhi. This was a step of complex significance, but plainly, from one aspect, it was a gesture of confidence on Britain's part, implying that there was no more need for a maritime escape-route.

Forster and Dickinson, and Liberals like them, at this period, scarcely envisaged independence for India. If they pictured such a thing at all, it was as a distant ideal; and they did not think of the home-rule movement as a serious force. The two friends, indeed, came to India in a mood of optimism, still believing in the power of disinterested social criticism. Both, in their own way, had made a special study of the jingoistic public-school-and-business type of Englishman, and, having observed him at home, meant now to witness him doing the work of empire. And, no doubt, they meant to twist his tail; but if so, in the name of a better England in which they still had faith.

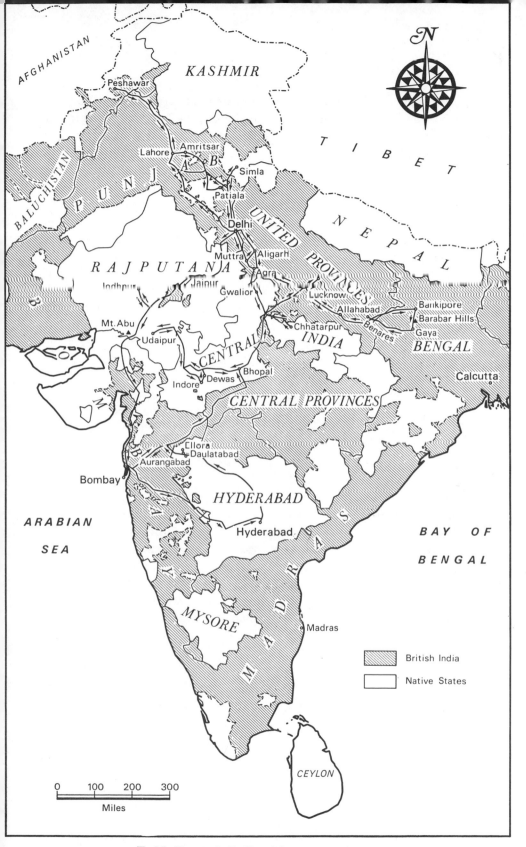

AFGHANISTAN

KASHMIR

Peshawar

TIBET

BALUCHISTAN

Lahore

Amritsar

A — B

Simla

P U N J

Patiala

R A J P U T A N A

Delhi

UNITED PROVINCES

NEPAL

Jodhpur

Jaipur

Muttra

Aligarh

Agra

Gwalior

Lucknow

Allahabad

Bankipore

Barabar Hills

Mt. Abu

Udaipur

CENTRAL

Chhatarpur

Benares

Gaya

BENGAL

INDIA

Indore

Dewas

Bhopal

CENTRAL PROVINCES

Calcutta

Ellora

Daulatabad

Aurangabad

Bombay

HYDERABAD

ARABIAN

SEA

Hyderabad

M A D R A S

BAY   OF

BENGAL

MYSORE

Madras

British India

Native States

0   100   200   300

Miles

CEYLON

E. M. Forster's Indian itinerary, 1912–13

In such respects their standpoints were much alike; and Forster, who was not a political thinker in the day-to-day sense, had taken many of his attitudes from Dickinson and his friends. In other respects, however, their approaches to India were very different – as different as they were as men. Dickinson was coming to India as a professional commentator. He planned to visit jails, and schools, factories, and religious establishments, and to collect views and data of all sorts. For him, as a systematic collector of ideas, the civilizations of the East were so many more ideas to set in place; and, partly as a result, he hated what he saw of India. He was appalled by its muddle and squalor and indifference to human life, as he was by the 'sense-lessness' and 'horribleness' of its sculpture and architecture; Forster remembered him cowering under the portals of a Hindu temple, with a look of horror on his face, 'as if a wind blew off them which might wither his soul.'[1] His visit brought him round to sympathy with the British officials. 'There is more in these men than appears,' he wrote on his return. 'They stand for . . . the energy of the world, for all, in this vast Nature, that is determinate and purposive, not passively repetitionary.'[2] India was such a contradiction of the Greek ideal that Dickinson could make no sense of it and felt that no Westerner could; and he went off to China with relief.

Forster came in a very different spirit: less political, more tentative, more exploratory. He had been drawn there by friendship and imagination, and he was ready for whatever the country might offer, with no very fixed idea as to what this might be. He kept an open mind, for instance, as to whether the spectacle of poverty in India would distress him intolerably. And, as things turned out, it did not do so – for which he was grateful, since (so he put it to himself) what he wanted was to get to know Indians, not to think about them as a problem. Coming in this mood, he quickly found himself at home in India and led the life he led anywhere, a life of mild human contacts and awakened imagination. To stake so much as he did on private life and private virtues won its reward; by means of his courtesy, his inconspicuousness, his desire to be liked, and his willingness to be bored, he did, as we shall see, break, or slip, through national barriers with remarkable success. He was a kind of Englishman unfamiliar to

[1] 'The Art and Architecture of India', *Listener*, 10 September 1953.
[2] G. L. Dickinson, *Appearances* (1914), p. 18.

Indians, and they greatly appreciated him. Anglo-Indians who had given their lives to the country often considered him prejudiced and superficial. This was natural on their part, and there was considerable truth in it, but a truth that does not seem, by comparison, of great significance.

*   *   *

He took ship on 7 October 1912, and four days later, at Port Said, he had his first glimpse of the East. It disappointed him: 'No minarets, only one dome, and the statue of Lesseps pointing with one hand to the canal and holding strings of sausages in the other.'[1] He was struck, however, by the spectacle of the coaling-barge, covered in black figures who 'awoke like an operatic chorus' and rushed on deck with baskets-full of coal. 'Quickest coaling station in the world,' he noted, 'but they had time to sing, fight and fondle.' After dark, when one of the coal-heavers stood with a lamp by the gangway, the East appeared to him as something 'happy and terrible'.

The ship was full of army officers and their wives, and the Cambridge group, with its highbrow chatter and explosions of giggles, was like nothing they had encountered. The sight of it sitting down, in a row, at tea was too much for the other passengers altogether – though, as Trevelyan kept remarking in a loud voice, no one was actually rude to them. At mealtimes Trevelyan would hold forth to the company in general upon such topics as the early Greek novelists and Nero's talents as stage-manager. Eventually, one of the passengers, goaded to madness, cried, 'But what is the use of all these scraps of information?' 'Why, to make amusing conversation as we're doing now,' replied Trevelyan blithely. On board ship there were endless deck-games and organized entertainments, and the great anxiety of the Cambridge group was to escape them. 'By what selection are the organizers of these things found?' Forster speculated. 'As if by magic, the appropriate colonel or captain is at the top. And is it by chance that the Indian has been drawn to play with the wife of his guardian, believed a semi Indian?'[2] As a gesture, however, Forster joined in a game called 'deck shovel', so as to show solidarity with two commercial travellers, whom the other passengers were boycotting – Trevelyan nicknamed them 'the pariahs'. Forster thought the women on board were 'pretty rotten, and vile on the

[1] Diary, 11 October 1912.
[2] Diary, 14 October 1912.

native question'. One of them, who had been a nurse in the Bhopal *purdahs*, complained to him, 'If our children stop in India they get to talk *chit chit*, and it is such a stigma.' They all agreed one must not speak politely to natives: 'they would despise you if you did'. When Forster told one he was going to stay with a 'native', she gave a little gasp and promptly changed the subject.

The solitary Indian passenger, who had been so tactfully handled by the Sports committee, turned out to have friends in common with Forster. However he proved tiresome, and Forster dropped him, and had almost forgotten him when, much later in the voyage, there was an odd development. The news went round that the Indian had accused his cabin-mate of threatening to throw him overboard; also more oddly, that the two were now friends again. The incident returned to Forster's mind forty years later, becoming the germ of that fine story of his old age, 'The Other Boat'.

Among the passengers was a fair-haired, Byronic-looking young army officer. Noticing him sitting alone, Forster got into conversation; and before long, the young officer, whose name was Searight, became confidential. He told Forster he was a poet; and, further, he declared himself an ardent and doctrinaire homosexual. He kept a diary full of Rousseauistic self-revelation and astonished Forster with some of his 'minorite' anecdotes. For the rest of the voyage he spent his time with the Cambridge group, and he made them all promise to visit him at his unit in Peshawar.

Despite the 'horrid' meals and the 'horrid' ship, the dances, gymkhanas, fancy-dress balls and prize-givings, Forster found the journey wonderful. When he tired of chatter, he would slip away to odd corners of the ship, to read and meditate.

> *18 October* . . . There was a concert but I sat reading by the sea, thinking now and then of the (apparent) happiness of sea-creatures: jelly fish, purple & scarlet, who float near the surface as soon as it is calmer, flying fish in parties, most frequent at rise and set of sun: what I believe still were water snakes asleep, though others say sea weed: and tracts of scarlet, hundreds of yards wide, said to be fishes' spawn. There is a sense of joy never conveyed by the air nor the dashing waters of the north. Coleridge knew of it.

On 21 October some yellow butterflies flew on board, and Forster claimed they had had their first sight of India. Trevelyan protested that butterflies were no more India than the Lascar deckhands, and, next day, he called Forster to the rail to witness the real India, which turned out to be a cloud-bank. Then they saw it at last: 'a queer red series of hills a little disquieting, as though Italy had been touched into the sinister'. They were rowed ashore in an open boat by an ugly crew, with beautiful skins, one of whom Forster thought 'resembled a stupider apostle'. On landing, his first act, as instructed by Kate and Maggie Preston, was to kiss his hand towards Madras, their childhood home. Trevelyan, seeing white-robed figures, insisted he was in ancient Greece.

Appropriately, India began for Forster with a muddle. Rupert Smith had engaged a servant for him, and he was there at the quayside to greet Forster: a Hindu called Baldeo, of indeterminate age, speaking not a word of English. Forster inspected his credentials, not focusing him very clearly in the glaring sun, and the party set off to find a hotel. The first they tried proved full, so they went on to another, telling the servant to follow with Forster's luggage. At this point he vanished, though the luggage mysteriously turned up, and the next two days Forster scoured Bombay for him, inventing innumerable explanations. Meanwhile one of the hotel servants proved remarkably attentive, even sleeping like a dog outside his room all night. It was Baldeo, who had slipped into the hotel unseen; Forster had pictured him as twenty years older. 'Poor chap – what must he have thought!' Forster wrote to his mother.

His friends and he were to go separate ways for a week or two: Dickinson and Trevelyan to Ellora and Ajanta to visit the cave-temples, and he himself to stay with Masood in Aligarh. He reported the 900-mile journey to his mother (October 1912) as 'the most comfortable and also the most expensive' he had ever taken.

> The moonlit country was beautiful, for we were crossing the hills; next morning it was not fine as scenery, but of course I was very excited. Sometimes it looked like Surrey – heaths with small hills, and 'blue distances'; but a 'blue distance' becomes very different when you see a camel walking across it or a palm tree growing against it, and a ploughed field over which women in crimson or blue are stalking, with beautiful pots of metal on their heads, becomes quite a new sort of ploughed field: I saw Bhopal, and Gwalior, which looks like a glorified Orvieto, rising sheer from the plain, and three magnificent elephants with hideous howdahs of

red and green. But the railway stations pleased me most – every
sort of dress and undress running up and down, and the children
with nothing on at all, bathing themselves solemnly under the
drinking water tap. Sweets like greasy tennis-balls, messes of every
colour, bread like pancakes, peacock-feather fans, plaster spaniel-
dogs – every sort of thing was being sold, and there were Hindu
sellers of food for the Hindus, so that they might not be defiled.

He missed his connection at Agra, so did not reach Aligarh till the
middle of the second night, being met on the platform by a flustered
Masood. They drove straight home to bed; but hardly had he shut
his eyes when the house filled with Masood's friends, so he had to
stagger out, in pyjamas, to drink tea and chew betel and be taken
for a drive. For the next week, this was to be the regular pattern;
friends flocked in from morning to night, and soon he was receiving
even in bed. He congratulated himself on landing so promptly in
the midst of Indian life, and Masood's friends were full of praise for
his English friend; the doctor declared that if more Englishmen were
like him all would be well with the world. 'I think,' Forster wrote to
his mother, 'he is so far right that the world would go wrong in a
different way.' Masood's mother kept strict *purdah*, so she felt
unable to see Forster, to Masood's embarrassment; however she
sent friendly messages and asked why he had not brought *his*
mother.

Masood arranged a country expedition, and at 4.30 a.m. the party –
Masood, Forster, the Professor of Mathematics and the Deputy
Collector – set off, jammed tight inside a *tikka gharry*; as they
travelled the moonlit road, Forster could discern on it the shadows
of many other passengers on the roof. Dawn broke as they passed the
great mosque of Koil, and an endless, featureless landscape stretched
before them: fields of cotton and linseed, high pampas grass and
'brushwood as if the downs had been ironed out flat'. It baffled
description, Forster thought, for there was nothing to describe, no
reason for the position of anything, nothing but 'the cultivated
earth extending for ever'. It was a response to the Indian landscape
which became habitual to him.

At a village in their route they were welcomed by a local dignitary,
who gave them tea and musk pills of his own making. Then they
transferred into bullock-carts, in which they stretched out at length
on bolsters; and at another village they were entertained to a feast,

after which they went to bed on their host's loggia, in full view of the assembled villagers. Forster sent Lily samples of the scents given to him by their host after dinner. 'Some were roses etc., but I chose you the queer ones. The one that smells of smoke is made out of earth. and the other is henna.'

In going to Aligarh, Forster had, more in fact than he could have realized, plunged into Indian politics; for at this time the M.A.O. College at Aligarh was the centre of Muslim nationalism and the training-ground for its leaders. This was a recent development, for Masood's grandfather, the founder of Aligarh, had been an ardent Anglophile and an opponent of Congress. At his death in 1898, however, the College had quickly fallen apart: there was continual bickering between the staff, who were mainly British, and the Muslim governing body, and the students likewise grew disaffected. These were the early days of the pan-Islamic and pro-Turkish movement among Indian Muslims, and the students formed secret Turcophile and anti-British societies. There were student strikes,* and the brothers Ali,[1] leading Muslim nationalist propagandists of the time, made play with the College's troubles in their journal the *Comrade*. Meanwhile the Government of India was quietly exploiting the College for its own ends, fostering Muslim separatism as a lever against the Hindus.† Forster sensed the drift of things there. 'Life at Aligarh shows many seams,' he noted in his diary (25 October 1912).

> The English staff complained that they were not trusted to give the help they had hoped to give, but would be turned adrift as soon as the Mahommedans cd. stand without them: they could make some way with the students – not much, owing to the influence of *The Comrade*, a forward-Islamic paper 'which told lies'; – and none at all with the governing body. The Mahommedans had an air of desperation, which may be habitual, but was impressive; why should Sir Edward Grey have been the *first* to recognise Italian rule in Tripoli,[2] they asked, and pertinently.

---

[1] Shaukat and Mohammed Ali were ex-students of Aligarh and later for a time became Gandhi's chief Muslim associates, being instrumental in raising him to the leadership of Congress in 1920. Their journal, the *Comrade*, sugared its anti-imperialism with verses, short stories and jokes and was much read in British official circles. It was suppressed in 1914, when Turkey entered the war against the Allies.

[2] By the Peace of Ouchy, 15 October 1912, Turkey recognized the Italian occupation of Tripoli, its erstwhile province.

He stayed at Aligarh for a week, and then Masood and he went on
to Delhi, to stay with a doctor friend of Masood's, M. A. Ansari.*
Ansari, though still a young man, was already an influential figure.
He was born in Hyderabad in 1880 and had studied medicine at
Edinburgh University, subsequently serving as House Surgeon at the
Lock Hospital in London, and at the present period he was very
nearly the only Muslim practising Western medicine in India. He was
also already prominent in Muslim nationalist politics and was later
to become leader of the Centre Party in Congress.

His private house was by the old city walls, near the Mori Gate.
It was tiny, so that Forster and Masood had to share a bedroom;
also – like all Indian houses, so it seemed to Forster – it was thronged
with unexplained visitors. Masood had just had a cholera inoculation,
and, being a hypochondriac, he took to his bed, worrying first at
feeling too ill and then at not feeling ill enough. Forster, in the
intervals of sight-seeing, would keep him company in the adjoining
bed, and before long the room would be overflowing with visitors –
sitting cross-legged on the beds, or on the luggage, or on one another's
laps, eating plates of rice, while three dogs, a cat and a cockatoo
roamed at large. Various poor relations sat apart humbly, and would
take messages and pick up fallen books. There seemed to be no set
mealtimes, but whenever Forster crossed the threshold, tea and
poached eggs would appear, while heaps of *pilau* rice lay cooling in
the dining-room. From time to time Ansari's wife, who kept *purdah*,
would send gifts of cigarettes, betel nut and scent. 'I am in the
middle of a very queer life,' Forster wrote to Florence Barger (2
November 1912); 'whether typically Oriental I have no means of
knowing, but it isn't English.'

Dr Ansari insisted on arranging a *nautch*, or party with dancing-
girls, for Forster's benefit. He would have liked to throw it at home,
but he lived next door to an Englishwoman, who – so he and his wife
feared – might make scandal about it and injure his practice. It was
to be held, therefore, in the house of a friend, in the middle of the
Old City. Forster was a little nervous at the prospect, not knowing
quite what to expect, and worrying about the expense.

This *nautch* led to a curious political incident. Both Masood and
Ansari were close friends of the Ali brothers and as such were much
concerned, as were Muslims generally, about the plight of Turkey, now
facing defeat in the Balkan war. (In December of this year, Ansari

would lead a Red Crescent medical mission to Turkey, partly
organized by the *Comrade*.) It so happened that the *nautch* was to
take place next to the *Comrade* offices, and on their way to it,
Masood and Forster called in there. They found Mohammed Ali in
great distress and threatening suicide. 'I am absolutely miserable,'
he exclaimed. 'The Bulgarian army is within twenty-five miles of
Constantinople.' Nearly weeping, he went with Masood into the next
room, crying, 'Let no quarter be asked and none given now. This is
the end.' Forster, though he found Ali 'a most untaking man', was
impressed by his emotion; and Masood, catching the infection, cried,
'This is the turning-point of my career. We shall give the Turks all
the money that we have collected for the University.' He insisted,
nevertheless, that Ali must come to the *nautch*, and when he made
difficulties, simply picked him up and lifted him bodily from the
room. Ali rashly told the story of this night to a fellow-journalist,
and not long afterwards, according to Ali, there appeared in the
London *Times* a report of how a leading Muslim agitator, on the very
eve of Turkey's defeat, had spent his evening at an 'orgy'.[1]

The 'orgy', in fact, turned out extremely decorous. There were
lengthy preliminaries, during which Forster found himself coolly
appraising the dancers' 'points'. 'One could easily "lapse" into an
oriental,' he reflected. He was taken with the leading performer, a
girl 'with a weak but very charming face and very charming manners'.

> Emotion came to me through the harsh voice and music, so that
> I enjoyed myself. The drum would thunder in on the last note:
> this excited us, though its function is only to beat time, and when
> the singer sank down in our midst, with her scarlet and golden
> robes spread round us, and sang love-songs, I realised what a
> Nautch must be to Indians.

Her companion, an unattractive girl, performed at great length, till
Forster nearly fell asleep, battered about the head by her screams.
Eventually, though, it dawned on him that the *nautch* would go on
as long as he was there, so he got up and made his excuses.

It was his last day in Delhi, and Masood and Ansari saw him off on
the night train to Lahore. Masood and he were now to part for a time,
Forster to stay with Malcolm Darling, now a magistrate in Lahore,

---

[1] See Mohammed Ali's autobiography *My Life: a Fragment* (Lahore, 1942),
in which Forster figures as Masood's 'fellow-Oxonian'.

and Masood to return to Bankipore, where his legal practice was. Lahore spelled Anglo-India, and after his dip into native life Forster found the transition chilling. The town of Lahore repelled him: it was anglicized and spaciously-planned but 'all unfinished and dreary, dissevered from home life and native.' The Darlings themselves were all he could have wished in sympathy with Indians, and he met many Indians at their table; but the tone of Darling's colleagues was depressing. It was the time of the Islington Commission,[1] which was sitting just then in Madras to discuss the opening of the higher civil service to Indians; perpetually, though, he heard the view that the educated 'native' didn't count, he was only a drop in the ocean. 'But every educated man is a drop', he protested to a friend of his. 'I am becoming quite a Padgett M.P.,[2] being full of good advice to everyone.' It convinced him of how unusual Malcolm and Josie were. He had been nervous of meeting Josie, but they got on well. She was mannish, an arch-tory, and rather exasperating, but a woman of great courage and integrity. Once he saw her, when a bullock-cart had overturned in the street, rush straightway and put her shoulder to the wheel to free the fallen bullock.

His weeks in India had taught him the pleasures of having a servant, even such a morose one as Baldeo. The Darlings approved of Baldeo; they said he 'kept to the custom' in the rate at which he cheated Forster. However, for form's sake, they told Forster, he should make a protest every now and then, so he took issue over some dusters, for which Baldeo had charged him 3d (in rupees)though they had only cost 2d. It was 'a rending scene', he told his mother (6 November 1912):

> He produced the dusters, which certainly were good ones. How-
> ever I wasn't there to be reasonable, and as I knew that the other
> charges were also a little higher than they should be, I kept to my
> point. He is said not to mind at all, and doesn't seem to.

Dickinson and Trevelyan were already in Lahore, and the former took Forster on a round of visits to schools and colleges. At what he

---

[1] The Commission included Ramsay MacDonald, Lord Ronaldshay, Valentine Chirol, Gokhale and Mr Justice Abdur Rahim. Dickinson attended some of its meetings.

[2] Character in Kipling's story, 'The Enlightenment of Padgett, M.P.', type of the meddlesome visiting English politician.

thought a Brahmo Samaj[1] college, Dickinson delivered an address, saying how warmly he had always felt towards the Brahmo Samaj, etc. – only to find that it wasn't Brahmo Samaj at all, but some kind of Christian institution. The audience was polite but sad. But in any case, Forster remarked to himself, 'it was a washy dirty little show.'

While in Lahore the three friends were to visit Peshawar, to stay with their shipboard acquaintance Searight. However, by the time they were due to leave, Bob, who was staying with an old school friend, developed German measles. He was put in a tent, for isolation purposes, but found the solitude torture. 'Well, if the whole regiment *did* get it,' he complained, 'what would it matter?'; and he cabled to his old nanny in England, 'Have I had German measles?' They left without him, but Forster told Dickinson, 'I'm sure Bob means mischief,' and when they arrived in Peshawar, sure enough a wire had preceded them: 'No measles. Am coming tomorrow.' The next day they all made an expedition to the Khyber Pass and 'sat watching Central Asia pass and repass'. Forster recorded the scene with detachment:

> Both sorts of camel, donkeys with hens and babies tied on their backs & sometimes quarreling. Costumes not brilliant, but a sense of splendour through dirt. Fine fierce youths. Finest effect returning when processions streamed over the broken ground like a divided river.[2]

It was a wonderful sight, he thought, 'but from a world too remote and savage to seem real. I could not mix with them as with a show in lower India. They were of the stage.'

Searight was an assiduous host, and Forster and Dickinson, who were in regimental guest-rooms, found their anti-military prejudices melting. It was guest-night, which meant dressing, and at the last moment Forster lost his collar-stud[3] and arrived ten minutes late, to find the whole mess waiting and the regimental band poised to play 'The Roast Beef of Old England'. He was in agonies for Searight, but the Colonel smoothed things over charmingly. 'Once in with the military,' Forster reflected, 'and they take one to their bosom. No gradations between hauteur and intimacy, as is natural with un-

---

[1] Theistic church founded by Ram Mohan Roy in the early nineteenth century.

[2] Diary, 8 November 1912.

[3] A detail turned to profit in Chapter 7 of *A Passage to India*.

reflecting men'. After dinner there was dancing. Searight was in tearing spirits and made Forster dance with him, then rushed about with Trevelyan pick-a-back on his shoulders. Whitewash was thrown, and uniforms got torn, and later, at supper, a charming and drunken youth made Forster and Dickinson drink prairie-oysters – 'quite the most horrible and senseless thing I ever swallowed,' Forster told his mother. Dickinson endured the horseplay benignly, being baptized 'The Don' by the young officers, who whispered to one another, 'I say, he will put you in a book.' On looking back, Forster thought it was on this evening that he first saw Dickinson as 'a solid figure, who had his own place in the world, and held it firmly'.[1]

In Lahore, the Darlings had introduced Forster to a lay missionary, George Douglas Turner, a very intelligent and high-minded man, who, until his recent marriage to the American novelist Mary Borden, had lived and worked in the native quarter. Forster sought him out on his return to Lahore, and Turner took him on a nocturnal tour of the city. They visited an opium den, about which Turner was very tolerant, and then they went to Turner's old house, where he was greeted delightedly by erstwhile neighbours. He told Forster how he used to hear them discussing him; one would say, 'He's a government spy,' another, 'No – he has committed some grave sin and is living among us as a punishment.' A young Indian barrister, a friend of Turner's, invited them home, and, sitting round his table, by the sputtering lamplight, they heard him describe his day.

> He had been defending a client who had bought a wife for 50 rupees from another man. 'Ah Krishna, Krishna!' said Turner, the missionary suddenly popping out. 'Did I not tell you that you would rue the day what you ever entered this damnable profession?' Mr Krishna smiled gently, and feeling that he ought to be confused, covered his face with his hands. Then he took us on to his balcony, which, like all the woodwork in the city, is beautifully carved, and we looked up and down the marvellous street and heard the conches and drums sounding from the temples and the chatter of the people.[2]

Forster's next destination was Simla. The novelist Sara Jeanette Duncan,[3] whom he had met for five minutes at the Morisons', had

---

[1] See Forster's *Goldsworthy Lowes Dickinson*, Chapter 11.
[2] Letter to his mother, 12 November 1912.
[3] Sara Jeanette Duncan (1862–1922), author of *A Social Departure* (1890) and other novels.

just written to invite him there, and he decided to follow his luck, leaving Dickinson and Trevelyan to return to Delhi. He told his mother he thought he was enjoying India much more than they were. Simla was half deserted, the season being over, but while there Forster attended a Muslim wedding conducted on rationalist lines. It was a curious scene: the bride, who was not veiled, sat with the bridegroom on a sofa on a dais, with the officiating *Moulvi* in an armchair beside them. The audience was restive, murmuring, 'This is totally contrary to Islamic law,' and a quarrel broke out between the *Moulvi* and the bridegroom's brother, who finally announced, in English, that the ceremony would begin with a verse from the Koran. After this a local poet recited verses in Urdu in praise of 'Conscience' – Conscience being a garden where the Bulbul of eloquence ever sang and the dew of oratory dropped continually. Having joined the couple, the *Moulvi* gave an address, saying that it was not important how one was married but how one behaved after marriage. It was all reminiscent, it struck Forster, of G. M. Trevelyan's rationalist wedding, with its marriage-service composed by Mrs Humphry Ward. He was saddened:

> It was depressing, almost heartrending, and the problem of India's future opened to me. For at one end of the garden burst a gramophone – 'I'd rather be busy with my little Lizzy' – and at the other, on a terrace before the house, about 20 orthodox Muslims had gathered for the evening prayer. Facing the sun, which sets over Mecca here, they went through their flexions, bowing down till they kissed the earth in adoration to God, while the gramophone burred ahead, and by a diabolic chance, reached the end of its song as they ended the prayer. They rejoined the other guests without self consciousness. But in them was the only beauty and dignity. The rest was hideous and tentative, entering a valley whose further side is still invisible.[1]

From Simla he made a *safari*, with two coolies, to Fagu, twelve miles up the Hindustan-Tibet road. He sat up late in his *dak* bungalow, gazing at the Himalayas, and in the night woke very unhappy: '. . . thought of him [Masood] who might be slipping away. In the morning the mountains were less wonderful.'

Dickinson and Trevelyan were expecting him, so he made his way back to join them in Agra, where they 'did' the Taj Mahal by daylight

---

[1] Diary, 18 November 1912.

and by moonlight. From there they moved on to Gwalior, a spectacular fortress-city on a rock, where they had an introduction to the
Finance Minister, who provided an elephant to take them up the
rock. 'It's an absurd way of moving,' Forster told his mother (26
November 1912):

> Nothing will hurry Elephant, and she is so huge that she has to
> take a great circuit round each corner. We were long before
> reaching the top and poor Dickinson had already a pain. Then we
> went down the opposite side of the Rock to see the statues, which
> oh! were wonderful. There is a deep chasm, full of water and trees,
> and in its side are cut naked Jain saints, very frightening, some
> of them thirty feet high. Some are in niches with a bar of rock left
> round their waists, like giants peeping out of a cage, and if they
> are very special, elephants pour water on their heads, attendants
> fan their feet to keep off the flies, and hundreds of little saints are
> cut all over their niche, as tiny as filigree.

Their friend, the Minister, invited them to tea, replying grandly,
when they asked where the house was, 'No matter. I will send my
servant to bring you. Do nothing.' So they did nothing; and at seven
o'clock, by which time still no servant had appeared and they were
growing distinctly irritable, their host drove up, demanding to know
what had happened to them. 'Oh I am so sorry,' he said, when they
explained; 'but anyone can tell you where my house is. I thought the
servant would not be necessary.' 'He quite saw his mistake,' wrote
Forster to his mother (26 November 1912); 'but how wonderful is the
oriental mind. There he sat, with a party of friends whom he had
asked to meet us, all wondering why we had not turned up.'

Bob was restless, constantly complaining that there was no time,
he would never see China at this rate, and Forster guessed that he
was bored. They therefore decided to cut short their stay in Gwalior
and make straight for Chhatarpur, to visit Morison's 'dear king'.
Their host, the Maharaja Vishnwarath Singh Bahadur (1866–1932),
has made various appearances in literature. Forster describes him in
his life of Dickinson, and he was the original of the 'Maharaja of
Chhokrapur' in J. R. Ackerley's *Hindoo Holiday*. One should picture
a little hobbling figure, dazzlingly dressed in a magenta frock coat,
diamond earrings and a velvet toque like Queen Mary's. He was
excessively ugly, with a face like a Pekinese's, his nose being completely bridgeless and his tongue a nasturtium-colour from habitual

betel-chewing. The passions of his life were philosophy, friendship
and beautiful boys. As a young man, under Theodore Morison's
tutelage, he had studied Plato and Herbert Spencer, and ever since
had been wont to ask himself 'What is God?' 'Is there an Absolute?'
and similar questions. He hoped to receive the answer from the West,
and was perpetually angling for some Englishman to come and live
with him and be his *guru*. Since he could not quite explain matters
thus to the British authorities, he would say he was looking for a
private secretary, or later on – as in the case of Ackerley – for a tutor
for his son. But the truth was, or so Ackerley thought, he simply
wanted someone to love him. (Once they were sitting together,
watching the sun set in a blaze of pink and gold, and the Maharaja
waved his hand towards it sadly, saying 'I want a friend like that.')
While the perfect friend delayed, he occupied himself with his private
theatre, for which he composed miracle plays. This entailed the
recruiting of boy-actors, a great interest and a great trial to him.
They cost a fortune, a point in which the British Political Agent took
a disagreeable interest, and all too often they turned out most
ungrateful boys.

He welcomed the Cambridge trio effusively, and, from the Guest
House, Forster wrote to Lily that now they had 'really done it'.
There they were, in the midst of the jungle, not another Englishman
for fifteen miles, tigers roaming close at hand and yellow apes
swinging from every tree. Even Bob was appeased.

Their day fell into a regular pattern. After breakfast the court
doctor and private secretary would take them sightseeing; then soon
after lunch the royal carriage arrived to take them to the Palace – a
carriage so crowded with attendants, in shabby uniforms, that the
horses could hardly draw it. The Maharaja could not invite Europeans
within his palace, so he received in the courtyard, squatting on a cane
lounge-chair, under a large and magnificent umbrella embroidered
with tigers and elephants. At his feet sat his Private Secretary,
cross-legged like the Buddha.

To begin with, the conversation would be philosophical. 'Tell me,
Mr Dickinson,' it would run, 'where is God? Can Herbert Spencer
lead me to him, or should I prefer George Henry Lewes? Oh when
will Krishna come and be my friend. Oh Mr Dickinson. . . !' Or again:
'If the soul has walked with the Gods, and if the Beloved on earth is
a staircase by which we can climb to Heaven again, then will you

tell me who has put the barriers in the way? Have I made myself plain?' The Maharaja regarded Dickinson as the most philosophical of the party, and the latter, though in agonies with diarrhoea, did his best to give good value. Books would be sent for, and the Englishmen called upon to explain them. Then the Maharaja would grow confidential. He gave them a witty review of all the seventeen Political Agents he had suffered under and showed them a quarrelsome letter he had written to the current one. They condemned it as 'unwise and undignified'.

Sometimes the 'Padre Sahib', an army chaplain from the neighbouring Nowgong cantonment, would join the party. His manner with the Prince was breezy. 'Now Maharaja,' he would roar, 'what is this I hear? You've made yourself ill by fasting. Don't you know you're transgressing the fundamental rule of religion?' His Highness would cast his eyes down, giggling gently. Forster thought the padre a bounder and a fool and commented in his diary (2 December 1912): 'His popularity here suggests, (i) how readily the Indian responds to kindness (ii) how incapable of distinguishing good European manners from bad.' As for the Maharaja himself, he was, at first, quite taken with him: 'He is so sensible and shrewd and full of fun,' he told his mother. 'He would be a remarkable man in any country, and out here he is very strange indeed.'

The Maharaja had a second palace, a romantic ruin in the middle of a lake, and he took his visitors to see it. It was here that he hoped to meet Krishna, the divine friend. 'It is true that he desires the impossible,' reflected Forster. 'But how unassuageable his sorrow, because it is a poet's and includes ours.' The Maharaja brought a sorcerer to make the palace walls speak, but the sorcerer had forgotten his incense, so no miracle was performed. In a tender mood, the Maharaja offered the palace to Forster, and two days later offered it to Dickinson.

In the evenings, on several occasions, the guests were allowed to watch the palace actors, a privilege not often granted to outsiders. The troupe performed some of the Maharaja's own plays, ceremonious little dance-dramas, full of endlessly-repeated incidents. In one, Vishnu visited Krishna in his cradle, disguised as a hermit, and, being driven away, was later recognized as a God. The plays bored Dickinson dreadfully, but Forster was delighted by them and by the whole unlooked-for experience.

Krishna and Radha wore black and gold. What to describe – their
motions or my emotions? Love in which there neither was nor
desired to be sensuality, though it was excited at the crisis and
reached ecstasy. From their quieter dancing, dignity and peace.
The motions are vulgarised by words – little steps, revolutions,
bounds, knee dancing – how clumsy it gets and will my memory
always breathe life into it? Radha was most beautiful and
animated, but a little touched by modernity; and Krishna,
hieratic, his face unmoved while his body whirled, soared highest.[1]

Getting away from Chhatarpur was not easy, for the Maharaja
invented innumerable objections. At last, however, the matter was
arranged. He insisted on their travelling on a Tuesday, which was
particularly auspicious for those, like Dickinson and Trevelyan, who
were journeying eastward. (The fact that Forster was travelling west
did not seem to trouble him.) The Cambridge party was now breaking up for good, and Forster had a fortnight of solitude before him,
before he was due at Dewas. He decided, therefore, to visit Rajputana,
making a loop through Bhopal and Ujjain on his way, and then
doubling back to Indore. 'I have steered a queer course through
India,' he told his mother. His description of his day's visit to
Ujjain[2] shows his deepest impressions of India already fixed: the
feeling that landscape in India had no shape, and the feeling that
time and history there took on a different meaning.

One confusion enveloped Ujjain and all things. Why differentiate?
I asked the driver what kind of trees those were, and he answered
'Trees', what was the name of that bird, and he said 'Bird'; and
the plain interminable, murmured, 'Old buildings are buildings,
ruins are ruins.'

India and the Indian landscape were pointing him towards a new
kind of novel, as he hinted in a letter to Forrest Reid from Bhopal
(13 December 1912). The letter was to acknowledge a copy of Reid's
new novel *Following Darkness*:

You are talking . . . about the chasms that surround us. You are
describing spiritual scenery, and though you are too skilled a
novelist to paint the figures in that landscape as generalities, they
are most significant when they remind us that we walk in it too . . .
    Now if you go on in this way, you'll find 'passing life' more and
more intractable.

---

[1] Diary, 8 December 1912.
[2] 'The Nine Gems of Ujjain', in *Abinger Harvest*.

He was, himself, as a novelist, to find 'passing life' increasingly intractable, or, at least, to feel that he was losing interest in it.

* * *

He reached Indore on 20 December and stayed there with a friend of Darling's, Major Luard, then private secretary to the Maharaja of Indore. Luard took him to the club one evening, and on his mentioning Forster's name aloud there, a 'bright and tiny young Indian' sprang up and wrung Forster warmly by both hands. It was the Maharaja of Dewas – the Indian who, next to Masood, was destined to have most influence on his life.

The Maharaja was then 24 years old and had been the active ruler of Dewas Senior for the last four years. He was a descendant of the Puars, a Rajput family of soldiers of fortune who, during the eighteenth century, had carved out a kingdom for themselves while in the service of the Mahrattas. The kingdom's first rulers, Tukoji Rao and Jiwaji Rao, having briefly attempted joint sovereignty, had agreed to divide the state between them; and possession of the twin states, now much shrunken, had been confirmed to their descendants by the British in 1818. The present Maharaja, Tukoji Rao III, had succeeded in 1899 – his aunt, the widow of the late Raja, having adopted him when her husband died without heir. The British had had much trouble with his predecessor, who had nearly bankrupted the state, and twice they had actually stripped him of his powers. Thus they took a particular interest in the young Raja, and had sent him to the Chiefs' College at Ajmere and subsequently on a course in administration. They had also provided him with a British tutor, Forster's friend Malcolm Darling, and, before his investiture in 1908, Darling and he had made a grand tour of India and Burma. No previous member of his house had received such an all-round education, and the Government of India hoped they possessed in him a loyal, new-style prince.*

Darling had grown fascinated by him, as Forster was to be. In physique Tukoji or 'H.H.' (His Highness), as Forster was accustomed to call him, was tiny, round-faced, with a long weeping moustache. He was vivid in manner, pulled one way and another by emotion: by turns kind-hearted and revengeful, confiding and secretive, regal and full of ridiculous schoolboy fun. The life of a Mahratta prince, he had found, was one long battle over status: the deepness of a bow or *salaam*, the height of a seat, or the relative number of steps he or another took, had been his constant preoccupation. There were elaborate manoeuvres over marriage, battles of protocol with other states or with Dewas Junior, as well as continual poisoning scares. The Dowager, having adopted Tukoji as her heir, had promptly regretted it and spent her time intriguing against his mother. The endless mischief-making often depressed H.H., who once or twice had threatened abdication. All the same, he enjoyed, as he said, 'cracking a nut' with a high official, and took a childish pride in his spy-system, which cost a fortune and served him extremely ill.

The phrase often on his lips, as a young man, was 'old-fashioned'. It was 'old-fashioned' to keep a mistress, he once told Darling's mother, rather disconcerting her. And when a fellow-Raja, angry at seeing himself lampooned on the stage, set fire to the theatre, this too, for him, was 'old-fashioned'. Whatever the phrase meant to him, his modernity rubbed off soon, and the ghosts of his ancestors possessed him. Already, as with his forefathers, his passion was for religion, and he devoted two, then three, then four hours a day to his prayers or *puja*. Having contrived to get himself recognized a *Kshatriya*, one of the three higher caste-groups, he had wrested control of religious affairs from the Brahmins, and from then on his chief interest became the state's religious ceremonies, which, while he could afford it, grew more elaborate every year.

He was profuse in regrets that, being here in Indore for a Mahratta chiefs' conference, he could not greet Forster on his arrival at Dewas. However, he promised a carriage to collect him. It did not arrive; so Luard – whom this did not surprise – sent Forster in his own Maharaja's car, and the court chamberlain at Dewas received him with ceremony and installed him in the Guest House. Josie Darling and her baby were already there, as well as Charles Goodall and his bride. Goodall was a Kingsman and now a director of the Bombay Company; Forster reported to his mother that there was 'great fun ahead', for the Goodalls were to be married again in Indian fashion, which would mean elephants and a great wedding banquet. Darling arrived the next day, with dramatic news of a bomb-attack on the Viceroy, Lord Hardinge, during his ceremonial entry into the new capital. According to Darling several high officials had wanted the troops to fire on the crowd and seemed almost sorry the Viceroy had not been killed, instead of only wounded, so as to give an excuse for reprisals.

Forster reported Dewas to his mother as not beautiful. However, he told her, 'there is a sacred hill above it, covered with chapels, which makes scenery interesting'. This was the Hill of Devi,[1] a bare conical eminence, surmounted very oddly by a sort of lid, like a bandsman's cap. On Christmas day the whole party climbed the hill. 'Oh hostile soil. Stones and sudden little holes at dark,' exclaimed Forster in his diary. Darling told him a story of princely intrigue which, somehow, chimed with his impression of the Dewas soil, and for a moment, put him out of temper with India.

> A land of petty treacheries, of reptiles moving about too cautious to strike each other. No line between the insolent & the servile in social intercourse: so at least it seems to me. In every remark and gesture, does not the Indian prince either decrease his own 'omertà' or that of his interlocutor? Is there civility with manliness here? And is conquest or national character to blame?

The Maharaja returned on Boxing Day, and, having made religious lustrations after his journey, devoted himself to his guests. 'Clever merry little face in a huge turban,' Forster noted. As it happened, their acquaintance began badly. At their first conversation H.H. made fun of the Maharaja of Chhatarpur and his sexual proclivities, which Forster considered bad manners on his part. 'Sorry he did,' he commented, 'as I was ready to like him and shall now dwell on his egotism and tortuousness.' He soon forgot his irritation, and found his host as engaging as Darling had described him. For the Goodalls' wedding banquet, the Maharaja insisted on his guests wearing Indian court costume. Darling later recalled that, of all the guests, Forster wore his with most dignity; he guessed that princely grandeur appealed to him. Forster gave his mother a cheerful and detailed account of the scene (1 January 1913):

> So many delights that I snatch with difficulty a moment to describe them to you. Garlanded with jasmine and roses I await the carriage that takes us to the Indian Theatre, erected for the Xmas season outside the Old Palace. But to proceed.
>
> On 29 Dec. the Rajah gave an Indian banquet to the newly married pair. I have both forgotten the time it was meant to be and the time it was. As usual they differed widely, but at all events, as darkness fell, the garden and road by the Guest House filled up with soldiers, policemen, horses, children, torch bearers,

---

[1] See Forster's *The Hill of Devi*, p. 51.

and a most gorgeous elephant. (There are two state elephants but
the other did not feel quite well.) Goodall was to wear Indian
dress, and I retired to my tent to put on my English evening
things. Baldeo, much excited by the splendour that surrounded
us, was making the best of my simple wardrobe and helping to
snip my shirt cuffs where they were frayed, when there was a cry
of 'may I come in', and enter the Rajah, bearing Indian raiment
for me also. A Sirdar (courtier) came with him, a very charming
boy, and they two aided Baldeo to undress me and re-dress me. It
was a very funny scene. At first nothing fitted, but the Rajah
sent for other garments off people's backs until I was suited. Let
me describe myself. Shoes – I had to take them off when the Palace
was reached, so they don't count. My legs were clad in Jodporos
made of white muslin. Hanging outside these was the youthful
Sirdar's white shirt, but it was concealed by a waistcoat the
colours of a Neapolitan ice – red, white, and green, and this was
almost concealed by my chief garment – a magnificent coat of
claret-coloured silk, trimmed with gold. I never found out to
whom this belonged. It came to below my knees and fitted round
my wrists closely and very well, and closely to my body. Cocked
rakishly over one ear was a Maratha Turban of scarlet and gold –
not to be confused with the ordinary turban; it is a made-up affair,
more like a cocked hat. Nor was this all. I carried in my left hand
a scarf of orange-coloured silk with gold ends, and before the
evening ended a mark like a loaf of bread was stamped on my
forehead in crimson, meaning that I was of the sect of Shiva.
Meanwhile the others too had been surprised with Indian costumes, Malcolm looking very fine in pink with a sword, and the
other man in purple. The ladies went as themselves. At last we
were ready, and really it was a glorious sight when the Goodalls
were perched on the elephant, sitting on real cloth of gold, with
torches around them and above splendid starlight. The band
played, the children cheered, and the Darlings' nice old Ayah
stood in the veranda invoking blessings from Heaven. We went
each in a carriage with Sirdars: I had two old men and one fat one,
all gorgeous, but conversation not as good as our clothes. An
elephant being pensive in its walk, we didn't reach the New
Palace for a long time, though it is close to the Guest House.
Hideous building! But it was too dark to see it. After the Rajah
had welcomed us we went to the Banquet Room. This again I
must try to describe to you.

We all sat on the floor, cross-legged, round the edge of a great
hall, the servants running about in the middle. Each was on a
legless chair and had in front a tray like a bed tray on which was
a metal tray, on which the foods were ranged. The Brahmins ate
no meat, and were waited on by special attendants, naked to the

waist. The rest of us had meat as well as the other dishes. Round each man's little domain an ornamental pattern was stencilled in chalk on the floor. My tray was arranged somewhat as follows, but 'Jane, Jane, however shall we recollect the dishes?' as Miss Bates remarked.

1. A mound of delicious rice – a great standby.
2. Brown tennis balls of sugar – not bad.
3. Golden curlicues – sweet to sickliness.
4. Little spicy rissoles.
5. Second mound of rice, mixed with spices and lentils.
6. Third mound of rice, full of sugar and sultanas – very nice.
7. Curry in metal saucer – to be mixed with rice no. 1.
8. Sauce, as if made from apples that felt poorly. Also to be mixed with rice, but only once by me.
9. Another sauce, chooey-booey and brown.
10, 11, 12. Three dreadful little dishes that tasted of nothing till they were well in your mouth, when your whole tongue suddenly burst into flame. I got to hate this side of the tray.
13. Long thin cake, like a brandy snap but salt.

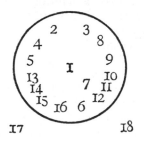

14. It may have been vermicelli.
15. As for canaries.
16. Fourth mound of rice to which I never came.
17. Water.
18. Native Bread – thin oat-cake type.

Some of these dishes had been cooked on the supposition that an elephant arrives punctually, and lay cooling on our trays when we joined them. Others were brought round hot by the servants who took a fistful and laid it down wherever there was room. Sometimes this was difficult, and the elder dishes had to be re-arranged, and accommodate themselves. When my sweet rice arrived a great pushing and squeezing and patting took place, which I rather resented, not knowing how attached I should become to the new comer. Everything had to be eaten with the

hand and with one hand – it is bad manners to use the left – and I
was in terror of spoiling my borrowed plumes. Much fell, but
mostly into the napkin, and the handkerchief that I had brought
with me. I also feared to kneel in the sauces or to trail my orange
scarf in the ornamental chalk border, which came off at the
slightest touch and actually did get on to the Jodpores. The cramp
too was now and then awful. The courtiers saw that I was in pain,
and told the servants to move the tray that I might stretch, but I
refused, nor would I touch the entire English dinner that was
handed round during the meal – roast chicken, vegetables, blanc-
mange &c. As each guest finished, he sang a little song from the
Vedas in praise of some god, and the Rajah was, as usual, charming He made the Goodalls feed each other five times and pronounce each other's name aloud. These are among their marriage
customs. Afterwards he, his brother, the Dewan, and all of us
went on to the Palace roof, where was champagne and betel nut,
and we danced in our grand clothes and our socks to the music of
the band which was playing down in the square. This suited me
very well. We were interrupted by a message from the Rani – she
desired to see us. This was a great surprise to me. The two ladies
went first, and then we, and had a lovely vision. She was extraordinarily beautiful, with dark 'gazelle' eyes. Having shaken
hands all round, she leant against the door-post and said nothing.
There was an awkward if respectful pause, and after Malcolm had
talked a little Urdu and received no answer, we went. Her dress
was on the negligée side, but she had not been intending to receive.
The Rajah was pleased she had sent for us. He longs to modernise
her, but she remains a lovely wild creature. We returned to the
hall below, sitting on the floor again and hearing a little singing
from nautch girls. We drove back to the Guest House to find Mrs
D. and Mrs G. in the most magnificent Indian dresses: the Rani
had dressed them and sent them back in a Purdah carriage. – So
ended a very charming evening, full of splendour yet free of
formality.

The Maharaja, in his element at the banquet, was another man
when, the next day (30 December 1912), he had to give a lunch to
the Agent to the Governor General and the Political Agent. He was
all anxieties. What would they think of him? Would it all go well?
Why *wouldn't* the servants bring lunch? It was the same lament as
Forster had heard from the Maharaja of Chhatarpur. 'It is odd that I
should have seen so much of the side of life that is hidden from most
English people,' Forster remarked. To entertain his guests, H.H. had
arranged an acrobatic performance in the Guest House garden and

later some theatricals, 'very tawdry and dull'. When at last his burdensome guests were gone, the Maharaja 'sported like a kitten'.

Two days later, Forster and his friends saw the Maharaja in another light again, holding his own durbar in the Old Palace, a fine eighteenth-century building in the middle of the town.

> Dressed in white, he sat on the 'Gaddi' – half bed, half throne – leaning against a white bolster with peacock-fans waving over his head. The court sat crosslegged all down the room on each side, we in an alcove on chairs: he would not have us squatting. All offered 'nazir' (homage) which he remitted to the servants. His expression changed as each came up: to the Sirdars he was dignified, to the Maratha guests courteous and warm: he laughed behind his hand when the Subahdar, his buffoon, came. (This is a puzzling unattractive man; a spy from Kolhapur[1] I am told. H.H. is always translating his droll speeches and I can't see their drollery: sometimes his turban is set on fire, which makes me wretched: he takes care of Lady, the flea-bitten little dog.) After each had paid homage, the Rajah made a long dull speech about the constitutional changes that he is making; a new advisory council; I believe it is important. No one was much pleased. Then scent and betel nut were distributed all round. The proceedings lasted two hours, and were impressive owing to the architecture of the fine little hall and to the dresses. But oh the pictures! The dear creature has not a glimmer of taste and on the dark wooden pillars are hung Love me Love my dog or Xmas plates from the Graphic. Even when the subjects are Hindu they are cheap prints, and he has actually put glass balls to swing from the ceiling. My heart aches, for he is an active and able ruler, and if he lives long Dewas will look like the Euston Road. Malcolm has asked him to take the balls away, and he will do so, but it's no good. Malcolm and Josie chose all the decorations for the New Palace, but the tints couldn't 'quite be matched', and the result is a nightmare of sickly green, proudly shown as an example of English taste. The Maharajah of Chhatarpur, on the other hand, seemed incapable of doing anything which wasn't beautiful.

Forster was in high spirits, and enchanted by his Indian Christmas. 'He loves the Raja and the Raja him,' Darling wrote to a sister. 'From start to finish he has just bubbled with whimsical, delightful humour, and from that old tin-kettle of a piano, which you may remember, he has drawn the most splendid music.' The Maharaja, for his part, had taken greatly to Forster and bitterly lamented the

---

[1] There was a bitter vendetta between Dewas and Kolhapur,

breaking-up of their party. They spent the last day picnicking by the Tank and played at marking one another's characters. The Maharaja was puzzled that one could earn marks for Passion; 'Is not Passion bad?' he asked apprehensively. It was a very happy day, and at the departure of the visitors the whole court assembled to garland them and sprinkle them with attar of roses.

Forster travelled back with the Darlings as far as Allahabad. Here the sacred Ganges and the Jumna rivers meet, and at their meeting-place, according to tradition, a third invisible stream springs up from the middle of the earth. This notion appealed to Forster, suggesting an allegory of human relationship, and, with a Muslim friend of Masood's, Ahmed Mirza,[1] he went to observe the miracle. There was no Ganges to be seen, however, only miles of fields and dry sand; and when they took a boat along the Jumna, the boatman got tired and said, first, that it was too far to the Ganges, then that they were in it already, and then that if they had been, the boat would have been swept away.

From Allahabad he proceeded to Benares, where he had an introduction to a schoolmaster, W. S. Armour. Armour insisted on putting him up, which was a misfortune, since, though a most well-intentioned man, he objected to all Forster's plans, saying that whatever it was 'wasn't done'. He lectured him incessantly, moreover, replying to every remark, archly, 'That's seditious', or earnestly, 'But the toiling *ryot* is the real India.' When they went for drives together, and the pedestrians would not get out of their way, he would sigh, 'They used to be quicker, they used to be far quicker than this.' Rothenstein had given Forster an introduction to a fakir, and at the cost of a quarrel with Armour, he went off to the riverside to find him. His first attempt led him to an empty bed of spikes, at which he left a visiting card. This turned out to be the wrong fakir, and the next day he found the right one, Nrusinh Sharma, who lived in a charming house and talked excellent English. Nrusinh Sharma showed Forster his sacred tea-things and a finger-painting by himself of Siva and Parvati. He compared Parvati to Queen Victoria, but Forster objected that the Queen would not have been sitting on her husband's knee but the other way round; the fakir laughed, and they rechristened them George and Mary. They went on to discuss

---

[1] See p. 202 and footnote.

inspiration and agreed on their experience of it. (A week or two before, Nrusinh had been visited by Dickinson and Trevelyan, and he wrote to Rothenstein,[1] thanking him for introducing him to 'noble types of humanity, whose hearts [were] as it were melting with love and fellow feeling and whom I would never forget because of the indescribable pleasure derived from their lucid conversation while sitting in my humble cottage'.) On his way home, Forster encountered the *wrong* fakir, a ferocious-looking character with face smeared with ashes and red paint, and he fled, 'like Hansel and Gretel from the witch'.

The time had arrived for him to rejoin Masood at Bankipore, and he set out there on 10 January – observing at a wayside station a tablet inscribed RIGHT IS MIGHT. MIGHT IS RIGHT. GOD SI LOVE. He found Masood established in a large bare house, which also served as his office. Outside, in a row of little sheds, lived numerous servants, 'each man squatting on his heels and muddling at something different'.[2] Masood was prospering, though he heartily disliked the law and was not to remain in it much longer. What finally sickened him with it, he would say later, was a client who cut off his own ear and brought it to Masood in a bottle as 'evidence' against his adversary. His English friends, like Morison, encouraged him to leave the profession, which they thought involved him too much in politics,[3] and were pulling strings to procure him a post in education. Meanwhile, as ever, he had a large array of friends, mostly young lawyers like himself, and Forster quickly made friends with some on his own account. With one, called Argawalla, he went every day for an early morning walk, and when Argawalla was troubled by a ghost, he spent the night in his house to assist in ghost-laying. Another, named Mahmoud, became the subject of his sketch 'The Suppliant'[4]: the gentle Indian who, when a villainous old man installs himself uninvited in his house and announces himself as his new clerk, is totally unable to tell him to go.

As for Bankipore itself, he found it 'horrible beyond words'. 'It

---

[1] His letter to Rothenstein, dated 3 February 1913, is preserved in the Houghton Library at Harvard University.

[2] Letter to his mother, 21 January 1913.

[3] He was employed as a junior counsel, on behalf of the arrested Muslim rioters, in the famous Cawnpore Mosque case of 1913.

[4] In 'Adrift in India' in *Abinger Harvest*.

consists of a street 14 miles long edged with hovels,' he told his mother (15 January 1913), 'from which it is impossible to escape because the Ganges stops you on one side and rice fields on the other. I wouldn't believe it until I took a bicycle ride and tried.' From Masood's roof, however, as he discovered, the city appeared transformed, miraculously, into a palm and lemon grove. Some of these details were remembered in his portrait of 'Chandrapore' in *A Passage to India*.

The new Indian provincial council[1] was just convening in Bankipore, and Masood took Forster to the opening. 'Towzled entry,' Forster noted in his diary (20 January 1913) 'All in funk of bombs.' The members made many loyal references to the bomb-attack on Lord Hardinge; but when this was mentioned later during a dinner-party, a British official exclaimed with flashing eyes, 'Deeds not words!' Among Masood's friends Forster figured, unusually for him, as a political authority. Questioned about Grey's foreign policy, he gave a lengthy exposition: 'Interests of British Empire so complex, policy based not on hatred of Islam but a fear of Germany,' etc. 'It is very easy to talk politics,' he told his mother (15 January 1913), 'when you meet someone who knows less than you. This has never happened to me before.' Masood's friends were impressed, and one of them said, with unction, that the British Empire might last for ever so long as it produced gentlemen like him.

There is no clue as to how things went between him and Masood during the fortnight. Unless, that is, an obscure entry, for his last day (28 January 1913) can be interpreted as a clue: 'Long and sad day . . . Aie-aie-aie – growing after tears. Mosquito net, fizzling lamp, high step between rooms. Then return and comfort a little.'

He was returning to Allahabad, since his friend Rupert Smith, now an Assistant Magistrate there, had invited him to see the annual bathing-fair. On his way, he visited the Buddhist sites of Buddh Gaya and the Barabar Hills, later to be a model for the 'Marabar Caves' in *A Passage to India*.[2] His first account (29 January 1913), even allowing that it was written to amuse his mother and aunt, is

---

[1] One of the changes announced by George V at his durbar was the forming of a new province of Bihar and Orissa, of which the capital was to be Bankipore.

[2] He said much later to the author that the caves were 'not all that remarkable' until they got into his book. He improved them.

remarkably blithe. He said in the Preface to *The Hill of Devi* that when he came to re-read his Indian letters, he felt they suffered from having been written for family circulation. He became too 'humorous and conciliatory' in them, too 'prone to turn rare and remote matters into suburban jokes'.

> Leaving Bankipore at an unearthly hour I was met at a little station called Bela by a friend of Masood's whose name is Nawab Syed Imdad Iam Saheb; I took it all down as I want to write to him. He was an active young man of seventy – rich, aimiable [*sic*], well read in English Poetry, and great on sport. He brought two nephews with him, who were not so nice and, it then being 10.0 o'clock, we mounted the elephant. It kneels down, You tread on its poor hind heel – that is the first step. For the next you tread in its tail which a servant holds looped in a festoon. The third step is more like a scramble. Ropes hang down from the Howdah over its person, and you haul yourself up by these. Then the final heave, and we have a fine view of the plain and the Barabar Hills where we are going. One of them, called The Crow's Swing, is this shape
>
> . Well I've exaggerated, but it is as steep as the Matterhorn though not so high, and as it comes straight out of the flat, looks amazing. It ends in a huge thumb shaped stone on the top of which stood a little one balanced so well that a crow could swing on it. Too heavy a bird must have tried, for it has fallen. On one side the rock comes down smooth and rounded like an inverted saucer and plunges into the earth of the plain. Beyond this – alas some way – were the other hills – and at their feet in a grove of palms, the tents were pitched. But breakfast – mockery of a name! – was not ready, and it was suggested we should visit the Buddhist caves while it was cooking. Here again were rocks, steps had been cut up them and in much heat and intense emptiness I climbed. The caves are cut out of the solid granite: a small square door way and an oval hall inside. This sounds dull, but the granite has been so splendidly polished that they rank very high among caves for cheerfulness. Date – 250 B.C.; as early as anything in India. One of them has a frieze of elephants over the door, but in the rest the only decoration is the fine Pali inscriptions on the sides of the entrance tunnel. Standing inside one sees them in the strong sunlight, and beyond the view. We lit candles which showed the grain of the granite and its reds and greys. The nephews also tried to wake the echoes, but whatever was said and in whatever voice the cave only returned a dignified roar:

Rupert Smith was in charge of the bathing-fair. He and his fellow officials were living in tents, in the middle of a mango-grove, and

every morning Forster rode out with him to the river-side, to observe
the swarm of naked pilgrims, sweet-sellers and fakirs. Whole villages
would enter the water at once, in long chains, 'like the Tonbridge
ladies at the Diamond Jubilee', Forster reported. By evening, seen
from above, the plain, clouded with dust and smoke, was 'like a pale
blue sea with people crawling as shrimps on the bottom'.

Four years of India had left their mark on Smith. He was curt and
insolent in court, wouldn't speak a word to Forster's friend Ahmed
Mirza when he came to lunch, and seemed, like his 'civilian' companions, to dislike every class of Indian except the peasant. One
evening Forster grew too depressed with the conversation and went
out to 'try to get through to the Mango trees & stars'. He was sad for
other reasons too, for he felt he was living through a glorious and
rare experience and yet was impotent as a writer. He wrote de-
jectedly to Forrest Reid that evening (2 February 1913):

> You ask me about my work. I feel you too sympathetic to keep
> silent. I am dried up. Not in my emotions, but in their expression.
> I cannot write at all. You say I helped you once – have a shot at
> helping me for I need it. Please do not mention this, as few people
> know. It often makes me very unhappy. I see beauty going by and
> have nothing to catch it in. The only book I have in my head is
> too like Howards End to interest me . . . I want something beyond
> the field of action and behaviour: the waters of the river that rises
> from the middle of the earth to join the Ganges and the Jumna
> where they join. India is full of such wonders, but she can't give
> them to me. – To have done good work is something and I don't
> the least doubt that I have done some.

There is a gap in his diary at the point. When we catch up with
him it is a month later, and he is once more in Lahore, where, one
Sunday evening, he is invited to a reception by the Brahmo Samaj
and meets a Mr Godbole, a Brahmin. ('What a name!' he exclaimed.)
After the reception, the two strolled in the public gardens, and Mr
Godbole sang to him. 'There are scales appropriate for all hours of the
day,' he noted. 'That for the evening was the scale of C major, but
with F♯ instead of F.'

From Lahore he made his way to Patiala, the Sikh capital, to
stay with the travel-writer Edmund Candler, and his plan on leaving
there was to revisit Rajputana. His arrangements were disturbed,
however, by the news that 'H.H.' was coming to Delhi, to attend a
Chiefs' conference. He wired to ask if they could meet, and the

Maharaja replied all delight. 'He was so sweet when I arrived,' Forster told his mother; 'darted up from behind and put his hands over my eyes.' Nothing would do for the Maharaja but that he should stay with the court; and the next three days passed for Forster in 'gentle oriental confusion', arrangements and mealtimes being equally vague. During these days the Maharaja and he, for the first time, had the chance of some serious conversation, and their talk turned towards religion. The Maharaja explained his belief that men, birds and everything in the universe were part of God, and that men had developed further than birds through coming nearer to this realization. And why had we ever been severed from God, asked Forster? Because, said the Raja, God became unconscious that we were part of him, his energies being concentrated elsewhere. 'So a man who is thinking of something else may become unconscious of the existence of his own hand for a time, and feel nothing when it is touched.' Every now and then during the conversation the Maharaja would break off to pray, tapping his forehead and going down on his knees. 'On days when one feels gratitude it is well to show it,' he said.

On his final day in Delhi Forster drove round with H.H. (sharing a seat with 'Lady' the elderly pug) while the Maharaja paid official calls. After the last of these the Maharaja bounced up and down with joy on the cushions, 'like a boy loose from school', and they went in search of amusement.

> We drove into the City, and came across his brother and various members of the court who had been shopping. Much excitement, and we drove on, but no sooner had we gone twenty yards than he thought it would be fun to have them all with us. But they had got into the electric tram to have the experience, which was new to them, and we followed madly in their wake, blocked by buffaloes and camels and goats and cows and sweetmeat sellers and pariah dogs. The tram was disappearing, but the coachman, at the Rajah's orders, leapt from the box and pursued it on foot, shouting. After five minutes he came back, leading the whole procession who got in, together with their purchases of briar-pipes, tobacco, mechanical monkeys for the children, writing-paper, ink, paper parcels of every size and shape. In all we were ten – the horses were strong and went slowly – it looked like a car in a carnival. I sat between the Rajah in a huge pale yellow turban and his brother whose turban was purple and who was trying to smoke his English pipe. Opposite were the doctor in red Maratha head-

dress, a secretary who wore an orange cup and saucer, and the court buffoon and spy, on whose knees Lady lay, indifferent to everything. Coachman, another attendant, and footman made three on the box, while the groom hung on behind. We attracted, as far as I could make out, no attention at all, though they all talked louder and louder as Indians do when they are happy.

After this diversion Forster, accompanied by Baldeo, pursued his way to Jaipur and Jodphur and thence to Bombay state, to visit Mount Abu and its famous Jain temples. An extract from his diary (17 March 1913) catches his style – responsive yet self-possessed – as a solitary sightseer.

Mount Abu is magical, with disorderly valleys full of rocks, palms, banyans, and a lake. Walked to Dilwana temples, for the hotel, civil if shifty, got me a permit. They were as I expected in effect, though the arrangement surprised: standing each in a small cloister; barbaric equestrian statues of kings who made them in a vestibule. Round cloister cells: in each a Tirthankara[1] with two comrades, or sometimes a party: the Indian gods have an air of confabulation; they were talking just before one walked in.

                              *   *   *

He now began the last lap of his journey, a visit to the Nizam's dominions. He had got in touch with a friend of Maimie Aylward's, May Wylde, who ran a school in Hyderabad city, and she arranged lodging for him there, and took him sightseeing in her car. May was an adventurous woman who had, against all sorts of opposition, set up a school for Indian girls, the first of its kind in the sub-continent. She had known Forster when they were both children, meeting him on his visits to Maimie, and had set him down in her mind as a mollycoddle, and later as an 'armchair Socialist'. On meeting him now she was, likewise, rather scornful of his pretentions to have sampled Indian life. She said later:[2] 'Morgan had got a few introductions to Indian homes in north India. Later on I heard one or two comments on his visits. They had wondered what the English visitor wanted to know. They did not find him as easy to talk to as the Englishmen who lived in India.' She also thought him prejudiced against the British official: too inclined to blame him for the lack of close intercourse between British and Indians, when the fault lay

---

[1] Traditionally, there were twenty-four *Tirthankaras*, or founders, of the Jain religion.
[2] In a letter to the present author.

with the *purdah*-system. She made efforts to correct his 'mistaken' ideas, but he took these in good part. Indeed, he warmed to her. He was amused at her breakneck driving and her very un-*memsahib* manner of squatting cross-legged in shops to haggle over prices. 'India attracts affinities,' he noted. He was lodging with friends of May's – a Mr Gamlen, director of the Mint, and his wife – and one evening they all went for a picnic on a rocky islet in a lake. Forster was cross-examined. *Mrs Gamlen.* 'What sort of novels do you write? Are they nice?' *Forster.* 'I can answer that – no.' *Mrs G.* 'Oh I see, they are modern?' *F.* 'Yes, that is the alternative.' *Mrs G.* 'Problem novels, I suppose. Well for my own part I think there are no problems left – they have all been written about.' *F.* 'Yes, they are old, but the writer's young.'

What had chiefly drawn Forster to the south was the cave-temples of Ellora. By good fortune Masood's friend Ahmed Mirza had a younger brother, Abu Saeed Mirza,[1] who lived in Aurangabad, a good jumping-off place for a visit to the caves, and Forster had secured an invitation from him. Abu Saeed, whom Forster had known slightly from Masood's London days, was now a *munsif* or junior magistrate and a dashing young fellow, with expensive tastes in horseflesh. He lived with two friends in a large, charming house which opened through arches, like those of the *Loggia dei Lanzi*, on to a garden of mango and lemon trees. So, 'Now I am plunged deep into the East again,' Forster told his mother. 'It is very nice to end up like this.'

Saeed took Forster to the courts, and in the sub-judge's court he heard part of a murder-case, during which, at the end of the table, a *punkah*-boy sat pulling his rope with 'the impassivity of Atropos'. They visited the jail, and then a nearby Mogul tomb, where the jail-inspector improvised a picnic, and the prisoners, in their chains, pulled carrots for them and shinned up trees to shake down catkins. 'It is impossible to take crime or punishment seriously in this country,' he told his mother (25 March 1913). 'The prisoners look like any body else and chatter all the time.'

In the evenings they would go riding, and Saeed would make his horse kick and curvet out of devilry. 'An amiable show off,' thought Forster. A horse, said to be very docile, was found for himself but

---

[1] See p. 202 and footnote.

promptly threw him. He fell on his behind, and Saeed, who was
'callous and sensible over illness', thanked God it was no worse.
Forster gave the horse a violent punch in the head, and after that
they got on better. All round them on their rides were relics of the
Mogul empire, tombs, mosques, dried-up fountains and ruined
palaces, and Saeed struck Forster as a remnant of that empire too.
'Many a young blood must have jogged through the evening before
him.' They talked of dominion and dynasties, and, climbing to the
summit of a fort, they surveyed the parched Deccan. Forster
wondered aloud what he would do with such a kingdom. Saeed was
all for ruling, 'though,' Forster guessed, 'not knowing what it
means.' He said: 'When I look down on walls I thought big from
below, I despise them.'

Another time they discussed marriage. 'I wonder what my auntie
will arrange?' said Saeed. 'I am in love with her already though I do
not know who she is . . . is that not strange? . . . With European girls
I must be very particular indeed – not even a little flirt . . . Then they
think I do not care about them and afterwards I have to explain . . .
I think ideal friendship with a woman is better than other things,
though it is love in a way, for one wants to kiss. That is my experience,
after trying all.'

Saeed was in debt, and Forster, who was worried about the expense
he himself was causing, lectured him about extravagance. He replied:
'God gives me food to eat. Brother and I were brought up by our
father[1] who gave us everything. We lived at a very happy time. Now
that I see my kids [he meant his nephews] I must give them a good
time too . . . They must want nothing.' 'But you must retrench
somewhere,' said Forster. 'Oh – everyone is in debt,' said Saeed; 'my
father died poor – I will die the same. Give your sons everything,
educate them, but leave no money lest law-suits come.' Forster
listened sadly, picturing how from 'these sweet strong impulses' might
spring the temptation to take bribes.[2]

On one of their rides Saeed burst out against the British. 'It may
be fifty or five hundred years,' he said, 'but we shall turn you out.'

---

[1] Their father had been Home Secretary to the Nizam. In 1909, as the result
of a court intrigue, he had had to leave the state, but on the accession of the
new Nizam in 1911 he had been persuaded to return.

[2] Forster's fears were not realized. Mr Abu Saeed Mirza had a distinguished
career, eventually becoming a Chief Justice. When I met him in 1970 he said

'He hates us far more than his brother,' reflected Forster, unoffended.

The cave-temples of Ellora, when Forster eventually visited them with Saeed, seemed to him 'More amazing than anything in a land where much amazes.' His chief impression was that they were diabolic, too diabolic to be beautiful; and since he refused to believe in the devil, he was unmoved by them – they were 'Satanic master-pieces to terrify others.' All the same, he determined to 'do' them thoroughly, staying on alone for a day or two for the purpose. The plan alarmed Saeed, who had seen his casual way of wandering off into pitch-dark cells, heedless of possible leopards or snakes. Anyway, as a Muslim, he had not much use for Hindu antiquities. He tried to dissuade Forster, who, always resenting interference, grew fretful, and they quarrelled. 'Am I irritable & offensive on these occasions?' Forster wondered. Saeed's final shot was: 'You have a wrong idea of the Indians: they are sensitive, but not foolishly sensitive.' This ended hostilities, and by the time of Forster's departure for Bombay – for the time had come for his return to England – they were on the best of terms again. As they parted on the platform Saeed embraced him warmly and garlanded him with marigolds. 'More charm than swagger in the boy,' Forster reflected. 'I like him and hope sense may be ripening in the undergrowth.' In Bombay he planned to buy some cakes, at a famous confectioner's, to send to Saeed, but the boat was leaving early, so he had to hurry aboard and leave his present unbought. 'It's as if I am to do nothing for him, however slight,' he sighed – consoling himself with Saeed's favourite saying, 'The accounts of friends are written in the heart.'

---

he had learned to think better of the British in later years. As for his youthful extravagance, he thought the house in Aurangabad might have given Forster a false impression; in fact they rented it very cheaply.

14 *Maurice*

Forster's letters from India had been studied assiduously at home. Lily would read them aloud to the maids and pass them round among the aunts; Kate and Maggie Preston offered to interpret the Indian references; and Aunt Laura had the letters typed for posterity. Thus his homecoming was quite a little event, and it remained in his memory afterwards as a happy moment in his life with his mother. He always remembered her gasp of joy when, having laid out his India presents in the dining-room, among silks and burning joss-sticks, he had called the maids and her in to view them.

For the first few weeks after his return he felt less imprisoned in his Weybridge existence. India had done much for him, he felt; it had broadened and matured him and distanced him from his youth. Nevertheless it had not done the thing most required; it had not restored his confidence as a novelist. He had formed a scheme for an Indian novel, and over the next few months he got several chapters down on paper, but he then found himself stalled. And before very long, whether as cause or result, he found himself facing his old problems: idleness, sexual frustration and a sense of ineffectiveness. He spent much time in erotic day-dreaming and, on his visits to London, would loiter in Hyde Park or visit public lavatories, half-heartedly hoping to make a pick-up. He refused to feel guilty about this; but it increased his sense of futility, and made him feel how much, for good or evil, he was condemned to self-consciousness. He went to see Nijinsky at Covent Garden, dancing nearly naked in *L'Après-midi d'un faune*, and found him very exciting – 'a humorous and alarming animal, free from the sentimentality of my stories.' It made him dream of missing his train and having adventures all night, but at the back of his mind he was aware of his own eye coldly judging him. Such as his problems were – and he was not always brooding over them – he began to feel they might be insoluble and recorded the fact with detachment: 'Growing sense of my own futility doesn't sadden me, though I shall grow queer & unpopular if I go on as I am now. I lack concentration even at the piano.'[1]

His mother, by now in her late fifties, was becoming crippled with rheumatism, and in September 1913 they decided to go to Harrogate, for her to take a cure. They were to be there for some weeks, and it occurred to Forster that, while in the north, he might pay a visit to Edward Carpenter. He had long planned to do this and had introductions from Dickinson, who was an old friend of Carpenter's; but apart from this, Carpenter's house at Millthorpe was a place of pilgrimage, much frequented by those, like himself, in quest of guidance.

Carpenter, the popularizer of the sandal and the 'Simple Life', was then at the height of his influence. His story was, in some ways, very representative of that of late-Victorian progressives. He had been born of well-to-do upper-middle-class parents, had gone to Cambridge and become a college fellow, taking orders in order to do so; and then, in his late twenties, he had lost his faith. This event made him feel that, not only his beliefs, but his whole way of life, were at fault and what he needed was 'to work down among the mass-people'. Accordingly he left Cambridge, becoming an extra-mural lecturer; and then, in 1883, on the strength of an inheritance, he bought some land at Millthorpe in Derbyshire and set up as a market-gardener – giving up meat-eating and alcohol, and embracing a life of open-air labour, sandal-making and writing. The first fruit of his emancipation was a long Whitmanesque poem, *Towards Democracy*, full of an ardent spiritualized humanism. It won him a following, and from now on, through his writings and his way of life, he became the leading exponent of the 'New Thought' – of Whitmanism, Tolstoyism, William Morris Socialism, Hindu mysticism, neo-paganism and sexual reform. Through books like *The Intermediate Sex* (1908) he campaigned for understanding of the homosexual, or 'Uranian', temperament; and for many visitors the most impressive feature of the Millthorpe household was that he openly lived with a male lover, George Merrill, a young man from the slums of Sheffield.

It is easy to chip away at Carpenter's personality: to say that he

---

[1] Diary, 26 June 1913.

remained parsonical all his life, and that within the serene sage, with
his vaunted 'Uranian' insight, lurked a rather irascible, humourless
and autocratic man, always in a pose of some sort and a very poor
judge of character. (His friend Henry Salt said so, very funnily though
not unkindly, in an obituary 'tribute'.[1]) However, what this misses is
that Carpenter was a healer, who worked through personal and
physical contact: he had what Forster later spoke of as 'the influence
which used to be called magnetic'.

On this first visit to Millthorpe, Forster felt the power intensely.
Carpenter, with his silkily-bearded features and still-youthful body –
though by now he was nearly seventy – conveyed calm and vitality,
He made Forster ashamed of his fidgetiness and self-consciousness.
To Forster's bright, intelligent remarks he would sometimes simply
answer 'Oh do sit quiet,' and Forster felt glad to sit quiet. He had
never before felt such power in another man, and he put it down to
Carpenter's breadth of humanity: 'He touched everyone everywhere.'
Forster liked George Merrill too, in a mild sort of way, though he
doubted if he were as devoted to wholesome toil as Carpenter
believed, and Merrill also touched people – in his case, usually on the
behind. He did so to Forster on this occasion; and his touch, or pinch,
had momentous results. 'The sensation was unusual,' Forster wrote
years later,[2] 'and I still remember it, as I remember the position of a
long vanished tooth. It was as much psychological as physical. It
seemed to go straight through the small of my back into my ideas,
without involving my thoughts. If it really did this, it would have
acted in strict accordance with Carpenter's yogified mysticism, and
would prove that at that precise moment I had conceived.'

What he had conceived was a novel about homosexual love – the
novel *Maurice* in fact. The entire outline, the three main characters
and the happy ending rushed into his mind, vivid and complete. He
went back to Harrogate in a state of exaltation, feeling that the fog
had cleared from his life. It was *this* he had been needing, he decided,
to cure his sterility; and he sat down to work at once. (It was the
only occasion that he would write a novel in this manner, without
lengthy planning and premeditation.) In the intervals of writing, he

---

[1] 'A Sage at Close Quarters', in *Edward Carpenter: an Appreciation*, ed.
Gilbert Beith (1931).
[2] Terminal Note to *Maurice*.

read Samuel Butler's *Life and Habit,* which, with its praise of instinct as the basis of right conduct, lent a kind of support to Carpenter's teaching. He had no intentions of publishing the novel; so long as he lived with his mother he thought it out of the question; and for the moment he did not even plan to show it to anyone. What was necessary, he told himself, was simply to write it.

His exaltation lasted three months and was only checked when, made reckless by it, he lent Dickinson one of his erotic stories. This was a false step, for Dickinson was shocked and disgusted. In Forster's mind, the stories, not being intended as serious literature, had no connection with *Maurice*; nevertheless, for the moment, this threw him back painfully on himself. 'So here I am with 3 unfinished novels on my hands,' he exclaimed in his diary (17 December 1913). 'Even mother must notice I'm played out soon.' He quickly overcame his discouragement, and his New Year's Eve review was chastened but not un-confident.

> To sum up: year has ended with 3 months of exaltation and India has made me more of a 'personage' – more able to defend my sterility against criticism, less swayed by the speaker of the moment. I think this is all. Forward rather than back.
> Edward Carpenter! Edward Carpenter! Edward Carpenter!

A more serious blow followed. He went in March to stay with Meredith, in Bangor, and showed him as much as he had written of *Maurice*, but H.O.M. was bored and indifferent and seemed to want to dismiss the whole subject. Forster, who in his novel had been drawing on memories of himself and Meredith, was wounded – so much so that he considered abandoning the novel. More, it made him reappraise Meredith. He told Florence Barger, 'Hugh can't again be in my life what he has been . . . To turn a hero into a jolly old boy is a ghastly task, but it must be done.'

He overcame this check too, and during the following spring he was very productive, writing his novel at speed as well as producing various articles on Indian themes for the *New Weekly*.[1] Writing was a useful refuge, since, for a month or two, his family life was in confusion. Lily, for some reason, had fallen out with Aunt Rosie, and his cousin Percy joined the quarrel, acting 'madly'. Then in April, Aunt Nellie had an alcoholic breakdown and took refuge with the

---

[1] Among them, the series 'Adrift in India', reprinted in *Abinger Harvest*.

Forsters, leaving her sister Georgie, with whom she lived, to 'sob and rage' in Putney. Forster prayed in his diary: 'O may mother not get ill. G[eorgie] works on her.' He busied himself as a peacemaker and go-between, though warning himself not to make it a principle to live for others; and amidst it all he progressed steadily with *Maurice*. By June he told Florence Barger that he had almost completed a long novel, though it could not be published 'until my death or England's.'

His theory had been that, having completed *Maurice*, his whole situation as a writer would be transformed and he would be able to get on with other creation: he might return to his two unfinished novels or embark on a new one. However, now, to his dismay, he discovered that life had played a trick on him. To have written an unpublishable novel, he found, was no help at all towards producing a publishable one. The realization dawned almost as soon as he had finished *Maurice*, and for the moment it crushed him. He had been depending on creation as his *raison d'être*, telling himself not to be seduced into 'living for others', and now after all it seemed that – in any useful sense – he could not create. Europe meanwhile was on the brink of war, and its onset found him full of self-contempt and irritability.

> *August 1st* . . . Civilisation as it topples carries my brain with it. Can do nothing, rotter that I am, and have *never* been more miserable than today. Irritable and callous. I would go away but for lecture on Butler[1] which I can't do. Perhaps I am ill. Only gaiety is bearable – I see, worthless. Mother is nice to me – I had to tell her my work is all wrong.
> *August 3rd* . . . Irritated not with war but with my relation to it. Narrowing circle of light. Mother happier since I confided I feel done up, & couldn't work, but respects me less.
> *August 4th* White faced boys guard the railway or walk arrogantly about . . .
> Wonder if I could get work in hospital.
> Feel the war exists on my account. If I died it would stop, but it is here to give me experiences if I choose to receive them.

He took the coming of war as a sign that, for the time being, he must give up all hope of creation; and as a token of this he decided to find a job: it would justify him in other people's eyes, and perhaps in

---

[1] He was due to give a lecture on Samuel Butler to the Ulster Arts Club, on a forthcoming visit to Hugh Meredith.

his own, too, and moreover he needed the money. He made inquiries here and there, and a Weybridge friend, Sir Charles Holroyd, who was Director of the National Gallery, offered him a post as a cataloguer at the gallery. The job entailed four days' work a week, plus an occasional night of firewatching. The more valuable paintings were being put in store. Thus, as he told his friends, if he were killed by bombs, he would die, appropriately, among second-rate masterpieces.

Volume Two

Polycrates' Ring

1914–1970

1 Facing Facts

The outbreak of the 1914–18 war found Forster in disarray, irritated and driven in upon himself. He was doubly disturbed – by the war itself, and by the inadequacy of his own response to it. He felt sure, indeed, that it was an unjust and unnecessary war, and so did his Cambridge and Bloomsbury friends. There was a general feeling on the part of the Bloomsbury group that it was not *their* war, and that all they had stood for, the new age of tolerance and enlightenment inaugurated in G. E. Moore's Cambridge, was about to be destroyed. Almost all were pacifists of one persuasion or another – some, like Bertrand Russell, militantly so – and in the week or two before the declaration of war they had been busy in the neutralist and anti-war cause. The war bound 'Bloomsbury' together, more than before, as a conscious *élite* and for a time a much-hated one. Russell later recalled sitting in a bus, soon after the outbreak of war, and reflecting: 'These people would tear me to pieces if they knew what I think about the war.'[1]

Forster, to the extent that he was a pacifist, was so by instinct rather than settled conviction. He was impressed by E. D. Morel and his Union of Democratic Control and distributed a few of the U.D.C.'s anti-war pamphlets, but his principal emotion was despair; he foresaw Britain handed over to all that he most feared – to panic and herd-instinct, to slogans and bogus 'cheeriness'. Nevertheless, for the moment he aligned himself wholeheartedly with his Bloomsbury friends. He guessed that there would have to be a 'sorting' of his friendships, and when his friend Malcolm Darling, in the Indian

---

[1] 'Some Psychological Difficulties of Pacifism in Wartime', in *We Did Not Fight*, ed. Julian Bell (1935).

Civil Service, wrote him a letter full of fire-breathing anti-Germanism, he feared for their relationship. 'I never would have been intimate with that pair if they hadn't been so sound about sex,' he reflected; 'and it's only a chance they are sound.' He wrote Malcolm a tart reply, meant also for his wife Josie's eyes, saying that Malcolm found in war what he had put there. Josie Darling came on a visit to England near the end of 1914, and she and Forster talked of the war. She thought him a 'dreamer' on the subject and challenged him to 'face facts'. 'Don't say "face facts" to me, Josie,' he answered, passionately. 'Everybody keeps saying it just now; but the fact is, it's impossible to face facts. They're like the walls of a room, all round you. If you face one wall, you must have your back to the other three.'

He pinned his hopes for the future, such as they were, upon friendship, as the sphere where decent feeling might survive. Recently he made a new acquaintance, with a schoolmaster named Lawrence Shuttleworth, a diffident and self-tormenting man, who, from some desire to 'test' himself, had enlisted as a trooper. Shuttleworth was eager for intimacy, and Forster, who feared for him, did his best to give it. They had an emotional conversation in the Café Royal, while Shuttleworth was on leave, in the course of which Forster said that it was not happiness one longed for but peace. Shuttleworth agreed.

> Long silence – during which did I feel happiness or peace? Another day we parted. He said 'You've been very good to me.' I, 'I know I wanted to.' He nodded. I: 'It's outside the category of give and take.' – As a trooper he has come near something real – had no one beneath him, and loved not 'the poor when they're nice' but the poor. I'm convinced he will be killed at the war – it is almost assumed in all either says. Have never seen my self ennobled in anyone before.[1]

Something of these feelings entered into a paper on 'Literature and the War' which he delivered to the Weybridge Literary Society near the end of the year, and subsequently at the Working Men's College. In his paper he argued that wartime was – as many were rightly saying – no time for reading; but it was a time for remembering what one had read, for learning more from great literature.

---

[1] Diary, 11 November 1914. Shuttleworth survived the war but committed suicide in 1925, a day after the death of his wife.

Literature does not teach us that War is either right or wrong,
these are questions outside our competence – but she does teach us
that hatred and revenge are wrong because they cloud the spirit.
It is not easy to love one's enemies – for my own part I find it
impossible – but one needn't be proud of not loving them, and she
does exhort us to that much. Love is an emotion, hatred an
excitement, and she is against excitement all along the line . . .
Such seems to me her [literature's] function in war time. She helps
us to abstain from fear and hatred, as far as our small minds will
permit . . . Against all such hysteria the voice of the immortal dead
protests . . . They have become one with Urania, the muse of
Divine Song, who has given them not happiness but peace.

His lecture, printed in the *Working Men's College Journal* reached
Rupert Brooke in the Dardanelles in March of the following year,
and Brooke wrote irritably about it to his friend Ka Cox.

It's odd seeing what the chrysalises think. You see I'm in it, and
the Ranee[1] (say)'s in it. But Forster's pathetically – where – on a
hundred verges: or behind them. But he seems far nicer than most
of them, though pathetically – outside. (The very point of war is
that it brings out their exteriority – which they have everywhere,
in the peacefullest of 1913 luncheons and nightmares.) They're like
nice and nasty children outside a circus, who alternately try to
peep under the flaps and explain to each other how they despise
circuses . . . he's nice about the soul of man. But ah! doesn't he
suspect that the nobilities he whinnies for, come out more in war
than in peace?

*   *   *

At the beginning of the war, Forster had decided that creation –
that is to say fiction – was for the moment impossible for him. As a
substitute, he resolved, in the autumn of 1914, to write a critical book
on Samuel Butler. (He was perhaps encouraged in this by Forrest
Reid, who had recently published such a book on W. B. Yeats.)
Butler had long been an interest of Forster's. *Erewhon*, he felt, was
a book that he might have written himself; and in *Howards End*
his handling of the money-theme, the Schlegel frankness about
money that so shocks the Wilcoxes, owed much to Butler.[2] His
interest had been quickened, too, when he met Butler's friend and
biographer, Henry Festing Jones. Jones had written to him in praise
of *Howards End* and had had 'incredible' things to relate about

[1] Family nickname of Brooke's mother.
[2] Mr Emerson in *A Room With a View* is probably partly based on Butler.

Butler.[1] Edward Arnold was encouraging about his project, and in December Forster negotiated a contract for it, bargaining rather toughly – so much so that Arnold said he hoped he didn't feel he was being exploited. Forster noted coolly in his diary: 'I have not been straight with him [Arnold], but do not mind.' For a little while the book interested him, but soon, in his words, 'a chill descended'. By June of the next year he had to tell Arnold that he was giving up 'in despair'.

His mother and he had taken in a Belgian refugee, a young man named Jules Quilley. He arrived at 'Harnham', their house in Weybridge, in November but did not last long, for Lily took against him, complaining that he ate up all the marmalade and never stopped playing the piano. After a few weeks Forster had to give him notice, at which Lily began to feel compunctious; Forster noted (15 December 1914): 'Mother interests herself in behaving well to Jules, while her heart harbours bitterness.' He felt it was a fitting end to a 'galling, undignified summer', and in his New Year's Eve review he found few gains to record to set against the year's losses. Among the gains was a closer intimacy with Lowes Dickinson, whom he still met often in Cambridge or London. 'I have drawn him to me,' he observed; 'it is odd to exercise power upon one whom one respects, and, tiresomely, doesn't increase the respect. The war has shattered him and inspired little more than a whimper. He feels himself old. – All the same, we are on a basis of comradeship at last.' He had shown Dickinson his homosexual novel, *Maurice*, completed earlier that year, and, to his enormous relief, Dickinson admired the book hugely. There were one or two more gains, like his new friendship with Shuttleworth; but against them had to be set the loss of Masood, who had got married during the year. Forster acknowledged an end to this chapter in his feelings:

> He never writes and I think of him seldom. There used never to pass a day. When I see him something, but not all, will revive. He stands at the close of my youth. I wish very much he had felt, if only once, what I felt for him, for I should have no sense of wasted time.

Early in the second year of the war, Forster's life received an unexpected enlargement. 'Oh my dear Reid, I have been in the most

---

[1] Presumably about his sex-life, which seems – in part anyway – to have been homosexual.

awful gloom lately,' he wrote to Forrest Reid (23 January 1915),
'and who do you think finally raised me from it? You will be so
contemptuous of me.[1] D. H. Lawrence. Not the novels, but their
author, a sandy haired passionate Nibelung, whom I met last
Thursday at a dinner party. He is really extraordinarily nice.' The
meeting had taken place at Lady Ottoline Morrell's. Lawrence was
her latest discovery, and the dinner party had been to 'launch'
Lawrence and Frieda. She had seated Forster and Lawrence together,
and they had taken greatly to each other. Lawrence had monopolized
the conversation; but Forster, when disposed, was an admirable
listener, and he had found Lawrence and his views wonderfully
attractive. He was, Forster had thought, so human, so personal; he
lived his views, with none of that pose of detachment that bored him
in Cambridge philosophizing. They had parted with the expectation
of meeting again the next day, Duncan Grant having invited them,
and others present, to tea in his studio. Meanwhile Forster wrote to
Lawrence, pursuing their dinner-table conversation, and repeating
the answers which – so he complained – Lawrence had refused to
listen to.

Lawrence and Frieda had recently moved to Greatham in Sussex,
where Viola Meynell had lent them a cottage. Lawrence was in the
process of systematizing his 'philosophy'. He had also, the previous
autumn, drawn up the constitution of his Utopia, Rananim, and was
on the look-out for recruits. He was thus, even more than usually, in
a proselytizing mood. Forster, who had found him so endearing, saw
a new side of him at their meeting in Duncan Grant's studio, when
Lawrence began a ferocious tirade against Grant's painting. It
rather alarmed Forster, who slipped away after a few minutes,
murmuring excuses about trains. Lawrence, however, when he came
to answer Forster's letter, was in a gentle frame of mind.

> Dear Forster,
>   Don't expect any sort of answer or attention from me today,
> because everything is so strange & I feel as if I'd just come out
> of the shell & hadn't got any feathers to protect me from the
> weather. It is very snowy here, & rather beautiful.
>   Will you come down next week-end & stay with us? I think

---

[1] Reid was scornful of Lawrence, as he was of most contemporary writers
apart from Yeats and Walter de la Mare.

nobody else will be here. As for my not listening to your answers, I've got a deep impression that you never made any.

I've only read one or two stories of yours, & should like *very much* to have the Celestial Omnibus.

This cottage is rather fine – a bit monastic – it was a cattle shed – now it is like a monks' refectory – the whole establishment is cloistral.

I'm glad you're not really Buddhistic – everybody said you were, I want somebody to come & make a league with me to sing the Chanson des Chansons – das Hohe Lied – and to war against the fussy Mammon, that pretends to be a tame pet now, & so devours us in our sleep.

But do come at the week end.

A weekend did not suit Forster, and he proposed coming some mid-week, meanwhile sending a copy of *The Celestial Omnibus*. Lawrence rejoined (28 January 1915) with a powerful homily, very definitely now suggesting a league between them and offering him membership of Rananim.

Very well, come when you can. I am so obsessed by this idea that you are always at the National Gallery,[1] like an attendant or a recording angel, that I can't conceive you free during the week. Come tomorrow or Monday or Tuesday or Wednesday or when you will – and stay one or two nights – as you will. Only let me know & say if you can walk 4 miles – & I'll meet you at Pulborough.

I don't belong to any class, now. As for your class, do you think it could tempt me? If I'm one of any lot, I am one of the common people. But I feel as if I'd known all classes now, & so am free of all . . .

In my Island, I wanted people to come without class or money, sacrificing nothing, but each coming with all his desires, yet knowing that his life is but a tiny section of a whole, so that he shall fulfil his life in relation to the whole. I wanted a real community, not built out of abstinence or equality, but out of many fulfilled individualities seeking greater fulfilment.

But I can't find anybody. Each man is so bent on his own private fulfilment – either he wants love of a woman, & can't get it complete, or he wants to influence his fellow men (for their good, of course), or he wants to satisfy his own soul with regard to his position in eternity. And they make me tired, these friends of

---

[1] Forster, at the outbreak of war, had taken a post as part-time cataloguer at the National Gallery. (See Vol. 1, p. 260.)

mine. They seem so childish & greedy; always the immediate
desire, always the particular outlook, no conception of the whole
horizon wheeling round.

What do you want for yourself? You used to want the fulfilment
of the natural animal in you – which is after all only an immediate
need. So you made the immediate need seem the ultimate necessity
– so you belied & betrayed yourself. I don't know where you've
got to after Howards End.

Don't think this priggish & conceited. I do feel every man must
have the devil of a struggle before he can have stuffed himself
full enough to have satisfied all his immediate needs, & can give
up, cease, & withdraw himself, yield himself up to his metamor-
phosis, his crucifixion, & so come to his new issuing, his wings,
his resurrection, his whole flesh shining like a mote in the sunshine,
fulfilled and now taking part in the fulfilment of the whole.

So I feel frightfully like weeping in a corner – not over myself –
but perhaps my own resurrection is too new, one must feel if the
scars are not there, & wince, & one must see the other people all
writhing & struggling & unable to give up.

How can there be a Celestial Omnibus? Is that satire? – like the
spiritual perambulators of a parson I knew – 'All of you want
wheeling to heaven in a spiritual perambulator' he said.

You are to take all this quite seriously.

There developed now quite a little imbroglio, for Frieda, in-
advisedly, had added a postscript. It ran:

This is a very angelic letter but I know the flapping of wings won't
quite make you overlook the little twisted horns and the hoof –
I thought you were 'good' to people – you listen so carefully, it
frightened me, because so many things are said thoughtlessly –
and you still listen with the whole of you – It is good of you. – I
have only read your Where Angels Fear to Tread, & felt like
turning somersaults and loved it – So you will come soon – I am
quite miserable over the Brontë sisters that I am reading – How
fond they were of each other.
                                    Yours sincerely,
                                    Frieda Lawrence.

A double act on the part of man and wife did not suit Forster, and
he replied tartly, refusing to 'have dealings with a firm'. Nevertheless,
he named a day for his visit (10 February) and lent them more of his
books.

Letters returned promptly from both the Lawrences. Lawrence's
own (3 February 1915) resumed the attack on Forster's life-aims:

. . . I have just read the Story of a Panic. You with your 'Only Connect' motto, I must say that you reach the limit of splitness here. You are bumping your nose on the end of the cul de sac.

My angels & devils are nothing compared with your Pan. Don't you see Pan is the undifferentiated root & stem drawing out of unfathomable darkness, & my Angels & Devils are old-fashioned symbols for the flower into which we strive to burst. Now no plant can live towards the root. That is the most split, perverse thing of all.

You see I know all about your Pan. He is not dead, he is the same forever. But you should not confuse him with universal love, as you tend to do. You are very confused. You give Pan great attributes of Christ.

All that dark, concentrated, complete, all-containing surge of which I am the fountain, and of which the well-head is my loins, is urging forward, like a plant to flower or a fountain to its parabola. And my angels and devils are a sort of old-fashioned flowering. I am just in love with medieval terms, that is all – & Fra Angelico & Cimabue & the Saints.

But your Pan is a stooping back to the well-head, a perverse pushing back the waters to their source, & saying the source is everything. Which is stupid & an annihilation – but very stupid. In these books, these last, you are intentional and perverse & not vitally interesting. One must live from the source, through all the racings & heats of Pan, and on to my beloved angels & devils, with their aureoles & their feet upon the flowers of lights, & with their red-mouthed despairs and destructions. However, we wait till you come. Don't be alarmed – I seem to 'stunt' because I use old terms for my feeling, because I am not inventive or creative enough.

> Auf wiedersehn,
> D. H. Lawrence

Frieda's letter (5 February 1915) was half-Lawrentian, half-diplomatic:

Thank you for Howards End – It got hold of me and not being a critical person I thank the Lord for it, and what he gives me. Only perhaps the end – broken Henrys remain Henrys as I know to my cost – It's a beautiful book, but now you must go further – We had violent discussions of your letters, L. and I – (Three cheers for the 'firm'.) What ails you modern men is that you put too high a value on ready-made consciousness, on the revealed things; because you cannot utter the 'unutterable' you are inclined to say it does not exist – Hope and that sort of thing is *not* your strong point – You are so frightened of being let down, as if one couldn't get up again! – As to the firm you *did* hit a little sore point with me – Poor author's wife, who does her little best and everybody wishes her to Jericho – Poor second fiddle, the surprise at her existence! She goes on playing her little accompaniment so bravely! Tut – tut, tra-la-la! Thank you again for Howards End, it had a bucking-up effect on me!

> Yours sincerely,
> die zweite Flöte
> And come soon.

Further messages followed, and Forster reached Greatham pleasantly keyed up, expecting much and feeling that much was expected of him. He had come for three days, and during the first day, again found Lawrence enchanting. Lawrence took him for a long walk on the downs, talking brilliantly and feelingly about his childhood and family – every now and then breaking off to look at birds or to pick catkins. In the evening, the three painted bee-boxes,[1] which was the Lawrences' craze just then. 'A fascinating employ-ment,' Forster wrote to Florence Barger (12 February 1915). 'You can be as post-impressionist or as virginal as you choose, and in any case all is over in an hour, and the design, if a failure, can be painted out in black, and recommenced.' He had brought a rumour that Boot's Library were refusing to supply Lawrence's *The Prussian Officer* and that Sir Jesse Boot, when pressed about it, sent sub-scribers a private copy in a special binding, so that they could see how disgusting the book was.[2] Lawrence raged at this and railed rather madly against 'respectability', but Forster felt much sympathy. 'I am getting awfully revolutionary in my old age,' he told Florence.

The second day turned out differently, for Lawrence was in a prophetic and denunciatory mood. He preached the need for a revolution, for the immediate nationalizing of industry, and the land, and the press. Then he began an attack on Forster, an interminable diatribe against his books, his philosophy, his whole way of life. In a way, Forster had been prepared for this, but not for the violence of it, which rather frightened him. He listened patiently, however; and when Lawrence insisted that, in order to come to life, he must change his whole existence, he merely asked, ruefully, 'How do you

---

[1] Boxes in which bees are transported.

[2] The ban, if it occurred, was probably motivated by anti-Germanism as much as prudery and may have looked forward to later police suspicions concerning the Lawrences' loyalty.

9

know I'm not dead?' Finally, after many hours of denunciation, he asked Lawrence if there were anything, anything at all, in his books that he could praise, and Lawrence, surprisingly, said yes, the character of Leonard Bast in *Howards End*.

It had been the confrontation that Forster had anticipated, and it left him angry but impressed, for he could see he counted for much in Lawrence's eyes, and he determined to be neither rattled nor conciliatory. Having heard Lawrence out – it was now late in the evening – he grasped his candlestick, muttering that he wasn't sure the Lawrences weren't 'just playing round his knees', and went to bed without saying goodnight. Lawrence liked this behaviour and wrote that night to his friend Barbara Low about him.

> Forster is here. He is very nice. I wonder if the grip has gone out of him.
>
> I get a feeling of acute misery from him – not that he does anything – but you know the acute, exquisite pain of cramp – I somehow feel that. I think I must get it by transference from him. He is going away in the morning. We have talked so hard – about a revolution – at least I have talked – it is my fate, God help me – and now I wonder, are my words gone like seed spilt on a hard floor, only reckoned an untidiness there. I must tell you I am very sad, as if it hurt very much.

Next day (12 February 1915) he also wrote to Bertrand Russell:

> We have had E. M. Forster here for three days. There is more in him than ever comes out. But he is not dead yet. I hope to see him pregnant with his own soul . . . He sucks his dummy – you know, those child's comforters – long after his age. But there is something very real in him, if he will not cause it to die. He is *much* more than his dummy-sucking, clever little habits allow him to be . . .
>
> Forster . . . is bound hand and foot bodily. Why? *Because he does not believe that any beauty or any divine utterance is any good any more.* Why? Because the world is suffering from bonds, and birds of foul desire which gnaw its liver. Forster knows, as every thinking man knows, that all his thinking and his passion for humanity amounts to no more than trying to soothe with poetry a man raging with pain which can be cured. Cure the pain, don't give the poetry. Will all the poetry in the world satisfy the manhood of Forster, when Forster knows that his implicit manhood is to be satisfied by nothing but immediate physical action. He tries to dodge himself – the sight is pitiful.
>
> But why can't he act? Why can't he take a woman and fight

clear to his own basic, primal being? Because he knows that self-realization is not his ultimate desire. His ultimate desire is for the continued action which has been called the social passion – the love for humanity – the desire to work for humanity.

True to his determination to take the quarrel seriously, Forster, on his return home, wrote the Lawrences a tough and rather rude letter, saying he had not enjoyed his stay. Lawrence was hurt, telling Forster 'Some things you should not say in your letters', and Frieda tried her hand at conciliation.

Dear Mr Forster,
   I have just read the book that came this morning – and I am still in the rotten hut of the decayed village where the last woman is crumbling to bits! And the boar with the big tusks coming in! It's grim, thank you for sending it – Your letter was not very nice – Of course you like us, even if you don't admit it. Neither L nor I are tout le monde, and what he preaches to you is just exactly what you say yourself in your books – But you are a suspicious person like Leonard Bast – Why? I have had such jolly conversations with you since you went, you weren't there to answer! No, you don't do L. or his work justice. God knows he is a fool, and undeveloped, but he is so genuine, a genuine force, inhuman like one also – and such a strain; but you ought to help him, he is really very inarticulate and *unformed* – Russell says of you, I expected great things of him – it makes me cross, they give up hope so soon, but it must be his own hopelessness that makes him doubt you – I felt you by no means dead and enjoyed your stay awfully and you ought to have enjoyed it more! Or have you the bad taste to prefer your Weybridge liter-society? I am sure you are a wonder to them and you are spoilt – very spoilt – And you are not to be suspicious – . . . L. is in London, so this is not a joint letter – I am *not* going to ask you to come again, you will have to come of your own free will – You are *not* to mind L's 'customs beastly, manners none'; think, *I* have to put up with them, and they have improved! I think you are both vile with each other, it was all the time on the brink of quarreling – watching each other like two tomcats! And there is the spring coming, and I feel so bruised and battered and I do so want to enjoy him (the spring) to the full! . . .

Lawrence, meanwhile, had inveighed to Lady Ottoline against Forster – or rather, against Forster's attitude to him, which he attributed partly to class-snobbery. She was excited, picturing herself in the role of peacemaker, and passed on Lawrence's complaint to Forster, and he replied asking her to tell Lawrence that he did not despise him.

> It's annoying enough that he should think this – it's worse he should think it's the contempt of the semi-detached villa for the cottage: I've looked up to the class that produced him for many years now.

Lady Ottoline then invited them together to her house, and they quickly made up their quarrel, while, unaware of this, she wandered from one to the other saying it was 'so dreadful' that two such writers should quarrel, then sighing 'I'm making it worse.'[1]

The friendship, in fact, had developed as far as it ever would. Lawrence wrote Forster no more long letters, though Frieda continued to, nor did he think any more of a 'league' between them. There was an incompatibility between them, partly to do with self-consciousness. Forster thought Lawrence too un-self-aware, or perhaps deliberately self-blinding. For one thing, or so Forster thought, Lawrence ignored his own homosexual side.[2] Forster wrote to Dent (6 March 1915) asking him if he had read Lawrence's *The White Peacock*:

> If not, do not, for you cannot, but read one chapter in it called a Poem of Friendship, which is most beautiful. The whole book is the queerest product of subconsciousness that I have yet struck – he has not a glimmering from first to last of what he's up to.

The blindness made for absurdity in their own relations. There was something stupid in being told by Lawrence to come to Rananim with his 'woman'. In addition, Forster found Frieda rather much to swallow. And a further wedge was driven between the two when, at some encounter, Lawrence spoke offensively about Edward Carpenter. It made Forster 'realize, with regret, that I cannot know him [i.e. Lawrence].'

Lawrence remained in a way attached to Forster and curious about him. In June he sent Forster 'The Crown', his philosophical testament, saying 'I can trust you to take me seriously, and really to read. Because whatever I may be, you *do* listen.' And Forster,

---

[1] Letter from Forster to Hilton Young, 4 March 1915.

[2] Forster did not do Lawrence justice here; see the remarkable suppressed Introduction to *Women in Love* published in *Phoenix II* (1968), pp. 92–108.

for his part, continued to do various commissions for the Lawrences, buying drawing-paper for Frieda and canvassing orders for their bee-boxes. (They were turning them to profit.) In the autumn, when Hugh Meredith published a volume of poems, Forster sent Lawrence a copy, and on the strength of this Meredith paid Lawrence a visit in Hampstead. Lawrence was amused by his self-dramatizing manner, reporting to Forster:

> He led off by saying 'I'm tired of language, both written and spoken.' Of course, after that, what was to be done? I asked him to turn cart wheels in the passage, or to gambol & bark like a dog on the rug. But he didn't rise to the occasion.
> Then suddenly he appeared at eleven at night,[1] the same night, for no reason whatever, and we talked till one o'clock. He says he's going mad. I say it's very undistinguished, because most folks are. We have a fireworky sort of conversation.
> There's no earthly reason why he *should* go mad, except the important one, that he wants to.

To Meredith himself he wrote a letter in apocalyptic vein, ending:

> One must try to save the quick, to send up the new shoots of a new era: a great utter revolution, and the dawn of a new historical epoch: either that or the vast amorphous dust. I can make nothing of the men, they are all dead. E.M. is dead *und schon verweste*. Perhaps the women – God knows, it is enough to send one mad.

*   *   *

The collision with Lawrence had one immediate effect on Forster; it made him determine to be more open in expressing feeling. Shuttleworth, one day when they were parting, said he thought he might commit suicide, and Forster answered him 'I'm not even here to tell you not to do that, but do realize that I love you.' Afterwards he reflected, 'It was my dressing down at the Lawrences that helped me to do this.' Similarly, it emboldened him to show *Maurice* to various friends, among them Dent, Forrest Reid and Lytton Strachey. Dent was enthusiastic, and Forster's confidence began to grow. 'You can scarcely imagine the loneliness of such an effort as this – a year's work!' he told Dent (6 March 1915).

---

[1] Calling uninvited was a Cambridge habit of Meredith's, which he practised till the end of his life. He would sometimes startle friends in Belfast by appearing at their house at breakfast-time.

> How one longs for praise shamelessly! You have given me the
> greatest comfort and pleasure. I wrote it neither for my friends nor
> the public, but because it was weighing on me: and my previous
> training made me write it as literature . . . I am much dependent
> on criticism, and now, backed by you and some others, do feel
> that I have created something absolutely new, even to the Greeks.

To Reid he sent the novel with trepidation, fearing that he might
be shocked; and, in fact the physical love-making in the novel,
though shadowy, did shock him, or at all events did not suit him.
Oddly, too, he claimed never even to have realized that Forster was
homosexual. Forster was roused to defence of the novel:

> I do want to raise these subjects out of the mists of theology:
> Male and Female created He not them. Ruling out underdeveloped
> people like Clive – or your youth, whom you advised most rightly
> – one is left with 'perverts' (an absurd word, because it assumes
> they were given a choice, but let's use it). Are these 'perverts'
> good or bad like normal men, their disproportionate tendency to
> badness (which I admit) being due to the criminal blindness of
> Society? Or are they inherently bad? You answer, as I do, that
> they are the former, but you answer with reluctance. I want you
> to answer *vehemently*! The man in my book is, roughly speaking,
> good, but Society nearly destroys him, he nearly slinks through
> his life furtive and afraid, and burdened with a sense of sin. You
> say 'if he had not met another man like him, what then?' What
> indeed? But blame Society not Maurice, and be thankful even in
> a novel when a man is left to lead the best life he is capable of
> leading!
>   This brings me to another point, and having gone bang at it,
> I will say farewell to sociology. Is it ever right that such a relation
> should include the physical? Yes – sometimes. If both people want
> it and both are old enough to know what they want – yes. I used
> not to think this, but now do. Maurice and Clive would have been
> wrong, Maurice and Dicky more so, M. and A. are all right, some
> people might never be right.
>   I know very well that argument does little, but perhaps it clears
> the air – we see better than before where we are fated to dwell.
> I've a world of the spirit that touches yours in places, but it trails
> down into earthly desires where we are severed, and though they
> tether me I don't even *want* to renounce those earthly desires. My
> defence at any Last Judgement would be 'I was trying to connect
> up and use all the fragments I was born with' – well you had it
> exhaustingly in Howards End, and Maurice, though his fragments
> are more scanty and more bizarre than Margaret's, is working at
> the same job.[1]

---

[1] Letter to Forrest Reid, 13 March 1915.

As for Lytton Strachey, Forster hardly hoped for his approval, knowing how little sentimentality, or at least his own version of it, was in Strachey's line. However, to his surprise, Lytton gave him high praise, mixed with some extremely sensible criticism.

> I enjoyed it very much indeed – I think really more than the others. The absence of the suburb-culture question was a relief. I wish I could talk to you about it – the difficulty and boredom of epistolary explanations is rather great.
>
> Qua story, first – I thought it seemed to go off at the end to some extent. The beginning – especially up to the successful combination of Maurice and Clive – I liked very much: it appeared solid and advanced properly from point to point. The psychology of both excellent. The Maurice-Alec affair didn't strike me as so successful. For one thing, the Class question is rather a red herring, I think. One suddenly learns that Maurice is exaggeratedly upper-classish – one wouldn't at all have expected it on the face of things – and then when the change comes, it seems to need more explanation. No doubt his falling in love with Alec was possible, but it's certainly queer as it happens – partly because the ground isn't enough prepared: and Alec's feelings I don't quite seize. As you describe it, I should be inclined to diagnose Maurice's state as simply lust and sentiment – a very wobbly affair; I should have prophesied a rupture after 6 months – chiefly as a result of lack of common interests owing to class differences – I believe even such a simple-minded fellow as Maurice would have felt this – and so your Sherwood Forest ending appears to me slightly mythical.[1] Perhaps it simply is that the position isn't elaborated enough. The writing gets staccato (for the first time) at the end of Ch. xliv – just at the crisis. 'Adamantine', too, can't be right.
>
> This is my main criticism of the story – I wonder if you'll see anything in it. A minor point is that I find it *very* difficult to believe that Maurice would have remained chaste during those 2 years with Clive. He was a strong healthy youth, and you say that, unless Clive had restrained him 'he would have surfeited passion' (Ch. xv). But how the Dickens could Clive restrain him? How could he have failed to have erections? Et après ça – ? Well! I suppose it's just conceivable, but I must say I think you seem to take it rather too much as a matter of course.
>
> I admire the cleverness very much. The opening scene with

---

[1] In the first version the novel contained an epilogue, set some years later, in which Maurice's sister Kitty encounters him and the gamekeeper Alec still living happily together and working as woodcutters – the world well lost. Forster's friends united in finding it preposterous, and taking their advice he suppressed it.

Mr Ducie is very good, and his reappearance 10 years later. The upper class conversations and that awful household in the country – how can you do it? Then the ingenuity of the machinery – e.g. the piano-moving incident – seems to me . . . 'supreme'! I like enormously Alec's letters. Is it true that the lower classes use 'share' in that sense? – I must find out.

There remains the general conception – about which I don't feel at all certain. I don't understand why the copulation question should be given so much importance. It's difficult to distinguish clearly your views from Maurice's sometimes, but so far as I can see, you go much too far in your disapproval of it. For instance, you apparently regard the Dickie incident with grave disapproval. Why? Then, à propos of Maurice tossing himself off (you call it a 'malpractice') (Ch. xxxii), you say – 'He knew what the price would be – a creeping apathy towards all things.' How did Maurice know that? And how do you? Surely the truth is that as often as not the effects are simply nil. Also (Ch. xxxi) you describe Maurice's thoughts in the railway carriage as 'ill-conditioned' – which appears to me the sort of word Mr Herbert Pembroke would have used.

It almost seems that you mean to indicate that Maurice's copulating with Alec is somehow *justified* by his falling in love with him. This alarms me considerably. I find the fatal sentence inserted (Ch. xliii – British Museum) – 'he loved Alec, loved him not as a second Dickie Barry, but deeply, tenderly, for his own sake, etc.' More distressing still, there is never a hint afterwards that Maurice's self-reproaches during that period were exaggerated. I think he had still a great deal to learn, and that the très-très-noble Alec could never teach it to him. What was wanted was a brief honeymoon with that charming young Frenchman who would have shown Mr Eel that it was possible to take the divagations of a prick too seriously.

Another thing is – perhaps even more important – that you really do make a difference between affairs between men and men and those between men and women. The chastity between Maurice and Clive for the 2 years during which they were in effect married you consider (a) as a very good thing and (b) as nothing *very* remarkable. You then make Clive marry (without any change in his high-falutin' views) and promptly, quite as a matter of course, have his wife. (So that when he said to Maurice 'I love you as if you were a woman,' he was telling a lie.) I really think the whole conception of male copulation in the book rather diseased – in fact morbid and unnatural. The speechification by which Maurice refuses to lie with Alec on the last night – no! – That is a sort of self-consciousness which would *only* arise when people were *not* being natural. It is surely beastly to think of copulation on such

an occasion – shall we copulate? shall we not? ought we to? etc. –
All one can think of is that one must embrace.
  I could write a great deal more – especially about 'the triviality
of contact for contact's sake' – but it's too difficult, and I feel half
the time that you have satisfactory answers. I wish we could talk.
I hope to be in London before very long. I hope this critique isn't
too much of a good thing, and will fit in nicely along with those of
Bob Trevy, Waterlow and Hilton Young.[1]

Forster replied that he found himself agreeing with Lytton more
than he would have liked. And, writing to Dickinson (13 December
1914), he put his finger on a central weakness in the novel, its wish-
fulfilment element, which lay deep in his whole motive for writing it:

  I might have been wiser to let that also [the Alec Scudder part of
  the novel] resolve into dust or mist, but the temptation's overwhelming to grant one's creations a happiness actual life does not
  supply. 'Why not?' I kept thinking. 'A little rearrangement, rather
  better luck' – but no doubt the rearrangement's fundamental.

He was by now seeing a good deal of Strachey. He would go to
stay with him at his cottage, The Lacket, in Wiltshire, and sometimes
Strachey would spend the day in London with Forster, visiting galleries. Strachey seemed to have revised his opinion of him, for the
better; Forster pretended to wonder if it was senility. In September
he went down to The Lacket for a weekend, at a time when Strachey,
not feeling he could face another country winter, was about to
abandon Wiltshire for London. 'By a stroke of genius,' Lytton reported to his brother James, he got Forster to stay behind and pack
for him, while he went off to visit other friends. Forster also cut his
hair for him. 'Your hair was a real weight off me,' Forster wrote to
him (27 September). They were now on very frank and comfortable
terms, and during the weekend they had talked a good deal about
Maurice and homosexual life. It gave Forster, afterwards, a twinge
of apprehension, and he warned Strachey: 'Oh, but do *not*, by the
way, reveal aught of me to the Lady O. [i.e. Ottoline], whom I
regard as a very high explosive, nor indeed to anyone.'

                    *   *   *

  His links with 'Bloomsbury' had grown stronger. He had got on to
friendly, if not intimate terms, with Virginia Woolf, and when her

[1] Letter to Forster, 12 March 1915.

novel, *The Voyage Out*, was published in the spring of 1915, he reviewed it in the *Daily News*, hailing it as a masterpiece. The book had chimed with his wishes for his own fiction, his desire for something more visionary, less restricted by satire and 'suburban' comedy. He wrote in his review: 'Human relations are no substitute for adventure because when real they are uncomfortable, and when comfortable they must be unreal. It is for a voyage into solitude that man was created.' Virginia Woolf, desperate for reassurance about her work, as she always continued to be, was profoundly grateful for his praise and from now on became very dependent on his opinion. He intrigued her as a person, too. She was impressed by his penetration and vision, and amused by the contrast between them and his old-maidish way of life. 'I saw Forster, who is timid as a mouse, but when he creeps out of his hole very charming,' she wrote to Margaret Llewellyn Davies (21 August 1915). 'He spends his time rowing old ladies upon the river, and isn't able to get on with his novel.' She liked him a good deal – rather more than, in his heart, he liked her. Throughout their friendship, which lasted till her death, he felt the need to be on his guard with her. 'One waited for her to snap,' he put it later. In the course of the last two years she had had several serious spells of insanity, and during her convalescence after one of these, Leonard Woolf invited Forster to lend her *Maurice*. He found an excuse for refusing.

*   *   *

The war, and the war-fever, weighed on him. In the May of 1915 he developed chicken-pox and was plunged into 'one of the simpler forms of war-malady', able to think of nothing but young men killing one another while old men praised them. He sent the Darlings the current war-gossip, about Zeppelin-raids and submarines, but, he told Josie Darling (20 June 1915), England was seeming to him 'tighter and tinier and shinier than ever – a very precious little party, I don't doubt, but most insistently an island, and there are times when one longs to sprawl over continents, as formerly'. Malcolm asked for his opinion of Rupert Brooke, whose death at Gallipoli in April had stirred so much patriotic emotion. His answer (2 August 1915) was sympathetic but debunking.

> You ask about *Rupert Brooke*. Considering we were on Christian names terms, I did not know him well, though enough to contradict the legends that the press are weaving round him. He was

serene, humorous, intelligent and beautiful – as charming an
acquaintance as one could desire – and latterly most friendly. But
he was essentially hard: his hatred of slosh went rather too deep
and affected the eternal water-springs, and I don't envy anyone
who applied to him for sympathy. The sonnets, on which his
reputation is evidently to be based, differ from all his previous
work, which was rebellious and unorthodox. They were inspired
by his romantic thoughts about war, not by his knowledge of it:
that also, had he been spared to gain it, he was hoping to express,
and, knowing his grim and grotesque realism, I feel sure that he
would have expressed something besides the Holiness in which –
to me so inappropriately – his work concludes. I don't know
whether the above conveys anything to you. If it erro on the side
of unkindness he himself wouldn't like it the less, for he was
extraordinarily free of conceit and sincerely desired to be done by
as he did. But he goes down to posterity as a sort of St Sebastian,
haloed by the Dean of St Paul's, and hymned by the Morning
Post as the evangelist of anti-Germanism. As far as I dare speak
for Rupert, how he would hate it, or rather laugh at it.

From time to time he received pinpricks over his failure to enlist,
or to do something more like 'war-work' than cataloguing paintings
at the National Gallery. Mrs Beveridge, mother of his old schoolfriend William,[1] wrote lecturing him on his lack of public spirit. Her
interference enraged him, and Lily much more so, and he replied
breaking off relations with her. Nevertheless, he felt uncomfortable
and began to consider some kind of non-combatant work at the
front. G. M. Trevelyan suggested he join an ambulance unit in
Italy, and he pondered this for some weeks. Then, in the autumn, a
better suggestion arose, which was that he should go to Alexandria
as a Red Cross 'searcher'.

The system of hospital 'searching' – that is to say, interviewing
the wounded in hospital for information about fellow-soldiers
reported 'missing' – had originated with Lord Robert Cecil, who had
formed a group for the purpose in the early days of the war. The
Red Cross had taken up the idea, setting up bodies of voluntary
searchers in all the main theatres of war; and with the Dardanelles
campaign, Alexandria had become a busy centre for this work.
Forster obtained an interview with Gertrude Bell, who was recruiting
'searchers'. She was somewhat snubbing, seeming not to want to
take him; and, piqued by this, he proceeded to pull every string he

[1] See Vol. I, p. 38.

could – a useful one being Percy Lubbock, who worked in the Red Cross 'Wounded and Missing' Bureau. 'I am leaving no stone a gentleman may turn to be sent to Egypt as a Searcher by the Red Cross,' he reported to Virginia Woolf (17 October 1915). 'Miss Gertrude Loathly Belle was greatly against me, but I do fancy is silenced at last.' Lubbock managed matters successfully, and a fortnight later Forster, wearing Red Cross uniform, embarked from England for Egypt expecting to be gone for three months.

2 Alexandria

With the war, Egypt had assumed great military importance for Britain. It was the supply base for the Dardanelles campaign, and a quarter of a million troops were stationed on its soil for the defence of the Suez Canal. Till then, Britain's position in Egypt had been very anomalous. For thirty years or so the British Consul-General had been the effective ruler of the country, yet formally speaking he had possessed very little power – no more than his French counterpart – and the country had still nominally been part of the Turkish Empire. It was only with Turkey's entry into the war, on the German side, that Britain had declared Egypt a protectorate, proceeding to depose the Khedive and replace him by a puppet Sultan.

Egypt, in fact, tended to be regarded as a rather second-rate part of the Empire. The British officials did not much like the place, nor – since the Denshawai incident of 1906[1] – were they much liked; there was little fraternization, on their part, either with the native Egyptians or with the cosmopolitan commercial and official classes. Even Lord Cromer, the so-called founder of modern Egypt, thought it a 'nondescript' place and considered the idea of its ruling itself as absurd as 'the nomination of some savage Red Indian Chief to be Governor-General of Canada'.[2]

Forster had been excited at the prospect of seeing Egypt, but at

---

[1] In June 1906 there was an affray between villagers at Denshawai, in the Delta, and a party of British Officers on a pigeon shooting expedition, one of the officers being murdered. The very severe reprisals – four of the accused Egyptians being executed – provoked much anti-British feeling.

[2] Letter to Lord Salisbury, quoted by the Marquess of Zetland in *Lord Cromer* (1932), p. 165.

first sight he too found it a disappointment. The landscape, as seen
from the train window, seemed to him 'a feebler India, as flat without
the sense of immensity'. And as for Alexandria: 'One can't dislike
Alex,' he wrote to his mother soon after arrival, '. . . because it is
impossible to dislike either the sea or stones. But it consists of nothing
else as far as I can gather: just a clean cosmopolitan town by some
blue water.' In fact, though he was to have important experiences in
Egypt and was, in one way or another, to write a good deal about it,
he never learned to love it or Alexandria. His standard was India,
and Egypt – the 'semi-East' or 'pseudo-East' – struck him as a
parody of it. The feeling had grown definite in a letter to Masood,
written a few weeks later (29 December 1915):

> I do not like Egypt much – or rather, I do not see it, for Alexandria
> is cosmopolitan. But what I have seen seems vastly inferior to
> India, for which I am always longing in the most persistent way,
> and where I still hope to die. It is only at sunset that Egypt
> surpasses India – at all other hours it is flat, unromantic, un-
> mysterious, and godless – the soil is mud, the inhabitants are of
> mud moving, and exasperating in the extreme: I feel as instinc-
> tively not at home among them as I feel instinctively at home
> among Indians.

The phrase 'mud moving' reappears in the opening paragraph of
A Passage to India as an evocation of India – albeit of the dreary
Chandrapore ('The very wood seems made of mud, the inhabitants
of mud moving'). Mud, the mud of the Nile, and moral 'muddiness'
were always to figure in his vision of Egypt. And in this and other
ways his experience there was taken up into his Indian novel.

On arriving in Alexandria, he reported at once to the head of
the Wounded and Missing Department, a Miss Victoria Grant Duff,
daughter of a sometime Governor of Madras: 'a youngish, slightly
shrewish lady,' Forster wrote of her to his mother, 'slightly distingué
and quite friendly and considerate.' His duties, as explained by her,
included daily searching in the wards of the various hospitals, and the
compiling, each evening, of a report – which might be quite lengthy –
for forwarding to the London Office. As a voluntary worker he had
'officer' status and was expected to find his own lodgings; so, for the
moment, he put up in a hotel, being kept company there by another
searcher, the historian D. A. Winstanley. There were two more full-
time searchers (as well as part-time helpers), but he gathered from

Winstanley that, 'through debauchery and age', they did not do much, and the bulk of the work would fall on themselves and Miss Grant Duff. The searchers, apart from their daily report, could organize their work as they liked. The amount of it depended on the arrival of convoys; and for the first week or two Forster found himself kept very busy.

He took to his Red Cross work and, before long, decided he was good at it. He found himself doing a good deal beside strict 'searching': he would play chess with the patients, take their watches to be mended, write their letters for them and act as unpaid solicitor. (It was a sort of serviceableness he enjoyed.) He was impressed by their lack of vindictiveness towards their Turkish adversaries. 'We fought every bit as dirty as what they did,' one said. Most of them were cynical about the fight for King and Country. He listened endlessly to their stories of war-horrors and, sporadically, compiled a collection of them:

> Pte. in the Herefords spoke of a dead Australian who was in the way when they were making a parapet, so they cut him at the neck and knees and fired through him.
> Private Davies 1/7 Royal Scots told me yesterday this.
> A Turk was mining and with a boulder they smashed the ladder down into his hole so got him. They were about to shoot but their officer went out of his mind and insisted they should bury the Turk alive instead. 'Bit too bad being buried alive' said the man in the next bed. 'I shouldn't mind being shot.'
> (A man who saw report of his own death.) He was a chap who was a regular comic and he said 'Well I never knew it before – I'll go and lie down.'
> Pte. Young 8 Mans., after giving careful evidence for 20 minutes: without reproof: 'I never like anyone to ask me about it – it leaves a bad taste in the mouth. I think of the days again, of the days again . . .'
> Our heroes. Sgt. Corrigan, Sussex Yeomanry. 'I often quarrel with myself as I lie here – don't quarrel with any one else – think of the foolish things I've done. Enlisting! King and Country. God's trewth! I'll watch them! I don't want to go into battle anymore. No place for me. They throw things at you and don't even say they're sorry.'

Miss Grant Duff praised his reports and told him that he was by far the best of her searchers. He also saw one of his reports reprinted by Lord Northcliffe in his book *At the War* as an example of the 'labour of love' by which the Red Cross were 'easing the sorest wounds of warfare'.

As soon as he had reached Alexandria, Forster had got in touch with an old King's acquaintance, Robin Furness,[1] who ran the Press Censorship Department. Furness was a close friend of Sheppard and Keynes: a very tall, elegant, sardonic man, learned about the poets of ancient Alexandria and with a line in extravagant bawdry.[2] He had a large and cosmopolitan acquaintance in Alexandria and introduced Forster among it, in particular to a Greek businessman, Pericles Anastassiades, a Syrian named George Antonius, and an elderly English major, Sir Bartle Frere. Pericles Anastassiades was an aesthete and amateur painter. He engaged Forster to give him English lessons (English being the fashionable language in the Greek community), and through him and Furness, Forster began to hear of, and before long met, the poet Cavafy, who was an old friend of Anastassiades'. Antonius worked in Furness's Censorship Department, later becoming a leading Arab nationalist and opponent of Zionism.[3] Forster struck up quite a friendship with him and sometimes, later, went for holidays with him; he liked him more than he trusted him, never knowing, as he said, 'which pair of back stairs he would next run up'. As for Sir Bartle Frere, he was, Forster told his mother, 'a kind, cultivated, unassuming, distinguished, aristocratic old gentleman, but oh! oh! oh! such a bore'. Sir Bartle became much attached to Forster, considering his jokes so witty that he would write them down to send to his sister in Gloucestershire. Through Furness and his friends Forster was also put up for a club, the Cercle Mohammed Aly – a smart and cosmopolitan establishment, with gaming-tables at which there was high play.

Another friend to whom Furness introduced him was Aïda Borchgrevink, the widow of a Norwegian judge. She was American by birth, the daughter of 'a corn-king', and before marriage had

---

[1] Sir Robert Allason Furness (1883–1954).

[2] He wrote to Keynes from Alexandria, 25 April 1907: 'I have long been a policeman or inspector of police in this disorderly town: daily I feed my disgusted eyes on drunken Welsh governesses and stabbed Circassian whores; I peer into the anus of catamites; I hold inquests upon beggars who die and are eaten by worms . . .'

[3] George Antonius (1891–1942). He acted as secretary-general to the Arab delegation at the Palestine Conference in London in 1939 and through his book *The Arab Awakening* had considerable influence on British policy.

trained as an opera-singer.[1] Furness had a passionate platonic
relationship with her; indeed, in a sense, she had been the 'making'
of him, and the polyglot group of workers in his Censorship Department were largely of her recruiting. She was an ebullient, romantic
woman, who sang Wagner at the top of her voice as she drove.
(Miss Grant Duff, who had a crush on her, used to address her as
'O Ocean Wave'.) She took a great fancy to Forster, whom she
insisted on calling 'Rickie'; and as her house, in the fashionable
eastern suburb of Ramleh, lay on his daily route, it was arranged
that he should take his lunch in her garden. She would leave fruit
and cold drinks in the summerhouse, and he in return would leave
a folded paper on the tray, containing a poem, a joke, or something
of the sort. Her daughter used to encounter him in the garden and
recalled him as a 'very pale, delicately-built young man, slightly
towzled and very shy, with a habit of standing on one leg and winding
the other round it.' Mrs Borchgrevink also subscribed to the 'shyness'
theory and would tell her daughter how this shy young man would
drop the oddest, most unforeseen remarks into the conversation,
Hearing that he was in uncomfortable lodgings, she found him a flat
with a former maid of hers, an Italian-speaking Greek named Irene.
Irene owned two houses, and was always moving from one to the
other, and when she did, she would take Forster with her. 'Lo porto
con me' she would say; it made him, he said, feel like a doll.

Three months came and went, with no suggestion of his returning;
nor had he any desire to return. Alexandria, prosaic, slightly debased,
and less hag-ridden by the war than England, suited his mood.
The weather was exquisite; he had taught himself to swim; and
he was busy and useful. 'I am here become cheeriness itself and
run from one little deed of kindness to another all the day,' he told
Leonard Woolf (12 February 1916).

> Little lists, little reports, little men – why are wounded soldiers so
> short? – then dinner in a little Italian restaurant & so to bed. The
> weather is perfect, the tennis courts of the Sporting Club thronged
> by day, the brothels by night . . . Invalids – opinions – and be-
> tween them a bottomless abyss. There you have it in a nutshell
> as the 119 Generals would say.

---

[1] She was baptised 'Ada', adopting the name 'Aïda' after attending a
performance of Verdi's *Aïda* during her honeymoon.

In June, however, his peace of mind was shattered. Three months before, the Government had introduced conscription, rescinding an earlier scheme under which men of military age were invited to 'attest' for future service; and, reacting to this, the Red Cross decided to release its able-bodied members for army service. The right to 'attest', thereby avoiding conscription proper, was due to expire in late June, and Forster was instructed to present himself for a medical examination before this, on the understanding that, if passed fit, he would 'attest'. He was horrified, and furious at what he thought a breach of faith; however, seeing no escape, he went for a medical inspection, having secured an undertaking that it would commit him to nothing, and expecting anyway to be classified as unfit. To his consternation, however, the new doctor reported him as suitable for active service. He was now in a serious dilemma. He was determined not to attest, yet could not easily explain his reasons – for he knew that, in a strict sense, he was not a conscientious objector. For a few days he was badly thrown by the contretemps, and – as once or twice later in life in times of stress – he developed a kind of falling sickness and had bouts of hurling himself against the furniture. His friends, luckily, were all on his side. And, bolstered by them (by Antonius in particular) he recovered and began half to relish a fight with authority. He wrote politely to the Chief Red Cross Commissioner, Sir Courtauld Thomson, asking to be excused from attesting, on conscientious grounds, and pointing out that, had he returned to England, he could have put his case to a tribunal. Sir Courtauld responded simply by sending a clerk to him with an attestation form, instructing him to report with it to the army within two hours. At this, Forster demanded and obtained an interview. When Sir Courtauld asked him his objections to attestation, he replied that they were not religious: he did not condemn anyone who joined the services – indeed, he considered them his superior. It was a matter of instinct, 'a very profound instinct which he could only call conscience and which presented the taking of the life of a fellow-creature as the most horrible thing he could do.' Sir Courtauld asked him to leave the room while he consulted, and on Forster's return said, unpleasantly, that conscientious objectors could not be considered at all. 'I see – they no longer exist?' said Forster, which made Sir Courtauld flush. They argued further; and eventually he obtained after all a grudging permission to return to England to

attend a tribunal. By now his friends were very busy on his behalf,
concerting plans to obtain him another medical examination. Miss
Grant Duff greatly disliked conscientious objectors but, illogically,
made an exception for Forster and urged his claims so vigorously to
army friends that a high-ranking officer intervened with Sir Courtauld,
telling him the army positively did not want Forster. 'I am quite
shameless over this wirepulling,' Forster wrote cheerfully to his
mother (10 July 1916):

> If I can't keep out of the army by fair means then hey for foul!
> Let alone that there conscience. I know I should be no good, and
> haven't the least desire to pacify the parrots who cry 'All must go.'
> One will lose a certain amount of friends of course, mainly female,
> and incidentally the approval and support of Uncle Horace![1]

The boat which was to take him to England was delayed. And
eventually, perhaps because of the friendly attitude of the army, the
'attestation' affair died down and was forgotten.

For Forster – though he did not realize the fact – it had a curious
sequel. On 29 July 1916 he had written to Masood, recounting the
recent drama, also reporting that he had recently had a letter from
the Maharaja of Dewas inviting him to come to India to be his
private secretary. In his letter, he had used the free, affectionate
style he always adopted with Masood. It ran:

> Dearest S.R.M.,
> I have a long unfinished letter to you somewhere. I remember
> the chief points:– (i) I had been dreaming of you and longed to see
> you – indeed woke up in the night to write. (ii) I was telling you
> how much I disliked the Egyptians and how inferior to the Indians
> I have found them, both in charm, intellect and morality. Now
> what shall I tell you in this letter? My longing to see you remains,
> but I grow frightfully pessimistic, frightfully. First the war must
> end, then freedom to travel must be re-established, and God knows
> how long this will take. I have had a long cable from Dewas asking
> me to be his Private Secretary and Right Hand. I should have
> accepted in normal times, partly because it would have given me
> the chance of seeing you. But it is impossible to leave the Red X
> at present. As it is they tried to hoof me into the Army, a disaster
> that I have hitherto avoided. I hope I shall be medically unfit,
> but they take everyone who isn't actually diseased I fancy. Except

---

[1] He disliked his uncle Horace Whichelo, considering him bullying and
overbearing. See Vol. 1, pp. 26–7.

for my nerves, which have got bad (chiefly owing to this enlistment worry) I am looking and feeling pretty fit . . .

Now where are you? I heard of the Hyderabad scheme back in England and am interested it has come off.[1] I loved the glimpse of Hyderabad I saw – also the Bidar work I got there. (You can give me a present of more if you like.) I loved the smells in the scent bazaar, and the Mosque and the Sagar on whose slot we picnicked by moonlight. It is nice to think of you among those things. Here there is only the pseudo-East – the pretentious, squalid, guttural Levant – and I shut my eyes to it on purpose, lest it spoil my pleasure in the true East, to which I shall one day return . . .

Much love, dearest Boy.
Morgan.

The letter was intercepted by the postal censor in Bombay, who was scandalized by it and forwarded it to the Bombay political department, remarking:

I took up a letter by the same writer to the same addressee last year to Special Officer. The letter was passed into the post. It was much of the same type as the present one, only it showed up the writer still more as a decadent coward and apparently a sexual pervert. I think the Political Secretary, Government of India, should see this letter as the writer does not seem to be fit to be employed in Dewas.[2]

The matter was referred to the central administration, in Simla, and the following exchange ensued:

The Hon'ble Mr J. B. Wood, C.I.E., I.C.S., Political Secretary to Govt. of India, Foreign and Political Department, Simla to O. V. B. Bosanquet, C.S.I., C.I.E., Agent to the Governor-General in Central India, Indore; 24 August 1916:

I send herewith a copy of a letter from Jukes with enclosures, which explain themselves. You will notice that the man Forster says that he has a cable from Dewas asking him to be his Private Secretary and Right Hand. It might be as well to ascertain which Dewas is referred to, and possibly to give him a hint that Forster is not altogether a desirable person.

---

[1] Through the efforts of his English friends, Masood had been diverted from the law, which he disliked, and which they thought politically dangerous, into education, obtaining the headmastership of a school in Patna (a post hitherto reserved for the British) and then becoming Director of Public Instruction in the state of Hyderabad.

[2] This, and the ensuing correspondence, are to be seen in the India Office library.

Bosanquet to Wood; 28 August 1916:

The intercepted letter . . . is from a man whom the Raja of Dewas, Senior Branch, was proposing to engage as his Private Secretary.

He is a novelist of some repute, who made the acquaintance of H.H. when he was travelling in India some time ago. He is evidently a poor creature; but Luard[1] who has met him thinks there is no foundation for the suggestion that he is a sexual pervert.

He declined the Raja's offer of an appointment, as he says in his letter, and we shall take steps to see that it is not renewed.

Forster's letter was allowed to proceed, and no whisper ever reached his ears of the stir that it had caused. Whether a word was spoken to the Maharaja is not clear; if it was, it had no effect.

*   *   *

As Forster's letter to Masood shows, he found it hard to like Egypt and the Egyptians. He, of course, knew hardly any Egyptians personally, there being almost no social contact between the alien 'upper classes', whether Greek, Turkish, French or British, and the indigenous community. Thus the dislike was largely an aesthetic not a personal one, but it disturbed him. He told Darling (6 August 1916):

I came inclined to be pleased and quite free from racial prejudice, but in 10 months I've acquired an instinctive dislike to the Arab voice, the Arab figure, the Arab way of looking or walking or pump shitting [sic] or eating or laughing or anything – exactly the emotion that I censured in the Anglo-Indian towards the natives. What does this mean? Am I old, or is it the war, or are these people intrinsically worse? Any how I better understand the Anglo-Indian irritation though I'm glad to say I'm as far as ever from respecting it! It's damnable and disgraceful and it's in me.

He had in fact got to know one Egyptian, an official in the Police Department, and with him he had an experience that seemed to him 'pure mud'. They had been to visit a hashish 'den', a sight which Forster was curious to see, having already visited an opium den in Lahore. Such 'dens' were illegal, but were generally run by aliens, so – under the Egyptian system of extra-territoriality[2] – they were

---

[1] Lt–Col C. E. Luard, an official in the political department and a distinguished archaeologist. He was a friend of Lowes Dickinson.

[2] One of the legacies of Turkish rule in Egypt was a system by which, by means of what were known as 'capitulations', Europeans in Egypt enjoyed extra-territorial rights.

not under police jurisdiction; indeed, not being able to at first find a 'den', Forster and his friend had asked help from a policeman, who had directed them to one kept by a Maltese. Forster described the visit in a letter (18 May 1916) to Edward Carpenter, who took a sociological interest in such matters.

> We went up pitch black stairs in a slum and scratched at a door at the top. 'No haschich here – hardly know what the word means etc.' We push in, and find a small and well mannered company smoking the drug, quiet and langorous. There was also an Arab girl, barefoot, very young and tired, and some boy attendants, playing cards together – not to speak of odd noises in unopened rooms. One of the boys made a sign to me. I did not respond, but he came and sat down by us on the bench. He was a young man really, of extraordinary beauty and charm, very big and well built and manly, despite delicacy of lip, and softness of eye. He wore garabia and tarboosh and wouldn't talk Italian and I no Arabic. The other boys – in European dress and less charming – also made signs. Every one – except ourselves – smoked. I would have smoked if I had been alone, but my friend, whom I knew very slightly, seemed puritanical, and we rather damped the evening. Three clients – dapper young men in straw hats, probably Italian shop assistants – came in and were horrified at our sight. Boys tried to sit on their knees, but they were not having any at all, and after drawing at the pipe once or twice went quietly away, as if this was all they had come for. – Well, with due regard for the censor, I have now indicated what was to me an interesting and even attractive evening. I felt curiously at ease in that haunt of vice, and didn't even realize I was behaving priggishly till afterwards. So perhaps I wasn't a prig really. However, no matter whether I was a prig or not. What matters is that I should give you first hand information. I hate, tho', to think of that young man immured in that den, for though haschich doesn't make people unpleasant it does rot them, there's no doubt, and youth can pay too heavily even for aphrodisiac power and the annihilation of time and space!

A few days after his visit, Forster learned from Furness that the Maltese proprietor of the 'den' had been reported to his consular authorities. He mentioned this to his Egyptian friend, to whom he was giving dinner, and to his astonishment, the Egyptian told him he had lodged the complaint himself. 'Oh yes,' he had said, smiling modestly, 'it was my duty. I am private gentleman in the evening but a member of the administration by day. I keep the two apart.'

Of the various nationalities in Alexandria, Forster came to the conclusion that he most liked the Greeks. 'There are other escapes – the Syrian, the Italian, the Bedouin etc. – but I prefer the Greeks,' he told Bob Trevelyan (6 August 1917).

> . . . the Greeks are the only community here that attempt to understand what they are talking about, and to be with them is to re-enter, however, imperfectly, the Academic world. They are the only important people east of Ventimiglia – dirty, dishonest, unaristocratic, roving, and warped by Hellenic and Byzantine dreams – but they do effervesce intellectually, they do have creative desires, and one comes round to them in the end . . .
> The Syrians dance.
> The Bedouins lay eggs.
> The French give lectures on Kultur to the French.
> The Italians build il nostro Consolato, nostro Consolato nuovo, ricco, grandioso, forte come il nostro Cadorna, profondo come il nostro mare, alto come il nostro cielo, che muove l'altre stelle, e tutto vicino al terminus Ramleh Tramways.[1]
> The English have witnessed 'Candida' or 'Vice Detected'.

His greatest discovery among the Greeks was the poet Cavafy. Cavafy was now in his early fifties. His parents had been Greeks from Constantinople, his father having been partner in a firm of wheat and cotton exporters, with branches in London and Alexandria. During the 1850s and 1860s the Cavafys had been leading members of the Greek community in Alexandria, living in style in the fashionable new Rue Chérif. With the death of Cavafy's father in 1870, however, the family fortunes had rapidly declined, the firm shortly afterwards going bankrupt; thus the poet and his brothers had been brought up with a feeling of vanished glories and lost status. At the time of the family ruin, Cavafy had been at school in England. He was, in consequence, more or less bilingual,[2] and on the strength of this he had, in 1892, obtained an ill-paid post as a civil servant, in what was called the 'Third Circle' of the Irrigation Department. It was a post he retained for the rest of his career, though – sharing the family feeling of being above work – he was never very industrious.

---

[1] 'Our Consulate, our new, rich, magnificent Consulate, strong as our [General] Cadorna, deep as our sea, lofty as our heaven that "moves the other stars", and quite convenient for the Ramleh Tramways terminus.'

[2] He spoke Greek with a faint English accent, and the Cavafy critic Robert Rowe has suggested that he 'thought' his poems in English.

(An office-colleague has given a nice account. of his ruses to conceal his late arrival from his British employers: 'He never used the lift, so as not to be scolded for being late. He climbed the stairs thoughtfully, ready to give some sort of justification if he were seen. What bothered him was his hat . . . sometimes he tried to get rid of it, or use it as an alibi. If he happened to meet one of the messengers when he arrived, he gave him his hat to hang up in his office before he himself came.'[1]) At the time of entering the British service, he was still living with his mother, whom he adored. After her death, in 1899, he had for a time shared a flat with his brother Paul, a society journalist; and when Paul had had to flee the country to escape his creditors, he had continued in the flat alone. It stood in the Rue Lepsius, a rather seedy street, otherwise mainly occupied by prostitutes and known among his English friends as the 'Rue Clapsius'.

He had been writing poetry from early years and in the early 1900s had published two pamphlets of verse containing one or two of his finest poems, including the famous 'Candles', and 'Waiting for the Barbarians'. It was not till 1911, however, that he felt he had perfected his true manner. The year represented a dividing-line in his career. He began then a new method of publishing his verse, distributing his poems one by one in the form of broadsheets or offprints, to a chosen circle of readers, for them to collect in folders; and about the same time he began to write more outspokenly on the subject of homosexual love. Since then, his fame as a poet had spread; and by 1917, when Forster got to know him, he was much discussed in literary circles in Alexandria, and to a lesser extent in Athens, though still totally unknown in non-Greek-speaking countries.

In person he was withdrawn, deliberate and rather over-polite in manner, and totally preoccupied with his own work and reputation. In his essay 'The Poetry of C. P. Cavafy',[2] Forster described how, after their first introduction, they would from time to time meet in the street. He would hear his name called out, in accents that seemed not so much to be greeting him as simply registering the fact of his existence. He would turn and would discover Cavafy, 'a Greek gentleman in a straw hat, standing absolutely motionless at a slight

[1] See Robert Liddell, *Cavafy* (1974), pp. 128–9.
[2] In *Pharos and Pharillon* (1923).

angle to the universe.' If the poet was going to his office, he would then disappear with a gesture of despair; but if he was on his way home, he might converse. He would begin an enormous, labyrinthine sentence, dealing with 'the tricky behaviour of the Emperor Alexius Comnenus in 1096, or with olives, their possibilities and price, or with the fortunes of friends, or George Eliot, or the dialects of the interior of Asia Minor', and before it had reached its conclusion Forster might find himself on Cavafy's doorstep or inside his flat. The flat was dark, with heavy Moorish hangings and elaborate carved candle-brackets, and was crammed with family furniture; outside in the passage there always stood a large garden-chair, chained to the wall. During one of his daily visits, Forster questioned Cavafy about his poetry, but Cavafy replied, discouragingly, 'You could never understand my poetry, my dear Forster, never.' Despite this, they looked together at 'The City', and Forster, with his scraps of public-school Greek, managed to grasp some of it. At this, Cavafy's interest in him rose. 'Oh but this is good, my dear Forster,' he exclaimed, 'this is very good indeed.' From then on they often talked about the poems, sometimes in the company of a friend of Cavafy's, George Valassopoulos, who was making translations. Cavafy was a man of rituals, and when the conversation flourished, he would jump up every now and then to light more candles. His own talk was mainly soliloquy. He would be caustic about his fellow Greeks. 'Aristocracy in modern Greece?' he once remarked to Forster. 'To be an aristocrat there is to have made a corner in coffee in the Piraeus in 1849.' For himself, he liked to be called a 'Hellene' rather than a Greek. 'Never forget about the Greeks,' he said to Forster, 'that we are bankrupt. That is the difference between us and the ancient Greeks, and, my dear Forster, between us and yourselves. Pray that you – you English with your capacity for adventure – never lose your capital, otherwise you will resemble us, restless, shifty, liars. . . .'[1] The vision that informed his conversation, a disbelief in racial purity and high valuing of 'bastardy' in civilization, fitted perfectly with Forster's own mood of the time, and he felt that in Cavafy he had found the epitome of Alexandria.

*   *   *

As the days went on, Forster began to find his 'searching' duties monotonous. Nevertheless he performed them conscientiously, and

---

[1] Quoted by Forster in a letter to Christopher Isherwood, 16 July 1933.

sometimes, as well, he would lend a hand in hospital entertainments. He worked up a lecture on ancient Alexandria, which he gave here and there to patients, with varying success. He also gave piano recitals and helped organize concerts of classical music. At one of these, at the Montazah Convalescent Hospital, he acted as master of ceremonies and felt pleased at the way he quieted several hundred catcalling troops. He wrote to Carpenter (23 April 1917):

> It was great fun quieting them down, and trying to talk sense about music instead of that damned superior art patronage; and I believe I was able to talk sense and quiet them because I loved them. They behaved perfectly through the programme and most of them stopped to the end. We had violins, tenor, and solo-piano: executants all first class. I can't help swanking over this concert. I felt that I had been burrowing under rubbish and touched something that was alive and had been trying to touch me. It is useless trying to touch something you don't want to touch: that is why all attempts to 'improve' people are vain.

He had himself convalesced from jaundice at Montazah and had come to love the place, often returning there for weekends. The hospital was in the Khedive's erstwhile palace and stood among tamarisk groves and oleanders, overlooking a bay where the patients bathed naked. This Edenic atmosphere, he felt, was just made for him. He wrote to Lowes Dickinson (28 July 1916):

> It makes me very happy yet very sad – they come from the unspeakable all these young gods, and in a fortnight at the latest they will return to it: the beauty of the crest of a wave . . . I came away from that place and time thinking 'Why not more of this?' Why not? What could it injure? Why not a world like this – its beauty of course impaired by death and old age and poverty and disease, but a world that should not torture itself by organized and artificial horrors?

From time to time, in the hospitals, he struck up a friendship with a soldier. Normally the acquaintance did not last, for the patient would soon return to his unit, but in one case something more enduring developed. This was with a young ship's steward, Frank Vicary. (It was a friendship that, later, would cause Forster a good deal of worry.) Vicary was a country boy from Herefordshire and before enlistment had worked as a cider-maker. He was small, vivid, rather gaunt and hollow-cheeked, but with bright blue eyes. He was an odd, independent character, with unexpected turns of phrase, and

quite widely read in a self-taught way: when Forster met him he was
reading William James. Their first meeting was in July 1916. Forster
was leaving his bedside, saying 'I know you're in the Navy, so we
won't have much to say to each other,' when Vicary, out of the blue,
exclaimed, 'I'm awfully interested in ideas – I'm more interested in
ideas than anything.' 'So am I,' said Forster, and sat down on the
bed again, whereupon Vicary talked charmingly and amusingly. He
told Forster of his first encounters with religion: at home, he said,
they had believed all one's cut toenails were resurrected on the Last
Day – though whether re-attached or in bags his grandfather could
not decide. Forster and he saw each other often in the next few weeks,
and when he was shipped home, the two agreed to write, and to meet
again in England.

Admirable though Forster had found Alexandria as an escape, it
had brought him no release from sexual frustration. He was attracted
by Vicary but could see no hope of a response there; nor could he from
any of his acquaintance. He wrote lamentingly to Carpenter (12 April
1916):

> Dear Edward, you continue the greatest comfort. I don't want to
> grouse, as so much is all right with me, but this physical loneliness
> has gone on for too many months, and with it springs and grows
> a wretched fastidiousness, so that even if the opportunity for
> which I yearn offered I fear I might refuse it. In such a refusal
> there is nothing spiritual – it is rather a sign that the spirit is
> being broken. I am sure that some of the decent people I see daily
> would be willing to save me if they knew, but they don't know,
> can't know . . . I sit leaning over them for a bit and there it ends
> – except for images that burn into my sleep; I know that though
> you have heard this and sadder cases 1000 times before, you will
> yet be sympathetic, and that is why you are such a comfort to me.
> It's awful to live with an unsatisfied craving, now and then
> smothering it but never killing it or even wanting to. If I could
> get one solid night it would be some thing.

However, a change was approaching in his sexual fortunes. In
October he had a casual escapade with a soldier on the beach. It was
his first full physical encounter, and he did not enjoy it greatly – not
so much because he found it squalid, as because it was so anonymous.
He reported it to Florence Barger, remarking 'It is as if (in the novel)
A[lec] had been ordered to come and then dismissed at once.'

Something more important was to follow. From time to time, on the Ramleh tram, he had noticed the conductor, a young, slightly negroid-looking Egyptian, and had felt faintly attracted. It struck him how carefully the young man threaded his way through the passengers, not trampling on their feet as was the general custom. Once, too, he observed him laughing with a soldier, and, as the two parted, holding one after another of the buttons on the soldier's uniform, as a kind of farewell – it struck him as rather charming. Then, one cold night as he was returning by tram to Irene's, the same conductor politely asked him to get up, as his coat was under Forster's seat. Forster was equally polite; and from now on, when they met on the tram, they half saluted each other. It was still nothing at all; but one evening the following March (1917), when Forster proferred his fare, the Egyptian said earnestly, 'You shall never pay! If you do not want that piastre in your hand, throw it into the road, or give it to some poor person as a charitable action. *I* will not have it.' Forster, perplexed, inquired why, and the conductor reminded him of the coat incident – he said he had not expected so much courtesy from an Englishman. Forster was greatly intrigued and took the same tram next evening, and again on the following one, hoping to see him, though without success; and before long he was spending hours every evening at the tram-stop. Eventually the desired tram and conductor appeared. He got on, the two chatted, and Forster offered a cigarette, receiving the reply, 'I seldom smoke – my Ministry of Finance does not permit it.' At this Forster, scenting a request for a tip, made an awkward little scene, insisting on paying his fare and making the conductor keep the change. The young man closed his fist, so that the coins scattered, and both had to get down on their knees to retrieve them. When at last the conductor, sulkily, had pocketed them, Forster said brightly: 'Now you can buy an English book.' 'The sum is too small,' answered the Egyptian coldly.[1]

Soon after this, the conductor saved Forster further loitering at tram-stops by telling him his hours; and now they frequently met and chatted. One day the Egyptian said to Forster: 'I want to ask you a question, which please answer truly, sir. Why do English people dislike Mohammedans?' 'They don't,' said Forster, with a twinge of

---

[1] It is noticeable that the offering and rejecting of money also figured in those two important incidents of Forster's early life, the occasion when he was sexually molested as a schoolboy and his encounter with a lame shepherd-boy in Wiltshire. See Vol. i, pp. 37 and 116–17.

guilt. 'They do, because I heard one soldier say to another in the tram, "That's a mosque for fucking (I beg your pardon) Mohammedans!" '

'They were joking, I think.'

'You think – you are not sure.'

'No, I am sure. One of my greatest friends is a Mohammedan. I went to India to see him.'

'That must have cost a great deal of money. With what you spent seeing your friend you could have bought many friends in England. You can get friends if you have money: except one or two.'

'But I enjoyed the travelling.'

'You would have been better employed at home making some useful invention, I think.'[1]

Their running dispute over Forster's fare ended in a crisis. One day an Inspector found Forster without a ticket and questioned the conductor, who made up some story that Forster was authorized to travel free. There was a violent altercation, in Arabic; and when finally the Inspector alighted, the conductor told Forster he was to be dismissed. 'But that's too awful, too appalling,' protested Forster. 'Why so? I have performed a good action,' said the young man, with dignity; adding, to make conversation, 'Please answer me a question. When you went to India, how many miles was it?' 'I don't know or care!' cried Forster. 'Whenever shall I see you again?' The conductor said, doubtfully, that perhaps they could meet one evening, if Forster would wear civilian clothes.

Forster was now much keyed up and went next day to Furness for advice. By good fortune Furness knew the Manager of the trams, who was under an obligation to him, and by mid-day he could report that the matter of the fare could be arranged. He was nervous, however, and urged Forster not to pursue the friendship – advice which Forster decided to ignore. He went to seek out the conductor with his good news, and the Egyptian, convinced that Forster had been to see the Manager himself, thanked him gravely. Forster once more asked if they could meet some evening. He replied, 'Any time, any place, any hour!' and they arranged a rendezvous at the Nouzha Gardens, on the outskirts of the city.

---

[1] This dialogue, and much of the detail of what follows, was recorded by Forster in a long 'letter' addressed to this Egyptian friend after the latter's death.

The Egyptian was there at the appointed time, smartly dressed and self-assured, and they found a bench. Forster, still imagining that bribes and gifts were required, had come furnished with chocolate and a large bag of sticky cakes. The Egyptian nibbled at these with disfavour (he told Forster later he thought they might be drugged) and remarked, 'I do not care for cakes. What did you pay for them?' Forster said he couldn't remember. 'No? How many centuries ago did you buy them? Next time you will put me to a similar expense.' Forster quoted the Greek proverb that 'The possessions of friends are in common,' but the Egyptian received this cynically. A little while later, he said, with a plunge: 'Would you like to see my Home of Misery? It will be *dreadful.*' This entailed a lengthy tram journey, and the Egyptian, forgetting his disapproval of the cakes, amused himself by handing them round among the passengers.

His room was very poor and bare, but they squatted on the bed and chatted amicably. The Egyptian told Forster his name, Mohammed el Adl, and one or two more facts about himself – that he had been born at Mansourah, a town in the Delta, and had learned English at the American Mission school. His parents were still in Mansourah – 'But I have always ate apart and lived apart and thought apart. Perhaps I am not my father's son.' Then, with another odd plunge, he insisted on showing Forster all his possessions, even turning out the contents of his trunk, exclaiming as he did so: 'Very little, but all clean!' Forster thought this a good omen. As they were parting, the Egyptian said, 'This is the very happiest evening of my life.'

They met again soon at the Home of Misery, and Forster met some of Mohammed's friends – a Syrian midwife, and a young Egyptian who ran a matrimonial agency – conversing with them in Italian. As he left, Mohammed said gravely, 'I have the honour to ask your name,' and Forster told him, though not what he did for a living.

On the next occasion, Mohammed came to Forster's room in Ramleh. They played chess and lay on the bed; and after a little while, they leaned towards each other and began to stroke each other's hair. Mohammed murmured, 'Beautiful hair,' and they kissed. Things now went wrong, for Forster, growing excited, made too fierce a grab at Mohammed, and there was a scuffle, during which Forster hurt his hand and Mohammed hurt his eye. It was not a serious quarrel, and next day, encountering on the tram, they compared their injuries and laughed.

38

Their next meeting, in the Home of Misery, was a more serious crisis, for Forster got it into his head that Mohammed was trying to insult him. He rose to leave, in a fury, glaring angrily at Mohammed. Mohammed, puzzled, said, 'What do you expect me to tell you?' – to which Forster replied, 'Let us be friendly when we meet on the trams, but we can never meet outside again.' His anger soon cooled. It was, he wrote to Florence Barger, 'curiously like Maurice towards the end of the book. I have found it so hard to believe he was neither traitor or cad.' Soon after this Mohammed was summoned to Mansourah, where his mother was dying. Forster, on his return, treated him with great gentleness and understanding, and this cemented their friendship. From now on it was understood that they would meet regularly.

Mohammed had a talent for friendship and found the right approaches with Forster. For one thing, from the start, he addressed him as 'Forster', which struck the desired note of comradeship; Forster first took it for naïveté, then came to the conclusion it was conscious tact. For another thing, Mohammed steadfastly refused gifts, so that Forster began to lose his embarrassment over money. His riches and Mohammed's poverty became a standing joke between them: Mohammed would take hold of Forster's sleeve, which was grubby, saying, 'You know, Forster, though I am poorer than you, I would never be seen in such a coat. I am not blaming you. No, I praise you. But I would never be seen so. And your hat has a hole, and your boot has a hole, and your socks have a hole. . . .' Forster would promise improvement, but Mohammed would say, no, clothes were an infectious disease, 'I had much better not care, and look like you, and so perhaps I will – but not in Alexandria.' They discussed the British character, and Mohammed, who on his tram had suffered many rudenesses from the British, was tolerant, holding that some British were good and others bad. Just about this time he had a fracas with a British officer. Mohammed had asked him either to get *on* the tram or off it, at which the officer had hit him with his cane. Despite this he remained not ill-disposed to the British.

They were not able to meet very often. And, to complicate matters, Forster's landlady, Irene, seemed to disapprove of Mohammed – when she first saw him in Forster's room she gave a little scream. It made Forster feel he could no longer have Mohammed to his flat; and then a brother came to stay with Mohammed, so they had no privacy in his room either. All that was left them was the public resorts, and they would meet at one or other of these once or twice a week. Mohammed was very accommodating, and agreed it would not be wise for them to be seen together too often.

For some time, he refused to go to bed with Forster. 'Never, never!' he exclaimed on one occasion: then he turned Forster's head away, saying 'I want to ask you a question. Do you never consider that your wish has led you to know a tram-conductor? And do you not think that a pity to you and a disgrace? While answering my question you are not to look at me.' Eventually he relented; and from now on, from time to time, they found the chance to spend a night together. Forster's happiness was now complete, and he determined to be grateful for his good fortune. 'Wish I was writing the latter half of *Maurice*. I now know so much more,' he told Florence Barger. 'It is awful to think of the thousands who go through youth without ever knowing. I have known in a way before, but never like this. My luck has been amazing.'

It was the realization of all his secret ambitions. He had, or so he felt, broken through the barriers of class and colour; and this had been the fruit of courage and persistency – of that 'athletic love', or taking trouble over relationships, which he had often preached. 'It isn't happiness,' he wrote to Florence Barger (1 June 1917); 'it's rather – offensive phrase – that I first feel a grown up man.'

> I felt the crisis coming just as I felt that very minor and grotesque episode coming last year. – This isn't a superstitious expression: it means that you feel faculties developing in you to grasp anything that comes. The practical difficulties – there is a big racial and social gulf – are great: but when you are offered affection, honesty and intelligence with all that you can possibly want in externals thrown in (including a delightful sense of humour), you surely have to take it or die spiritually.

Florence was thrilled by the romance and responded to his weekly letters with ardent advice; and other friends in England, like Dickinson, Carpenter and Lytton Strachey, wrote applaudingly. 'Your situation sounds all that could be wished,' Strachey told him; 'though I suppose you may suppress the drawbacks. And perhaps you exaggerate the Romance – for my benefit – or your own.' Forster longed for a confidant to talk to, but there seemed none in Alexandria. Furness, the likeliest choice, still seemed alarmed and unwilling to be involved. Indeed, Forster felt he was no longer such an object of interest to his friends, like Furness and Mrs Borchgrevink, as he had been at the time of the C.O. affair. Partly for this reason, he began to feel alienated from his own class. 'Our table manners remain identical, but little else,' he told Carpenter (22 July 1917); and in a letter to Dickinson (5 May 1917) he gave him what he called a 'helpful tip':

> You can remain a patriot if you will become a snob. Realize that the lower class, not the middle, is the typical Englishman, and you can love our race without difficulty. Officers, stockbrokers, politicians, grocers – they run us, but they are not England numerically, and their self righteousness is not our national characteristic. Shuttleworth[1] and I have decided to be snobs. We shrink, consciously, from such people, just as they shrink unconsciously from the lower class whom we love. We want to pretend we shrink from no one. But it's no good. Middle class people smell.

Mohammed earned a miserable wage on the trams, two shillings or so a day, and Forster decided he must help him find a better job. He made cautious inquiries among his friends, cursing the fact that he could not be more open, but could hear of nothing in Alexandria. Eventually, however, Furness, who had been moved to Cairo, found an opening for Mohammed with the army in the Canal Zone. It was a species of low-level 'intelligence' work. Mohammed was cynical when he heard of it: 'In other words, I am to be a spy?' However, he could hardly refuse, nor did Forster feel he could ask him to. Thus the fact had to be faced that they would be separated, and in war conditions there was no telling when they might meet again. They planned a farewell holiday, but were balked of this too, and late in October Mohammed left for the Canal.

*   *   *

Just about the time of Mohammed's departure, a quarrel developed between Forster and Miss Grant Duff. Usually he was skilful at avoiding quarrels, or settling them by a swift manoeuvre, but once or twice in his life a quarrel got out of hand, and then, for a time, it quite obsessed him. It did so on this occasion. Up to now, he and Miss Grant Duff had got on admirably. This war-work was her first job, and she took it with great seriousness and had frequently hymned Forster's praises as her one truly faithful assistant; he suspected, in

---

[1] Lawrence Shuttleworth (see p. 2) had been stationed in Alexandria for a few months, and Forster and he had met.

fact, that she was a little in love with him. Now, however, the London office, which also thought highly of his work, wrote giving him general control of the searchers in Alexandria and Cairo, with powers of appointment and dismissal. He was gratified, welcoming a change from 'searching'. Miss Grant Duff, however, spoke of it as 'a slap in the face'; she threatened resignation and at once set herself to thwart him all she could in his duties. He tried his best to avoid an open quarrel, knowing his over-reaction to quarrels; moreover, he was sorry for her. Thus, for some while they conducted a silent battle. She would open official letters addressed to him and answer them and would keep the searchers' reports to herself; meanwhile, as he told his mother, he 'acted like a perfect gentleman', pretending to notice nothing. To escape from her, and to console himself for Mohammed's absence, he took some leave, going to visit the Nile temples and the Pyramids, but on his return matters were as bad as ever. At this, he proposed to the Red Cross Commissioner that he should give up his new powers, or at any rate exercise them under Miss Grant Duff's direction. A meeting between them was arranged in the Commissioner's office, and Miss Grant Duff, on hearing the proposal, murmured frostily, 'Kind!' She was not placated, however, and went on exactly as before. Forster also discovered that she had given up her own searching. He attacked her over this, receiving a confused reply; and for some weeks afterwards she refused even to speak to him, wincing and biting her lips when their paths crossed. By now Forster felt quite ill with anxiety and irritation. It had aroused his latent misogyny, and he wrote to the London office, demanding to be rescued from Miss Grant Duff by whatever means. The authorities took his side, and letters came back from Percy Lubbock, reprimanding her and giving him total support. Even after this, though, the affair dragged on for several months, and Miss Grant Duff, though now more or less idle, would still haunt the office 'with the air of Iphigenia or Jeptha's daughter'. Forster felt enraged and saddened. 'She is only one of thousands whose characters have fallen to pieces during the war,' he told his mother. 'She is of course in great pain – a tragic figure, but I have suffered too much from her to feel any pity. My sensations with regard to her have all dried up.'[1]

---

[1] She was, in truth, a tragic figure. After the war she lingered on in Egypt and fell on hard times. She spent her remaining money on a racehorse, and would lead it about on a string, smelling strongly of the stable herself; once,

In Mohammed's absence, he occupied himself writing for the local press, in particular the *Egyptian Mail*. The articles made a hit with the British community – probably, he told R. C. Trevelyan in a letter, because they were too facetious. There was 'Our Diversions', a series about the films, concerts and concert-parties of Alexandria; 'Gippo English'; 'Handel in Egypt', about a local performance of *The Messiah* (for him, the quintessence of sentimental Englishness in music); and 'Royalty', a satirical account of a visit by the Sultan of Egypt. When Pericles Anastassiades took him to visit the Bourse, he wrote up the experience in an article, 'Cotton from the Outside':[1]

'Oh Heaven help us! What is that dreadful noise! Run, run! Has somebody been killed?'
'Do not distress yourself, kind hearted sir. It is only the merchants of Alexandria, buying cotton.'
'But they are murdering one another, surely?'
'Not so. They merely gesticulate.'
'Does any place exist where one could view their gestures in safety?'
'There is such a place.'
'I shall come to no bodily harm there?'
'None. None.'
'Then conduct me, pray . . .'

In March of 1918 he was, for the first time, taken flying, by an acquaintance in the Royal Flying Corps, named Eversden,[2] and this, too, provided copy for an article.[3] Eversden, who was a religious man, told Forster that the experience would 'take the sarcasm out of him'; and, in fact, as well as amusing and scaring him, the flight filled him with delighted awe.

And this was flying, this was what scientists had aimed at and poets dreamed of for centuries. Even Shelley never flew . . . How is it possible to describe that reality to people who have never left the earth? I think it is not possible. There is nothing mystic in aviation, but no earthly pleasure resembles it. It has opened a new kingdom of material beauty . . .

---

to test a theory that iron shoes were cruel, she had horseshoes fitted to her own shoes. Eventually she was kicked by the horse and died of her injury.

[1] Reprinted in a volume of his Egyptian writings, *Pharos and Pharillon* (1923).
[2] He had once been secretary to Oscar Browning.
[3] 'Higher Aspects' (*Egyptian Mail*, 5 May 1918).

For all this, it remained true that he did not respond to Egypt imaginatively; and in compensation he withdrew, in imagination, into a vision of ancient Alexandria. He gradually formed the plan of writing a book about it (eventually published in 1922 as *Alexandria: a History and a Guide*) in which he would reconstruct 'an immense ghost city'. He began to read widely in histories of the Ptolemaic and Christian periods and to reconstruct the topography of the ancient city. Practically nothing remained in the way of monuments, at most a few ruined walls and cisterns and a tall classical column known as 'Pompey's Pillar'; even the outlines of the harbour had changed, through silting. Thus, much had to be done by guesswork and by inference from the modern street-plan, and he spent his off-duty hours peregrinating the streets, sometimes in the company of an elderly friend, G. H. Ludolf. Ludolf was an official in the Post Office, who did part-time searching; he knew the city well and got Forster the *entrée* to places, such as mosques, normally closed to visitors. Meanwhile Forster read about Plotinus and Philo, and the controversies of Athanasius and Arius, receiving encouragement and reading-lists from Cavafy, who had constructed his own 'ghost city' of Alexandria. 'I am reading about Philo and the logos at present,' Forster wrote to Florence Barger:

> Philo's god is in a great predicament. He can only say I AM – no he can't even say that – can't speak or be spoken to (like a servant who has given notice). Just undiluted amminess. Under these circumstances the thought occurs to him to create a useful fetch-and-carry called the Logos. Adam and Eve next come into being, learn to say, among other things, HE IS, and God is well pleased.

The enterprise gripped him increasingly; he was 'touring in time', he told Florence Barger, 'since space is a military zone'. He wanted to get it 'lucid and dignified', he wrote to Reid; 'the spirit of a procession is to inform it, if so I can contrive.'

He was weary of the actual Alexandria, but every now and then added a new friend, of one nationality or another, to his little circle. He got to know a Jewish lawyer and theosophist, named Leveaux, sometimes giving talks to Leveaux's Theosophical Society; also an Italian composer called Terni,[1] with whom he would go bathing. (Terni was or had been a Wagnerian, and they sang *Leitmotiven* to

---

[1] E. Terni. He published an atonal quartet in 1925.

each other under the water.) Leveaux passed on to him a young
English acquaintance, Robert Sencourt,[1] and Sencourt took rooms
in the same house and for a time saw a good deal of Forster. Forster
read him some of his abortive Indian novel, which Sencourt thought
'the most amusing satire on Anglo-India that had ever been written.'
Sencourt, however, criticized certain descriptive passages for
'incompetent management of sound', recommending Forster to read
Stevenson on the art of writing. Forster, he recalled, was a little taken
aback, 'but seemed to feel there might be something in the idea'.

At about the same time, Forster also saw something of E. K.
('Francis') Bennett,[2] his friend from the Working Men's College.
Bennett, a gentle, benign and vulnerable man, loathed the army. (He
told Forster his fellow-recruits had pissed in his boots.) He was indeed,
for the moment, in great gloom, though was shortly afterwards, in
Jerusalem, to receive a kind of revelation.[3] Forster, so far, thought
him rather uninteresting, a 'kindly vegetable'. Nevertheless, he
confided in him about Mohammed, and, after Bennett had left for
Palestine, he received from him 'a most beautiful and affectionate
letter'. He had never dreamed there was so much in Bennett, and
thereafter, for the rest of their lives, the two were close friends. 'He's
got *creative* unselfishness,' Forster wrote of him, 'as opposed to the
"never mind me" unselfishness, which springs from idleness and lack
of vitality.'[4]

          *   *   *

Forster had come to feel that the war would never end, or that if it
did, human nature would take centuries to recover. He sent Dickinson
(5 May 1917) what he called his 'Notes on Human Nature Under
War Conditions':

> When a man makes a statement now, it seldom has any relation
> to facts or even to what he supposes to be the facts. He is merely
> functioning – generally under the stimulus of fear or sorrow.
> Realize this, and he will puzzle you less.
>   Most men are unhappy and restless without Faith, and, to cover
> up the path that led them to it, give out that Faith is splendid

---

[1] Robert Sencourt (1890–1969), biographer and critic.

[2] See Vol. I, p. 176.

[3] He recorded it in *Built in Jerusalem's Wall* (1920), published under the
pseudonym of Francis Keppel. The chapters were dedicated to various
friends, including Forster.

[4] Letter to G. H. Ludolf, 8 May 1920.

and arduous and only fully attained by the elect. They can most agreeably believe in an enlarged and everlasting man. Hence 'God' in the past and the 'Nation' now. Either is the reflection of man; weakness upon a cloud.

It is easier to personify an enemy-nation than one's own, owing to one's greater ignorance of the items that compose it. Only by believing in a Germany have we become patriotic, just as we remained religious only so long as we could believe in a Devil. A menace essential to Faith . . .

Privately most men attain to love and unselfishness and insight and a priori one would expect them to display these qualities in their social life, for they certainly bring earnestness of purpose to it. But some psychological hitch takes place, whose nature is not easy to determine: could it be removed we should be free from all evils except disease and death. An observer from another planet who watched not only the earth's wars but its public institutions would never infer what sweetness and nobility there can be in intercourse between individuals.

Dickinson had spent the war in black despair, ostracized by some of his old friends in Cambridge because of his pacifism, and deliberately isolating himself from others.[1] Forster did his best in his letters to comfort him but admitted to his own 'hard little theory' – that all rational and philosophic effort towards a good society was futile. 'But then,' he told him, 'I have never had the energy or intelligence to understand contemporary civilization, have never done more than loaf through it and jump out of its way when it seemed likely to hurt me.' In so far as he saw hope for the post-war world, it was along the lines of Bertrand Russell's *Principles of Social Reconstruction* (1917). He recommended it to friends as a 'brave and splendid book', but to Russell himself he wrote (28 July 1918) that the book, with its faith in social progress, left him unconvinced.

> For a time I thought you would shake me out of my formula – that though of course there is a connection between civilization and our private desires and impulses and actions, it is a connection as meaningless as that between a word and the letters that make it up. But the formula holds. The war will only end through exhaustion and nausea. All that is good in humanity must be sweated and vomited out together with what is bad.

---

[1] He told C. R. Ashbee, when Ashbee was going off to Egypt in 1917, that he was not envious and wanted to stay in Britain to feel the hideousness of things to the very full.

Some time during 1917 he received a letter from Siegfried Sassoon, a letter of homage and desire for friendship written out of the stress of Sassoon's disgust with the war. (It was during this year that Sassoon published his anti-war *Soldier's Declaration* and flung his M.C. ribbon into the Mersey.) The letter impressed Forster – he told Sassoon later that it had 'wound him up' when he had run down. A correspondence developed; and in the following year, when Sassoon (who by now had rejoined his regiment) was returning from Palestine, they made an attempt to meet. It was frustrated; and, next day, Sassoon wrote to Forster from the boat:

1 May 1918

Dear Mr E.M.F.,

I am awfully disappointed because I have been unable to go ashore; we came straight on board from the train; the last Division who left here for France behaved so badly that we are not allowed to leave the boat – licentious soldiery! It is indeed a disaster that two eminent authors must be so cruelly isolated!

But, if you could see the officers' smoking room an hour or two after dinner, you would understand that there is a reason for these restrictions on liberty.

When I see a large number of officers herded together with facilities for enjoying themselves I simply loathe them as a class. The quiet ones sit in corners and are absolutely swamped by the odious vulgarity of the remainder.

I wish I had your power of reproducing conversations. A novel dealing with the bad side of the officer class in wartime would add something to the indictment against militarism. There are several generals and their staffs on board; – fairly quiet; but most of them look like tailor's advertisements. One hears them talking in their superior, self-possessed voices – 'I myself think . . .', 'My own opinion is . . .', and so on . . . But 'red tabs' always 'get my goat' as the troops say. The troops! I wish you could see them asleep on the decks at night, with a few violet, dim lights glowing overhead. They are crowded and overcrowded – many more than there is room for. And their patience & simplicity make me hate being an officer. But the troops are the only thing in the war that moves me deeply. When I see them in large masses they seem like the whole tradition of suffering humanity. They are like a single soul. Officers are merely nasty individuals who drink cocktails all day, and are touched by 'Because', 'The Rosary', & 'I Hear You Calling Me', & read 'The Tatler' & 'The London Mail', & put their own comfort before anything else . . .

Forster, equally disappointed, replied (2 May 1918):

Dear Sassoon,

Damn you. I suppose for writing such a letter and for not being ill. I settled when I saw the Ras el Tin postmark that you were in hospital there and that I should come to see you. How one longs for people to be ill. It's a great disappointment to me that we shan't meet. I have read those 4 poems. I like possessing them. I am writing for more of you to England.

I began a short story about officers.[1] It is called 'Inferior'. Two of them take cigarettes round their men in a Hospital, and come across a man whom one of them had shot at for 'cowardice'. But it was an inferior story. It's not that I'm off writing, but I can't any more put words between inverted commas and join them together with 'said' and an imaginary proper name. The atmosphere of the story, had it attained one, was exactly what your letter describes, though the officers only got their Rosaries and Cocktails as the curtains fell. I have seen more officers than usual lately. What *is* it? What *is* it? I believe it's the possession of power. Give a man power over other men, and he deteriorates at once. The 'troops' are decent and charming, I believe, not because they suffer but because they are powerless. – And the devil who rules this planet has contrived that those who are powerless shall suffer.

I expect to stop here until combed out . . . There are things in these last two years that I can never be too grateful for, never. My work here is obscure and occasionally humiliating. Never mind. It's been worth my while. Petulant rather than puffy one steals ahead – the whole act of living seems one continuous theft now . . .

In another letter to Sassoon he told him how he could see 'geographically, scars across Europe and Asia, into which, from both sides, all forms of life – men camels vegetables sugar – are being pushed by the respective governments.' To this horror, he continued to think, the only decent response was 'decadence', epicureanism or *fainéantisme*. On a visit to Furness in Cairo he sprained his ankle badly and had to lie up for a week or two in Furness's brother's house, and, searching for something to read in his idleness, he happened on T. S. Eliot's *Prufrock and Other Observations*, recently published by the Egoist Press. It hit his mood to perfection. 'Here was a protest, and a feeble protest, and the more congenial for being feeble,' he wrote later.[2] 'For what, in that world of gigantic horror, was tolerable except the slighter gestures of dissent?'

So endless did the war seem, he half felt that he might never see

---

[1] It has not survived.
[2] 'T. S. Eliot', in *Abinger Harvest*.

England again – or at least that, before he did so, he might somehow
find his way to India. Home began to seem unreal – the more so that,
in his letters home, he had to watch himself continually to keep out
hints of Mohammed. None the less, he followed his mother's doings
anxiously, and implored Florence to keep an eye on her. Maimie
Aylward fell ill and was clearly dying, and Lily, who went to Salisbury
to nurse her, wanted Maimie to spend her last days in Weybridge.
Hearing this, Forster told her to empty his study and sell his furniture, so as to make an extra bedroom; further – guessing that she
was short of money – he even urged her to sell his typewriter. He
struggled to imagine England, with its air-raids and food queues, and
for a time, out of an impulse of solidarity, made a principle of
refusing dinner-invitations. Nevertheless, he told Florence Barger
(14 May 1918), it was as if Mohammed had 'fallen like some lovely
cloud' between himself and the war. 'Were he to rise I should see it
again. He has hidden my home life too.'

Mohammed got a few days' leave in May 1918 and came to see
Forster in Alexandria. Forster was still convinced he could not have
him to his flat. He told Florence Barger that it would be different if
his landlady were disobliging: 'But when a perfect person turns odd
and huffed you have to notice it.' Florence asked him why he didn't
simply move. But this he was not inclined to do, so he and Mohammed had to meet where they could, at the house of Mohammed's
friend the matrimonial agent, or on a hillside near Mex, where they
sat 'as Maurice and Clive sat at Cambridge'. Forster told Mohammed
he should give up his job and come back to Alexandria and take an
allowance from himself till he found work, but Mohammed refused.
He said, philosophically, 'Two days have passed like two minutes,
yet I think perhaps it is best so, for if I walk with the same friend
every day I have sometimes wanted another. Now we shall again be
anxious for one another for six months and then have this time of
happiness.'

Shortly afterwards, Mohammed did in fact give up his job, to avoid
signing on for the duration; and it so happened that, at about the
same time, his father died and his brother was drowned in a bathing
accident. As a consequence, he inherited the family house at Mansourah and a little money – just enough to consider setting up in
business. The best possibility seemed to be the cotton trade – that is
to say, buying cotton in the villages for sale in the Cairo market. He

had a prospective partner who, Mohammed told Forster, 'I think cannot pull Mohammed's leg.' Forster offered to lend him £70 capital, and, after some pressing, he accepted – also sending Forster on various business errands in Alexandria, such as enquiring the current price of cotton-bags. Being now a householder, Mohammed also decided to get married. His first idea was that he should marry his brother's widow. This fell through, but thereupon he quickly found another match.

In July, before the marriage, Forster came to stay with him in the family house. It was a little slum dwelling, in a muddy lane overrun with ducks and chickens, and Mohammed had let most of it; thus they had to live in one room – a room so crammed that, on entering, they had to jump straight on to the sofa. To wash, they stripped in a grimy stone-floored passage and poured tins of water over each other. Forster told Florence Barger (16 July 1918) that he blessed his adaptability: 'Where would I be if I had gone in for "requiring" things like Plugs and Plates?' They spent their two days visiting among Mohammed's friends. Mohammed still refused gifts, but they exchanged various cast-off clothes and went together to a tailor, for Mohammed to be measured for a suit (a little too large for him) which they could possess in common. In bed at night they played the fool like children, Mohammed declaring 'Morgan I will hurt you! – Edward I will kill you!' Mohammed was in high spirits, looking forward, he said, to 'living as a happy man in my own paternal home'. Forster felt happy for him and was not jealous of the coming marriage.

Not long after his return, however, he received a desolate letter from Mohammed. It said that he was ill, had been losing weight and spitting blood, and fairly certainly had consumption. 'I do not trouble much about my illness,' he wrote. 'I believe that only the death is my relief from this troublesome world.' He went on with his marriage-plans, and the wedding took place on 1 October 1918, but his letters continued gloomy; he was ill, his business was doing badly, and he had been in trouble with the police over selling some bags of rotted cotton. By the last days of the same month, with the defeat and surrender of Turkey, Forster's Red Cross work more or less came to an end, and he had to tell Mohammed that he would be leaving Egypt in January.[1] The news added to Mohammed's depression. He wrote:

---

[1] 'What a time of mad joy!' wrote his Aunt Eliza Fowler to Lily, at this time, apropos of the armistice with Germany. 'Miss Roberts was much

I feel very feeble and I am looking for anything to strengthen me
but I have not found any here. I believe I am growing thinner
and thinner . . . I was looking for a bottle of that oil of this fish
but they ask a great sum of money, moreover it is not I think
from the best kind . . . I am not looking forward to my future nor
to my career.

> Your miserable friend,
> Moh. el Adl.

According to Mohammedan custom, it would not be proper for
Forster to stay with Mohammed after his marriage; however, in
defiance of this, he came for a farewell visit and found things better
than he had feared. Mohammed was enjoying marriage, claiming that
before it 'he had not been in the world'. Forster only caught glimpses
of his wife, Gamila, but told Florence Barger that she was very young,
simple, and charming. He enjoyed hearing her and Mohammed laugh
together:

> She is like some tame and pretty country animal, and he will be
> kind to her as to all, but the idea of companionship never seems to
> have entered his head . . . He differs from the northerner in being
> unsentimental, and in keeping his senses apart from his mind.

He asked Mohammed to obtain him some of the locally-made flutes
or panpipes, to take as presents for Florence's children. To this
Mohammed replied: 'Why do you not take them costlier gifts? Why
not take them a pair of Egyptians?'

---

affected with the downfall of the viper, so like him to run away, but his time
is to come, the shameful boasting bubble . . . Now the great joy is to come dear
Lily to you. Morgan will soon I hope be with you, for goodness sake for a little
time keep the frothy women off.'

3 Sins of Empire

Forster returned to England at the end of January 1919. His mother treated his homecoming as a solemn occasion, insisting, for the first time since his boyhood, on reading family prayers in his presence. The gesture pleased him, and later he was to reflect that a little more ritual in their life together might have helped them. He soon found, though, that contrary to his hopes, nothing much had changed in their relationship. He had imagined that his three years' absence, together with his release from sexual 'apprenticeship', might have given him independence, but, for good or evil, he found himself still in her power: he loved her, knew he could not be frank with her, yet still needed her good opinion and feared to be despised or pitied by her. One morning at breakfast, soon after his return, he broke down after reading a letter from Mohammed, and was angry at himself afterwards. 'Very unwise,' he noted in his diary, 'for it puts me in mother's power. She is *very* sweet, but it is never safe to be seen in pieces.' The solution, he had learned, was not to be too long in her company at one time; and within days of his return he departed on a round of visits, going to stay with the Bargers in Englefield Green, with the Merediths, in Belfast, and then to Lyme Regis for a holiday with Lowes Dickinson.

He also, during the next month or two, renewed contact with Frank Vicary, his friend from hospital-searching days, and invited him to stay at Weybridge. Vicary was now a miner, working in the Kent coalfields. As before, Forster found him very charming—odd, imaginative, unexpected – and Lily took to him also. It was an inter-class friendship of the kind that Forster found romantic. He warned himself to make no sexual approaches, but fell into the role of protector towards Frank, helping him with advice and money. After a little while, he even arranged to give him a small regular allowance.

It was a difficult moment for him in his own career. At the time of the success of *Howards End* he had asked himself whether, when his reputation declined, as it probably would, he would begin to feel envious towards other writers: and now the test had come. He was not forgotten, it is true; during 1919 Arnold's reissued *A Room With a View* and *Howards End* and Alfred Knopf published the first American edition of *Where Angels Fear to Tread*. All these were quite small printings, however. His was no longer a really famous name, as it had been briefly before the war certainly not a household word like that of Wells or Bennett or Galsworthy. As things proved, the fact aroused no envy in him at all – he was always to be immune to envy as an emotion. Nor did it, as might have been natural, make him begin to doubt his own worth. He was quite clear, for instance – when he thought of the matter – that Galsworthy was his inferior. When asked this year to review a novel by Galsworthy, he refused, saying 'I can't patronize novelists who once were or might have been my fellows. And I can't look up to them.'[1] Similarly, when he heard from Hugh Walpole that Knopf wanted Walpole to write an Introduction to *Where Angels Fear to Tread*, he squashed the idea briskly.

> My dear Walpole,
>   Damn those people – oh look here – in the first place I don't want to be introduced at all; in the second place I don't want you to introduce me, for the reason that you are natu minor and the veteran business does, just here, come in I find . . .

Nevertheless he had to face the fact that his career as a novelist was probably finished and he would have to find some other purpose in life. It was necessary even from the money viewpoint, for his investments had suffered during the war, and his royalties had dwindled. He might eventually have to consider finding a full-time job. Meanwhile the obvious course was literary journalism. He was much in demand as a reviewer, so there were plenty of congenial openings for him – for instance the *Nation* and the *Daily News*, with both of which he had a long-standing connection. He was also being pressed by Siegfried Sassoon to review for the *Herald* – recently reconstituted as a daily with Sassoon as its literary editor. Forster

---

[1] Letter to Siegfried Sassoon, 18 October 1919.

had admired the *Herald*'s radical and pacifist stand during the war and liked the notion of writing for it – though as he told Sassoon, he wasn't sure if he knew what the Common People wanted, his own past having been uniformly refined. The *Athenaeum* was also eager for work from him. This, the most famous of the Victorian weeklies, had briefly converted itself into a monthly, with Middleton Murry as its literary editor. Forster particularly liked the *Athenaeum*. 'Here at last,' he wrote later, 'was a paper which it was a pleasure to read and an honour to write for, and which linked up literature and life.' He wrote a good deal for it in the next two years, beginning his campaign for Cavafy in its pages, and for a time he acted as its theatre critic. In all, in these and other journals during the years 1919–20, he would produce something like a hundred reviews and articles. It was a decent substitute for creation, and he enjoyed it, though in gloomier moments it gave him feelings of futility:

> *12 Aug. 1919.* I am happiest when busy. How fatuous! I see my middle age as clearly as middle age can be seen. Always working, never creating. Pleasant to all, trusting no one. A mixture of cowardice and sympathy. Blaming civilization for my failure. At the end of these activities begins a great pain, after which death, but I cannot realize such things. I do not bother about keeping young since my triumph with M. I long for something of which youth was only a part. I don't see what it is clearly yet, but know what keeps me from it. I am not vain, but I am sensitive to praise and blame: this is bad. Is it just the aimiable [*sic*] journalist – who can't even write as soon as he looks into his own mind?

Soon after his return to England he had had his long-delayed meeting with Siegfried Sassoon, finding him very engaging, and evidently eager for his friendship. Sassoon was now in his early thirties. He was attractive and impressive in appearance: tall, beaky-nosed and hawk-faced, with abundant reddish-brown hair. In manner he was a mixture of *hauteur* and naïveté, sometimes voluble, some-times taciturn, egocentric in an ingenuous way, and full of disordered opinions. His talk came out in little spurts and was often almost inaudible. He took to Forster, as Forster had taken to him, and the two quickly became intimate, meeting and dining out frequently during Forster's London visits. Forster, from the first, took a paternal and admonitory tone towards Sassoon, thinking him muddled in his ambitions and relationships and altogether, as he once told him, 'wanting rather more than the world's economy can provide'.

Out of reaction to the war, Sassoon had become a Socialist. He had done some campaigning for Philip Snowden in the 1918 election and talked with violence against the idle rich – especially against his own millionaire Sassoon cousins. By now, too, he had made the round of literary society. He was intimate with most of the surviving 'Georgian' poets, and with the Sitwell circle. He also had various friends among the older generation – among them Gosse, Robert Bridges and Thomas Hardy. He saw it as his function to bring the literary generations together; it was under his auspices that, later this year, Forster paid a first visit to Hardy at Max Gate.

For all this, Sassoon liked sometimes to think of himself as a simple-hearted fox-hunting man, astray among Bohemians. Once, in these early days of his friendship with Forster, he wrote to him, defensively, 'You *must* realize that I am *not* an intellectual.' Forster, amused, replied: 'I had no idea that you were not an intellectual. I used to think I was not. Now I think I am. It makes, of course, not the least difference to one's enjoyment or one's insight or any thing else.'[1] As a poet, Sassoon was finding himself in difficulties, uncertain of his direction, Forster urged him not to type himself as a satirist: 'As for satire,' he wrote to him, 'for God's sake only write if it amuses you or if savage indignation impels you; the satirical *habit* means slow death of the most ignoble kind. I should have thought that, once out of the army, you would have lost interest in satire.'[2]

Sassoon revealed, or perhaps Forster had already learned from gossip, that he was homosexual. He was secretive and rather anguished about his love-life,[3] but became confiding with Forster, who from time to time would offer him advice. In one such letter, Forster wrote to him:

> . . . you ought to drop your Catholic. I think the objection is even greater than in the case of Colin. If *you* were involved, that's another matter, but it's merely your (too stupid to find right words) – inquisitiveness and so to speak vanity that are involved, while him you may get into a most frightful casuistical tangle.

[1] Undated letter, probably *circa* June 1919.
[2] Undated letter, probably *circa* June 1919.
[3] According to his friend Sam Behrman, when Sassoon was in America in 1920 giving readings from his war-poems, he was bitterly hurt by a reported remark of Edna St Vincent Millay's: 'I wonder whether he would have cared so much if it were a thousand virgins who had been slaughtered.' (S. N. Behrman, *Tribulations and Laughter* (1972), p. 116.)

> Not to have confessed the 'certain difficulties' is I suppose a sin,
> and anything that from our point of view would be better, would
> be infinitely worse.[1]

Sassoon had written some 'unpublishable' writings, and he showed
them to Forster, who, in return, lent him *Maurice*.

Forster, since the war, had been without a London club,[2] and
Sassoon introduced him to one – just then very popular with the radical intelligentsia – the 1917 Club in Soho. It had been founded by
Ramsay MacDonald and friends of his, in honour of the Russian revolution and as a place in which to talk freely without fear of DORA.[3]
It had premises, very grubby ones, in Gerrard Street, a street occupied
otherwise by prostitutes, and was frequented by every kind of
progressive: labour politicians, pacifists and communists, vegetarians,
free lovers and theosophists. Many leftish writers belonged, the Sit-
wells, Aldous Huxley and the Woolfs all being members. Virginia
Woolf used to find that her friends, Forster among them, would, in
her phrase, 'gather to a bunch' at the club most weekdays at teatime.

She and Forster gradually were growing a little more intimate. She
was drawn to him, though sometimes feeling that he shrank from her
misogynistically, as 'a woman, a clever woman, an up to date woman'.
Seeing him one day at the 1917 Club, beside Clive Bell, she was
struck by the contrast they made. 'Clive showed as gaslight beside
Morgan's normal day – his day not sunny or tempestuous but a day
of pure light, capable of showing up the rouge and powder, the dust
and wrinkles, the cracks and contortions of my poor parakeet.'[4]
When her *Kew Gardens* and *The Mark on the Wall* came out in the
summer of 1919, Forster gave them a very appreciative and imaginative review. It made her realize, once again, how much she valued
his approval; and when he disparaged *Night and Day* to her, it caused
her to reflect that even his blame made her happier than other
people's praise. He impressed her as very detached, very sure of
himself, but timid, with no intensity or rapidity about him, and easily
drowned by Bloomsbury vociferation. He resembled, she thought, 'a

---

[1] Undated letter, probably June or July 1919.
[2] Before the war he had for a short time belonged to the Savile Club,
resigning, so he said, because the Brussels sprouts were cold (probably,
actually, because of the expense).
[3] The much hated *Defence of the Realm Act*.
[4] Virginia Woolf's diary, 10 January 1920.

vaguely rambling butterfly', and was as hard to catch or pin down as a butterfly. She liked his odd, direct way of explaining things: how he only had £26 in the bank and would come to stay with her and Leonard in Sussex if they paid his fare; how he hated Stevenson; how he made up his novels as he went along. . . . She felt there was a lot to say about him, though she didn't yet know how to say it.

Forster, before leaving Egypt, had found a publisher for his *Alexandria: a History and a Guide,* and was expecting proofs. Meanwhile, he was doing some journalism about Egypt and, partly on Mohammed's account, was following the news from there with a sense of personal involvement. Soon after his return there had been serious disturbances in Egypt. The country was still under martial law, but there was now an organized nationalist party, and its leader, Zagloul, had asked permission to lead a political delegation to Britain. The request had been refused, contemptuously; and thereupon Zagloul had declared a campaign for total independence for Egypt, to which Britain had responded by deporting him to Malta. As a result, in March 1919 there were strikes and rioting in Egypt, several British being murdered and their deaths being followed by very harsh reprisals. The events prompted Forster to write to the *Manchester Guardian* (29 March 1919), condemning Britain's record in Egypt and her wartime policy over the Egyptian Labour Corps.

> Sir:
>   May I after over three years in Egypt, confirm the main statements in Captain Guest's[1] account of conditions there? As he points out, the causes of the present unrest must be sought for in something deeper than the grievances of the Nationalist party. The *fellahin* have become embittered, for the first time in the history of our occupation, and there is no doubt that the military authorities of the E.E.F. are mainly to blame for this. Recruiting for the Egyptian Labour Corps and similar bodies was at first popular, for the pay is good. But before long the supply of volunteers ran low, and then the military authorities gradually adopted a system of compulsion. The governor (*mudir*) of each province was required to supply so many men; he assigned the various districts to his subordinates, and they informed the head

---

[1] His letter followed an article by L. Haden Guest in the issue for 25 March, in which Guest blamed the disturbances on Britain's mishandling of the Egyptian Labour Corps during the war and on uncertainty among Muslims over British intentions in the Middle East.

man (*omdeh*) of each village how many *fellahin* he must provide. The system was absolutely secret. The districts that suffered most were the country ones, where public opinion could least express itself. It was extended to the towns as the needs of the army grew, until at last only Cairo and Alexandria were exempt. No doubt it would have reached them but for our victories in Palestine – victories to which, according to all accounts, the work of our Egyptian auxiliaries substantially contributed.

With regard to the treatment of these 'volunteers' while they were in health opinions vary, but several British soldiers have informed me, unasked, that it was brutal. With regard to their treatment in sickness there is only one opinion. It was disgraceful. Insufficient in number, ill-equipped, unsupervised, the hospitals promoted rather than checked the typhus epidemics that were raging. The official view, apparently, was that the Egyptians are never ill, but if ill are certain to die, and treatment seems scarcely to have existed. In a case for the facts of which I can vouch, a native was sent into one of these hospitals with some slight ailment and at once caught a fever which almost carried him off. He had to bribe an orderly for everything, including a bed, and around him men were dying unattended. Small wonder that the hospitals were regarded by our own troops as centres of infection, and that they dreaded being camped in their vicinity.

We can never replace the *fellahin* whom we have so needlessly destroyed, but we can perhaps enter into the feelings of the survivors and realize why the present disturbances have occurred quite as much in country as in the towns. When I arrived in Egypt the people were invariably friendly, but in 1918 there was marked change – silence from the adults, and from the children an occasional hooting which, trivial in itself, showed how the wind was blowing. And just at the time of our victories a plaintive little popular song was born and sung to a minor tune about the street –

My native town, oh my native town!
The military authorities have taken my boy.

A week or two after this letter, there arrived from India the first news of the Amritsar massacre. *The Times* reported the event briefly and non-committally: 'At Amritsar, on April 13, the mob defied the proclamation forbidding public meetings. Firing ensued, and 200 casualties occurred.' There was also some comment in a leader, and the following week the *Nation* ran an article on the shootings, but for the moment the affair did not make much stir in Britain. (Indeed it did not become a national issue till next year, when the Hunter Committee published its report.) The news, however, coming on top of the reprisals in Egypt, fed in Forster a general sense of indignation against his country – still run, so it seemed, by the old gang, made more powerful and irresponsible by the war. He expressed his feelings in an ironical letter to the *Daily Herald*,[1] headed 'Hawkeritis';

> Sir,
>
> Europe is starving. In Egypt the native population is being arrested wholesale. Similarly in India. In Russia our troops are being employed on some unknown adventure. At home prices are rising, unrest is increasing, our homes are full of the wreckage of four years war. Are we downhearted? No. Do we clamour for facts, for the removal of the censorship, for the repeal of DORA? No; a thousand times no. In Paris a handful of generals and diplomats are deciding the future of the world. Are we interested in their decision? Not the least. Give us something to shout about. That's all we want.
>
> Mr Hawker comes along. He has done for money what thousands of other airmen have done for nothing – namely, made a dangerous flight. And, unlike thousands of others, he has got through. One is glad that he is all right, just as one is glad that Mrs Hawker possesses a fawn-coloured skirt. They appear to be an amiable young couple, and one wishes them well. But why in the name of goodness, should we get Hawkeritis? This planet is passing through the supreme crisis of its history. It is being decided whether we shall be governed openly, like a free people, or secretly as in the past. And how the cynics who govern us secretly must have gloated over the hysterics of last Tuesday! 'There goes the mob!' they must have thought; 'just the same as ever after four years of suffering – indifferent to truth, incapable of thought, and keen only on trifles. As long as we arrange for an occasional Hawker to be shouted at and boomed in the newspapers we can manage them as easily as ever.'
>
> The 'mob' will not be governed as easily as the cynics think. On the other hand, we shall never conquer unless we divert our enthusiasms to worthy things, the real things. Until a people is serious it will never be free.

This letter was published on 30 May, and meanwhile, from a friend of Mohammed's in Egypt, he had received some very disturbing news – that Mohammed had been arrested and was in prison. For a

---

[1] *Daily Herald*, 30 May 1919. The flying-feat referred to was the first, and unsuccessful, attempt to fly the Atlantic, made by Harry G. Hawker and Mackenzie Grieve. Their plane came down into the sea 740 miles short of Ireland but they were rescued by a Danish steamer. The newspapers were full of the story for many days.

time he could discover no more. Pretty clearly, the arrest had some connection with the recent disorders in Egypt; but the only other clear fact he could gather, for the moment, was that by paying a £10 fine he could have Mohammed's sentence curtailed by three months. He duly sent the money, but otherwise he felt helpless, anguished on Mohammed's behalf, and cursing his own ill-management in not finding a better 'agent' in Egypt.

While in this anxious frame of mind, daily awaiting news from Egypt, he received a long and impassioned letter from Malcolm Darling about the Amritsar affair. Darling had been in the Punjab at the time of the massacre, and it had disturbed him profoundly, shaking for the moment both his patriotism and his love for India. In the days just before the shootings, there had occurred two brutal assaults on Englishwomen, and he had witnessed the resulting hysteria and closing of ranks among the British. In fact, he had suffered under them painfully himself. When the news arrived of the first disturbances at Amritsar, he and Josie had been at the nearby town of Gurdaspur, preparing to go on a tour of co-operative societies.[1] The Superintendent of Police, alarmed by the news, had urged him to stay in Gurdaspur and cancel his tour, but Darling, thinking this would give a bad appearance, had set out as planned. This was on 11 April, two days before the massacre in the Jallianwallah Bagh, and, on returning to Lahore after his week's tour, he had found himself accused of dereliction of duty – that is to say, of refusing help to a colleague in time of emergency. The gossip in the Club was that he had shown cowardice.

The affair had been smoothed over, and for the moment he did not tell Forster of it, and wrote only of the general tragedy. 'The world for the moment has gone mad,' he wrote (11 July 1919):

> Ever since the Armistice I have grown more and more pro-German to use the cant phase of those, the largest number, that still see red. If the Germans hated us before, they will hate us twice as much now. Said my ever ardent Josie tonight – if I were German I would long for boys to bring up to avenge this peace. – We have, I fear, missed a great opportunity . . .
> But what of India you say. Why talk of things you know nothing about, when there are 30,000 things I want to know about India? Well, we're in a bit of a mess out here too. Racial hatred

---

[1] Darling's main work in India was in the field of agricultural co-operation.

in towns leaping in a twink to pillage and murder, murder too of the most horrible kind. Then panic and cruelty – the two go together. I understand now why Germans did those terrible things in Belgium, they got cold feet passing thru and fell blindly upon the people whom they feared. So with us (with a big difference of course). We did not rape and hack to pieces, but one day in Amritsar they shot down hundreds, mostly zemindars, there by religious hazard (Bhaisakh Day). I have seen the place – a death trap. 5 or 6,000 there, the kernel of them thoroughly seditious, but the majority lookers on, mooching about as zemindars do. Enter infuriated general – 'I took 30 seconds to make up my mind', said he to Watkin – and then – 1500 rounds. God it makes me sick to think of it. Yet I was told by my chief 10 days later – 'people at the Club (Lahore) say you ought to be court martialled for criticizing.' Surprising the number of Englishmen who got the wind up those days. Our D.C. – Supdt of Police[1] notably. Many others too. Josie was magnificent – refused to go up to the Hills, came out into Camp with me when everyone else was huddling at Headquarters. It was undoubtedly a bad quarter of an hour, actually about 10 days, that they gave us – but for Martial Law things might have pitched us all onto the bonfire. The zemindars were luckily absorbed in their harvest but in some Districts they found time to burn quite a lot of stations. Wires cut everywhere of course as in Egypt. Heaven knows what produced so sudden a flare. Literally everyone was caught napping. Some say it's Bolshevist gold, others that it was all spontaneous. One thing is clear – the big towns hate us. Martial Law (kept on much too long) has cowed them (easily done out here) but the old bitterness remains, embittered. On the other side you can guess the effect of the Amritsar murders. They were awful Morgan. Two of the men I knew slightly. But it was the way they tried to batter the women to death. One, a friend of Josie's, who had ridden into the City to save *Indian* girls (Christian) was set upon and knocked down ½ dozen times before she was left for dead. Mon Dieu, it's a bad world . . . And now, what's going to happen. What the Statesman's panacea? Dyarchy or Democracy. For India, with her 300 million illiterates – God's truth, we must be possessed. The Gadarene swine are not in it. Yet I almost believe it's the only way out of the mess Montagu[2] and his gang have got us into. Home Rule is so much in the air, that now the only way is to let them have it. Let 'em taste the poison they long for. It's the only way to cure them. It can't last, any more than a sand castle before a rising tide.

---

[1] see p. 60.

[2] Edwin Samuel Montagu, Secretary of State for India 1917–22. See p. 68.

In Forster's present mood, this letter came home to him powerfully. He searched the papers for details of the Amritsar affair and questioned Darling further about it when he came on leave; and in his emotions, Egypt and India became more and more identified.

Through his journalism, he now counted as an expert on Egypt, and in the autumn the idea occurred to Leonard Woolf, who was secretary to the Labour Research Department, to invite him to contribute to a Fabian pamphlet on the Egyptian question. He accepted with hesitation but grew confident – he told Woolf – as he found 'how easy it is to write impressively about politics'. What he was composing was a historical Introduction to the pamphlet, relating the story of the British occupation of Egypt. He told himself he was writing it for Mohammed's sake, and he drew on his own experiences. 'The mild and cheerful Egyptians,' he wrote, 'seemed – especially to one who had known Indians – an easy people to live with.' They had been alienated by British high-handedness: by forced recruitment to the Labour Corps, the commandeering of supplies, and an absurd wartime censorship; and, in general, by officials who 'had a profound distrust of orientals'. He considered four solutions to the Egyptian problem and came down, without much conviction, in favour of a mandate under the League of Nations. A meeting was called to discuss his pamphlet, and everyone, including Bernard Shaw,* was very approving, wanting him to do more work for the Fabians. The trouble with this, he wrote to Reid, was that he didn't want to join the Labour party, or any party.

Mohammed had been due for release in October, and for a week or two, when the month had passed without news, Forster fell into acute distress. At last, late in November, a letter arrived from Mohammed, announcing his release and beginning to relate the story of his arrest. (It took him several letters to tell.) What had happened was that back in March, during the disturbances, there had been a railway strike in Egypt. As a result there had been food shortages, and it had occurred to Mohammed and a friend to undertake a little profiteering enterprise, going by boat to Cairo to buy beans and returning to sell them at inflated prices in Mansourah. All had seemed to go well; 'I thought the time after looking at me always cross began to smile,' Mohammed wrote. However, his partner, while selling their beans on the street, had been accosted by two Australian soldiers, who wanted to sell him an army revolver. Mohammed, who had been at lunch,

returned at this juncture and, according to his account, had stopped
the transaction. The soldiers had gone off, swearing; but two hours
later they had returned with an order for the arrest of Mohammed and
his friend for attempting to buy firearms. Under martial law this was
a serious offence. And to make matters worse, Mohammed, under
questioning, had pretended to know nothing about the revolver and
had told the absurd story that the soldiers had accosted them for
'baksheesh'. The soldiers ('those animals') had stuck to their account;
and as a result Mohammed had been tried by a military court and
sentenced to six months' hard labour (and his friend to four). So
'They shaved the hair they used a filthy basket instead of a towel,
took off my civil clothes and gave me a prisoner's clothes, a jacket
and a pair of trousers and a filthy Libda.' There had been bullying
and ill-treatment in the prison, and the food had been uneatable – he
had nearly starved till, at the cost of all his savings, he had bribed a
guard to fetch food from his home. The experience had made him at
last violently anti-British. At his trial he had exclaimed that he knew
an Englishman who said the English were just and he had believed him,
but 'now I found myself that I was about to make a great mistake'.

The story, long-awaited, stirred Forster's indignation. He guessed
that, in Mohammed's state of health, prison had done him fatal
injury, and his anger swelled against an empire that – here as in
India – made such injustices possible. In his New Year's Eve review
he recorded that Mohammed's imprisonment had 'really wrecked'
him this year.

*   *   *

Early in the New Year, Siegfried Sassoon went to the United
States, on a poetry-reading tour, and it was arranged that from March,
Forster should take his place as literary editor on the *Daily Herald*.
The job entailed two days' work a week, for which he was paid £5.
He found the work entertaining, and was glad, especially, to be able
to give reviewing work to Forrest Reid, whose name, he thought,
needed pushing.[1] Before long, however, he found himself engaged in
a battle to defend his page. He complained to Reid (18 April 1920)
that 'A "conference" consisting of the General, Assistant, Foreign

---

[1] He published reviews by, among others: Francis Birrell, David Garnett,
Gerald Gould, Aldous Huxley, H. J. Massingham, Forrest Reid, Bertrand
Russell, C. K. Scott Moncrieff, Frank Swinnerton, Rebecca West and Leonard
Woolf.

News-, Boxing-, Childrens-, and Sub-Editors, indeed all of the Editors except the Literary Editor, decides the length and quality of my Reviews, or attempts to.' He resisted vigorously, being resolved on resigning if he did not get his way, and in fact won his point. He got a feeling, however, that he was not popular in the *Herald* office, and after two months he gave the job up.

It was a continuing chagrin to him that he was not creating. He lamented it in a letter to Reid, who replied by speculating – rather more intimately than Forster quite liked – about the causes of his sterility. Forster told Reid (3 March 1920) that there was no one he would rather have such a letter from, but 'it is not the sort of letter I want to be appropriate to my troubles'.

> Why is it that one so dreads any discussion of the unconscious within one? It obscurely attacks one's pride, I suppose. I know that though I try to write back to you frankly, I shall probably fail.
>
> I think that I've stopped creating rather than become un-creative: you are quite right there. I have never felt I'm used up. It's rather that the scraps of imagination and observation in me won't coalesce as they used to. Whether I'm happy or sad or well or unwell (and I've been all in the last 8 years, *very* sad, *very* happy) the internal condition doesn't change. I'm sure that the Psycho-Analysts would nip on to it, and might possibly diagnose a toad. But I mistrust not so much their judgement as their influence. I should be very reluctant to let them meddle with me and make me change my estimate as to what is within myself. What they call a toad may be something that I call a precious stone . . . These people have no sense of literature and art and I regard with foreboding and resentment their offers to turn an artist upside down.

It was no longer a secret among his friends that he felt dried up as a novelist, and from time to time they would suggest other careers. Sydney Waterlow, who had re-entered the Foreign Service, was full of schemes on his behalf, and in the autumn of 1919 procured him the offer of a post in the Inter-Allied Commission in Germany. It was a well-paid job and attracted him in some ways – he felt he might be a good administrator – and he vacillated unhappily for some weeks before refusing. Then in the following spring, Sydney arranged an opening for him in the Foreign Office. Again he agonized for some time before refusing; and soon after this, on his own initiative, he wrote to the Maharaja of Dewas asking if there might be a post for

him at his court. This was a notion they had discussed earlier[1]
and – were it to be realized – it would be a considerable adventure;
all the same his letter was in a sense an admission of defeat, and while
he awaited an answer he fell into depression. It was quite acute, but
he was rescued from it – decisively, for the moment – by an old
Cambridge friend of his, Hilton Young.[2]

Young, a much-decorated war-hero, was now Parliamentary
Secretary to H. A. L. Fisher, the Minister for Education. Forster
and he rarely met, but there was a bond between them, a memory of
an exchange, 'not erotic but affectionate and mysterious', of many
years before.[3] Young, so different from himself in almost all ways
worldly, 'Wilcoxian', true-blue – was someone he felt he could profit
from; and, during an hours-long talk one day in October, Young did
him more good, he felt, than any psychoanalyst could have achieved.

> Oct. 28. Hilton Young: tea and dinner with him a week ago. He
> gave me carefully and considerately, with great sensitiveness and
> affection, some advice . . . Surmising the artist from the egoist –
> he ranks himself as the latter – he thought that the path to
> creation is to be found not by looking about one, but by peering
> into the lumber room of one's mind. 'It's a dark difficult place to
> see in – but presently something may catch your eye that will do.'
> His words impressed me deeply as did their sequel. He rose and
> looked at the book case, evidently daring himself. 'And one stocks
> the lumber room by –' The exact phrase I forget but the thought
> was familiar because it had struck me in By Sea and Land.[4] The
> point is that one must think and do and frequent what is decent.
> What a man has lived with he will have to die with. Exactly at
> what in my life Hilton may be hitting does not concern me, and
> this indicates the bigness of his personality. I am generally so
> worried lest people should not approve, and not content until I
> have defined their criticism and tried to cap it with a counter-
> criticism. He raised the interview high above fencing. It was

---

[1] See pp. 27–9.

[2] Edward Hilton Young (later Lord Kennet), 1879–1960. He was a Liberal,
and later a Conservative, politician, becoming Minister of Health 1931–5.
He had many friends in Bloomsbury.

[3] At the time of Hilton Young's death in 1960, Forster noted in his diary
(15 July 1960): 'As for H – , I remember something passing between us
over ½ century ago in Malcolm's mother's drawing-room, something not
erotic but affectionate and mysterious. . . . He referred to it afterwards, and
from that time I regarded him without fear.'

[4] Hilton Young's book of that name, published in 1920.

> practical and helpful in the sense that it has sunk deep. Even if I
> don't and can't resume creation he has made me vaster and more
> happy . . . No one, in a direct talk, has ever helped me more, and
> I think my gratitude got through, he is so acute and subtle. Since,
> I have street-walked and entertained idleness and indecencies,
> but the ground beneath them seem to have worn thinner.

Talking to Hilton Young had made him feel larger, 'vaster'. By
contrast, his Bloomsbury friends, though he liked and admired them,
tended to make him feel smaller, and he was wondering just now
about his relations with them. 'I don't think those people are little,'
he told himself, 'but they belittle all who come into their power.'
At the Woolfs' invitation he had recently joined the newly-formed
Memoir Club. Members of the club met three or four times a year,
dining at a restaurant and then moving on to one or other's home to
read autobiographical papers, which had to be of total frankness. It
was a reincarnation of a pre-war society, the Novel Club,[1] and
included many of the same members; the Woolfs, the Bells, the
MacCarthys, Keynes, Roger Fry and Duncan Grant. Forster enjoyed
the club and sometimes shone at it,[2] adopting a special, rather hard
and brittle style for his papers to it. Nevertheless, he had qualms
about it. He was present in February 1921 when Keynes read his
memoir on the Versailles peace negotiations[3] and thought it 'most
wonderful' and a privilege to listen to. He even enjoyed Clive Bell's
paper, the same evening, about his 'copulations'. All the same, not
for the last time, he half thought he might be wise to resign.

In the February of 1921, as two years before, he went for a holiday
with Dickinson in Lyme Regis. He described the scene to Forrest
Reid (17 February 1921):

> I am with Lowes Dickinson, who has forgotten the League of
> Nations, the Vienna University Relief Fund, the famine in China,
> the French in Syria, the depreciation of the Mark, the lynching
> of negroes in America, the depopulation of the South Sea Islands,
> and the unrest in Ireland for a little, and sits in a little mandarin's
> cap translating Faust with satisfaction and rapidity. All is peace

---

[1] The Novel Club was founded in 1913, with the professed aim of inducing
Desmond MacCarthy to write a novel.
[2] Virginia Woolf noted in her diary, 5 December 1920: 'The Memoir Club
was fearfully brilliant. Morgan very professional.'
[3] Published in Keynes's *Two Memoirs* (1949).

and pearly greyness, and the cat and dog, both female, lie down to
sleep in each other's arms or sit on the deserted parade and watch
the gulls.

Amid this scene of harmony, he received a cable from the Maharaja
of Dewas, summoning him to India. The invitation was rather vague
– Forster told Reid he was asked to go 'as Prime Minister or something' – but one point was clear: he was to come for a period of six
months or so, to replace another Englishman who was on sick-leave.
The Maharaja wanted him at once, and he accepted at once, cabling
a reply the same day. As soon as he got home from Lyme, he made his
travel arrangements, securing a berth on a P. & O. ship for 4 March,
and he wrote to Muhammed, proposing that they should snatch a
meeting as he passed through Port Said. His friends speculated
variously about his plan. 'Morgan goes to India and I think forever,'
recorded Virginia Woolf in her diary (1 March 1921). 'He will become
a mystic, sit by the roadside and forget Europe . . . we shan't see him
again.' The prospect of his departure depressed Lily, and during his
last weeks at home she was scratchy and difficult, but he saw this as
inevitable and was patient with her; and on the evening of his going,
she wrote him a tender letter (one of the very few of her letters to
him that have survived).

> I feel I want a little chat with you before I go to bed. I feel I got up
> days ago, and that you have been gone a very long time. The
> house seems sorrowing for you – such a desolate feeling as if it
> knew you had really gone and were not in London for the day or
> away on a visit. I must try to be a brave mammy and keep cheerful
> and look forward to your return. I shall come and meet you in a
> new garment of very radiant hues. I felt in a dream when I was
> out, rather as I felt when war was declared.

4 The Maharaja's Secretary

He was going to India at a time of high political drama. In the summer of 1918, the British Government had published what was known as the Montagu–Chelmsford report,[1] a set of proposals for India based on the principle of 'dyarchy', or the sharing of government between British and Indians. According to this scheme, the administration in the provinces would be divided into two parts, 'law and order' matters being reserved, as before, to the Governor and his appointed councillors, but other, so-called 'nation-building', matters being placed in the hands of native ministers, responsible to elected provincial councils. The proposals were rather paternalistic, the suggestion being that further freedoms for Indians would have to be earned by good behaviour. Nevertheless, they represented a fundamental change in British policy, and they had been received by the Congress leaders with guarded approval. A few weeks after this, however, there had been published another important document, very different in character. It was the report of a committee, known after its chairman[2] as the 'Rowlatt Committee', appointed by the Government of India to inquire into seditious crime. It was alarmist in tone, painted a lurid picture of new revolutionary threats and techniques, and recommended very repressive legislation. The relative timing of the two reports was disastrous. The goodwill earned by the Montagu–Chelmsford proposals was instantly dissipated. And worse, long before these proposals could become law, the

---

[1] After its sponsors, the Secretary of State for India, Edwin Montagu, and the Viceroy, Lord Chelmsford.

[2] A judge named Sir Sydney Rowlatt.

Government of India had taken action on the Rowlatt report, passing, early in 1919, Acts denying political prisoners the right to trial by jury and giving provincial governments the power of internment. Resentment in India had been intense. Gandhi, who emerged as a leader at this moment, had organized *hartals*[1] in protest against the Rowlatt Acts; the *hartals* had led to riots and to the fatal events at Amritsar; and these, and the vicious punitive measures which followed – public floggings, 'crawling orders'[2] and the like – had transformed the whole nature of Indian politics. Congress, hitherto an association of middle-class intellectuals, had in these few months become a mass movement. And Hindus and Muslims, to the alarm and incredulity of the British, had joined in a common front.

The Muslims nursed their own quite separate grievance against Britain. They believed her, and with reason, to be plotting the dismemberment of the Turkish empire – which, as being the seat of the Caliphate, was still the spiritual head of Islam. During the period of the Versailles peace negotiations, feeling over this had grown fierce, and a nationwide *Khilafat*[3] campaign had been launched in India. It was, in many ways, an unrealistic movement. Its leaders made wild and unfulfillable promises to Turkey, and at one stage set in motion an abortive exodus of Muslims to Afghanistan, with very tragic results. Nevertheless the movement gained a large following; and when the terms of the Treaty of Sèvres became known, with their very harsh treatment of Turkey, the *Khilafat* leaders had looked round for some positive action. It was the chance that Gandhi had been waiting for – 'the moment of moments', as he said, for creating a united party and country. He pledged Hindu support for the *Khilafat* campaign. Congress and the Muslim League merged, for the moment, more or less into a single party. And in September 1920, at a special meeting of Congress at Calcutta, Gandhi, with full Muslim backing, had declared a policy of 'non-co-operation' with the British.

*   *   *

No more on his present visit to India than on his earlier one did Forster come for political purposes, or with politics uppermost in his

---

[1] Days of national mourning, when business was suspended.

[2] The street in which a woman missionary had been attacked was declared a 'crawling lane', and Indians wishing to pass through it had to do so on their hands and knees.

[3] i.e. 'Caliphate'.

mind. His attitude was still, and in a sense always remained, the one expressed in his 'Salute to the Orient': '. . . we who seek the truth are only concerned with politics when they deflect us from it.' In so far as he had one special motive for coming, it was simply that having hitherto mixed mainly with Muslims, he wanted to see more of Hindus. Nevertheless the events of these years 1919–20, both in India and in Egypt, had affected him powerfully and they would be echoed in all sorts of ways[1] in his *A Passage to India*. The novel, whatever its original conception, was profoundly influenced and changed by them.

*   *   *

Forster, who set out for India on 4 March, managed his meeting with Mohammed as arranged. He was still on board ship at Port Said, wondering how to get to their rendezvous, when Mohammed appeared on deck, beaming and excited, having bribed his way on board. They went to a dockside café, where Mohammed, still wearing various cast-off clothes of Forster's, gave him a box of expensive cigarettes – no longer full, as some had had to go in bribes. He was thinner, and, as they talked, it became plain that things were going badly with him; however, having only a few hours together, they agreed to talk of cheerful subjects. Mohammed was impressed by Forster's palace appointment, but he warned him against pride. By now Forster, in a guarded way, had revealed Mohammed's existence to his mother, and they composed a joint postcard to her. All seemed the same between them as it had been two years ago, and they agreed to spend a week or two together on Forster's return from India.

He had been hoping to be met by Masood in Bombay. However, on his arrival there, he found neither Masood nor any message for him. Nor was there an emissary from Dewas, as had been promised, so he felt rather at a loss, and for the moment went to stay with his friends the Goodalls.[2] A day or two later, as he was standing in the Post Office, two nobles from Dewas, their faces painted red for *Holi*, rushed up to him, having been searching for him for days at a wrong address. Various further confusions ensued, but the party got off the same evening for Dewas, and at Indore a palace car was awaiting them. As they travelled the dull *chaussée*, edged with stunted trees,

---

[1] They have been analysed by Dr G. K. Das in his *E. M. Forster's India*.
[2] See Vol. 1, pp. 239–43.

that ran from Indore to Dewas, Forster was musing about his sex-life. He remembered how censoriously he had heard the Maharaja once speak of homosexuality, and he said to himself, 'The least I can do is to give him no trouble.' Then, from the car window, he noticed a dead cow with vultures gathering round it. It seemed an evil omen, and the thought occurred to him, 'That's how it will end.'

The Maharaja was at the palace entrance when they arrived, bare-headed and capering with glee. His first action was to dictate a cable to Malcolm Darling, and another to Forster's mother. He then handed Forster over to the major-domo, who showed him his rooms. These were on the first floor of the palace and quite extensive, comprising three rooms and a bathroom. In the evening, courtiers fitted Forster out with Indian clothes, and he was taken to the Cavalry Barracks, where a visiting troupe of actors were performing.

The following day the Maharaja instructed him as to his duties. The first step in this was a lengthy explanation of the court and its hierarchy. Forster learned that there were four grades of dignitaries: the ruling family, which included H.H. himself, his brother Bhau Sabib and his son Vikramsinha; the great Maratha nobles; the secondary nobles; and the lesser nobles, among whom Forster would belong. To his superiors at court Forster was to salaam with both hands and the whole hand, and he was to do likewise with the British A.G.G. and P.A.[1]; in dealing with these latter he was to regard himself as an Indian. The Maharaja wrote him out a list of the court nobles, with comments on their characters, and went on, confusingly, to describe a whole string of further personalities, such as 'Horse Doctor' and 'Eighteen Offices'. Forster also learned that there was a Council of State, though H.H. was vague about its workings.

His own sphere of action was to be the palace garden and tennis courts, the Guest-House arrangements, and the garages and 'electric house'; in addition, all mail was to pass through his hands; and apart from this – and most important of his functions – he was to give the Maharaja as much of his company as was possible and sometimes read aloud to him. Forster, who had been picturing himself as some kind of high diplomatic aide or counsellor, was a little taken aback at his duties and not sure how he would cope with motorcars and electric generators. He was told that his predecessor, Colonel Leslie, had been

---

[1] Agent to the Governor-General, and Political Agent.

a great expert in all such matters, as well as being fluent in several Indian languages; so he would hardly shine by comparison. Of course, he could take advice, for instance from the mayor of the palace, Malarao Sahib, or from the chief Indian secretary, Deolekr Sahib; but Deolekr spoke only broken English and Malarao hardly any English at all. As for himself, he spoke a little Urdu – enough to explain himself to servants and taxi-drivers – but knew no Marathi, which was the court language. He wrote to Masood (1 April 1921) that he thought he would be lonely in Dewas.

Still, he told himself, there would be the Maharaja himself, and there he foresaw much friendship and fascination. It was true, he had guessed by now that H.H. was not the 'dear, and a competent dear' that he had first imagined, but, in many ways, a great muddler. But if so, he might be a help to him. At all events, he had come to deepen his knowledge of India, and here was his perfect opportunity. He had learned from Darling, and from his own talks with H.H., that religion was all-important to the Maharaja, so, in studying his character, he determined to see what case it made for religion.

Holi was still at its height. It is the festival of the Sudras, the lowest of the caste-groups, and a time for horseplay and misrule. The Maharaja loved such things and had imported dancers and actors from the Deccan for the occasion – it was they whom Forster had seen perform on his first evening. He had found the play, a bawdy farce, stupid and disagreeable. He described it to Dickinson (14 April 1921):

> . . . Husband and wife. She: 'Can I go and see my people?' He: 'Dangerous for you – and for me – and morality generally.' She persists, and as soon as she goes the husband says 'I want a eunuch – *at once*.' – A tall scraggy man with a moustache then came on, in a pink sari, and paid attention to such members of the audience as His Highness indicated. (This is a recognized turn, the boy-dancers did it too.) The 'eunuch' squatted beside his victim and sang 'do not hurt me' – or 'I am not too old yet to remember what we did as boys' – and tried to kiss him amid laughter from the court. Resuming the drama he danced indecently before the husband, made 'terms' with him, bought him sweets, and was coming to a conclusion when the news is brought to the ill-advised wife. She returns from her parents. 'How can you ruin your health by such a proceeding?' is her argument; & I think that's where this particular indecency ended.

Forster was puzzled by this palace vein of 'naughtiness', for apart from this the tone of the court was strict, and (in theory anyway) actual sexual misbehaviour was frowned on. He supposed it was some kind of release, but it struck him as out of key and surmised that it was 'queered' – made distasteful – by religion. The Maharaja, when he discussed it with him, said: 'If a girl had been acting, it wouldn't have done, it would have been too much. As it is, it was all right.'

April Fool's Day arrived, reinforcing *Holi*, and Forster had to submit to exploding cigarettes and sofas that gave an electric shock. He was also, which pleased him more, given the chance to witness *Holi* observances in the country. Malarao took him to his own native village, accompanied by his cousin (a noble at present out of favour at court) and by Deolekr, who drove. As they were picnicking, villagers approached, singing, and showered them with red powder, and then a group of women emerged through the mud-wall of the village with strange cries. He wrote to his mother (6 April 1921):

> They, like the red powder, were part of a Hindu festivity, and squatting at a little distance, looking very Omega-like, they made a bright spot in the dust. The men continued their songs – one about the coming of Europeans to India, the other about the coming of Man to the Earth. Then my companions made me give the company Rupees (which they afterwards replaced stealthily in my pocket). I chose a site for a house, and we passed into the village by the seated ladies who abused us violently – so violently that even the young Sirdar[1] could not understand what was said. This abuse is of course traditional and has nothing personal in it: 3000 years ago in Greece the women did just the same thing at certain festivals.

During the same expedition they took a walk along Dewas's one river, the Sipra, and there occurred an incident which, to Forster, seemed emblematical of India:

> Our train of villagers stopped and pointed to the opposite bank with cries of a snake. At last I saw it – a black thing reared up to the height of three feet and motionless. I said 'It looks a small dead tree' and was told 'Oh no,' and exact species and habits of snake were indicated – not a cobra, but very fierce and revengeful, and if we shot it would pursue us several days later all the way to Dewas. We then took stones and threw them across the Sipra ($\frac{1}{2}$ the width of Weybridge Thames) in order to make the snake crawl

---

[1] Officer.

away. Still he didn't move and when a stone hit his base still didn't move. He *was* a small dead tree. All the villagers shrieked with laughter. The young Sirdar told them I was much disappointed and displeased about the snake, and that they must find a real one. So they dispersed anxiously for a few moments over the country, after which all was forgotten. – I call the adventure 'typical' because it is even more difficult here than in England to get at the rights of a matter. Every thing that happens is said to be one thing and proves to be another, and as it is further said in an unknown tongue I live in a haze.[1]

Despite his fears of loneliness, Forster was where he most wanted to be, in the midst of an Indian existence. He had written to Rupert Smith to send him his old servant, and Baldeo arrived in Dewas, more wizened, more morose than ever. Forster's life soon fell into a pattern. Baldeo would make his bed on the roof and serve him breakfast there at 6.30 a.m. From 8.00 to 10.30 a.m. he would work in his office or go on a tour of inspection of the garages, the 'electric house' and the gardens. Lunch was at 10.30, and the two following hours were devoted to the Maharaja, after which he took a siesta, followed by afternoon tea and then tennis or a drive. Dinner was at 8 p.m. and after it there would be conversation or music, or the courtiers would play cards in the palace courtyard, with decanters of whisky and port to hand. It was very hot, and growing hotter (reaching 108° F), but the atmosphere was dry and healthy, and he felt well and vigorous. Dewas was an ugly place, a poor and mean town in a parched and treeless landscape; but he learned to console himself with the magnificent night-sky and the constellation of Scorpio hanging down the whole of the eastern heaven. The proofs of his *Alexandria: a History and a Guide* had followed him to Dewas, and at odd intervals he would correct them, feeling that the book was now remote from him. From time to time, too, now and throughout his stay, he would take out his Indian novel, despairing at the discrepancy between it and the India around him.

Messages from Masood began at last to arrive; he had been on a tour of schools and had only just received Forster's cables. Forster had asked him for money, and he now despatched it in such quantity that the Dewas post office had to deal with it in instalments. A few days later, at the Maharaja's invitation, he arrived in person,

---

[1] Letter to his mother, 6 April 1921.

74

attended by a private secretary and two servants. His coming was
quite an event, for he had never before been a private guest in a
Hindu court, nor did Dewas often receive a Mohammedan visitor.
The Maharaja was at his most gracious. It was almost like the
meeting of two princes, and Masood told Forster that, in addition
to the outward ceremonies, H.H. showed him niceties of respect that
only another Indian could appreciate. Forster thought Masood's
public manner excessively pompous. However, it seemed to go down
well, and in private he was as companionable as ever.

To entertain them, the Maharaja arranged an expedition up the
sacred hill of Devi, providing an elephant for the occasion. Half way
up to the summit, the elephant's howdah began to slip, at which
Masood got off, remarking grandly: 'I prefer not to be on a tower
when the base totters.' Another day the Maharaja sent them in a
car to the holy city of Ujjain. There, on the riverside, they beheld a
swarm of ash-coloured *saddhus* (fakirs), seated on spikes – some
laughing, some quarrelling, others serving tea to one another. The
scene was too much for Masood, who expostulated to Forster, as if
he were responsible: 'My dear chap, I ask you!' A good deal that he
saw at Dewas, like the ill-organized building activities, bothered
him too, and he told Forster they were a crying example of his
country's inadequacy.

The Maharaja enjoyed Masood's visit and was more and more
delighted with the company of his 'dear Morgan'. He was full of
solicitude for his comfort, and soon became confiding. Much had
happened since Forster's last visit. For one thing, he had separated
from his queen. She was the daughter of the Maharaja of Kolhapur,
the senior Maratha prince, and the marriage, which had taken place
in 1908, had thus been a grand alliance. It had gone disastrously
wrong, however, and in 1915 the Marahani had been sent, or had
fled, back to her home state. As a result, the rich and powerful
Kolhapur and the tiny state of Dewas had become implacable
enemies and spent much of their time and revenue in spying on one
another. There was a child, Vikramsinha, from the marriage, now
some ten years old (he was away in the hills during Forster's stay).
But since the separation the Maharaja had taken another wife,
named Bai Saheba – wife or mistress, for her status was unclear –
H.H. called her his 'Diamond Concubine.' She had borne him children;
thus dynastic problems were arising, and they were to do so more

seriously when she gave birth to a son. For reasons of protocol, Bai Saheba did not live in the palace but had a tumbledown house of her own near the gates of the city. She had abandoned purdah and, as Forster described it to Dickinson (14 April 1921), 'lay about on carpets in a farm yard, with men and lamps scattered about her.' Forster took to her, finding her intelligent and amusing, and the Maharaja, pleased by this, encouraged him to pay daily visits. A few days after his arrival, her youngest daughter fell ill, and the Maharaja, who idolized Bai Saheba, went to sleep at her house. In his absence, life in the palace fell into confusion, and it was left to Forster to think of sending food down to him. 'Sometimes I feel I am no use to him,' he told his mother (4 April 1921), 'at others that I am the saving of his life.'

The more Forster saw of the Maharaja, the more he longed to be of help to him, and the more of a problem it appeared to find the way. There was no doubt in his mind that the Maharaja needed help: affairs in Dewas seemed in considerable confusion. The new palace, already under construction when he was there in 1912, was still unfinished, while parts erected ten years ago were already collapsing; and meanwhile, to pay for it and for his other extravagances, H.H. was borrowing heavily on the security of next year's revenues. The spectacle of waste and disorder distressed Forster, and he wrote to his mother (1 April 1921) in baffled tones:

> You would weep at the destruction, expense, and hideousness, and I do almost. We live amongst rubble and mortar & excavations whence six men carry a basket of earth as big as Verouka's[1] twenty yards once in five minutes. I have not yet discovered who loosens the earth, but am familiar with the boy who scrabbles it into the basket with his fingers, the man who bears it on his head along the bottom of the chasm, the next man – very chatty and almost naked – who receives it from him and, merely turning round, places it on the head of No 4. No 4 begins the ascent, No 5 continues it, and No 6 who is immensely old totters along the surface and drops the earth on to a heap which will have some day to be cleared away. And the basket has to be passed back. This is the scene under my window, but for acres around the soil is pitted with similar efforts, slabs of marble lie about, roads lead nowhere, costly fruit trees die for want of water, and I have discovered incidentally that £1,000 worth (figure accurate) of electric

---

[1] The Forsters' cat.

batteries lie in a room near at hand and will spoil unless fixed promptly. I can't start on the inside of the house – two pianos (one a grand) a harmonium, and a 'dulciphone', all new and all unplayable, their notes sticking and their frames cracked by the dryness. I look into a room – dozens of warped towel horses are stabled there, or a new suite of drawing room chairs with their insides gushing out. I open a cupboard near the bath and find it full of tea-pots. I ask for a book case and it bows like a Kafouzleum[1] and lies rattling on the floor. And so on and so forth. I don't know what to do about it all, and scarcely what to feel. It's no good trying to make something different out of it, for it is as profoundly Indian as an Indian temple.

The real danger for the Maharaja, Forster could perceive, was that things had moved on politically in India. Thus, if H.H. were ruining his state, as he appeared to be, he would now, in the age of Gandhi and Non-co-operation, have not only the British to answer to, but Indian politicians and an Indian press. The Maharaja was in fact alarmed at these developments and complained of British India as the home, not so much of autocracy and tyranny, as of sedition. He managed to exclude Gandhi-supporters from Dewas Senior, but there was a railway station in Dewas Junior where they would alight and shout slogans across the frontier. Like several of his fellow-princes, the Maharaja, as a gesture to democracy, was drawing up a written Constitution for his state, but this was fairly plainly only window-dressing. Forster would try to reason with H.H., and urge prudence, without much success. There was a little incident, over the palace motorcars, which brought out H.H.'s attitude revealingly. The cars were always breaking down, so Forster got hold of a garage-mechanic, in Indore, to come and overhaul them; however, it turned out, the mechanic (an Englishman) had been summoned before and complained that the Dewas drivers would follow none of his instructions. Forster reported this to the Maharaja, but what interested him was not the cars but the domestic politics of the matter. 'Oh that's all right, Morgan,' he said. 'I have him out so that the drivers may see that I *can* have him out; and he on the other hand – it's a very good thing he should see he is not indispensable.'

Forster felt at a loss – also rather a fraud as compared with his predecessor, Colonel Leslie – and cast about in his mind for some

---

[1] A Victorian toy (of the doll type, I believe; but I have not been able to identify it exactly).

sphere of useful action. He could not really comprehend the state finances, though he guessed they were in a bad state, but he determined at least to do something about the smaller bills and salaries, which were generally months or even years in arrears. He became an expert at this, going to the appropriate officials, making what he called 'a loud lamentation', and acquiring a bag, or several bags, of silver coins, which Baldeo would take and hide in his bedroom till they were required. Sometimes not even a bag was provided, and he had to take the coins in handfuls, depositing them in a pile in the courtyard, amid a crowd of onlookers, while Baldeo went to fetch boot-bags.

Then there were the gardens. The Palace gardens had been the passion of Colonel Leslie, and, in conception anyway, they were extensive and magnificent, comprising various lotus-ponds, some eighty flowerbeds, pits for mangoes and lemon-trees, and grand ornamental terraces. Nothing much grew in them, however, and what did was liable to be eaten by cows. Periodically a law against straying animals was proclaimed by torchlight, to the sounds of drums; and Forster learned to be vigilant for cows, rushing out with the gardeners to lassoo them and send them to the pound. The next stage would be the arrival of their owner – always a poor man and in tears, for when a rich man's cow was caught he would hire a poor man to weep for him. Forster learned to ignore the tears and imposed the law with severity. A further trouble was the water-supply. Colonel Leslie's arrangements looked impressive. Down every border there ran a pipe, with standard taps, connected to a large and hideous water-tank, and in theory water to supply the tank could be raised from a nearby well: in theory only, for the well was practically dry in summer, and the pump was quite inadequate for its task. When Forster first complained of this, he was told of a marvellous well, a well that never dried up, known as 'The Water that Speaks', and when evening came, he went off to inspect it. 'It lay in a deep hole on the further side of the raised *chaussée*,' he wrote in a later reminiscence.

> We scrabbled down to it over rubble, warning one another against a huge black snake which was said to live close by. 'It is beautiful water, but I don't see how we can use it for the garden,' I said – all had waited for me to express an opinion. 'The road is in the way for one thing. We can't pump it up in the cistern, and we can't carry it across in skins.' 'No we can't, we can't, it has been a

mistake', agreed the others pleasantly. We returned to the palace in a pensive and friendly mood.[1]

In spite of all difficulties, he planted his seeds, not very hopefully, and wrote a sixteen-page letter to Colonel Leslie, giving him the best news he could of his beloved garden, and the Colonel replied politely.

Colonel Leslie's letters to the Maharaja were in a different tone. He wrote (H.H. showed Forster the letter) that he was greatly disappointed to hear that his works were not being continued. 'So all my plans are set aside. In all the years that I served Queen Victoria (of sainted memory) I have never experienced one fraction of the mortification and humiliation that I underwent while serving you, my dear White Prince. Your heartbroken Father William.' Another letter ran: 'When H.R.H. the Prince of Wales comes to India, does he propose to visit Dewas? If he does, I shall cut my throat. To see the Palace and Grounds that you planned as a monument of piety become a dung hill and a rubbish heap and a laughing stock of those vile sneering Politicals from Indore, is more than my soul can bear, as your saintly mother and mine, both together with God, well know.' Leslie also, so Forster discovered, was writing to Malcolm Darling, who was an old friend of his, to complain of Forster: he was particularly incensed at Forster's dismissing one of the palace chauffeurs. Forster began to be curious about Colonel Leslie. On his arrival, the refrain had been how admirable, how amusing, how energetic the Colonel was: such a great hunter – he had tamed every animal in India except the crocodile; such a dear friend of H.H.'s – they were Father William and White Prince to each other, and when he had had his accident (he had fallen between a train and the platform and been crushed) the Maharaja had gone in person to nurse him. Now, however, as Forster pressed his inquiries, the picture altered: it appeared, or so H.H. said, that Leslie had quarrelled with practically everyone (but especially Deolekr), and had had affairs with the wives of several local residents. Forster asked the Maharaja how he knew this, and the Maharaja explained that one day 'for a joke', he had opened Leslie's letters and found one from a local lady, beginning 'My own darling'. 'But that was bad of you,' said Forster. 'Yes, Morgan,' said H.H., 'I know it was bad of me and I said so. I

---

[1] 'Woodlanders on Devi', *New Statesman*, 6 May 1939.

repented, still I did it, and that's how I know.' The Maharaja was pledged to have Leslie back in the autumn and felt he could not break his promise. Plaintive messages would arrive from Leslie, saying 'I am sure you prefer Morgan Forster,' whereupon he would send expensive telegrams saying 'I love you more than ever and long to have you with me'; but he looked forward gloomily to the prospect and told Forster 'He will notice a great change in my manner.'

Early in May, Bai Saheba gave birth to a baby, another girl, and everything was in upheaval at court, custom demanding that for the next fifteen days the mother should be serenaded by day and by night. For the first five days H.H. was not allowed to see Bai Saheba but camped in the compound of her house, amid a crowd of friends, attendants and cows. The court musicians played, there were fireworks, the army fired rifle-volleys, and *nautch* girls and boys in girls' clothing performed dialogues and dances. At night-time Forster came to join the Maharaja in his encampment and slept beside him, sometimes with his head propped against a bullock's flanks. The din was appalling and usually lasted till the small hours, but one night, about 3 a.m. he was woken by music that he recognized as rare and beautiful, an endless *raga*, performed by a singer and a drummer, that seemed to him 'like Western music reflected in trembling water'.

The finale of the festivities was an elaborate present-giving. Forster described it at length in a letter to his mother (17 May 1921):

> H.H. was so very nice – told me about it, so that I might not be left out, and secretly assisted me in my choice. I rested in the morning, and drove down to Bai Saheba's to change into Indian clothes, then drove on with my gifts to join forces with the Commander-in-Chief and his gifts. Malarao, the Chief of Police, etc., etc., swelled the party, and we marched back to Bai Saheba's on foot, first the army, playing the British Grenadiers, then servants, bearing gifts on platters, then ourselves, hand in hand in affable converse, then a huge crowd, and finally the Commander-in-Chief's lady in a Purdah carriage. As we reached Bai Saheba's, two other bands struck up, one military but making Indian sounds, the other the violent bang-bang of the Sweepers, outcastes but loyal subjects who stood at the side of the road hitting sieves with shovels. We swept into the courtyard, then melted into nothing, as is the Indian spirit. There was no grand crisis or reception. The gifts were dumped on a durry, where, very anxious, sat H.H. among clerical assistants. For he had to give back to each donor a gift of equal value, and quickly to guess what each

present cost. I gave the lady a sari for day wear and a piece of silk for a jacket, and to the baby a deplorable piece of pink material. This was a respectable minimum gift: near relatives added coconuts, silver ornaments, and rice. While we all messed on the durry, the ladies kept arriving, mostly in covered ox wagons, and were decanted into the purdah tent beside us. The gifts couldn't be taken in because of the Dowager Maharani, who as always was late. A cradle arrived, made by the state carpenters, and very dizzy in its action. H.H. had meant to get me almost into the purdah tent, but desisted, as a few old-fashioned people would have minded. We went into the house behind, against which the tent backed, and I sat by the door and peeped over his shoulder, but saw little. He worked like an underwaiter in a Soho restaurant. The platters came out through the door of the purdah tent, containing the gifts that had been submitted and approved, and he upset them – clothes, coconuts, and all – upon the floor where we sat, in order to leave the platter free for the return service. His return gift was popped on, and back it went into purdah to the wife of the man who made the original gift. Having no wife – or none on the spot – I got my return present direct. I had chosen it beforehand – a goldified turban which he told me was the proper monetary equivalent of what I had given. I was pleased: not so the Dowager Maharani, who rejected her return present because she thought it only cost Rs 200, whereas there was precedent for Rs 250. This, and other bad news kept leaking out through the folds of the tent. H.H. was sad but philosophic: 'I spend all this money in the hope they would be happy, but they quarrel   it always happens . . . yes, the Dowager Maharani has been rude, but how can I take any notice? They will think it revenge for her behaviour in the past to me and she is defenceless now. I shall invite her later on for the singing . . .' all the time pouring valuables on to the dusty floor.

*   *   *

During the birth-festivities Forster, for most of the day, was left on his own in the palace, with little to do and no one to talk to. The heat was intense. It did not upset him, but its effect, combined with idleness and solitude, was to fill him with sexual desire: during the long siesta period, especially, it became almost intolerable, and masturbation gave no relief. He began to feel he would be ill, and his good resolutions towards the Maharaja gradually weakened. He guessed that among the various palace hangers-on he could find someone he might have sex with. Two, he thought, had already guessed what he wanted: a young Mohammedan who acted as his postilion; and one of the palace workmen, a Hindu of about eighteen. When the Hindu salaamed him – very respectfully, using both hands – Forster would respond with his whole attention, and when the boy brought him a chair he would thank him with a smile. The coolie took his meaning and found an ingenious method of declaring himself: he took a leather strap and lashed the floor of the Hall with it, hard, startling Forster and making him look in his direction; he lashed the floor a second time, hard; and then a third time, gently, so that Forster would only look round if he wanted to; and when he did so, the boy smiled. After that, for some days the two eyed each other in the corridors, and when the coolie disappeared round a corner, Forster could see from his shadow that he was waiting for him to follow. As he drove to Bai Saheba's, in the scorching heat, the other servant – the postilion – used various tricks to catch his attention. It was as if nothing existed except lust.[1]

His resolve held out no longer, and he sought some way of talking with the Hindu coolie. This was not an easy problem, for there were onlookers everywhere; however he hit on a solution. He let it be known that the *tattie*[2] on his bedroom door needed watering, dropping a hint that the coolie should volunteer for the task. The hint was taken, the Hindu came, and, pretending to show him how to throw the water, Forster stroked his wrist. The coolie smiled happily, and Forster said 'Meet me at 7.30 on the road near the Guest House.' Some ten minutes later, to his dismay, he heard two excited voices outside his door. The first said 'The *burra* [master] sahib has given orders to come at night.' 'At night?' said the other. 'Yes, and he will give me money.' Their voices then mingled with those of other workmen, leaving Forster in a panic of terror and shame. His thought was: 'H.H. has had me out from England because I am Malcolm's friend and as one of the few he can trust, and this is what I do.' To make matters worse, when he looked out of the window, he saw a flurry below and one of the senior clerks of the palace jumping into a bullock-cart. He felt sure the clerk had gone to report the scandal to the Maharaja; and when H.H. himself returned an hour later, his manner – merry, but slightly malicious and hard – seemed to confirm it. As they passed a servant painting the wainscoting, H.H. ex-

---

[1] In what follows I have drawn on an unpublished Ms. entitled 'K—'.
[2] A screen made of grass-roots, kept wet as a form of air-conditioning.

claimed impatiently: 'everywhere . . . I cannot get away from them.'
Forster sensed a sting in the words; and later that evening, in front
of the assembled courtiers, the Maharaja said severely that he meant
to banish all catamites from his court: 'What is the good of such
people?' He was very silent when, late the same night, Forster joined
him, and Forster was now finally convinced that he knew of his
escapade. Worse, he felt sure that all the courtiers knew; he got the
impression that they were mocking him and no longer held him in
respect.

For four days he swallowed his trouble, taking care to avoid or
ignore the coolie, but at last he could bear it no longer and asked the
Maharaja for a private interview. 'As I think you know, I am in great
trouble,' he said.

'Tell me, Morgan,' H.H. replied. 'I have noticed you were worried.'

'I have tried to have carnal intercourse with one of the coolies and
it has become known.'

'With a coolie-girl?'

'No, with a man. You know about it, and if you agree I think I
ought to resign.'

'But Morgan, I know nothing about it,' said the Maharaja. 'This
is the first I have heard of it.'

Forster wished he were dead: he need never have confessed, and he
guessed that the confession would do him no good in H.H.'s eyes.
For a time, he thought the Maharaja must be lying, but H.H. found
harmless explanations for all that had perturbed him. He questioned
Forster further, kindly and seriously.

'Why a man and not a woman? Is not a woman more natural?'

'Not in my case. I have no feeling for women.'

'Oh but that alters everything. You are not to blame.'

'I don't know what "natural" is.'

'You are quite right, Morgan – I ought never to have used the
word. No, don't worry – don't worry. I am only distressed you did
not tell me everything before – I might have saved you so much pain.
May I know all about this coolie now?'

When he heard that nothing physical had actually taken place,
the Maharaja was reassuring: there was nothing to fear, he said.
'Only always come to me when you are in difficulties like this. I
would have found you someone reliable among the hereditary
servants, and you could have had him quietly in your room. Yes, yes,

it's true I don't encourage those people, but it's entirely different in your case and you must not masturbate – that's awful.'

Forster was so touched and relieved that when he tried to apologize he broke down. The Maharaja nearly broke down too, crying 'Oh devil! Don't do that Morgan – the only way with a thing like this is to take it laughing.' And he threw himself with zest into schemes for finding Forster a bed-companion. Forster – quite cured of desire for the moment – insisted that he did not want one, that he would abstain from all forms of sex now, only coming to H.H. for advice if lust should trouble him again. The Maharaja would have none of this. God had made Forster the way he was, he said; he was his country's guest and his own honoured assistant; there must be no talk of vows or remorse. Throughout their talk, Forster thought afterwards, H.H. had acted perfectly, like the saint that he suspected him of being. Perfectly in all but one detail: the Maharaja wanted to blame Forster's 'perversion' on Egypt – it pleased him to ascribe all vice to Mohammedans – and he had tried to question Forster about his Egyptian experiences. Forster had felt this impertinent and had fobbed him off with lies.

His virtuous resolutions did not persist, and he began to hope that the Maharaja would renew his offers to procure for him, but H.H. seemed to avoid the whole topic. At last, one evening, H.H. remarked that a palace barber called K—, who had the reputation of a male 'tart', was loitering too much in the palace and that this must stop: it was bad for the other servants. On an impulse, Forster said: 'I wish you could get a boy for me.' The Maharaja responded without hesitation: 'I was waiting for you to mention it, Morgan – not the least difficulty; get K— come and shave you – no possible suspicion – he often comes, indeed he's budgeted for – we'll fix it up now, and I'll have his salary increased.' Forster agreed, somewhat nervously, and a visit from the barber was arranged for noon the next day, a time when Baldeo would be away at dinner. K— proved pretty, overdressed and amiable. He paid a second visit, and on this occasion, as he was shaving Forster, the latter drew K— to him and kissed him. He took it with the greatest calm, and Forster proceeded to bolt the door; but at this point a bucket of water came crashing against the door of the verandah. It was Baldeo, who had come back early from his lunch. As he went on noisily sluicing the *tattie*, Forster hurried K— out by the other entrance.

The Maharaja, when told of this mishap, advised Forster to lose no time on the next occasion: once something definite had taken place, he said, K— would be discreet. All that he begged Forster was that he would do nothing that savoured of passivity: a rumour of that would be harmful. Forster started to tell him the time of his next rendezvous, but H.H. cried 'I don't want to hear, because when the hour comes I shall think of you, and that I don't want.'

All went well on this next meeting, and after it the Maharaja complimented Forster on his improved appearance and sent K— a gratuity of 25 rupees – this was better, he said, than Forster paying K— himself. As was natural with Forster, having had sex with K—, he began to feel a friendly interest in him and wanted to establish some kind of intimacy, but here he found himself baffled: K— was smiling and cheerful but totally blank – there seemed no possibility of human contact with him. The two, moreover, were rather at cross purposes, K— being terrified of the Maharaja, whilst for Forster he was the one person he need not fear.

The arrangement continued, and Forster felt the better for it, but it needed expert management. Baldeo became suspicious and took to cutting short his lunch-hour; and, since K— was unpunctual, Forster was on thorns the whole time – watching for K—'s arrival, watching for Baldeo's return, and, when K— left, watching to see that he did not loiter and gossip. Once they tried meeting in the Guest House Garden, but K—, slinking after Forster in the dark, was mistaken for a thief, and next day there were reports from the gardeners that by their courage and vigilance they had repelled a dangerous gang of robbers. When the Maharaja was told the true story, he devised a new system, by which they should meet in a disused suite of the palace.

The fact that homosexual jokes, though not homosexual acts, were so much a feature of court life, made some gossip inevitable, and H.H. instructed Forster as to his best tactic. This was, he said, to agree cheerfully to every innuendo. Forster took his advice, and when Malarao, who had no idea of the truth, teased him about K—'s visits, he responded gaily, accusing Malarao of jealousy. H.H. assisted by casually letting out Forster's age, which was forty-two – an age at which any normally-constructed Indian might be expected to be impotent. Forster mentioned his philanderings in a letter to Moham-med (26 August 1921), who replied 'I got nothing to say except that

you are so silly. I am very sad for that game and I have just understood why the (what you call them bad) people oppose you . . . I am
looking forward to see you and to blame you about your foolish
deeds, foolish deeds. . . . Your sad friend, Moh el Adl.'

In July Forster was granted ten days leave and went to stay with
Masood in Hyderabad. He told K— to avoid the palace in his
absence, but on his return H.H. broke the news to him that scandal
had begun: K— had boasted in Deolekr's house that he was under
Forster's protection. 'Sahib's fond of boys,' he had said, and the
story had spread. Forster attacked K—, who begged forgiveness, but
the harm was done; and he suspected that Deolekr, with whom he
did not get on very well, might deliberately have fomented the
scandal. And now, what he had imagined earlier, became the fact:
the courtiers treated him less respectfully, and with an air of 'You're
no better than we are, after all' – there was, he thought, a touch of
racial vengeance in it. It bothered him less now, matters having gone
so far. He felt in a vigorous and attacking mood; and when he heard
that Bidwai, the Brahmin – one of the few courtiers he respected –
knew of the scandal, he took him for a long walk, talking resolutely
on indifferent topics, to show him he was determined to remain
friends.

*   *   *

Just about this time, the Agent to the Governor General came on
a state visit to Dewas, and, as a result, Forster figured in a diplomatic
incident. According to custom, the Maharaja began civilities by
calling on the A.G.G. and his aides at the Guest House – much
protocol being involved as to who took how many paces towards
whom. The Dewas courtiers, Forster among them, then attended in
the A.G.G.'s tent, where the visiting British ceremonially offered *itr*[1]
and *pan*.[2] By now Forster's position at court had received official
approval, but there was some doubt whether, on such a visitation,
he should receive *itr* and *pan* at the hands of a British or of an
Indian official. In the event, he was passed over by both. H.H., when
he was told this, was furious. He took it as a calculated insult,
designed to cast doubts on his right to employ a European, and the
rest of the visit passed in glacial hostility. He told Forster to remove
himself for a time, and when the P.A. inquired where he was, he

---

[1] Perfume.
[2] A masticatory composed of betel-leaf, areca nut and lime etc.

replied that he wasn't sure if he would return, he was 'rather out of spirits' – at which glances were exchanged among the British. When Forster finally did appear, he sat well away from the visitors. By contagion, he had begun to feel that he *had*, personally, been insulted, and when sought out by the P.A. and his Chief of Staff, he received their remarks about the weather with frigidity. A cheerless banquet and cinema-show followed; and when the A.G.G. who had hitherto ignored him[1] came to bid farewell, Forster pretended not to see his hand till it was offered a second time.

Next day there came an embarrassed apology from the Political Agent. H.H., however, was not appeased and took the matters to higher quarters, and the affair rumbled on for some months. He had a relish for such disputes – a fact which, in the end, helped to bring about his ruin. For Forster, the affair was opportune. He had, for a day, embodied the court's honour, and his stock rose in consequence.

*   *   *

There was now approaching the festival of *Gokul Ashtami*, an eight-day festival in honour of Krishna. The religious festivals were not all now kept up so lavishly at Dewas as once they had been, but *Gokul Ashtami*, the crowning event of the year, was still celebrated with much pomp, and the whole life of the state stopped for it. It was a festival in which priests took little part, the emphasis lying on *bhakti*, or direct union with the Divine through love, and much of the local ritual was of H.H.'s own invention. Each day had a different *mise-en-scène*, devised, in a sort of rivalry, by one or other of the state authorities – the Public Works Dept, the Army, the Dewan (Prime Minister) or the Maharaja himself. For the period of the festival the Court moved down to the Old Palace, which stood in the middle of the town. It was a fine eighteenth-century building, with a frescoed cloister and a grand Temple Room and Durbar Hall – though, to Forster's distress, the walls were hung with appalling chromolithographs cut from illustrated magazines. A room in the Old Palace was set aside for him, though the Maharaja urged him not to feel bound to attend the festival. Nothing might be killed during the eight days, but he was told he might eat tinned food if he consumed it elsewhere than in the Palace.

The preparations amused him and irritated him in about equal

---

[1] It is, of course, just conceivable that some echo had reached the A.G.G. of the fuss over Forster's intercepted letter to Masood (see pp. 28–9).

measure. He was feeling fretted and baffled by India and wrote to his Alexandrian friend Ludolf (28 July 1921) that he wished he were ten years younger, or that what he found so interesting did not also seem so silly.

> The day before yesterday H.H., his wife, the Commander in Chief, etc., etc. sat on the floor for three hours choosing costumes for the Lord of the Universe, whose birthday falls next month. Luckily he is only six inches high, but he needs eight costumes of increasing splendour, and he has various companions of larger size, who have also to be dressed, and he has to have a bed, and he has to have a mosquito curtain, and the costumes will cost over £30 and the electric light will cost over £100, and his breakfast and dinner will cost a hell of a lot more and I just want a broom to sweep it all away, for it seems to me neither instructive or beautiful.

Nevertheless, as he knew, it was an extraordinary privilege to witness the coming scenes, and he determined to make the most of it, spending most of his days and nights at the Old Palace and, as activities began, adjusting his ears as best he could to the unceasing, fantastic, nerve-shattering din. His letters home, printed in *The Hill of Devi*, are deservedly famous. Here is one for 24 August 1921:

> Old Palace
> 24 August
> This ought to be an interesting letter. It is the fourth day of the Festival and I am getting along all right though I collapsed at first. The noise is so appalling. Hymns are sung to the altar downstairs without ceasing. The singers, in groups of eight, accompany themselves on cymbals and a harmonium. At the end of two hours a new group pushes in from the back. The altar has also a ritual which is independent of the singing. A great many gods are on visit and they all get up at 4.30 a.m. – they are not supposed to be asleep during the Festival, which is reasonable considering the din, but to be enjoying themselves. They have a bath and are anointed and take a meal, which is over about 9.0 a.m. At 12.0 is another service, during which three bands play simultaneously in the little courtyard, two native bands and one European, affecting a merry polka, while these united strains are pierced by an enormous curved horn, rather fine, which is blown whenever incense is offered. And still I am only at the beginning of the noise. Children play games all over the place, officials shout. Last night I had a dreadful dream about Verouka. I thought I had shown him a mechanical doll that frightened him so that he went mad and raced round and round in a room overhead. I woke up to find

it was the thudding of the old steam engine which we have
tinkered up to drive our electric light – As I said, the noise was
too much at first, but Bapu Sahib's[1] kindness and foresight for
others never fail. I can always retire to the Guest House which is
peaceful and now very beautiful since the Tank is full, and there
is a complete staff of servants there and European food. I needn't
stay here a moment longer than I like.

Well, what's it all about? It's called Gokul Ashtami – i.e. the
8 days feast in honour of Krishna who was born at Gokul near
Muttra, and I cannot yet discover how much of it is traditional
and how much due to H.H. What troubles me is that every detail,
almost without exception, is fatuous and in bad taste. The altar is
a mess of little objects, stifled with rose leaves, the walls are hung
with deplorable oleographs, the chandeliers, draperies – everything bad. Only one thing is beautiful – the expression on the faces
of the people as they bow to the shrine, and he himself is, as
always, successful in his odd role. I have never seen religious
ecstasy before and don't take to it more than I expected I should,
but he manages not to be absurd. Whereas the other groups of
singers stand quiet, he is dancing all the time, like David before
the ark, jigging up and down with a happy expression on his face,
and twanging a stringed instrument that hangs by a scarf round
his neck. At the end of his two hours he gets wound up and begins
composing poetry which is copied down by a clerk, and yesterday
he flung himself flat on his face on the carpet. Ten minutes
afterwards I saw him as usual, in ordinary life. He complained of
indigestion but seemed normal and discussed arrangements connected with the motor-cars. I cannot see the point of this, or rather
in what it differs from ordinary mundane intoxication. I suppose
that if you believe your drunkenness proceeds from God it becomes more enjoyable. Yet I am very much muddled in my own
mind about it all, for H.H. has what one understands by the
religious sense and it comes out all through his life. He is always
thinking of others and refusing to take advantage of his position
in his dealings with them; and believing that his God acts
similarly towards him.

The Old Palace is built round a courtyard about 50 feet square,
the Temple-Hall being along one side on the ground floor. The Hall
is open to the court and divided into three or four aisles by thick
pillars. The singers stand at one end of the chief aisle, the shrine
is at the other end, red carpet between. The public squats against
the pillars and is controlled, of course incompetently, by schoolboy
volunteers. The heat is immense and, since H.H. disdains adven-
titious comforts, he has the electric fans turned off when his time

[1] i.e. the Maharaja.

comes to sing. – I don't think I can describe it better than this, and it is difficult to make vivid what seems so fatuous. There is no dignity, no taste, no form, and though I am dressed as a Hindu I shall never become one. I don't think one ought to be irritated with Idolatry because one can see from the faces of the people that it touches something very deep in their hearts. But it is natural that Missionaries, who think these ceremonies wrong as well as inartistic, should lose their tempers.

Next week I shall have the crisis of the Festival to describe – the announcement of Krishna's birth (for he is not born yet!) and the procession from the Old Palace to the Tank, where a clay model of the village of Gokul will be thrown into the waters, and so it will end. Before I forget, though, we none of us wear shoes or socks inside the O.P. My feet suffered at first, but they can walk over heaps of coal now, as they have to whenever the Electric Light goes wrong. The costume is a turban (sāfar), a long coat, and a dhoti, which last resembles a voluminous yet not entirely efficient pair of bathing drawers. I have learnt to tie my own dhoti – the turban is much more difficult and I cannot acquire the knack. If you get the dhoti too short it is not thought elegant and if you get it too long you catch your bare foot in the folds and fall down.

My bedroom at the Old Palace is secluded (except for noise) since it is upstairs, through the Durbar Hall. This is fine – I described it in a letter eight years ago – and it is now free from mess, which has been carried below to adorn the Temple, so one can see its proportions. Nothing remains in it except the Gaddi, a sacred feather-bed with which the fortunes of the Dynasty are mysteriously connected. I am told – and I can well believe it – that some of the stuffing has been in that bed for generations. A row of little roses are placed on the bolster every day, and there are two lamps at night. H.H. comes up once in every twenty-four hours to worship the bed: except for this excursion he is forbidden to leave the ground floor of the Palace. I shall never be at an end of the queernesses. But give every place its due. There are no smells and (as far as I can testify) no bugs. It is the noise, the noise, the noise, the noise which sucks one into a whirlpool, from which there is no re-emerging. The whole of what one understands by music seems lost for ever, or rather seems never to have existed.

I am finishing at the Guest House! The Tank looks so pretty and if it does not rain I shall take the boat out.

*   *   *

During the festival, Forster discovered, K—'s indiscretion had taken a further turn; forming higher ambitions than his post with

Forster, he had made advances to the Maharaja himself. One night H.H. had found K— lying in the corner of his own bedroom. He had thought nothing of it – for in the Court no one, not even a prince, expected privacy – and had lain down to sleep, but after a few minutes K— had approached and begun massaging his feet, the conventional prelude to asking a favour. 'Sirkar,' he said, 'can I have employment at the Palace?' 'But you have it already,' the Maharaja had replied. 'You are Forster Sahib's barber.' 'Sirkar, I want employment with you. I want more employment. Sahib goes to bed with me.' At this the Maharaja had bellowed 'How dare you?' and K— had fled in terror.

When H.H. told Forster, his fury at K—'s silliness overflowed, and the next time K— came, he boxed his ears, at which K— fell on the carpet, kissed his feet and loudly prayed for mercy. He then shaved Forster in the usual way, and Forster sent him away, determined to have no more to do with him. However, when he told H.H. this, H.H. warned him against too brusque a dismissal – it might arouse suspicion. Thus K— was allowed to continue his visits, and Forster resumed relations with him – finding, to his surprise and distaste, that he enjoyed giving K— pain. He did not really hurt him, but the emotion seemed to him a bad one, and harmful to himself. It was a feeling of omnipotence – himself a despot, whom no one could call to account, and K— his slave. The trouble was, he thought, K— had the soul of a slave.

A few days after *Gokul Ashtami*, H.H. set forth on tour. He was bound first for Nagpur, capital of the Central Provinces, where he was to preside over an All India Maratha Educational Conference – which, Forster surmised to Dickinson (30 August 1921), would mean 'a damned lot of Marathas and bloody little education'. Nagpur was in British India, and the Dewas party made a triumphal entry there, mounted upon elephants and with a train of camels and riderless horses hung with rich caparisons. At the Fort, to H.H.'s gratification, they were received with a salute of fifteen guns. 'A pathetic pageant,' Forster wrote to his mother. 'Under our feet were crowds of the Nagpur people, at present the most fanatical and anti-British in India, all contemptuous or indifferent, and many of them wearing the white Gandhi cap.' Forster had the arranging of a garden party, a vast and successful affair, and when he brought garlands for the departing guests, the Maharaja turned and garlanded him with them instead. The royal party then set off for Simla, where the Maharaja had business with the Viceroy, hoping to persuade him to come to Dewas to inaugurate his Constitution. Forster, meanwhile, had been granted some leave and went off to stay with Rupert Smith in Agra.

Smith was now a Collector. He was married and was living in a large house in the civil station – a house he was rather proud of and was later annoyed to see vilified in *A Passage to India*.[1] Forster found him changed and, as he thought, much improved, no longer barking at his Indian subordinates: indeed the Smiths actually had an Indian friend staying in their house. The alteration struck Forster as symbolic. As he knew, a directive had gone out to the British that, in the new climate of liberal reform and 'dyarchy', they must be correct and courteous in all personal dealings with Indians. Masood was cynical about the change,[2] and Forster, likewise, considered it as 'a hasty and ungraceful change of position', too obviously inspired by fear of Gandhi. The new note in Anglo-Indian voices, he wrote to Dickinson (25 September 1921), was 'tragic resignation'. 'People pretend that they are leaving the country shortly, and so no longer feel it their duty to be rude to its inhabitants.' Later in the year he was to write an article[3] for the *Nation and Athenaeum* on the theme of 'Too Late?':

> The Indian has taken up a new attitude. Ten or fifteen years ago he would have welcomed attention, not only because the English man in India had power, but because the etiquette and customs of the West, his inevitable destiny, were new to him and he needed a sympathetic introducer. He has never been introduced to the

---

[1] 'Then they reached their [the Turtons'] bungalow, low and enormous, the oldest and most uncomfortable bungalow in the civil station, with a sunk soup plate of a lawn.' (*A Passage to India*, chapter 3.)

[2] He told Forster a story which Forster repeated in 'Reflections in India'. (*The Nation and Athenaeum*, 21 January 1922.) He had got into a railway carriage, occupied by an English officer, and – as against his experiences in earlier days – the officer had sprung up politely, and begun to shift his kit, saying, 'Here, take my berth, it's the best; I'm getting out soon.' 'No, why should I?' said Masood. 'Oh, no, take it, man, that's all right; this is your country, not mine,' said the officer. Masood rejoined grimly: 'Don't do this sort of thing, please. We don't appreciate it any more than the old sort. We know that you have been told you must do it.'

[3] 'Reflections in India, 1: Too Late? (By our Indian correspondent)', *Nation & Athenaeum*, 21 January 1922.

West in the social sense, as to a possible friend. We have thrown
grammars and neckties at him, and smiled when he put them on
wrongly – that is all. For a time he suffered . . . Today he has
ceased to suffer. He has learnt to put on neckties the right way,
or his own way, or whatever one is supposed to do with a necktie.

For the remaining week of his leave, Forster had invited himself
to Chhatarpur. He had been in correspondence with Chhatarpur for
some months. The Maharaja,[1] hearing of his appointment at Dewas,
had instantly set his heart on Forster's coming to his own court
instead, offering him twice the salary. Forster's refusal had piqued
him, and he had shown no great enthusiasm for Forster's projected
visit. He greeted Forster with effusion, however. He called on him at
6 a.m. on the morning after his arrival and launched at once upon his
favourite topic, his quest for a companion. Recently he had been
much struck by the hero Olaf in Rider Haggard's novel *The Wanderer's
Necklace* and had written to the author begging him to find him a
secretary as like to Olaf as possible. Rider Haggard had done as he
was asked, but his protégé had had to withdraw, and the Maharaja
had then written to Sir Theodore Morison, in Weybridge, asking him
to suggest a candidate. Sir Theodore, however, had not replied. The
court astrologers were of the opinion that the letter had not reached
him, but Forster told Dickinson, 'My mother gives a different
account.'

There had been changes in Chhatarpur. The Maharaja had been
forced to give up most of his retinue of boy-actors, retaining (or so
he said) only one beautiful and melancholy-looking youth known as
'the last of the Krishnas'. Even to employ the last of the Krishnas
required discretion. The Maharaja sent him to visit Forster at the
Guest House but punished him when he learned with what ostentation
he had gone – accompanied by a horse (which he could not ride) and
wearing diamond earrings. Forster enquired, 'Has he any friends of
his own age?' The Maharaja replied, with great satisfaction: 'None.'

Forster and the Maharaja had philosophical conversations in
which, Forster told Dickinson, he cut more of a figure in Dickinson's
absence. The Maharaja had been corresponding with Bertrand
Russell, and the letters were fetched for Forster's inspection. Russell
was 'helpful but firm', Forster told Dickinson (25 September 1921):

---

[1] See Vol. I, pp. 234–7.

> – regretted that he had not read G. H. Lewes but believed him to
> be inferior to Herbert Spencer – denied that the universe has any
> consideration for man but equally denied to man the right to
> neglect his own hopes and ideals since this would be 'to bow before
> an alien power'. He left the Maharajah in a tight hole in fact. But
> every Indian hole has at least two exits . . .

Chhatarpur and its environs seemed even more beautiful to Forster
than on his visit nine years before. 'You cannot imagine what
aesthetic peace I am finding here,' he wrote to Dickinson. 'The sense
of beauty, which Dewas daily outrages, is soothed by every turn of
the architecture, every clean floor, and white washed wall. It is like
those first ten minutes after a toothache has stopped.' After many
false starts, an expedition was made to the famous temples at
Khajuraho; and on another day the Maharaja took Forster once
more to the ruined lake-palace at Mau, of which he had once offered
him the possession.

On their homeward journey from Mau, a mild frost developed
between Forster and his host. Forster refused to answer some
questions about a third party, causing the Maharaja to say that he
was not his friend. Then a woodpecker cried from an ill-omened
direction, and the Maharaja, shuddering, pulled the whole of the
travelling-rug away from Forster and wrapped himself up in it. On
their arrival back in Chhatarpur, the Maharaja left Forster to walk
the slope up to the Guest House instead of driving him to the door,
and Forster, knowing that this 'would not do' in India, riposted with
a note cutting short his visit. All was quickly forgotten, however, and
in a letter which followed Forster to Dewas, the Maharaja wrote that
the days he had spent in Forster's company were 'as if I had been in
the company of an angle!!' (Forster noted on the letter, 'I felt one
some times, too.')

Upon his return to Dewas, Forster found awaiting him a letter
from Colonel Leslie, his predecessor as private secretary, a letter
which amazed him greatly and even more greatly enraged him. It ran:

London
6 September 1921

Dear Mr Forster,
    In thanking you for your note received about a week ago, I am
sorry I have no time to reply except on a very important subject.
    You enclosed the contents of a cover addressed to me by name,
and with no mention even of my official job.

I know that some people feel when they get east of Suez that not only the ten commandments are obsolete but also the obligations and etiquette of English society. You had twice before opened my private letters, but on the second occasion – a letter addressed most obviously by an English lady – you felt some qualms as to your action and I refrained from remark. These qualms now seem to have subsided. I can only think that the hypnotic power of your surroundings has affected you, but as I may now have a number of private letters awaiting my arrival, may I ask you most kindly to refrain from opening them, and if you think H.H. wishes you to act otherwise kindly obtain written authority in each case.

Yours sincerely
W. Leslie

The letter 'threw' Forster badly. He had felt some sympathy for the colonel, but this all dissolved now in desire for revenge. He went straight with the letter to the Maharaja, who met him with the news that Leslie was coming to Dewas – sailing on the same boat as the Darlings. Leslie had written, said H.H., that he meant to do no more administrative work, as it was plainly not appreciated, but he would continue to supervise the young Prince's education. 'It's an unpleasant letter,' said H.H. 'So is this,' said Forster grimly, showing him his own. H.H., reading it, was all concern. He insisted on Forster's taking another holiday and sent him off in a Palace car to visit a cousin, the Maharaja of Dhar. Thus for two days Forster went sightseeing, visiting the ruined city of Mandu, a romantic and magnificent site high up in the Vindhya mountains; but all day long what occupied his mind was not scenery but the answer he should return to Colonel Leslie. Should it be elaborately ironical, he wondered? Or genial and facetious? Neither, he decided; and on his return he composed what he called 'a stinker'.

Dewas Senior
7 October 1921

Dear Colonel Leslie,
    I have received your letter of September 6th and will hand to H.H. any of your correspondence that may precede you at Dewas. Your bicycle and lamp, hitherto in my room, will be given to Malarao Sahib.
    As regards your private letters, opened by me, I herewith make the following statement. I opened them in the belief that they were of an official nature, bearing on my work. Finding that they were not, I did not read them. I have no knowledge as to their

contents, nor, until you informed me, was I aware of the sex of your correspondents.

   If you believe the above statement, I demand from you a full and unqualified apology for your letter of September 6th, as regards both its matter and its manner. If you do not believe it, I neither expect nor desire to hear from you again.

   A copy of this correspondence will be forwarded to Mr Darling. It is on his account that I provide you with this opportunity for apologizing.

Yours sincerely,
E. M. Forster.

Since Leslie was coming to Dewas, he himself, Forster told H.H., must clearly go, for it would not do for them to meet. H.H. agreed – though regretfully, for he was as delighted as ever with Forster's company. It was a harassing time all round for the Maharaja. He had at last had to admit the disastrous state of his finances. He had countermanded all work on the Palace and its gardens and had spent a humiliating day in Indore chaffering with money-lenders. Then, it appeared that the Viceroy would *not* come to inaugurate his Constitution. Also the Dowager Maharani was, as usual, stirring up trouble. And he was much worried as to what Malcolm Darling, such a close friend of Colonel Leslie's, would think of the quarrel and of his own behaviour to Leslie. Yet another festival, *Dessera*, was approaching, and H.H. felt in no mood for it. He told Forster that, for the festivities, he meant to dress in white, the symbol of depression.

   Dessera, traditionally, marked the return of the cold weather, when warfare might begin again, and it celebrated the nation's possessions and its military might. It would be a shabby affair this year – nothing to the splendid spectacle which Darling had witnessed fourteen years before. The central event was a torchlight procession to a Tree of Victory, planted for the occasion outside the city boundary. Beneath this tree the Dewan sat and recited the list of the state's possessions – which, according to his statement, included an enormous army, thousands of bows and millions of arrows, and numerous battle elephants. The Maharaja's empire, according to the Dewan, extended from Lahore in the north to Poona in the south and Bengal in the east; Forster asked H.H. why he did not, as did the Maharaja of Udaipur, claim the whole of India while he was about it, but H.H. said there was 'no precedent' for this. During the festival,

Forster had to officiate as a priest. Under the direction of his clerk, he first worshipped a pen, an inkpot and a wastepaper basket, offering them and his clerk a sacrament of cocoanut; then, proceeding to the Electric House, he did the same for the switchboard, dynamo and battery, and for the mechanics. 'One has not to say anything, still less to feel,' he told Florence Barger (13 October 1921). 'Just wave incense and sprinkle water and dab with red powder anything you like. V. easy.'

Meanwhile, there had been a fresh development in the Leslie affair. Messages came that he was not travelling on the Darlings' boat, but the following one, and – though this was to be a secret – that he was engaged to be married. 'Am I to support his wife too?' H.H. asked indignantly; and he determined, if he could, to prevent Leslie from coming. This could not be done without consulting Darling; thus, someone would have to meet the Darlings' boat at Bombay; and since H.H. was busy, the emissary had to be Forster. It proved a curious expedition. The ship arrived at Bombay on the Sunday, and at midnight, while it still stood out in the harbour, Forster hired a boat and went on board, bearing numerous garlands.[1] Darling, when Forster showed him the letters between Leslie and himself, looked grave. 'A lamentable correspondence,' he said; and there was worse to follow, for Forster had to explain that H.H. now refused to have Leslie back in Dewas. Darling grew heated at this, declaring that it would kill Leslie, or at any rate break his heart; and moreover it was too late – he was already on his way. Many telegrams flew between the ship and Dewas, and, since Darling was due in the Punjab, it was arranged that Forster and the Darlings should get on the Punjab Mail, and that H.H. should join them up the line, for further discussions. The Maharaja did duly join the train – 'almost alone', as he had promised – that is to say with five courtiers and several servants – and the whole party travelled aimlessly onwards across India, debating the Leslie problem. 'Answer this one question, Malcolm,' said H.H. 'If I put him off now, shall I be behaving in an ungentlemanly fashion?' Malcolm considered and

[1] There were nine brides on board, he told his mother (25 October 1921), and he was mistaken by each of them for the bridegroom of one of the other eight. 'Josie is sure that the marriage of all will be permanently embittered by the remembrance; each will think, whenever she looks at her husband, "He failed to board the boat when a stray man succeeded".'

replied: 'I know nothing you do could be ungentlemanly, but it will certainly be considered so by other English people who hear of it.' 'No matter,' replied H.H. imperiously. 'Their opinion is not of the least importance. I cable at the next stopping-place.' The Darlings received this frostily, and the Dewas party got out at a remote station, where Forster was made to draft the cable. It was long but began: 'Owing to temporary financial difficulties in my state am reluctantly compelled to forgo pleasure of having European officer.'

This confused episode was the last of Forster's experiences as a courtier. He returned to Dewas with H.H., but mainly in order to pack – his plan being to spend some last weeks in India with Masood in Hyderabad. The Maharaja was eager for him to stay, now that the way was clear; however, it was not certain that their telegram would reach Leslie, or that it would stop him if it did.[1] Moreover it seemed to Forster the right moment to go; his usefulness to H.H., never very great, was at an end. The Maharaja was disconsolate, making many speeches of affection and decorating him with the Tukojirao III Gold Medal, the second highest honour of the State. Forster was dissatisfied with himself. He felt he had been a trouble to H.H. – though it was true, this had brought them together, which was a gain. He was disturbed, too, by the memory of his own panic and disorder. Also, he foresaw with distress that H.H., so rare, so brilliant, so incompetent, was doomed to disaster. 'We were very melancholy,' he wrote to his mother (12 November 1921):

> I hated leaving him, but it is his tragedy not to know how to employ people, and I could not feel it any use to go on muddling with work that gave me no satisfaction, and was of no essential importance to him. The things of this life mean so little to him – mean something so different anyway – I never feel certain what he likes, or even whether he likes me: consideration for others so often simulates affection in him. I only know that he is one of the sweetest and saintliest men I have ever known . . .

*   *   *

After the heat and confusions of Dewas, Forster's last two months in India were a relief, and a very carefree and delightful time. The relief came, partly, from his being among Mohammedans. He felt he

---

[1] The telegram seems to have done its work, for Col. Leslie never reappeared in Dewas.

understood Mohammedans, as he did not understand Hindus. 'The Hindu character is almost incomprehensible to us,' he wrote to his Aunt Laura Forster (6 November 1921):

> The more I know the less I understand. With the Mohammedans it is different. When after the nightmare of Gokul Ashtami, I stood on the minaret of the Taj in Agra, and hear the evening call to prayer from the adjacent mosque, I knew at all events *where* I stood and *what* I heard; it was a land that was not merely atmosphere but had definite outlines and horizons. So with the Mohammedan friends of Masood whom I am meeting now. They may not be as subtle or suggestive as the Hindus, but I can follow what they are saying.

He found Masood in tearing spirits, surrounded by friends, busy with all sorts of schemes and full of plans for his own entertainment. Masood was now an influential personage in Hyderabad, and, as Director of Public Instruction, was well placed to continue his grandfather's work for the Muslim cause. (He was playing a large part in the planning of Hyderabad's new Osmania University, the first Indian university to employ a native language – Urdu – for its teaching.) His wife Zorah and children were away when Forster arrived, so the two had the run of the house and lived in the zenana, sleeping side by side on a vine-shaded verandah. In the morning, clients and suppliants arrived in throngs, by bicycle, horse, carriage or motorcar, until the front drive looked like the approach to a racecourse.

Masood had commanded various old companions, like Sherwani and the Mirza brothers,[1] to join him in Hyderabad. Apart from them, his closest friends were Sir Akbar Hydari and his wife Amina Bibi. Sir Akbar was the Nizam's Finance Minister and one of the most powerful figures in the state.[2] He had been the instigator of the Osmania University. Though hostile to Congress, he was a modernizer, and he and his wife had fought the *purdah* system; her abandonment of *purdah* was still a scandal to their neighbours, who would spy on her with binoculars. Forster became friendly with both, but especially with Amina Bibi, a humourless and censorious but exceedingly kind and sensitive woman. The Hydaris and their children, Forster told

---

[1] See Vol. 1, p. 202 and *passim*.
[2] His name became known outside India when he led the Hyderabad delegation to the Round Table Conference in 1930–2.

his mother, were the plainest family he had ever seen: '. . . thick lips, huge chins, and noses on which gold spectacles do rest, crimped black hair, clumsy feet.' Another friend among the high officials was the Nawab Nizameth Jung. Forster was taken to dinner with him and was struck by his perfect impersonation of the English gentleman and scholar. They dined in the garden, where the Nawab was building a 'retreat' in the style of the Parthenon, 'He is an oracular and cultured talker,' Forster told his mother (1 December 1921), 'and his idea of happiness is to exclude reality, which may indicate a guilty conscience. We praised Marcus Aurelius and Epictetus and other celebrated back numbers and stuffed ourselves full of pilau, also discussing the stars.'

The favourite topic of the Nawab and the Hydaris, as of everyone else, was the appallingness of the Nizam: his meanness, his cruelty, his tyranny and misgovernment. Even court officials spoke quite openly on the subject, though the Nizam employed innumerable spies, no important household being without one. (At the Masoods, the chauffeur and two other servants were known spies.) The fact was, Forster reported to his mother, 'the cat can't be more out of the bag than it is'. Moreover, the spies' reports were so voluminous, and implicated so many people, the Palace could scarcely have acted on them all even had it wanted to.

There was much talk everywhere of the forthcoming visit of the Prince of Wales, due to begin in November. Almost all Masood's friends, though they were pro-British, thought the visit a mistake. And in fact, from the moment of the Prince's coming, it proved a disaster, riots and boycottings being provoked by it, and the Prince, on several occasions, having to make a royal progress through empty streets.[1] There was a ripple of protest in Hyderabad itself, the boys at a local school absenting themselves *en masse* on the day of the Prince's arrival. Forster wrote to his mother (20 December 1921):

> To the educated Indian, whatever his opinions, this ill-omened visit does seem an impertinence. You can't solve real complicated and ancient troubles by sending out a good-tempered boy; besides, this naive slap-the-back method, though the very thing for our colonies, scarcely goes down in the East. People talk about his

---

[1] The Prince wrote to the Secretary of State for India, Edwin Montagu, complaining 'India is no longer a place for the white man to live in.' (S. D. Waley, *Edwin Montagu* (1964), p. 262.)

safety – but not about what he *is* or *says* or *does*: all that is ignored. It is just a piece of luggage that must be carried about carefully.

He published a biting article on this theme, 'The Prince's Progress', in the *Nation and Athenaeum* in January, describing the Prince as 'the chatty, handy type of monarch, which the West is producing rather against time, and of which the King of the Belgians is the leading example.'

He was eager to see Bidar and to buy some of its famous inlaid metal work, and Masood took him on a three-day trip there, leaving Forster to go sight-seeing while he and a colleague, Ali Akbar, inspected local schools. Forster remembered it as a time of great happiness, wandering alone in this red walled city, its ancient cannon half smothered in cactuses and the air thronged with brilliant birds and butterflies. He was studying the Indian birds and would be out of doors in the early morning, before Masood and his friend had woken, identifying species in his *Birds of India*.

In December, when Masood made a visitation of schools in south-western Hyderabad, the three of them made a longer trip together, witnessing the ruins of many empires: Hindu, Moslem and British. The scene at Lingsagur, till 1860 a British cantonment, impressed Forster. He wrote to Ludolf (11 December 1921):

> A civilization, however silly, is touching as soon as it passes away, and I sit on the stucco curve of what was once a band stand, or wander through ruined halls of bungalows that once smelt of whisky and echoed to giggles, or read in the tombs in the cemetery that the 'dearly beloved sweet gentle wife of Captain Pedley' has 'gone before'.

Masood's tour ended at Gangavati – crowds gathering there to cheer this eminent visitor – and then, in bullock-carts lent by the Rani of Anegundi, they set out for Hampi, the ancient capital of the Vijaya-nagar kings, crossing the Tungabhadra river – a fierce and rocky stream in a gorge – in 'immense bowls of wicker work, coated with leather and propelled by a savage with a paddle'. On this trip, Forster came out as a most determined sightseer. On their way to Gangavati they noticed a fort on the top of a hill, and he insisted on their visiting it. They enquired the way from a policeman, who said the path was entirely blocked by cactuses; however, Forster was not to be deterred, saying curtly: 'I will take the risk.' Masood began to get angry: 'Morgan, you are impossible,' he said. 'You can go if you like, but Akbar and I are not coming.' So, with the policeman and a couple of villagers, Forster set off up the hill. Twenty minutes later he was back, groaning and covered from head to foot in cactus thorns, and they had to hurry him off to a doctor.[1]

It was altogether a cheerful time for Forster. By now – it was a comfort – he felt he need have no secrets about his sex-life from Masood and told him the K— episode. Masood gave him advice, and would tease him in a way he enjoyed: 'Morgan, will you never change? . . . Morgan, the time has come for me to take you to a woman,' etc. They bickered amicably. Masood told Forster he was impossibly wilful. Also, he complained, he was too taciturn and would not put himself out in company. On Christmas day, taking Forster to dinner with an English colleague, he implored him; 'Do try to be a success this time.' 'So I pulled myself together,' Forster told his mother (28 December 1921), 'drank plenty of wine, and interrupted everyone's conversation, which is, I have discovered, the simplest way of producing animation, and they were all delighted. If Masood gave me wine I should be noisier at his parties, but that he does not know.' On his birthday, there was a charming scene, which he reported to his mother:

> As I lay in bed drinking tea at 7.30, fortunately in my grand dressing-gown – Masood reclining near – three small boys in white robes and astrachan caps entered throwing roses, followed by 2 young men doing ditto, 2 ditto Mohammedan maidens, 3 Moham-medan matrons, and finally old Hydari, and another gentleman and a tray of oranges, apples, bananas, sweets, and (but this didn't come off) a bomb which ought to have exploded under my bed-room window and didn't.

The same evening, returning from a banquet at the Hydaris, he found his room like a bridal chamber: flowering shrubs pinned on the curtains, and his whole bed and dressing-table strewn and festooned with rose-leaves. He did not yet feel India a 'success', in the sense of restoring his power of writing, but – remembering his chagrins at Dewas – he told himself 'I never thought to end this year so well.'

*　　*　　*

[1] Related by Ali Akbar in an article, 'E. M. Forster in India', in the *Illustrated Weekly of India*, 18 October 1970.

He had booked his return passage for early in January, planning to spend a week or two with Mohammed in Egypt. Egypt was in state of crisis, with daily shootings and anti-British demonstrations – so much so that he wondered if he would be allowed to land. He put off his journey for a little, but in the end there seemed no point in waiting, and – much fêted and garlanded by Masood and his friends – he set off, reaching Port Said on the 23rd. There was no trouble about landing, but what greeted him was grim. Instead of Mohammed in person he found a letter from him announcing that he was ill, and, on making his way to Mohammed's home at Mansourah, he found him far gone in consumption and evidently dying. He took him off to Cairo, to see a specialist, but the doctor gave no hope at all, and they had to face the fact that in a few weeks or months he would be dead.

It remained for Forster to do what he could for Mohammed in the days left to him. Mohammed's daughter was also ill, and was in hospital, so, leaving Gamila to look after her, Forster took Mohammed off to Helouan, a health-resort on the Nile above Cairo, and found some furnished lodgings for them, where the family could join him later. Mohammed was penniless, and Forster wondered how best to help him over money, guessing that if he gave him a lump sum the doctors would soon strip him of it. The best plan was a monthly allowance, and he again cursed his failure to find an 'agent' to transmit money and relay news: Furness had proved useless, and he wrote to the kindly Ludolf to prepare him for the role. He felt strong and capable and angry at the political forces which, so he felt, had helped to kill Mohammed. He wrote to Dickinson (28 January 1922): 'I can look no Egyptian in the face. Their hostility is obvious, and they obstruct one in various little ways, and would do more if they dared. It is odious being in this country. India absolutely different, for there we have committed no comprehensive wrong.'

His few days with Mohammed at Helouan turned out unexpectedly happy. Mohammed was well enough to come for brief expeditions, and on one of them they bought Gamila a silk shawl, proposing to pretend that Forster had brought it for her from India. Forster asked Mohammed why he did not educate her more, but he replied contentedly: 'She is very nice and good to me, and I enjoy her talk and am most fond of her, but her head is empty and it is too late to fill it.' 'But you are filling it with lies,' said Forster. 'All is the same,' said Mohammed, 'as long as she gets the silk.' Forster described the scene in their room on one of these last days, in a letter to Florence Barger:

> He is asleep now – tried to read the proofs of my Alexandrian book with excellent effect. Now and then I shoo the flies off his face which is unaltered and a very nice one. You wouldn't know that he is ill . . .
>
> Feel very fit and damned competent.

5 *A Passage to India*

It proved a difficult homecoming for him. Mohammed's coming death lay heavy on his mind. He awaited it calmly, but it was painful concealing his feelings about it from his mother. The pain was another reminder of his imprisonment with her, and in his present mood his home, and the sight of England generally, depressed him. He wrote to Ludolf: 'It's like a person who has folded her hands and stands waiting. I do think that during the war something in this country got killed.'

His deepest trouble lay in the knowledge that even now, he was still balked as a novelist and that India had not released him. Calling on the Woolfs a week or so after his return, he struck Virginia as 'depressed to the verge of inanition'. He chatted with them dispiritedly about the sparrows that flew about the Dewas palace ('I used to shout at them sometimes') and how squirrels sat on the piano. He told them he didn't believe any more in native states but felt no enthusiasm at seeing the cliffs of England again. Then, wrote Virginia Woolf (12 March 1922), 'Off he went, carrying a very heavy metal plate, to dine with Aunt Rosalie at Putney.' She felt sorry for him.

> To come back to Weybridge, to come back to an ugly house a mile from the station, an old, fussy, exacting mother, to come back having lost your Rajah, without a novel, and with no power to write one – this is dismal, I expect, at the age of 43. The middle age of buggers is not to be contemplated without horror . . .

Over the next fortnight his depression grew, becoming crippling, so that he felt he could hardly face people. It seemed to him his life was at a crisis; and he asked advice from Leonard Woolf, always a support to friends in such moments. Woolf gave him lunch and talked to him at length, arguing that at all costs he must go on with his half-written novel, regardless whether it could be published or not, for if he did not do so, he could never be sure it was a failure. This was probably the advice he wanted. At all events, he took it and now summoned up all his courage to resume writing. As a first step, on Woolf's advice, he gave up reviewing. But he also took a more drastic step: he decided to burn his indecent short stories. The burning took place early in April and was done, he told himself,[1] not as a moral repentance but out of a feeling that the stories 'clogged' him artistically. They were 'a wrong channel' for his pen.

The novel now began slowly to advance. The fact that he had begun it before the war presented a difficulty – for, of course, Anglo-India had changed very fast over the last decade. But it was also a challenge. And he resolved the problem by making it a novel 'out of time' – neither precisely pre-war nor precisely post-war, and deliberately free from direct political reference. In tone it would be darker than the novel originally planned – for he felt bitterer against the British after Amritsar, and less in love with Indians too. He wrote to Masood (27 September 1922):

> When I began the book I thought of it as a little bridge of sym-
> pathy between East and West, but this conception has had to go,
> my sense of truth forbids anything so comfortable. I think that
> most Indians, like most English people, are shits, and I am not
> interested whether they sympathize with one another or not. Not
> interested as an artist; of course the journalistic side of me still
> gets roused over these questions . . .

What he could not change was the manners and tone of his Anglo-Indians, and these – as critics were to point out – remained irredeemably pre-war.

A different kind of difficulty was that he had come to feel bored with orthodox fictional form. He told Dickinson (8 May 1922) that he was tired of the convention that one must view the action through the mind of one of the characters.

> If you can pretend you can get inside one character, why not
> pretend it about all the characters? I see why. The illusion of life
> may vanish, and the creator degenerate into the showman. Yet
> some change of the sort must be made. The studied ignorance of
> novelists grows wearisome.

---

[1] Diary, 8 April 1922.

There may have been, here, some influence from Proust, for, while in Marseilles on his return from India, he had bought *Du Côté de Chez Swann* and had read it with excitement. In his diary for 7 May he noted: 'Have made careful & uninspiring additions to my Indian novel, influenced by Proust.' Sometimes, too, he felt there was a basic defect in his Indian novel. It was that, as he told Ludolf (13 June 1922), 'the characters are not sufficiently interesting for the atmosphere. This tempts me to emphasize the atmosphere, and so to produce a meditation rather than a drama.'

He pressed on doggedly with the writing, wanting at times to 'spit or scream like a maniac'; and by mid-May he was able to show some two-thirds of the novel to Arnold's, who were enthusiastic. The following month he received an unexpected boost to his confidence. *The Times* reviewer, writing of 'Lucas Malet'[1] and her latest volume, *Da Silva's Widow, and Other Stories*, remarked that there was hardly one of her stories which did not carry a reminder of some other author, and in one or two cases the author was 'Mr E. M. Forster of *The Celestial Omnibus*.' 'Lucas Malet' replied (8 June 1922), saying that she could hardly be guilty of plagiarism from E. M. Forster, since she had never heard of him. And at this, several admirers of Forster wrote in, testifying to their love and admiration for his books. Frank Sidgwick, profiting from the occasion, offered to send a free copy of *The Celestial Omnibus* (1911) to any British novelist 'who, in our judgement, is as distinguished a writer as "Lucas Malet", if that novelist will make a similar public confession in your columns that he or she has never heard of Mr E. M. Forster'; and *The Times*, on 17 June 1922, published a rather solemn profile or 'Medallion' of him. It said that 'Mr Forster of *Howards End* and the short stories is a man who has something of the vision that has received its most unhesitating and masterful expression in the music of Beethoven.' As a result of this unlooked-for publicity, Forster received a stream of enquiries from agents and publishers and many letters from unknown admirers.

* * *

The news of Mohammed continued to be melancholy. In March he wrote, telling Forster 'I think we shall meet each other if not in the world it will be in the heaven'; and in April there was another gloomy

[1] Pseudonym of the novelist Mary St Leger Harrison.

letter, causing Forster to confide in his diary, with self-knowledge:
'I want him to tell me that he is dead, and so set me free to make an
image of him. Latterly my great love prevents my feeling he is real.'
In the same realistic vein, he noted, a few days later: 'Determined my
life should contain one success I have concealed from myself and
others M's frequent coldness to me. And his occasional warmth may
be due to politeness, gratitude, or pity. The prospect of his death
gives me no pain.'

A despairing letter from Mohammed arrived, dated 6 May:

> Dear Morgan
> I am sending you the photograph
> I am very bad
> I got nothing more to say
> The family are good. My compliments to mother
> My love to you
> My love to you
> My love to you
> do not forget your ever friend
>
> Moh el adl

It was followed by another, dated two days later:

> Dear Morgan
> I have got the mony today from you and thank you very much
> for it. I am absolutely bad I don't go out I can't stand
> I am very weak
> How are you no more today
> My love to you
> My love to you

By the time that Forster received the letters, Mohammed was in fact
already dead. Forster had guessed as much; and on 17 May there
arrived a letter from Mohammed's brother to confirm it. In further
letters, Forster was told that Mohammed had died possessed of
three houses and £60. He did not believe it about the houses; all the
same, it crossed his mind that Mohammed might not have been
straight with him over money. He noted on 17 June (perhaps
recording a dream): 'His ghost as one needing forgiveness came out
from the curtain in a sort of way, conceived of as taller than normal.'
Mohammed had bequeathed him a ring, and he wrote to a friend of
Mohammed's asking him to forward it. Inwardly, however, he told
himself that he did not much mind if it came. 'The affair has treated
me very gently.'

Alexandria: a History and a Guide had even now not appeared. He had written the publishers various 'stingers' and had set Ludolf on to them, but to no avail. By now he had ceased to speculate when it might come out and had decided that, in any event, there should be no English edition. The thought, however, occurred to him that he might construct a second Alexandrian book, making use of his wartime journalism in the *Egyptian Mail* and elsewhere. He suggested the project to the Woolfs, who were enthusiastic, and it was agreed that they should publish it at the Hogarth Press under the title of *Pharos and Pharillon*. For him it represented a kind of tribute to Mohammed, and he gave the book a dedication – ' Ἑρμῇ ψυχοπομπῷ ' (To Hermes, leader of souls)' which alluded cryptically to him. This concept of Hermes was a cherished private cult of Forster's, symbolizing the aid that one soul can give another. It had first been inspired, it may be guessed, by the Greek sculpture in the British Museum of a beautiful Hermes escorting Alcestis to the underworld.[1]

He was now outwardly much restored in spirits. Virginia Woolf found him 'very calm, serene, like a kettle boiling by some private fire'.[2] He saw a good deal of the Woolfs at this time, on business or otherwise, and was active in the Memoir Club. On a weekend at the Bells' house at Charleston he went for a walk with Duncan Grant and, rather uncharacteristically, talked about his own work: how his new novel was to have a great central nave, a succession of side chapels and a lady-chapel at the end.[3]

In May, Lady Ottoline Morrell invited him to come to Garsington for a weekend, giving him the choice of meeting Eliot or Wyndham Lewis. He replied (perhaps associating her in his mind with Mme Verdurin) in the style of *A la recherche du temps perdu*.

> Dear Lady Ottoline,
>   I come.
>   I have always wanted to see both Lewis and Eliot, and though the longer I see them the unlikelier I am to meet them, this is after all but a subordinate clause in the career of one who, despite considerable delay, (due partly to idleness, partly to impecuniosity, partly to the hope that the object of this sentence – who will finally be mentioned in strict accordance with the rules of Grammar,

----

[1] Conceivably this was the 'wonderful boy with the broken arm' which he refers to in his diary in 1904. (See Vol. I, p. 110.)

[2] Virginia Woolf's diary, 2 June 1922.

[3] Information from Duncan Grant.

and possibly even upon this page – would have been forgotten in Europe before the subject of it returned to Asia) is reading Proust. I shall eat, I shall eat, I shall eat, and, then, quite suddenly and naturally, I shall break silence by a little noise which is really the height of Oriental good manners, but which Lewis will regard as insolent, and consequently respect. And all will be well . . .

He chose the Wyndham Lewis weekend and found Lewis, as he had foreseen, 'a curious mixture of insolence and nervousness'. They got on amicably, however. On the first day, at least thirty guests were expected to tea, and Forster and Lewis, though expected to 'perform', escaped and went for a walk. Lady Ottoline was piqued. 'So like life,' she murmured. Mark Gertler the painter was also there – 'a little East End Jew, very amusing and clever', Forster told his mother; 'exactly like a street boy who makes faces at the people in carriages and imitates their gestures. He and W[yndham] L[ewis] were frightened of, and frightened, the high-born undergraduates, who motored out, gasping and undulating, from Oxford.' H. J. Massingham, the editor of the *Nation*, was expected next day, and, since Lewis had quarrelled with him, Lady Ottoline was expecting explosions. She drifted about, 'wondering what will happen, wishes she could *understand* people, wishes they were more simple etc., clad the meantime herself in elaborate floating dresses of all the colours of the rainbow.' Lady Ottoline had heard rumours of Mohammed and kept loudly fishing for confidences, evidently regarding it as an occasion for Bloomsbury truth-telling. Forster was upset and resentful, and in the succeeding months he begged friends, such as Sassoon, never to discuss him at Garsington. 'Whenever you want information about me,' he told Sassoon (26 March 1923), 'it is always to be had at first hand.'

Forster's acquaintance with the Hardys, engineered by Sassoon, had flourished, and this July, as several times later, he went down on a visit to Max Gate. He wondered about his own motives, a little; for as a conversationalist he found Hardy very boring. Especially so about books. Forster determined, on this visit, to keep the talk away from books, and he did quite well, with topics like the discomfort of charabancs and whether 'chicken' was a singular or a plural. However, eventually Hardy sensed his drift and, Forster told Sassoon, 'with commendable pique he insisted on revealing the secrets of his art'. Forster noticed how anxious Hardy was to make a good impression, no matter upon whom. While they were having tea, a reporter was announced, at which Hardy sprang up with alacrity, saying 'Reporters are very important people, you know.' Being very deaf, he had not heard the reporter's knock, but the dog 'Wessie', who had, had given a bark: Hardy, in a tone of significance, said *They* know,' as if Wessie had displayed some preternatural faculty. Someone had said that Wessie looked like Robert Bridges, and Hardy, who was envious of Bridges, repeated this with relish. (Forster later remembered this with pleasure, when Bridges, who was envious of Hardy, said to him, when preparing an anthology of recent verse: 'I tried to find two poems by Hardy to include, but I couldn't, you know, I really couldn't.'[1]) Hardy showed Forster the graves of his pets, each with a headstone, now overgrown with ivy. They all seemed to have come to violent ends: 'This is Snowball – she was run over by a train. . . . This is Pella, the same thing happened to her. . . . This is Kitkin, she was cut clean in two . . .' Forster asked: 'How is it, Mr Hardy, that so many of your cats have been run over? Is the railway near?' 'Not at all near, not at all near. I don't know how it is. . . . But of course we have only buried those pets whose bodies were recovered. Many were never seen again.' Forster, reporting the scene to his mother (19 July 1922), said he could hardly keep grave, it was so like one of Hardy's novels or poems.

*   *   *

All through 1922, as he worked on his novel, the British empire and its misdeeds were much on Forster's mind. During September Lloyd George nearly brought the country to war with Turkey, over her seizure of Chanak, a British outpost in the neutralized zone of the Straits. The war, so it was said in some quarters, was a debt owed to the British war-dead in the Dardanelles. This chauvinist appeal

---

[1] When Bridges refused to be a pall-bearer at Hardy's funeral, Forster wrote some lines on the occasion, in a letter to Roger Fry, later copied into his Commonplace Book:

Twas breakfast at Boar's Hill one January morn;
Woe wimples the housewife, awake to the menace
Of burial bell from far Peter's monastery,
Where with undue pomp and excessive attendance
Of Jack and his apes rhymster Hodge is enterrèd.
All windows she hath shut, all newspapers withheld,
Blaming this icy weather or postman's laggardness.
Surl husband sits silent still, ah but for how long?

was ridiculed by A. A. Milne, in the *Daily News* (4 October 1922), in an article which impressed Forster:

> They have almost brought it off, the War to End Peace, for which they have been striving for three years. What an incredible joke! A war 'to defend the freedom of the Straits and the sanctity of our graves in Gallipoli', says *Punch* magnificently. Of course you can think of it like that, and it sounds quite dignified and natural. But you may also think, as I do, of those five or ten or twenty men, our chosen statesmen, sitting round a table; the same old statesmen; each with his war memories thick upon him; each knowing his own utter incompetence to maintain a war or to end a war . . .'

Forster, taking up Milne's title, 'Another Little War', wrote five days later:

> Sir, – Mr A. A. Milne's brilliant article deserves special thanks for its scathing analysis of 'the sanctity of our graves in Gallipoli'. Our rulers knew that their policy would not be popular, and in the hope of stampeding us into it they permitted this vile appeal – the viler because the sentiment that it tries to pervert is a noble one and purifies the life of a nation when directed rightly. The bodies of the young men who are buried out there have no quarrel with one another now, no part in our quarrels or interest in our patronage, no craving for holocausts of more young men. Anyone who has himself entered, however feebly, into the life of the spirit, can realize this.
>
> It is only the elderly ghouls of Whitehall who exhume the dead for the purpose of party propaganda and employ them as a bait to catch the living.
>
> > Peace would do wrong to our undying dead, –
> > The sons we offered might regret they died
> > If we got nothing lasting in their stead.
> > We must be solidly indemnified.
>
> Thus wrote Wilfred Owen, a month before he was killed on the Sambre Canal. The men about whom he wrote it are still in office, still pleasantly busied in their task of finding graves for heroes. At the next election can we not provide them with a quiet retreat of their own? Its sanctity should be inviolable.

In the same vein he wrote for the *New Leader* a bitter imaginary dialogue 'Our Graves in Gallipoli',[1] in which two anonymous graves – one, so it turns out, of a British soldier and one of a Turkish – speak

---

[1] 20 October 1922. It was reprinted in *Abinger Harvest*.

to each other about the strange interest taken once more, after seven years' silence, in 'the sanctity of our graves in Gallipoli'. The dialogue made scathing mock-Homeric play with the names of 'Lloyd George, prudent in counsels, and lion-hearted Churchill'. Churchill was the one politician whom Forster truly detested and he was jubilant when, in the November election, Churchill lost his seat.

*   *   *

Alexandria: a History and a Guide finally appeared in the December of this year, and its fate now took an even odder turn. Soon after its publication, Forster received a regretful letter from Whitehead Morris & Co., informing him that there had been a fire in the warehouse and that the entire stock of *Alexandria* had been burnt. Fortunately, they said, it had been insured, and they enclosed a substantial cheque in compensation. A few weeks later he received another letter from the publishers. It was even more regretful. It said that, upon further search, the books had been found intact, in a cellar which had escaped the flames. This, in view of the insurance money, his publishers wrote, had created a most awkward situation, and they had taken the only way out – namely, to burn the books deliberately.[1]

*   *   *

Mohammed's death had preoccupied his thoughts all the year, and in August he had begun a long and impassioned 'letter' or book addressed to him, meaning to record in it every moment of their friendship.

August 5th 1922

Dear Mohammed,

    This book is for you and me – I wish I could distinguish more clearly between us, but it was always difficult, and now you are not here to correct me when I think of you not as you are but as I should like to think you. I write it with my mind on you and with the illusion that your mind still exists and attends. I pretend that you are still alive, because it only is thus that I can think of you as real, although I know that a putrid scrap in the Mansourah burial ground is all that was you. I write for my own comfort and to recall the past, but also because I am professionally a writer and want to pay you this last honour, although there is much that you will not understand, and some things that you will not agree with . . .

---

[1] There was not another edition until 1938.

The letter was written in stages. He resumed in November:

> Mohammed I try to keep this real, but my own words get in the
> way, and you are decayed to terrible things by this time – dead
> six months. I do not mind that, but I fear you becoming unreal,
> so that all our talks and the occasional nights we have slept in one
> bed will seem to belong to other people . . . Dear boy, I want those
> memories to be of you, not stained by me. I do not want to prate
> of perfect love, only to write to you as if you are real. So I try to
> think of your putrescence in your grave sometimes. It is real, and
> contemporary with me, it leads me back to the real you.

He dreamed of Mohammed most nights, and one dream expressed
much self-knowledge:

> I passed a young man in black with a slight but well defined
> moustache. He was and was not Mohammed – not he outwardly
> but he in the intensity, the quality of the emotion caused in my
> heart. I knew I ought to follow him but delayed – my character –
> and when I tried to do so my legs were weighted, I heard he was
> catching a train. Painfully I arrive, a bath being filled with hot
> water. I was in time, the train had not gone, others in the bath
> room left us alone, he lent against the edge of the bath, half sitting,
> half standing, entirely naked, his dark bush distinct, and he
> smiled. The effect was not physical nor was my awakening ghastly
> except that I awoke.[1]

The dream throws light on the story that he wrote at about this time,
called 'The Life to Come'.[2] The story began merely as one of his
'indecencies', but turned into something very different. It concerns
a handsome young missionary who once sleeps with a young native
chieftain, with the result that the chieftain takes their love to be that
'love of God' which is spoken of by Christians and promptly announces
the conversion of his tribe. The missionary is appalled but is too
prudent to give up this brilliant conversion, so he cheats his uncomprehending disciple, who wishes to enjoy more such love, with
shadowy promises. Years pass, and the chieftain, broken-hearted at
the postponement, and finding himself robbed not only of his religion
but of his lands and royal authority, falls mortally ill. The missionary,
now dried-up and middle-aged, comes to visit him on his deathbed,
finding him lying alone and naked on his house-roof. He feels it safe
now to venture a Christian embrace and tells the dying Vithobai of

---

[1] Diary, 20 December 1923.
[2] Published in *'The Life to Come' and Other Stories* (1972).

the joys of the life to come. 'And will there be love?' asks Vithobai. 'In the real and true sense, there will,' answers the missionary. 'The life to come,' shouts Vithobai. 'Life, life, eternal life. Wait for me in it'; and he stabs the missionary through the heart and hurls himself, victoriously, over the parapet.

The story was written, Forster said, 'in indignation'. By which, he meant, partly, indignation against British imperialism; but he was hitting, too, at some suspected over-cautiousness in himself. It was a story, eloquent but over-romantic though it is, which always meant a lot to him.

He had received Mohammed's ring, and would put it on once a day. In the spring of 1923 he went for a walk in Chertsey Meads and put it on his finger, hoping to recapture Mohammed's image but finding him grown even more unreal. 'What was so appalling on the Meads,' he noted (25 March 1923), 'was the belief that I had *better* forget my friend: this had never come to me before.' He added more words to his letter to Mohammed:

> You are dead, Mohammed, and Morgan is alive and thinks more about himself and less of you every word he writes. You called out my name at Beebit el Hagar station after we had seen that ruined temple about two miles from it that no one but us seems to have seen. It was dark and I heard an Egyptian shouting who had lost his friend: Margan, Margan – you calling me and I felt we belonged to each other, you had made me an Egyptian. When I call you on the downs now, I cannot make you alive, nor can I belong to you because you own nothing. I shall not belong to you when I die – only be like you.

*   *   *

Pharos and Pharillon came out in May 1923. It was very well received, and, as he had hoped, the section on Cavafy's poetry aroused interest, various publishers and agents writing to him to ask for more Cavafy poems. He had, meanwhile, succeeded in interesting T. S. Eliot and Arnold Toynbee in Cavafy and had placed one or two poems in the *Nation* and the *Criterion*. The problem, he found, was not so much to provoke interest in Cavafy as to galvanize Valassopoulos, the translator he most favoured, into activity. He wrote and wrote again to him, but little or nothing came. (According to Robert Liddell, Cavafy's biographer, the trouble was that Valassopoulos did not like Cavafy's erotic poems.) He also wrote frequently to Cavafy, receiving back grateful, but very stiff and impersonal, replies.

He liked to take such trouble for other authors. Serviceability always appealed to him; and efforts of this kind, it seemed to him, were one of the duties of a man of letters. Quite often, he wrote long letters out of the blue to unknown authors, when something of theirs had interested him. He wrote such a letter, full of praise and painstaking criticism, to J. R. Ackerley, about a poem of his called 'Ghosts' which had been published in the *London Mercury* in April 1922. The theme of the letter was Memory, a Proustian subject rather on Forster's mind just then:

> This business of remembering a past incident. The horror, beauty, depth, emotional and mental insecurity, that is thus introduced into our lives, and that we can neither avoid or recall. I have been reading Proust who knows all about it too and like you rejects the ordinary explanation . . . I don't know whether you and Proust are right in your explanations. 'Out of death lead no ways' is more probably the fact. But being right is of little importance. What you have done is to drive home the strangeness of a creature who is apparently allowed neither to remember nor to forget and who sees in the stream of his daily life, piteously disordered, the recurrence of something that is beautiful and that passes as inevitably away now as it did then . . . The moment a memory is registered by the intellect is its last moment.

Ackerley, then totally unknown as a writer, was flattered by this attention from Forster, and the letter was the beginning of a friendship important to both.

Ackerley was then twenty-six. He had fought on the Western Front as a junior officer, had been wounded and taken prisoner, and had subsequently been interned in Switzerland. After the war he had gone to Cambridge; and he was now in London, trying to write, while living on an allowance from his father. The father, Roger Ackerley, was a director of Elder and Fyffes, the banana-importers, and the family lived in some style, in a substantial mansion on Richmond Hill. Joe was the darling of both parents.[1] They encouraged him in his writing, and regarded it with some awe – a fact which embarrassed him, for so far he had not achieved very much. He had drafted a play about his internment experience, but this was hanging fire, and he was having even less success with some Henry-James-type short stories and a historical drama in verse. So far, his only publication of any size was a long poem printed in the *English Review* in 1916.

---

[1] See his posthumous autobiography, *My Father and Myself* (1968).

Forster and he met a few months after exchanging letters, and it amused them to find that, in a remote degree, they were family connections; for Mr Aylward, the music teacher whom Maimie Preston had married, was, by a former marriage, Joe Ackerley's great-grandfather.[1] Forster was attracted by Ackerley. He was exceedingly good-looking, in a romantically-English way: tall and golden-haired, though with something thin-lipped and pike-like about the mouth. He was charming and gay and funny,[2] with an extravagant comic imagination, a sympathy for the underdog, and a mania for telling the painful or awful truth. 'I think people *ought* to be upset,' he would say. He quickly and ostentatiously announced that he was homosexual, and, as Forster soon gathered, led an intensely promiscuous, and very disaster-prone, love life. (In his own mind, however, it did not appear as promiscuity but as a devoted quest for the Ideal Friend.) There was no question of an affair between him and Forster; and indeed – though this was common with Forster – the friendship took some time to develop; as late as a year after their first meeting, Forster noted in his diary (14 October 1923): 'I don't quite like A. though he has intelligence and charm. I suspect him of cruelty.' Meanwhile, it occurred to him that here, in Ackerley, might be the private secretary that the Maharaja of Chhatarpur[3] had so long been looking for – or rather, for he knew Ackerley felt unsettled, here was a post which might suit him and give him rewarding experience. Ackerley rose to the suggestion; and a long and confused correspondence with India ensued, leading eventually, in October 1923, to Ackerley's appointment. Forster gave him much good advice, both before and after his departure, ending one letter to him in India (29 January 1924): 'As for being bored, don't mind it – more than the unpleasantness I mean: don't think you are wasting your time. You will never get hold of anything in India unless you experience Indian boredom.' Ackerley, after his arrival, sent him many long and entertaining letters,[4] and Forster,

---

[1] Or as Forster put it to Ackerley: 'Henrietta Synnot, as the second sister of the first husband of your great grandfather's second wife, was my first cousin once removed.'

[2] 'I do think he had more charm than anyone I ever knew,' said his friend Gerald Heard of him later.

[3] See p. 93.

[4] Two of them may be read in *The Ackerley Letters*, ed. N. Braybrooke (1975), pp. 6–13.

in one of his replies, told him: 'Your letters were a godsend to my etiolated novel. I copied in passages and it became ripe for publication immediately.'

With the death of Mohammed, Forster had felt that for the moment he wanted no new intimacy – also that, perhaps, he was incapable of attracting one. His experience at Dewas, had, he felt, left him 'both cuter and stupider' – more wary, but less capable of connection with people. Nevertheless, in this same year, he began another of the major friendships of his later life, with Sebastian Sprott.[1] Sprott, the son of a country solicitor, was by now twenty-five and was studying psychology in Cambridge, having done some war-service before going to the university. Forster had got to know him through the Apostles, and by the time that he did so, Sprott was already well known in Bloomsbury, the friend and lover of Maynard Keynes and an intimate of Lady Ottoline Morrell. Outwardly he was almost an 'exquisite': he fluttered, dressed elegantly and spoke in very Bloomsbury accents – the voice shooting up and down the scale or suddenly pouncing on some selected word. His style was, in a way, misleading, for his true wish was not for a 'gilded' Cambridge existence but for a hearty, egalitarian, sexually promiscuous low-life. A year or two later, being then a lecturer in psychology at Nottingham university, he had taken a house in a slum and had made for himself a largely working-class circle of friends, half of them regularly in and out of jail.

Sprott was a tender-hearted, loquacious and impractical young man, facing the world with a frown of pretended truculence. His comic insouciance made Forster laugh a good deal. There was never an 'affair' between them, but from the first Forster felt a kind of protectiveness towards him, regarding him as too harebrained to make a success of his career. Sprott, who was open-handed, was constantly hard up, and quite soon Forster was making him an allowance – something in the order of £100 a year. Sprott developed a great loyalty and affection towards Forster and, to amuse him, would write him long picaresque accounts of his escapades and

---

[1] Walter John Herbert Sprott (1897–1971). A Cambridge friend, A. T. Bartholomew, was once telling him that 'Jack Sprott' was too short and insignificant a name, when Dent came into the room carrying some music by J. S. Bach, and it was decided there and then to call him 'Sebastian'. In later years he reverted to 'Jack'.

seductions: they were some of the few letters that Forster, an habitual burner of letters, never destroyed. One, belonging to the later 1920s, runs: 'And now for a warning, Forster old chap, – don't you ever use a heap of chaff as a double bed. It is a long story . . .'

Forster's work on *A Passage to India* had continued steadily throughout 1923. In 1920 Masood, no doubt through Forster's arranging, had published an article on 'Some Aspects of Urdu Poetry' in the *Athenaeum*, and Forster drew on it – using some of Masood's very quotations* – when depicting Aziz and his friends and their love of flowery and melancholy verse. Forster had much trouble with the trial scenes in the novel, not being sure of his legal detail and doubting – with reason, as it turned out – whether a case as important as that of Aziz would have been tried in a subordinate court. He wrote about it to Masood, and Masood offered to check such details throughout the novel. When Forster finally sent him the typescript, however, his only reply was, unhelpfully, 'It is magnificent. Do not alter a word.'

The final pages of the novel were assisted not only by Proust and Joe Ackerley, but by T. E. Lawrence's *Seven Pillars of Wisdom*. Forster had received an introduction (or rather a re-introduction[1]) to Lawrence through Siegfried Sassoon. It began by Sassoon's lending him, at his own request and with Lawrence's approval, a copy of the privately-printed 'Oxford' text of *Seven Pillars*.[2] He had guessed instinctively that Lawrence's book would prove important to him: 'It is exactly what I want,' he told Sassoon on 12 December 1923, before he had even seen it. It proved to be so beyond expectation. The book astonished him, and supported him in a cherished belief, that sensitiveness and introspection could exist side by side

---

[1] He had encountered Lawrence two years earlier. George Antonius, Forster's old friend from Alexandrian days, had come to London on the Emir Feisal's staff and invited Forster to a luncheon with Feisal at a hotel in Berkeley Square. The meal took place on 22 February 1921. Feisal was absent during most of it, on business at the Colonial Office, but had returned near the end of it in the company of T. E. Lawrence, whom Forster remembered as 'a small fair-haired boy' who 'rapped out encouraging words about the Middle East'. He had been excited by this meeting and had written to Lawrence, receiving no reply. (See *T. E. Lawrence By His Friends*, ed. A. W. Lawrence (1937), p. 235.)
[2] During 1922 Lawrence had had eight copies printed on the presses of the *Oxford Times*.

with vigour, active heroism and largeness of vision. He wrote a fervent panegyric to Sassoon on 31 December:

> Fancy people still discussing whether the Nation or the Adelphi is in the right, whether the Sitwells have genius or merely talent, whether Riceyman Steps is up to the level of Clayhanger or of the Old Wives' Tale, whether De la Mare is more or less imaginative than Yeats, and all the time a book like this is being written. It moves me so deeply that I nearly cry, but my emotion is not entangled with any affection for the author – who is well able to look after himself – and so it is disinterested and so durable. I have read straight ahead as far as the meeting with Feisal, and have dipped much elsewhere: the effect is far greater when one reads straight on, and the cumulation will surely be tremendous: greater for me than for you because you have not this romantic passion for the East which chance or temperament has allotted me, and which L's scenery, or characters, evoke with almost intolerable violence.

The book affected him not only as a man but as a writer. He wrote the two final chapters of *A Passage to India* under its influence, completing them, and the novel, in a burst of confident energy. With his novel finished, Forster sent Lawrence one of his admirable and painstaking letters of criticism. It ran to many pages and was by no means all adulation. It drew a distinction between the 'fluid' and the 'granular' methods in writing: Lawrence's was the granular – as opposed to Tolstoy's, which was the fluid.

> I see people on camels, motionless; I look again and they are in a new position which I can connect with its predecessor, but is similarly immobile. There never can have been a Movement with so little motion in it! It all goes on, never unreal, practically every sentence and word is alive, but life unprintable in the spaces between the words is absent.

There were, he told Lawrence, certain subjects that the granular method was adapted to and others which it was not; it was suited to scenery, and also to pathos, but it did not suit men, or animals. He also found fault with what he called Lawrence's 'pseudo-reflective vein': 'I don't always see that which you are willing to reveal, but rather your hand straying towards the black heap of words.' For all this, he told Lawrence, 'You will never show it to anyone who will like it more than I do.' Lawrence was excited by this letter, writing to Forster (20 February 1924) that it had been brought to him while he was in bed with influenza and had instantly cured him. His own letter, as often in the future, was in a tone of extravagant self-abasement: 'I feel profoundly dejected over it all. It reads to me inferior to nearly every book which I have found patience to read ...'

At this period Lawrence was serving, under the name of T. E. Shaw, as a private in the Royal Tank Corps. It was the second of his attempts to escape his own identity – the first, when he enlisted in the R.A.F. as 'Aircraftman Ross', having been thwarted. He disliked the army, and within a year or so, through influence in high places, he was to secure a transfer back to the R.A.F. Meanwhile he was stationed at Bovington, in Dorset, working in the company stores and spending his spare time in a nearby cottage that he rented, called Cloude Hill. He invited Forster to visit him there, and the visit, which took place in March, went very well; indeed, Forster told Sassoon (25 March 1924) that he 'nearly fell to pieces before Lawrence'. He found him, 'a rare remote creature, uncanny, yet attractive', with sudden and disconcerting shifts of role – one moment he was the aspiring writer, the next a 'close-lipped Oxford M.A.' or a 'dashing freebooter'. He noticed he had a bad handshake, a clammy and limp one, and, perhaps partly for this reason, he suspected him of 'practices'. (By this he meant something of the Yoga kind; but it was a shrewd observation, considering what is now known about Lawrence's devices to have himself beaten.[1]) As for Lawrence's present way of life, and his explanations of it, they struck Forster as preposterous. 'He is inside a membrane of absurdity which has worn so thin that it is amazing he cannot see the light,' he wrote to Sassoon (25 March 1924). 'Those damned Arabs are all right and he knows it.' They had got on to the subject of 'unpublishable' writings – Lawrence remarked that *Seven Pillars* would have been unpublishable a year or two previously – and Forster, after his return, sent him 'The Life to Come'. This caused a momentary hitch in their relations, for Lawrence's reaction to the story, so he told Forster, was to want to 'laugh and laugh'. It seemed a very odd remark to Forster, and he never forgot it.

At the end of April, Forster and his mother received news from Abinger that his Aunt Laura Forster had collapsed and was probably dying. They went down at once to West Hackhurst and found his

---

[1] See P. Knightley and Colin Simpson, *The Secret Lives of Lawrence of Arabia* (1969).

aunt wandering in her mind, but able to recognize them. To Forster's surprise and pleasure, she kept saying nice things about Lily; it seemed that, having for forty years resented Lily as an intruder in the family, she now wanted, on her death-bed, to make amends. She died peacefully within a fortnight, leaving instructions for all her animals to be killed after her; and on the day of her funeral her friends and relations had a gay and noisy lunch, drinking several bottles of her wine.

Her death was a significant event for Forster. His feeling for her had been more of a family one than personal: she had been too masterful, and too boring a conversationalist, for real affection. Still, she had been his benefactor all his life, and he was now to inherit West Hackhurst, the house that his father had built for her. (He half regretted the inheritance, for her love for her house had appealed to him, and he wished in a way it could be buried with her.) His inheritance was bound, he felt, to make a change in his way of life. It meant he had become one of the 'landed gentry', and the prospect repelled and intrigued him. To friends, he wrote about it ruefully. 'I have to visit my estates,' he told Carrington (27 June 1924). 'They are no pleasure, but a bitterness and dreariness.' He was not really sure if he would ever occupy the house; but meanwhile there were months of work ahead, sorting through his aunt's possessions. 'I am tearing up letters of the last 150 years, all uninteresting,' he wrote to Sassoon (17 June 1924), 'or wondering what is to be done with George Richmond heads, each more insipid than his sister.'

A Passage to India was due to appear on 4 June. It was an appropriate moment for it, for the rights and wrongs of the British *raj* were much in the news throughout May and early June, by reason of the O'Dwyer case. Sir Michael O'Dwyer, who had been in charge in the Punjab at the time of the Amritsar massacre, had brought a libel action against an Indian official, Sir Sankaran Nair, over the latter's book *Gandhi and Anarchy* (1922). The book was mainly an attack on Gandhi, but incidentally it accused O'Dwyer of 'terrorism' in wartime recruiting and of ultimate responsibility for the 1919 massacre. General Dyer, the officer who had actually ordered the shooting, was too ill to give evidence, but the judge, H. A. McCardie, took the occasion to revive the whole Dyer controversy. Forster followed the case with excitement; and as it happened, he got an inside view of proceedings, for Harold Laski, whom he knew slightly, was on the jury. Laski was an expert on all aspects of the Amritsar affair, and the trial became a duel between him and McCardie. All through, the judge was extremely partisan in Dyer and O'Dwyer's favour, cutting many waggish jokes at the expense of Indian politics and politicians and going so far, in his summing-up, as to say that 'General Dyer, in the grave and exceptional circumstances, acted rightly, and in my opinion he was wrongly punished by the Secretary of State for India.' The jury duly found for O'Dwyer, awarding him £500 damages (some of them had wanted to give him £20,000), and they were violent against Laski, the sole dissenting juror. One of them, he told Forster, said to him, 'I am sorry for your poor wife and hope she will never speak to you again.' Forster wrote to Darling (17 June 1924) in fury at the verdict:

> It looks to me so sinister and so simple, but probably it is neither. Thus: – Sir S. Nair, a shit, writes a book against Gandhi, which incidentally contains a sentence libelling O'D. Besides being a shit, he is a Moderate so O'D takes the opportunity of discrediting that party by bringing an action, and wrecking our last hopes of coming to terms with India. – Is this correct? It is impossible to suppose O'D minded the attack personally, moreover only 3 copies of N's book ever came to this country. God, I have been enraged. A dirty political manoeuvre. There may be some other reason but I can see none.

Out of pure resentment, he sent McCardie a copy of his novel, and to his bafflement received a courteous acknowledgement from the judge, saying it had been an 'inspiration' and a 'help'.

Up to the last moment, he had been assailed by doubts and despairs about his novel, but its reception removed all his fears. The book suited the moment, and friends and reviewers alike called it a masterpiece and his finest achievement. Ralph Wright, reviewing it in the *New Statesman* said: 'We have had a long time to wait since *Howards End*, and if Mr Forster continues to write like this the waiting is worth it. *A Passage to India* is a better book than any earlier ones. It is as sensitive as they were, it is far better proportioned, and the mind which made it is more mature.' He was echoed by Rose Macaulay, writing in the *Daily News*. She said:

> He has quite lost the touch of preciousness, of exaggerated care for nature and the relationships of human beings, that faintly irritate some readers of his earlier books. He used once to write at times too much as a graduate (even occasionally as an under-

graduate) of King's College, Cambridge (perhaps the most civilized place in the world), who has had an amour with Italy and another with the god Pan. In *A Passage to India* (as, indeed, in *Howards End*), Pan is only implicit, the mysticism is more diffused, the imagination at once richer, less fantastic, and more restrained. It is a novel that from most novelists would be an amazing piece of work. Coming from Mr. Forster, it is not amazing, but it is, I think, the best and most interesting book he has written.

The allusion to 'King's' values chimed with Forster's own thoughts. He wrote to Darling (15 September 1924):

I have wondered – not whether I was getting down or up, which is too difficult, but whether I had moved at all since King's. King's stands for personal relationships, and these still seem to me the most real things on the surface of the earth, but I have acquired a feeling that people must go away from each other (spiritually) every now and then, and improve themselves if the relationship is to develop or even endure. A Passage to India describes such a going away – preparatory to the next advance, which I am not capable of describing. It seems to me that individuals progress alternately by loneliness and intimacy, and that legend of the multiplied Krishna (which I got, like so much that is precious to me, by intercourse with Bapu Sahib[1]) serves as a symbol of a state where the two might be combined. The 'King's' view over-simplified people: that I think was its defect. We are more complicated, also richer, than it knew, and affection grows more difficult than it used to be, and also more glorious.

He had sent a copy to D. H. Lawrence, in New Mexico, and it was this theme of 'going away from each other' that most struck Lawrence. He wrote (23 July 1924):

. . . I don't care about Bou-oum – Nor all the universe. Only the dark ahead & the silence into which we haven't yet spoken our impertinent echoes. – You saying human relationships don't matter, then after all hingeing your book on a very unsatisfactory friendship between two men! *Carito*! – After one's primary relation to the X – I don't know what to call it, but not god or the universe – only human relations matter.

Various readers and reviewers, Dickinson among them, objected to the mystery of the Caves scene, but, for the moment at least,[2] he had his answer ready. He wrote to Dickinson: (26 June 1924):

[1] i.e. the Maharaja of Dewas.
[2] In later years he somewhat revised his opinion. Writing to William Plomer in 1934, he told him that what was wrong with Plomer's latest novel was the

> In the cave it is *either* a man, or the supernatural, *or* an illusion. And even if I know! My writing mind therefore is a blur here – i.e. I will it to remain a blur, and to be uncertain, as I am of many facts in daily life. This isn't a philosophy of aesthetics. It's a particular trick I felt justified in trying because my theme was India. It sprang straight from my subject matter. I wouldn't have attempted it in other countries, which though they contain mysteries or muddles, manage to draw rings round them.

Not to his surprise, different readers took every possible different view as to the fairness of his treatment of Indian problems. Some Tory-minded readers were incensed at the book. Bob and Bessie Trevelyan showed Forster a copy with annotations by their neighbour, Major Lugard,[1] saying 'Horrid!' 'The man's a bounder,' and so on, and Rupert Smith wrote him a violent letter, more or less breaking off their friendship.[2] A rumour also reached Forster that the book was thought 'highly dangerous' in certain official circles. Indian students took quite the opposite viewpoint: they complained of the slighting portrait of Indians and of his making Aziz a 'libertine'. Marmaduke Pickthall[3] thought his Indians unreal but said his Anglo-Indians were all too lifelike; but there were those, too, who thought just the opposite, Then, there were readers like Edmund Candler and Edward Carpenter who thought him scrupulously fair to both sides; and Sir Horace Plunkett[4] even said that the book would save India for the empire. Beatrice Webb wrote to him that the novel 'entirely expresses our own view of the situation'.

He had thought much about 'fairness' himself and had come to the conclusion, or so he told himself, that he was bored with it. He wrote to his old friend E. V. Thompson[5] (22 June 1924):

---

thing he found wrong in *A Passage to India*. 'I tried to show that India is an unexplainable muddle by introducing an unexplained muddle – Miss Quested's experience in the cave. When asked what happened there, I *don't know*. And you, expecting to show the untidiness of London, have left your book untidy. – Some fallacy, not a serious one, has seduced us both, some confusion between the dish and the dinner.'

[1] A relative of the famous Lord Lugard, Governor of Nigeria.

[2] The two did not renew their friendship for thirty years.

[3] Marmaduke Pickthall (1875–1936), author of novels on oriental themes admired by Forster.

[4] Sir Horace Curzon Plunkett (1854–1932), founder of the Irish co-operative movement. He was a friend and neighbour of Forster's in Weybridge.

[5] See Vol. 1, p. 138.

It is a very fair-minded book. Now I am a bit worried at this, for my deepest feeling is that you are all the most awful shits at the Club, and are to blame for the muddle: but so well have I damped this down that the Northcliffe Press and officials purr.

I like being with Indians. It isn't broad mindedness but an ideosyncracy [*sic*]. Over the Anglo Indians I have to stretch and bust myself blue. I loathe them and should have been more honest to say so. Honesty and fairness are so different. Isn't it a pity.

He returned to the theme in a letter (26 June 1924) to Dickinson, who was a specialist in seeing both sides to questions:

Isn't 'fair-mindedness' dreary! A rare achievement, and a valuable one, you will tell me, but how sterile in one's own soul. I fall in love with Orientals, with Anglo-Indians – no: that is roughly my internal condition, and all the time I had to repress the consequences, or fail to hold the scales. Where is truth? It makes me so sad that I could not give the beloved a better show. One's deepest emotions count for so little as soon as one tries to describe external life honestly, or even readably. Scarcely anyone has seen that I hoped Aziz would be charming . . .

The two criticisms that impressed him most were, in fact, attacks, severe but well-informed ones, by Anglo-Indian experts. The first came from H. H. Shipley, a retired Indian 'civilian' of thirty years' experience. 'You will, I trust, forgive me,' he wrote, 'for saying that you have treated the English officials very unfairly. Not one among them is even a decent fellow.'

Frankly, your Collector is impossible. There is not a Collector in India – not an English Collector – who would behave as he does. No Collector in his senses would go to the railway station to witness the arrest of a Native Asst. Surgeon. Nor would he discuss a case 'pendente lite' publicly at the Club. Nor (incidentally) do Collectors clap their hands at such meetings to enforce silence or attract attention. The arrest was absolutely illegal. A warrant is indispensable except in certain cases where the offender is taken 'flagrante delicto'. Even assuming its legality, no Superintendent would be such a fool as to carry it out so publicly; he would go quietly to the man's house. Superintendents don't ask for trouble like that! The meeting at the Club is impossible, too; Clubs are not used for such purposes in India. If a Collector behaved as Turton did he would be written down as a madman. And pardon me if I say that the idea of the members rising to their feet at Heaslop's entrance made me roar with laughter. In our Indian Clubs a member is a member, not a God, whether he be Collector or

Merchant's Assistant. We are not such bum-suckers as that, if you
will excuse the expression.

There was much more on the same lines, and Forster replied with
asperity. 'Even if my technical errors over the arrest and trial were
corrected, even if the alleged social solecisms (though these of course
are more disputable) were altered to your liking, you would still
dislike the book as a whole because of its reading of English psychology. The reading according to my lights is true, and I am not disposed to modify it, nor does anything in your letter, either explicit
or implicit, dispose me to modify it.' Shipley replied civilly and at
length, making a further defence of the British in India, and concluding:

> It is a feature of the stay-at-home Englishman that he is intensely
> suspicious of his countrymen who are engaged in the administra-
> tion of the dark races. Possibly it comes from an uneasy fear of
> what he himself might do in circumstances; possibly from a too
> rigid belief in the saying that onlookers see most of the game,
> forgetting that 'cœlum non animum mutant' etc. I have often
> puzzled over it & am no nearer a solution . . . That is another
> reason why I think it deplorable that a man should consider
> himself well-equipped for writing about India after a superficial
> study of its conditions.

Forster thanked him for his more friendly tone and answered:

> . . . As to what qualifies a man to write a novel dealing with India,
> to what extent blue-book accuracy is desirable, to what extent
> intensity of impression and sensitiveness, is a controversial
> question, and one on which gibes are apt to be exchanged. I have
> only been to the country twice (year & a half in all), and only been
> acquainted with Indians for eighteen years, yet I believe
> that I have seen certain important truths that have been hidden
> from you despite your thirty years service on the spot, and
> despite your highly specialized training. 'Padgett M.P.'[1] you will
> retort. We must leave it at that. But several times in your letters
> when you lay down that certain things can't happen I am
> reminded from experiences that they can: and when you select
> for special censure the atmosphere of 'boorishness' in my court
> scene, I think of the precisely similar atmosphere that appears to
> have prevailed in the O'Dwyer libel trial, which occurred after
> my book had gone to press.

---

[1] Character in Kipling's story of that name; type of the opinionated and
ignorant visitor to India.

The second attack came in a long letter from E. A. Horne, published in the *New Statesman* for 16 August 1924. Horne, whom Forster knew a little, had served in the Indian education service and was author of *The Political System of British India* (1922). His letter began with praise, especially of the portraits of Indians in the novel. It was, said Horne, when one turned to Forster's Anglo-Indians that one was 'confronted by the strangest sense of unreality'.

> Where have they come from? What planet do they inhabit? One rubs one's eyes. They are not even good caricatures, for an artist must see his original clearly before he can successfully caricature it . . .
>
> Even about the general background, however, there is a slight air of unreality. This is partly because the picture is out of date. The period is obviously before the war. Not that this matters, provided it is clearly understood. It is not only that Lieutenant-Governors and dog-carts are out of date. All the fuss about the 'bridge' party will strike the Anglo-Indian reader as hopelessly out of date, it being nowadays very much the fashion – not in Delhi and Simla only, but in the humble mofussil [rural] station also – to entertain and cultivate Indians of good social standing.
>
> But it is of Mr Forster's Anglo-Indian men and women that I wish to speak. Of Turton, the Collector, who is addressed individually and in chorus, and at every turn – as by children in school – as 'Burra Sahib'; and about whom all the other Europeans scrape and cringe. Turton, who is for ever hectoring Fielding, a man not much his junior in years and occupying a sufficiently important official position, telling him (speaking 'officially', whatever that may mean) to stand up, or 'to leave this room at once', or to be at the club at six, always addressing him as 'Mr' Fielding. 'Pray, Mr Fielding, what induced you to speak to me in such a tone?' This man is not an Indian civilian; he is a college don, and ridiculous enough at that . . . And what is one to make of the women? But I think they are scarcely worth discussing, so inhuman are they without exception. And if these people are preposterous, equally preposterous are the scenes which they enact . . .
>
> And why is this? Why are these people and these incidents so wildly improbable and unreal? The explanation is a singular but a simple one. Mr Forster went out to India to see, and to study, and to make friends of Indians. He did not go out to India to see Anglo-Indians; and most of what he knows about them, their ways and their catchwords, and has put into his book, he has picked up from the stale gossip of Indians, just as the average Englishman who goes out to India picks up most of what he

knows about Indians from other Englishmen. It is a curious
revenge that the Indian enjoys in the pages of Mr Forster's novel
which profess to deal with Anglo-Indian life and manners; and
some would say a just one. All the same . . . we venture to suggest
to him, next time he goes to India: 'Try seeing Anglo-Indians.'

He added that there was yet another reason why Forster's picture
was distorted, a reason symbolized by the fact that Fielding can
forgive Aziz for bitter offences but has no forgiveness for the European club. 'I have said that Fielding is Mr Forster's mouthpiece; and
nobody can describe people as they really are unless he has some
affection for them.'

Forster wrote him, in private, an amicable answer (19 August
1924):

> . . . Your letter has interested me more than any printed criticism
> I have read. I have gone through it several times and am very
> grateful to you. Like it all? – no! but I am held from first to last,
> and do appreciate your consideration – in all senses of that word.
>
> Let's take the praise as read – read with delight and pride – and
> come to the last four paragraphs. The novel is full of mistakes in
> fact – naturally, for I've only been twice to India, and neither you
> nor I will lay stress on them. There is no reason I should not
> correct or omit the various details you criticise – e.g. I have
> already been told about 'Burra Sahib' and have cut it out in the
> next edition, and I could make it clear that Turton habitually
> said 'Fielding' and only stuck on 'Mr' when he was in a temper,
> and I could make Mrs McBryde's children have measles and call
> her to the Hills suddenly, thus decreasing the enormity of her
> husband's conduct. But even if I made these and similar changes,
> you still wouldn't feel the Anglo-Indian picture fair. The facts
> might be right, but the accent would remain, and how on earth is
> one to do away with one's accent? I tried, but knew I'd failed . . .
> you have hit the nail on the head. I don't like Anglo-Indians as a
> class. I tried to suppress this and be fair to them, but my lack of
> sympathy came through.
>
> You say I don't like them because I don't really know them.
> But how can I ever like them when I happen to like the Indians
> and they don't? They don't (this part of my picture you do not
> challenge) – so what am I to do? Sympathy is finite – at least mine
> is, alas, – so that as the rope is pulled into the right hand it slips
> out of the left. If I saw more of Anglo-India at work (or shared
> its work, which is the only sympathetic seeing) I should of course
> realize its difficulties and loyalties better and write about it from
> within. Well and good, but you forget the price to be paid: I

should begin to write about Indians from without. My statements about them might be the same, but the accent would have altered.

That is why I feel your letter so fair and so unfair at the same time. You say that I am always prejudiced and frequently preposterous – quite right, I am (if by prejudice you mean honest prejudice, blindness temporary or congenital, and I think you do). But you haven't seen that this lack of balance is inherent in the Indian tangle, and that if I got the Club sympathetically true, Aziz's shanty would ring false and no longer move you. Perhaps we shall get the perfect, the unaccented book some day, and all my theory of an Indian tangle prove mere Cambridge. Perhaps the book will come – from you . . .

There were further letters in the *New Statesman*, but he did not make any public reply. He was not seriously troubled by the criticisms, though he cursed Masood for the errors of Indian detail. Essentially, he was at last at ease about the novel and no longer acutely sensitive to praise or blame; moreover, it was selling extremely well – especially in America, where sales reached 30,000 within the first month. With his coming royalties and his inheritance from Aunt Laura he felt himself, for the first time in his life, to be becoming prosperous, and his thoughts turned, as usual with him, to sharing his good fortune. Over the next year or two he was to make many large gifts of money to his relatives, and to friends like Forrest Reid, Frank Vicary and the Bargers.

He was enjoying his success and fame, but, as in earlier years, they disturbed him too, and he did not quite know what to do with them. 'Have pains in my heart, so that I may not be able to carry vegetables home to Weybridge,' he noted in his diary (31 August 1924). 'Too much good luck, and too late. I cannot live up to it.'

6 A Section House in Hammersmith

Underlying his various reflections about the success of *A Passage to India* was the most important of all: that he would never write another novel. This was an instinct and prognostication rather than a vow or decision: however, it proved correct, and we must search for the explanation. One thing is plain, we have to go back in time at least to *Howards End*, for it was after the publication of *Howards End* that his difficulties as a writer began. I suggested in my pages on 'The Year of *Howards End*' (Vol. I, Chapter 11) that he was of the type defined by Freud as 'Those wrecked by success': that he was one of those who, on realizing their dearest wishes, are afflicted and inhibited by superstitious fears – the fears in his case taking the form of a conviction of sterility. One must not build too much on this theory: for one thing, 'wrecked' is too dramatic a word for what happened to him. Nevertheless it could be one part of the explanation. Forster, though a rationalist, was certainly by temperament a superstitious man: one who, having been especially and royally favoured as a child, had magical feelings about his own life. The plots of his novels, where they involve children, have, from one point of view, the air of being miraculous 'nativity-stories' about himself: how such a favoured child came to be born (*Howards End*), or how, with a little less good fortune, he might have been deprived of life (*Where Angels Fear to Tread*). Similarly, the excess of sudden deaths in those early novels, which are otherwise so joyful in tone, suggests some kind of superstitious propitiation. We can easily imagine such a man experiencing irrational fears at the realization of very deep wishes. And indeed there is evidence that he did so. A year or two after the period we have now reached, he experienced spectacular success and acclaim with his lectures on 'Aspects of the Novel',[1] and again he found it half-painful. He told T. E. Lawrence: 'A sort of nervousness – glancing at my stomach for beginnings of cancer – seems to gather in me.' He asked Lawrence, at this time, what he thought of the story of Polycrates and his ring.[2] The story runs that Polycrates, tyrant of Samos, was so invariably successful in all his enterprises, that his friend the king of Egypt, fearing so much good fortune for him, told him he should sacrifice something of value to himself. Accordingly he threw a precious ring into the sea; but a few days later, a fish was brought to him at table and the ring was found in its stomach. At this, his friend abandoned him, as being clearly doomed by the gods. Forster told Lawrence he regarded it as an allegory, 'and more helpful than most'.[3]

He himself sometimes gave a much more practical reason for giving up novel-writing: namely, that, being a homosexual, he grew bored with writing about marriage and the relations of men and women. This must have been an important part of the truth; and one can add to it the various frustrations attaching to *Maurice* – to have written a novel that could not be published (for it is certainly true that in 1914 it could not have been[4]); to know at the back of his mind that it might have been a better novel if it had been written for publication; to find that, having written it, he was, after all, no nearer to writing a publishable novel; and finally, to reflect, as he must have done then, that he had written about homosexual love-affairs as a substitute for having one. There is no need to look further for the 'cramp' that D. H. Lawrence diagnosed in him in 1915, and this 'cramp' must have some bearing on our problem.

But there is a third consideration, more general than either, and that is that Forster was one of those who have 'only one novel to write'. I don't mean this in the vulgar sense that he repeated himself: I mean that he received his whole inspiration – a vision, a kind of plot, a message – all at once, in early manhood. He became an artist because of that early experience, an experience of salvation, and his inspiration as a novelist always harked back to that moment of enlightenment. For this reason he was content to use and re-use

---

[1] See p. 143.
[2] It is related by Herodotus, *History*, Book 3, Chapter 40.
[3] Letter to T. E. Lawrence, 18 March 1927.
[4] It was not published till after his death, in 1971.

many of the same plot-materials: for instance the jaded traveller unable (for what reason he cannot tell) to respond to the scenes he or she has come to visit; or the picnic or party of pleasure invaded by panic forces. (Mrs Moore in *A Passage to India* is, again, clearly a reworking and elaboration of Mrs Wilcox in *Howards End*.) For the same reason, the social types and manners which ruled his imagination were those of his Edwardian youth. This was no small difficulty for a realistic novelist, though it would not have arisen for a poet. He already found it so with *A Passage to India*, and evidently it was bound to grow with every year or decade.

It seems likely that all these factors were present in his mind in the year that we have reached. At any rate, though in the years that were to follow his thoughts did sometimes turn towards a new novel, they did so surprisingly rarely, and the most that ever took shape was a brief synopsis. The knowledge of his situation did not make him so anxious as it had done in earlier days, though sometimes he would lament that he 'felt like a dummy, from whom real life has been withdrawn'.[1] Creation had always represented for him the supreme pleasure, but he refused to regard it as his sole *raison d'être* in life; he told himself he had other resources and must make do with them.

*   *   *

The immediate problem facing him was what to do about West Hackhurst. For one thing, only thirteen years of the lease were left to run. Moreover, the prospect of moving filled his mother with gloom and despair. For her it symbolized her supersession, since it would be his house, not hers; moreover, or so Forster guessed, she pictured it as her 'last home', a token of her coming death. She suggested at first that they should occupy both houses, then that she should 'retire' to Weybridge, leaving him in sole charge of West Hackhurst. They vacillated all summer, before making up their minds to the move and to the selling of Harnham.

He had, meanwhile, begun an adventure, though one that seemed unlikely to prosper. He had casually got into conversation with the driver of a Weybridge bus. The young man had attracted him, reminding him vaguely of Mohammed – partly, no doubt, because of his occupation; also he was rather amusing in a Cockney-humour vein.

---

[1] Letter to G. H. Ludolf, 11 July 1926.

After one or two more encounters, the driver, who was called Arthur B—, surprised Forster by inviting him home, 'to have a crack'. It turned out he had a wife and child; but Forster enjoyed his evening with them, and, since Arthur seemed eager for friendship, he invited him back to Harnham, explaining to his mother that he was giving him French lessons. Lily told Forster that B— had mistaken his class and would be intimidated when he saw their house; however B—, when he came, surveyed their hall and its carpet without emotion. ('Perhaps I don't look like a gentleman, or the house like property,' Forster told Ackerley.) After the first visit, B— gave Forster his photograph, and this provoked another sharp remark from Lily: 'How like the lower classes to give you his photograph at a first call. They always think one in love with them after the slightest civility.'

Forster began to build hopes on this new acquaintance and arranged further French lessons, planning them for when his mother would be away in Abinger. He told Florence that he had better pursue the affair, if 'affair' it should prove, while he was able to, since it would not suit with the 'pseudo-feudalism' of Abinger. However, B— now began to break appointments, and eventually Forster realized that his wife Madge was interfering. He resigned himself to failure, telling Joe 'It is not my policy, even were it within my power, to break up homes.' It left him a little cast down, and with the thought that, with all his success, he was missing the thing he most desired and was not likely to achieve it. In his New Year's summing-up he addressed himself and his appearance with discomfiture:

> Jan 2. Famous, wealthy, miserable, physically ugly – red nose enormous, round patch in middle of scalp which I forget less than I did and which is brown when I don't wash my head and pink when I do. Face in the distance – mirrors of Reform Club[1] – is toad-like and pallid, with a tiny rim of hair along the top of the triangle. My stoop must be appalling yet I don't think much of it, indeed I still don't think often. *Now* I do, and am surprised I don't repel more generally: I can still get to know any one I want and have that illusion that I am charming and beautiful. Take no bother over nails or teeth but would powder my nose if I wasn't found out. Stomach increases, but not yet visible under waistcoat.

---

[1] He had joined the Reform Club in 1922, being sponsored by Siegfried Sassoon.

The anus is clotted with hairs, and there is a great loss of sexual
power – it was very violent 1921–22. Eyes & probably hearing
weaker.

Lily was particularly trying, just at this time. The New Year was
always a bad period with her, and the move had exacerbated matters.
She would be peevish, and then he would hear her sobbing. Once,
hearing her, he took some pennies out of his pocket and hurled them
all over the floor, noting 'This is the 8th or 9th time I have lost
control in the last 3 months. I am not afraid of madness for it's a
gesture not a mood but I am afraid of doing something extensive.'[1]
What he actually did was to decide to find himself some rooms in
London. It was an obvious solution, and one which he could well
afford, and he began the search at once. Bloomsbury seemed the
obvious choice as an area; and with Vanessa Bell's help he succeeded
in finding a flat at 27 Brunswick Square, in the house of Mrs M. A.
Marshall, widow of an architect and a friend of many of the 'Bloomsbury' circle.[2] Lily took the development surprisingly coolly; and very
soon the pattern was established that he should sleep a night or two
every week in London. (Even on these weekly visits, he would keep
in touch with her by postcards.)

*   *   *

Joe Ackerley had by now returned from India. He greatly approved
of Forster's move towards London, and the two began to see a good
deal of each other, falling into the habit of discussing all their doings.
Ackerley even wanted to live with Forster, but Forster did not wish
this. For the time being Ackerley had returned to his parents' home in
Richmond, but he felt restless there, and guilty at his parents' in-
dulgence towards him as a 'writer'. His mother would tap timidly at
his 'sacred' door, fearing to interrupt, and he would snap at her,
knowing there was nothing to interrupt.

He had a variety of friends among writers and actors, and Forster
and he would often meet them at lunch at a favourite Soho restaurant
(for some time, it was Chez Victor in Wardour Street). Forster thus

---

[1] Diary, 2 January 1925. – 'Poor dear, how she figures!' he wrote a year or
so later, on re-reading this entry. 'In my memory she does not cause me all
that pain.'
[2] She was the mother of Ray Marshall, who married David Garnett, and of
Frances Marshall, who married Ralph Partridge.

acquired a new circle. He began to see a good deal, for instance, of Leo Charlton.[1] Charlton was a First World War general, now an Air Commodore, and had recently resigned as Chief of Air Staff in Iraq, in protest against the bombing of defenceless tribesmen. He came from an old Northumbrian Catholic family and, in manner, was very much the old-style army officer: tall, large-nosed, dictatorial, with a flat tweed cap pulled well down over his eyes in guardsman fashion. He wrote boys' books (later becoming the *New Statesman's* air correspondent) and lived with a young ex-aircraftman boyfriend named Tom Wichelo[2] – carrying this fact off among his fellow-officers with great insouciance, though saying 'One is always dreading the sound of parental hooves up the garden path.' Another of their friends was Gerald Heard,[3] just then making his name as a scientific journalist. He was reputed to read two thousand books a year and had an extraordinary flow of information about hygiene, sex, para-normal phenomena and the probable destiny of mankind. He was a dress-fetishist, favouring purple suède shoes and leather jackets with leopard-skin collars, and he had his eyelids painted with what looked like mascara (actually a specific against conjunctivitis). Strangers thought of him, nervously, as a sort of Wellsian supermind or 'man of the future'. These and other friends represented for Forster a new aspect of London life – as it were the higher Bohemia. He enjoyed great prestige and affection among them, though he was felt not in all respects to belong. Leo Charlton once said: 'Have you noticed how Morgan's friends always drop their voices when they talk of him, as if he were Jesus Christ?'

Joe Ackerley himself was living a more and more busy and con-fused love-life. As one of his friends described it, he would encounter a foreign waiter at lunch at the Café Royal, take him home in the afternoon, give him a gold trinket as a seal of undying friendship, quarrel with him irrevocably, and return him, with tragic dignity, to the Café Royal in time for dinner. Forster was amused, for Joe made an excellent comedy of it all; then he became disquieted. Before long he was noting: 'Joe I am worried by, for I and his other friends are

---

[1] L. E. O. Charlton (1879–1958), author of *Charlton* (1931), *More Charlton* (1940).

[2] No relation of Forster's own family.

[3] Henry FitzGerald Heard (1889–1971), author of *The Ascent of Humanity* (1929), *Pain, Sex and Time* (1939) etc.

inclined to be critical of him, having first encouraged him to be what he is.' When Dickinson, to whom he had introduced Ackerley, showed signs of falling in love, Forster warned him against it, telling him that Ackerley was scared of response: 'It accounts for his having had less than what seems obvious in the way of happiness.' He made the same remark to Ackerley himself on one occasion;[1]

> I think you are scared or bored by response. Here my lecture ends, for how you are to alter yourself I know not; but sometimes the comment of an outsider helps so I make it. I think love is beautiful and important – anyhow I have found it so in spite of all the pain – and it will sadden me if you fail in this particular way.

Ackerley did not resent such homilies, indeed he had quickly developed a strong devotion to Forster. Forster was the father-figure he wanted: a man he could revere, who was solid and gave wise and objective advice – not that he took it – and yet with whom he could be frank and easy, as he could not with his own father. He began to take over Forster's attitudes; so much so that for a time, so his friends said, he became almost Forster's puppet. In return he, like Sprott, perceived a service he might render Forster, by modernizing his still-Edwardian ideas about the homosexual life. Forster was very ready to learn, and this too became a bond between them.

Ackerley was Forster's confidant when, unexpectedly, his acquaintance with Arthur B— turned into an affair. It happened during the move to West Hackhurst, and Forster, on his return-visits to Weybridge, enjoyed several cheerful and successful assignations with Arthur in the half-empty rooms of Harnham. It was 'a queer ending to my 20 years' sojourn in this suburb', he told Joe. He did not quite like deceiving his mother in this particular way; nor could he decide if he were doing something foolish or was 'a wise man trying to do a difficult thing'. Hitherto he had looked for 'love' in any affair, and here it did not arise. Arthur was affectionate and made Forster laugh, and that was as far as matters went, emotionally. Forster generalized to himself:[2] 'Coarseness and tenderness have kissed one another, but imaginative passion, love, doesn't exist with the lower classes. Lust & goodwill – is any thing more wanted?' Arthur told Forster it was the first time he had made love with a man. However, Forster did not

---

[1] Letter quoted by Ackerley in *My Father and Myself* (1968), p. 131.
[2] Diary, 24 March 1925.

place much faith in that, for he had perceived that, in a harmless way, Arthur was a compulsive liar. There was even doubt about his name: first it was 'Arthur', then it was 'Sid', now it seemed to be 'Ted'. He took 'Ted' to Wembley and found him very good company. 'It's been a vernon bruiser all day,' said Ted; and, seeing a van being loaded with parcels: 'Look at the Owards End being lifted in packages for export.'

*   *   *

In his writing life, since *A Passage to India*, Forster had been occupied with various small tasks. He was doing some reviewing for the *Nation and Athenaeum* and the *New Leader* and had completed an edition of the travel letters of Eliza Fay for the Hogarth Press. He was also busy over Cavafy, having at last received from Valassopoulos some fifty or so further translations, which he was reworking. Since the successful completion of *A Passage to India* he had resumed his indecent story-writing – occasionally lamenting the burning of earlier stories – and had found an audience for them with Lytton Strachey and 'Carrington',[1] to whom he would read them when he stayed at Ham Spray.

A French translation of *A Passage to India* was in hand, by a young writer named Charles Mauron, living in Tarascon. He and his wife Marie were Roger Fry's discovery. He had trained as a scientist, but, being threatened with blindness, had had to give up a career in the government service and had turned to literary criticism and translation – being encouraged by Roger Fry, who urged his claims as a translator in Bloomsbury and helped with the Forster translation himself. Forster and Mauron had corresponded, and it was arranged that Forster should go and stay with him in April, to work over the translation with him. In prospect, the visit made him nervous, for he had gathered that Mauron was 'shatteringly' intellectual. However, it turned out extremely happily. Mauron proved gentle and disarming, though certainly very high-mindedly literary and philosophical (he was constructing a theory called *psycho-critique*, later expounded in books on Mallarmé and Nerval). He and his wife Marie were both provincials, Charles's father being a peasant farmer who wrote poems in Provençal and had been mayor of St Rémy. The two

---

[1] The painter Dora Partridge, *née* Carrington (1893–1932). She and her husband Ralph Partridge lived with Strachey, in a complex *ménage à trois*, at Ham Spray House in Berkshire.

were very poor, cheerful and energetic – Marie worked as the village postmistress and wrote romantic novels. Altogether, Forster told Ackerley (16 May 1925), they were a great find. 'They have no furniture, and the most exquisite food which Madame cooks and serves with gestures of despair.' Charles was in difficulties with his publishers, who were critical of his translation and demanded extensive changes. Forster, suspecting Parisian snobbery towards provincials, encouraged Mauron not to yield and promised to take the line that, if Mauron's translation were not accepted, he would rather the novel was not published in France at all.

*   *   *

Joe Ackerley's literary career at last took a turn for the better. His play *Prisoners of War*, now six years old, was accepted for production at the Court Theatre by a group called the 'Three Hundred Club'. It had its *première* on 5 July 1925 and received very warm reviews – from *The Times* especially. Their reviewer said:

> The facts are dark, it may be, but the treatment is full of light –
> the light of which no audience can fail to be continuously aware
> when a man, who is deeply and sincerely moved by his subject,
> writes with a superb naturalness and a real control of the stage ...

Forster was impressed too, and told Ackerley he thought the play was moving and 'big'.

This original staging of the play was only a club production, but Nigel Playfair interested himself in it, and in late August he gave it a commercial production at the Playhouse in Hammersmith, with quite a distinguished cast. It so happened that at about this time Ackerley had taken a flat in Hammersmith (6 Hammersmith Terrace, one of a row of pretty Georgian houses overlooking the river). One morning, going to collect his milk, he got into conversation with a young policeman; by chance he mentioned his name, and, to his surprise, the policeman asked if he was the author of *Prisoners of War*. It was a flattering and somehow delightful occurrence, and on the strength of it the two became friends. The policeman was named Harry Daley, and he is the key to much that follows in the present chapter.[1]

Daley was the son of a Lowestoft fisherman. His father had been

---

[1] I got to know him in 1968 and had many talks with him before his death three years later.

drowned when he was still a boy, and during the 1914–18 war the family had moved to Dorking in Surrey, where Harry, on leaving school, had become a grocer's roundsman.[1] He was now twenty-four, having joined the police the previous year. He was plump, curly-headed, genial and rather cocky in manner: very intelligent, with a taste for music and opera, and a brilliant *raconteur*.

He was homosexual and made no secret of it; indeed he was wildly indiscreet. His closest friends, and lovers, were mainly criminals: cat-burglars, gang-leaders and the like. The police knew this very well and not only did not object but encouraged it, the sergeant in charge of his Section House allowing his friends to use the police gymnasium. Daley rarely made an arrest and took pride in this fact, but, being a keen photographer, he would sometimes stage the 'arrest' of one of his criminal friends in the station-yard – his victim peering pathetically through the bars of the Black Maria or held by Harry in a masterful grip.

Joe Ackerley and he, though never lovers, soon became intimate. It was Ackerley's *entrée* to Hammersmith and its working-class life, as it was Daley's *entrée* to literary and artistic society, and their respective friends would mingle at 6 Hammersmith Terrace. Ackerley's own circle was by now quite extensive, and Daley by this means became friendly with various writers and artists – among them Forster, Raymond Mortimer, Duncan Grant and Gerald Heard. The police, as always, were hospitable to Daley's friends, and he would throw breakfast or supper-parties for them at the Section House, cooking them bacon and eggs and then taking them off to an opera or a boxing-match. It was a life of some stresses for him, for, the next day he might find himself the policeman on duty at some fashionable Mayfair party and meet the same friends, exchanging embarrassed winks with them. It made him extremely touchy and prone to imagine slights, and his life was littered with quarrels and reconciliations.

The friendship altered Ackerley's way of life and outlook. Half of Daley's friends were unemployed, and Ackerley would befriend them, helping them with money in ingenious and delicate ways, and – with philanthropic friends like Gerald Heard – concerting schemes for

---

[1] He had often called for orders at West Hackhurst, during Laura Forster's lifetime.

finding them work.[1] He got his father interested in a friend of Daley's, called Fred J—, and his father was about to give him a job, when it came to his ears that Fred had been a striker, and at this he would have no more to do with him. Ackerley told Daley the news with bitterness, saying – about his father – 'You see, Harry, he's a different sort of person from you and me.' Through his new way of life he was acquiring social conscience, and he adopted left-wing attitudes and style. Previously he had been rather a dandy, but he now took to corduroys, and, in his flat, adopted the austere Section-House style – bare scrubbed tables and milk served straight from the bottle.

Fred J— had a sailor brother, Albert, who was away at sea when Ackerley and Daley first met but was due home in six months. It seemed fated that Ackerley, who had become popular with the whole family, should fall in love with this brother, and so it turned out. He had little difficulty in winning Albert, when he returned to England, and – for one of the few times in his career – he now began a serious relationship. Albert was an excellent character: charming and modest, as well as extremely good-looking. He was also a naval boxing champion and a reckless gambler, but Joe persuaded himself that he was a helpless boy who needed protecting from the world.

Forster, as Ackerley's close companion, often met Harry Daley and became friendly with him. He would take him to plays and concerts, and, since Daley was independent about money, he would also – though it worried him – sometimes go at Harry's expense. The friendship developed, and eventually it became an affair. Forster's letter to Daley (18 July 1926) after they had first gone to bed together harped concernedly on the money issue:

> After leaving you and having some food, I found myself too excited to do anything but walk about – it is the happiest day I have spent for a very long time. But as regards the theatre, this is what I wouldn't say at the time, because it would have spoiled things: – It is this: – Those tickets cost 4/9 each I believe – well you mustn't ever spend so much on me again. Make 2/6 the limit, either for a theatre or a meal. Will you agree? Isn't this common sense – given your present salary? And is anything in it contrary to friendship? I don't think so.

---

[1] Heard found that hotel and domestic service were less affected by the depression than other occupations, and he and his friends would pay the fees to send unemployed acquaintances to the Westminster School of Catering. It became the fashion to lunch at the restaurant attached to the school and eat food cooked by one's *protégés*.

Forster was attentive to Daley. He would write him innumerable little notes and, having got to know his duty-hours, would always be proposing brief meetings, or a stroll or a meal or a visit to a play. Sometimes he would walk with Daley along his beat, and Daley would introduce him to his costermonger and burglar friends. He was alarmed by Arthur G—, the leader of the 'coffee-house gang', though he told Daley he could understand Daley's liking him, but he approved of Fred J—. 'He spoke my language,' he told Daley. It was all an education to him in working-class life. In one slum café he was intrigued by a notice saying 'Nothing but the Best Margarine Served in this Restaurant'. 'What on earth can they have been accused of serving?' he asked, wonderingly. He found it hard to relinquish philanthropic worries about money. Once, they had a meal in a café run by Italian friends of Daley's. The proprietor wanted to treat them, but Forster insisted vehemently on paying, and this riled Daley, who said: 'Next time you take me to tea with your friends, I shall insist on paying.' They could never get this money issue right. Once Daley borrowed a pound from him, repaying it next pay-day, and then a month or two later asked for another, which Forster sent, but this time with a letter of conditions: Harry must not fritter his money away, he must not buy Forster expensive meals, etc. Daley returned the pound with a rude letter, saying he could easily borrow it elsewhere, but as it turned out, he was unable to – whereupon Forster, characteristically, sent it back again without conditions.

Daley made it a principle of life to say what came into his mind. Forster would tell him he was frightened what he would say next, adding that this was not a complaint, for the great Russian novelists considered people like Harry, spontaneous people, the best in the world. Privately, though, he thought Daley sometimes rather brash. And other friends of his could be ruffled by him. On first being introduced to Forrest Reid, Daley chatted, as he constantly did, about life on the Hammersmith Streets: how Hennekey's stored their cider in old rum or brandy bottles and the local Irish would run mad drunk, by hundreds, on sixpennyworth. 'But don't you find the Irish navvy lovable in his honesty and simplicity?' asked Reid. 'No I don't,' said Daley. 'They come in fighting drunk; when you search them they've got nothing but pawntickets and rosaries; and then they are sick all over you.' Reid took a strong dislike to Daley and warned Forster against him.

Forster got to know Daley's family in Dorking and would go and chat with his mother, whom he liked, and bring her presents of vegetables. When she fell seriously ill, Joe Ackerley paid for her to see a specialist, who said she must have an operation. The expense worried her, for she knew that Ackerley was not rich; and, hearing this, Forster insisted upon paying all fees himself. Harry wrote to him, vowing eternal gratitude; but by the same post he wrote to his mother – saying, to reassure her, 'Don't worry; old Morgan's got plenty of money' – and contrived to put the letters in the wrong envelopes. Forster was greatly affronted; and, since it was a fixed principle with him never to explain or apologize, or to allow others to do so,[1] the incident rankled on both sides.

*   *   *

In the Spring of 1926 Forster received an invitation from Trinity College in Cambridge to give the annual Clark Lectures. It pleased him, for these lectures, 'on some period or periods of English literature not earlier than Chaucer', were a distinguished series. (The previous Clark lecturer had been T. S. Eliot.) He agreed without much hesitation, and it was arranged that the lectures should be delivered in the following spring and should take the form of a general discussion of the novel as a *genre*. Over the years, in letters to friends and fellow-novelists, he had sketched many half-formed theories on the subject; however, as he knew, there were vast gaps in his reading, and he now set about filling them. One large gap was the eighteenth century, in which he had done little reading since his undergraduate days – once shocking Virginia Woolf by admitting he had never read Defoe. He now wrote to her for help (17 May 1926):

> I am going to give some lectures in Cambridge. I suppose on the novel but am a good deal hung up, & should be very grateful indeed if I might consult you about them . . . Please tell me the names of the best novels – I have only just read Tristram Shandy and Moll Flanders, so you see.

It was the moment, also, when he must decide his attitude to the *avant-garde* in fiction. It was and would remain to some extent an outsider's attitude. He had not been able to make much of *Ulysses*.

---

[1] The theory underlying this, I assume, was that whatever actually happens always reveals a truth, if not necessarily the one intended. There is a connection, here, with his habit, when correcting himself in a letter, of deliberately leaving the cancelled words visible.

143

And when he now read Gide, he found him somewhat disappointing.
He wrote to Virginia Woolf (19 November 1926):

> Les Faux-Monnayeurs proves not to be a new sort of novel after
> all – only the throwing-up of an old sponge. There is no punch
> or colour in it – only more and more interesting, most most
> interesting.

As for Virginia Woolf's own work, he had, in a recent lecture on
her, defined a problem which, he had said, 'would inaugurate a new
literature if solved'; it was for her to 'retain her own wonderful new
method and form, and yet allow her readers to inhabit each character
with Victorian thoroughness.'

He did much of the actual writing of the lectures in the Isle of
Wight, while on a visit with his mother to the Preston sisters. It was
to be their last visit, for Kate and Maggie died soon afterwards, and
it was a sad one. 'Illness and old age are the sole topics,' he told
Masood (26 September 1926), 'and whatever is said is repeated 10,000
times. In the midst of it all, on a small lodging house table, I endea-
vour to prepare my lectures.'

The eight lectures were delivered between January and March
1927. They were very much in a 'Bloomsbury' style – anti-academic,
playful, full of odd, brilliant metaphoric flights – and he exploited
his habitual simplifying technique, presenting complex matters in
the homeliest and most 'bread-and-butter' terms. He was by now a
very experienced platform-performer, and the lectures, and their
manner – grave, charming, precise, but full of little surprises of
nuance and inflection – made a great hit with his Cambridge audience.[1]
Audiences grew larger and larger, and by the concluding lecture he
was reporting to T. E. Lawrence that the series had been the *greatest*
success and his 'constant rise to fame' had impeded him from letter-
writing. (As we have seen, he found the fame mildly disturbing.) On
the strength of this success, King's College offered him a three-year
fellowship, which he accepted, on the understanding that he need
not reside for more than six weeks in a year.

---

[1] He was giving them at a time when Cambridge was witnessing the rise of
a very different style of criticism. F. R. Leavis, a temperate admirer of
Forster's novels, attended the lectures and was enraged by them, finding them
'intellectually null' and their success 'gruesome' and evidence of 'the potent
orthodoxy of enlightenment'. (See a letter from Leavis to Oliver Stallybrass
in the Introduction to the Abinger edition of *Aspects of the Novel*.)

In the summer of the same year, Virginia Woolf published *To the Lighthouse*, and it made Forster feel that that 'new literature', which he had said was within her grasp, had arrived. At any rate he thought it her best novel, exciting in its formal innovations but at the same time humanly interesting and compelling. He wrote to her (5 June 1927):

> It's awfully sad, very beautiful both in (non-radiant) colour and shape; it stirs me much more to questions of whether & why than any thing else you have written. The uneasiness of life seems to well up between all the words, the excitement of life on the other hand to be observed, stated

The praise delighted her; but at this time, the two had a clash. She had written an article[1] on Forster's own work, the main theme of which was the problem of reconciling realism with vision. Forster, she said, faced the same problem as Ibsen: he worked with realism and minute observation, but 'his reality must at certain points become irradiated: his brick must be lit up; we must see the whole building irradiated with light.' Ibsen achieved this, Forster did not quite succeed in it – for the reason that 'that admirable gift of his for observation has served him too well. He has recorded too much and too literally.'

> If he were less scrupulous, less just, less sensitively aware of the different aspects of every case, he could, we feel, come down with greater force on one precise point. As it is, the strength of his blow is dissipated. He is like a light sleeper who is always being woken by something in the room. The poet is twitched away by the satirist; the comedian is tapped on the shoulder by the moralist; he never loses himself or forgets himself for long in sheer delight in the beauty or the interest of things as they are.

Forster was shown a draft of the article and was ruffled by it. (Part of the trouble, though he didn't tell her so, was that he neither wanted to show her *Maurice* nor to have his work summed up without it.) He wrote to her (28 June 1927):

> . . . *I don't believe my method's wrong!* The trouble is I can't work it: through simple lack of the co-ordinating power that Ibsen had. My novels will be either almost-successes or failures: – probably in the future almost-successes, because experience enables one to substitute cleverness for force with increasing verisimilitude.

---

[1] It was published in the *Saturday Review of Literature*, 17 December 1927.

He wrote again, several times indeed, though telling Leonard Woolf that Virginia must be sure not to spoil the article by softening or omitting anything: 'There is no individual phrase that I "mind" in the least.' Virginia was surprised, remarking to herself: 'Here is this self-possessed aloof man taking every word to heart . . . writing again & again to ask about it.'

When, a few months later, his lectures were published as *Aspects of the Novel*, Virginia Woolf reviewed it in the *Nation and Athenaeum*, and her article[1] succeeded more definitely in annoying Forster. Their difference, it now became clear, was one about 'life', a fictional concept dear to both of them. 'There is something – we hesitate to be more precise – which he calls "life",' she wrote in her article:

> It is to this that he brings the book of Meredith, Hardy or James for comparison. Always their failure is some failure in relation to life. It is the humane as opposed to the aesthetic view of fiction . . .
>
> But at this point the pertinacious pupil may demand: 'What is this "Life" that keeps on cropping up so mysteriously and so complacently in books about fiction? Why is it absent in a pattern and present in a tea party? Why is the pleasure that we get from the pattern in *The Golden Bowl* less valuable than the emotion which Trollope gives us when he describes a lady drinking tea in a parsonage?'

Forster wrote a piqued rejoinder the next day:

> Your article inspires me to the happiest repartee. This vague truth about life. Exactly. But what of the talk about art? Each sentence leads to an exquisitely fashioned casket of which the key has unfortunately been mislaid & until you can find your bunch I shall cease to hunt very anxiously for my own . . . I find the continentals greater than the English not because Flaubert got hung up but because Tolstoy etc., could vitalize guillotines etc., as well as tea-tables, could command certain moods or deeds which our domesticity leads us to shun as false. And why do you complain that no critic in England will judge a novel as a work of art? Percy Lubbock does nothing else. Yet he does not altogether satisfy you. Why?

On the subject of Percy Lubbock, he had, in *Aspects of the Novel* if not here, been a little disingenuous, crediting Lubbock's *The Craft of Fiction* with 'genius and insight', whereas privately he thought it

---

[1] Reprinted in *The Death of the Moth and Other Essays* (1942).

not much good, 'a sensitive yet poor-spirited book'. Virginia Woolf
evidently guessed this. She replied (16 November 1927):

> I'm not particularly inspired to repartee by your letter. But I
> reply: – You say 'Each sentence leads to . . . a casket of which the
> key has unfortunately been mislaid, and until you can find your
> bunch I shall cease to hunt very anxiously for my own.'
>
> Very well – but then I'm not writing a book about fiction. If I
> were, I think I should hunt a little. As a reviewer, which is all I
> am, it seems to be within my province to point out that both
> bunches are lost . . .
>
> No; Percy Lubbock doesn't 'altogether' satisfy me. But then
> I don't agree with you that he is a critic of genius. An able and
> painstaking pedant I should call him, who doesn't know what
> art is.
>
> . . . The above is official & impersonal. Unofficially & personally
> I'm afraid I've hurt or annoyed you (perhaps I imagine it). I didn't
> mean to. The article was cut down to fit the Nation and the weight
> all fell in the same place . . .

*   *   *

Forster was in continual correspondence with T. E. Lawrence.
Lawrence, having at last in 1925 secured a transfer back to the R.A.F.,
had been serving as an instructor to the Cadets' College at Cranwell,
and at the end of the following year he had been posted to Karachi.
The friendship between him and Forster had prospered by letter. It
had grown clear that what Lawrence wanted was, essentially, a
literary friendship – one between an aspiring but self-doubting writer
and, as he termed Forster, a 'lord of the pen'. 'I've always stood in
the plain, like an ant-hill,' he told Forster, 'watching the mountain
and wishing to be one.' As a parting present he had given Forster a
copy of *Seven Pillars of Wisdom* complete with the Eric Kennington
illustrations, promising to inscribe it on his return. 'The inscription
I had meant to write,' he told Forster (11 January 1927), 'was
"To a swift runner. From one who walks. EMF from TES." But I
don't think it fits perfectly. I will use these five years to think of
something really good. Can you suggest the attitude of a moon to
Jupiter?'

Forster gladly fulfilled his allotted role. Lawrence, while at Cranwell, had produced a revised and slightly shortened version of
Seven Pillars, and Forster, still zealous on the book's behalf, volunteered to collate this with the 'Oxford' version and adjudicate

between them. (The task was to employ him, on and off, for several years, and his final verdict, expressed with much delicacy of discrimination, was in favour of the earlier one.[1]) He wanted in all ways to be serviceable to Lawrence and went to some lengths to aid a soldier friend of Lawrence's, 'Posh' Palmer, finding a buyer for his proof-copy of *Seven Pillars* and acting as his 'banker' with the proceeds. Altogether, Forster felt much affection and concern for Lawrence. 'I believe that reading, thinking, sitting in an aerodrome, are all right for you, and that suddenly you will find the world endurable,' he told him (9 August 1927). 'I wish I could give you my pelt, but if indeed I have one it cannot of course be given.'

Lawrence was re-reading Forster's books, with the idea of writing a critical article on him. 'They beat me,' he told Forster (14 July 1927). 'All over them are sayings (generally terrible) which I feel are bursting out from your heart, and represent yourself; but when I put together a sheet of these, the portrait they make is not the least like you, as I've sat at tea with you.' Forster (9 August 1927) told him not to bother about reconciling the statements in his books with his conduct at the tea-table. 'See whether you can reconcile the statements with each other, and you will find that you cannot, alas that you cannot. And even Virginia Woolf has discovered this.' He had been writing a new story, 'Dr Woolacott', but he did not at once offer to send it, being puzzled by Lawrence's attitude to his homosexual writings. 'Do you remember,' he asked Lawrence, '. . . a novel I mentioned to you. I offered you the reading of it when you were in England, but you did not seem keen. I did not understand why. There are items which you must have in your mind if you want to sum me up. Virginia Woolf, deprived of the items, has just made the attempt.' Lawrence's answer (8 September 1927) was revealing.

> I wanted to read your long novel, & was afraid to. It was like your last keep, I felt: and if I read it I had you: and supposing I hadn't

---

[1] Letter to T. E. Lawrence, 18 January 1931. 'What I was trying to say is that you can handle a theme (write a book), describe an action or state of mind (write a chapter), and write sentences that are awfully good as sentences, but which are sometimes too carefully wrought, with the result that the context, and the paragraph, suffers. "Then the chapter and through it the book suffers." No, literature isn't so logical. The desiccatedness blows off by the time we get to the larger items, and in the smallest (the sentences) it sparkles as individual crystals; but the intermediate, the paragraphs, occasionally bear a brunt, and move a little slowly and dryly . . .'

liked it? I'm so funnily made up, sexually. At present you are in all respects right, in my eyes: that's because you reserve so very much, as I do. If you knew all about me (perhaps you do: your subtlety is very great: shall I put it 'if I knew that you knew . . .'?) you'd think very little of me. And I wouldn't like to feel that I was on the way to being able to know about you.

Forster told Lawrence he liked his reasons for not wanting to read *Maurice*. Nevertheless, at Lawrence's request, he sent him 'Dr Woolacott',[1] and Lawrence's response to the story was rapturous. He told Forster, 'It's the most powerful thing I ever read . . . more charged with the real high explosive than anything I've ever met yet. And the odd extraordinary thing is that you go about talking quite carefully to us ordinary people . . .' Forster, always anxious for reassurance about his homosexual writings, was proportionately grateful, and wrote (17 November 1927):

Yes, I know Doctor Woolacott is the best thing I've done and also unlike any one else's work. I am very glad it got you. I hope you will write again and at length. I wanted to know, among other things when you first guessed the oncomer was a spook. Not until the cupboard or before? The story makes me happy. It gives bodily ecstacy outside time and place. I shall never be able to give it again, and once is something.

Odd that in my daily life I should be so timid and ingratiating and consequently so subject to pain. Your letter helps me a lot. I have gone through the story today in my mind, with the knowledge you have read it, and this [comforts me strengthens] hardens (got it!) me.

I believe, as you know, that you are a 'greater genius than myself' to use the dreary phrase, and put this in here to explain my attitude to you and the things I say. Not for any other reason. Don't contradict me – only wastes time. Write again about Doctor Woolacott.

From your friend: –

Edward Morgan Forster

Lawrence duly sent a long letter, ending:

There is a strange cleansing beauty about the whole piece of writing. So passionate, of course: so indecent people might say: but I must confess that is has made me change my point of view. I had not before believed that such a thing could be presented – and so credited. I suppose you will not print it? Not that it

---

[1] Published in *The Life to Come and Other Stories* (1972).

anywhere says too much: but it shows far more than it says: and
these things are mysteries. The Turks, as you probably know (or
have guessed, through the reticences of the Seven Pillars) did it to
me, by force: and since then I have gone about whimpering to
myself unclean, unclean. Now I don't know. Perhaps there is
another side, your side, to the story. I couldn't ever do it, I believe:
the impulse strong enough to make me touch another creature
has not yet been born in me: but perhaps in surrender to such a
figure as your Death there might be a greater realization – and
thereby a more final destruction – of the body than any loneliness
can reach.

Meanwhile I am in your debt for an experience of such strength
and sweetness and bitterness and hope as seldom comes to anyone.
I wish my account of it were not so vaguely inadequate: and I
cannot suggest 'more when we meet' for it will be hard to speak
of these things without dragging our own conduct and bodies into
the argument: and that's too late, in my case.

Forster agreed to the 'not more when we meet'. He told Lawrence,
'It is natural for me to drag my own body and conduct into an
argument (should be dotty and sterile but for these and other
outlets), so you may every now and then have to fend me off, but I
shall never feel snubbed when you do.' Lawrence's feeling for the
story became, for Forster, a permanent bond between them. He told
Lawrence, 'It is the experience of a lifetime to get such praise and
I don't think of it as praise . . . What you have *written* has the effect
of something absolute on me.'

A month or two later, it was his own turn to give encouragement.
Lawrence, back in 1922, had kept some notes on his first experience
of barrack life – indeed, to do so had been one of his motives
for enlisting as an 'other rank'. Now, with Edward Garnett's encouragement, he was considering converting the notes into a book,
and he asked Forster to borrow them from Garnett and give his
opinion on them. There ensued, on a smaller scale, the experience of
Seven Pillars. Forster read the notes (later to become *The Mint*),
and admired them very greatly, sending Lawrence a letter that he
found 'wonderful' and that strengthened his resolve to complete the
book. 'If I just say "book's good – masterpiece" you'll be neither
helped or amused,' wrote Forster:

> The first two parts are superbly written – the third part is a little
> odd: will come to it later. The style is constricted yet fresh –
> exactly what is needed to express the guts of men, and they have

never been expressed before: spiritual or scientific detachment or
licentious sympathy have all three had their try and all failed. You
have got the new view point and the words in which can be put . . .

Now you give good reasons both for the style (epistolary) and
for the matter of Part III, so what I am about to say is empty but
what I wish is that you could have taken up your narrative from
the moment when you left the depot, described your dismissal,
touched on the Tanks, described your readmission, and then gone
ahead. Plenty of reasons, dynastic and personal, against this no
doubt: I am only saying what I wish. As it is the transition is into
another medium, into a sort of comforting bath water, where I
sat contented and surprised, but not convinced that I was being
cleansed. You hadn't, that is to say, communicated your happiness
to me. Which is difficult to do, we know. But I think more could
have been done if you hadn't made the big leap in time and could
also have put away from your heart and head the notion that you
ought to be fair, and emphasize the pleasanter side of the R.A.F.
before laying down your pen. 'For fairness' sake' (p. 122) were the
words that caused me to prick my literary ears, and I am trying
to keep to literature for the reason that I am unlikely to be useful
as any other sort of animal.

Summing up as such, I inform you that *The Mint* is not as great
a work as *The Seven Pillars*, either in colour or form; but it is
more new, more startling and more heartening than either *The
S.P.* or anything else I've read . . . It's heartening because it shows
that cruelty is accidental and abnormal, not basic: I have known
this sitting in drawing rooms and gardens, but you have gone to
places where I should smash and scream in 30 seconds, and bring
back the same news. A world of infinite suffering, but of limited
cruelty: that's what one has to face.

*   *   *

From time to time, since his last visit to India, Forster had
received news from Dewas. The Maharaja rarely wrote letters now,
but every now and then he would despatch a friendly cable or send
messages through the Darlings to 'that noblest specimen of humanity,
Morgan'. Josie Darling, in her capacity as the Maharaja's 'sister',
had gone to visit him on her own in 1924, finding him as fascinating
as ever but, she thought, unwise and neglectful in his handling of his
son Vikramsinha. He rarely saw Vikramsinha, who was now thirteen
years old, and left him in the charge of a tutor called Sharma, well
known to be a Kolhapur spy.[1] It seemed great folly to her, and she

---

[1] The Darlings had long disliked Sharma. When Vikramsinha came to stay
with them for the summer of 1916 in Dalhousie, they sent Sharma packing.

made what protest she could, writing to Malcolm, in German for fear her letter should be opened: 'Du lieber Gott, was kann mann thun darüber – muss ich von Merz am meiner Bruder sprechen.'

Her anxiety was well-founded, for in January 1928 news of an appalling scandal appeared in the press. Vikramsinha, who was by now married, had fled from Dewas, in the company of Sharma, accusing his father of trying to seduce his wife and to poison him.[1] He had taken sanctuary with the British Resident at Indore, going a day or two later to join his mother in Kolhapur, and the newspapers carried a lengthy story of intrigue at Dewas, depicting the Maharaja as under the evil influence of a 'dancing-girl' (i.e. Bai Saheba). Forster, after a week or two, received confirmation of the flight from the Darlings. Malcolm had gone at once to Dewas and had found the Maharaja distraught, begging for Malcolm's advice but paying not the slightest attention to it, and raging against his 'enemies', who now in his eyes included the British. So far as Darling could make out, he was innocent of all crime; but he was doing everything he could to blacken himself further – showing vindictiveness towards Vikramsinha, proposing absurd bargains over Vikramsinha's guardianship, and insisting there must be no official enquiry into the flight. Josie wrote Forster a long analysis of the affair, as she and Malcolm interpreted it, concluding: 'If the villain of the plot has been Sharma in the pay of Kolhapur, the Ikonoklast which has wrecked Tukoji's[2] reputation has been that fearful blob – "The dignity of an Indian Prince: the honour of my state".'[3] Meanwhile Darling had interceded with the Resident at Indore and had written to the *Times of India* on the Maharaja's behalf. He urged Forster to do what he could in the English press, and Forster wrote to various newspapers in the Maharaja's defence, his letter being printed in the *Daily News* for 16 January, under the heading 'THE SCANDAL IN DEWAS'.

> Sir, – I have read with amazement and incredulity the account of the alleged conduct of the Maharajah of Dewas (Senior Branch) as reported by your Bombay Correspondent in your issue of January 10, and would respectfully suggest that your readers should reserve their judgement until they have heard the other

---

[1] Vikramsinha, who eventually succeeded to the throne of Kolhapur, came in later years to think that he had misjudged his father.

[2] i.e. the Maharaja.

[3] Letter dated 2 February 1928.

side. Your correspondent, though of course he reports in good faith, has clearly come under the influences that have proved so sinister in Dewas in the past.

I have known his Highness for nearly sixteen years now. I have lived in his State and seen a little of the intrigues against which he has had to contend and the forbearance that he has exercised. He is a true friend, a great gentleman, and a saint. He has incidentally, one of the finest minds in India. The notion that such a man should persecute his daughter-in-law and attempt to poison his son and heir is perfectly preposterous.

Neither his nor Darling's efforts could achieve much. The harm was done, and the Maharaja's reputation was in ruins.[1]

*   *   *

The tiff, such as it had been, between Forster and Virginia Woolf had soon subsided, and in the course of 1928 the two became allies in the *Well of Loneliness* case. The notorious Lesbian novel by Radclyffe Hall had been published in July 1928, and a few weeks later the *Sunday Express* had made a front-page story of it, as being a threat to the nation's morals. ('I would rather,' said the editor, 'give a healthy boy or a healthy girl a phial of prussic acid than this novel.') The publishers, Jonathan Cape, published a letter in next day's *Daily Express* defending the book as decent and sincere, but saying they were sending copies to the Home Office and the Public Prosecutor and promising to withdraw the novel from circulation if either found it objectionable. The Home Secretary, 'Jix',[2] did object, so the book was duly withdrawn; and at this point various of the *Nation* circle, the Woolfs and Forster among them, grew interested in the case. Forster, reminded of his own 'unpublishable' novel, saw it as a challenge and responded energetically. With Leonard Woolf's help he drafted a public letter of protest, persuading various literary friends and acquaintences, like Lytton Strachey and Arnold Bennett, to sign it; and at the same time he got in touch with Radclyffe Hall. And here difficulty began. For his proposed letter dealt merely with the legal aspect of the suppression, saying 'We offer no opinion on either the merits or the decency of the book.' This would not do for the author at all. She wanted her book to be championed and sent Forster her own version of how his letter ought to run. He now went to see her, and, to begin with, the monocled and lounge-suited novelist

---

[1] See Appendix (pp. 333–6) for further details.
[2] Sir William Joynson-Hicks, first Viscount Brentford (1865–1932).

was all friendliness and gratitude; however, at some point in the conversation, Forster incautiously hinted a mild criticism of her novel, and at this she grew violent, refusing all support from him and his friends unless her book were proclaimed not only pure but a masterpiece. This was more than he had bargained for, for he thought the book ill-written and pretentious, and he wondered how to proceed. He reported the meeting to his friends; and Arnold Bennett, though he had described the book in the *Evening Standard* as 'honest, convincing and extremely courageous', turned out privately to share Forster's feelings about it. He told Forster he would not sign such a letter as she desired 'even if the co-signatories were all the swells in the world', and he advised Forster to drop the matter. 'You have behaved in a noble manner, and she will perceive this later on, when she gets calmer.'

Forster wished himself out of the affair, but, having begun, he felt he must persist. The round-robin having been abandoned, he published in the *Nation and Athenaeum* for 1 September an anonymous article entitled 'The New Censorship', condemning the suppression as 'an insidious blow at the liberties of the public' and saying that 'further attacks may be anticipated unless an effective protest can be made now.' The article brought some response, and in the following issue Forster and Virginia Woolf signed a joint letter, saying that the *Well* had evidently been suppressed, not for indecency, but simply because of its theme.

> The subject-matter of the book exists as a fact among the many other facts of life. It is recognized by science and recognizable in history. It forms, of course, an extremely small fraction of the sum-total of human emotions, it enters personally into very few lives, and it is uninteresting or repellent to the majority; nevertheless it exists, and novelists in England have now been forbidden to mention it by Sir W. Joynson-Hicks. May they mention it incidentally? Although it is forbidden as a main theme, may it be alluded to, or ascribed to subsidiary characters? Perhaps the Home Secretary will issue further orders on this point. And is it the only taboo, or are there others? What of the other subjects known to be more or less unpopular in Whitehall, such as birth-control, suicide, and pacifism? May we mention these? We await our instructions! . . .

At about this time, he went down for a weekend with the Woolfs in Sussex, and, prompted by the *Well* affair, the conversation turned to male and female homosexuality. Forster told the Woolfs that a certain Doctor Head claimed to be able to 'convert' homosexuals. 'And would you like to be converted?' asked Leonard. 'No,' said Forster, without hesitation. From this they got on to lesbianism. He and Virginia were both a little tipsy, and with a queer burst of frankness he told her he found it disgusting – partly out of conventionality, and partly because he 'disliked the idea of women being independent of men'. Virginia was not outraged. Indeed, this weekend, they were unusually in harmony, and to her diary she confided that he was 'timid, touchy, infinitely charming'.

Soon after this, the police brought a prosecution against *The Well of Loneliness*. The case was to be heard at Bow Street in November, and Forster busied himself recruiting fellow-writers to appear as expert witnesses. Meanwhile Radclyffe Hall herself, having secured public declarations on her behalf from Shaw and Wells, was – as she told Forster – rallying the support of the 'working people', obtaining signed protests from the National Union of Railwaymen and the South Wales Miners' Federation. On the day of the trial, a distinguished array of writers had assembled at Bow Street, and all seemed set for a dramatic confrontation – a *Lady Chatterley* trial thirty years before its time – but, in the event, the magistrate refused to call expert evidence and pronounced the book obscene on his own authority.

Forster felt flat at this outcome to his campaign; still he did not feel it had been profitless. It had, moreover, given him a feeling of usefulness. As a non-practising novelist, he had been feeling the need for some outlet into public activity, and the *Well* case had given him his line. From now on he would often be heard on the censorship issue, and, by extension from this, on civil liberties generally.

During this year, too, he became active in the International P.E.N. club. The P.E.N., an association for established authors, dedicated to 'the freedom of literature and the friendship of nations', had been founded in 1921, with Galsworthy as its first President. Forster had joined in 1927, and, in the present year, he became the first president of a new and subsidiary body called the 'Young P.E.N.', a club for young and unknown writers. At its inaugural meeting, in the University of London club in Gower Street, he gave a semi-autobiographical talk about 'Inspiration', and in the following year he took the chair at the annual dinner (finding it rather 'tiresome', and taking a dislike to the guest of honour, J. B. Priestley).

*   *   *

Masood had arrived in England in the autumn of 1928; he had brought with him his sons Anwar and Akbar, and they had all been to stay at West Hackhurst. His affairs were in confusion. His marriage had broken down, and his wife Zorah had gone back to her parents' home in Aligarh; on the boat to England he had announced to the children that he was divorcing her. He was also in some kind of indefinite retirement from his post in Hyderabad. With Forster's help, he found places for the boys at the Perse School in Cambridge, and spoke vaguely of settling in Europe. Forster was worried on his behalf – also a little irritated. 'Masood is here,' he wrote to Sprott (23 September 1928). 'He has cut himself off from his own country in masterly fashion and for good reasons, and now the reaction starts. Boys placed at school, Jaeger underclothing bought, presents given to old friends. What next? I recommend Paris feebly – to take a flat there was his ideal once.' Masood followed his advice and went to Paris, and from there, after a while, he moved on to Frankfurt. There he fell ill with Spanish 'flu; and from his sickbed he wrote forlornly to his friends that he was 'standing alone in the midst of the ruin of my life' and had nothing in the world to cheer him 'except the memory of things and deeds now long dead'. He sounded in serious straits, and in December Forster went over to Germany to see him, finding him quite recovered and cheerfully lunching and dining about town in the company of seven Germans, an Indian and a Czech.

Masood continued on his travels during the early months of 1929 – living, so Forster thought, with monstrous extravagance – and then, in the stock-market crash of that year, he found himself ruined. His situation now looked bleak. However, at this juncture, he received the offer of a high political post in Hyderabad; and, while he was considering this, there arrived a cable inviting him to become Vice-Chancellor of the M.A.O. University at Aligarh – the famous college founded by his grandfather, raised in 1920 to university status. The choice puzzled him. The post at Aligarh would be much the less well paid, and Forster urged him to refuse it because of the painfulness of Zorah's presence at Aligarh. However, his guardian Sir Theodore Morison insisted that he had no choice. He must accept Aligarh – the more so that the University was in a bad way, being very nearly bankrupt and widely accused of corruptly selling its degrees. 'This is the call of your blood,' Sir Theodore told him; and – unwisely as it turned out – Masood took his advice.

There remained the problem of the children. Anwar was now thirteen and Akbar eleven. They were both very charming, intelligent and enterprising boys (physically very large like their father – Anwar was almost a giant), and Lily and Forster had been much taken with them. Forster promised to keep a close eye on them, and over the next few years they could come for long stays at West Hackhurst during the school holidays, treating Forster as a sort of parent.

*   *   *

By the present year Forster's affair with Harry Daley had cooled. The truth was, they were not well matched. Daley was too indiscreet for Forster, who told Ackerley he was sure Harry would one day have them all in the dock. Also he was too uncertain-tempered and prone to writing abusive letters. Moreover, so Forster thought, Harry aimed at too many roles: intellectual, man of the people, socialite, sexual emancipator and so on. 'Harry never could do things in style,' he told Ackerley; 'he places too many models before himself.' As for Harry, he was irked at being 'mothered' by Forster – exploding once to a friend, 'He's whimsical *and* interfering. It's not fair!' He also formed the impression, which was correct, that Forster employed Ackerley as a go-between, deputing him to ask Harry questions as if on his own behalf and to report the answers. Harry once complained to them: 'It isn't a friendship, it's a conspiracy!' at which Forster merely smiled and wagged his head. There was no dramatic rupture between them at this time, though there was to be later, and – as Ackerley's friend rather than his own – Forster still saw him quite often. During 1928 Ackerley had at last taken a job, as a director in the B.B.C.'s newly-formed Talks Department. He had responsibility for a series called 'The Day's Work', and Forster and he coached Daley, and other of their working-class friends, to appear on it. Daley gave several talks about a policeman's life, winning for a time some mild fame as a broadcaster, and beginning, with less success, to write short stories and articles.

As for Forster himself, he was feeling rather 'off' literature. He told Sassoon (9 January 1929) that if he could say something which would help avert another war, or give men more courage in their daily lives, he would say it, but anything else seemed to him mere 'pattern-weaving' and self-expression. He had been reading Edding-ton's *The Nature of the Physical World* and thought that it put mere literary speculation to shame. In a Commonplace Book, begun a year or two before, he made on 5 January 1929 a long entry on Eddington, saying that he wanted to record, 'like the extra sounds one catches immediately after one's ear is squirted out', his first sensations on realizing that matter was not solid, that one knew everything through measurements only, that his own 'spasmodic instincts and confusions about Time' had a value, and that one thing only – the quantum – had existence in the physical world.

> Coming at a moment when I felt literature and myself were played out, the book has convinced me that there is life in the latter-named yet, while it had increased my mistrust of thoughtful generalizations about poetry, philosophic by-the-ways, and all that, and even of that fancifulness which in my own writing, may have justified such solemnities. The seriousness of a large housefly can't be taken very seriously. I don't think literature will be purged until its philosophic pretentiousness is extruded, and I shan't live to see that purge, nor perhaps when it has happened will anything survive. I think if a new race would be born, un-bothered by sunsets etc., a new literature *might* be born, but the spurious clouds of glory still trail round the writer and prevent him either accepting or rejecting the second law of thermo-dynamics.

He was also rather 'off' Cambridge. At least, he did not altogether enjoy his official life as a fellow, though, personally, he liked both the dons and the undergraduates and felt he was a success with them. The trouble was, he had no real or settled work in Cambridge. Also, the place cut him off from his working-class friends – for he did not feel he could well have them to stay there. Moreover such London friends as he did invite seemed to dislike both King's and Cambridge. Joe Ackerley went quite silent and gloomy when he came on a visit, and Leo Charlton, after he had come to stay, wrote warning Forster not 'to exchange your pleasant sunny bow-window upon life for a Norman arrow-head looking north'.

His London friends wanted him to live in Hammersmith, but this prospect did not attract him either. Hammersmith life, as lived by Joe Ackerley and his friends, seemed to him to have a fatal flaw; it was destroyed by gossip, which wrecked both human relationships and work. 'Why need you meet Harry?' he had once asked Sebastian

Sprott. 'Why must everyone meet everyone? I am sick of it.' He felt
sure that Joe Ackerley would never write anything while he lived
this life. His own few years of it had given him a vision of what he
named the 'cat circus'. 'I have got a sort of cat-ring feeling,' he told
Ackerley; 'so many Dicks, so many Toms . . . I suppose there is something secretive about me – unless I am merely growing old and don't
secrete enough.'

What he would have liked for himself, at least in fantasy, was
something more on the Edward Carpenter lines, a rustic and working-
class idyll. He still half thought of Frank Vicary as the key to it. He
often went to see Frank in the country, feeling relief at the escape
from 'gentility'. Vicary had given up his job as a miner some years
before, for health reasons, and had become a ship's steward. Next he
had taken a fancy for farming, and Forster had set him up as a pig-
breeder, buying him some land and a cottage in Gloucestershire. The
farm had not flourished – nothing of Frank's ever did – and then, in
1928, one of his children died accidentally and horribly, being scalded
in his bath. The tragedy more or less destroyed Vicary, who became
feckless and morose. Later in the same year Forster discovered that
Vicary was badly in debt and, without telling him, had raised a large
mortgage on the farm. Forster was shocked and blamed himself for
having let Frank drift. Frank was still so charming and, every now
and then, still said such original, imaginative things, that he had not
wanted to face the truth about him. The farm, too, he recognized
ruefully, had been a solace to his own day-dreams. He had pictured
himself 'toddling there in old age, looked after by the robust and
grateful lower classes'.

*   *   *

In this year, 1929, he was, in fact, rather at a loose end – doing a
little reviewing and lecturing (he toured the Midlands in February,
giving a centenary lecture on Ibsen), but planning no book. Thus
when the Bargers invited him to come to South Africa with them, on
a cruise organized by the British Association, he accepted for want
of a good reason for refusing. Having accepted, he became apprehensive. He would not exactly be in his element, amid a party of four
or five hundred scientists, and it would be the sort of official tour he
had no liking for: they would, he guessed, 'be shown everything and
see nothing'. Moreover, he had a feeling – it was a recurrent fear with
him – that he was losing his power of taking in new experiences.

It was to be an extensive tour. They would stop first at the Cape, then make their way to Johannesburg and to Rhodesia, and proceed thence by ship to Kenya, visiting Zanzibar *en route*. And from Kenya Forster planned to make his own way home, spending some days in Egypt. They set off in late June. Florence was in high spirits, praising everything, despite George's quenching remarks, and thrilled at the prospect of long *tête-à-têtes* with her adored Morgan. Forster was not in such high spirits; and, though he loved Florence, he now, intermittently, found her a bore – too voluble, too appreciative, too high-minded and sentimental. He concealed this and danced attendance on her very loyally, but the cruise turned out, as he had feared, only a half-enjoyed experience. He kept a diary, and through it there runs a note of jadedness – a mixture of rational distaste for some of the scenes he observed and a private vision of savourless, joyless middle age.[1]

He received, none the less, a few intense experiences, one being the island of St Helena, where they called on the voyage out. This strange island, so rocky and inhospitable but inhabited by gentle birds and gentle people, captured his imagination. 'Views over crags of lava and the soft radiant sea, and birds of fairy-white called "love-terns" nest in the crevices. . . . Have seldom seen such a touching island,' he wrote to Joe Ackerley; 'all the volcanic sternness and the live things perched about in it, longing for kindness and company. Some day we will go and give it to them.' He was impressed powerfully too, as by a kind of hellish contrast to this gentle vision, by the Kimberley diamond mines:

> *29 July*. Kimberley or the Kingdom of Antichrist. Four tram loads of us in the grey morning rolling past barbed wire, more inventive than I've ever seen – loops ◖═◗ and even crowns ⌀, quite beautiful. Some fences ended abruptly, as if run up for the infernal joy of the thing, others both sides of a ditch, at one place tram plunged through a cutting. Led into an enclosure where a few black-and-red jerseyed convicts were at work, and to a shed containing piles of the imbecile stones . . .

---

[1] The note recurs in his essay, 'Luncheon at Pretoria', in *Two Cheers for Democracy*. 'We went into the drawing-room and talked a little, and then went into the dining-room and talked a little more and ate and drank a little. It would be unjust to call us a set of dull dogs. We were not dogs, we were not even dull. We were not amusing or bored or critical or cross or anything. We were just a collection of well-fed people who did not know one another well and did not want to . . .'

On his return to England he sold his African mining shares.

In general, Africa saddened him. 'Most of the African peoples seem simply heart-broken,' he told Joe Ackerley (9 September 1929); 'they wander about as if their lives were lost; trade and Christianity together have done them in.' He was moved – almost to tears, he told Ackerley – by the new Union Government buildings at Pretoria. They struck him as genuinely noble, in their way, and a fine gesture of English and Boer *rapprochement*; but 'such an empty gesture, for beneath and beyond both English and Dutch are these millions of blacks whom one never speaks to and whose existence one assumes as one does electric bells! That was why I nearly cried at Pretoria. It is Valhalla, and the dwarfs haven't been paid.'

His spirits did not really rise till he was back in Egypt, and, then, he told Joe Ackerley, having been 250 years old a fortnight back, he could now knock off the nought. Once more on his own, he enjoyed himself in the manner that suited him, going to see Cavafy and his other friends, and paying a nostalgic visit to the 'Home of Misery'. 'Egypt after the British Empire,' he told Joe, 'is more wonderful, beautiful and amusing than can well be imagined.'

His spirits rose even higher when, on his way home, he had an enjoyable sexual escapade with a French sailor, named Achille, in Toulon. He had planned to stay some more days in France, visiting the Maurons, but, on collecting his mail from England, he found a letter from Joe Ackerley, and the news it contained brought him hurrying home. It was that Ackerley's father had died, and that, from a letter marked 'Only in the case of my death,' Joe had learned that his father had been supporting a second family, secreting them in a house only a mile or two from Richmond; and that, partly in consequence, Joe and his mother and sister would be left nearly penniless.[1] 'This house of cards has indeed come tumbling about my ears with Dad's death, a month ago today,' he wrote (3 October 1929). 'There isn't really – I'd better forewarn you – even a chink of sky to be seen; the wreckage is so overwhelming and complete.'

Forster, on his return to England, gave Ackerley what advice and support he could. 'Your best friends, i.e. Leo and self, walked about

---

[1] The story is related in Ackerley's *My Father and Myself* (1968) and from another angle in *The Secret Orchard of Roger Ackerley* (1975) by Diana Petre, one of Ackerley's half-sisters.

here [West Hackhurst] yesterday, important and thoughtful but completely futile,' he told him (12 October 1929). 'The dog came too. We all felt that you would not realize you have no money till the trades people won't send you any food.' Ackerley was faced with a moral problem: his father had left word asking him to give his mistress the benefit of a £2,000 insurance policy – one of his few remaining assets – but his father's business partners were scornful of this 'sentimental blackmail' and refused to give his mother any sort of pension unless he ignored it. Joe discussed the matter, uncomfortably, with Forster and others, but in the end could see no alternative but to acquiesce in the partners' demand. He moved his mother into a smaller house; and in a little while the drama subsided, and was supplanted in his mind by his miseries over Albert J—.

His affair with Albert was breaking up. It was, his friends thought, largely his fault. He mishandled Albert, growing absurdly possessive, and unreasonably resentful when, as sometimes happened, Albert broke appointments. He was both excited by and wanted to ignore the fact that Albert was working-class, and this, his friends thought, was unfair on Albert. Forster read him many homilies on the class-issue. He wrote to him early on in the affair:

> You must go very easily on Albert. The standards which are so obvious to you are very remote to him and his class, and he was bound to lapse from them sooner or later. And by standards I mean not only conventional methods of feeling. He can be quite deeply attached to you and yet suddenly find the journey up too much of a fag. It is difficult for us with our middle class training to realize this, but it is so.

For a time, impatient at only seeing Albert at weekends, Ackerley took rooms in Portsmouth in order to play the faithful housewife to him – only succeeding by this in irritating and boring Albert. Soon afterwards, they had a more-or-less final quarrel. It reduced Ackerley to such a plight that he would barge blindly into people in the street.

The fundamental trouble, Forster thought, was that Ackerley was one of those who can learn nothing from experience. As for himself, he could and did learn from experience. After two or three years of casual affairs, he had come to look at them more dispassionately. 'I'm not romantic, not like you – at least not any more,' he wrote to Ackerley (25 January 1930). 'I like these flowers, and life would be lovely if a new one sprouted every day, but I've learnt how they wither. Here and there stands something solid and *conscious* . . . but the rest wither, whether I pick them or not.'

*   *   *

Over the years, Forster had kept up a remote contact with D. H. Lawrence, sending him his books as they were published and receiving back brief but affectionate letters. 'Yes I think of you,' Lawrence wrote from New Mexico (22 September 1922); 'of you saying to me, on top of the downs in Sussex – "How do you know I'm not dead?" – Well, you can't be dead, since here's your script. But I think you *did* make a nearly deadly mistake glorifying those *business* people in Howards End. Business is no good.' Two years later, he wrote from Baden Baden to thank Forster for *Pharos and Pharillon*: 'Sad as ever, like a lost soul calling Ichabod. But I prefer the sadness to the Stracheyism. To me you are the last Englishman. And I am the one after that.' In his letter acknowledging *A Passage to India* (23 July 1924), Lawrence told Forster, '. . . there's not a soul in England says a word to me – save your whisper through the willow boughs.' From time to time during these years, Forster would read another of Lawrence's novels – forming a preference for *The Plumed Serpent*. He regarded their friendship as one of his 'failures' and did not often think of Lawrence, but when he did it was with admiration, and he was moved by the news of his death in 1930 and angered by the hostility of the obituaries.[1] The latter stirred him to write to the *Nation and Athenaeum* (29 March 1930):

> . . . Now he is dead, and the low-brows whom he scandalized have united with the high-brows whom he bored to ignore his greatness. This cannot be helped; no one who alienates both Mrs Grundy and Aspatia [*sic*] can hope for a good obituary press. All that we can do . . . is to say straight out that he was the greatest imaginative novelist of our generation. The rest must be left where he would have wished it to be left – in the hands of the young.

---

[1] *The Times* obituary said: '. . . There was that in his intellect which might have made him one of England's greatest writers, and did indeed make him the writer of some things worthy of the best of English literature. But as time went on and his disease took a firmer hold, his rage and his fear grew upon him. He confused decency with hypocrisy, and honesty with the free and public use of vulgar words. At once fascinated and horrified by physical passion, he paraded his disgust and fear in the trappings of a showy masculinity.'

His letter, together with an appreciative tribute to Lawrence by Lady Ottoline Morrell,[1] stirred up a controversy. T. S. Eliot wrote in the next week's issue, in his most niggling manner:

> I am the last person to wish to disparage the genius of Lawrence, or to disapprove when a writer of the eminence of Mr. Forster speaks 'straight out'. But the virtue of speaking straight out is somewhat diminished if what one speaks is not sense. And unless we know exactly what Mr Forster means by *greatest*, *imaginative*, and *novelist*, I submit that this judgement is meaningless. For there are at least three 'novelists' of 'our generation' – two of whom are living – for whom a similar claim might be made.

This exhibited a side to Eliot that Forster had always disliked,* and – being a skilled controversialist when occasion demanded – he transfixed Eliot in the following issue with a few quiet and devastating words:

> Mr Eliot duly entangles me in his web. He asks what exactly I mean by 'greatest', 'imaginative' and 'novelist' and I cannot say. Worst still, I cannot even say what 'exactly' means – only that there are occasions when I would rather feel like a fly than a spider, and that the death of D. H. Lawrence is one of these.

Lawrence was not much liked in Bloomsbury, and Clive Bell now joined the controversy, with a rather foolish and tetchy letter, asking Forster what he meant by 'straight out' and by 'high-brow'. Perhaps, he said, speaking 'straight out' merely meant being uncritical: 'That, I admit, is a quality which Mr Forster may have reason to admire.' Forster demolished him equally effortlessly, replying:

> I cannot tell Mr Clive Bell the meaning of 'straight out' and 'high-brow' until he has defined what he means by 'meaning'; but I would like to remind your other readers that my letter, which occasions his questions, was occasioned by the death of D. H. Lawrence. They may not have agreed with what I said . . . but they will scarcely misunderstand it or bark their shins on every word unless they are expert controversialists. These, very properly, form a race apart, with difficulties and methods of their own . . .

He received a letter from Frieda, giving an exalted and eloquent account of Lawrence's death. He had, however, never quite liked

---

[1] 'D. H. Lawrence, 1885–1930: By one of his friends', *Nation and Athenaeum*, 22 March 1930.

Frieda's Laurentianism, or indeed Frieda herself, and her letter did
not change his attitude. When, soon afterwards, she came to see him,
he recorded the visit wryly in his Commonplace Book.

> D. H. Lawrence's Frieda, seen last week after an interval of 15
> years, still uttered the old war cries . . . but her manner was
> nervous, almost propitiatory, and I realize that she, and perhaps
> he, were as afraid of me as I could have been of them. There was
> something both pretentious and rotten about her, as in his
> pictures. She would rebuke me for disobeying the Message and
> then stop and watch me with a shy smile. Very proud of having
> no friends, equally so of her apparatus for collecting and compel-
> ling them. – And the tripe without the poetry was not attractive,
> and I retired unashamed into my academic tower. He and she
> haven't had a bad life, but it seems vulgar when they proclaim it
> as Ensample and a Mystery.

*   *   *

Every year, since his move to riverside Hammersmith, Joe
Ackerley had held a party on the day of the Oxford *v.* Cambridge
boatrace. They were large, miscellaneous gatherings, attended by all
his friends: writers, actors and B.B.C. acquaintances, policemen and
guardsmen, his mother, his aunt and neighbours. Forster came
regularly, and during the one in 1930 he was introduced to a police
constable named Bob Buckingham. He was one of Harry Daley's
fellow-policemen from the Hammersmith Section House: a large,
genial, good-looking young man, with a nose flattened in the boxing-
ring and a resounding bass laugh. They chatted about the river, a
subject which Buckingham was knowledgeable upon, and also about
books. Buckingham said he had been reading Dostoevsky, and
Forster promised, when they met again, to lend him Joyce's *Portrait
of the Artist* and his own *A Passage to India*. He was taken with
Buckingham, and, more to the point, Buckingham seemed taken with
him. Forster invited him to Brunswick Square,[1] a few days hence,
when he duly lent him the books; and before long they were meeting
often. Buckingham proved as good a talker, in his way, as Harry
had been, conversing very knowledgeably about the life of the
Hammersmith streets. They discussed books a little, too. Till now,
despite Dostoevsky, Buckingham had not been much of a reader,

---

[1] At about this time he had had to give up his flat at 27 Brunswick Square
(his landlady Mrs Marshall having been unable to renew the lease of the house)
and had moved next door, to No. 26.

but he showed himself eager to learn, and Forster enjoyed taking charge of his reading. Before long, Buckingham became confiding, and from there on they would talk about his life and problems.

Bob Buckingham, who was to become very important in Forster's life, was now twenty-eight. He came from a large and very poor family, living in Somerstown, and before joining the police he had had countless other occupations: docker, loader for a parcel-delivery firm, apprentice instrument-maker, mechanic, boot-and-shoe salesman. Much of the time, too, he had been out of work, living – as did many of his friends – on cocoa and dripping-toast, and earning a few shillings at Christmas by sweeping snow. His father was a bad provider, often absent for months at a time, and, from early on, Bob had tended to take his place, supporting his brothers and sisters as best he could on his meagre earnings. He was, or had been born, one of the very poor who in *Howards End* are described as 'unthinkable'.

He had survived with great resilience, becoming a warm-hearted, broad-minded, responsible man, with a patronizing manner – a manner which could sometimes annoy people. He loved to be in the know (a *trait* of the police generally) and was very quick to pick up a new tone. Up to now he had been essentially a 'hearty', fond of blue jokes, and mad on sports and games, which he played with furious concentration; but, having got to know Forster, he changed. Harry Daley, who was jealous over Forster, would remark, maliciously, what a highbrow Bob had become of a sudden – how Bob would affect an interesting stutter and tell his friends what was wrong with the Albert Memorial and what they should look out for at the Tate Gallery. Bob, for his part, treated Harry as a sort of licensed lunatic. He refused to countenance Harry's gaolbird friends, but not censoriously, merely treating Harry as a hopeless case. He would put his arm round him affectionately, sighing, 'Oh Harry, you *are* a fool.'

It went with much else in Bob Buckingham that, having once attached himself to Forster, he did the thing with thoroughness and became intensely loyal, demanding a similar faithfulness. This suited Forster admirably, and in the early days of their friendship he trod very cautiously, doing his best to prevent gossip among the 'cat-ring'. 'I must re-emphasize the need of silence about Bob,' he told Ackerley, some months after their first meeting. 'The results of his kindness rather disconcerted him, I think, and I am most anxious that nothing shall get about to vex him.' Not long after this, matters between them took a definite step forward. Forster reported to Sprott that Bob had 'fallen very violently in liking with him', and he began to wonder if he, himself, were not falling in love. He did not really want to, but before long he had done so; and the two, at this time, plighted some kind of troth.

Matters between him and Buckingham being now on a firm footing, Forster relaxed his caution and began to go about with him among his own friends. He introduced him to Florence Barger, who liked him and was soon forming schemes for improving his mind. He also took him to West Hackhurst, where Buckingham, who was a handyman, tactfully exerted himself doing odd jobs. Lily, however, was jealous and took against him. 'How ugly Mr Bucknam is!' she remarked; to which Forster replied, hypocritically: 'Well *I* think so.' She never really got to like Buckingham or learned to pronounce his name, persisting to the end in calling him 'Bucknam'.

Forster wondered sometimes if he were not now tending to show Bob off, like a trophy. Also, and conversely, he noted: 'When one takes someone one loves to pay a call, one assumes that a great impression will be made for good or bad. It is surprising to learn from a fourth party that his visit was scarcely noticed.'[1] When Buckingham had a few days' leave in the early summer, they hired a car and went for a brief tour in the West Country, calling on their way on Lytton Strachey and Carrington. Carrington, who greatly liked Forster – half wishing, indeed, that she could be his *confidante* – observed Buckingham with all the attention Forster could have wished, writing to Sebastian Sprott:

> Morgan, & Bob (?) have just left me. They dropt in about 3 o'ck – Then went off across the Downs to see Monkey-wife-author,[2] found him out so came back here to tea – I found Policeman Bob very charming and attractive to look at, & 'easy to get on with', as they say. I couldn't quite remember past history, but I think I do . . . He told me he looked up your name in the 3 swans, where they had lunch. – Morgan seemed very happy. He had hired a very old Essex motor car & was going for a tour in the West with his sweetie. But *why not* buy a new car, & make Bob the chauffeur sez I to myself after they had been trying to start up the old thing

---

[1] Commonplace Book, p. 97.
[2] John Collier, author of the novel *His Monkey Wife* (1930).

for 20 mins in a piercing cold wind in the drive, & Boy Bob only in a thin mackintosh.

I suppose the love of the Policeman is too much for Morgan. – Query? Why don't females have affairs with female policewomen.

Forster was now confident that he had found a lasting relationship; and one wonders what sort of relationship it actually was – that is to say, how much, in fact, it was a physical one. Strangely enough, it is not easy to decide. Carrington, and most of Forster's other friends, assumed, of course, that the two went to bed together; but against this there is a curious piece of evidence. During the 1960s Forster, being then in hospital and believing himself to be dying, spoke to Buckingham about his physical passion for him, and Bob was, or so he said, greatly upset: according to him, it was the first he had known of Forster's real feelings, even the first time he had known Forster was homosexual. By this time there were difficulties between them, so it could well be that he was lying – to others or to himself. And certainly, considering Forster's circle, and the knowledge of life acquired by a London policeman, it does seem incredible that Bob should not have known Forster was homosexual. But that they were never – anyway in Buckingham's view – 'lovers' in the physical sense is quite conceivable. Forster was by now middle-aged, and less troubled by physical desire. He would have derived intense pleasure – physical pleasure – from Bob's presence. And Bob, who was an affectionate man, would have given him embraces; no doubt on holidays they would have sometimes shared a bed. It could be that Forster, having fallen profoundly in love, decided not to risk wrecking things by demanding more. I would guess myself that, in early days, there was somewhat more to it than this, but of a kind easily forgotten by Buckingham in later years. The nearest thing to evidence that has survived is a letter from Forster to Sprott (16 July 1931):

> . . . I'm quite sure that his [Buckingham's] feeling for me is something he has never had before. It's a spiritual feeling which has extended to my physique – pardon, cher maitre, such nomenclature; I desire to convey that it's something he calls MORGAN he's got hold of, so that my lack of youth and presence which in other relationships might hinder or depress me, are here no disadvantage, in fact the reverse.

Whatever their relationship, there was one major threat to it. Buckingham, when he first met Forster, had just broken with a girl-

friend, but since then he had found another, a hospital nurse named
May Hockey, and it seemed that they might be marrying soon. It was
a prospect that had to be faced, and Forster faced it as gracefully as
he could, even lending Bob a key to his flat so that he could meet May
there. As for meeting May himself, his heart sank at the prospect. 'I
wish there wasn't this horrid nurse – I assume she's horrid,'[1] he told
Reid (17 July 1931). 'At present she is longing to meet me, but one
knows what that means and how it ends.' The encounter eventually
took place, and he was forced to admit that May was probably 'a
good sort' and nice-looking. 'But *oh* the voice!' he told Sprott. 'Oh
the proprietary screams at Bob!' His own feelings were every bit as
proprietary. By facing the likelihood of their marriage he did not
mean renouncing any of his rights in Bob, either over his affections or
his time. May, as it turned out, made no difficulties over this; indeed
she showed herself full of good will. Thus for a year or so the three
arranged their lives very amicably, and in 1932 Forster, in his
Commonplace Book, addressed a message to posterity:

Happiness
I have been happy for two years.
It mayn't be over yet, but I want to write it down before it gets
spoiled by pain – which is the chief thing pain can do in the inside
life: spoil the lovely things that had got in there first.
Happiness can come in one's natural growth and not queerly, as
religious people think. From 51 to 53 I have been happy, and
would like to remind others that their turn can come too. It is the
only message worth giving.

[1] There was irony in her being a nurse, considering his and his mother's
prejudices about nurses. (See Vol. 1, p. 83.)

7 'Saving Civilization'

By this time Forster had come to be in demand as a broadcaster. His connection with the B.B.C. went back to 1928, when he had delivered a talk on 'Railway Bridges', and since then, through his friendship with Joe Ackerley, he had exercised some behind-the-scenes influence in the Talks Department.[1] He had formed a strong sense of the importance of the B.B.C., both for good and for evil. It had struck him how Dickinson, in his old age, had become a successful broadcaster, beginning to win the sort of following he had failed of as a writer. And he sensed, too, the various pressures on the B.B.C., some of them sinister, and suspected the Government of wanting to exploit it for its own ends.

Now during 1931, he received an invitation to give a regular fortnightly series of broadcast book-reviews. The year was one of some significance in the B.B.C.'s history. When the B.B.C. had first received its charter, in 1927, it had been forbidden to broadcast discussions on controversial topics, only securing the right after some tough fighting by its Director-General Sir John Reith. Reith, having won his battle, had appointed an energetic Talks Director, Hilda Matheson, and she had brought various prominent controversialists to the microphone. They had, however – to Reith's discomfort – been mainly of a leftish tinge: and by 1931, a year of national crisis and 'red scares', the B.B.C. was under attack from all sides, but

---

[1] Lionel Fielden, a Talks producer at this time, wrote: 'I remember best the trinity of E. M. Forster, Desmond MacCarthy and H. G. Wells, who gave us freely of their time and wise counsels, and would sit round our gas fires at Savoy Hill, talking of the problems and possibilities of broadcasting' (*The Natural Bent*, 1960, p. 105).

especially from the right, and was in danger of forfeiting its independence.

There occurred, for instance, a ludicrous episode when a radio play about General Nobile's Polar expedition was withdrawn at the last moment, under government pressure, for no better reason than that it featured a rescue by a *Russian* icebreaker. Forster, who had not yet begun his book-talks, was provoked by this incident to write an article, 'The Freedom of the B.B.C.', for the *New Statesman* (4 April 1931). Till recently, he argued in it, attacks on the B.B.C. had been harmless, a matter of old ladies removing their earphones and shouting 'Rubbish' into them, under the impression that their words were transmitted back to the B.B.C., or of old gentlemen scrawling postcards saying 'Is this music? If so, I or it are mad.' Now, however, the attacks were on new lines: 'The aim is suppression. When suppression has been achieved, control may be attempted, but suppression is the immediate objective.' The B.B.C. – by which he meant Sir John Reith – took the line of dignity: it was too grand to take notice of press attacks. 'Unfortunately its dignity is only superficial. It does yield to criticism, and to bad criticism, and it yields in advance – the most pernicious of surrenders.'

Reith by now was at war with Hilda Matheson, his Talks Director. He would send her sharp little notes, suggesting that such-and-such a speaker was 'subversive' or eccentric or an anarchist. He also tried to prevent Harold Nicolson, a friend of Hilda Matheson and one of her star broadcasters, from referring to Joyce's *Ulysses* in his book-talks. Thus, before Forster began his own book-talks, Reith summoned him to Savoy Hill to explain his policy and certain 'formulae'. It was stiff little interview, and after it Reith wrote (1 October 1931) reaffirming his standpoint:

> We cannot clearly define the 'limitations' under which a broadcast critic should work. I felt that you both understood and agreed with our sense of responsibility in the control of this great influence. That, and the character of the audience more or less determine what should be said. I think you agreed with me that in talking to such an audience – all ages, all grades of intelligence, and perhaps particularly all standards of stability – one has to be careful not to disrupt and leave disruption. The works of certain writers such as those whom we happened to mention may be of interest, and may even be of importance, but with many people they are not, in these days especially, helpful. And I am not sure

that being helpful, in a comprehensive sense of the term, is not a fairly good criterion.

The 'unhelpful' writers whom he hoped Forster would not mention were Aldous Huxley and Bertrand Russell. Forster replied diplomatically, saying that he was glad that Reith's 'formulae' were not to be applied rigidly, for otherwise 'I could not conscientiously apply for the post'.

Soon afterwards Reith discontinued Harold Nicolson's contract, and, partly as a result of this, Hilda Matheson resigned. Nicolson then wrote a vituperative article in the *Spectator*, describing the B.B.C.'s board of governors as 'a pack of ninnies . . . too prone to listen to letters from angry clergymen', and Forster wrote in his support, saying that the reason why Hilda Matheson had resigned must be because the B.B.C. was too cautious. 'A timid B.B.C. is an appalling prospect,' he said, 'because, though timid, it will always be influential, and it will confirm thousands of us in our congenial habit of avoiding unwelcome truths.'

No reprisals followed from his intervention, and it was arranged that he should begin his book-talks in October 1932, alternating week by week with G. K. Chesterton. He also, in the preceding February, broadcast a dialogue with Bob Buckingham, in a series called 'Conversations in the Train'. In this, the two meet as strangers on a train. There is a little *contretemps*, when Forster tries to throw Buckingham's suitcase out of the window, under the impression that another traveller has left it. As a result, they fall into conversation, and, discovering each other's occupation, they quarrel amicably about the Police versus the Public. Buckingham demolishes various misconceptions about the police – that they are ignorant flat-foots, that they get promotion solely by making arrests, and so on. He describes the new educational system for policemen, at which Forster, asks: 'This excellent education they give you, this Peel House, and all the rest of it: does it make you human?'Buckingham answers, 'I should hope not. . . . The public doesn't want us to be human beings, with human faults. It wants us to be a machine on which it can rely – a machine that will stop traffic for it when it wants, and pick it up when it faints and show it the way when it's an old lady who's lost and guard its house when it's got one. . . .' Growing heated, he continues: 'If I may say so, isn't it rather a pity to keep on grumbling against the

Police and everything the way you do? You don't help us nor yourself either.' At this Forster rounds on him:

> *F.* It is not a pity and I shall continue to grumble. And I'll tell you why. This bickering ungenerous attitude of the general public whom I represent; this endless uninformed ungracious criticism of the Police and their ways; I suggest to you it's much more valuable than you think. It keeps you up to the mark –
> *B.* Well I'm blessed.
> *F.* Our mark, not yours. It counteracts your officialism. It helps you to be human beings and at the bottom of your hearts you should be grateful for it.

*   *   *

Forster's commitment to the P.E.N. had never been more than temperate. In 1930 he had been invited for the third time to be president of the Young P.E.N. but had refused, saying 'All institutions benefit by a change of officials (even when the officials do as little as I have done!)' Then, early in the following year he had a fracas with the P.E.N. – rather a characteristic one. Two years previously a scheme had been concerted between the P.E.N. centres to erect a memorial to Rupert Brooke, on the island of Skyros. It was to be in the form of a bronze, commissioned for the purpose from a Greek sculptor, and Forster had made a small subscription towards the cost. The monument was to be unveiled in April 1931, and Forster was duly sent a circular about the ceremony; however, with it there was enclosed a brochure from a travel agency, advertising a cruise to Skyros for Rupert Brooke admirers. Forster was scandalized by this advertisement, which seemed to him the most vulgar piece of commercialism. He returned it to the P.E.N. Secretary, Hermon Ould, with a severe little note, saying that the manner and the matter of it were 'equally deplorable', and announcing his resignation from the P.E.N. Ould, somewhat bewildered, replied denying any personal responsibility for the cruise and asking Forster to make it clearer 'why you think the P.E.N. deserves your resignation': Forster however, was not to be shifted. Nor was he appeased by a letter from Galsworthy, who wrote;'Honestly I don't think there's often been an association that has kept itself clearer from commercial notions.' The break with the P.E.N. was not, even at the time, very drastic, for when, next year, he visited Romania, the P.E.N. gave a dinner in his honour in Bucharest. (It left him feeling slightly dashed, since none of those present had actually read, or even, it seemed, heard of his novels.) All the same he never forgot the Skyros cruise. He would say that, after it, he had never taken the P.E.N. very seriously. In later years, his tone about it was indulgent but dismissive. 'A very harmless club . . . never very brilliant or commanding. . . . When you heard of a person who belonged, you thought that was the sort of thing he *would* do.'[1]

The Romanian visit was his first taste of the Balkans. He went as the guest of an old friend from Weybridge days, Sir Alec Randall, now First Secretary at the embassy at Bucharest. Randall was an enterprising host.[2] Forster was taken on 'intensely romantic' expeditions in the sub-Carpathians, lunching in the woods upon trout, and sheep's cheese packed in pine-bark, and descending the slopes in a brakeless railway timber-truck. He wrote dithy-rambically to Ackerley of 'The scenery, the gorgeous rough costumes, the peasants and workmen sprawling in the brilliant sun, the wolves bears and boars lurking to pounce upon them from the beeches birches larches and spruces and to dapple with their rich gore their couches of pansies and thyme.' He also made the discovery of Sibiu, an ancient fortress-town in Transylvania, still half German-speaking, and very curious and charming in its architecture – its houseroofs being pierced with dormers like elongated eyes. It prompted an article, 'The Eyes of Sibiu',[3] in which he played with the fancy that its inhabitants were the children led through the mountain by the Pied Piper. From Rumania he travelled on alone to Cracow, and this too caught his fancy. 'What other town,' he wrote later, 'has threaded a golden crown on the spire of its church, or has installed a trumpeter to play every hour and to end his tune with a gasp because, centuries ago, a trumpeter was shot through the throat by the Mongols.[4] He found it altogether a strange place and witnessed there a game of chess played with human pieces.

He had come to Cracow with an introduction to an English-

---

[1] Conversation with the author in 1969.

[2] See Sir Alec Randall's memoir 'Forster in Rumania', in *Aspects of E. M. Forster*, ed. O. Stallybrass (1969).

[3] *Spectator*, 25 June 1932.

[4] 'Chess at Cracow'; *Time and Tide*, 13 August 1932, reprinted in *Abinger Harvest*.

speaking Polish lady, Mrs Myslakowska. She proved to be young, large and beautiful, 'a perfect Juno of a woman', and he was entertained by her several times at her flat. She was a translator, and the idea soon occurred to them that she might translate his novels.[1] Before long she became confiding, and Forster heard about her troubles with her husband, who had recently threatened her with a revolver. She was longing for a divorce; and on Forster's return to England, he received a letter from Mrs Myslakowska containing – more or less – a proposal of marriage. Forster made what reply he could, and Lily said he seemed to have left the Continent only just in time. However, a few weeks later, Mrs Myslakowska appeared in England in person. Forster was by now somewhat nervous, but he invited her to West Hackhurst; and during a walk in his wood, she vigorously repeated the marriage-proposal – also alarming him by suggesting they lie down under the trees. He found himself in an awkward situation; and it was made worse by the fact that Lily had taken a great fancy to their visitor. She sang her praises so loudly, Forster half suspected she wanted to marry him off.

In the event he extricated himself from the affair with fair grace, even retaining the friendship of Mrs Myslakowska. But it had added a grain or two to his misogyny. During the same year he made a long entry on Women in his Commonplace Book.

> . . . One can run away from women, turn them out, or give in to them. No fourth course.
> Men sometimes want to be without women. Ah why is the converse not equally true? ('Yes – it is – don't you be so conceited' – even as I write the above I hear the insincere unfriendly shriek.) Destruction of Club Life – women will not rest till it is complete . . .
> Indeed this note need never end. I must set against it the occasional beauty of their voices in singing. The male, even at his best, has a fruity complacency. A woman can forget herself here.

*   *   *

Since 1931 Lowes Dickinson's life had been in decline. He was now over seventy and was suffering from prostate trouble, and he told Forster he wondered how much longer he wanted to cling on to life. In July 1932 he had to go into hospital for major surgery. He kept the fact a secret from his sisters but gave Forster letters to deliver in the

---

[1] In 1938 she published a translation into Polish of *A Passage to India*.

case of his death; and a few days after the operation he died. It was a momentous event for Forster, who still felt strong emotions of discipleship. 'Who will not miss him?' he wrote to Darling (24 August 1932). 'Mrs Newman his bedmaker said "He was the best man who ever lived," and I would write that on his tomb, if he needed one.' Dickinson had appointed Forster his literary executor; and on the strength of this the Dickinson sisters[1] invited him to write their brother's biography. It seemed to him a fitting idea, indeed in a way a duty, and he agreed, setting to work within a few months.

The experience of reading early letters and of reviving his own now far-off Cambridge youth seemed at first, he told a friend, 'like opening a tomb'. He guessed that his younger friends, like Ackerley and Bob Buckingham, would find his book old-fashioned, but, so he told Buckingham, he did not want 'to be up-to-date at someone else's expense'. The problem about old-fashionedness was preoccupying him just then, and he wrote words about Dickinson that applied partly to himself:

> One may almost say of him that he held nineteenth-century opinions in a twentieth-century way . . . he felt the questions of personal immortality and the existence of God to be so important he never got fussed over them . . . One can contrast him, here, with another academic speculator, Henry Sidgwick. Sidgwick wanted to believe in God, and his inability to do so caused him a constant strain. Dickinson, equally conscientious, was somehow freer and less glum. It would never have occurred to him as it did to Sidgwick to compose his own funeral service. As soon as it came to the question of his own death, his own fate, he turned easy and modern . . .[2]

Dickinson's letters were not only illegible but mostly very dull, and as he laboured through them, he told Ackerley, he imagined he heard Dickinson's voice sighing: 'Really my dear Morgan, that you should have to do this.' More and more, as he progressed, he had the illusion of Dickinson speaking to him in person. Dickinson had left an autobiography in manuscript, and Forster used it as a framework for his own book, omitting however, the very frank sexual confessions which, with his encouragement, Dickinson had written in his last years. It set his mind running on his own future biographer. 'I get

---

[1] i.e. May and Hester, Janet having died in 1924.
[2] *Goldsworthy Lowes Dickinson* (1934), chapter 10.

more absorbed in the book on Goldie,' he told Joe Ackerley (10 January 1933). 'I wish I could get one written about me after I die, but I should want every thing told, everything, and there's so far so little. Goldie, because one's condemned to omissions, looms larger.'

                              *   *   *

That 'easiness' and 'modernity' Forster had defined in Dickinson, he possessed himself in a larger share, and they did duty in place of more conscious literary 'modernism'. As a result of the war, there had been a vogue for hatred of old men, every evil in the world being blamed on the old; but, by some exception, Forster had escaped and was regarded by the young as an 'old man' deserving of respect and love. In fact, despite his only half-welcoming attitude towards the literary *avant-garde*, he had become an influence on young writers. There is a passage in Christopher Isherwood's autobiography *Lions and Shadows* in which a Cambridge friend of his called 'Chalmers' (in real life, Edward Upward) announces the discovery of Forster's modernity. The year is 1926, and 'Chalmers' and Isherwood are collaborating on a novel. Chalmers writes:

> I saw it all suddenly while I was reading *Howards End* . . . Forster's the only one who understands what the modern novel ought to be . . . Our frightful mistake was that we believed in tragedy: the point is, tragedy's quite impossible nowadays . . . We ought to aim at being essentially comic writers . . . The whole of Forster's technique is based on the tea-table: instead of trying to screw all his scenes up to the highest possible pitch, he tones them down until they sound like mothers'-meeting gossip . . . In fact, there's actually *less* emphasis laid on the big scenes than on the unimportant ones: that's what's so utterly terrific. It's the completely new kind of accentuation – like a person talking a different language . . .

The phrase 'tea-tabling' got about and became current among critics as the way of defining Forster's fictional method.

Isherwood himself had felt Forster's influence. He had written his first novel *All the Conspirators* in 1926, and in revising it during the following year he gave it the 'tea-tabling' treatment. Looking back later on this period he saw himself as influenced both by Forster's 'rejection of the humbug that still predominated in English society', and by the casual easy tone of his novels. He wrote: 'One of the most revolutionary (opening) sentences to a working novelist was "One may as well begin with Helen's letters''.'[1] For him, as for Upward, Forster represented a kind of modernity, and the two were greatly excited by Forster's account of Gide's *Les Faux-monnayeurs* in *Aspects of the Novel* – finding the actual novel, when they read it, rather an anti-climax.

*   *   *

The year of Dickinson's death was, as it happened, one in which Forster formed friendships with several of the younger novelists. It was at this time, for instance, that he got to know William Plomer. Plomer had made his name a few years before with his first novel, *Turbott Wolfe*, an impassioned tract about black–white relations in South Africa, written while he was still a very young man and working as a trader and farmer in Zululand. It had caused much scandal in South Africa, and on the strength of its success he had joined Roy Campbell in launching a literary magazine; then in 1927, on a whim, he had gone to Japan for two years, scraping a living there by teaching, and producing a volume of short stories on Japanese themes. Since that time he had been in London, living with a painter friend named Anthony Butts. Forster had known him casually through the Woolfs, who had published *Turbott Wolfe*, and also through Joe Ackerley, who was a close friend of Plomer's; and now, rather suddenly, the two became intimate.

Plomer was an ironic, rather secretive and mystery-loving man, with a collector's passion for oddities – for suburban house-names, public statues and human eccentrics. In manner he was precise and sedate, with a teasing and foxy aplomb. It was a manner at odds with his life, which at this time was almost as frenetic a homosexual chase as Joe Ackerley's: Forster told Sprott that he had only gained Plomer's friendship because he happened to catch him in an 'unguardeed' moment. There was in fact some split in him between irony and feeling, for he was at heart deeply sentimental – indeed, his friends said, he allowed sentiment to destroy his life. Like most of his circle he was an admirer of Forster's work, and as he got to know Forster he conceived a strong respect and amused affection for him as a man. He once said to Virginia Woolf: 'I not only like him very much, I esteem him.' (The remark made her laugh. 'That's a most *extraordinary* word,' she said.) During the early days of their friend-

---

[1] First words of *Howards End*.

ship, Forster invited him to tea to meet Somerset Maugham and
Herbert Read. The occasion went disastrously, Read becoming very
pugnacious towards Maugham, referring to 'Contemptible people
who write for money, like you.' When the party had dispersed,
Forster said reproachfully to Plomer: 'Well, I did think you would
have intervened'; to which Plomer replied, sincerely, that a young
man like himself could hardly have ventured to.

Plomer was a friend of Christopher Isherwood, at this period
living in Berlin, and persuaded Forster to read Isherwood's recently-
published novel *The Memorial*. It impressed him enough for him to
want to meet the author, and, on one of Isherwood's visits to London,
in September 1932, Plomer brought him along to meet Forster.
Isherwood was excited and awed and adopted the attitude of a
disciple. ('Christopher made a good disciple,' he wrote of himself
later;[1] 'like most arrogant people he loved to bow down uncondition-
ally from time to time.') They talked, among other things, of T. E.
Lawrence, and, at parting, Forster lent Isherwood his illustrated
copy of *Seven Pillars of Wisdom*. The two began to correspond,
and in a letter written soon after their first meeting Isherwood told
Forster he was writing 'an indecent bumptious stupid sort of novel
about Berlin', which he feared Forster would not like. 'It's strange,
I long to do very moving Dickensy scenes with tears, and when it
comes to the point I dry up like a stone and write something
venomous. It's as if I had some nasty green poison in my system.'

At much the same period, Forster also made the acquaintance of
'John Hampson' – in real life, John Simpson – the author of a much-
praised though now forgotten novel of provincial life, *Saturday Night
at the Greyhound*. Simpson, who was now in his late thirties, lived
with a family named Wilson, near Birmingham. He was tiny, and in
appearance rather grotesque, with a cow-lick and a Hapsburg chin
and dressing from head to foot in brown. (He had a mania for the
colour brown, writing in brown ink on nearly-brown paper.) The
Wilsons employed Simpson as nurse to Mrs Wilson's idiot brother,
Ronald. Before taking this post he had worked in hotel kitchens and
had supported himself for a time as a book-thief – though, as he said,
'only taking the best books'. Forster met him through the Woolfs,
who had published his novel, and took to him greatly, considering

---

[1] In *Christopher and his Kind* (1976).

him a most admirable and saint-like character. He soon became a frequent visitor to him and the Wilsons, growing quite fond of the idiot, Ronald, a good-humoured giant who could not talk but would imitate cows mooing and horses neighing. Forster said that every family should have an idiot.

*   *   *

So far as his London life was concerned, his closest companion was still Joe Ackerley. He was very fond of Ackerley, perpetually amused by him, and had no secrets from him. Ackerley had at last, in a mood of desperation, completed a book, *Hindoo Holiday*, based on his experiences at Chhatarpur. It received a glowing press, Evelyn Waugh writing of it in the *Spectator* (16 April 1932) that it was 'difficult to control one's enthusiasm and praise it temperately'. It did his reputation in the B.B.C. much good, with the effect that a year or two later he would be appointed literary editor of the *Listener*.

To Forster's relief, Ackerley was for the moment seeing less of Harry Daley. In fact, the Hammersmith circle was breaking up, and there had begun a general exodus of Forster's friends to Maida Vale: Plomer, Ackerley and Leo Charlton and Tom Wichelo all moved there during the autumn of 1933, and they were joined by Stephen Spender and, briefly, by Auden. Jokes began to be made about the 'Maida Vale School' of writers, and Virginia Woolf decided to name them 'The Lilies of the Valley'.

For some years, Forster had seen little of Siegfried Sassoon. For one thing, Sassoon was not often in London, having bought himself a large mansion, Heytesbury House, in Wiltshire. For another, he was growing prickly and reclusive, inclined to cut old friends in the street and to break appointments. There was an occasion during the mid-1920s when he invited Forster to tea in his London flat and not only was he not there to receive Forster, but the rock cakes provided for his tea were stale. The cakes were the sort of detail Forster's mind fastened on, and not long after this he delivered Sassoon a homily (20 March 1927):

> I enjoyed seeing you the other day, and as I probably shan't see you again for 18 months am moved to write you a line. I think your anti-social and self-centred life has a good deal to say for it if you will face its consequences, and not hanker after the best of two worlds. You are full of illusions and they are worrying you and

perhaps stopping your work. You think you want people to come and see you, then you funk their arrival and go out and don't even provide rock cakes that are fresh for their tea. I know you're different from the majority and this isn't a scold – only a tentative tip.

Yours to a street corner,
E.M.F.

Sassoon swallowed the reproof, and the two continued to correspond, intermittently but affectionately, and Forster had once or twice been to stay at Heytesbury. Thus it was with some amazement that in *The Times* for 6 November 1933, he read the announcement of Sassoon's marriage. With amazement and annoyance, for the news puzzled him, and he was hurt to have had to learn it from a newspaper, and on impulse he wrote to Sassoon what he described as 'a line of affection and good wishes and (in a sense) of farewell'. Sassoon, taking this more literally than it was meant, replied anxiously, and at this Forster wrote again (8 November 1933):

> Have just had your affectionate letter. I don't think you quite understood mine but you saw it too was affectionate which is what matters. I didn't suppose you had acted other than rightly, and I shan't seek T.E.'s or anyone else's opinion on her, and I shall like to meet her. But Siegfried you mustn't expect me at my age to take on new intimacies. I am wonderfully pliable but I am nearly 55. You are entwined with my past and with my future so far as I can connect it with that past.
>
> To ask what doctors might call 'a certain question', and which I shouldn't ask unless I was very fond of you – Have you had an emotional and physical overturn? Your news, though I accept it as good news, startles me. (Not a question that has to be answered.)
>
> Then as to that rock bun, it never stuck in my throat, and it has only made me laugh . . .

There was much gossip in Bloomsbury about the news, and Virginia Woolf was ribald about the 'great sorrow' in Maida Vale over Sassoon's 'defection'.[1] Forster, before long, accepted an invitation to stay with Sassoon and his wife Hester,[2] and was, in the event, greatly taken with Hester. He told Plomer (March 1935) that he was 'half in love with her – she is so intelligent, simple and gentle.'

*   *   *

Dickinson's death had been memorable for Forster in another way

---

[1] Letter from Virginia Woolf to Quentin Bell, 21 December 1933.
[2] Hester Gatty.

than the obvious one, for at the memorial service in King's Bob Buckingham had told him that he and May Hockey were to get married.[1] Forster received the news quietly, but it hit him hard, and during the next few days he felt, he told Sprott, as if 'hourly rolled upon a shingle beach'. The wedding took place in August at a registry office – Forster, and one of Buckingham's fellow-policemen, acting as witnesses; he refused to stay for the celebration and went back to his flat in gloom. The next few months in his life were bitter for him. The Buckinghams had taken a flat in Shepherd's Bush, and he helped them a little with money, wondering for an instant whether he should, as it were, bargain for Bob's time. All depended, for his peace of mind, on how often he could still get Bob alone; and since Bob, preoccupied with May, was also working for his sergeant's examination, he became unreliable about appointments. It was what Forster had dreaded, and he would have flares of misogny and would rail against May to friends: 'The woman is domineering, sly and *knowing*.' As before, at moments of extreme stress, he suffered hysterical rages, when he would throw himself against the furniture. He wrote about them to Sprott (4 October 1932), asking him, in his capacity as psychologist, for a diagnosis or cure. He described them cynically:

> Attacks take the form of sudden yelps, contortions, pretence fainting-fits, and the hitting of parts of my body that don't hurt against objects in the room that aren't valuable, and always the feeling that I could have 'helped' it, indeed I often have helped it . . . I don't like calling them attacks, but regard them as part of my character.

He began to feel that he must make a break with Bob, or perhaps go abroad to escape. Even at this time, he saw Bob often for brief meetings, at the Section House or in Brunswick Square. Bob's line was 'We've got to go without pleasure for a bit'; and Forster had to acknowledge that, to an onlooker, it would seem Bob was acting very responsibly. Eventually, in December, he plucked up courage to pay the Buckinghams a visit. It went not too uncomfortably. The worst was now over, from his point of view, and soon he began to frequent their flat and was involving himself in their joint life.

Bob Buckingham now found himself a prize disputed between two

[1] Much of the information in the present chapter comes from May Buckingham and the late Robert Buckingham.

determined claimants. The great issue was his leisure-time. Forster
felt he had a claim on it, or at any rate he meant to assert one. It was
a silent fight between him and May, and to a good extent he was the
winner, making Bob give him his half-days-off and other odd hours
during the week. In a way he had the upper hand, for Bob was
fascinated by him: fond of him, flattered by the attachment and
excited by the *entrée* into a new kind of life. It made May feel
neglected and jealous, also a little bewildered, but she kept her
feelings to herself. She behaved, in fact, with great staunchness and
shrewdness, refusing to listen when Harry Daley told her that
Forster was breaking up her marriage. She realized the danger of
interfering and reflected that maybe it was better than a husband
who ran after other women. Moreover, even at this stage, she liked
Forster and could half understand Bob's infatuation. Very occasionally, she would rebel, usually over Bob's free time, and then Forster
and she would quarrel. He fought her toughly – even, sometimes,
asking her to leave the room, in her own house, so that he might talk
privately with Bob.

As for Bob Buckingham himself, he was both flattered and confused by the duel fought over him. His life was exciting when he did
not scrutinize it closely, but when he paused to examine it, he began
to feel bewildered – wondering about his class-situation, and about
his position in Forster's circle. It was pleasant, but faintly unreal, to
be on Christian-names terms with Siegfried Sassoon and T. E.
Lawrence; it was nice, but also galling, to be an object of interest and
philanthropy and to be encouraged to paint and to learn German –
though indeed he enjoyed painting and thought he had a talent for it.
He was a sanguine and unreflective man and was enjoying a happy
marriage, so he did not often brood on the situation; but every now
and then he would feel lost, and as if he were only at home in his
rowing-club. He managed to escape quite often to the club, winning
sundry cups for rowing and causing Joe Ackerley, on Forster's behalf,
to reproach him for neglecting his friends.

For all this, he held his own in his friendship with Forster. He was
himself fairly left-wing, once having been active in the Unemployed
Workers Association, and he would attack Forster over class-
attitudes. Once he lectured Forster for talking too much about
money, in an 'amusing' way. The criticism went home. 'It is true, but
how to cure myself at 55?' Forster noted in his Commonplace Book:

> The ugly habit has crept on me. I bring myself to the front by
> saying jokingly that I am rich, poor, have made good terms in
> America, paid a lot at a restaurant; and a man who has had real
> worries over money rebukes me. 'A thing to use if one's got it' – I
> have always preached that, yet I am letting it use me, and take
> hold of me where I feel safest, through my sense of humour.

Through Siegfried Sassoon they had got to know Stephen Tennant,
a nephew of Margot Asquith and a well-known aesthete of the period.
They would go to stay weekends with him in his house, Wilsford
Manor, near Salisbury. Tennant made a cult of things marine; his
vast mock-Tudor baronial hall was hung with lobster-pots and
fishing-nets, and Forster and Buckingham would be given the Sailor
Suite, which was furnished with portholes opening on to painted
seascapes. The two much liked Tennant but, bridging their own class-
difference, suspected him of upper-class caprice. (There was an occasion, a few years later, when Bob held forth at dinner about crime
and criminal horrors, and, in a fury, Tennant rushed from the
room, extinguishing all the candles.) From time to time, Forster
would send Tennant a reproof, which he would accept with melancholy grace. He admired Forster extravagantly, considering him a
'mage' and 'a sublime malcontent', and noticing – percipiently –
Forster's suppressed love of the exotic. (They would talk about
Persian poetry.) He collected Forster's sayings – 'Nothing lasts' (a
frequent remark); 'I like fellows who fib'; 'I can't ever hear enough
festering superstitions'; and 'One is conscious of traits in oneself that
are not very admirable – but one deals with them'. When Tennant
praised a passage in one of Forster's novels, he said to him 'That was
one of my little swallow-flights into Proust.'[1]

* * *

On 21 April 1933 May had a baby; and at a party in Brunswick
Square the next day, Forster, Buckingham, Joe Ackerley and
Christopher Isherwood toasted the child's health in champagne. It
was a boy and was to be named 'Robert Morgan', and Forster was
to be godfather – a fact which excited him, for he had always wanted
a son. He now had a further foothold in the Buckingham household,
and in June, less than two months after May's confinement, he
managed to commandeer Bob for the whole of Bob's annual holidays.
They had arranged to borrow Sprott's car and make another tour of

[1] Information given to the author by Stephen Tennant in 1975.

the West country. Forster told Sprott [n.d.] 'I have been "watching"
him [Buckingham] over this holiday, but he advances blandly
towards it, apparently not thinking it will be too long with me or
wanting to be with his wife.' Sprott applauded Forster's enterprise,
writing (17 August 1933):

> What you have to do is to fight against anything that savours of
> fidelity to his wife. It can't crop up in such old-fashioned dress as
> 'FIDELITY' – *nous avons changé* . . . – but there is a nice line of
> fancy dress at its disposal. 'It wouldn't be fair . . .' 'If one builds a
> home, it's only right that one should stop in it.' 'She is so miserable
> when I am away.' And so on. Well then you have a nice line in
> counter-arguments, and among them FREEDOM, which is much
> thought of by any who want to appear modern.

Joe Ackerley and Sebastian Sprott were, as always, solicitous about
Forster's love-life. On first hearing of Forster's happiness with Bob
Buckingham, Sprott had written in terms of great devotion:

> I've just re-read your letter for the 4th time – you can't think
> how very glad I am to hear of your happiness. You give so much
> to me and other people. I believe you are about the only person
> whose happiness makes me really feel happy – not a mere 'say so'.
> I have a faint feeling of good will to most people, a feeling of envy
> towards many, but nothing but strong wishes about you and no
> envy in an unpleasant sense whatever, nothing but wholehearted
> pleasure at hearing of your success, and reading that you are
> *gonflé d'amour*.[1]

He and Ackerley were still keen, none the less, to do some friendly
pandering for Forster, and though, since the advent of Bob, Forster
was less interested in casual affairs, he would every now and then
spend an evening with one or other of their *protégés* – guardsmen,
window-cleaners, reformed or unreformed burglars or the out-of-
work. He grew friendly with several of them, keeping up with them
as friends in a desultory way for years. They would sometimes call
unannounced, and he would take them out to supper and, if asked,
give them a very small loan. He became an expert in cheap restau-
rants: at any time there was some transport café or fish-and-chip
diner which he extolled, to the disadvantage of places like Boulestin's,
where, he would say, one ate 'scented muck'. Since these callers were
genuine friends of Sprott's or Ackerley's, he felt in no danger. On one

---

[1] Undated letter, presumably 1931.

occasion he was robbed, but of nothing of great value, and it did not perturb him. On another, in 1934 or thereabouts, an out-of-work acquaintance described to him how he had been enrolled in Mosley's Blackshirts and given a weekly dole by them. Forster felt he must do something about this and reported the details to Beatrice Webb.

Every now and then he would hear from Achille, the sailor he had picked up in Toulon in 1929. Achille wrote very good letters, though usually they included a request for a loan; and sometimes a letter would come from a friend, regretting that Achille was in prison *pour une petite escroquerie* and asking for a few francs, which Forster sent or did not send as his mood inclined. Achille had returned to his home in Forbach, in the Saar, and was working as a waiter there. He kept pressing Forster to come and see him; and in November 1934, being *en route* for the Maurons, Forster went to spend two days with him. To explain Forster's presence to his friends, Achille passed him off as an uncle in the clothes trade, long domiciled in England – in a small way of business, Achille added, to account for Forster's dowdy appearance. Achille relished the drama of the occasion. He put Forster up in a hotel but made rules, such as that they must never leave the hotel together, or look out of the window, since the restaurant opposite was kept by a cousin. Forster, enjoying himself, reflected that nothing like this had happened to him in his youth.

*   *   *

As for some time, and more keenly now with the menace of fascism, he felt the urge to involve himself in public activities. Bob Buckingham, who thought him too retiring, encouraged him in this. And in the spring of 1934 there presented itself a cause very much suited to him, when the recently-founded National Council for Civil Liberties invited him to become their first president. The Council was the creation of Ronald Kidd (1889–1942), a freelance journalist of crusading tendencies, much influenced in his youth by Edward Carpenter and Havelock Ellis. The immediate *raison d'être* of the Council had been the Hunger Marches. At the last appearance of the hunger marchers in London it had been widely rumoured that the police had used foul means in handling them, employing *agents provocateurs* and the like. Kidd had been vocal in the press* on the subject, and had eventually decided that what was needed was an organized body of impartial and reputable observers, to be present at such demonstrations and report illegalities or police misconduct.

Kidd was an earnest and saint-like man, with wide connections among left-wing lawyers and journalists. He and his friends – among them Kingsley Martin and Claud Cockburn – had founded the Council in February 1934, at a meeting in the crypt of St Martin's-in-the-Fields.[1] They had practically no funds, so for a headquarters it was decided to use Kidd's own flat, a cheerless hovel in Dansey Place, off Shaftesbury Avenue. A month or so after their foundation, another hunger march had taken place and Kidd had organized a distinguished corps of observers for the occasion. including Julian Huxley, Vera Brittain, H. G. Wells* and Forster. The newspapers had taken up the story, and as a result the N.C.C.L, had become famous. As Claud Cockburn related: 'People from far and wide who felt themselves spurned by bureaucrats, menaced by tyrannical authorities, or just generally kicked about and done down, came rushing to Dansey Place with such enthusiasm that part of the staircase gave way and people looking for Civil Liberty had to jump.'

The Council's first choice as president had been H. W. Nevinson. Nevinson had declined, on grounds of age and ill-health, and it had been he (most probably) who proposed Forster's name. The declared aims of the N.C.C.L. were entirely Forster's own, and he felt he could hardly refuse the invitation. Some of his friends warned him that the Council was crypto-communist,* but for the moment he did not believe this. And Kidd himself – grave-mannered, single-minded, and imperturbable – impressed Forster. He thought Kidd a genuinely selfless man. 'Very serious and pushful,' was his later phrase for him.

The business of the Council was transacted in an Executive Committee, which met monthly, and a General Purposes Sub-Committee, which met weekly, both being chaired by W. H. Thompson, a genial, brusque and philistine solicitor of the radical left. Forster became a regular attendant at the Executive Committee. He was not, as a rule, very vocal at its meetings, his habit being to listen

---

[1] There were a dozen or so present at the founding meeting, including Kingsley Martin, Claud Cockburn, Edith Summerskill, Amabel Williams-Ellis, Mrs Haden Guest, Dudley Collard, Geoffrey Bing, David Freeman, Ambrose Appelbe, Alun Thomas of the International Labour Defence, Professor George Catlin (Vera Brittain's husband), Professor W. E. Le Gros Clark, Douglas Goldring, and Sylvia Crowther-Smith (later Scaffardi).

carefully and then put his own views in letters to Ronald Kidd.

Shortly after accepting the presidency, Forster invited Kidd for the day to West Hackhurst and, after some hesitation, mentioned that he had a close friend in the police force and asked Kidd if this might prejudice his position as president. Kidd, for whom the enemy was not the police themselves but those who misused them for political purposes, reassured him; and before long Forster was finding Bob Buckingham a useful informant on police behaviour.[1]

Within a few weeks of his becoming president the N.C.C.L. became involved in one of its most important campaigns, against the 'Sedition Bill'. The National Government, alarmed at the circulation of Communist journals among the armed forces, had introduced a Bill making it an offence to disseminate, or even to be in possession of, literature 'liable to seduce soldiers or sailors from their duty or allegiance'. In effect, the Bill reintroduced 'general warrants', which had been illegal since the days of Wilkes. There was excitement in the press, and within forty-eight hours of the Bill's publication, the N.C.C.L. circulated an analysis of it, and of its threats to liberty, to every member of the House of Commons. It also, immediately, began to organize protest meetings, first of its own members, then of representatives from various political parties, churches and pacifist organizations. Forster, who was strongly convinced of the evils of the Bill, found himself extremely busy, despatching innumerable canvassing letters and taking part in a deputation to the Attorney-General, Sir Thomas Inskip.

The agitation was kept up all the summer. A mass meeting, to be held in the Central Hall, Westminster, was planned for 18 October, just before the re-opening of Parliament, and Forster ('by pure personal charm', as he reported to John Simpson) secured H. G. Wells, J. B. Priestley, Bishop Barnes and Hannen Swaffer as speakers; he also helped organize a giant petition, to be presented in Parliament by Eleanor Rathbone. Kidd and his friends had meanwhile devised an ingenious tactic, according to which members were to pledge themselves, should the Bill become law, to go to the military establishment at Aldershot and distribute copies of 'seditious' speeches

---

[1] On 9 September of this year Mosley's Blackshirts and the Anti-fascists held rival rallies in Hyde Park. Bob Buckingham was detailed for duty in the Park, and Forster got him to write a detailed account of events.

made by the present prime minister, Ramsay MacDonald, at the time of the First World War and the General Strike. Forster disliked this 'pledge'. He took advice from Leonard Woolf and others, and from this it appeared to him that the gesture might expose them to prosecution even under existing laws. The matter worried him, for the idea was to make the pledge a test of allegiance to the N.C.C.L.; and eventually, after some heart-searching, he wrote to Kidd (6 October 1934) offering to resign if the pledge were made compulsory. He did not expect his resignation to be accepted, nor was it; and he appeared and spoke, though without taking the chair, at the meeting on 18 October. The star speaker was H. G. Wells. Wells had just returned from the Soviet Union, in a very bad temper, and he insisted on talking not about the Bill but about the suppression of free speech in totalitarian countries. For this he was barracked by some communists in the audience, and Kingsley Martin, who was in the chair, handled the interruptions in a clumsy and schoolmasterly fashion. As a result the few newspapers that covered the meeting reported the whole occasion as a mainly communist demonstration.

Forster, indignant at the press treatment of the meeting, now put to use his position as journalist. In the summer of this year he had been given a regular column in *Time and Tide* (in a series called 'Notes on the Way') and in the issue for 27 October he contributed an editorial, headed 'Still the Sedition Bill', in which he accused the press and the B.B.C. of deliberately suppressing news of the meeting of the 18th. He urged readers to join the N.C.C.L., and to attend an open-air rally against the Bill in Trafalgar Square the next day; also to get into touch with their M.P. 'And,' he said, 'if their M.P. happens to be Ramsay MacDonald, will they not ask him why the General Search Warrant, which he condemned very sarcastically in 1925, is being fastened on us by him in 1934, and where, in 1935, he would find himself if the Bill functioned retrospectively?' He did not appear in Trafalgar Square himself, but he prescribed tactics to Kidd, telling him he hoped speakers had strict orders to stick to the Bill itself and not be drawn into anti-fascist demonstrations. 'Up to the end of the month, the Government and nothing else is our objective, and nothing else should be allowed to intervene.'

By now no one even in the Government much liked the Bill, and it had been considerably modified in committee. It did in fact become law in November, and one or two minor prosecutions were brought under it; but the agitation had for the moment effectively discredited it.* The N.C.C.L. had proved its efficacy, and it began to form branches up and down the country.

* * *

Forster's *Time and Tide* articles had, in his own phrase, given him a 'pulpit', and from now on he was to be much heard and listened to on political and social issues. He had devised a successful poise for these polemics, writing with much verve and witty phrase-making, but managing at the same time, to raise, with honesty and simplicity, questions that were nagging at ordinary readers' minds. They came down to the question, which bothered him much personally: did it really *matter* what the average, intelligent, but powerless citizen felt about war, or rearmament, or fascism, or communism? The answer he gave was: yes, it mattered just a little. And he defined his own feelings and views unpretentiously and with candour. Of communism: 'It would destroy nearly every thing I understand and like, and I want the present economic and social order to continue. If the present order breaks, communism seems the only hopeful alternative.' And was there anything the same citizen could actually do about these issues? Yes, he answered, some very small things. He might at least boycott the Aldershot Tattoo and the Royal Tournament, and all such institutions which glorified war: 'War has moved from chivalry to chemicals. It is time that we left the Royal Gas Tournament and considered the gas.' He might, too, sell any shares he happened to have in firms that would profit from war.

> Some people will say that my scruples are groundless, others that they are futile. Others – and they will be the majority who read these notes – will blame me for not acting before. In no case am I in a position to preach. But I do think that another little thing the private individual can do against war is to look through his investment list and make sure he isn't financing it *directly*.[1]

His articles gained him a new following, and he received a stream of grateful letters; they also gained him some violent abuse, for instance in a letter to the editor on 23 June 1934:

---

[1] He sold his own I.C.I. shares at this time and gave the money to anti-war organizations.

Sir. – Mr E. M. Forster in the course of the pathetic disclosures of his terrors and of his despair, says that 'no political creed except communism offers an intelligent man any hope.'

Further on, he commends to our notice a body called the Council for Civil Liberties.

It might be dangerous for Mr Forster to imagine the amount of Civil Liberty that he would enjoy in a Communist society, unless there were at hand whole hogsheads of the liberty anodyne to which he turns in emergencies, and in which he particularizes . . .

*   *   *

That the N.C.C.L. itself was simply a front organization for the Communist party was a rumour always in the air, and sometimes the rumour grew loud. Forster did all he could to quiet it and made efforts to attract right-wing, as well as genuinely non-party, members. In January 1935 the Council drew up a declaration of principles, and Forster managed, against much opposition, to impose his own non-party sentiments on it. The draft declaration had referred, vaguely, to the threat to civil liberty 'from whatever quarter', but he had this changed to 'the threat from left or right.' He told Kidd (21 January 1935): 'To my mind the fact that "right or left" has been used by the Conservatives ought not to preclude us from using it. – I should have thought indeed that we would gain rather than lose by stealing their thunder.' The other main line he pressed on the Council was that it should not disperse its energies upon European issues, or even on the troubles in Northern Ireland.[1] It was not strong enough, or well-endowed enough, to do so, and should stick to domestic issues. One of the issues he was interested in was the obscene publication laws, a matter much on his mind ever since the *Well of Loneliness* case. In March 1935 James Hanley's novel *Boy*, published four years before, was condemned as obscene at the Manchester Assizes and its publisher fined £400. Forster, who knew Hanley a little,[2] was greatly indignant and campaigned through the N.C.C.L. for a change in the law.

*   *   *

---

[1] His advice over this was not followed. The N.C.C.L. set up a commission of enquiry into abuses of the Special Powers Act (1922) in Northern Ireland, and its report, which came out in 1936, made a considerable stir.

[2] He had been introduced to Hanley's work by T. E. Lawrence in 1931, greatly admiring his *A Passion Before Death*.

With his prestige, and his concerned but non-party political stance, Forster was an attractive prize for cultural organizations, and in the spring of 1935 he was invited to head the British delegation to an International Congress of Writers in Paris. The Congress, which was dedicated to the 'Defence of Culture', had been planned by a group of French communist writers originally associated with Henri Barbusse. The effective organizer was André Malraux; and it was part of Malraux's scheme for the Congress to exploit the prestige of his friend André Gide, a recent and illustrious convert to communism. The actual occasion of the Congress, or so Malraux explained it to Gide, was that the Soviet Union, being frequently accused of neglecting or stifling culture, wanted a public opportunity for its writers to expound their ideas. The Congress was to be on a large scale. The Russians were sending a strong delegation, headed by Gorki. Among the French speakers, as well as Malraux and Gide, there were to be Benda, Crevel, Louis Aragon, Barbusse and André Breton. Various leading central-European anti-fascists were to attend, including Brecht, Toller, Musil, Capek and Heinrich Mann; and among the English delegation would be Forster, Aldous Huxley, John Strachey, Ralph Fox and Amabel Williams-Ellis.

As the Congress approached, numerous dramas and intrigues developed. Gorki withdrew for 'health reasons', and a hasty invitation had to be sent to Pasternak and Isaac Babel; Ilya Ehrenburg demanded that the invitation be withdrawn from André Breton, on the grounds that Breton had recently physically assaulted him: and René Crevel, who was on the organizing committee, committed suicide. Forster was for the moment ignorant of these developments, but Malraux wrote to him repeatedly about his own speech, asking him to say this and to say that – causing him to reply that if he could not do things his own way he would not speak at all. He told Malraux he was willing to speak on 'The Cultural Heritage' or 'Liberty of Expression in Society', but whichever the subject he would give the same speech. He had persuaded Charles Mauron to keep him company in Paris and to act as his translator, telling him that not much was to be expected from the Congress beyond 'the smaller writers sidling up to the larger ones and the larger ones sliding away.' In fact, despite his irony, he thought of it as an important occasion, and he did what he could to persuade friends and fellow-writers, James Hanley, the Woolfs, J. B. Priestley and John Lehmann and others, to come to

orence Barger

E. M. Forster on the beach at Alexandria, circa *1916*

stantine Cavafy

Mohammed el Adl

Siegfried Sassoon

Goldsworthy Lowes Dickinson

E. M. Forster, in Mahratta turban

he Royal Palace at Chhatarpur

ard-players in the Palace courtyard at Dewas. From left, 3 The Maharaja, 5 E. M. orster.

E. M. Forster, by Jessica Dismorr: 19 February 1926

From left to right, Edward Hilton Young, later Lord Kennet, with son; 1929. J. R. Ackerley, in his flat at 6 Hammersmith Terrace. W. J. H. ('Sebastian') Sprott

At Garsington, 1926. (From the left, unidentified, Mark Gertler, E. M. Forster, Julian Morrell)

Tom Wichelo and L. E. O. Charlton

Gerald Heard

Harry Daley and 'prisoner'

R. J. Buckingham

R. J. Buckingham in Section House

Boat-race Day party at 6 Hammersmith Terrace. Front row, 2 Anwar Masood (?), 3 Tom Wichelo, 4 Mrs Ackerley, 5 L. E. O. Charlton, 6 Akbar Masood, 8 J. R. Ackerley, 9 E. M. Forster.

May Buckingham, early 1930s

Garden at West Hackhurst

Lily Forster in her '80s

Paris. 'I do beg you to come, if only for a day or two,' he wrote to
Virginia Woolf (6 June 1935). 'I don't suppose the conference is of
any use – things have gone too far. But I have no doubt as to the
importance of people like ourselves *inside* the conference. We do
represent the last utterances of the civilized.'

The five-day Congress opened at the Palais de la Mutualité on
21 June, in sweltering heat. There were some 2,000 in the audience,
and many more listening to speeches over the loudspeaker system in
adjoining halls and bars; everywhere there were reporters, photo-
graphers and cartoonists, and there was a continual coming-and-
going in an underground headquarters, where the confidential business of the Congress was transacted. Forster had travelled to Paris
with James Hanley and was staying at a hotel with Charles Mauron.
He spoke early on the first day of the Congress, entitling his speech
'Liberty in England'. English freedom, he said, was race-bound and
class-bound; it meant freedom for Englishmen, not for Indians and
Africans, and freedom for the well-off, not for the down-and-out for
whom it 'did not signify a plate of fish and chips.' Nevertheless, he
said, he believed in liberty, and he thought that the type that had
developed in Great Britain might still be useful, both to the British
and to the world. As for his politics, the audience would have guessed
he was not a fascist ('Fascism does evil that evil may come'), and
it might have guessed that he was not a Communist either – 'though
perhaps I might be one if I was a younger and a braver man, for in
Communism I can see hope. It does many things which I think evil,
but I know that it intends good.' For Britain, he said, the danger,
except in the case of war, was not really from fascism, but from something more insidious: 'Fabio-fascism.' Fabio-fascism was the dictator-
spirit 'working quietly away behind the façade of constitutional
forms, passing a little law (like the Sedition Act) here, endorsing a
departmental tyranny there, emphasizing the national need of
secrecy everywhere, and whispering and cooing the so-called "news"
every evening over the wireless, until opposition is tamed and gulled.'
As an example, he described the workings of the Obscene Publications laws and related the story of the James Hanley prosecution.

He spoke, he said, only for himself, and not for the rest of the
English delegation:

> My colleagues probably agree with my account of the situation in
> our country, but they may disagree with my old-fashioned

attitude over it, and may feel that it is a waste of time to talk about freedom and tradition when the economic structure of society is unsatisfactory. They may say that if there is another war writers of the individualistic and liberalizing type, like myself and Mr Aldous Huxley, will be swept away. I am sure that we shall be swept away, and I think furthermore that there may be another war. It seems to me that if nations keep on amassing armaments, they can no more help discharging their filth than an animal, which keeps on eating, can stop from excreting. This being so, my job, and the job of those who feel with me, is an interim job. We have just to go on tinkering as well as we can with our old tools, until the crash comes. When the crash comes, nothing is any good. After it – if there is an after – the task of civilization will be carried on by people whose training has been different from my own.

The speech, with its Englishness and gentleness, mystified and exasperated his young and mainly communist audience. (Though indeed, since he refused, or had not learnt, to use the microphone, they heard very little of it, and had mainly to depend on Charles Mauron's translation.) The American novelist, Katherine Anne Porter, was in the audience, and – though she was an ardent admirer of Forster – she recalled it as a dispiriting episode:

I think it was just after André Malraux – then as dogmatic in communism as he is now in some other faith – had leaped to the microphone barking like a fox to halt the applause for Julien Benda's speech, that a little slender man with a large forehead and a shy chin rose, was introduced and began to read his paper carefully prepared for this occasion. He paid no attention to the microphone, but wove back and forth, and from side to side, gently, and every time his face passed the mouthpiece I caught a high-voiced syllable or two, never a whole word, only a thin recurring sound like the wind down a chimney as Mr Forster's pleasant good countenance advanced and retreated and returned. Then, surprisingly, once he came to a moment's pause before the instrument and there sounded into the hall clearly but wistfully a complete sentence; 'I DO believe in liberty!'
The applause at the end was barely polite, but it covered the antics of that part of the audience near me; a whole pantomime of malignant ridicule, meaning that Mr Forster and all his kind were already as extinct as the dodo. It was a discouraging moment.[1]

---

[1] *The Days Before* (1953), pp. 117–18.

Gide spoke to a very different and rapturous reception, declaring his belief that 'individuals and their peculiarities can best flourish in a communist society' and prophesying a day 'when great literature could be made not, as till now, out of men's sufferings, but out of their joy'. The rest of the five days were filled with interminable harangues, interspersed with disturbances from the Surrealists and scuffles with the Trotskyites, who chanted the name of Victor Serge[1] and at one point tried to rush the platform and seize the microphone. The Russian delegation retorted with the official explanation of the Victor Serge affair, but so implausibly that Gide complained afterwards to the Russian ambassador, who assured him his letter would be put in the hands of Stalin himself. Aldous Huxley, meanwhile, wrote to Gide, complaining of the endless communist demagogery, where there might have been 'serious, technical discussions'. Forster reported the Congress, equivocally, in the *New Statesman* (6 July 1935), saying that 'Some of the speakers appeared to be journalists rather than creative artists, and some were Congress-addicts who would travel any distance for their drug. Yet it remained an impressive affair which only a common danger could have created.' A permanent bureau had been set up to continue the work of the Congress, and he urged fellow-writers to support it, for, he said, it was in danger of becoming 'a chapel of the One True Revolution', and English writers, though as a rule they 'cut so little ice on the Continent', might help to prevent this.

The phrase about 'cutting little ice' was written feelingly, for one of the attractions of the Congress, for him, had been the expectation of meeting Gide, with whom he had corresponded some years before and whose autobiography *Si le grain ne meurt* had impressed and astonished him. Thus he had been pleased when Gide and Malraux had invited him out to dinner. However, the very moment the meal had been consumed, the two French writers had got up and left – presenting Forster, so he said, with 'the spectacle of their distinguished backs'. Despite this, he wrote a glowing account of Gide's speech, in his *New Statesman* article, describing how Gide, who began

---

[1] Victor Serge, a Franco-Russian novelist and polemicist, was arrested by the G.P.U. in 1933, on trumped-up charges of Trotskyite activities, and sentenced to enforced exile in Orenbourg. As a result of the agitation at the Congress, aided by a personal plea to Stalin from Romain Rolland, he was released the same year and allowed to leave Russia.

with 'Airs and archery' had gradually forgotten himself, and 'his style became fluid as his thought soared and sentimentality passed into affection.'

In all, Forster did not feel his effort had been wasted, though believing, as he told John Lehmann (12 July 1935), that 'It is only at this particular moment of civilization that such a show is likely to be held. Next year every one may know their own minds.' He had accepted election to the committee of the Permanent Bureau and wrote to various writers of his acquaintance, including Bernard Shaw, to join. Shaw, who was going through a flirtation with totalitarianism, returned a brusque retort:

> Dear Forster,
>   I am very much obliged to you indeed for calling my attention to the fact that this International Association of Writers, which I have been officially invited to join, is a political conspiracy against Fascism: that is, against the German and Italian Governments and, in effect, against all governments which have discarded Liberal party parliamentarianism. An Italian writer who is a supporter of Mussolini will not join. An Italian writer who is anti-Fascist dare not join for fear of being sent to the Lipari islands. German writers, Polish writers, Hungarian writers, Turkish writers are similarly excluded.
>   I will have nothing to do with such an exhibition of political imbecility and incorrigible Anarchism. And I strenuously advise you to follow my example.
>   Fortunately the silly business can do no harm because it can do nothing. It has cut its own throat with the first stroke of its pen.
>   Have you ever thought of the Committee for Intellectual Co-operation of the League of Nations as a possible instrument lying ready to our hands and quite neglected by us? I am too old to start on it; but if I were a beginner I should certainly organize an attempt to capture it. It is just dying to be taken notice of.

8 Trees

Even now, at the height of his public life, the larger part of Forster's existence was spent with his mother in Abinger. Their style of life had not been changed much by the move to West Hackhurst. Neither was very active in the village. Lily had acquired one or two 'pensioners' in the village, but it was not her style, nor was it Forster's, to play a great part in local functions. They were, of course, not without friends. There was a long-standing friendship between them and the local builder, William King, and his wife; and they were on chatting terms with various other neighbours – for instance with the Broyds at Hackhurst Farm, from whom they bought their milk. Forster was also friendly with the butcher's son, Ernest Read.[1] Read was an amateur archaeologist, and the two would go for walks together, searching for flint arrow-heads, and Forster would invite him back to supper in his study. In general, nevertheless, the Forsters were regarded in Abinger as a little aloof; and Forster himself, though liked, was considered by some as distinctly odd. Mrs Broyd once said, 'He's rather simple, isn't he?', and the remark had gone round. As for Ernest Read, he suspected a secret, and, when Forster had gone to South Africa in 1929, he had thought it must be on some 'hush-hush' work.

In 1934, however, Forster was drawn somewhat into village activities. It had been decided to stage a pageant in Abinger, in aid of the church-restoration fund, and the pageant-committee invited Forster to write the 'book'. The pageant was under the auspices of the Farrers of Abinger Hall (the family with whom many years

---

[1] He is mentioned in 'The Last of Abinger', in *Two Cheers for Democracy*.

before Lily had been a governess). The committee was headed by Lord Farrer,[1] who had offered the grounds of Abinger Hall for rehearsals, and Vaughan Williams, who lived nearby in Dorking and was a family connection of the Farrers[2] had agreed to provide the music. The producer was to be a young man of the village, named Tom Harrison, aided by an artistic adviser, Miss Gwen Lally. Harrison, with the aid of one of Lord Farrer's daughters, had drawn up a scenario, and it was to be Forster's function to write the speeches and the programme notes.

He applied himself dutifully to the task, sighing a little at the prospect. 'I have promised to write the Book of the Abinger Church Pageant,' he wrote to Sprott (30 April 1934). 'How I wish I could speak to Miss Velda [Sprott's sister] about it. Our producer, Mr T. Harrison, thinks very badly of Miss Gwen Lally's work indeed. He strikes me as a silly puppy, but I am unused to local efforts, and we know how very good they can be don't we . . .?' The pageant was to contain the usual ingredients: ancient Britons in skins gathering fuel in the Abinger woods; a cry of 'Romans, the Romans!'; arrival of the Saxons and of the Normans; the news of the Spanish Armada brought to Abinger; and so on. One aspect, however, caught Forster's imagination. Tom Harrison had suggested that the pageant should stress the theme of woods and trees, and Forster was much taken with this notion of a 'Pageant of Trees'[3] and put his narration in the mouth of an Abinger woodman. In the Prologue, the Woodman addressed the audience thus:

> Welcome to our village and our woods. I welcome you first to our woods, because they are the oldest. Before there were men in Abinger, there were trees. Thousands of years before the Britons came, the ash grew at High Ashes and the holly at Holmwood and the oak at Blindoak Gate; there were yew and juniper and box on the downs before ever the Pilgrims came along the Pilgrims' way. They greet you, and our village greets you.
>
> What shall we show you? History? Yes, but the history of a village lost in the woods. Do not expect great deeds and grand

---

[1] Thomas Cecil Farrer, 2nd Baron (1859–1940).

[2] His mother was first cousin of Katherine Euphemia Farrer, second wife of the first Lord Farrer.

[3] After the first performance, Forster wrote a letter to *The Times*, thanking the editor for the 'sympathetic' review of it, but regretting its failure to mention Tom Harrison; 'It is to him that the conception of a Pageant of Trees is due.'

people here. Lord and Ladies, warriors and priests will pass, but this is not their home, they will pass like the leaves in autumn but the trees remain. The trees built our first houses and our first church, they roof our church today, they are with us from the cradle to the grave.

Forster, from childhood, had had a passionate fondness for trees, and such landowning instincts as he possessed were largely concerned with woods and trees. Adjoining West Hackhurst there lay a wood, of some four acres, called Piney Copse, and soon after he had settled there he had discovered that the wood was threatened, and on an impulse he had bought it, for the sum of £450. By doing so he had forestalled Lord Farrer, who would have liked to buy the wood himself, but Farrer had made way for Forster gracefully. The timber in Piney Copse had mostly been felled during the 1914–18 war, only a few straggling oaks remaining, and Forster had set to work to replant it. He did not much like oaks, because of their too-patriotic associations, and in restocking the wood he introduced a variety of other species: birch, rowan, beech, sweet chestnuts, horse chestnuts, wild cherries, crab-trees and conifers. At the thought of trees his mind became irrepressibly allegorical. He saw important virtues in a wood's being mixed in species – in its being, as one might say, a sort of Alexandria, cosmopolitan and racially mixed. Again, he approved of the spectacle of self-sown saplings – trees which had grown 'only because it occurred to them to do so'. For some reason the squirrels seemed to leave such saplings unharmed, and he reflected that the self-sown and the humble do sometimes escape in this way. He felt proud of his wood: even secretly patriotic, as though by means of it he were helping to maintain England. It had also drawn him just a little into village society, for he would throw the wood open for an annual school treat, going about it on the previous evening hanging the trees with toys, bags of sweets, and swatches of bananas.

From the beginning, he foresaw the effect that the wood might have on him, depicting this satirically in an essay, 'My Wood', published in the *New Leader* in 1926. In the first place (the essay ran) the wood made him feel heavy and laden and a 'man of weight', like the one who failed to get into the kingdom of Heaven. In the second place, it made him feel it ought to be larger.

The other day I heard a twig snap on it. I was annoyed at first, for I thought that someone was blackberrying, and depreciating the value of the undergrowth. On coming nearer, I saw it was not a man who had trodden on the twig and snapped it, but a bird, and I felt pleased. My bird. The bird was not equally pleased. Ignoring the relation between us, it took fright as soon as it saw the shape of my face, and flew straight over the boundary hedge into a field, the property of Mrs Hennessy, where it sat down with a loud squawk. It had become Mrs Hennessy's bird. Something seemed grossly amiss here, something that would not have occurred had the wood been larger. I could not afford to buy Mrs Hennessy out, I dared not murder her, and limitations of this sort beset me on every side. Ahab did not want that vineyard – he only needed it to round off his property preparatory to plotting a new curve – and all the land around my wood has become necessary to me in order to round off the wood. A boundary protects. But – poor little thing – the boundary ought in turn to be protected.

The essay was prophetic, for he was eventually to be parted both from his house and his wood, partly through his own fault, and was made to reflect ruefully on the influence of property on his character.

How he came to lose his property is a long, petty and slow-moving country tale. From the time of Aunt Laura's first acquiring land from her friends the Farrers in 1877, the latters' lawyers (who were Farrers themselves) had disliked the transaction, regarding her proposed house as an evil. Thus, though she wanted to buy the land freehold, she was only allowed to take a lease; and, having been advised that she might begin building before formalities were all settled, she had found, too late, that the lease would be only for the very short term of sixty years. The lease was also hard on her in other ways, and friends told her it was iniquitous, but she had decided that her only plan was silence,[1] since any complaint might injure her friendship with Lady Farrer.[2]

Her friendship with the Farrers had thus continued; indeed it had strengthened, so that, during the second Lord Farrer's brief widowhood, she would sometimes act as hostess at his table. After Thomas Farrer's remarriage relations cooled a little, and during her last years, Forster gained the impression that she felt neglected. However, she never admitted it; and, to the eyes of the world at least,

---

[1] This at least was her own account. Many years later, the Farrers' agent told Forster that, on the contrary, she had written 'vitriolic' letters.
[2] Euphemia Farrer, née Wedgwood, second wife of the first Lord Farrer.

she had remained till her death the close and honoured friend of the Farrer family.

Thus, when Forster inherited West Hackhurst, he assumed that, should he and his mother decide to occupy the house, Lord Farrer, out of friendship, would not insist strictly on the terms of the lease. To make sure, he put the question tactfully to him, and Farrer had replied, reasonably, that if he were still alive in 1937 he would be glad to consider an extension of the lease, but he did not feel he could bind his heirs. Forster, still anxious, pressed for stronger assurances, and to this Farrer answered, more frostily, that he did not understand what Forster wanted him to do.

From the beginning, therefore, of Forster and his mother's residence in Abinger there was some uneasiness in their minds over the house – also a faint edginess towards the Farrers personally. The Farrers owned most of the parish, and Tom Farrer played the lord of the manor in a rather heavy-handed fashion. Nevertheless, as connections of Aunt Laura's, Forster and Lily expected some notice from them, and it seemed slow in coming. Lily, indeed – being shy at the memory that she had once been a governess at Abinger Hall – would say that when the Farrers invited them to dinner she would not accept and would let Forster go on his own, for it would be him they really wanted. She need not have worried, for the invitation never came. The Farrers were cordial when encountered by chance, but otherwise they were silent. Or rather, so the Forsters said to themselves, they were silent till they wanted something, such as a subscription or a personal favour. A daughter of Lord Farrer asked Lily one day, in a breezy fashion, whether they were using Aunt Laura's old coachhouse, and if not, might she use it for her car? Lily refused rather sharply, saying it was full of furniture.

All this was insignificant, and the Forsters would merely say to each other, from time to time: 'Do you notice how little we hear of the Farrers?', or 'Really, the Farrers mightn't be there.' Then the day came when Forster went to Abinger Hall on a philanthropic errand. It was on behalf of his gardener, Henry Bone, whose brother Charles was in trouble, having been sent to prison for sexual assault. Lady Farrer,[1] who was a magistrate, had shown kindness and enterprise over the affair and had pulled strings for Charles Bone to be

[1] Evangeline Farrer, *née* Knox (*d.* 1968).

transferred to a mental hospital. However, there had arisen a question as to which mental hospital he should go to. The Bone family had heard bad reports of the one of Lady Farrer's choice, and Forster had come to urge the claims of one at Brookwood.

He never felt at his best in Abinger Hall. He became, he thought, too ingratiating, and at the same time anxious to be 'independent and interesting'. Also, perhaps, too Bohemian. Unthinkingly, on the present visit, he sat, as he often did, perched sideways on the edge of his chair, with one knee on the floor, and it occurred to him, too late, that Lady Farrer might despise him for this. He wondered, too, whether scandal about his London life might not have reached her ears. He was thus in a selfconscious mood on this occasion, and the interview turned out badly. After much smiling debate, about personal relationships versus 'the interests of the community as a whole', Lady Farrer lost her temper and snubbed him: 'You cannot expect a separate institution for each case,' she said crushingly. He showed no reaction but, after an interval, snubbed her back. 'I quite agree, Lady Farrer,' he said, 'with what you were just saying about the impossibility of a separate institution for each person; but perhaps you will agree with me that when there are two institutions, one wants to choose the more suitable of the two?' He gained his point, and Charles Bone was sent to Brookwood as he wished, but the little clash was not forgotten.

Another ensued. When the lease of West Hackhurst was near to running out, Forster reminded Lord Farrer of his promise, and Farrer declared himself ready to honour his promise and continue the lease during Lily's lifetime. There was a snag, however. The lease would only be renewed on condition that Forster sold Lord Farrer Piney Copse. It was a reasonable proposal, for he was to retain the right to rent it during his lifetime. None the less it incensed Forster, who by now loved his wood dearly – feeling that in buying it he had shown himself independent, not a mere humble continuer of his aunt's traditions. Moreover, he did not like the declension in Lord Farrer's letters from 'Morgan' to 'Forster' to 'Mr Forster'. His lawyers told him he had no redress, but he pondered, and a cunning stratagem occurred to him. Lord Farrer was on the committee of the National Trust. What if he, Forster, were to undertake to leave the wood to the National Trust in his will? His lawyers could see no flaw in the plan. (They looked cross when he suggested it, which he thought a good omen.) And accordingly a letter was concocted, saying that Mr Forster had a strong sentimental feeling for Piney Copse, as his one piece of freehold property, and was not disposed to sell it. Nevertheless, he realized that it affected the amenities of West Hackhurst, so he proposed to leave it to the National Trust, a body which, he knew, had Lord Farrer's warmest support. A silence ensued, lasting several months, and then at last a letter came, agreeing to the arrangement.

Two months later he was involved with the Farrers in a battle about a footpath. There was a field running down from West Hackhurst to the village, and Forster rented this, as Aunt Laura had done before him, for the sake of a path across it which provided the most direct route to the village. He had no other use for the field and when, some years before, the Cecil Farrers, Lord Farrer's son and daughter-in-law, had come to live nearby at High Hackhurst, Forster had renounced the upper half of the field to them. Now, however, he received a letter in the guise of a poem, supposedly from Mrs Farrer's horse May Moon, complaining that May Moon felt cramped for pasture, and asking, would not the kind Mr Forster give her the rest of the field? Forster returned a stinger, addressed to Cecil himself, saying that, while he commended his wife's literary skill, he felt in no mood to appreciate this informal approach, after the anxieties he had been put to over Piney Copse. Cecil replied that it was his wife's affair, not his, and could not Forster and she meet on the disputed territory for further discussion? They did so, and Mrs Farrer pointed out the new route she envisaged for the Forsters' path. It was much longer and ran past a slaughterhouse and through a bed of nettles, and Forster said he was afraid it would not suit his mother, who was now such a poor walker. Mrs Farrer, not listening, continued: 'There should be some pegs. Yes, here they are.' 'Pegs?' exclaimed Forster, 'How did they get there?' and she explained that Cecil and she had gone into the field in his absence and marked out the proposed new path. With hauteur he replied, 'I own myself greatly surprised'; and the two walked back uphill, and parted, without another word. No more was heard about the path for some years, so Forster had won another battle.

A battle, however, presupposes a war, and the thought of war seems to have originated on Forster's rather than on the Farrers' side. There was some anti-upper-class feeling involved. He com-

plained to Bob Buckingham, at the time of the footpath row: 'These
are the people who will be heirs to a considerable property and were
educated at Eton . . .' etc. And combined with this there was the
growth in his own landowning and proprietorial feelings. He came
later to see them as having been unsuitable for him: they had not,
he reflected, made him more tolerant and civilized. In a memoir,[1]
written in bitterness after his expulsion from West Hackhurst, he
scathingly recorded a memory of them:

> Once I attended at Dorking a meeting of landowners who were
> trying to obstruct rural development. I was humble in their
> company and watched with awe an arrogant old hag come totter-
> ing on the arm of her cockaded chauffeur. Our aim was to make
> the country inaccessible to common people. Elbow to elbow,
> acre to acre, we were to stand firm. The old lady spoke almost
> inaudibly, and her remarks were respectfully megaphoned to the
> chairman. She signalled, the chauffeur was summoned, and she
> tottered away. A feeling of well-being came over me, yes, I was
> among my own sort at last, and I beamed at Tom Farrer, who
> made no acknowledgement. That was my nearest approach to
> feudalism. My next nearest had been at the age of fourteen, in the
> Howards End house in Hertfordshire. We were turned out of it.
> If the land had welcomed me then, if it had welcomed me more
> effectively at West Hackhurst, the Tory side of my character
> would have developed, and my liberalisms been atrophied.

---

[1] 'West Hackhurst: a Surrey Ramble.' The present chapter is largely based
on this memoir.

9 The Last Parade

The contest over Bob Buckingham had continued but was now less near the surface. For one thing, May was preoccupied with her son Robin. And apart from this, she had long accepted that Bob should have a separate life with Forster and Forster's friends. It had not wrecked their marriage. Indeed the marriage had proved a most successful one. They had a cheerful social life in Shepherd's Bush, had become mildly 'artistic', and were very up-to-date as parents; Rob's sleep-time and the temperature of his food were calculated according to the latest theories. They became quite censorious of a young policeman friend and his wife upstairs, over their old-fashioned methods of child-rearing.

Then, at the beginning of 1935, it was discovered that May was suffering from tuberculosis. She was quite seriously ill and would have to go to a sanatorium for at least a year. Forster was greatly concerned at the news. By now, for better for worse, he was firmly established as the family friend, and he took part in all the discussions and arrangements. It was decided to send Robin to a sister of May's; and since Bob, who was a hypochondriac, was persuading himself he might be tubercular too, Forster made a pact with May to watch over him and report to her. May had laughed at the torrent of notes from him to Bob that had flowed through their letter-box. Now she began to receive such a stream too. Forster sent her books and suggestions for reading, offered her pictures and photographs for the walls of her room at the sanatorium, and gave her much sympathetic advice. 'The great thing,' he wrote (10 April 1935), ' is that you and R. should worry about one another as little as possible – mutual worry is like holding up two looking glasses in front of each other, so that a thing gets reflected to infinity.' He went sometimes to see her at the sanatorium at Pinewood (though, as he remarked to Bob, he found he got on better with her by letter), and he recruited various friends of his to visit her too. For some time now he had come to revise his opinion of her, admitting grudgingly that she was 'a decent sort' and inventing the theory that it was a case of a good person (Bob) – together with the baby – transforming an inferior one. Now he began actually to warm to her; and she, who had always wanted his friendship, responded with great good will. By imperceptible degrees during this year, the two became friends and allies.

*   *   *

T. E. Lawrence had returned from India in 1929, having once more been hunted out from a retreat by newspaper reports, which said, this time, that he was Britain's 'top spy' and had been fomenting a revolt in Afghanistan.[1] He had been posted first to Plymouth, to work on R.A.F. flying-boats, going subsequently to Southampton, where he had been employed in experimental work on speedboat design. He was, meanwhile, conducting a behind-the-scenes campaign for the improvement of conditions in the Services. He had aged and was less restless, though still half-toying with visions of himself as a national saviour.[2] Forster would go down to see him at Plymouth or Southampton from time to time and would be taken for trips in Lawrence's speedboat. When Frederic Manning's outspoken novel of trench-life, *Her Privates We,* was published in 1930, Lawrence, who was a friend of Manning's, induced Forster to read it, and Forster, who was greatly impressed, went to some lengths to promote Manning's reputation. Lawrence made much of Forster's friendship, telling Robert Graves, in 1933: 'I think Frederic Manning and an Armenian called Altounyan,[3] and E. M. Forster are the three I most care for, since Hogarth[4] died.'

---

[1] He may have helped to spread the rumours himself.

[2] Winston Churchill wanted him, when he retired from the R.A.F., to help to re-organize the nation's defences.

[3] Ernest Altounyan (1889–1962). He was a doctor and poet and published a sequence of poems *Ornament of Honour* (1937) in memory of Lawrence. Forster was very friendly with him round about 1915 but they were later estranged.

[4] D. G. Hogarth (1862–1927), the archaeologist and orientalist, a major influence on Lawrence's career.

Lawrence received his discharge from the R.A.F. in 1935 and was planning to spend his retirement in his Clouds Hill cottage. He wrote to Forster (26 November 1934) that he was looking forward 'fantastically' to receiving him at Clouds Hill. 'There are no beds (but two sleeping bags embroidered MEUM and TUUM) no food, no drains: nightjars (outdoor pattern) and wood fires and slow talk. Many good records upstairs, and a windy gramophone.' Forster offered himself for the 13th of the following May, receiving back a postcard (bearing the printed legend: 'To tell you that in future I shall write very few letters. T.E.S.'[1]) to say that his arrival would be marked by the setting of a white stone into a newly-built wall. On the very day, however, that Forster was to arrive, he received the news of Lawrence's fatal motor-cycle accident.

The affair, like so much else in Lawrence's life, was surrounded with mystery and official secrecy, and it affected Forster powerfully. He did not attend the funeral, but went down to Clouds Hill a few days afterwards, in the company of Sassoon and his wife, and was shown by a young neighbour and friend of Lawrence's, Pat Knowles, the preparations Lawrence and Knowles had made for Forster's visit. 'Every thing very grey and quiet and touching in the rhododendron dell,' Forster wrote to Isherwood (1 June 1935), 'but outside I knew Lord Lloyd[2] was waiting. S. said he looked absolutely foul at the funeral. Well he must vomit for someone else now.'

The thought of Lawrence, his complex personality and his strange fate, stayed with Forster. He felt it possible that, if Lawrence had not died, some reactionary group might have got hold of him and tried to turn him into a leader. (It was an idea shared by Christopher Isherwood, whose next literary undertaking was *The Ascent of F.6*, a play – written jointly with Auden – about a Lawrence-like 'leader-figure' of this kind.) Lawrence's brother and executor, Professor A. W. Lawrence, did not want a biography written. Instead, he proposed a large edition of Lawrence's letters, and, knowing of Forster's friendship with his brother, he invited Forster to edit the volume. The notion excited Forster, and he accepted, feeling pleased to be labouring once more on Lawrence's behalf. The book was to be an

[1] i.e. 'T. E. Shaw'.
[2] Lord Lloyd of Dolobran (1879–1941), High Commissioner in Egypt 1925–9 and a friend of Lawrence's for many years. The reason for Forster's hostility is not clear.

ambitious affair, and he pondered how to shape it. Desmond Mac-Carthy advised him to divide the letters into thematic groups, supplying a separate commentary to each group – the whole to lead gradually to a final grand character-portrait and estimate of Lawrence. It seemed a promising scheme, and he adopted it, finding the portrait of Lawrence soon growing under his hands.

> . . . if when the schoolboy grows up he takes to archaeology seriously, he seldom loses this primitive excitement, this thrill of adventure, reinforcing the thrill of research. The trespassing-spirit persists, the angry farmer becomes an Arab with a gun, the clergyman and the policeman coalesce into a foreign government, which it is a pleasure to fool and a duty to spy on. It is not surprising that so many archaeologists take to secret service and do well in it. Their mentality as well as their opportunities qualifies them.
> . . . Those who get the best out of orientals usually despise the East, but he was always able to respect while he controlled them; it was one of his great virtues. And at Carchemish the idea of a crusade, vaguely conceived amongst medieval oddments, takes a bold habitation and a non-Christian character: he will free the Arabs.
> . . . The notion of a crusade, of a body of men leaving one country to do noble deeds in another, now possessed him, and I think it never left him, though the locality of the other country varied: at one time it was Arabia, later on it was the air. Had he been a Christian, his medieval equipment would have been complete and thought-proof: he would have possessed a positive faith and been happier: he would have been the 'parfit gentil knight', the defender of orthodoxy, instead of the troubled and troublous genius who fascinated his generation and failed to fit into it. He would have been much smaller.

*   *   *

Forster was now in close touch with Isherwood. By this time he had given Isherwood *Maurice* to read, and this had helped cement their friendship. Isherwood had been impressed by the novel and to Forster's enquiry 'Does it date?' had answered 'Why *shouldn't* it date?' From then on it had become a favourite occupation of theirs to devise endings to the novel.[1] Isherwood's own new novel *Mr Norris Changes Trains* had come out early in 1935, and Forster wrote to

---

[1] See Isherwood's *Christopher and his Kind* (1976), pp. 125–7.

him about it (11 May 1935) with a mixture of admiration and reserve:

> Have now read Mr Norris twice and have had much admiration
> and enjoyment. I liked it less the first time because it is not
> altogether my sort of book – dwells on contradictions rather than
> the complexities of character and seems to reveal people facet by
> facet whereas the Memorial if my memory serves tackled strata.
> However I got over that and managed to read what you've
> written, I think. The construction is fine and Margot was a
> complete surprise to me. It's marvellous too the way you've
> maintained standards of right and wrong and yet left Norris an
> endearing person. And you've made him both silly and witty,
> like a character in Congreve. He's awfully good. The necessity of
> combining knowingness and honesty in William renders him more
> of a problem, for in art these are uneasy bedfellows. However you
> bring him through pretty well. I was a little worried in Switzerland
> to what extent he was paying his employer's way with the Baron.
> Did he go the whole hog or turn a pig-skin cheek? I don't the least
> mind, but feel that in the first case he would violate the fastidious-
> ness and in the second the integrity of his character. – Still perhaps
> I needn't worry, for he was only hired to make the Baron move,
> not to make him happy . . .

Isherwood was living with a young German named Heinz. Heinz had
fled Germany to escape conscription, and, partly for this reason, the
two were continually on their travels, moving from Greece to the
Canary Isles to Brussels to Amsterdam in quest of some alternative
citizenship for Heinz. From one country or another Isherwood
repeatedly urged Forster to join them, and this summer – May
Buckingham being still in the sanatorium – Forster took Bob
Buckingham to stay with Isherwood in Amsterdam. The city was
then a resort for anti-fascist writers, forming a circle round Klaus
Mann, who was running a newspaper there. Stephen Spender and
Brian Howard were in Amsterdam when Forster arrived, as was
Gerald Hamilton, the original or part-original, of Isherwood's 'Mr
Norris'. The English party, Forster and Buckingham among them,
went about Holland on a sightseeing tour, talking loudly against
Hitler wherever they went. In a restaurant in The Hague (in which
there was a large lady with a whip) they became aware of two
detectives or spies listening to their conversation. The detectives
followed them through the Mauritshuis gallery, then disappeared in
the wake of Hamilton, who took the train for Rotterdam; but the

same evening in Amsterdam, another spy attached himself to the party in a café. At least, Bob thought it was a spy, Forster reported to May Buckingham, 'It may have been mere honest curiosity – you know how Stephen Spender squeals and giggles, and his sounds must have been carrying far through the night.'

*   *   *

For much of the autumn of 1935 Forster was going through old articles of his, making a selection for the volume *Abinger Harvest*. He gave a good deal of creative thought to the shaping of the volume, also taking advice from friends, especially William Plomer. As late as the proof stage he was writing to Plomer (24 November 1935): 'Can you support me in withdrawing from Part I: Kipling, Edward VII and the Clemenceau novel[1] they are all good, but weaken the section. They cannot go into Part II, because nothing is ragged there. – Roger Fry also interpolates; he might close Part III but I don't think so.' There had been argument about a title for the book, and, he told Plomer, people made 'a face like a shrew mouse' when they heard what he had chosen.

He was working under difficulties. For a year or two he had been suffering from a bladder disorder, and he had now begun to have sick headaches. Eventually, in December, he was told that he must have an operation on the prostate. His mother, though usually calm in the face of illness, was alarmist and convinced herself he would die under the operation. He, remembering Dickinson, thought this quite likely himself. Half an hour before leaving for the nursing-home, he wrote Bob Buckingham a tender letter, telling him he felt cheerful and calm but 'have an open mind whether I shall get through or not. I don't feel afraid of anything, and it is your love that has made me like this.'

The first part of the operation was performed on 18 December and, soon after it, blithe messages were arriving from him. To Bob Buckingham, 'Tell May that I have started re-reading "Mansfield Park" and not Lady Bertram could feel more tranquil.' To Bessie Trevelyan, 'I write to most people in pencil if at all, to underline how ill I am, but ink is more convenient really . . .' The second and main part of the operation was performed in February. It was again quite successful, but the wound took long to heal, so that he remained in

---

[1] Review of *The Strongest*, by Georges Clemenceau, in the *Athenaeum*, 27 February 1920.

the nursing-home all through March. He was full of plans for what
he would do on his recovery. He meant, he told Isherwood (25
February 1936), to 'visit the English Lakes, Portugal and Dorsetshire,
reform the Police Courts, read all Milton, not lift a finger to hinder
the next world-war, be very kind, very selfish, and incidentally write
masterpieces.' However, a fortnight after his release from the
nursing-home, he received a new and different kind of blow: Arnold's
wrote to tell him that he was to be sued for libel.

The occasion was an article, 'A Flood in the Office' – one of those
from his Egyptian period, which he had reprinted in *Abinger Harvest*.
It was a review of a pamphlet in which Sir William Willcocks, an
engineer in the Egyptian administration, had attacked a fellow-
engineer, Sir Murdoch MacDonald, over his projects for the Nile
waters. It was an entertaining piece, picturing the two sources of the
Nile as another pair of warring old gentlemen, and it came down
strongly on Sir William's side. However, as it now appeared, Sir
Murdoch had, in the meantime, sued Sir William for libel in an
Egyptian court and won his case; thus Forster, by reprinting the
article, had unwittingly but indisputably repeated a libel. At first it
seemed as if Sir Murdoch would settle for the withdrawal of *Abinger
Harvest* in its present form, combined perhaps with a formal apology
and a token payment to charity. 'We staged him as a nice cross old
gentleman,' Forster told Isherwood. However, it turned out that
Sir Murdoch was an unforgiving old gentleman and was out for heavy
damages, and Forster and Arnold's had, in the end, to pay £500 in
damages plus costs. This, with the considerable expense of withdrawing and reissuing *Abinger Harvest* without the offending article,
was a serious blow to Forster. In his state of physical weakness he
took it very hard. He began to worry about libel dangers in his work
on T. E. Lawrence, which indeed were considerable, and tried to
extract a guarantee of immunity from the Lawrence trustees. They
were sympathetic but could not give him the full assurance that he
wanted, and after protracted negotiations, he decided to resign from
the editorship of the letters. It left him feeling sore – not with the
Lawrence trustees, but with the libel laws. It had discouraged and
thwarted him in his writing hopes, and as a result he did not undertake another book for fifteen or more years.

*   *   *

During July, while he was still convalescing, he went with his mother to stay in Dover, in some lodgings rented by Joe Ackerley. Dover had begun to be a vogue among his friends. William Plomer spent a whole year at about this period in a flat at the West end of the promenade. He was followed by Joe Ackerley, who took rooms there for several summers. Isherwood and W. H. Auden[1] would come there for briefer periods, and Leo Charlton and Tom Wichelo eventually deserted Maida Vale to settle in Dover permanently (or, in Leo's fruity phrase, to 'pitch camp beneath the lintel of England's continental doorway').

It was a pretty place, a barrack-town of fine early-Victorian terraces crowned by a Norman castle and encircled by grassy hills. Tourists did not visit it much, and the streets were quiet by day, while at evening the pubs filled up with soldiers from the four regiments garrisoned there. Plomer in his memoirs[2] describes the 'frou-frou' of kilts in the streets, and Auden also evoked the spectacle in his poem 'Dover':

> Soldiers crowd into the pubs in their pretty clothes,
> As pink and as silly as girls from a high-class academy.

The soldiers were a leading attraction, especially for Charlton and Ackerley, who would comb the pubs in the evening.[3] But, apart from this, the place was convenient for habitual travellers like Isherwood and Auden, who would stay with friends there on their way to Brussels or Amsterdam or would arrange meetings with them at the nearby Ostend. Further, the place had a symbolical or allegorical significance. To live in Dover, the last extremity of England, had a flavour of Europeanism. (This aspect was likewise caught in Auden's poem:

---

[1] Auden would come there to write and would work with the blinds drawn against the daylight. May Buckingham, who sometimes stayed there as Forster's guest, remembered Auden emerging from his rooms, with white face, blinking like an owl. It also worried her how appallingly he bit his nails.

[2] *At Home* (1958), p. 154.

[3] Oddly, however, in *More Charlton* (1940), Leo Charlton wrote with sanctimonious severity of those who came to Dover for 'the satisfaction of unwholesome appetites'.

> From London, from neighbouring resorts, men would appear who were clearly recognizable for what they were. Flabby features, an effeminate bulk of body, a mincing gait, furtive glances and a curious clipped pronunciation marked the type, whose prey was youth and whose bait was silver coin.

Aeroplanes drone through the new European air
On the edge of a sky that makes England of minor importance.)

Forster became fond of the place and the life that had developed
there, and over this and the following two summers he came there
repeatedly, bringing his mother or the Buckinghams or friends like
John Simpson and Sprott. He took lodgings with the same landladies
as Joe Ackerley, two friendly but very 'correct' sisters nicknamed by
Leo Charlton 'the Holy Ladies'.

At Dover, and elsewhere, he was now seeing something of W. H.
Auden. Auden, the previous year, had married Erika Mann, Thomas
Mann's daughter, as a device to procure her a British passport, and
he wanted other homosexuals to make similar marriages. ('What
are buggers for?' he would say.) With Forster's help, he recruited
John Simpson, arranging for him to marry a German actress friend
of Erika's, Therese Giehse. The marriage took place in a registry
office in Solihull. (Auden – in striped trousers and with a carnation –
took charge with great zest, answering all the clerk's questions on
the bride's behalf and standing double brandies all round after the
ceremony, declaring 'It's on Thomas Mann'.) Auden and Isherwood
had completed their play, *The Ascent of F.6*. It was published in book
form in October 1936, receiving a flattering review from Forster in
the *Listener*, and a stage-production by Rupert Doone's Group
Theatre company was arranged at the Mercury Theatre in Notting
Hill Gate for the following February. It was an important occasion
for them and their group. Benjamin Britten, then twenty-three, had
been engaged to write incidental music, and Auden's friend, the
painter Robert Medley, was to design the sets. Forster came to a
dress-rehearsal and witnessed an angry scene between Britten and
Rupert Doone, when Doone – a very *prima donna*-ish director –
demanded last-minute cuts in Britten's score. He brought Bob
Buckingham and John Simpson to the opening night. Isherwood was
in high excitement before the curtain rose. 'Oh dear! Oh dear!' he
kept saying, 'What shall I do? I don't think I can sit down,' till Bob
Buckingham took him out for a drink in a nearby pub. Next day,
Forster wrote him a detailed critique of the production:

> ... Act I – splendid. My only query was Mrs R's circumambulation,
> the discussion about the two sons, and the shrinking away of
> Levantine James: 'But this will come clear later on.'

Act II – kept me more critical. The *monk* – not good nor good to look at. Presages are not interesting in themselves, and Ransom's, which is interesting, comes out well enough in his ensuing talk with the Abbot. John S[impson] and I felt the monk could be cut.

The *Abbot* – the finest scene in the whole play. Quite marvellous. Then troubles gather, for which the meagre scenery isn't wholly responsible. The elimination of Lamp made me wonder 'How will they get rid of the other two?' Ian's was good – jealousy does carry one along. David's too slow. Then Ransom – falling into the audience almost, realistic, panting 'I will kill the demon' – it wouldn't live in that theatrical bleakness, nor would Mrs R's rocking chair.

He had disliked the Freudian *coup de théâtre* in the last act, in which the hero, on the mountain-top, is spectrally confronted by his mother, seated in her rocking-chair. He told Isherwood: 'Mother on the ice-throne, not rocking-chair. The rocking-chair is the sounder, but it won't come across. It's a moment when you *must* sacrifice psychological propriety to poetry.' Others too had objected to this scene, and for the next week or so they tried out a different ending each night. When Auden, who had been in Spain, eventually came to see the play, he exclaimed to Isherwood in a loud and carrying whisper: 'My *dear*, what have you *done* to it?'

Forster admired, and rather idealized, Isherwood's anxious efforts on behalf of Heinz, which seemed to him an epitome of friendship's role in the present state of Europe. A month or two after the play, he had a chance to give Heinz a helping hand himself. Heinz was alone in Paris, penniless and in trouble with the police, and Forster and Auden, who happened to be in Paris at the time, went about borrowing money from friends to get him out of the country and into Luxembourg. It was nearly the end of Heinz's wanderings, for shortly afterwards, as part of an expensive (and possibly quite phantasmal) plan concocted by Gerald Hamilton to procure him a Mexican passport, he ventured into German-occupied Trier and was at once arrested.

*   *   *

Steadily, the crisis in Europe invaded Forster's thoughts. '. . . the collapse of civilization seems to eat up from below in to any thing I do', he recorded in his Commonplace Book (5 September 1936). He recalled how Machiavelli and certain Chinese sages had believed that, to tranquillize the mind before reading and writing, one must perform prescribed rituals, reflecting how contemptuous he would once have been of such weakness. Now he felt differently:

> A clean table and proper lighting made me solider, I find. Tonight I have swept all the rubbish off my board and read some of Oedipus Tyrannus with only the lamp and two vases in sight. One vase had four roses, the other a spray of oak leaves: the acorns, when the sun falls on them, have a blue bloom.

When, on 5 January 1937, he read the news of the landing of 10,500 Italian troops in Spain, he wrote to Isherwood telling him he felt the world to be 'close to the edge'. In the present time, he said, the passage in literature which most satisfied him was the one in *War and Peace* about the Russians after the fall of Moscow: '. . . Those who were striving to understand the general course of events, and trying by self-sacrifice and heroism to take a hand in it, were the most useless members of society; they saw everything upside down, and all they did for the common good proved to be futile and absurd.'[1]

There was much going-and-coming of his younger left-wing friends between England and Spain, and the spectacle impressed him as dubious and frivolous. 'Did you know that Christopher, Stephen, Auden and some more geese were going to a literary conference at Valencia including a day at *Madrid*?' he wrote to Bob Buckingham in June 1937. 'I never heard such nonsense, and the Foreign Office fortunately shares my feelings and has refused them visas.' When, at a party, one of his friends asked him why he wasn't going to Spain himself, he answered, deflatingly, 'Afraid to!' By contrast, when Stephen Spender wrote to him in distress over his friend Tony Hyndman,[2] who had joined the International Brigade, and asked Forster to use his influence with Harry Pollitt[3] to get Hyndman released, he persuaded Spender that he should go to Hyndman's rescue himself.

Now that his waking thoughts were hag-ridden by international affairs, he found himself living a more and more vivid nocturnal dream-life, repeatedly waking with a dream-sentence on his lips. He made a collection of such sentences in his Commonplace Book: 'The

---

[1] *War and Peace*, trans. Rosemary Edmonds; Book 4, Part I, Section iv.
[2] See Spender's *World Within World* (1951) for a long account of this episode.
[3] General Secretary of the Communist Party in Great Britain.

proud treacherous night has almost puzzled me'; 'How country-simple the white mice! How very young . . .'; 'A pretty face, An eager pleasure to become the bride of either snoozling soldier'; 'I merely told you the intelligent talk of an important husband'; 'Oh I always do admire the royal family of your foolery'. He welcomed the dreams, which gave him a sense of freshness and richness, but he told Isher-wood he thought them a proof that as a novelist he had 'gone under-ground'. Occasionally, too, in his waking hours, he had moments of a pure and mystical self-forgetfulness in which – as was always the tendency of Forster's imagination – the world seemed to become more real rather than less.[1] A note, headed 'Bunch of Sensations', records one such moment:

> Listening in the late dusk to gramophone records I did not know; smoking; the quarter moon shone as the light faded, and brought out sections of my books; motors coming down the Felday road shone through the window and flung the tulip tree and pane shadows on the wallpaper near the fireplace. When the music stopped I felt something had arrived in the room; the sense of a world that asks to be noticed rather than explained was again upon me.

His life with his mother continued much as before, a mixture of devotion and exasperation. At eighty, Lily had grown dumpy, solid and matriarchal – not a dragon, but someone whose wishes were to be obeyed. She was soft-voiced and outwardly serene, making a joke of anything she disliked, and caricaturing her own intolerances. She once told her nephew, Philip Whichelo,[2] how a young girl had said to her, 'Oh don't be silly.' 'That dished her,' said Lily. In late years she had become a wireless-addict, saying that the wireless had cured her loneliness, and if bored or irritated she would clamp on her ear-phones. Florence Barger, who believed in serious conversation, com-plained: 'I think you would listen to nonsense on that thing, rather than not listen.' 'Well yes, dear,' answered Lily, 'I think that at my age I would.'

---

[1] In Forster's descriptive passage in his novels, he constantly writes as though inanimate nature had purposes and volitions of its own. I remember him in the last year of his life saying, during a car-drive, that ancient roads 'still consented to move him'.

[2] Philip Whichelo (1905–), son of Lily's brother Horace. He became an artist and stage-designer.

To Forster's London friends she was always very pleasant – even, with an effort, showing graciousness to Bob Buckingham, whom she resented, and making quite a friendship with May Buckingham. Of Sprott and Plomer she had a high opinion. When, a year or two later, Plomer published a description of Forster,[1] mentioning his dowdy appearance, she was delighted. 'You see, Morgie, what Mr Plomer says about you,' she said. 'How often have I told you to brush your coat.' Joe Ackerley pleased her less. She thought him not quite the thing. Once he came to lunch at West Hackhurst in an open-necked short-sleeved shirt, and she remarked afterwards, 'Wasn't that an *extraordinary* thing to do?' Ackerley was scurrilous about her, referring to her, to Forster, as 'Your mouldy old mother.'

To outside observers she and Forster seemed very close, almost as if sharing a private language. He would play up to her with, as he called it, 'bright prankishness' and was endlessly solicitous for her welfare, hinting to visitors how they might give her pleasure. ('I think she would be very interested in that.') He knew her fears and did his best to protect her from them. Once, when he was visiting his Aunt Rosalie in Putney, his aunt said she had just written to Lily, reporting that Nellie was ill and must go to hospital. He was angry, thinking this an inconsiderate way to break the news, and, putting down his teacup, instantly set off home to forestall the letter. In a way, now that his fate as a writer was settled, his dependence on Lily irked him less deeply, and he could see more clearly what he owed her. 'I wonder whether women are important to one's comfort and stability,' he wrote to Ackerley at about this period:

> I am inclined to think that may be. Although my mother has been intermittently tiresome for the last thirty years, cramped and warped my genius, hindered my career, blocked and buggered up my house, and boycotted my beloved, I have to admit that she has provided a sort of rich subsoil where I have been able to rest and grow. That, rather than sex or wifiness, seems to be women's special gift to men.

*   *   *

In the space of six months, during 1937, Forster lost the two closest of his Indian friends, Masood and Tukoji, the now-deposed Maharaja of Dewas. (In a way, their fates had a certain resemblance.) Masood,

---

[1] Later incorporated in his autobiography *At Home* (1958), p. 107.

having accepted the Vice-Chancellorship at Aligarh in 1929, had thrown himself into his role with energy. He was a skilful fund-raiser and had done much to restore the University's reputation. Nevertheless, from the start, he had had powerful enemies in Aligarh, both political and private ones, and he was not well equipped to cope with opposition; he was too high-handed, too inclined to ask 'Are you for me or against me?' He had, moreover, from quite early on, offended the British authorities, by inviting Gandhi and Nehru to speak at Aligarh. The opposition to him had grown, and in 1934 he had been outvoted in the University Court over the matter of a staff appointment. His friends told him that the meeting had been deliberately packed with 'flunkeys' of the government, flown in for the occasion by chartered plane, and in dudgeon he had resigned. This defeat, taking place in the University created by his own grandfather, had more or less wrecked him. His friend and colleague Sherwani saw him the day before he left Aligarh, sitting forlornly in his dismantled drawing-room; he cried to Sherwani, 'I persuaded you to come here. I was wrong to do so. It is no place for any self-respecting person.'[1]

His friend the Begum of Bhopal had come to his aid, giving him a post as Minister of Education in her state, but he had never recovered his spirits; he was, so Sherwani said, a 'bathos' in his last years, even intellectually. He died of kidney-disease on 30 July 1937, at the age of forty-seven, and his body was flown back to Aligarh and buried in the University mosque. While at Bhopal, Masood had found a place at court for his old friend the poet Iqbal, and Iqbal inscribed on his tomb some lines in Persian originally intended for his own epitaph. He also wrote an elegy on Masood, describing him as 'the most precious possession of the nation's caravan.'[2]

Forster and Masood had drifted apart in recent years – Forster had found Masood 'too pompous and reticent'. Nevertheless, the brief announcement of the death in *The Times* came as a deep shock to Forster. Masood's son Akbar hurried back from France to join him, and for a few days the two waited anxiously for further news; there seemed to be some mystery about the death and, now or later,

[1] Information from Professor Sherwani.
[2] In the years to come, Masood came to be honoured as one of the heroes of Pakistan, and a 'Ross Masood Education and Culture Society' was founded in Karachi. A symposium on him, *Muraqqa-e-Masood*, edited by Jalil A. Kidwai, was published in Karachi on 'Ross Masood Day' in 1966.

vague rumours of poisoning. Eventually Forster bought Akbar an
air-ticket and saw him off to India, guessing – rightly – that he would
find much family dissension and little in the way of inheritance. Soon
after the death, there was a memorial number in Masood's honour in
the Urdu journal *Anjuman-e-Taraqqi-e-Urdu* and Forster contributed a loving account of him.[1] 'There never was anyone like him,'
it said, 'and there never will be anyone like him.' He never forgot
Masood or what their friendship had meant to him. A year or so later
he was visiting Akbar at Oxford, in his college rooms, and saw a
drawing of Masood on the wall. He told Akbar it was so lifelike, he
could not bear to sit with it, and asked if they could go out.[2]

The Maharaja of Dewas died in December of the same year, and
his final years were a tragedy on a vaster scale. Tukoji's reputation
and fortunes had never really recovered from the scandal of 1928. At
about the same time as this scandal, there had been complaints by
the peasants of Dewas of illegal exactions on his part. A commission
of inquiry had been demanded. And meanwhile, the Maharaja of
Kolhapur, Tukoji's chief enemy, had gained the ear of the Governor-
General of Bombay and had filled it with rumours: that Tukoji was
deliberately ruining his state, so as to embarrass his son on his
accession, or alternatively that he was trying to oust his son from the
succession in favour of a son by his second wife, Bai Saheba.[3] The
Maharaja of Kolhapur was even allowed to propose what terms the
British should offer Dewas and claimed that, if they were refused, he
had evidence to discredit Tukoji entirely.

From year to year, the situation had grown worse. Tukoji had
temporized, repaired some of the worse failings in his administration,
had chaffered for loans from his fellow-princes and, growing desperate,
had invited a British friend, a doctor named Sir James Roberts, to
help him put his State in order. Eventually, though, the authorities
had lost patience and, as their phrase went, had decided to 'put this
Maharaja out of business'. And at this point, the most dramatic
developments had taken place. The Maharaja, under pretext of going
on pilgrimage to South India, had absconded from his State, bearing
with him its remaining treasures, and had taken refuge in Pondicherry
in French India. The move, whether conceived as vengeance or as

---

[1] Reprinted in *Two Cheers for Democracy*.
[2] Told to the author by the late Akbar Masood.
[3] The erstwhile 'Diamond concubine', now Maharani.

diplomacy, had been quite fatal for the Maharaja, the completest *débâcle* imaginable. He had lived on for four miserable years, dishonoured, almost destitute, crowded with his large family into a shabby little house in Pondicherry, despatching innumerable and interminable telegrams to the Viceroy and to English politicians. Malcolm Darling had gone to see him in 1934, after he had been on a weeks-long penitential fast. It was a touching reunion. The Maharaja, a grey-bearded holy man, had laid his head in Darling's lap and wept. None the less, as soon as his 'case' came up, he had been as intransigent as ever. He declared: 'I am a Rajput and I should be false to all my traditions if I compromised my honour. I would much rather die than do that.' The tender-hearted Darling, after his departure, had sent the Maharaja a cheque, for more money than he could well afford, and had continued to intercede on his behalf with the British authorities – being rebuffed for his pains. He knew that, to the outside observer, the Maharaja had put himself hopelessly in the wrong. Yet he felt, and imbued Forster with the feeling, that he had been mishandled by the British. They had been 'impeccably correct' in their behaviour, and 'absolutely wrong'.[1]

On the Maharaja's death, *The Times* gave him a censorious obituary. It ran: 'He came of an ancient and renowned dynasty, and in the earlier years of his rule gave some promise of doing well, but an ungovernable temper and self-indulgence led to serious deterioration. . . .' The obituary enraged Forster, who thought it 'a model of ungenerous and prim indignation', and, in a letter published on 28 December, he did what he could in the way of rehabilitation. He wrote:

SIR TUKOJI RAO PUAR

As a friend of exactly twenty-five years' standing, may I be allowed to add a tribute of affection to the account published in your columns of the late Maharaja of Dewas (Senior Branch). Whatever his weaknesses as ruler, he possessed incomparable qualities as an individual: he was witty, gay, charming, hospitable, imaginative, and devoted, and he had above all a living sense of religion which enabled him to transcend the barriers of his creed and to make contact with all the forms of belief and disbelief. I am not the only English person who will mourn 'Bapu Sahib',

---

[1] *The Hill of Devi* (1953), p. 171. The last paragraph of Darling's autobiography *Apprentice to Power* (1966), which voices similar sentiments, was partly drafted by Forster. For further details of the affair, see Appendix, pp. 333–6.

as we called him, and who will never forget his vivid and unique
personality or cease to remember him with love.

*   *   *

Since his illness Forster had been less active on the public scene.
The illness had forced him to resign the presidency of the N.C.C.L.;
and his work for the Permanent Bureau of Malraux's *Writers in
Defence of Culture* did not amount to much, though once or twice he
did some peace-making between the French and English branches.
In the summer of 1937, however, he agreed to take part in an
entretien organized by the League of Nation's Committee for Intellectual Co operation. This was the body which Bernard Shaw had
advised him to exploit; it had been conceived early in the 1920s by
Henri Bergson, to be an expression of 'the deepest spirit of the
League', and recently had been taken up with enthusiasm by Gilbert
Murray, who had become president. The *entretien*, on 'The Immediate
Future of Literature', was a four-day affair beginning in July and
chaired alternately by Paul Valéry and Gilbert Murray. Forster spoke
(or rather delivered a written paper in French) on the theme of the
special situation of the writer. The writer, he said, differed from other
citizens in having a double duty: to promote the general welfare; but
also to express his own personality.

> It is not a plain straightforward opposition between art, a good
> thing, and government, an evil thing. It is rather an opposition
> between two cosmogonies, the spontaneous and the administra-
> tive, each with its rival conception of civilization, and at the
> moment the administrative is winning . . .

He found the *entretien* a very polite, very official French occasion and
rather futile. The most burning question, the treatment of writers in
totalitarian counties, was discreetly played down, and the one ripple
of animation, amongst the gilt chairs and the tapestries of the Palais
Royal, was a parochial French dispute over state aid for literature.[1]

It was the time of the great Paris Exhibition, and Bob Buckingham
came over to Paris to visit it with him. Forster had been invited by
John Lehmann to report on it for *New Writing*, and in the resulting
article, 'The Last Parade', he evoked, out of the neon-lights and
fireworks of the Exhibition, a vision of the coming war – an aerial

---

[1] See 'A Conversation', *Spectator*, 13 August 1937, and *Le destin prochain
des lettres* (League of Nations, Paris, 1938).

war of poison-gas and 'vesicant dew' – and of the approaching extinction of civilization.

> O splendour unequalled! Splendour ever to be surpassed? Probably never to be surpassed. The German and Russian Pavilions, the Chinese and Japanese Pavilions, the British and Italian Pavilions, and all of the pavilions will see to that. The Eiffel Tower sings louder, a scientific swan. Rosy chemicals stimulate her spine, she can scarcely bear the voltage, the joy, the pain . . . The emotion goes to her tiny head, it turns crimson and vomits fiery serpents . . . the rockets fall, the senses disentangle. There is silence, there are various types of silences, and during one of them the Angel of the Laboratory speaks. 'Au revoir, mes enfants,' she says. 'I hope you have enjoyed yourselves. We shall meet again shortly, and in different conditions.'

His vision had grown more despairing, and his hopes, such as they had ever been, of writers' congresses and declarations of 'commitment', had dwindled. When Rosamund Lehmann invited him to speak at one such occasion, he refused. 'These gatherings of worried writers,' he wrote (27 April 1938), 'serve, it seems to me, no further purpose than this showing where one stands. Neither the Government nor official Labour, nor any other organization with power behind it, will pay the least attention to them. Their only chance is to *do* something – instead of meeting one another and one another's hangers-on. And I don't know what they should do, or what I, as one of them should do. If I did I would come and say.' (When, in the Café Royal, on the eve of the Munich crisis, Goronwy Rees[1] challenged him, saying 'Why have you given up politics?' he replied, 'Because I want just a *little* result.')

In January 1938 Auden and Isherwood set off for China, to collect material for a book about the Sino-Japanese war. Forster and Bob Buckingham attended a sending-off party at the painter Julian Trevelyan's[2] house in Hammersmith. It was a large affair, stage-managed by Rupert Doone, and, for the occasion, Britten and Auden had composed songs for the cabaret-singer Hedli Andersen and Trevelyan had decorated his walls with *collage* pictures made from lumps of wool and frying-pans. Forster told Isherwood that he and Bob enjoyed it, 'though I believe it wasn't the general verdict and

---

[1] Morgan Goronwy Rees (1909–), then assistant editor of the *Spectator*.
[2] Julian Otto Trevelyan (1910–), son of R. C. Trevelyan.

the wine-cup vile and Rupert Doone an obvious crook.' A few days before it, Isherwood had come on a visit to West Hackhurst and had talked about the China expedition in terms of the 'Test' and the need for the 'Truly Weak Man'[1] to prove himself. Forster received this with cynicism, writing to Isherwood (17 February 1938) after his departure:

> *Bother the Test* – am so certain I shall fail mine that I can't think about it. Now and then I get towards facing facts, but get too tired to keep on at it. I only hope I shan't let any one down badly: *that* thought does precise itself rather alarmingly.

However, if he had lost his trust in political gestures, he felt a growing desire to define his personal faith and philosophy. He received a stimulus to do so from reading an 'Open Letter' to himself by Julian Bell,[2] written shortly before Bell's death in the Spanish civil war. Julian Bell's brief career had been significant both as a product of, and as a revolt against, Bloomsbury values. Brought up among pacifists and 'liberal humanists', he had reacted into a cult of 'hardness' and the military virtues, deserting from pacifism to his own brand of militant Fabianism.[3] While at Cambridge in the early 1930s he had achieved some minor success as a poet, but he had fallen out with the prevailing poetic school of Auden, Day Lewis and Spender, and accused them of 'homosexual worker-worship'. The Spanish civil war had come as a challenge to him. By the time that it broke out, he had been in China, teaching literature, but he had felt compelled to return and take part in the war; and on the boat-journey home, early in 1937, he had drawn up a general statement of his beliefs in the form of three 'Letters': to Roger Fry, C. Day Lewis and Forster. In the letter to Forster his argument – or a part of it – was that war was going to come anyway, 'and the terror, hate and enthusiasm of war, and the narrow-mindedness, the orthodoxy, the hatred of liberty and doubt'; so how one would face it was merely a choice of two evils. For himself, he would choose the military virtues:

---

[1] See Isherwood's autobiography *Lions and Shadows* (1938), chapter 2, for his theory of the 'Test'.

[2] Julian Bell (1908–37), eldest son of Clive and Vanessa Bell.

[3] Characteristically, for the purposes of an anti-war demonstration in Cambridge on Armistice Day 1933, he converted his old Morris car into an 'armoured vehicle'.

This both because they alone will help us in practice, and because they offer us an attitude tolerably proof against disaster and emotion. The soldier's is not perhaps the best of lives for many people: it may not offer a very great number of highly valued states of mind.[1] But it can be a good life, and is similar to the kind of good life I have described, as the saint's and enthusiast's is not: it is secular and rational.

Julian Bell knew Forster and the letter was half affectionate in tone and half truculent. In a private letter to his brother Quentin he had written that his 'Letters' were meant to cause pain to intellectuals: 'thought if possible, but pain anyway. It's no use persuading woollies and softies and c.p. hysterics into being honourable and common-sense soldiers. But it's just worth publishing my reflections for those who are capable, but want to lead.'

Forster had liked Julian and had been upset by his death, but he considered him callow and muddle-headed, and he took the attack coolly. The 'Letters' were published in a memorial volume,[2] edited by Julian's brother, and for this Forster composed some 'Notes for a Reply'. What had been Julian's motive in the Letter, he speculated. Most likely, not to rebuke him, but simply to ride a hobby-horse: 'More an attitude than an ideology. And how can you argue with an attitude?' And what had Julian wanted him to do? Not to 'chuck gentleness', he supposed. At all events, he did not feel induced to do so. 'If one has been gentle, semi-idealistic, and semi-cynical, kind, tolerant, demure and generally speaking a liberal for nearly sixty years, it is wiser to stick to one's outfit.'

Round about the same spring of 1938, he was invited by the New York *Nation* to contribute the first of a series entitled 'Living Philosophies'. He agreed; and the resulting article, originally called 'Two Cheers for Democracy' and later 'What I Believe', developed into a comprehensive statement of his beliefs. ('As for me, I am trying to construct a philosophy,' he wrote to Plomer, 9 January 1938.) It is an essay full of memorable sayings. It contains the famous '. . . if I had to choose between betraying my country and betraying my friends, I hope I should have the guts to betray my country.' Also:

---

[1] An allusion to G. E. Moore's ethical theories, so important to the Cambridge 'Apostles' of the previous generation.

[2] *Julian Bell. Essays, Poems and Letters*, ed. Q. Bell (1938).

> The people I respect must behave as if they were immortal and as
> if society was eternal. Both assumptions are false: both of them
> must be accepted as true if we are to go on eating and working
> and loving, and are to keep open a few breathing holes for the
> human spirit.

And:

> I believe in aristocracy . . . Not an aristocracy of power, based
> upon rank and influence, but an aristocracy of the sensitive, the
> considerate and the plucky.

The essay, so deeply felt, and so disconcerting in its tactics, made a
considerable impression. It annoyed many, both orthodox patriots
and orthodox Marxists, but they felt outmanoeuvred by it. And
many others, sickened of 'commitment' by the betrayals and confusions of the Spanish civil war, found it a great support and recognized a heroism in its facing of limitations. Philip Toynbee, reviewing
it together with Spender's *The Trial of a Judge* and Rex Warner's
The Professor, wrote that Forster was one of the very few members
of the pre-First-World-War generation who had honestly confronted
the limitations their period imposed on them. 'He is a Liberal in
every sense of the word and he has no illusions about the sad condition of Liberalism in the modern world. . . . Mr Forster's beliefs are
very few and very simple, but all of them are denied and repudiated
by the modern *Zeitgeist*.'[1]

Forster had decided that, in his everyday life, his best attitude to
the crisis in Europe was an 'alternation of fuss and calm'. ('Keeping
calm and cheerful,' he told Florence Barger, 'is one of one's unshake-
able functions.') He was planning no large work but did some reviewing and broadcasting and wrote the text of another village pageant,
in aid of the Dorking and Leith Hill Preservation Society. The
pageant this time was entirely of his own devising. Its central idea
was a parallel between the eighteenth-century Enclosures, which had
robbed the peasantry of their common land, and the twentieth-
century Death-duties, which, in theory, returned their land to them –
in theory, but not in practice, for 'Squire Jeremiah', the 'improving'
London landlord who had once despoiled 'Jack' and 'Jill', had been
reincarnated as a property-developer, 'Jerry the Builder', to rob
them all over again. Vaughan Williams, once again, had agreed to

---

[1] 'Too Good for This World', *Town Crier*, 9 December 1938.

provide the music, and the two had cheerful planning sessions, conducted amid gales of laughter. He had always liked and admired Vaughan Williams and would speak of him as a 'noble' man, though he thought him chuckle-headed – a 'goose' – in matters of judgement.[1]

The pageant's sponsors included Dukes, Earls and the Lord Lieutenant of the County, but, to the general surprise, Lord Farrer refused to be a patron; indeed, he now actually resigned from the presidency of the Preservation Society. It suggested to Forster that his disputes with the Farrer family had not been forgotten; though it also occurred to him that it might merely be that the pageant, which featured the Labourers' Revolt of 1830, was too 'Bolshie' for Lord Farrer. Whiffs of local gossip reached him, about resentment against the pageant-organizers in the village. He told Bob Buckingham (4 July 1938): 'It has opened my eyes a little to the suspicions and jealousies which are moving everywhere beneath the social surface.'

He did some of the writing of the pageant at Dover. It was to be the last of his Dover visits, for Joe Ackerley's activities had finally been too much for the 'Holy Ladies'. They had asked him to leave; and Forster, in the circumstances, felt obliged to leave with him, reporting to Sprott that 'Dover is, alas, henceforward a Closed Port.' Ackerley felt compunctious on Forster's behalf, but Forster told him not to worry on this score. 'But what does concern me is that you won't face up to the fact that, to the average person, this sort of thing is disgusting, especially when it obtrudes its creaks and sheets end first upon their notice.'

Isherwood came back to London in August, via New York, and was working on his part of *Journey to a War*. As a result of the Spanish civil war, and its failures and betrayals, he and Auden were both in reaction against their earlier political attitudes. They had gone to China less in an ideological frame of mind than to prepare themselves imaginatively for the coming European war*; and in China, Auden had begun to turn against the belief that poetry could have political effect or could be an agent in history. On their journey,

---

[1] A friend of mine, O. W. Neighbour, remembers talking to Forster about Vaughan Williams and the comic vehemence and violent shaking of the head with which Forster said: 'If he [Vaughan Williams] got an idea in his head, *you – could –* NOT get it out!'

he and Isherwood argued sometimes about religion. Isherwood denied so violently that he possessed a soul that Auden would tell him, teasingly, that he must be on the brink of a conversion; and at this Isherwood would invoke Forster, saying that Morgan Forster was incapable of having truck with 'such Fascist filth'.[1] Auden was in a new mood of quasi-religious pessimism, and to him, too, the figure of Forster, so unpolitical yet 'committed', appeared now in an exemplary light. He composed a sonnet to him, which became the dedication of the book. It ran:

> TO E. M. FORSTER
> Though Italy and King's are far away,
> And Truth a subject only bombs discuss,
> Our ears unfriendly, still you speak to us,
> Insisting that the inner life can pay.
>
> As we dash down the slope of hate with gladness,
> You trip us up like an unnoticed stone,
> And, just when we are closeted with madness,
> You interrupt us like the telephone.
>
> Yes, we are Lucy, Turton, Philip: we
> Wish international evil, are delighted
> To join the jolly ranks of the benighted
>
> Where reason is denied and love ignored,
> But, as we swear our lie, Miss Avery
> Comes out into the garden with the sword.[2]

The concluding verse-sequence of *Journey to a War* was also unmistakably Forsterian, speaking of the need for the heart to be made 'awkward and alive':

---

[1] Isherwood writes in *Christopher and his Kind*: 'I wonder, now, if Wystan then believed what he stated in a letter to Christopher many years later in explanation of Forster's declared agnosticism. "As I see him, Morgan is a person who is so accustomed to the Presence of God that he is unaware of it: he has never known what it feels like when the Presence is withdrawn." '

[2] See *Howards End*, chapter 41:
> They laid Leonard, who was dead, on the gravel; Helen poured water over him.
> 'That's enough,' said Charles.
> 'Yes, murder's enough,' said Miss Avery, coming out of the house with the sword.

Ruffle the perfect manners of the frozen heart,
And once again compel it to be awkward and alive,
To all it suffered once a weeping witness.

Clear from the head the masses of impressive rubbish;
Rally the lost and trembling forces of the will . . .

Forster particularly admired these poems of Auden's in *Journey to a War*. Later he wrote of Auden: 'He elicits a response which I cannot always explain. Because he once wrote "We must love one another or die", he can command me to follow him.'[1] He also once said that Auden's 'In Memory of Sigmund Freud' was the best poem ever written.

As for Isherwood, he had returned to England in a mood of confusion and self-disgust. The truth was, as he related later, he had totally lost his political faith. The 'line' he had to take in the China book – 'united front', resistance to the Japanese, etc. – had lost all meaning for him and had become mere slogans. He confided to his diary bitterly (31 August 1938): 'And yet I still slip into the slogan-language when I write, and I talk it quite shamelessly on the lecture-platform, where I strut mock-modestly, playing the hero for the benefit of anyone attractive who may happen to be in the audience.' He felt poisoned by his crisis-fears, compulsively buying ten newspapers a day, but feeling, under all his various moods, a 'cold rock-bottom resentment': 'I resent being forced by the crisis to read the newspapers: they are *always* trash, no matter what they have to report.'[2] When he heard that Chamberlain had flown to Berchtesgaden and a friend said that England would lose prestige by this, he said to himself: 'What do I care? At least the showdown is postponed.' By now moreover he, like Auden, had privately decided to migrate to America.

Forster took Isherwood out to lunch during the Munich crisis, telling Bob Buckingham afterwards (26 September 1938); 'Cheered poor Christopher a bit: war is particularly awful for him, owing to Heinz being on the other side. I think he would rather kill himself than kill a German.' He told Isherwood he was afraid of going mad – of suddenly turning and running away from people in the street. 'But,

---

[1] Ironically, by the time that he came to write this, in a review of *The Enchafèd Flood* in 1951, Auden had grown embarrassed by the line and had jettisoned it.

[2] *Down There on a Visit* (1962), p. 176.

actually,' Isherwood wrote in his diary, 'he's the last person who'd
ever go mad; he's far saner than anyone else I know. And immensely,
superhumanly strong. He's strong because he doesn't try to be a
stiff-lipped stoic, like the rest of us; and so he'll never crack. He's
absolutely flexible. He lives by love, not by will.'[1] While they were
eating, the manager came over to tell them he had just heard on the
radio that Hitler had allowed six days for the evacuation of the
Sudeten areas. It seemed to Isherwood an almost indefinite reprieve,
and he ordered champagne, which set Forster off making silly and
charming jokes. More and more, in Isherwood's eyes, as in those of
a few others who knew him closely, Forster grew into a symbol and a
hero. 'When the newspapers compare Chamberlain to Abe Lincoln
and Jesus Christ,' wrote Isherwood in his diary, 'they aren't being
in the least sacrilegious; because *their* Lincoln and *their* Christ are
utter phonies, anyhow. The newspapers are moved to tears by the
spectacle of a gentleman standing his ground against a non-gentle-
man. So they call him "England" '.

> Well – *my* 'England' is E.M.; the anti-heroic hero, with his
> straggly straw moustache, his light gay blue baby-eyes and his
> elderly stoop. Instead of a folded umbrella or a brown uniform,
> his emblems are his tweed cap (which is too small for him) and the
> odd-shaped brown paper parcels in which he carries his belongings
> from country to town and back again. While the others tell their
> followers to be ready to die, he advises us to live as if we were
> immortal. And he really does this himself, although he is as
> anxious and afraid as any of us, and never for an instant pretends
> not to be. He and his books and what they stand for are all that is
> truly worth saving from Hitler; and the vast majority of people
> on this island aren't even aware that he exists.[2]

---

[1] *Down There on a Visit* (1962), p. 192.
[2] *Ibid.*, p. 177.

10 A Visit to Ferney

The Munich pact made Forster ashamed for his country. Life in the months after it seemed to him to have a new character, confused, ambiguous and ignoble. 'This post-Munich world may not last long,' he wrote in an article, 'The 1939 State', in the *New Statesman*.[1]

> We have to make the best of an unexplored and equivocal state, and we are more likely to succeed if we give up any hope of simplicity. 'Prepare, prepare!' does not do for a slogan. No more does 'Business as usual'. Both of them are untrue to the spirit of 1939, the spirit which is half-afraid and half-thinking about something else . . . the imperfect and blemished lamb, as he stands at the foot of the altar, is partly atremble because of the on-coming knife, and partly thinking of other things.

The dilemma facing his country, so it seemed to him, was that to defeat totalitarianism it would have to become totalitarian itself. By now he feared Communist totalitarianism as well as the Nazi kind. In a letter (30 October 1938) to C. Day Lewis, who had dedicated *Overtures to Death* to him, he wrote that the poems offered the possibility of heroic action and that many would be satisfied with that, but not Lewis or himself.

> . . . since I spoke up for Communism in Paris three years ago, I have had disillusionments which don't altogether proceed from my own weaknesses. Russia, perhaps from no fault of her own, seems to be going in the wrong direction, too much conformity and too much bloodshed. Perhaps – and perhaps under another name – Communism will restart life after the next European

---

[1] *New Statesman and Nation*, 10 June 1939. It was reprinted in *Two Cheers for Democracy* as 'Post-Munich'.

catastrophe and do better. Indeed a vision sometimes comes to me that it will start again and again, always more strongly, and in the end be too strong for catastrophes. But that won't be in our time, nor perhaps in Europe's. If *that* is the way I think my own job is to fall out and die by the way side.

For the immediate future, Forster foresaw an era of censorship and suppression of liberty, the history of which, when some satirist came to write it, would be entitled 'They Hold Their Tongues'.[1] It renewed his sense of the importance of the N.C.C.L., and he once more became active on its executive committee. The issue most concerning the N.C.C.L. just now was the Official Secrets Act of 1920, and especially its Clause 6, which made it the duty of a citizen to supply, on demand, information relating to breaches of official secrecy. There had been discussion of the Act in Parliament during 1938. The Act was ostensibly aimed at spies, but recently there had been a tendency to use it more widely, and it had been invoked by the police against a journalist, in connection with a 'wanted' man,[2] and by the Attorney-General when Duncan Sandys had asked permission to put a question in the House about London's anti-aircraft defences. The Sandys case had aroused violent controversy, leading to an investigation by a Select Committee, and the N.C.C.L. and the National Union of Journalists had launched a joint campaign for amendments to the law. A deputation to the Home Secretary, Sir Samuel Hoare,[3] was arranged during December, and Forster went as one of the two N.C.C.L. representatives. He took against Hoare, who struck him as civil but shifty, and he wrote an article for the *New Statesman*[4] about the interview, in which he analysed the technique of the ministerial snub:

> They carry on like this: begin a sentence deeply, gruffly, gently; it moves along like a large friendly animal: then it twitters, turns acid and thin and passes right overhead with a sort of whistling sound.

The agitation had some effect, for next year the Government brought in a bill to amend Clause 6, restricting its use to cases of espionage.

---

[1] 'They Hold Their Tongues'; *New Statesman and Nation*, 30 September 1938.

[2] *Rex v. Cattle*. Cattle was convicted under Clause 6.

[3] Samuel John Gurney Hoare, 1st Viscount Templewood (1880–1959), joint author of the much-vilified Hoare-Laval pact over Abyssinia in 1935.

[4] 'Comment and Dream: On a Deputation'; *New Statesman and Nation*, 14 January 1939.

Being a prominent figure in all civil liberties matters, he was invited early in the following year to serve on a Lord Chancellor's committee on the laws of libel. He was still smarting over 'A Flood in the Office' and accepted with enthusiasm, getting the P.E.N. Club to brief him with case-histories of fellow-writers victimized under the present laws. The Committee, under the chairmanship of Lord Porter,[1] sat for several years, being reconvened after the war, and its report eventually helped to secure some protection to authors in cases of inadvertent libel. Forster attended regularly, and at the session on 27 July 1939 he led the examination of witnesses. It was the day when the Society of Authors, represented by Ernest Raymond, Alec Waugh and the Society's Secretary, Kilham Roberts, was giving evidence. Forster extracted a declaration from Kilham Roberts that 'the libel law had murdered, or killed, a great many books' and from Ernest Raymond that the law 'tended if not to dry up the springs of creation, at least to dilute them'. He then proceeded to describe his own experience over the Lawrence letters, presenting it as an instance where the libel law had stopped a book from being written. Finally, he brought up the theory, often heard, that in cases of inadvertent libel 'the author hardly ever pays'. It was, he said, quite false; and he related the story of 'A Flood in the Office'[2] and various other incidents, some quite recent, when innocent authors had had to pay heavy libel damages.

*   *   *

In January 1939 Isherwood and Auden had emigrated to America. They had briefly shared a flat in New York; then in May Isherwood had moved on to California, partly in order to discuss pacifism, and his own situation in case of a war, with Gerald Heard. (Like many of his friends he revered Heard as a mentor and sage.) He was in a mood of confusion and self-doubt, wondering if he had made a mistake in deserting England, and he wrote asking Forster for his opinion – telling him how much he learned from him in the past. Forster replied (14 May 1939) that he wondered he should have taught him anything:

---

[1] Samuel Lowry Porter (1877–1956), Lord of Appeal 1938–54.
[2] See p. 211.

. . . but it is quite true that I don't hate a lot, if that is at all exemplary. It is partly idleness, partly an attempt to avoid being hated, but partly an impulse towards love . . .

But what are you to do dear Christopher? I don't see, after what happened to Heinz that you can help hating, and I hope G. Heard won't try to persuade you out of it. If you can come to love in your own way that's all right of course. But don't feel worried at being bitter.

I have still not told dear Christopher what he is to do. Well *I* in your shoes would not return to England unless the social scene normalizes.

For his own part, as the crisis in Europe prolonged itself, Forster felt it absurd to pretend any longer to measure up to it – to 'echo its crescendo with a personal one'. It was better, he decided, to try to keep in temper, even if it meant not 'facing reality', and to provision one's soul against the coming war. In this spirit he went in June to join Charles Mauron in Geneva, to see the exhibition of paintings from the Prado museum. In both their minds it was a sort of farewell to civilized enjoyments; and for Mauron it was a farewell in another sense too, for he was on the verge of total blindness. In this valedictory mood they paid a visit to Voltaire's Ferney. The chateau was not open to visitors, but they peered in through the fence and got a view of it and of the chapel, with its tablet 'Deo erexit VOLTAIRE' – the lettering of 'VOLTAIRE', they were pleased to notice, being twice the size of the Deity's. What the place seemed to say to Forster was 'Civilization, Humanity, Enjoyment'. As Mauron and he peered, they clung to the bars of the fence, and, when he wrote about it later,[1] he had a vision of them as monkeys, soon to return to separate and locked cages.

'I am content to have seen Ferney,' remarked Charles, as he dusted his paws. I popped the object into my pouch for future use. One never knows, and I had no idea how precious it would become to me in a year's time, nor how I should take it out, and discover that it has turned faintly radioactive.

*   *   *

The outbreak of war in September 1939 left him calm though pessimistic, convinced that Britain would be defeated. His mother

---

[1] 'Happy Ending', *New Statesman and Nation*, 2 November 1940; reprinted in *Two Cheers for Democracy* as 'Ferney'.

took it well; she was keyed up but not painfully so. However, he wished she were out of it; and he looked forward gloomily to the prospect of his own imprisonment in Abinger. Bob Buckingham had persuaded him to give up his Bloomsbury flat and to take one nearer to himself and had found him one in Chiswick (9 Arlington Park Mansions). Nevertheless Forster imagined that, as soon as air-raids began, London would be closed to him; and even were it not, Bob Buckingham would be busy day and night. Thinking thus, a day or two before war broke out, he bade Bob a farewell. 'Bob twice k'd me on Waterloo entrance No. 3 platform, 8 p.m., then walked away firmly, his broad shoulders in bluish sports coat last seen by me.'

In Abinger, he told John Simpson, he prepared himself for 'comforting my mother through bottling fruit and Armageddon.' His cousin Percy Whichelo and Percy's wife Dutchie had come to live at West Hackhurst, supposedly for the duration. Percy, who had shared a tutor with Forster fifty years before,[1] was a retired official of the Ecclesiastical Commission: rather pompous and touchy and a great writer to the newspapers. His and Dutchie's stay was not a success. 'Dutchie is upset,' Forster wrote to Bob Buckingham, soon after their arrival, 'because mother has contradicted her about some lion cubs. Percy because he has been spoken to too sharply about an apron.' They left in dudgeon in November, and were replaced by Forster's Uncle Philip, now very old and frail, and by Lily's old friend Mrs Mawe. At first, matters did not go very well with Mrs Mawe either. Lily was fond of her, but the two often exasperated each other: 'At times, much as I love Mrs Mawe, I could tear her to ribbons and use a chopper besides,' wrote Lily once, in her slashing manner. 'She tosses erroneous statements in the air like an aimless cow.' Tempers grew frayed, Mrs Mawe left, and her daughter Elaine wrote rebuking Lily. The letter delighted Lily, Forster told Ackerley, 'because Elaine has told her of the misfortunes of Bunny, her daughter and made her feel important,' and as a result peace was made and Mrs Mawe returned. A little later, in September 1940, Florence Barger was bombed out of her house in Hampstead and came to join them. It was an intensely old-fashioned household. They still had no telephone, nor electric light. There were not even any baths, so that Agnes, old and bent double with rheumatism, still had to carry hot

---

[1] See Vol. I, p. 30.

water up to bedrooms in heavy brass cans; in her cap, apron and
streamers she was, friends said, 'the last parlourmaid in England.'
Lily herself, born in 1855, was by now an old woman and in continual
pain from rheumatism – so much so that she stood rather than sat
whenever possible and would write her letters standing. More and
more she refused to spend money on herself; and day in and day out,
she would wear the same ancient grey coat, full of holes.

During these early war months, Forster busied himself with
journalism. In November 1939 he wrote a review of Jan Struther's
Mrs Miniver,[1] a novel glorifying the whimsical humour and heroism
of the English upper middle classes. It was a very funny and deflating review – concluding on a more sober note that national
characters, English or otherwise, were not likely to be of much
importance in the future, though 'they have a factitious value,
especially in wartime, because they are exploited by rival governmental gangs.' The review annoyed his friend Hilton Young (now
Lord Kennet) who wrote that it was untimely and unpatriotic. 'I am
against criticism,' he told Forster. 'In our race and society and time
it is the besetting sin.' Forster retorted with some friendly digs at
Kennet's own way of life and outlook, and this brought from Kennet
an enormous letter, expounding his own Tory philosophy, and
defending his decision, now that he was on the shelf politically,[2] to
devote himself not to literature but to money-making. Forster,
impressed, replied (15 February 1940) with an *apologia* almost as
long:

> . . . you do believe that a society which encourages money-
> making is good, and that good men should try to make money
> in it, and you have faith (which I don't share) that the Youngs
> rather than the Kylsants[3] will come on top. Your other motives
> I follow pretty well, and some of them I even imitate: I too want
> to be comfortable when I'm old, and to keep up my little family
> tradition – though I don't believe that the present fabric of
> society is going to survive. I love my books as dearly as you can

---

[1] 'The Top Drawer But One', *New Statesman and Nation*, 4 November 1939.
It was reprinted in *Two Cheers for Democracy* as 'Mrs. Miniver'.
[2] He was Minister of Health in Ramsay MacDonald's second National
Government (1931–5), thereafter losing office and being relegated to the
House of Lords.
[3] In 1931, in a case of much notoriety, Lord Kylsant, a well-known shipping
magnate, was sent to prison for publishing a fraudulent company prospectus.

love yours, but it is typical of us that when you should stick in
armorial bookplates I should only write in mine 'E. M. Forster,
at West Hackhurst'. I don't feel *of* any where. I wish I did. It is
not that I am déraciné. It is that the soil is being washed away.

. . . I suppose you feel you can serve, fulfil, nourish yourself
better by making a large income – I use these words in a sort of
16th century Renaissance sense of course, and I felt while reading
your letter that you belonged to the Renaissance.

. . . The parts of Communism and of Christianity that interest
me are *not* their boring egalitarianisms, but their attempts to cut
out money. I do think money is dangerous, and I know more
about its dangers than you suppose, for my great grandfather was
quite a famous banker, and some of his canniness runs in my
blood, and tempts me to prefer money to the things it buys.

. . . I cling to criticism, much as you cling to that still mistier
abstraction, justice . . . Why should you think that just *now* dumb
obedience is best? It might be if we were sure it wasn't the
Kylsants who were giving the orders.

*   *   *

For Forster there was no doubt that anti-semitism was the worst
and most shocking of all things. It was the one evil, as he wrote,[1]
that no one had foreseen at the end of the First World War; and it
dominated his attitude to the present one, making it impossible for
him to be a pacifist. He detected Jew-consciousness in the air even in
England. 'A nasty side of our nation's character has been scratched
up – the sniggering side,' he wrote. 'People who would not ill-treat
Jews themselves, or even be rude to them, enjoy tittering over their
misfortunes.' When, in May of this year, he heard that a young
policeman friend of his and Bob's had been talking anti-semitism,
he at once despatched him a stinging letter. He wrote that he was
surprised that E—of all people should be anti-Jewish, pointed out
the evil effect of such opinions, and ended with a list of the names of
great Jews. E— was hurt; for in fact the rumour had been unfair –
he had merely remarked that it was a pity certain Jews had involved
themselves just now in an insurance scandal, at the moment when
their race was in such peril. He complained to Harry Daley, and
Daley, attributing the rumour to Bob Buckingham, wrote Forster a
furious and violent letter, telling him his rebuke to E— had been
impertinent, and blaming him for betraying his working-class

---

[1] 'Jew-consciousness', *New Statesman*, 7 January 1939; reprinted in *Two
Cheers for Democracy*.

admirers by deserting pacifism. It was the last letter to pass between the two, and Daley was later ashamed of it. Forster did not reply and now finally wiped Harry off the list of his friends.*

Isherwood wrote often from California. He had become a declared pacifist, and, under the influence of Heard and Heard's *guru*, the Vedantist monk Prabhavananda, he had begun a conversion to Hindu mystical beliefs. (As he grew firmer in his beliefs, he attempted to explain them in his letters to Forster but received a discouraging response; Forster said he 'couldn't imagine' the belief that God could help him.) Even before the war, in the English press, there had been sporadic attacks on Isherwood and his fellow-exiles but Forster had advised ignoring them. 'I very much hope that you and everyone will try to keep away,' he wrote to Isherwood (10 July 1939), '– it is clearly your job to see us sink from a distance, if sink we do.' The attacks had continued, and during the spring of 1940 they swelled into a chorus. Cyril Connolly in the second number of *Horizon* (February 1940) gave cynical praise to Isherwood and his friends for their opportunism in deserting 'the sinking ship of European democracy'. And in an article in the *Spectator* for 19 April Harold Nicolson speculated as to why Auden, Isherwood, Heard and Aldous Huxley should have 'retired within the ivory tower':

> These men have been my friends. For nearly a quarter of a century I have admired Aldous Huxley as one of the most intelligent of our authors and as a man who possesses a brilliant, inquisitive and enfranchised mind. I have looked on Gerald Heard as the most delightful of companions and as one of the most saintly men that I have known, I have seen Wystan Auden playing upon the Malvern Hills, and Christopher Isherwood shyly and slyly observing human behaviour from a retired seat in a Berlin café. Huxley has exercised, and still exercises, a great influence upon my own and the succeeding generation; Heard has brought novelties of science within the scope of the ordinary man; W. H. Auden is rightly regarded as among the most gifted of our younger poets; and with Isherwood rests, to my mind, the future of the English novel. Why should these four eminent Georgians have flown? . . .
> It is not so much that the absence of these four men from Europe will cause us to lose the Second German War. It is that their presence in the United States may lead American opinion, which is all too prone to doubt the righteousness of our cause, to find comfort in their company . . . How can we proclaim over

237

there that we are fighting for the liberated mind, when four of our most liberated intellectuals refuse to identify themselves either with those who fight or with those who oppose the battle?

On 13 June 1940 a question was asked in Parliament about Auden and Isherwood and their situation as regards war-service,* and next day the *Spectator* printed a vicious epigram, signed 'W.R.M.', addressed 'To Certain Intellectuals Safe in America':

> 'This Europe stinks', you cried – swift to desert
>   Your stricken country in her sore distress.
> You may not care, but still I will assert,
>   Since you have left us, here the stink is less.[1]

Forster, already irritated by Harold Nicolson's article, countered this epigram with a letter[2] which carried the war into the opposing camp.

THESE 'LOST LEADERS'

Sir, W.R.M.'s epigram in your issue of June 21st impels me to ask whether there could not now be a close time for snarling at absent intellectuals. About half a dozen of them – not more – are away in America, and week after week their fellow-authors go for them in the newspapers. The attacks are highly moral and patriotic in tone, but their continuance raises the uneasy feeling that there must be something else behind them, namely, unconscious envy; they are like the snarl of an unfortunate schoolboy who has been 'kept in' and is aggrieved because the whole of his class has not been kept in too, and therefore complains and complains about those stinkers out in the playground instead of concentrating on his own inescapable task.

And there is a further objection to this undignified nagging: it diverts public attention from certain Englishmen who really are a danger to the country. They too, are few in number – perhaps again not more than half a dozen – but they have influence, wealth and position, which intellectuals have not, and they shelter not in the United States, but in the City and the aristocracy. Our literary lampoonists can here find a foe worthier of their powers. Let them leave their absent colleagues alone for the next fortnight, and denounce our resident Quislings instead. The consequences may be unpleasant to them, for Quislings sometimes hit back. But they will have had the satisfaction of exposing a genuine menace instead of a faked one, and this should be sufficient reward.

---

[1] Forster, writing to John Simpson (10 July 1940), said he had heard that 'W.R.M.' was W. R. Matthews, the Dean of St Paul's.

[2] *Spectator*, 5 July 1940.

He told John Simpson (10 July 1940) that he would have liked to
defend his friends but thought attack the better tactic.

*   *   *

Bob Buckingham, till now a pacifist, was beginning to waver in
his views, deciding that should the police be armed to fight invaders
he would fight with them, though if he were called up he would
try to choose some non-combatant service. He was having a
tough and heroic time on duty in the London blitz. In a way he was
enjoying it. 'I just couldn't bear to be away from London as things
are,' he wrote to Forster (in September or thereabouts). 'I don't think
it is anything to do with courage at all, rather I feel that the Police
are really doing a fine job and I at least get a wonderful feeling of
having accomplished something which was worth doing, and of
course it is exciting.' He was bitter against the amateurism of the
air-raid rescue services and wanted something done to 'pull down this
curtain of sham heroism' which the newspapers put round them.
Forster asked Bob to let him know of any special cases of need among
the air-raid victims. He was curious to see the devastation, and got
Bob to take him on a tour of the blitzed areas. His main reaction,
however, was a sort of chagrin at not feeling more. After the great
raid on the docks, on 7 September 1940, he noted cheerlessly in his
diary:

> *Sept. 8* London Burning! I watched this event from my Chiswick
> flat last night with disgust and indignation, but with no intensity
> though the spectacle was superb. I thought 'It is nothing like the
> burning of Troy.' Yet the Surrey Docks were ablaze at the back
> with towers and spires outlined against them, greenish yellow
> searchlights swept the sky in futile agony, crimson shells burst
> behind the spire of Turnham Green church. This is all that a world
> catastrophe amounts to. Something which one is too sad and
> sullen to appreciate.

*   *   *

Believing, as he had told Hilton Young, that 'criticism' should be
his public function, Forster kept a close eye on the B.B.C. He had
made quite a study of the B.B.C. and its tactics in imposing itself as
'the voice of the Nation', and, remembering the odious behaviour of
the press during the 1914–18 war, he distrusted its wartime influence.
He had many friends in it, including George Barnes, shortly to
become head of the Talks department. Thus he was kept well

informed about developments; and during the course of the war he had several victorious brushes with the B.B.C. One was over the treatment given to literature in its programmes. It had struck him that, since the war began, almost no time at all was given to literature – at most five hours a week out of a hundred and fifteen on the Home Service, and none at all on the Forces programme. He spoke privately to George Barnes on the subject with no result; then, later in 1940, he was invited by a Talks producer, C. V. Salmon, to appear in a series of interviews with writers. This gave him the chance for his protest. 'I think the suggested series would have been very suitable,' he replied, 'if the B.B.C.'s attitude to literature had been different':

> But what has *it* done of recent years to bring the public into relation with writers either dead or alive? What attempt has it made to treat our national heritage in letters seriously? With its miserable record, I don't think it's in a position to invite authors to chat!
> I am sure that individual officials and probably individual directors too, think English literature a valuable national asset. And they control an organization which is exempted from the financial anxieties which vex the ordinary publisher, and which can address the public, on one wavelength alone, for over a hundred hours a week. They have convictions and they have power, and my God look at their performance.
> If the performance had been different, it would have been fun to discuss who could be compèred at the microphone and how. As it is, I feel it is too wry a jest.

The B.B.C. took notice of this and, in March 1941, convened a meeting to discuss the matter, to which Forster led a delegation from the Society of Authors. His intervention bore fruit, and various literary features were thereupon introduced into the wartime programmes.

By now Forster was a very frequent broadcaster. Soon after the outbreak of war Malcolm Darling had resigned from the Indian Civil Service to take charge of broadcasting to India,[1] and as one of his first actions at the B.B.C. he had engaged Forster to give regular weekly or fortnightly talks to India. Forster talked mainly about books; and, reflecting that Indians would have had English literature stuffed down their throats, he devoted as much time as he could to

---

[1] Darling was knighted in 1939.

continental literature. With intervals he continued to deliver these talks throughout the rest of the war and for a year or two after it.

He had, thus, become a valuable property to the B.B.C. And when in March 1941 he was involved in a serious clash with the Corporation, he put his position to use. The dispute was over governmental interference in broadcasting. At the beginning of the war, the B.B.C. had divested itself of most of its governing body, in the name of increased efficiency. The dismissed governors were said to have approved of their dismissal (though one of them, H. A. L. Fisher, wrote to the newspapers denying it), and more recently the B.B.C. had accepted, in their place, two governmental 'advisers', of dubious status and powers. Now, this March, it became known that the B.B.C. was blacklisting performers (and in one case a composer, Alan Bush) because of their political activities. Specifically, they were being banned if they belonged to the 'People's Convention' – a Communist-run body, founded the previous year, which was campaigning for friendship with the Soviet Union and a 'People's Peace'. Questions about the ban were asked in the House of Commons, and the Minister of Information, Duff Cooper, defended it, asserting that to be employed by the B.B.C. was a 'privilege' and not a right, and that artistes who took part in public agitations could not expect to receive this 'great privilege'. From this it seemed plain the Government had had a hand in the blacklisting; and the N.C.C.L. (many of whose members belonged to the People's Convention) launched a protest campaign, attacking the whole relationship of Government to broadcasting. A mass meeting was staged for 17 March, at the Conway Hall in Bloomsbury, and Forster was one of the main speakers.[1] 'Who is responsible for this dastardly attack upon our democracy?' he asked.

> One's first impression was that it must be the officials of the B.B.C., and this was the nimble idea of G. B. Shaw.[2]
> But it is most unlikely that the Director General of the B.B.C.[3] could have been responsible, because he is a man of integrity and he came from Belfast with a great reputation for moral courage.

---

[1] Among the other speakers were Beatrix Lehmann, Michael Redgrave and the Archdeacon of Westminster, Canon Donaldson.

[2] A message from Shaw was received at the meeting, saying that the whole managing staff of the B.B.C. should be sacked instantly.

[3] Sir Frederick Ogilvie (1893–1949), Reith's successor as Director-General.

The two Government officials are more sinister – Sir Alan Powell, who was a Conservative ex-Mayor of Kensington, and Captain Millis. They are probably not indeed the initiators but the willing agents.

The true villain, he suggested, was Duff Cooper:

There is an extraordinary priggishness and fatuousness in his saying that it is a privilege to the artist to come to the microphone. I would rather say that it is a privilege to us to listen to these artists. Mr Duff Cooper has got it all upside down. Logic indeed is not his strong point. He told us in the past that we were not to talk and then he organized questioners to find out what we were saying.

He and his friends, Forster said, were not asking for much. They were not asking for freedom of speech at the microphone, but freedom of speech away from the microphone; and if what they did there was illegal, that was a matter for the courts to decide, and not the Ministry of Information or the B.B.C.

In making this protest I think we should be chiefly concerned for the smaller people. Because when important people are thrown overboard they make a big splash. We all rush to the edge and say 'my goodness we must make a row'. The whole affair is brought up to the front. But the smaller people don't make a splash; they vanish silently and the injustice never comes to light.

He read out a letter from Vaughan Williams to the B.B.C., protesting against the victimization of Alan Bush and withdrawing permission for one of his own works to be performed on the air. Forster said he was following this 'magnificent lead' and was withdrawing his labour also.

It was an effective campaign. Three days later, Churchill promised in the House that the ban should be removed, and twelve days after that Duff Cooper announced the reconstitution of the B.B.C.'s Board of Governors. Asked whether 'in the reasonable restrictions of war, this enlightened Board of Governors would be allowed to exercise genuine freedom', he replied, 'Yes, certainly.'

The cry was growing louder that the N.C.C.L. was Communist-run, and Forster found himself fighting a double battle, defending the N.C.C.L. to the world outside and combating Communist influence within it. A little before the B.B.C. affair, the Council had run a campaign for freedom of the press, prompted partly by the

banning of the *Daily Worker*.[1] It had called a conference, and
on the eve of this, Forster received various telegrams from Communists, challenging him to make a public stand in favour of the
Daily Worker. Despite this, when helping to frame the conference
resolution, he did his best, as he told Sprott (2 February 1941), 'to
find a formula for protest which should give the Communists no
pleasure.'

The Communist issue was involving him in some awkward publicity. The N.C.C.L. had convened a conference to consider, among
other questions, the position of the trade unions under war-time
legislation, and the National Council of Labour had issued a circular
denying the N.C.C.L.'s right to interfere in trade union affairs. The
matter had come up at the Labour Party's annual conference, and
A. M. Wall, Secretary of the London Society of Compositors, had
attacked the N.C.C.L., saying that 'some of us know quite well that
the National Council for Civil Liberties is not entirely removed from
the Communist Solar System, and for the last few months has been
almost mainly under its control.' The N.C.C.L. responded with a
letter to the press, signed by Forster among others, denying Wall's
charges 'categorically'. It appeared, among other places, in *Time and
Tide* on 21 June 1941, and 'Four Winds' (most probably the editor,
Lady Rhondda) commented in his Diary, in the same issue:

> The little quarrel which is proceeding between the N.C.C.L. and
> Mr A. M. Wall, Secretary of the London Society of Compositors,
> who before he held his present office was for 12 years Secretary of
> the London Trades Council, is an entertaining one. Presidents are
> chosen for their probity, but probity can sometimes go with some
> degree of innocence. Men of the calibre of Mr H. W. Nevinson[2]
> and Mr E. M. Forster would never knowingly sign anything false,
> but unless they make their presidential work a whole-time job
> they might not always know what is true. I am bound to say that
> I would sooner trust to Mr A. M. Wall's knowledge than that of
> Mr H. W. Nevinson in a matter of this kind. I had myself already
> noticed two odd things about the N.C.C.L.: (a) that it appears to
> be totally unaware that there is a war in progress; (b) that all the

---

[1] The *Daily Worker* was suppressed on 21 January 1941, under Regulation
2D of the Defence Regulations, on the grounds of its 'systematic publication
of matter calculated to foment opposition to the prosecution of the war to a
successful conclusion'.

[2] Nevinson was now president of the N.C.C.L.

same a number of its recent activities have been calculated to hinder rather than to help the war effort.

Forster and Kidd replied separately in the following week's issue, Forster's letter running:

> Sir,
>
> In your issue of June 21st you imply that I am not a Communist. That is correct. And my general attitude towards this war is probably more or less your own: it is set out in a pamphlet called *Nordic Twilight*.
>
> But in the same issue you imply that the N.C.C.L., an organization of which I was once president and on whose platform I have lately spoken, is mainly Communist-controlled, and that I have been tricked into supporting it.
>
> By whom have I been tricked?
>
> By our secretary, Mr Ronald Kidd, who invited me to join it about ten years ago? And if not by him, then by whom have Mr Kidd and I both been tricked? Would you please give the name?

Time and Tide commented in its leader that it would not have chosen this week, when Russia had just entered the war on the Allied side, to pursue the matter of the N.C.C.L.; but 'a challenge has been made. It must be answered. Mr E. M. Forster has asked a straight question. And Mr Kidd protests too much to be ignored.'

> Mr Forster has asked us who has tricked him. The answer lies not in one name but in a whole system.
>
> We would, in our turn, ask Mr Forster three questions.
>
> (1) Does he know how many Communists there are on the Executive Committee of the National Council for Civil Liberties?
> (2) Has he got particulars as to how many of these are publicly known as Communists, and how many are secret members of the Communist Party?
> (3) Can he deny that at a meeting of the Executive Committee of the N.C.C.L. held last February, two leading members were obliged to protest against the Communist trend of a policy suggested?[1]

Forster replied that to speak vaguely of 'a whole system' was no answer to his question and to this the editor rejoined with further remarks about the 'system': it was, she said, the system known as

---

[1] It is conceivable that *Time and Tide*'s informant was Kingsley Martin, who tended to blow hot and cold towards the N.C.C.L.

'white-anting', by which 'a determined and energetic minority uses the broadly humanitarian objects of recognized societies as a cover for its own political ends.' In the same issue (5 July 1941), Rebecca West wrote, describing the mental state of the N.C.C.L. as 'dewy, cloistered, nun-like'. She herself, she wrote, had been a Vice-President but had resigned the previous year in protest against the Council's campaign – run purely for Communist ends, so it seemed to her – over conditions in French internment camps. The Council, she said, had seemed quite astonished by her resignation, and by the suggestion that they were under Communist control.

> They treated the allegation as if it was sheer perversity on my part, a quaint and ugly fancy. Their best friends had, apparently, never told them.
> With such simplicity it is not for us to argue. I will offer no prize for a delineation of the Committee as I have seen it in my mind's eye ever since. I will say that I hope none will doubt that I ever suspected the integrity of Mr Nevinson or Mr Forster, who seem to me two of the most distinguished and also lovable Englishmen we have looked on in our time. But I was not prepared to find the whole society cut of the same cloth, white samite, mystic, wonderful . . .

For the moment Forster did not let himself be swayed by these attacks, and in the following year, on the death of H. W. Nevinson, he briefly resumed the Presidency.

*   *   *

In 1943 the influential American critic Lionel Trilling published a book on Forster. It made large and persuasive claims for him. Forster, he said, was for him 'the only living novelist who can be read again and again and who, after each reading, gives me what few writers can give us after our first days of novel-reading, the sensation of having learned something.' Forster was a liberal 'at war with the liberal imagination'. He had, what the liberal in general lacks, 'moral realism', the power to envisage not just good and evil but good-and-evil.

> He is content with the human possibility and content with its limitations. The way of human action of course does not satisfy him, but he does not believe there are any new virtues to be discovered; not by becoming better, he says, but by ordering and distributing his native goodness can man live as befits him . . .
> He is one of the thinking people who were never led by thought

245

to suppose they could be more than human and who, in bad times, will not become less.[1]

Trilling's book did much to increase Forster's reputation in America. Various other American critics wrote on him,[2] and E. K. Brown said that he 'stands in this country as the greatest living English master of the novel'.

As a result of this boom, and through his expatriate contacts, he now began to acquire American friends. Isherwood wrote to him, somewhere about Christmas 1943, that he had a 'present' for him. The present was a young American actor named William Roerick, who was coming to London in a show called *This is the Army*. Roerick – engaging, good-looking, loquacious – charmed Forster, and the two quickly struck up a friendship. Roerick, who was in corporal's uniform, had brought for Forster in his cartridge-belt two acorns from the New World, to be planted in the Old. He also showered Forster with other presents: chocolate, soap, lemon-essence, American books and tickets for his show. ('I must say I liked being pelted by such a storm,' Forster wrote to Plomer.) After a few weeks, Roerick left with his show for Italy; meanwhile however, he had put Forster and the Buckinghams on a list of gifts from America, and before long quite a stream of parcels and fan-letters was arriving for Forster. In particular he was in touch with the painter Paul Cadmus, in New York, with Edith Oliver, who worked for the *New Yorker*, and with Mr and Mrs Edward Root, patrons of Roerick's *alma mater*, Hamilton College in upper New York State. Hamilton College adopted the village school in Abinger, sending it pencils, crayons and exercise-books.

From Bob Buckingham, still employed on street-duty, Forster heard stories of the horrors and petty crime that flourished among the ruins of London. It seemed to Forster the Dark Ages returned, and he sought interpretation of it in the fourth and fifth centuries, reading quite extensively in St Augustine, St Jerome and other early Fathers. The thought of Rome invaded his experience of blitzed London. 'What a wilderness south of St Paul's', he recorded in his Commonplace Book.

---

[1] *E. M. Forster: a Study* (1943), Chapter 1.
[2] Among them were Clifton Fadiman, Newton Arvin and Morton Dauwen Zabel.

> I stood (Feb. 1943) by St Augustine's – a tiny Wren – and saw the
> tower of St Nicholas Cole rising from the plain. Two dirty little
> boys had discovered an echo born in the desolation (as in the
> Coliseum's) and were inclined to exploit it commercially. 'The
> old man doesn't know where it comes from.' The sun had set
> coldish. A few birds whistled. In the portico of the Cathedral
> hundreds squeaked. Full of my own desolation, I thought 'It will
> never get straightened out,' also 'Here is beauty.' O I long for
> public mourning in the sense of recognition of what has happened.

For one of his Indian broadcasts, he agreed to write the last instal-
ment of a five-part serial story, by different hands, set in the London
of the blitz. The story featured a disgruntled intellectual, Moss, and
an old enemy of his, Coburn, who had ruined his life and career.
Moss finds Coburn lying in a bombed house and is about to murder
him, when he notices that in the shadows, a pickpocket is waiting.
Here Forster took up the narrative. For him, the interest of the story
lay in the pickpocket, Stan, 'a creature of burning doorways, crashing
beams, rubble heaps and spouting drains . . . his sort had haunted
London ever since the foundation of the city, and 1940 seemed to
bring it into its own.' Stan has a knuckle-duster, acquired while he
was employed by the Mosleyites. 'It had been a happy episode –
plenty of food, a bed to sleep in at the local centre, and ten shillings
a week. "We will cleanse this city of London," he had been told. "We
will hack our way through to power." Well, and why not? And he
had taken part in one or two purity drives, and had hit one or two
people whose noses were the wrong shape.'

In Forster's continuation, Coburn, recovering consciousness, takes
Moss outside into the Park to talk over their past differences, and
he eventually reveals that, to expiate his own behaviour towards
Moss, he had gone to fight in the Spanish civil war. At this, Moss is
reconciled, and the two shake hands. The pickpocket meanwhile had
been eavesdropping. He is discovered; there is a fight; and Moss and
Coburn, without compunction or interest, leave him for dead. In an
epilogue, Forster said:

> I've shifted the interest from Coburn and Moss to the pickpocket,
> and I've tried to show how their fine sentiments would appear to
> that sort of man. He doesn't care about snobbery or outraged
> feelings or moral redemption or heroism in Spain, or hopes for the
> world's future. He can't see either why the two mugs quarrelled or
> why they make it up. And when they punish him – which they do

> pretty thoroughly – they can't see that he too has a way of life,
> and a way which, in our present chaos, may possibly flourish.

*   *   *

Still at the centre of his London life were Bob Buckingham and Joe Ackerley. Buckingham was by now burning to get into the services. 'I'm sick of hanging about,' he would say. 'I shall never forgive myself if I don't go.' Forster tried to dissuade him, but when, in 1943, the police were allowed to volunteer for service on bombers, Buckingham applied; and when turned down for defective eyesight, he tried, again without success, to join the Navy. Forster considered him boyish and irresponsible in his attitude, noting a few months later, after the beginning of the flying bombs, that he had matured. 'He has changed in the last week,' he wrote to Plomer (26 February 1944) '– I can't say for the worse, since his attitude is now my own. All the desire to give it back to the Germans has died in him. He is outwardly very grave.'

Ackerley, under the influence of the war, had been writing verse again. He wrote several poems to soldier friends killed in the war, depicting them as the obscure victims of an unjust society. He also wrote a long poem 'Micheldever', published in *Horizon* in August 1940, about a Hampshire ploughboy hanged for his part in the Labourers' Revolt of 1830; and this too, in its final section, became a comment of the present war:

> The struggle still goes on. We give it names
> You'd never comprehend and we defend
> What you contested, but the fight's the same;
> You fought at the beginning, we at the end.
>
> And all are in it now; across the world
> The dikes are down; in intricate dismay
> Gainer and loser both in the flood are hurled:
> Those tears you shed, we drown in them today.

Ackerley had been a success as a literary editor, and the *Listener*'s book and art pages had now a high reputation, rivalling the *New Statesman*'s. He would take great pains with his contributors and would write them pages-long critiques of their work, with much insistence on painful frankness. Forster enjoyed writing for Ackerley and for some years the bulk of his reviewing had been done for the *Listener*. Nevertheless he worried about Ackerley. He would write wryly about him to Bob Buckingham: 'Joe came yesterday, very gloomy – trouble with the new editor[1] and muddle with the new guardsman. He now goes in for scientific introspection and analysis of his pre-natal state. . . . I'm afraid there's something really wrong with him.'[2] 'Joe very low. Nothing teaches him.'[3] He would still give him admonitions, but more from habit than in hope of changing him: 'Joe, you must give up looking for gold in coal-mines,' he wrote to him (18 August 1939); 'it merely prevents you from getting amusement out of a nice piece of coal.'

Some time about 1943 Ackerley got involved with a new soldier and began an affair which was to have far-reaching and, in a way, disastrous consequences for him. The soldier, X—, who was married and had a child, was extremely good-looking, but vague, dishonest and feckless. Most of Ackerley's friends disliked him. Ackerley, however, insisted that he was a youth of great sensibility and beauty of character. X—'s mother had told Ackerley how, as a child, he had climbed a heap of dirt in the backyard, saying 'I am king of the cath'le'; 'I'm not surprised,' Ackerley had cried – 'He walks like a king!' X— was an incipient deserter, continually going absent without leave, and Ackerley vacillated over this, alternately lecturing him and encouraging him – buying him a railway-ticket back to his unit and then begging him not to use it. Soon, X— got involved in petty theft and house-breaking, and Ackerley found himself harbouring stolen property. Eventually, for X—'s own good, he reported him to the military police – making efforts through X—'s commanding officer, whom he happened to know, to have him punished lightly.

Forster had lunch with Ackerley at the height of this first crisis of his affair and became exasperated by Ackerley's self-absorption. 'A very Balzacian lunch with Joe,' he wrote to Plomer (12 June 1943). 'Since he could take no interest in any one or any subject, I asked about X—, and he then settled himself in his treadmill and ground out "And . . . er, and . . . er, ander" for the rest of our time together. Such a story of woe, weakness and muddle, and so ardently claimed by him as such! In some ways it must have been worse for me than

---

[1] Alan Thomas.
[2] Letter to R. J. Buckingham, 16 August 1939.
[3] Letter to R. J. Buckingham, April 1939.

for him, since he cannot realize how much he has altered.' In addition to irritation he felt anxiety lest the police should make a raid on Ackerley's flat and seize his own letters. He tried to persuade Ackerley to return them, but without success. Before long, as the result of another lunch, an actual quarrel developed, and he wrote Ackerley a cutting letter (16 August 1943):

> D.M.J.[1]
> Mind you let me know if I can help you with tea or other things in your problems. I am any how good for ¼lb of the first-named commodity.
>
> As for my own news, I don't think I shall be telling you any more of it unless it is arrestingly bad or good, and this letter is, in that limited sense, a farewell.

Ackerley wrote placatingly, and Forster was soon mollified, writing again, two days later: 'I got so cross at my trivialities falling flat when they had had such encouraging reception for so many years. Now that I have said this I shall keep my temper better when I revert to them, as I am sure to do, and they fall flat again.'

*　　*　　*

In Abinger, Forster did a little 'war work'. He served on the Dorking Refugee Committee and, during most of 1942, attended each week at a local Searchlight Unit to lead discussions with the soldiers. For some time, too, he helped a friend, Mrs King the builder's wife, give a weekly party for Italian prisoners of war.

The war threw him and his mother together with one or two local celebrities. They got to know Marie Stopes, who lived at Norbury Park, near Dorking. She came to tea at West Hackhurst and, so Forster told Ackerley, 'proved very friendly and domestic'. Forster knew that Ackerley had asked her to review a current 'Penguin' on Sex, and he left a copy about to see if it would ruffle her, which it did. When he went to tea with her she said 'I told the Roman Catholic Church years ago it must do one of three things: Kill me, or go to pieces, or follow me. It tried to kill me but failed; it did not want to go to pieces; so it had followed me, and brings out books every word of which is copied from me.' She believed herself to be 'banned' by the B.B.C., and, hearing this, Forster took up her cause with George Barnes. Visits and courtesies continued: 'My mother has eaten an

---

[1] i.e. 'Dearest My Joe'.

egg kindly laid for her by Dr Marie Stopes and is not feeling very
well,' Forster wrote to Plomer (18 April 1942).

Forster also saw something of Max Beerbohm, who, at the outset
of the war, had taken refuge with his wife in a cottage in Abinger, lent
them by Sydney Schiff. Beerbohm and he had been brought into
contact by a neighbour, Sylvia Sprigge, who – with the assistance of
R. C. Trevelyan – ran a literary journal called the *Abinger Chronicle*
and had recruited them both to write for it.[1] Forster and Beerbohm
liked each other and respected each other's work. Forster, it is true,
considered Beerbohm's Rede Lecture on Lytton Strachey a failure;
he told Sprott 'you can't quite do literary criticism on social sensitiveness and flair.' And Beerbohm, persuaded by Sylvia Sprigge to
read *Howards End* for the first time, had found it a very strange book
indeed: 'a book beautiful and delightful throughout the first half of
it,' he told Violet Schiff (5 June 1940), '– and then falling away ever
so far beneath contempt. . . .'

> I felt as though I had been taken up for an air-joyride by an
> 'ace' aeronaut, and had mounted high and far, seeing far below
> me a charming conspectus of things as they are, and had
> immensely enjoyed the sight, until suddenly the machine began
> to jerk and wobble, and I looked at the ace, and his face had
> turned pale green, and his jaw had dropped, and I said 'Is any-
> thing the matter?' and he gasped 'Yes, I'm afraid I—', and at
> that moment the machine gave a nose-dive, and, a few sickening
> moments later, I and my trusted pilot were no more.

For Beerbohm's seventieth birthday in 1942 a 'Maximilian Society'
was founded, and the members presented him with a large gift of
wine. Forster, as a member of the society, went one afternoon to help
him drink it and was greatly intrigued that Beerbohm, with some
ostentation, warmed a white burgundy in front of the fire. Neither
then nor later could he decide if it had been a hoax.

*   *   *

The household at West Hackhurst diminished. Mrs Mawe died in
the course of 1942, and Florence Barger returned to London in May
of the same year, finding herself a new house in Golders Green. Her
stay had been a success: she had helped in the village school, had
kept peace among the other inmates, and had been a support during

---

[1] Forster contributed 'Luncheon at Pretoria', 'The Last of Abinger',
'The C Minor of That Life' and 'Mon Camarade est Anglais'.

Uncle Philip's last illness. Lily missed her, and so did Forster. He told Forrest Reid (4 September 1942) that his mother kept well and active but was 'terribly authoritarian'. 'Old women frighten me when I think of them: they are really giving all those orders and prohibitions to Death, and ordering Him to keep away from them and from their house.'

To keep himself in good temper at home, Forster established certain disciplines. Each morning, 'before the world of worries and kindnesses gathers strength,' he would write for a little in his Commonplace Book. It was what he called *recueillement*, and he warned himself not to confuse it with creation. One Sunday morning, sitting with his Commonplace Book before him, he realized that, for once, he was experiencing perfect silence. To complete it, he stopped the clock, and recorded his *recueillement*:

> Listen out for silence! The mind is so accustomed to noise that it goes on imagining it even when there is no message from the ear.
>
> The eye even in darkness and blindness (Charles)[1] sees something. The ear *can* hear nothing, can register the last vibration of a note and enter a state of negation, of absence, which should please the mystics. But the state is best reached when there is something to listen *for*, when the window is open as now and the vast landscape might pop and seethe but does not. Silence would be unsatisfactory in a cell.
>
> Has any creature except a man had such thoughts as above, or attempted to record them?

The fate of Charles Mauron, enduring who could tell what sufferings and dangers in France, took on a symbolic importance for him. 'I disapprove of feeling intimidated,' he wrote to John Simpson (13 February 1941), 'and Charles Mauron's "Vain de se lamenter (et un peu dégoûtant)",[2] keeps ringing in my ears and helps to steady me.' He would re-read the letters of his 'loved and lost Charles', copying portions out into his Commonplace Book, and felt that they fortified him. Early on in the war, at Mauron's instigation (or at least with his approval) he had begun writing an analysis of Beethoven's piano sonatas. 'I'm keen on a vision of Beethoven reached through playing him as well as listening to and based upon details,' he wrote about it to Forrest Reid (30 September 1940). The work was done at

---

[1] i.e. Charles Mauron.
[2] 'Useless to complain (and even a little disgusting).'

the keyboard, with the aid of the gramophone for sonatas too difficult for him to play, and over several years he made notes on this or that work or movement as the fancy took him. He copied out a sample note for Reid:

Beethoven   Op. 90   *Sonata in E Minor*
First Movement
1–81 a single gigantic gesture, although there are pauses in it and changes of theme. Lyric emotion until 65 when there is a good little growl, repeated in 71, which *might* introduce a fiercer mood. It doesn't, the gesture dies, the hand falls in peace. Though the actual sounds are less delicious than the 1st movement of Op. 101, the general effect is sweeter because the flow isn't interrupted or in spurts. I find lovely the continuation: the bars 82–84 echoing 79–81; minims echoing crochets; I feel sure they belong to what comes after, not to what has gone, though I don't know how to prove this. The original motive returns in 84 but pricked with quavers; it becomes a little scholarly-harsh, and I don't enjoy myself so much until 108, when it has done its stuff and the first motive (or rather the second theme in it; 8 originally) comes in at 108, and itself turns very scholarly in the base [*sic*].
     Movement almost in the front rank. So exciting and touching that I am always surprised to get to the end. One of the many Beethoven pieces that couldn't be any other piece.

Bob Buckingham, from time to time, told Forster he must at all costs write another novel. He attacked him vehemently on this theme on 8 March 1943: 'Repeat yourself: it doesn't matter, the conditions are so changed. Say again that you believe in human relationships and disbelieve in power.' The words came home to Forster:

Yes – I am drawn into trivialities (home life) and diverted to unimportancies (Civil Liberties, B.B.C.) yet I can still write well and I am wise . . . I consider my age, 64, my family record of idleness, inability to start, and three years of war which have weighed down my spirits, like everyone's, so that I no longer hit out vivid similes or make big jokes. And my mind would slip off into cynicism, or – more readily – into affection for Bob for bothering to attack me. But his voice! 'Leave all that out and start a new novel at once' cuts at me. So easy to reflect that he is crude and was a bit alcoholic. The plea remains . . .[1]

He had had another brush with the Farrers, over the field and the footpath, and this time had been worsted. It had taken place in the

---

[1] Commonplace Book, p. 162.

second year of the war. He had begun to feel qualms that the field was not being cultivated, and had said as much to Mrs Cecil Farrer; however, incautiously, he let slip the fact that his sole interest in the field was the diagonal footpath across it. The Cecil Farrers had seized on this, and had manoeuvred him into giving up the field, on the understanding that he retained the use of the footpath. He had signed an agreement to this effect, though in fury; and having done so, he had written the Cecil Farrers two very sharp letters. The dispute was beginning to obsess him. He felt he must do something to curb the obsession, and, fired by a meeting of the Memoir Club, he decided to write a history of West Hackhurst and its Farrer neighbours. 'I am writing as quickly as Trollope and as badly as Balzac,' he told Plomer, 'but the sensation is novel. Do not mention this to any one. I am not mentioning it to any one else.' By October 1943 he had completed a substantial portion of 'West Hackhurst: a Country Ramble'. It was, he told Forrest Reid (16 October 1943), 'clever, bitter, not valuable.'

*   *   *

During the summer of 1944 German flying-bombs fell round Abinger. Forster and Lily took them calmly – too calmly, Forster tended to feel. 'Life is certainly odd,' he wrote (21 August 1944) to Paul Cadmus, one of his new-found American friends, 'and what I resent is that it must be making *me* so odd, and people elsewhere (e.g. in Poland) still odder. It does not seem natural that I should have interrupted this letter to call out to my mother (aged 88) to keep away from glass, that she should have transmitted the warning in calm tones while packing me up some margarine, and that I should have gone on with this letter equally calmly. One adapts oneself to conditions, and it is depressing that one should, for it means that one is failing to notice them.' He blamed himself and his friends for not making more imaginatively of the world's amazing situation. 'I do a little thinking about the Flying Bombs, though,' he wrote to Isherwood (7 July 1944). 'I believe they are going to be important psychologically. They will bitch the Romance of the Air – war's last beauty-parlour.'

As best he could, he kept busy. He was up in London most weeks for his Indian broadcasts and was doing some lecturing, delivering a paper on 'Literature Between the Wars' at various places, including Glasgow University. The P.E.N. had organized a five-day conference in August, in honour of the tercentenary of Milton's 'Areopagitica',

and he agreed to preside. Its theme was to be 'The Future Spiritual
and Economic Values of Humanity'. 'A neat little subject,' he
remarked to Paul Cadmus, promising to write again when he had
cooked the Spiritual and Economic Geese of Humanity. 'There will
be a great dispute as to whether they can be got into the same oven.'
In his own addresses[1] to the conference he continued his campaign
against secrecy in national life and against censorship. Would Milton
have approved of the 'wireless', he asked?

> Yes and No. He would have been enthusiastic over the possibilities
> of broadcasting, and have endorsed much it does, but he would
> not approve of the 'agreed script' from which broadcasters are
> obliged to read for security reasons . . . You can argue that the
> present supervision of broadcasters is necessary and reasonable,
> and that a silly or cranky speaker might do endless harm on the
> air. But if you feel like that, you must modify your approval of
> the *Areopagitica*.

*   *   *

In December 1944 letters began at last to arrive from France,
among them a long one from Charles and Marie Mauron. They were
safe and well (though Charles, as Forster learned later, had been
active in the Resistance and several times had been in great danger).
The Germans had just decamped from the neighbourhood, and
Charles, though now quite blind, had been appointed *maire* of St
Rémy, as his father had been before him. For Forster, the renewed
contact with Charles and with France seemed the ending of a five
years' imprisonment.

Not long after this Lily, who was now ninety, fell ill, and by March
it was plain she was dying. On 5 March she would not get up; a day
or two later she had a fall from her bed; and then early in the night
of 10 March she had another fall. Forster slept for the rest of this
night in the passage outside her bedroom, and the next day they had
a tender farewell conversation. Lily said: 'I shan't be long with you,'
to which he replied, 'But your love will.' At 1.30 p.m., as he was
giving her some beef broth from a spoon, she fell back and was dead.

'Yes – sad news. My mouldy mother, as you once called her, is
dead,' he wrote to Joe Ackerley (13 March), 'and I expect now to

---

[1] i.e. his opening address, and a talk 'The Tercentenary of the "Areopagitica",' reprinted in *Two Cheers for Democracy*. The proceedings of the conference
were recorded in a symposium, *Freedom of Expression* (1945), edited by
Hermon Ould.

start mouldering myself, in accordance with the laws.' Florence Barger and his Aunt Rosalie came down to West Hackhurst, in alternation, over the next few weeks, to give him company, and Agnes the maid looked after him with great solicitude: '. . . entirely admirable, helpful, feeling,' he described her to Ackerley (13 March 1945), 'yet never pretending that she and mistress have liked each other.' He was calm, though at moments grieving bitterly and feeling that he could not face life alone. His diary recorded:

> 5 April. Churchyard with blossoms. Broke down returning.
> 6 April. Bob to W.H. Happy.
> 10 April. Broke down returning to W.H.
> 13 April. Went to Dorking. Broke down.
> 11–13 May. May and Robin here. Happy.

He felt he must begin clearing the house. Both his aunt Laura and his mother had been hoarders – the one from family piety, the other from inertia – so that the house was stuffed and overflowing with possessions. For the moment he could not face his mother's room, but he made a start on the papers and letters, some of them dating back 150 years, and all though April he was reading and tearing them up and putting them on bonfires. He also went away for a visit or two, going down at the end of April to stay with Ted B— and his wife Madge in Surrey. The B—s were running a pub, and he spent a cheerful Saturday evening in the bar while Madge served and Ted thumped the piano, helping afterwards with washing the glasses. The thought occurred to him that it was the first time he had really enjoyed himself in a pub. After a few weeks he was able to resume his broadcasting to India. And by June he had become involved in the making of a film, *Diary for Timothy*, for the Ministry of Information. (It was a not-too-successful essay in the 'What-kind-of-world-shall-we-be-making-after-the-war?' style, in which, impersonated by Michael Redgrave, he addressed a baby, Timothy Perkins, born exactly five years after the beginning of the war.[1])

Intermittently, remembering the loss of his mother, he was still drowned by waves of despair. On the day after the Japanese surrender he woke feeling that he couldn't 'live to himself', and all through the day he found himself repeating 'I cannot go on, simply

---

[1] The film, made by the Crown Film Unit, was directed by Humphrey Jennings and was distributed in November.

E. M. Forster and Christopher Isherwood, at Ostende June 1937 (?)

E. M. Forster and R. J. Buckingham 1930s

Ronald Kidd

John Simpson ('John Hampson')

R. J. Buckingham, E. M. Forster,
J. R. Ackerley

J. R. Ackerley and William Plomer

AT DOVER, *circa* 1937

E. M. Forster and J. R. Ackerley

E. M. Forster at International Congress of Writers, Paris 1935.

At the Abinger Pageant, 1938: Lady Allen, E. M. Forster, R. Vaughan Williams, bandmaster.

E. M. Forster, late 1930s (?)

E. K. ('Francis') Bennett

*Unveiling plaque to Forrest Reid at 13 Ormington Crescent, Belfast; 10 October 1952.
From left, H. O. Meredith, Lennox Robinson, Eric Ashby, Lord Mayor, E. M. Forster,
S. Knox Cunningham*

E. M. Forster, Benjamin Britten and William Burrell, in Burrell's boat

E. M. Forster and Eric Crozier, at Crag House, Aldeburgh, 1949

W. J. H. Sprott and J. R. Ackerley, 195(

ay Buckingham, E. M. Forster, J. R. Ackerley and Robin Buckingham, at 129
endell Road, Shepherd's Bush; early 1950s

M. Forster and Charles Mauron, at
Rémy, 1950s

E. M. Forster and William Roerick,
late 1960s

E. M. Forster in his rooms at King's, 1950s

Drawing-room at West Hackhurst, date unknown

cannot,' and then, 'surely she will give up being dead now?' In this emergency, an old instinct came to his aid, and, as often in the past in times of stress, he deliberately sought relief in erotic fantasies. During August he made another visit to the B—s and to Walton Regatta, where Bob Buckingham was rowing, and in his diary afterwards (13 August 1945) he arranged his impressions in the form of an erotic film-scenario:

> Sun sex and a little pain because Bob was rough and sarcastic to me on his boat. Otherwise flowers and trousers opening. Want a film. Boys sleep in the shadow of a car by the tow-path, bare to the middle one of them, and the other's arm round him from behind. Yorkshire boy by the bridge selling soft drinks and filling up my glass when it spilt down my trousers: 'looks like something else.' Youth in lav at night, asks me time, accepts cig, is a brick-layer, drunk? Little M. Ted and a quick one on the Morrison.[1] Cock and one ball of a policeman in shorts seen from the boat below, the sun shining full into their tranquillity. I gazed while he talked to the company. Once or twice he hitched, but they sidled back into view. May kissed me so affectionately when I left, that helped, so did a farming lad with a splinter in his finger. All warmth and willingness. Words – adjectives especially – too formal. All smiles, lightings up, clothes pushed back, soft curves, every where the brightness on young men's faces usually reserved for girls. In the faces & glances, readiness. I in a way wasn't there at all except during Bob's unkindness – and what a rest to be absent! I was the light up the big policeman's shorts and what it touched. I was the splinter up the farm lad's nail. All this needs putting without 'I', so where is a film of people seeing and touch-ing bits of each other in the sun, and not thinking about love or lust. Each night my sleep was stronger, and when I woke with that fatal clear-sighted jump, I had more control over my thoughts than Dame Worry. Should this be in the lovely film too – sensuous angels so driving off Worry that we don't know they protect us? Sun and sex – O teach us no lesson, teach us nothing, come again and open trousers and flowers till – O no last word! Yes, it is warmth, and one's own warmth, and will be there until death and perhaps a little after . . . Don't ever look back at the sun and the sex. Get them into your blood, and they will shine in your eyes. Be impatient and irritable if it helps you turn the right way . . .

A day or two later William Plomer came to spend a night at West Hackhurst and found Forster composed and cheerful. It was a day of

---

[1] Perhaps an allusion to a Morrison air-raid shelter?

national peace-celebrations, and Forster had hung out flags dating from Queen Victoria's diamond jubilee. He took Plomer blackberrying in Piney Copse, showed him some material for a book he was projecting on his Thornton ancestors,[1] and gave him a gold-and-white tea-service. He told Plomer he wished he hadn't 'so many memories, plans and principles.' On 17 August he recorded in his diary: 'I am better, and it *is* the sunshine.'

---

[1] i.e. the future *Marianne Thornton* (1956).

11 The Reluctant Lion

Forster at present had no particular plans for his life, indeed he was trying not to look ahead. Thus when this summer he received an invitation from the All-India P.E.N. to attend a conference of writers in Jaipur, he accepted eagerly. To revisit India at this moment, he felt, would be the ideal diversion, and he blessed his fame for procuring him it. All his friends wanted him to go, he wrote to Isherwood (26 August 1945), 'and some may be glad to get rid of me, for I partly died when my mother did, and must smell sometimes of the grave. – I have noticed and disliked that smell in others occasionally.' He was to be flown to India at the British Council's expense, in the company of Hermon Ould, Secretary of the English P.E.N.; and plane reservations – hard to come by for ordinary travellers – were to be arranged for them by the Secretary of State for India. It worried Forster a little that he should be leaving Agnes alone in the house. However, she was not perturbed, saying 'no one would run away with her', and Joe Ackerley and Sebastian Sprott volunteered to come down from time to time to see her and attend to his mail.

He set out on 5 October 1945, leaving a spray of honeysuckle on his mother's pillow. It was his first air-journey of any length, and the experience excited him. It struck him that, during its two days, he would have recapitulated forty years of his life – France, Sicily, Egypt, India. 'Few people alive can have such culture – practically all the Englishman's tradition.' He was made to feel guilty by the endless lavish meals and was faintly repelled by his companions, all 'priority' travellers like himself.

> How they chatter while the Sunderland sways exactly like a boat.
> Up 5000 feet above the tortured earth, rushing on with masses of
> uneaten and spoiling food. I was relieved to see the man-indifferent
> desert of Sinai, which frightened Ould. Me Sardinia frightened
> with Mussolini's salt colonies, ruled on the ugly liver-coloured
> earth which would have been glad to kill me![1]

He was met in Delhi, as arranged, by a novelist friend Ahmed Ali,
a distant relative of Masood. Ahmed Ali and he had first met in
London just before the war. (Forster thought him a good writer, as
well as a 'perfect charmer', and had helped find a publisher for his
first novel, *Twilight in Delhi* (1940).) Ali put him up for a day or two
in his sister's house in Delhi, and then, since the Conference was not
to begin for twelve days, the two set out on a sightseeing tour.
Forster was moved by the experience. 'I feel like a sponge which has
been dropped back into an ocean whose existence it had forgotten,'
he wrote to Bob Buckingham (8 October 1945). 'I have a swelling
soul, and it is not the same as a swollen head.'

His stay in India, he knew, would be a different sort of thing from
his earlier wanderings. For one thing, as he soon found, he was never
alone – being constantly attended by 'a Gide entourage, who do
every thing for me, fetch, carry, plan, pay, walk, fight.' He was a
public figure, a famous Englishman, fêted and interviewed, and
expected to give talks and broadcasts, and to sign autograph-books,
wherever he went. Invariably, he was asked what changes had struck
him in India since his last visit, and he grew fluent with his answer,
which was 'a higher level of general conversation' and 'the disap-
pearance of *purdah*'. 'If this is fame, I can bear it,' he wrote to Sprott
(12 October 1945). Nevertheless, he longed for solitude, and he seized
such chances of it as offered. As he and his party were driving to
Jaipur, they stopped to visit a ruined Pathan mosque by the wayside,
and Forster remained inside for half an hour in meditation. Ahmed
Ali, who kept him company in silence, remembered that, as they
emerged, his face was radiant. Several more times during Forster's
stay, friends saw him go down on his knees in mosques, like a
believer.

The Jaipur Conference, attended by a thousand or more, took
place in the town hall, in a vast apartment looking out, through
arches, on to the roofs and trees of the Maharaja's palace. On the

---

[1] Travel-diary, 7 October 1945.

platform with Forster were the Prime Minister of Jaipur and Mrs
Sarojini Naidu, famous as a poet and associate of Gandhi. ('Loveliest
of toads,' Forster called her in his diary.)

During the three days of the conference they heard speeches on the
future of the Indian languages, on the Indian copyright act, on a
scheme for an encyclopaedia, and on 'Literature as a unifying force'.
Forster himself gave a version of his talk on 'Literature Between the
Two World Wars'. He thought the conference went well, as such
things go, and was an event that would not have been possible
twenty-five years back. As the speech-making went on, he noticed
above a movement of dim figures, a 'sort of cloud-movement high
up in the thickness of the wall', which he realized to be women
watching from the *purdah*-gallery. 'We might be the future,' he wrote
later,[1] 'but we were observed by the past.'

A week or two after the conference, he set out with Ahmed Ali for
Calcutta. Either by accident or design, it was the first time he had
visited Bengal – most likely by design, for Bengal was the home of
nationalist politics and also of the Tagore cult, neither of which
attracted him. The ten days he now spent there proved the least
enjoyable of his stay, and Calcutta as a city seemed to him quite
desolating. He was staying a few miles outside, with his old friend
Hashim Ali,[2] but spent his days in the city, attending official functions and meeting innumerable writers, half of whom he suspected to
be gate-crashers. More enjoyably, he was also taken for a tour of
painters' studios, and bought a painting from the prolific Jamini
Roy.[3] He was invited to lunch at Government House, and wrote to
Sprott (14 November 1945):

> Yes, yes, India is changing. Past the throne of Warren Hastings,
> down apartments renovated by Curzon, trots a straightforward
> Australian dame, thanking you for coming, and knowing, she too,
> all about Jamini Roy, and Gopal Gosh.[4] Outside the chaprassis
> fling wide the magnificent iron gates to Morgan and worse – guests
> of Mrs Casey in dhotis and saris – and mutter to one another that
> there was a time when *lat* sahibs were *lat* sahibs.

[1] In a broadcast talk, 'India After Twenty-five Years', reprinted in *Two
Cheers for Democracy* as 'India Again'.

[2] Hashim was a cousin of Ahmed Ali.

[3] Forster became friendly with Jamini Roy and opened an exhibition of
his paintings in London the following year.

[4] Another artist whose studio he had visited and who gave him a drawing
he much liked.

During his stay in Bengal, he spent a night at Santiniketan, the university or 'Home of Peace' founded by Tagore. He was pleasantly surprised by it: 'I came to sneer, I remained to sleep,' he wrote to Sprott. 'It really is an agreeable place, and the Great Spirit was referred to by his disciples quite sensibly.'

His next destination was Hyderabad. It was expected that he should stay at the Government Guest House, but, being weary of playing the public man, he escaped to the home of his friend Sajjad Mirza,[1] now the state's Education Secretary. His few days in Hyderabad were a time full of feeling for him. 'I had not realized how much of my heart had gone into this place,' he noted (17 November 1945).

> Such happy days when Masood and the Hydaris were friends and at their best. I visited yesterday Sir Amin Jung[2] too. Both moved, and sitting at his feet I had the peace that comes from Indian old men.

He was living much in memory. One day while there, he asked Sajjad Mirza to drive him to a certain palm-covered hillside at sunset and leave him alone for a while; when Sajjad returned, he told him he had been thinking of Egypt.

Meanwhile the Resident had been ringing for Forster at the Guest House, in vain. Tiring of this, he asked Sajjad Mirza, who he knew was a friend of Forster's, if he could locate him and deliver an invitation to him. 'And did he include you in it?' asked Forster, when he heard. 'No,' said Mirza. 'Then I shan't go. These people have no manners'; and a message was sent that Forster was unwell.[3]

While he was in Hyderabad state, he took the chance, which he had bungled previously, of visiting Ajanta and its famous Buddhist cave-frescoes. The paintings proved all that he had been told or could have hoped, and they gave a happier turn to his mourning for his mother. He noted in his travel-journal (23 November 1945):

> As a rule, I only receive impressions when I forget my grief. But the paintings have fused sadness with interest in the outer world, and have helped me towards doing the same. It is not the loss but the shut-up feeling that is so horrid. The paintings (caves 1 & 2) have not been overpraised, and have gone further towards fusion

---

[1] Brother to Ahmed and Abu Saeed Mirza; see Vol. 1, p. 202, and *passim*.
[2] A friend from his 1921 visit, once Private Secretary to the Nizam.
[3] Later, the Resident's wife rang at Mirza's house and asked to speak to Forster. 'So the game was up,' related Mirza, and Forster went for a meal.

than the Italian 14th & 15th cent. art to which it is natural to
compare them. They are not mystic – geese, Bhils, elephants eating lotus, do not go wispy. But they have found a connection
(unconscious) between my two worlds.

The last month of his stay he spent mostly in Bombay, in the house
of Mrs Wadia, the Secretary of the All-India P.E.N. He enjoyed
Bombay – it was 'grand, fascinating and Levantine,' he told Sprott –
and he performed his public duties there with zeal, lecturing to the
Bombay Rotarians, to the Gujarat Vernacular Society and so on,
also broadcasting on 'Has India Changed?' He felt well and vigorous
and believed that, as regards India at least, he had deserved his
fame. Every now and then, though, the thought came to him that he
was now empty, 'a shell'. On the plane home, he meditated a little
sadly:

> I have failed to do what I might. The only first class thing about
> me now is my grief. With dissatisfaction I look back upon myself
> in India, humorous, conciliatory, an old dear, whose lavish
> gestures gave away very little, and has been too idle to record the
> honest-to-God facts. . . . The day after tomorrow shall be 67. O
> lovely world, teach others to expound you as I have not been able
> to do!

*   *   *

In London, on the morning after his return, he rang Bob Buckingham at the Section House to announce his arrival. Buckingham
sounded mysterious. 'Lots of things have happened since you left,'
he said; 'some good, some bad.' 'What are the bad things?' asked
Forster at once. 'Tell you when I see you,' said Buckingham. He
came round during the day and to Forster's instant inquiry, 'What's
the bad news?' replied breezily: 'Oh it's West Hackhurst. You've got
to leave in nine months or something. Jack Sprott will tell you all
about it.'

This way of breaking the news, Forster soon discovered, had been
stage-managed by Sprott. A few days after Forster's departure for
India, Sprott had found in Forster's mail a letter from the Farrer
solicitors, saying that Lady Bridges (the late Lord Farrer's daughter)
would regretfully have to ask Forster to leave West Hackhurst, since
the house was needed for a relative. He had taken it to Forster's
solicitors, thinking there might be some protection under the Rent
Restriction Act; however they could offer little hope, so, having

debated whether to tell Forster, he had decided to keep the news for his return.[1]

Buoyed by his Indian trip, Forster took the news coolly, and for a few weeks, he went about telling his friends and himself, with a liberal's 'fairmindedness', that there was really no reason why he shouldn't be told to go. By this time he had been given formal notice to quit, in a year's time; and when a further letter arrived from the Farrers' lawyers, he sent a gracious reply, thanking Lady Bridges for giving him so much advance warning. (It occurred to him he might as well not antagonize her, as he had not kept the house in good repair and might be liable for dilapidations.) He told the news to Agnes, who was scared, and to Bone the gardener, who said merely 'Well . . .' and 'Well, I'm sorry.' Neither told anyone else, so for the moment the rumour did not reach the village. Nor, for the time being, could Forster guess who was to supplant him at West Hackhurst.

He began to consider where he might go, when he left Abinger. His first thought was Stevenage, his childhood home and the place where, if anywhere, he could imagine he had roots. But now he discovered a new aspect to his plight: the Labour Government had just declared Stevenage the site of a 'new town'. He was thwarted equally by 'feudalism' and by Socialism, and it seemed as if from now on he were not meant to have 'roots'. Of course, he could forget 'roots', and buy himself a house without associations. A friend of Bob Buckingham's sent him word of a property at East Molesey, and he went to view it. It was small, modern and semi-detached, very trim and convenient; but confronted with it he simply could not imagine himself or his furniture in it. This was almost his sole effort at house-hunting; and for want of a better plan, he began to consider going to America for a long stay.

At this juncture, he heard from J. T. Sheppard, now the Provost of King's College, to say that the College wished to make him an Honorary Fellow. He was gratified; and in his letter of acceptance he remarked casually that he would soon be homeless, so that it would be pleasant to feel he had some connection somewhere. It was a fortunate remark. Sheppard passed it on. And as a result, the Governing Body asked him if he would like to come and 'reside' in

---

[1] 'And great praise I got for this,' he said later, to the author.

College. This was a quite unusual offer; however he was highly regarded in King's and was felt to have peculiar claims on it. He accepted gratefully, not knowing if he should enjoy a life in College rooms, but telling himself it would give him a respite, time in which to look about him.

By this time, his feelings over West Hackhurst had grown rancorous and bitter. In February he was invited by Keynes, who was chairman of the Covent Garden Opera Trust, to the *première* of *The Sleeping Beauty*. It was a lavish occasion, marking the re-opening of the opera-house. He went with May Buckingham, and for the length of the first act he forgot all his chagrins, telling himself with elation that it was the end of wartime gloom and austerity. However, during the interval, while they were having supper with the Keyneses in a private room, he found himself being introduced to Lady Bridges. They shook hands. And the physical contact brought all his bitterness in a flood. For the rest of the evening, oblivious to the ballet, he was composing crushing letters to his Farrer 'enemies'.

Two days later, he received a letter from Lady Bridges's sister, Miss Frances Farrer, telling him she was to be the new tenant of West Hackhurst and asking if they might meet to discuss arrangements. She said how much she regretted inconveniencing him. 'But my roots are very deep in Abinger, and we can no longer afford to stay on at the Hall.' He said to himself, it was an example of the Farrer 'friendliness' technique – the word had passed between the sisters that he could be got round – and, egged on by Joe Ackerley, he replied that, from his own point of view, he could think of nothing requiring immediate discussion; 'and to be frank I should prefer to be undisturbed by callers during the remainder of my tenancy.' To further requests, that Lady Bridges might be allowed to come and measure the rooms, he replied that he would be happy to receive her in six months' time. Meanwhile, he told Agnes and Bone to turn away unwanted callers.

He had fallen into an irrational state of mind over the affair. He knew this himself. For one thing, he had never felt particularly at home in West Hackhurst, having continued half-consciously to regard it as his aunt's house. For another, he could hardly have hoped to go on running it with only Agnes to help him – Agnes, worn out in his service, old, bent double and with bad feet. And what younger servant would come to a house so impossibly inconvenient? But the matter had passed beyond reason. It had come at a moment when, with his mother's death, he was feeling emotionally 'homeless'. And it had disturbed profound and complicated class-feelings, springing from the social difference between his mother's and his father's families. With all his ironies about 'feudalism' and 'visiting his estates', he was not indifferent to his status in Abinger. It was part of his place in the world, the place he had won for himself as a writer, and he felt his expulsion as an attack on it.

*   *   *

It remained for him to sort his possessions, deciding what to take to Cambridge, what to give to friends, and what to sell or burn. The task, when he addressed himself to it, appeared enormous. The house contained the accumulations not just of his Aunt Laura's life and his own and his mother's, but of the whole Thornton past. There was a whole coach-house full of furniture. There were wicker dress-baskets full of letters dating back to the time of Wilberforce and before; innumerable books; seventy pieces of Wedgwood china; and rolls of silk brought back by him from India, never opened and rotting at the folds. He could, of course, have an auction at the house; but that would mean deciding what to keep, which he could not at once do; so all through the year of 1946 he continued sorting and reading and giving away and sending to jumble-sales. The dining-room mantelpiece, designed by his father, was removed and sent up to Cambridge, to be installed in his rooms there, and the sundial on the lawn was uprooted and moved to the parish churchyard, as a memorial to his mother. He even, as he had done fifty years before on leaving Rooksnest, drew up a plan of the kitchen garden. The task took hold of his imagination. During his rummaging he found, he wrote to Plomer (3 July 1946), a box full of gold and jewels, including a locket 'disclosing two unknown people inside who had been facing one another in the darkness all this time'. He took the task seriously. 'I see myself as a historic figure, if not a very important one: the last survivor, the last possessor, of a particular tradition,' he told Plomer (28 July 1946). 'Your family got their clearing up finished a little earlier. Osbert,[1] whose second volume I am now at, will have to start his when I am done.' He was instinctively spinning his removal out, as a protection against other thoughts, and he was still engaged upon

---

[1] Osbert Sitwell (1892–1969), who published an autobiography in five volumes between 1944 and 1950.

it when, in September, he received a letter from Harvard University, inviting him to America the following spring to take part in a Symposium on Music Criticism. The invitation seemed to him a reprieve, and he sent his acceptance the same morning.

Meanwhile, during the same month, Miss Farrer at last paid her visit to West Hackhurst, in the company of an architect. She came prepared to be friendly, but Forster had chosen his line, which was to be, as he later put it, 'courtesy and personal hatefulness'. He ignored her half-proffered hand, received an allusion to her childhood in stony silence, refused to sell her his hens or to solicit Bone to stay on as her gardener – all this with implacable politeness, received of course with equal politeness by Miss Farrer. He made one tiny 'score': the architect caught sight of a plaque in the north verandah and read it out (stumblingly, because of the fancy lettering): 'Edward Morgan Llewellyn Forster. . . . Is that anything to do with you?' he asked. 'My father,' replied Forster; and he thought he noticed Miss Farrer wince. After the visit, Agnes said she hoped Miss Farrer would never get a proper meal.

So far as he could gauge it, feeling in the village seemed to be on his side. For one thing, the Farrers, though in general good landlords, were felt to be a little domineering – this anyway was the reputation of the previous Lord Farrer, who had so alarmed certain of the timider villagers that they would hide from his sight. Forster's own local friends, the Kings, the Reads, the Meade family at the Rectory, naturally supported him; and as his departure drew near, Mrs Meade organized a farewell party for him in the Village Hall. There was dancing, and musical chairs, and the Rector gave a speech about him – a very bad one, Forster thought – after which he presented him with a book in which most of the village had signed their names. Forster then made a speech of his own, in which he exhorted the company to defend their field-paths and rights of way. This, too, did not go down very well, or so he thought: it was too didactic for the occasion. None the less, he felt himself popular. One of the young women of the village said to him, 'You belong here always,' and in his present mood this enchanted him. For years to come he would think sentimentally of this evening.

His prolonged removal came at last to an end. There were final sales, bonfires and distributions of possessions. Agnes had found a home for her retirement, in the house of a niece in Barnet, and Forster, who went to look at it, felt satisfied she would be comfortable there. She was to take with her the cat Tinka; and Forster, in his diary, recorded the last night of Tinka's companion, Toma, who was to be 'put to sleep'.

> *Oct 22*. . . . Much affection during drawing room supper and returned for more. How little I mind his cankered ear. Yesterday morning this very sweet cat, disliking Tinka on my bed, but desirous to honour me, sat on my knee and clawed my pyjama breast. What pleasure these cats have been and felt – years of purring, my creation. Tomorrow he will 'sleep' in 'mother's pocket'. Rubbishy word, sleep.

*   *   *

He arrived in Cambridge in the first days of November. The arrangement was that he should occupy a room in the front court of King's – to his pleasure, it had been that of his old friend and tutor Wedd. And, in addition, partly so as to protect his privacy, he should have some lodgings outside the college, in the house of the Senior Tutor, Patrick Wilkinson.[1] He was, he realized, very fortunate – comfortably lodged, cared for, and surrounded by friends – and his College room, spacious and full of his own furniture, already had a look of West Hackhurst. For some weeks, nevertheless, he felt dazed and miserable. As soon as his presence in Cambridge had become known, people had made efforts to meet and lionize him, but for the moment he did not feel equal to it. He thought he must escape; '. . . there is no privacy,' he complained to May Buckingham, 'and people are always pestering one to be interesting.' He could not imagine what life he should make for himself in Cambridge, nor how long he should remain there. Indeed the one definite prospect in his mind was his coming visit to America. His best support for the moment was his old friend Francis Bennett[2] at Caius College. He would go round to Bennett's rooms daily and lament his fate: it was, he said later, one of Bennett's great charms that one could complain to him without good cause.

By the next term, he had begun to look more kindly on Cambridge. He had re-established contact with the Apostles Society – now active again after a long interval – and had invited them to meet in his room, taking an interest in the society's 'births'. He also began a

---

[1] L. P. Wilkinson (1907–), author of *Horace and his Lyric Poetry* (1945), etc.
[2] See p. 45.

little college teaching in English literature. The word spread that he was accessible, and he began to receive and accept invitations to undergraduate parties.

He had been intending, as soon as he had settled in, to go for a stay with Forrest Reid in Belfast. All through the years he had kept up with Reid, encouraging him, consoling him in his solitude, and helping him to find reviewing. He was much attached to Reid – 'I have a constant and remote love for you which began when I first read the Bracknells,' he once wrote to him – though, privately, he thought his later novels thin. Just as he was preparing for his visit, however, he heard through a friend that Reid was dying; and a few days later the news came of his death. He had always thought Reid neglected by Belfast, and in an affectionate obituary article on him he wrote:

> He was the most important person in Belfast, and, though it would be too much to say that Belfast knew him not, I have sometimes smiled to think how little that great city, engaged in its own ponderous purposes, dreamed of him or indeed of anything.

*   *   *

On 14 April 1947 he set off by plane for the United States. He meant so far as possible to make it a private visit. In India, two years before, he had felt it his duty sometimes to play the great man, but here he would have no such duty. There was, of course, his Harvard lecture to deliver, and he had agreed to give some readings from his novels here and there about the country. Essentially, however, his aims were to see friends – especially Bill Roerick, who had appointed himself Forster's host and guide – and, above all, to go sightseeing. With Roerick's help he had formed an ambitious plan of travel, encompassing the length and breadth of the continent.

Roerick was there to meet him at the airport in New York. He took Forster to stay at his mother's house, on Marble Hill Avenue, and, for the next three days, he and his friend Tom Coley drove Forster about the city, sightseeing and visiting. In Forster's mind there lingered Lowes Dickinson's diatribes against America, and he found New York 'more gracious and benevolent' than he had expected. They met various of Roerick and Coley's actor friends and spent a cheerful and tipsy evening with Edith Oliver, drinking 'May Wine' (hock with woodruff and strawberries in it). On another evening, his friends took him to *Annie Get Your Gun*, his first American musical. To start with, as Roerick recalled, Ethel Merman's yelling quite baffled Forster: then, at her number, 'I'm an Indian too!', in which Annie tries clumsily to move and dance as a Sioux, he became much taken with her. 'But she was so civil to the Indians!' he exclaimed.[1]

Soon after his arrival in New York, he paid a call on Paul Cadmus, at the studio in Greenwich Village which he shared with another painter, Jared French, and his wife. It was a 'perfect' meeting, Forster told Bob Buckingham – his visit having taken them by surprise, before they could 'make suitable arrangements for entertaining the Great Writer'. His hosts fetched wine and delicatessen from a nearby restaurant, and, as he told Bob, he 'ate, drank and talked enormously' – learning from them later that he was rumoured in America to be a man who never spoke. French showed him a painting of his own, an allegory entitled 'Learning', and Forster, after a pause, remarked: 'Isn't it odd that we think of men of the past as heads only but those of the future as having bodies also?' 'Not a stupid comment,' wrote French afterwards,[2] 'and, poor dear, he was put to it to say something; and with the artist beside him!' Cadmus and the Frenches were to be out of New York by the time that he planned his return there, and they insisted he must use their flat, as well as coming to see them in their summer retreat at Provincetown.

It had been agreed between him and Roerick that, in the interval before the Harvard Symposium, they should spend a week or so at Tyringham, a remote spot in the Berkshires where Roerick had a dilapidated farmhouse; he had wanted this quiet spell to 'ease' him into the country, also to give him the chance to revise his Harvard lecture.

The farmhouse itself was uninhabitable in cold weather, so they stayed nearby, in the house of some friends named Rudd. The view from the windows made Forster feel he was living in *Ethan Frome*. '. . . scenery between Switzerland and Hindhead, half covered with snow, milky white birch stems,' he wrote of the place to Sprott; 'in two words New England, nostalgic, a little meagre, a little starved, shelving and rising towards the grandiose, checked, and the Houstonic flowing not quite in a gorge.' On their first evening in the house,

---

[1] See W. Roerick, 'Forster and America', in *Aspects of E. M. Forster*, ed. O. Stallybrass (1969), pp. 61–72.

[2] In a letter to the author, 17 February 1972.

Forster read Roerick his Harvard lecture, and Roerick told him it
had no shape, so they set to work to reconstruct it. 'You have put the
spade into the soil and turned it over,' Forster told Roerick when he
saw his proposed revisions. 'It had to be turned over, but you cut
through all those worms, which must now be sewn together or
destroyed.'

Tyringham was in Shaker country, the Rudds' house itself being
Shaker-built, and he was taken on a visit to the Shaker colony at
Mount Lebanon. Only a handful of occupants remained, all old and
some a little crazed, and for some years there had been no 'shaking' –
indeed no religious activity at all. Forster chatted with the Elderess,
who, to the envy of his friends, gave him a home-made ruler. He felt
no great romance in the place. The most interesting thing about it,
he noted in his Journal, was how it interested and excited his
American friends, filling them with a desire for the primitive. 'It is a
country (say I after 5 days) with an intense *feeling* for the past: much
more so than India.'

During his stay at Tyringham, he was interviewed by a journalist
from the *New Yorker*. 'We found him a shy, apprehensive Edwardian
gentleman of sixty-eight, with a long sensitive nose and tousled tan
mustache,' the reporter wrote.

> He was alone and huddled over a thundering grate fire in a room
> full of cool Shaker furniture when we arrived. He welcomed us
> with a shiver, a blush, and an uneasy chortle. 'I'm really a frightful
> old bore,' he said, twisting the collar of a loose brown sweater. 'I
> have no intention of being bright. Not that I mind being bright
> you know, but I can never seem to accomplish it.' He gave an
> explosive laugh and lapsed into a rather forbidding silence.

They talked about sightseeing, and Forster told him he expected to
go up the Empire State Building.

> 'I think I'll pass up the Niagara Falls, though, I've seen Victoria
> Falls, you know, and I expect one lot of water falling over a ledge
> is rather like another.' An expression of anxiety suddenly appeared
> on his face. 'I say,' he said, 'I do hope that won't annoy anybody.
> I've heard that there's a great controversy between the Niagara
> and the Victoria people.'

The subject of his writings came up, and Forster told the reporter
that Americans had been 'awfully kind' to his books.

> But admiration can be a little frightening, you know. I understand
> there are some very deep readers of mine at Harvard, and I'm a
> bit uneasy about facing them.

The interview was published on 3 May, and Forster told Bob
Buckingham to look out for it, saying it was proving a sort of test:
'Every decent sensible person dislikes it. Everyone who is a fool, a
snob, or a shit congratulates me on it. I don't altogether dislike it
myself. What may be deduced?'

He was due in Harvard on 29 April, and on his way there he took
the chance to visit Hamilton College, the home of his wartime
benefactors the Edward Roots. There was much talk of their gifts
and food-parcels, and he gave a public talk on the subject, telling
his audience that the English in the post-war period, were now 'not
starving but bored, not ragged but dingy'.

At Harvard he was the guest of Professor Finlay. He was the star
performer and opening speaker of the three-day symposium (1–3
May), and in his talk. 'The Raison D'Etre of Criticism in the Arts',[1]
he gently needled the 'deep readers' he associated with Harvard.
The 'critical state', he said, had many merits; it employed 'some of
the highest and subtlest faculties of man'; but it was 'grotesquely
remote from the state responsible for the works it affects to expound'.
Criticism did not have 'spiritual parity' with creation, and 'his main
conclusion on it had therefore to be unfavourable'.

The Finlays gave a reception, at which Forster and T. S. Eliot
were guests of honour. The two writers took up position in front of
the fireplace, but very soon a vociferous group had collected round
Eliot, and had pinned him down on a sofa, for questioning, leaving
Forster more or less deserted. An eyewitness, George Martin, recalled
that Forster was quite unabashed, looking on at the scene with
amusement. Martin and he exchanged glances. He came over. And,
while Harry Levin was grilling Eliot on his Theory of Language,
Forster made mild chit-chat about travel in America.

His own major travels were now to begin, and on 10 May he set
off by plane for the West. A day or two later he was descending the
Grand Canyon on mule-back. He had been wondering, as so often,
whether he were still able to respond to travel-experience, and here
he found himself answered. The Canyon astonished him more than

---

[1] Published in *Two Cheers for Democracy*.

any object that he had ever seen. The same evening, from his 'ranch'
on the Canyon-bottom, he wrote with excitement to Bob Buckingham
(15 May 1947):

> I am half way through a two days' ride on a mule called Monkey,
> so do not expect a normal letter. If it gets posted you will know
> that I have returned to the surface safely. The Canyon is one mile
> deep, and we zigzagged down 8 miles before we reached the
> Colorado or saw it – an incredible story-book river 400 ft across,
> the colour of cement, and so violent that when it passes a beach it
> throws up regular waves sideways like a sea. As a rule it is roaring
> between dark red precipices. . . . The picture above[1] – of the
> chaotic upper surface – gives no impression of the world hidden in
> the depths and throbbing with the mad river. I only decided to
> make the plunge an hour before the mules started. Thought it
> would be 'too much' for me, also bad weather. But the last named
> has only made the descent more romantic, storms and clouds
> doing occasional ballet-dances, and the sun returning. Our guide,
> James, rides first, I last, and he only knows me as 'Gentleman on
> Monkey'. He is a lean cinematographic cow-boy, not much
> interested in us, as why should he be? I should think a guide got
> bored with anyone, even the loveliest young girls. He has to help
> me on and off, am sorry to say. I can never remember *where* I am
> heavy, always assume it is my head. . . . one can't write a letter
> about everything, so I had better try to tell you what the picture
> on this note paper looks like. Imagine a number of sphinxes, each
> over ½ mile high, with white heads and draped in crimson shawls
> which usually leave their paws free. I can't do better for the
> Canyon than that, nor go on for the numerous objects which do
> not resemble sphinxes – a hill like this 〰 which James calls a
> battleship or an extraordinary ⌐‸⌐ like the lid of a
> giantess' work basket. All in a crack occurring in dull level
> country, small fir trees rather like Woking – crack from 1 to 14
> miles across . . .
>
> I hear music – James or someone strumming a guitar and
> looking handsome no doubt, but *must* go to bed now.
>
> All sorts of water are rushing about outside in the dark and.
> someone is singing.

From Colorado he travelled on to Berkeley, in California, to stay
with Noel Voges, an American acquaintance acquired during the
war,[2] and Voges' wife Marietta. Voges was now teaching in the

---

[1] i.e. on the hotel notepaper.

[2] Bob Buckingham and he had met by chance on the Thames riverside,
and when Voges happened to mention his admiration for Forster's work, Bob
had arranged an introduction.

Modern Languages department at the university. He proved to be an excellent host. Also, he interested Forster as a character: the under-privileged American who had 'made good' – most generous and kindly in practice, but hard and strength-worshipping in theory. 'He has an irritability towards weakness,' Forster noted, 'of which he is not proud but is too honest to conceal.' Apart from Voges, nothing in Forster's stay in California made a lasting impression on him. He found the West makeshift and rootless: 'No indigenous civilization to clamp it down. The Indian are thinnest ghosts, the Mexicans, who would clamp, too infrequent, Spain too phoney.'

There followed a series of immense train-journeys: over the Rockies to Salt Lake City; across the Great Plains to Chicago; and – for he had changed his mind about Niagara Falls – north across the border to Ontario. Scenically it was full of wonders for him, and he adjured himself to remember, especially, three sights:

> (i) the Moonlit Assyrian Bull seen by chance in the first ascent of the Rockies; so narrow it was, so tall, so sudden the light-change when we reached it, that I gasped as rarely (ii) a low doorway of cloudy light in the thunder cloud overhanging Salt Lake (iii) the V of the Great Plains . . . what beside it is the Rift Valley from Kenya?

He had been awed, too, by Boulder Dam, which had given him 'a vision of a transformed world'; and by a contrasting spectacle in the Arizona desert – an array of obsolete aircraft, thousand upon thousand of them, awaiting destruction. 'When you reflect that each plane carries a wireless set which will also be destroyed,' he wrote, 'you begin to realize the other side of the Spirit of America – the Spirit of Waste.' Certain oddities and surprises stayed with him as well: the five separate locks on his host's[1] door in Chicago; a lady Saint reeling drunk in the streets of Salt Lake City: and the chamber-maid in the hotel there, who told him, when he offered her a tip, 'I don't like to take your money, brother; you need it more than I do.'

There were many invitations awaiting him on his return to New York, and during the next week or two he did much dining out and party-going, also giving several public readings and lectures. He made the acquaintance of Lionel Trilling, spending an evening with him and his wife Diana, during which they discussed – as Forster put

---

[1] Professor Morton Dauwen Zabel.

it – 'the liberalism which stultifies itself in the name of liberalism'. Trilling arranged a lecture for him, then discovered it to be a 'communist trap' and persuaded him to withdraw. ('I do hate traps,' Forster wrote to Bob Buckingham, 'I never know whether I ought to fall into them or not.') He felt much respect for Trilling, and the Trillings were greatly charmed with him. They later recalled, particularly, one tiny incident. They had given him their young baby to hold, and, thinking to please the child, he had swept its face into a bunch of sweet-smelling lilacs. The baby had yelled with rage; and instantly his sole concern had been for the child, not even remotely for his own *amour-propre*.

While he was in the flat at St Luke's Place he happened to read some stories, partly on homosexual themes, by a twenty-eight-year-old friend of Cadmus named Donald Windham. He was struck with them and got Cadmus to give him an introduction to Windham, who lived in New York, and he began with him one of those relationships of friendship, professional helpfulness and careful (sometimes severe) literary advice that he was skilled in.[1] Some years later he wrote an Introduction to Windham's collection of stories *The Warm Country* (1960), saying that the most important thing about Windham was that he 'believed in warmth'. 'He knows that human beings are not statues but contain flesh and blood and a heart, and he believes that creatures so constituted must contact one another or they will decay.'[2]

The Indian ambassador to the U.S.A., Asaf Ali, an old acquaintance of Forster's, had invited him to Washington, and during June he stayed for five days there in the Indian embassy. It gave him an experience – alarming to him – of the cocktail-party circuit. ' "To meet you meet you meet you" sings a bird outside my . . . window this early morning . . .,' he noted, 'well symbolizing Washington Society.' He was treated with much attention at Washington parties – but often on the assumption that he was C. S. Forester, and he grew hardened to being thanked by strangers for his immortal Captain Hornblower.

It amazed him how deeply Washington was obsessed with the

---

[1] See *E. M. Forster's Letters to Donald Windham* (Verona, 1975).

[2] He wrote, more equivocally, to Eric Fletcher (12 December 1960) that a friend (Ted Gillott) had liked the stories very much. 'He thinks they are about people who gave themselves away too much. I think they are about people who gave themselves away too little.'

Russians. At a dinner at the embassy, given in his honour, one of the guests, a journalist, proposed the dropping of an atomic bomb on Russia without warning. 'Stone dead hath no fellow . . . That's good, isn't it Tom?' he called to another journalist, and the two shouted and chanted the phrase to each other for the rest of the evening. Forster was disgusted. 'Had not expected such an experience at Washington or in an embassy,' he noted disapprovingly.

During his stay in Washington he visited the National Gallery, and, as a privilege, he was shown the treasures of the Kaiser Friedrich Museum of Berlin – removed by the American army from a salt-mine in the Russian zone and now kept in secrecy in a locked cellar. The sight of these imprisoned spoils impressed him. 'I have seen the great art-crime of the age,' he reflected. 'Napoleon's nothing to it.'

Bill Roerick was at Tyringham, acting in a stock company, and Forster paid a return visit there, this time living in 'Lost Farm' itself. It was very rough and bare, reminding him of Clouds Hill. 'Don't let the ladies make it cottage-chintzy,' he told Roerick. 'They will want to.' The chores at the cottage were shared, Forster's being to fetch two pails of water each morning from the brook. The peace and loneliness pleased him, and he found something touching in this gentle, so-nearly English landscape. 'Saw a bobolink in the meadows,' he noted. 'What a quaint pet, and what a pretty song! How wrong the English have gone in their contempt of the American country scene and their denial of distinction.'

These last days in America were a happy time for him. He had felt he had 'had the America he wanted' and reflected, gratefully, how much he had been cosseted by his American friends – perhaps too much for his own good. He was loth to go and told himself at moments, especially on waking, that he had nothing to go back to. Paul Cadmus came to New York to see him off and shopped and packed for him, while he gave another interview and had his portrait drawn by Bernard Perkin. He took the plane home on 12 July 1947, with no expectation of ever returning. 'Last night in the kindest of lands,' he noted. 'Last night on earth always a possibility too.'

12 Writing Again

The life in Cambridge to which he returned began to present attractions. He had been accustomed to say that Cambridge was a place for the very young or the very old, and now that he was old he found that in many ways it suited him well. He was looked after; he was among friends; he knew the way of life and loved the city and its buildings; and at his age it was convenient, though it had its disadvantages, to live somewhere he might easily be visited. The idea of finding a house elsewhere gradually faded.

A new element had entered his life: the duties belonging to great fame. His daily post was enormous: there poured in invitations and requests for interviews, letters of praise or abuse from strangers, begging letters, business letters (for he employed no agent), theses on him sent for his comments, or books sent, unsolicited, for him to autograph. He found it a curse, and he reproached himself for idleness in answering; but it went with a stream of public praise and affection, for which he was grateful.

Now that he was known to reside in Cambridge, many people were burning to meet him. He was an object of pilgrimage, particularly, for visiting Indians. This pleased him, and he made several valued friends in this way, though also acquiring one or two pests or parasites, on whom he would keep a 'file'. He was very generous towards Indian acquaintances, often helping them with money and writing numerous prefaces to books by Indian writers.[1]

The young generally were eager for his acquaintance. Some of them sought it out of curiosity, as one might want to see the Pope or the

---

[1] For instance to *Hali* by G. V. Desani (1950), *Maura* by Huthi Singh (1951) and *Zohra* by Zeenuth Futehally (1951).

Pyramids; others out of lion-hunting; and others again to sit at his feet, or consult him as an oracle, or bring him their personal problems. All this seemed very natural to him, and he was skilful in dealing with it. He felt he had duties in the matter. In his books, he had played the mentor or sage, so it was to be expected that in life also he should be sought after as a sage; and indeed he thought he had wisdom, though he did not believe it could be communicated.[1] He knew, too, that – to a rather special degree – people fell in love with him through his books. Admittedly, the person they fell in love with in this way was to some extent imaginary. Still, he had wanted this love and felt it wrong to reject it.

Further, he had not given up wanting new friendships, especially with young men, and his fame helped him in making new ones. At about the time, he struck up a very warm friendship with a King's undergraduate named Eric Fletcher, a miner's son from Doncaster. He wrote about Fletcher to William Plomer (7 November 1948), in the early days of their acquaintance: 'He's working class (very much so in his speech) . . . I like him for his outlook as well as for himself – humanist, humanitarian, openly agnostic, whereas most people up here, young or old, hedge, and sometimes turn into quick set hedges.' Fletcher, for his part, became greatly devoted to Forster. He left Cambridge in 1948, marrying and becoming Principal of a Teachers' Training College. Forster and he continued to meet and stay with each other, and over the coming years, Forster wrote him several hundred letters of gossip, affection and advice.

Among the senior members of the College, Forster had acquired one close friend, Kenneth Harrison – a biochemist, and lay Dean of the College – generous, warm-hearted and freakish in his conversation. Apart from this, his relations with the King's dons were affectionate but unintimate, and he would sometimes rebuke himself for not contributing more to college life. He suspected that the smarter dons avoided him, finding him too uninteresting despite his fame – 'so distinguished yet so undistinguished'. One evening he caused amusement by playing Patience in the Combination Room. 'They liked seeing me do something,' he noted. 'I do too little and bore

---

[1] He noted in his Commonplace Book in 1943: '*Wisdom*, when acquired, proves incommunicable and useless and goes with our learning into the grave. The edges of it occasionally impinge on people, though, and strike a little awe into them.'

them.' The present Provost of the College was J. T. Sheppard, a friend
of Forster's from undergraduate days.[1] He was by now rather a vain
old man, with Quilp-like body and flowing white locks – a figure much
revered by strangers to Cambridge, but in private teasing and
malicious; Forster would have little brushes with him from time to
time, and would dissect his character in his diary. Sheppard made a
cult of Bob Buckingham, doing him many real kindnesses and
declaring loudly, for the benefit of his colleagues, 'if half my dons
were as intelligent as you we should have a most splendid College!'
Bob considered the Provost a great friend, but Forster suspected him
of devious motives.

The chief objection to great fame, Forster was finding, was that it
helped to keep him idle. 'Being an important person is a full time
job,' he reflected, 'and is bound to generate *some* inward futility and
pretentiousness. "You need not do any thing – you've arrived." And
I don't.' There were those who spotted his indolence. Simon Raven,
who came up to King's as an undergraduate at about this time, wrote
later, in a caustic article,[2] that 'Morgan Forster was (or seemed to be)
bone idle . . . He was for ever pottering from nowhere in particular to
nowhere else, so that very often, if he happened on friends by the
way, he would turn round and go wherever they were going instead.'

Forster wished dearly that he could settle to some solid piece of
work, while he was still capable of it, and one project he considered
intermittently was that he should write up his Dewas experiences, or
at least such part of them as was publishable. He felt that the
moment to do so had come; and during 1948 he had his letters from
Dewas typed and wrote to Darling asking for his own reminiscences
of that 'vanished magic and muddle'.

*   *   *

He still kept up an active London existence and, most weeks,
would spend a day or two in his Chiswick flat, seeing friends. Always
he would travel with a small Gladstone bag, which would contain his
pyjamas (usually not a pair), a sponge, and, for his breakfast, a screw
of melting butter, an egg (wrapped up in his socks), and some bread
(or he might be intending to ask some friend for 'a bit of bread'). All
his travelling in London, whatever the weather or the hour, would be

---

[1] His Apostles paper, 'King's or Trinity', may, I have suggested, have had
some influence on *The Longest Journey*. (See Vol. 1, pp. 104–7.)

[2] 'The Strangeness of E. M. Forster', *Spectator*, 5 September 1970.

done by Tube or bus, taxis being in his view a vulgar extravagance.

The friends he would most regularly see were Joe Ackerley and the Buckinghams. There had been a change in Ackerley. Some time in 1945 his deserter friend, X—, had been arrested – as it so happened, by Bob Buckingham – and had been sent to prison. Ackerley had done all he could for X—,[1] forming an uneasy alliance with X—'s wife over prison visits, and going regularly to see his parents. On one of these later occasions he had seen and taken pity on X—'s dog, a beautiful young Alsatian bitch named Queenie. No one in the household took Queenie for walks, so he had volunteered to do so himself, journeying at weekends all the way from Putney to east London for the purpose, and this had had a curious sequel, for his affections had gradually transferred themselves from X— to the dog. Eventually he had bought her from X—, and she had revolutionized his life. No longer during the office day did his mind run on the evening's chase, but on the welcome awaiting him from Queenie – on her walk, the problem of food for her supper, her sex-life and her ailments. It was a bother to Ackerley's friends – if only because Queenie, who was possessive and hysterical, barked ceaselessly in company, wrecking all attempts at conversation.* Forster was both worried and irritated by Joe's obsession. ('Just off to lunch with doggy Joe, and hope he will bore *and shock* me less than he did last time,' he wrote to Sprott during 1946.) He was gentle about it to Ackerley, but very occasionally teased him: Ackerley, on one occasion asked how any one could enjoy seeing a baby, 'except its fond parents', to which Forster replied 'Considering how *some* people dislike *some* animals, your rejection of all babies is somewhat of a challenge.' Once, when Queenie barked at Forster's landlady, he broke out 'That *bloody* dog!' but instantly apologized to Joe, saying earnestly 'But it was so *rude.*'

* * *

For some years Forster had not been active in the National Council for Civil Liberties. Friends like Leonard Woolf had continued to warn him about its Communist leanings, and an incident at the annual

---

[1] His friends had the greatest difficulty in preventing him from appearing in court and making dramatic appeals on X—'s behalf – which, as they told him, would infallibly give a homosexual flavour to the affair, would probably earn X— a heavier sentence, and might very well land him in gaol too.

general meeting in March 1948 finally brought him round to their opinion. The Government had recently announced a purge of Communists from the civil service, and at the meeting a motion condemning this action had been passed, amid a good deal of cheering and howling-down of objectors. Forster made it the occasion to resign, on the grounds that the motion was not a civil liberties one but a political one. His letter to the *New Statesman* announcing his decision (15 May 1948) was a mild one, saying he resigned only 'after careful consideration and with much regret' and paying tribute to the memory of Ronald Kidd.

*   *   *

During the summer of this year the first Aldeburgh Festival took place, and Forster was invited by Benjamin Britten to give a lecture at it, on the poet George Crabbe. There was a curious history behind the invitation. Britten and Forster had known each other since the days of *The Ascent of F.6* (see p. 213), and, through a happy accident, Forster had had considerable influence on Britten's career. Britten had followed Auden to America in 1939, planning to apply for American citizenship, but by 1941 he had begun to feel doubts about his decision. In this mood of uncertainty, he had happened to pick up a copy of the *Listener*, containing an article by Forster on Crabbe. It began 'To think of Crabbe is to think of England.' To Britten, who had been born in Crabbe's part of Suffolk, it had come home intensely, and it had precipitated his decision to return to England. It had also set him reading Crabbe, especially the poem 'Peter Grimes' which Forster had discussed in his article, and when, shortly afterwards, he received a grant from the Koussevitsky Foundation to write an opera, he chose 'Peter Grimes' as a subject.

Since Britten's return from America, the two had occasionally met and had corresponded. At a National Gallery Concert in 1944 Forster had heard Britten and Peter Pears perform Britten's *Michelangelo Sonnets* and had been much impressed, buying himself records of the work. Hearing of this, Britten had presented him with a score; and a year or two later he made Forster the present of a gramophone, with an admiring inscription. It was agreed that, for the Festival, Forster should stay with Britten and Pears at their house in Aldeburgh. He went a few days in advance of the opening, to do some exploration of the Crabbe countryside, and in the evenings Britten and Pears played and sang for him and improvised musical parodies at the piano. He was enchanted by his whole stay and told Plomer that his hosts were 'the sweetest people'. The lecture that he gave was on 'George Crabbe and *Peter Grimes*', and in it he speculated as to what sort of opera *Peter Grimes* would have been if he had been the librettist. Certainly a rather different affair, he said; it would have been more faithful to Crabbe and would have featured ghosts, hell-fire and a spine-chilling curtain-scene like the one in *Don Giovanni*.

* * *

During the autumn of 1948 Forster fell into depression – one of the acutest depressions of his life. There were a number of factors contributing. He was nearly seventy, thus on the threshold of old age. He was still obsessed by his 'homelessness' and his 'expulsion' from Abinger. He felt unproductive and, as it were, living from hand to mouth intellectually. And, as happened from time to time, there was a hitch in his friendship with Bob Buckingham. Earlier in the year, he had helped the Buckinghams buy a house in Shepherd's Bush, but since then, Bob – or so Forster thought – had been 'boorish' and ungracious and had neglected him. The thought gnawed him that he could no longer interest or impress Bob. The perennial fear of his life, constantly dispelled and constantly returning, was that his imaginative life should dry up; but under this, and allied to it, lay a worse fear – that he should lose the power to feel about people or take interest in them. He had evoked this fear in *A Passage to India*, when depicting Mrs Moore's collapse after her visit to the Marabar caves, and it now took hold of him. 'I open this book in fulfilment of a vow,' he wrote miserably in his diary for 8 October.

> After three miserable days in London I believed that I must address myself. For I cannot speak to others of my worst trouble, which is that I have got tired of people and personal relationships. I don't avoid people who are in my way, but I want to see no one – except Rosie, E. K. Bennett and Bob, and the young who are different. Unless I can manage to settle down to some work this year, I may go wrong in my head. I feel so desolate and useless, and observant people see it in my face. A 'red-Indian' slapped me on the arm in Tottenham Court Road saying 'be cheerful.' . . . Part of my disintegration is old age, over which I need not waste time. Will self-communing check the other part? . . . I am writing this in No. 3 Trumpington Street, one of my many unsatisfactory 'homes'. It has not brought me nearer to myself so far. I feel scared. If human beings have failed me, what is left?

The desolation soon left him, and it was never to return with such acuteness. By December he was recording that he had been very happy lately. Bob Buckingham was affectionate once more, and the world seemed conspiring to treat him with kindness and flattery. For his seventieth birthday Plomer and Ackerley organized a party in a Soho restaurant, inviting various of his closest friends.[1] There were birthday tributes to him in the papers, and many private letters. Bennett wrote to him:

> To me you are my *wise* friend as well as being my loving friend, and this being a suitable occasion I want to say how much my life owes to you . . . it is not only the 'me' of today but also the poor boy to whom you were kind forty years ago who thanks you now.

Forster told himself that the word had gone round that 'I am old and must be spoilt.'

*   *   *

There was a further reason for his contentment. Britten, so it seemed, had remembered the half-conscious hint he had dropped in his Aldeburgh lecture. Since then, Britten had been invited to write an opera for the Festival of Britain, and he suggested they should collaborate. Forster was greatly excited at the prospect. At first he hesitated, feeling his lack of theatrical experience. However, then it was suggested that he should have a helper, Eric Crozier – an experienced librettist and man of the theatre who had already collaborated with Britten on an opera[2] – and at this, he accepted. It was exactly the stimulus he needed. And, as it proved, it was the beginning for him of ten or so very contented and productive years.

It remained to find a subject for the opera: and after a good deal of fruitless discussion, Britten and Forster, almost simultaneously, hit on the idea of Herman Melville's *Billy Budd*. It seemed to them, instantly, the right, the perfect choice. They sent a telegram to Crozier, summoning him to them at Aldeburgh; and when Crozier suggested difficulties, pointing out that it meant an exclusively male cast, they were too impatient to listen.

Crozier overcame his doubts, and Forster found him an admirable

---

[1] The guests were Anwar Masood and his wife, the Buckinghams, the Wilkinsons, Rose Macaulay, Elizabeth Poston, Hugh Meredith, E. K. Bennett, Sebastian Sprott and his friend Charles Lovett, and John Simpson.
[2] He wrote the libretto of *Albert Herring* (1947).

collaborator. Together, in the course of sixteen days at Britten's house[1] in March 1949, they roughed out a good deal of a first draft of the libretto. Melville's story concerns a handsome and innocent-hearted naval rating, Billy Budd, hanged for striking and accidentally killing his persecutor, a malevolent petty officer, Claggart. As Melville wrote it, the weight lies not so much on Billy as on the ship's captain, Vere, who, though knowing Billy's innocence, feels it his duty to condemn him. The problem Forster and Crozier set themselves, Forster told Plomer, was to 'rescue Vere from Melville', that is to say to correct Melville's excessive respect for authority and discipline, as embodied in Captain Vere – in fact to make Billy the hero rather than Vere. Apart from this major change, Forster decided to make one important addition to Melville's text: a soliloquy or *credo* for Billy's persecutor, Claggart. In writing it, he took a hint from a remark made by William Plomer, in a preface to Melville's story,[2] to the effect that 'natural depravity' is not the same as absolute evil. 'We were anxious to avoid competition with Iago's monologue in Verdi's Otello,' he told Plomer (10 March 1949), 'and this aids us – Iago being absolutely evil, and quite chirpy in consequence.' He was pleased at his monologue, thinking it his best achievement as a librettist. It was a grand-opera effect; and in general he thought in terms of grand opera, being anxious, he told Britten (20 November 1948) that the work should be mounted 'clearly and grandly' – 'I seem to have the fear of a lot of symbolic and inexpensive scenery.'

In May, Forster went for a second and briefer visit to America. He went this time with Bob Buckingham, staying at 'Lost Farm' and in Greenwich Village and revisiting Hamilton College to receive an honorary degree. On his return he at once resumed work on the opera, and by August he and Crozier had completed their first draft, altering it from a three-act to a four-act shape. He was enjoying the experience of creation and felt a growing excitement about the work. 'An enormous amount of stuff has got caught and fixed,' he told Ackerley (21 August 1949), 'partly out of Melville, partly out of the inversions of his absurdities.' Britten, as usual with him, was involved in half-a-dozen other projects and had not yet begun composing. Forster grew impatient: 'I do wish Ben would get on,' he would remark fretfully to Crozier. However, at this point, his plans fell into confusion, for

---

[1] Crag House, overlooking the seafront.
[2] Introduction to *Billy Budd* (John Lehmann, 1947).

he had a revival of his old prostate trouble and was told he must have another operation. His chief regret, when he heard this, was that he might be leaving *Billy Budd* unfinished.

The operation was fixed for December, in a nursing-home in Sloane Square, and May Buckingham volunteered to come in to the nursing-home and act as his nurse. The gesture touched and delighted him and became another bond between them. It was also fortunate, for – or so his doctor told him afterwards – by her quickness in reporting some symptom she saved his life.

For his convalescence, Britten had invited him to Aldeburgh. He stayed there some months, being looked after with much tenderness by Britten. By now Britten had begun work on the opera, and, as soon as Forster's strength returned, the two worked on it together, doing several very productive weeks of work. As recreation they would sometimes go sailing in the boat of a fisherman friend, Bill Burrell, a handsome and good-natured young man with a 'noble savage' quality faintly evocative of Billy Budd's. (In later years Forster would sometimes go to stay with Burrell and his wife.)

The friendship of Forster and Britten had been a quick and intense one, and these weeks were, in a sense, its peak. Soon minor frictions began to develop. Forster, feeling himself fruitfully employed at last, could not understand Britten's breaking off at every moment to play in concerts or attend conferences. Vexed by this, he left Aldeburgh rather earlier than he had planned; and soon afterwards, on a visit of Britten's to Cambridge, he got it into his head that Britten had treated him off-handedly and told him so very sharply. (Crozier, who was present, was astonished at his fierceness; 'he berated him [Britten] like a schoolboy,' he related.) There was a mild estrangement for a time, repaired partly through Crozier's efforts. Forster blamed himself for his part in it. 'I am rather a fierce old man at the moment,' he confessed to his diary (31 December 1950), 'and he is rather a spoilt boy, and certainly a busy one.'

A little later there was a further jar between them. Forster, who in general thought the *Billy Budd* music magnificent, wrote to Britten criticizing the setting of Claggart's monologue. He said:

> It is my most important piece of writing and I did not, at my first hearing, feel it sufficiently important musically ... I want *passion* – love constricted, perverted, poisoned, but never the less *flowing* down its agonizing channel; a sexual discharge gone evil. Not

> soggy depression or growling remorse. I seemed turning from one
> musical discomfort to another, and was dissatisfied. I looked for
> an aria perhaps, for a more recognizable form.

Britten, though Forster did not know this, was intensely touchy about criticism and, as Forster heard from Crozier, was badly offended by the letter. Forster made efforts to repair his mistake, and before long matters were mended. By now he felt certain they were engaged upon a masterpiece.

*   *   *

He was at Aldeburgh again several times during 1951, and in June, while climbing the belfry of the parish church, he fell and broke his ankle. It was quite a serious fracture. With his foot in plaster, and being unhandy with crutches, he was left more or less helpless by it, and the Buckinghams insisted, for the moment, on his coming to live with them. It was several months before he could walk again, and, as May Buckingham recalled, he was a bad invalid. Annoyed that the specialist was, as he thought, neglecting him, he asked May to make a boot to go over his plaster, to get him walking again. 'Well, I made the boot as instructed,' she related, 'and was trying it on, and Morgan got absolutely furious and threw the boot at me. And he never learned to use his crutches. Rose Macaulay came, and "It's easy, Morgan," she said, and she was going up and down the room, showing him how easy it was – but he never tried. We've got those crutches still.'

To occupy himself in his helpless state, Forster turned his mind to his projected book of Indian memoirs. It was a difficult task in some ways. The material was delicate politically and bristling with libel dangers. Also, he would not be able to discuss his own sexual escapades – not that he wanted to do so, for their own sake; but it was they that brought him closest to the Maharaja and were his grounds for considering him a saint. This was a weakness that the book must always suffer; and, despite it, *The Hill of Devi* gradually began to take shape. He sought and obtained much advice from Darling, and, to his good fortune, Darling managed to find a graphic letter written by himself from Pondicherry, describing the Maharaja in his despair and exile. Forster felt happy to be dwelling upon Dewas, a place which still had mystery for him. He wrote to Darling: 'Sometimes I think of Dewas as a hole going down (beneficently) to the centre of the earth.'

The end of 1951 was a little peak of fame for him. During the past year he had assembled a new collection of his reviews and essays, under the title of *Two Cheers for Democracy*, and this was published in November, gaining a particularly enthusiastic and admiring reception. There was a feeling that, over the last decades, he had somehow kept his nerve better than most of his contemporaries. Reviewers praised the cunning of his style and his strategies. Jocelyn Brooke, in the *Spectator* (9 November 1951), wrote that 'The oblique, sinuous sentences worm their way into one's mind, apparently so off-hand, yet carrying a weight of meaning which seems disproportionate to their spare and elegant scaffolding.' V. S. Pritchett, in the *New Statesman* (13 November 1951) noted: 'The streak of personal inadequacy is carefully, cunningly put in; the astutely dated slang plays its part in the masked battery of weakness.' The reviewers were agreed, too, in recognizing a new firmness in his tone. 'He is consistent, he is tough,' wrote P. H. Newby in the *Listener* (1 November 1951), 'he is quite unlike the person described under his name in the *Concise Cambridge History of English Literature* as being "at heart a scholar" whose work has a "shy unworldly quality".'

The following month, the première of *Billy Budd* took place at Covent Garden. It had a generally enthusiastic, if not rapturous, reception, several critics praising Britten's genius for creating 'music of the sea' though one or two others complaining of his failure at this, many complimenting Forster and Crozier on the intelligence and distinction of their libretto but some others accusing it of a lack of dramatic life.

*   *   *

In 1951 Bob Buckingham reached the police retiring age. He was only fifty, young enough to begin a new career, and, with Forster's encouragement, he decided he would try to get into the probation service. It turned out, there was some prejudice against ex-policemen in the service, but Forster used his influence with Margery Fry and others, and Buckingham was accepted for training. However, when, two years later, he came to apply for jobs, he was told that he could not be employed in London, and as a result he had to take a post in Coventry. This was a blow for Forster. During his long stay in the Buckinghams' house, he had come to think of it as a home, and since then he had often come to stay there, and the house had become a meeting-place for his friends. Each summer, since 1951, the Buckinghams and he had thrown a large party there, and streams of famous people had filled the garden at Wendell Road. It now seemed that, once again, he was to lose a home. At first he was against Buckingham taking the job. For the last time in their lives, there was a fierce quarrel between him and May Buckingham; and when she and Bob began house-hunting in Coventry, he began to reclaim this or that piece of his furniture from them, declaring that it had only been lent. His resentment quickly subsided; and when, near the end of 1953, they found a house, he helped them very handsomely in buying it, as well as towards buying a car. Very soon he was paying them frequent visits in their new home, a semi-detached house in the Coventry suburbs. He told Plomer that it was very nice – if one didn't look out of the windows, for the garden 'forecast an allotment in hell'.

At about the same time he had to give up his rooms with the Wilkinsons in Cambridge. In lieu of them, the College gave him a bedroom, but he felt it as one more dispossession. 'I see my furniture everywhere, my home nowhere,' he lamented. By this time, his friends were feeling he made too much of his homelessness, and eventually Bob Buckingham attacked him on it, telling him he was making himself unhappy to no purpose. He took the advice to heart, and, with some pangs, he now made a formal renunciation of 'homes' and 'roots in the land'.

*   *   *

He was by this time a grand old man of letters and might expect to receive national honours. A year or two before, he had been offered a knighthood but had refused it, telling his friends that 'it wasn't good enough for him'.[1] In 1952, however, he was approached by the Palace with the offer of a C.H. This seemed to him more suitable, and he accepted, remarking in his letter that he preferred honours that came after his name. The award was announced in the New Year's Honours for 1953, and he went to Buckingham Palace for the investiture the following month. It was quite a lengthy audience, in the course of which the Queen said how sad it was he had published no book for so long – upon which he politely corrected

---

[1] He took an independent line towards honours. On one occasion he was informed by Oxford that an honorary degree was to be bestowed on him and that he should present himself to receive it on such-and-such a day. He considered the tone of this presumptuous and replied that he must refuse the honour, since it would not be convenient for him to be in Oxford on that day.

her. As he left, he brandished the insignia to an equerry, exclaiming brightly 'Well, I got my little toy,' and was received with freezing glances. They failed to chill him, and he returned to Cambridge in a glow of loyalty, declaring that if the Queen had been a boy he would have fallen in love with her. Lengthy accounts of the occasion were sent to his aunts Nellie and Rosalie and the maid Agnes.

Once or twice every year he would pay a nostalgic visit to Abinger, to take a distant view of West Hackhurst and to call on Bone the gardener. Rose Macaulay, an old friend and author of a book about him,[1] drove him there for his mother's birthday in February 1952. They took flowers to the churchyard, and Rose was amused at his method with them. 'He was rather nice,' she wrote to a friend.[2]

> He distributed sprays of mimosa also to the graves of his aunt, close by, and other deceased acquaintances, according to their deserts, taking some away when he recalled tiresome things they had once done, and being very careful to raise no jealousies; it seems that even in the grave, feuds rage in country villages.

With his renunciation of 'homes' and 'roots', his chagrin and obsession over West Hackhurst faded, and with it his resentment against the Farrers; when he heard of a suicide in their family, he felt a twinge of guilt at ever having wished them harm. At the time, his expulsion had offended his family pride. And now pride – or at any rate interest in his Thornton ancestors grew in him, and he renewed connection with one or two surviving Thornton relatives. He discovered that his cousin Sir Hugh Thornton and Sir Hugh's wife May also took an interest in family history, and he exchanged information with them and went with them on expeditions to Clapham. Meanwhile he was still burrowing through his mass of old letters and papers, puzzling as to what to keep and what to destroy. The letters were mostly very dull, but – as he felt increasingly – they represented a tradition; and though he rejected patriotism and had renounced 'roots in the land', he believed in tradition. He also believed in, and had a deep imaginative feeling for, inheritance and post-humous influence. As he read, the character of his great-aunt Marianne impressed him more and more, and he began to speculate about her

---

[1] *The Writings of E. M. Forster* (1938). He did not think very highly of it.
[2] See Rose Macaulay, *Letters to a Friend*, ed. C. Babington-Smith (1961), p. 261.

influence on him. Her legacy had, at any rate in the material sense, been the making of his career as a novelist, and the inheritance could be seen in a spiritual aspect too. There was a theme here: how, through Aunt Monie's love and hopes for him, so Philistine a family as the Thorntons should in the end have produced an artist. He saw his way to a substantial book, and, during 1953, having completed *The Hill of Devi*,[1] he set to work upon it. In form, it developed into a fourfold biography of Marianne Thornton: as Daughter, Sister, Aunt and Great-Aunt. Houses loomed large in it; and as he came to write of the time in the 1850s when, through family disputes, the house in Battersea Rise had stood vacant, he composedly drew a parallel with his own experience.

> They did not know whether they wished the house to be sold and to vanish off the spiritual face of the earth, or to stand as it was, an empty and dishonoured shell. I understand many of their feelings: it has so happened that I have been deprived of a house myself. They will not be understood by the present generation.[2]

---

[1] It was published in October 1953.
[2] *Marianne Thornton* (1956), p. 188.

13 E. M. Forster Described

I got to know Forster myself early in 1947, a few months after he had arrived in Cambridge. I was then twenty-seven and had just become a fellow of Emmanuel College. We met at the Apostles, and a day or two after our first encounter he called on me in my rooms uninvited. It was a sort of 'apostolic' visit, very charmingly conducted on his part, and on the strength of it, during the coming year, we got on to terms of friendship. I left Cambridge a few years later, to work in London, but we continued to meet and to correspond; and eventually, a year or two before his death, he asked me if I would like to write a book about him.

I will try in this chapter to describe him as he was when I first knew him. It is easiest to picture him in his College room. This was on the first staircase of the front court of King's: a spacious, high-ceilinged room with tall Victorian-gothic windows, looking out on to a little inner court. The first thing that caught one's eye in the room was the mantelpiece, designed by his father,[1] an elaborate oaken structure with blue china in its niches and, on its topmost shelf, some vases and three large beaten-copper platters. Above it hung portraits and engravings of his Thornton ancestors, by George Richmond and others;* and in front stood a long sofa with a padded rail, rather shabby, flanked by two William Morris armchairs, also shabby, and swathed in knitted shawls.[2] Behind these were a mahogany dining-

---

[1] It was presumably designed for Forster's parents' house in Melcombe Place and accompanied him all his life, being transported from one home to another.

[2] They were knitted, or rather crocheted, by Sebastian Sprott, who learned crocheting from Lady Ottoline Morrell.

table,[1] an upright piano and a free-standing mahogany bookcase,[2] containing handsome, unread-looking, morocco-bound volumes; and round the walls ran other assorted bookcases, some solid and Victorian, others cheap modern shelving. On the right as you entered there was a fine Georgian bureau; near it hung an imitation 'Turner'[3] of a castle on a lake, in a heavy gilt frame; and over the further door was a framed reproduction of Picasso's 'Boy leading a horse'. On the tables and ledges, about the room, lay a variety of ornaments and knicknacks: Bidar-work pots and trays, painted-leather runners, Victorian posy-glasses, a Zoëtrope and a solitaire-board.

It was a charming room, full of objects but not cluttered, untidy but not disorderly, settled but changing a little from month to month as a table or vase was shifted, a picture rehung or some new gift or memento exhibited or put away. When one called on Forster, one would generally find him in the further armchair, a tiny vase of flowers at his side, a shawl over his knees if it were winter, and letters, opened and unopened, strewn in quantities round him. There would be a moment of doubt or suspicion, until he recognized the visitor, and then a very warm, solicitous welcome, decorated by airy mutterings. 'How are you, Morgan?' 'I am functioning with great precision, though coldified. An *excellent* instrument . . .' He would throw himself back in his chair, in rather a sack-like way, and address himself benevolently, with an air of leisure, to conversation. There might be a pause at this point. Pauses played a considerable part in his conversation.

He was a fairly large and plumpish man, dressed ordinarily in a dowdy suit, cheap shirt and nonedescript tie. Straggling hair, broad brow, a long reddish nose, and under it a wispy moustache; fine eyes, in steel-rimmed glasses, and a most expressive and sensitive mouth, by turns tremulous, amused, morally reproving or full of scorn. It was the mouth, one felt, of a man defending the right to be sensitive. Physically he was awkward, limp and stiff at the same time. He would stand rather askew, as it were holding himself together by

---

[1] It was the nursery table from Battersea Rise.

[2] The bookcase, and its contents, had belonged to his grandfather, Charles Forster, and is described by Forster in his essay 'In My Library' in *Two Cheers for Democracy*.

[3] It was painted by Forster's great-great-uncle John Whichelo and had been given to Forster's mother by Henry Festing Jones.

gripping his left hand in his right. By contrast his gestures were most graceful; he had a beautiful blessing gesture of the hand, and a curious and charming habit, when drinking tea, of describing a little circling motion with the cup. On occasion, if he happened to be touched or grateful, he would kiss a friend's hand with great beauty of manner.

With a little pushing, on such a visit as I am describing, he could be got chatting freely, and, in a desultory way, his conversation would range widely – though always with lapses and hiatuses. Suddenly, he would let a subject drop, whereupon no effort could revive it. There would be a good deal of mild gossip, in exactly the same style whether one knew the characters in the story or not. These stories, dramatizing some absurd little scene or contretemps, were very funny and living, and, at the end, he would explode with laughter himself; he laughed as if it hurt him, convulsed, giving a wail from a mirthless face. Sometimes, after some ridiculous tale, he would hang his head in pretended despair, with a cry of 'Oh!' – meaning, 'What *was* there to be done?'[1] Whatever the subject his talk had odd glints and tiny surprises in it, a queer precision of vocabulary, a perpetual slight displacement of the expected emphasis. The voice went into the air with charm and decision: a minute pause, and then a beautifully-formed, idiosyncratic phrase or just-hinted comic idea. 'Did you do any acting when you were young, Morgan?' 'No never – I – no, that wasn't acting – I played the triangle once . . .'[2]

There was always a great quickness in his response: not so much quickness of wit, though he could be witty, but quickness in 'placing' someone else's remark, in instantly seeing its drift, its motive, its upshot. His mind would race so quickly round the remark, that the topic was exhausted as soon as begun. As a part of this trait, he had a peculiar faculty for listening. Many acquaintances, throughout his life, remarked how intently he listened – seeming to attend not so much to what was said as to the underlying meaning or drift.[3] It

---

[1] For instance, he had 'been told' to laugh at a certain film, and had done so, being rebuked for it by a foreigner in a nearby seat ('We do not share your humour.') At the end of the film, the foreigner told him that now he regretted not having laughed himself. 'Oh!' exclaimed Forster relating it, hanging his head.

[2] Scrap recorded by Eardley Knollys.

[3] J. R. Ackerley, in his memoir *E. M. Forster: a Portrait* (1970), wrote: '. . . when I was alone with him and his unselfconscious listening attention

gave a special virtue to friendship with him, but for the un-self-confident it could be unnerving, and they would often find their words freezing on their lips.

He was at his best in a *tête-à-tête*. In company, even among close friends, he could be taciturn and would spark up only intermittently. He did not make much effort in general conversation; also he would never argue. Among strangers, though courteous, he could on occasion be very blank, shades of boredom and simulated benignity flitting over his face as he spoke, very carefully, of trivialities. Sometimes strangers found him altogether disappointing; others were charmed by him but could remember nothing he had said.

He had certain rather oriental forms of courtesy. Once he called on me, carrying a large bunch of flowers intended for someone else, and when I praised the flowers he instantly felt bound to give them to me; whereupon, of course, I was faced with the problem of finding him some more flowers. He would listen complaisantly to any suggestion, however preposterous, and only afterwards, and by faint indications, convey that perhaps, just possibly, something might be urged against it. Similarly, he would gravely consider, or seem to consider, the most hackneyed remarks about his own work – for instance, that there were too many sudden deaths in *The Longest Journey* – as if he were hearing them for the first time. This courtesy of his went together, however, with some unnerving plain speaking. Once a fellow-guest at a party, having conversed with him for some time, remarked: 'But I mustn't keep you from more distinguished guests.' 'No, you mustn't,' replied Forster.[1]

At any social gathering in these late days, he was exposed to much adulation and lionization. It was a phenomenon he understood very well, and he did not pretend to think it strange that people, especially the young, should reverence him or feel awe at meeting him. It could grow tiresome, however, and he developed ways of deflecting it. For instance, at a party, he might single out some stranger and spend most of the evening in quiet conversation with him. He would choose the stranger because he or she attracted him, or because the stranger

was turned upon me – an attention which, I felt, was hearing not only the thing said but the motive in saying it – I experienced a sense of strain, as though more and better were expected of me than I really believed myself to contain. To be *really* listened to is a very serious matter.'

[1] Anecdote related of a friend by Arthur Crook.

looked lonely – and if the latter, it was done partly to shame his host or hostess. Whatever the motive, however, when he set out to please in this way, he did it whole-heartedly, occasionally getting snubbed for his pains – which enraged him greatly – but often making a new friend. These and similar habits of behaviour earned him a reputation for humility, and many anecdotes circulated of his 'humbleness' and unassumingness. It was in a sense a misunderstanding, for he had a very accurate idea of his own worth and was not slow to resent slights upon it. The truth was, rather, that he was modest – that is to say, had profoundly good manners, manners that were the fruit of his lifetime of moral self-cultivation.

The central preoccupation of his life, it was plain to see, was friendship, and he had a rather special attitude towards friendship. He never casually dropped friends, as most people do, out of forget-fulness or through change of circumstance – though, as has been seen, he might drop one with perfect deliberateness, if the friend had offended him in some vital way; and when this happened, he was unforgiving. Otherwise, if someone became a friend of his, he might expect to remain so for life, though perhaps gravitating over the years from one grade of his friendships to another. He believed – literally, and as more than a sentimental cliché – that the true history of the human race was the history of human affection. And for this reason it was a principle with him to keep his friendships in mind and to be continually reflecting on them. Also, to the end of his life, he was on the look-out for new friends and showed great enterprise in finding them.

He was frequently described as 'shy', but this too was a mis-nomer. What was certainly true was that he was timid: that is to say, he did not like to be hurt and took elaborate precautions not to be hurt. He was, and wished to be, sensitive; and since sensitiveness made him vulnerable, he had equipped himself with innumerable defensive weapons. He could withdraw into himself, be evasive, be over-polite, be silent and let others flounder. On extreme occasions he could speak out angrily, and his anger was frightening – but it did not often come to this, for he was not easily cornered. And all these defences could be lowered; he was not encased in Edwardian courtesy and could play the fool and laughed delightedly at plain speaking. He did not avoid intimacies, indeed he courted them. On the other hand, he did remorselessly *manage* them and was not ready to 'give himself'

295

unreservedly in friendship. For one thing, he greatly disliked being laughed at. He would swallow it sometimes, for friendship's sake, but for him it was no part at all of the pleasures of friendship, and he winced and bristled so visibly under teasing that people did not usually try it twice. Equally, as has been seen, he was bad at quarrels – that is to say, they assumed too vast proportions for him. He nerved himself up to a quarrel with painful effort and remembered it for years afterwards, still brooding about it at intervals and perhaps keeping a *dossier* on it. He had curious ways of describing a quarrel. If he were not involved personally, he spoke as though he were – 'Tom got angry with Bill, and then we were all in trouble . . .' And if he were involved personally, he would put the whole thing between inverted commas. 'I have been *insulted!*' he might say, as if he had only just thought of the name for what had taken place. He could not conceive of quarrels as a natural part of a relationship, and when married friends, like the Buckinghams, had a quarrel, he felt sure their marriage must be breaking up. There was great sense of duty, and great loyalty and benevolence, in his relationships, but also something self-pleasing and managing; he was responsive, but never in the least pliable. Even with his closest friends, he took on the role of a mentor; he was a stickler, they could feel his eye on them, and sometimes, with those less intimate, his governessy side caused serious offence.[1]

What was involved in this aspect of him was not bossiness but the determination to judge. A good way of visualizing Forster, I have found, is to imagine him being introduced to a dog or a cat. I never witnessed this, but can picture it. He would put himself on a level with the animal, approaching it tolerantly but non-committally. It *might* be a nice animal, but then again it might not; it was a mistake to have preconceptions on such matters; and at all events it didn't matter *much* what character an animal had – but it mattered a little. That would be his tone, I think; and he would shoot glances at the

---

[1] It did so with Lionel and Diana Trilling, though this was partly a case of Anglo–American misunderstanding. They brought their young son to see him at King's, sometime during the 1960s, and at tea the boy said he would have some more cake – to which Forster replied severely, as his mother might have done, 'You will have some when you are offered it.' The Trillings, who had been greatly attached to Forster, thought the snub intolerable and could never feel quite the same towards him again.

animal in the intervals of conversation, examining it from various angles till he had made up his mind about it. His mind was a vast breeding-ground for judgements and discriminations. He endlessly picked and chose and could distinguish one blade of grass from another. Similarly, no one ever made such *restrictive* remarks, giving and then drawing a limit to what was to be given. 'X—, with an intelligent face, fairly,' he might say; or 'I am devoted to Y—'s son, slightly.'

One could imagine, knowing him, that he had a 'secret'. It is a sentimental notion, but one that occurred to many of his acquaintances. It had to do with the fact that, to a rather special degree, he lived the imaginative life and, whether in company or in solitude, was attending to imaginative impressions. He did this consciously, feared to lose the power of doing so, and rebuked himself for slackness in it. It was, to him, the rule and aim of his existence and was entwined with his sense for what – for want of a better word – he called 'life'. He felt as if, on occasion, he could see through to 'life': could hear its wing-beat, could grasp it not just as a generality but as a palpable presence. The feeling communicated itself. I remember him, once, describing Masood's children, and their love for their companion Cotter Morison,[1] who was not quite right in the head. He spoke of it in a delighted tone, as if that was what life was made up of: the whole of life was present in it, and there was nothing beyond. I remember too, another even tinier incident. For some reason we were sharing a hotel bedroom, and as he undressed, the coins dropped out of his pocket, chinking as they fell, and he said, in a tone of mock-superstitious resignation: 'When they begin to sing, it's all over with them.' There was the same joyful note in his voice, and it was oddly ghostly and impressive, as if he truly had insight into the workings of Providence.

*   *   *

I started to keep a diary in 1952 and used to record meetings with him in it. Here follow a few extracts.

5.8.52. Tea with M.;[2] he described the plum cake as a *dire* one. Said what he liked about Aldeburgh, where he had been staying,

---

[1] Son of Masood's guardian Sir Theodore Morison.
[2] i.e. 'Morgan'.

was that it was so *athletic*; the air flowed by one, one didn't have to *fend* it from one. Spoke of Angus Wilson's *Hemlock and After* and said the opening chapter was good as construction in two ways. He had been reading ghost-stories, and what was bad about them was, they were so slow. About writing: he said that he enjoyed it so much himself that he would be thinking about what he was writing at odd times and didn't listen to the clever things people said.

Later, in the Combination Room, he said, apropos of the papers (the *Daily Worker* and the *Tablet*), that he liked to have something of which you could say 'That's Communist,' 'That's Catholic,' and then you could think on from there. He didn't like it when they infiltrated.

28.8.52. Supper with M., Francis Bennett and Joseph S.,[1] at Joseph's expense. M. defined smoked salmon as 'the pork of the deeps'. He had been dining recently with Bob Buckingham at 'that nice, costly place,' the Red Lion at Grantchester. 'Everything very nice, and turns out more expensive than you thought. It is excellent. Bob's eyes shone.' He said, 'I have an Indian staying with me, who is going to get better.' I laughed a little too loudly at this, and he was faintly annoyed: 'Look at him! Laughing all over his face. It is perfectly ordinary English conversation.' He complained that no one in Cambridge was interested in India, nor did either Indians nor English people know about its history.

1.1.53. With M. in Francis Haskell's rooms. He described visiting his Aunt Rosalie and Aunt Nellie, now living near each other. Rosalie hissed, as he went on from her to Nellie: 'You won't get anything to eat *there*!' We discussed literary biography and whether a critic had any right to draw on biographical facts. M. said he often felt like wanting readers to know only what he chose to tell them about himself. This was probably just selfishness – it was because it made things *socially* more comfortable. The question to ask oneself was, how far removed is the author's state of mind, when writing, from what it is normally. If it is very different then what is true of his life will not be true of his writings. 'Is the state always the same for you?' I asked. 'You can only define it negatively,' he said. 'It is interfered with by the same things.' (His was always completely changed by people coming into the room.) He remarked: 'I find I sit down in the best chair: it is a little habit I have nowadays . . . Or perhaps I always had it. My New Year's resolution was to enjoy myself more and more in every way.' (Sadly) 'And now I am looking round for ways of doing it.'

4.1.53. M. to tea. He said 'Orgies are so important, and they are

---

[1] Yugoslav friend of E. K. Bennett.

things one knows *nothing* about.' We talked of the unhappiness of wealthy people who fear they are only loved for their money and are always wanting *real* love. He said it wasn't only wealthy people, it happened to others too (meaning himself). 'I suppose one answer is not to keep wanting people to love you . . . but it's difficult. It's more *practical* not to have devotions – to be independent. You do less damage, I suppose. Of course, it's customary to suspect devotion. I read an absurd book on someone – who was it? – who was happily married, and the author thought that very suspicious: 'There's something psychological there! It wants looking into.'

6.5.53. M. just returned from France, where he had been touring with Bill Roerick and Tom Coley.[1] It was marvellous travelling with them, he said, something was always happening. Bill drew people out, went in the restaurant kitchen and got the menu changed, made great friends with the organist at Angoulême. 'I used to do it a bit,' said M. 'So I liked it. Once Tom got angry with Bill, and then we were all in trouble.'

24.6.53. M. for a drink. 'How lamentable I find other people's limitations,' he said. He had been visiting Siegfried Sassoon. 'Lives alone in a vast house, and can't see anyone in case it should happen to annoy the housekeeper.' Sassoon had talked all the time, and been so charming, overwhelmingly so, and such a bore too. (M. imitated him.)

8.9.53. M. at lunch in the Garden House Hotel. He talked about the High Table at King's. He had a technique for snubbing the Vice-Provost when he 'shouted' at dinner. M. 'happened' to know the private ailments of most of the elderly dons and would lean across the table and ask them quietly 'How was it at Addenbrooke's[2] today?' He called this 'flaunting the realities at him [the Vice-Provost]'. He said: 'We complain of the dullness at High Table, but then think "What have I contributed?" One isn't interested and sits there munching the nourishing food and saying nothing.'

20.11.53. M. to tea. He had been meeting Stephen Potter[3] and found it dispiriting. Potter oughn't to spraddle in front of the fire, as he did, seeing that he had sold himself to Schweppes' advertisements. Potter kept improvising etymologies, at which he fancied himself; then he would go to the dictionary to confirm them and exclaim 'No, I'm wrong, ha, ha!' – he always was.

1.12.53. M. has been having an exchange of letters with Lord

---

[1] See pp. 246, 269.

[2] Hospital in Cambridge.

[3] Stephen Potter (1900–69); literary critic and author of *Gamesmanship* (1947) and *One-Upmanship* (1952).

Samuel* over homosexuality. He tried to define Lord Samuel:
'Morally weighty, and actually a windbag. I think that's it, isn't
it?'

12.7.54. Dinner with M. at the Reform Club. M.: 'It's so lovely
when people are kind. Did you notice, she [the waitress] gave me
a little touch on the shoulder.'

28.10.55. Went with M. to the Portuguese Art Exhibition [at
Burlington House]. He stood for some minutes in front of the
Goncalves 'Portrait of a Young Man', which we had seen in
Lisbon,[1] and murmured 'Beautiful creature!' At dinner at the
Reform we talked about old age. He said he felt things with more
acute excitement than ever, but in disconnection. Recently he
had been greatly excited by some carving on the choir-stalls in
King's Chapel, but it had all gone by the time he left, and he
couldn't remember what it had been about. Talked about slang
and vogue-words. He said the expression 'I couldn't care less' was
wrong, 'morally wrong.'

16.2.56. Had M. to supper. We talked of Portugal. He said Francis
Haskell[2] had penetrated the inner Catholic circles of Portuguese
society, and he wondered what it would be like . . . 'Inside that
rose of mysticism and royalty and looking out towards one's own
Protestantism.' He had been seeing his Aunt Nellie, who 'was not
often to be seen, but very effective when she was.' When her
sister Rosalie projected marriage with Bob Alford, she said she
wouldn't marry Bob 'if every hair of his head were hung with
diamonds'. He talked about Ramsey's suicide[3] at King's; said he
thought the villain of the piece had been Sheppard, who used to
'needle' Ramsey. As for poor Ramsey, he was 'a goose'.

26.3.56. Tea with M. at the Reform. He said what a worry stealing
was. He often has the feeling of wanting to steal, and thinking
how clever it would be of him.

By the end of 1955, he had completed *Marianne Thornton*.[4] He had
enjoyed writing it, and for a moment he considered attempting some
further book of family memoirs, then he decided he must not
'maunder on' about his ancestors. He wondered what else he might
write and, with simplicity, wrote to Leonard Woolf asking what he
would suggest. Woolf advised him to write his autobiography, but

---

[1] We had gone to Portugal together for a holiday in the summer of 1953.

[2] F. J. H. Haskell (1928–); subsequently Professor of Art History in
Oxford.

[3] I. E. St Clair Ramsey, Dean of King's College, had committed suicide
by throwing himself off the roof of the Chapel.

[4] It was published in May 1956.

this was not advice he felt he could take. He thought he might be able to handle isolated incidents but he did not understand his own life sufficiently to describe it as a whole.

Then a quite different scheme occurred to him. Forty years before, he had written the first chapter of a novel, never to be continued, in which he depicted an 'Anglo-Indian' family – a widow, Mrs March, and her young children – returning on a boat from India. The children, with their mother's grudging permission, take up with a half-caste playmate, called 'Cocoanut'. At first, being white *Sahibs*, they order Coco about, which he rather enjoys. Then they let him lead them off on a mysterious game or errand of his own invention, and their mother catches sight of them on a distant deck, playing hatless in the mid-day sun. It is still the era of the solar *topi* and of the fear of sunstroke, and she rushes off to put a stop to their game, becoming involved in a curious little drama, full of confusion and cross-purposes. Suddenly, hot, tired and worried about the future, she becomes hysterical and vents her hysteria in rage against the half-caste: 'You're a silly little boy and I shall complain to the stewardess about you,' she breaks out at him angrily. 'You never will play any game properly and you stop the others. You're a silly idle useless unmanly little boy.'

Forster came upon the manuscript during his move to Cambridge and showed it to Ackerley, who was impressed by it and published it in the *Listener*.[1] Forster thought well of it himself, and, over the next few years, his mind continued to run on the characters – on that triangle of the mother, her eldest son Lionel and the half-caste, 'Cocoanut'. What would have happened, he asked himself, if Lionel and Coco had met again in adult life and the faint attraction between them had revived and turned into a sexual affair? It was a different development from the one planned originally, but quite plausible. Other buried material came to his mind, like that bizarre incident during his first boat-trip to India, when an Indian accused his cabin-mate of threatening to throw him overboard and the two were later mysteriously reconciled. He found himself with the plot, not of a novel but of a long, tragic short story, and, during the summer of 1956, he decided to try writing it. It was a different sort of writing from his facetious short stories, and to begin with he doubted his

---

[1] 'Entrance to an Unwritten Novel', *Listener*, 23 December 1948.

powers. He need not have doubted. To his excitement, he found he was producing something at his very best level and, in a way, of a new kind for him. This story, published posthumously as 'The Other Boat',[1] occupied him intermittently over the next year or two.

I will continue here with my diary.

> *2.4.57.* M. is writing a long short story, a sequel to his fragment of forty years before about children on board a ship returning from India. The half-caste, ten years later, is determined to get the English officer, the 'marvellous creature', and arranges for them to share a cabin . . . 'It is easy to write tragedy, I find', M. said. 'No need to tidy everything up as you have to do with comedy.'
> *18.8.57.* Went to see M. in Cambridge. He lent me Frank Sargeson's[2] novel *I Saw in my Dream*. He said it had a real plot as well as a mechanical one: 'a theme which reverberated.' 'Does it move on, as well as reverberate?' I asked. He replied with precision: 'The theme returns at intervals, on each occasion more forcibly.' He had just been interviewed by Angus Wilson, for *Encounter*.[3] Wilson had liked everything in his room, except the petunias.
> *28.8.57.* M. came with his new story. He said: 'Of course, I suppose I don't write so well as I used to, but I find writing more fascinat-than ever.' 'Making this fit with that?' I asked. 'Making things work, yes,' he replied. He read me the story. Said T. E. Lawrence had told him that all one of M.'s unpublishable stories[4] had done was to make him laugh: he was anxious for the new story not to run this danger.
> *29.8.57.* M. last night, worried whether his story might not seem too 'clinical', especially when it came to the mother. He said you could only depict people *enjoying* making love if it was within a framework of tragedy. I said: 'Is that because otherwise it would make the reader envious?' He replied, severely: 'That was not the reason I had in mind. I meant that the reader would get bored.' He said people found his indecent stories monotonous: they ran to type. Whenever the same tall athletic figure came on the scene, eroticism started. This was limiting.
> *18.10.57.* Dinner with M. at the Reform. He said Florence Barger was eighty now, and not always *compos mentis*. They had been at Covent Garden the night before, with Francis Bennett, and

---

[1] In *'The Life to Come' and Other Stories* (1972).

[2] Frank Sargeson (1903–), New Zealand novelist. Forster who had been put on to Sargeson's work by William Plomer, wrote to him in 1949 in high praise of *I Saw in My Dream*. A correspondence ensued, and Forster wrote a brief Introduction to Sargeson's *Collected Stories* (1965, second impression).

[3] See 'A Conversation with E. M. Forster', *Encounter*, November 1957.

[4] 'The Life to Come'; see p. 121.

Florence had asked: 'Who is that old man who has attached himself to us?' 'But Florence, he's Francis Bennett.' 'If you say so, then I will accept it,' she said stiffly. 'She keeps her surface,' M. said; 'but I don't know if there is much beneath.' She looked at her *Times* every day, but he didn't think she read it.[1]

6.3.58. M. to the flat tonight. He said Joe Ackerley had objected to the letter with which his new story begins. If the young man remembered all his mother had said and thought about Coco (the half-caste), he wouldn't have written this letter. 'Of course he wouldn't,' said M. 'But then one is up against the trouble of story-telling, and has to use devices. Not that Joseph Conrad didn't resort to far worse.' (He chuckled gleefully.)

7.3.58. Francis Bennett, according to M., is to have electrical shock-treatment, as a cure for depression; M. had written him what may have been a 'pushing' or patronizing letter.

23.3.58. M. came to collect his story, which I had been retyping. I said that I guessed that the added violence in the new climax was what he had originally intended: he said 'No, I've been unstable about it all the time.' Said that Francis, after his shock-treatment, was more like *that* – indicating jerky, nervous movements. Speaking of his book on his Thornton ancestors, he said: 'I try to make religion as dull as possible.'

15.6.58. M., at the Reform, told me that Francis Bennett had died.

5.7.58. M. said that on the night of Francis' death, a picture fell off the wall of his (M.'s) bedroom, and he had felt absolutely furiously angry.

21.10.58. M., at the Reform last night, told me he had been to Aldeburgh and described the home of his fisherman friend, Billy Burrell.[2] The front of the house was a beauty-parlour, and the back was used by fishermen in filthy oilskins: the smells sometimes met in the middle, and the effect was appalling. There were 'enormous intrusions of adorable fishermen'.

He had been reading *Dr Zhivago* and thought it became good after page 200. Pasternak was not good on people, so it was absurd to compare him with Tolstoy. He liked the two railway journeys very much, and the whole evocation of the Revolution: 'It makes you feel a revolution is *never* worth it.'

Said he thought the tragic theme of 'The Other Boat' – two people made to destroy each other – was more interesting than the theme of salvation, the rescuer from 'otherwhere', the generic Alec. That was a fake. People could help one another, yes; but they were not decisive for each other like that.

---

[1] She died in 1960.
[2] Burrell's wife kept a hair-dressing shop.

The writing of 'The Other Boat' had revived Forster's interest in his own career and reputation. At about this time he made one of his periodic siftings of his unpublished stories, and I typed some of them for him, also persuading him to have more copies of *Maurice* made. A friend of mine, O. W. Neighbour, had asked if he could read *Maurice*, and he raised a question about the *dénouement*. As it stood, Maurice, seeing Alec Scudder's boat depart for the Argentine without Scudder aboard, turns his face towards England in a brave blur of exalted hope. But how, asked Neighbour, was he actually going to find Alec? The point worried Forster, and during the next year or so he did some substantial revision to the end, adding a passage in which Maurice is brought safely to Alec's arms. He had no intention of publishing *Maurice* during his lifetime and now was not certain whether it ought to be published at all. He thought it might seem dated and, as he said, 'give such a dim report'. Also, one or two friends to whom he had recently shown it had responded rather coolly.

His literary executor, according to present arrangements, was to be Sebastian Sprott, and, failing him, Bob Buckingham. He meant whoever undertook the post to enjoy his posthumous royalties, and the idea now entered his mind of appointing Buckingham in Sprott's place, as an insurance for his future. It was not a firm plan, but it served him as a pretext for trying – as fifteen years before – to retrieve his letters from Joe Ackerley. 'Bob wouldn't be worried over my literary remains,' he wrote to Ackerley (21 August 1958). 'He might be worried by anything that made his work awkward. I am for that reason collecting such letters written by myself as may be available, and storing them here, where they would be safe. I asked you some years ago, I remember, about my letters to you and you said they were stored with Herbert Read.' Ackerley suspected, probably correctly, that what Forster really wanted was to destroy the letters, or most of them, and he refused to surrender them, telling Forster they were back in his own possession and 'he would not care for them to be anywhere else.' At this, Forster dropped the subject. 'How good he is,' Ackerley noted:

> He would have felt safer, even in death, to have had his letters returned, he thinks he is not a good letter-writer and betrays himself and others. It may be that he *is* not a good letter-writer, but whether he is or not, his letters, and his friendship, have been

the major influence in my life from Cambridge onwards; if I gave
up his letters I should give up one of the foundations of my life.
I expect he knows that, he knows everything; he tried it on out
of nervousness, and has easily let it go.

* * *

In January 1959 Forster was eighty, and to mark the occasion
King's College organized a large birthday luncheon in the College
Hall, attended by more than a hundred guests – friends, relatives,
writers and dons. Bill Roerick, Tom Coley and Edith Oliver came
over from America for it, and Charles Mauron and his second wife
from France. Forster was happy and in high spirits. He heard himself
referred to by the Provost, Noël Annan, as 'the greatest living
Kingsman' and invited by him to 'ruminate and emanate' for long
years to come, and in his reply he made mild pleasantries about old
age, his own and the college's, concluding:

> I had something else to say – can't remember. I would anyhow
> like to mention my Aunt Nellie,[1] Miss Nellie Whichelo, who had
> to decline her invitation to this party because she is 96, and now
> sits at her own fireside drinking our health in Bristol Cream. I
> would also like to read this cable which I have just had from my
> friend Auden. It is entirely to my credit, but no matter. –
> Dear Morgan, Wish I could be with you in more than spirit
> Stop May you long continue what you already are Stop Old
> famous loved yet not a sacred cow Stop Love and gratitude.
> I certainly don't want to be a sacred anything, and may be
> going a little further than Wystan here . . .*

Writing to William Plomer a year later (16 December 1959), he told
Plomer: 'Another 80th Birthday lunch today. To Charles Tennyson.
Oh a very small affair in comparison.'

* * *

My diary continues:

> *19.12.58.* Spent night of Tuesday in M.'s Chiswick flat. We
> approached across the roof and over a little shaky iron bridge.
> He said he felt nervous of going to the flat alone nowadays. He
> had had an attack of deafness, could not listen to his new
> gramophone, and had told the doctor he needed 'psychological

---

[1] His aunt Rosalie had died in 1957.

re-adjustment'. 'They don't like getting their language back at them,' he chuckled.

3.4.59. Dinner with M. He said his spirits were not high, and at last he had discovered what it was: it was something quite absurd: he was *affronted*, that was the word: Bob and May weren't near enough, Rob and Sylvia had moved further away, and Eric Fletcher had gone to the depths of Yorkshire. But the real trouble was the loss of Francis: one could go to him with complaints that *weren't* justified. Told me of Francis's affair with one of the waiters in his college: 'very grand and sly' it had been. Said of his own obituary on Francis in *The Caian*[1] that it was 'all right – too smiley'. We discussed Canon Vidler[2], who proclaimed great freedom of thought and had joined the Rationalist Association. I said, 'But is it all genuine?' 'Well, there we are!' said M., lifting up his hands to convey how reasonable the doubt was, how little he committed himself, save just to indicate the faint possibility . . .

22.4.59. Lunched with M. last Friday. We talked about Christ. He said he didn't feel he wanted to know Christ: this had been an important factor in his loss of faith. If Christ were in the next room, would he want to go and meet him? Could one like someone who never laughed? Also, he lacked intellectual power: could one put up with the lack of that?

8.5.59. Dinner with M. at Reform. He had been to see his Aunt Nellie, who had collapsed and could not speak or write, but had asked for him. She and her home had been tidied up: her dirty old curtains pulled down, her face washed ; 'it looked much smaller' – her toenails cut. M. banged the side of his chair to convey her indignation. He had arrived ready to 'condemn her to destruction', but his feeling had changed when he saw her. He supplied her with the swear-words she could not utter.

29.5.59. M. for lunch in restaurant, to collect *Maurice*,[3] which I had been having retyped for him. 'Such a nice thing I've found,' he said; 'Francis's *Tales of Sarras*.[4] I'm so pleased.' Then, recollecting himself: 'Actually I found the writing disappointing.'

9.10.59. M., at dinner at Reform, said he had been reading letters from his mother to his grandmother, and they were not very pleasant about him. His mother always accused him of helpless-

---

[1] Caius College magazine. The obituary appeared in the number for the Michaelmas Term, 1958.

[2] Alexander Roper Vidler (1899–); Canon of St George's Chapel, Windsor and prolific author of theological polemics.

[3] I had encouraged him to get more copies made and had found him a typist in London.

[4] A volume of stories by E. K. Bennett, privately printed in 1934 under his pseudonym of 'Francis Keppel'.

ness, but he had hoped she talked differently to others. When he broke his arm, falling on the steps of St Peter's, this had been taken as a signal example of his helplessness.

4.11.59. Saw M. off to Italy. In the Club last night Lord Beveridge[1] greeted him: they clasped hands and discussed the dispute over the India Office papers.[2] 'What a charmer,' he said to me afterwards; then a little later, recollecting himself, 'What an ill-informed distinguished old man.'

14.11.59. M., the other day, said that Kipling was one of the few people he deeply regretted not having known. He had lectured on him, admiringly, in India, and his audience, though polite, hadn't believed a word of it: they knew it could not be true of that monolithic imperialist.

12.12.59. M. back from Italy, looking young in a new grey suit. He had been taken to see the newly-discovered 'Cave of Tiberius' and there had been a violent row, in Italian, between the British Council men and a rough country fellow who would not let them in. At last he gave in, and the British Council men said 'He was only doing his duty, you know. We mustn't let ourselves get annoyed with these chaps,' and they offered him money. To M.'s glee, the man refused. M. talked about Thomas Hardy. What he most remembered was staying at T. E. Lawrence's cottage, and 'that bald head' emerging suddenly through the loft trapdoor. When they put electric pylons on Egdon Heath, Hardy said, '*We* never thought Egdon was any use to anyone, and now you see, we were wrong.'

18.12.59. Dinner at Reform with M. and Joe Ackerley. Joe was writing a novel,[3] and the publishers had said he must alter its locale, to avoid libel, so he had been investigating North London suburbs. He questioned shopkeepers, he said; and when, as sometimes happened, they said 'Why do you want to know?' he would answer, very irascibly, 'What's it got to do with you?' He had spotted an elderly porter who he thought might be useful as an informant. 'You've got grey hairs,' he had called out to him; 'You're the man I want.' – 'You use interesting approaches,' remarked M.

19.1.60. In Oxford yesterday, to see the dramatization of *A*

---

[1] William Henry Beveridge, 1st Baron (1879–1963), Director of the London School of Economics 1919–37 and author of the Beveridge Report of 1942 on *Social Insurance and Allied Services*. He and Forster were at preparatory school together.

[2] The governments of India and Pakistan were demanding the return of the India Office Library, having already made the same request, and been refused, four years before.

[3] *We Think the World of You*; published, after various vicissitudes, by Bodley Head in 1960.

Passage to India.[1] After the performance M. came on the stage to make a speech, holding his arms drooping in front of him, in an odd posture: was struck by the commanding upper-middle-class voice emerging from the slightly awkward figure. He said: 'Though you might not think so, this is not the first time I have trodden the stage. On the previous occasion it was that of Covent Garden: then I only had to bow. Tonight's undertaking is more difficult . . . How good the actors were. And how pleased I was that there were so many of them. I am so used to seeing the sort of play which deals with one man and two women. They do not leave me with the feeling I have made a full theatrical meal. They are excellent in many ways, but they do not give me the impression of the multiplicity of life . . . As a member of the audience I have on occasion been thanked by the actors for being so good. It did not arouse in me any great emotion. All the same, it is a pretty thought, so I will give you my bow.' Talking today, he said it was absurd to say, as the *Times* review had done, that he was writing about the incompatibility of East and West. He was really concerned with the difficulty of living in the universe.

---

[1] By Santha Rama Rau. This was its première.

14 Last Years

By the 1950s there had begun for Forster a period of idolization. He had come to be honoured for personal goodness and sanctity, to an extent that perhaps few writers have known. In 1957 the American writer Dorothy Parker, in an interview in the *Paris Review*, remarked: 'Somerset Maugham once said to me, "We have a novelist here, E. M. Forster, though I don't expect he's familiar to you." Well I could have kicked him. Did he think I carried a papoose on my back? Why I'd go on my hands and knees to get to Forster.'[1] There were others who spoke of him almost as extravagantly. And moreover, in print at least, he had remarkably few detractors.[2] His friends were not all so reverent. Lord Kennet reported an exchange between Forster and Percy Lubbock in 1955.

> *Lubbock:* It's too funny your becoming the holy man of letters. You're really a spiteful old thing. Why haven't people found you out, and run you down?
> *Forster* (cheerfully): They're beginning.

Nevertheless, even with many of his friends, 'holiness' entered into their conception of him.

He was meanwhile, till the end of the 1950s, an active and influen-

---

[1] He drafted a grateful reply to her, which he never despatched.

[2] His most formidable detractor was Graham Greene. Greene caricatured him in *The Third Man* as the old-maidish writer Benjamin Dexter, who 'took a passionate interest in embroidery' and calmed 'a not very tumultuous mind with tatting'. He also attacked him in *Why Do I Write?* as an irresponsible liberal, a typical member of the PEN Club, always signing appeals in *The Times*. 'So long as he [i.e. such a writer] had eased his conscience publicly in print, and in good company, he was not concerned with the consequences of his letter.'

tial writer. During his visit to Italy in 1959 he had heard much talk of the novel *Il Gattopardo* (*The Leopard*) and of its author, the Prince of Lampedusa, who had died recently. He bought it and read it in Italian and found it wonderful, a life-affirming book after his own heart. The book, so he said later, had enlarged his own life, for all that that life was now in its eighties: 'Reading and rereading it has made me realize how many ways there are of being alive, how many doors there are, close to one, which someone else's touch may open.'[1] When the English translation, by Archibald Colquhoun, came out in the following year, he reviewed it at some length in the *Spectator* (13 May 1960). It was an eloquent and feeling review, responsive especially to the novel's enlightened attude to death:

> What a tribute to the urbanity of death! The whole [last] chapter scintillates with power and with a tenderness that is untroubled by pity. There is no summing up, nor moral balancing, though before his consciousness weakens the dying man thinks what has happened to him and employs himself in separating the good moments from the bad.

This was to be the last major review that Forster would write.[2] He now found it difficult to concentrate. He complained that his life was all in pieces and scraps, and the tone of these complaints, which were not new with him, was changing from self-rebuke to resignation. 'Going to Bits' was the heading of an entry in his Commonplace Book for 31 January 1961:

> This phrase describes me today and is indeed the one I have been looking for: not tragic, not mortal disintegration, only a central weakness which prevents me from concentrating or settling down. I have so wanted to write and write ahead. The phrase 'obligatory creation' has haunted me. I have so wanted to get out of my morning bath promptly: I have decided to do so beforehand, and have then laid in it as usual and watched myself not getting out. It looks as if there is a physical as well as a moral break in the orders I send out. I have plenty of interesting thoughts but keep losing them like the post cards I have written, or like my cap . . .

---

[1] Introduction to Lampedusa's *Two Stories and a Memory*, trans. A. Colquhoun (1962).

[2] His very last review was of Leonard Woolf's *Growing* in the *Observer*, 5 November 1961.

He knew, without too much sadness, that his career was more or less at an end, and the knowledge revived in him thoughts of a biography of himself. Sometimes it seemed to him, his life was too uneventful to be written, but at other times he felt eager for it. At all events, he guessed that someone would attempt a *Life*, so he decided to make preparations. Sprott suggested that he should invite William Plomer to write something on him – either a full-dress *Life* or a shorter sketch, and he put the idea to Plomer, who agreed. This was in August 1960, and over the next year or so, in a desultory way, Plomer questioned Forster about his life and career and Forster wrote notes for him.

                              *   *   *

In November 1960 Forster appeared as a witness in the *Lady Chatterley* trial at the Old Bailey. A new Obscene Publications Act had been passed the previous year, and under this a book, though admitted to be obscene, might now be defended on the grounds that its publication was for the public good, as being 'in the interests of science, literature, art, or learning' – the Courts being required to hear expert witnesses on this issue. The prosecution of Penguin Books for publishing the unexpurgated *Lady Chatterley's Lover* was the first brought under the new Act and was thus a test case.[1] Forster, one of thirty-five expert witnesses, spoke on the third day of the trial – coming after the decisive cross-examination of Richard Hoggart, in which Hoggart had maintained Lawrence's book to be 'highly virtuous and if anything, puritanical'. Jeremy Hutchinson, the defence counsel, asked Forster where he would place Lawrence in literature.

   F. In all the literature of the day, do you mean; in all contem-
       porary literature?
   H. Yes.
   F. I should place him enormously high. When one comes to the
       upper ten novels, then one has to begin to think a little of the
       order, but compared with all the novels which come out, the
       novels he wrote dominate terrifically.

---

[1] The Director of Public Prosecutions, Sir Theobald Mathew, had been shown Penguins' advertisement for their forthcoming edition of *Lady Chatterley*, and ordered the police to buy a copy, upon publication, in the Charing Cross Road. However, Penguin's solicitor forestalled this by inviting the police to call round at the Penguin offices and collect as many copies as they wanted – thus removing the need to implicate a bookseller.

> *H.* When he died I think you described him as the greatest imaginative novelist of your generation?
>
> *F.* Yes, I would still hold to it.
>
> *H.* You have read *Lady Chatterley's Lover*?
>
> *F.* Yes.
>
> *H.* Judging it in the same way, what would you say as to its literary merit?
>
> *F.* Judging it in the same way, I should say that it had very high literary merit. It is, perhaps I might add, not the novel of Lawrence which I most admire. That would be *Sons and Lovers*, I think.
>
> *H.* Lawrence has been described as forming part of the great Puritan stream of writers in this country. Have you any comment to make on that?
>
> *F.* I think the description is a correct one, though I understand that at first people would think it paradoxical. But when I was thinking over this matter beforehand, I considered his relationship to Bunyan. They both were preachers. They both believed intensely in what they preached. I would say, if I may speak of antecedents, of great names, Bunyan on the one hand and Blake on the other; Lawrence too had this passionate opinion of the world and what it ought to be, but is not.

Forster, remembering the *Well of Loneliness* case, was elated when the trial went in favour of Penguin Books. He told Ackerley (4 December 1960) that it felt odd to be on the winning side. He intended, he said, to go to Penguins' victory party, though it ought to have been a dinner party 'considering all we have put in their pockets . . .'[1] 'By the way, did D. H. Lawrence ever do anything for anybody? Now that we have been sweating ourselves to help him, the idea occurs.'

* * *

Despite the fact that Plomer was writing his *Life*, the close-knit alliance between himself, Plomer, Sprott and Ackerley was falling a little apart. For one thing, Plomer had in 1953 left London for Sussex, settling in a seaside bungalow at Rustington with a friend of his, Charles Erdman. In the normal way Forster and Plomer did not now meet very often. Moreover, though Plomer was to write his *Life*, he had grown by this time less in sympathy with some of Forster's attitudes. He had himself become religious, which created a

---

[1] The sales of the Penguin *Lady Chatterley* proved, as expected, enormous.

barrier; also, he disliked Forster's indecent stories, considering them unworthy of him, and Forster guessed this.

Sprott and Forster, likewise, saw each other much less often. The days had gone by when, every few weeks, Sprott would be borrowing Forster's London flat. And, dearly as Forster loved Sprott, he found visits to Nottingham a trial: the house was so cold, and so grimy, and Sprott would talk so much. Also more serious, he would drink so much. Sprott, a professor since 1948, had made more of his career than Forster had expected. His book *Human Groups* (1958) was quite widely known, and his lectures had a large following. (They were a great technical display. He would stop on time to the very second – vanishing instantly, still talking at colossal speed – and would resume next week as if completing the same sentence.) Nevertheless, the drinking worried Forster. It did so on Sprott's account; and, since Sprott was his literary executor, on his own also.

He still regularly saw Joe Ackerley, but here too there was a change. Ackerley claimed that his years with his dog Queenie, who died in 1961, had been the happiest of his life. But, happy or not, they had made him a misanthrope, committed to the cause of animals as against the human race. ('Everyone in the long run must decide which side he is on,' he said to Harry Daley.) He had espoused the cause of animals with fanaticism, constantly writing to the press on their behalf.[1] If he heard that friends were leaving their cat alone at the weekend, he might quite likely go and keep it company. To Forster, who had once called the saying *Plus que je vois les hommes plus j'aime les chiens* 'one of the most hopeless and ignoble maxims ever uttered',[2] it seemed a tragic madness, and it separated him a little from Ackerley.

Ackerley, for his part, was growing critical of Forster. He would pick holes in Forster's books, saying how much he 'got away with' in *Howards End* and that he enjoyed his own *Hindoo Holiday* more than *The Hill of Devi*. Forster's fussy ways began to irritate him, and he would grumble at Forster's referring to him as 'Ackerly' in *Marianne*

---

[1] Some swans on Barnes common once hissed at Queenie, and Ackerley at once wrote to the mayor. His letter, according to William Plomer, ran: 'I have something very disgraceful to report. You have some quite undisciplined swans on the Common: they have threatened my Alsatian in a most serious manner. I can't answer for the state of her nerves if it occurs again . . . etc.'

[2] 'Notes on the Way'; *Time and Tide*, 23 June 1934. His article asked 'Can we take on the animals?'

Thornton. ('After all these years, he couldn't even spell my name!') It was an irritation not so much against Forster as against his own long self-imposed prostration before him, which he felt had hindered his own writing. By now, he was active again as a writer, and in 1956 had published *My Dog Tulip*, an account of his life with Queenie. It had had quite a success, and Forster himself had praised it in public, though privately admitting to Ackerley that parts of it had shocked him. Despite his success, Ackerley was in low spirits. In 1959 he had been retired from the *Listener*, and it had left him feeling at a loose end. He was hard up, was drinking too much for his pocket, and – with Queenie and his Aunt Bunnie in his flat, and his sister Nancy in lodgings nearby – he saw himself, in gloomier moments, as marooned among jealous and possessive females.[1] In the winter of 1960–61 he had gone to Japan, at Forster's expense, and for a moment he had been cheered, then had suffered an emotional 'disaster', of the kind that his life was littered with, and had returned no more cheerful than he set out.

* * *

In April 1961, a few months after Ackerley's return from Japan, Forster visited him in his flat at Putney and had a fall on the threshold, breaking his wrist and suffering shock. ('No one else had ever done it,' said Ackerley, in a grumbling tone, 'but Morgan chose to.') Bob Buckingham was summoned and brought Forster back to Cambridge, and he spent a night or two in hospital. All went well with his wrist, but a few days later he felt ill and had to return to hospital and was told he might have suffered damage to his heart or lungs.

The news left him philosophical. He wrote to Bob Buckingham, 'We must not worry about my failing powers . . . To me decay is so natural in a universe that admits growth, and it puzzles me that so great a man as Hardy should have wasted so many of his poems in saying "I am not what I was. Boo!" ' None the less, he took it as a warning of approaching death, and his thoughts turned once more to posthumous arrangements. Joe Ackerley had recently said to him that Sprott and himself were 'a couple of alcoholics'. It had been a joke, but it had worried Forster, and in his present frail condition he wrote Sprott a needling and rather unkind letter (20 April 1961):

[1] See his sketch 'A Summer Evening', *London Magazine*, October 1969, describing an evening in 1958.

Joe – or has he got it wrong again? – tells me that you and he are
Y addicts[1] – two classes above or below the Master of the Rolls,
he naturally forgets which. Long may you both continue to swill
and I to sip in your wakes. What about addicts as exors [*sic*]? It
seems to me that they are perfectly suitable in most matters –
acceptance of property, payment of legacies, winding up of estates
etc. – but that of a literary exorship might be different. *You* are
perfectly and equally suitable for that too in the immediate future,
but no one wants you to act immediately and if you had to do it
in 5 or 8 years time, when you might be a Y + or –, might you
not find it remote, boring, vexatious?

Do you think there is anything in the following device? To leave
you as general exor and residuary legatee, if you will be so good
and sweet as to remain, *but* to make a literary exor out of Bob?
I am sure that he would do the job, though it is outside his own
line, and that a 'certain element' in unpublished Mss. would not
disconcert him.

The letter, naturally, caused a flurry. 'What have you been saying
to Morgan?' asked Sprott; and Ackerley, in reply, complained bitterly
of Forster's interferingness. Nothing ensued about the executorship;
and Forster had earned so much devotion from the friends that they
did not quarrel with him; indeed Sprott, an unresentful person,
soon forgot it. With Ackerley, however, it rankled.

Meanwhile, Forster had collapsed once more and had been rushed
into hospital. He was suffering from a blood-deficiency, and for a day
or two, before this was diagnosed, his life was in danger. Later, in his
Commonplace Book, he recorded the experience, which had confirmed
him in his belief that death was 'nothing if you can approach it as
such'.

No pain, no fear, no thought of eternity, infinity, fate, love, sin,
humanity or any of the usuals. Only weakness,. and too weak to
be aware of any thing but weakness. 'I shan't be here if I get
weaker than this' was the nearest approach to a thought. I knew
that Bob and May were to my right and left – they had been
summoned by the Police and arrived about 4.0 – and was not
surprised and liked touching them: Bob's little finger pressed
mine and pursued it when it shifted. This I shall never forget.

A story about him went the round at this time. It was that he had
been put in the public ward of the hospital, next to a jaundice-patient
very yellow in the face, and when it was suggested that he move to

---

[1] An abbreviation for 'Winos'.

a private ward, he said anxiously that he did not like to – the person in the next bed might think it racial prejudice.

*   *   *

He had a strong constitution, and after two months or so he had returned to more or less normal health. He was able to go about visiting, and to travel, and during the next year or two he went on several foreign holidays – to Italy with a young Cambridge friend Tim Leggatt in 1962, to St Rémy to stay with Charles Mauron (also to Paris and Switzerland) in 1963, and again to St Rémy, with the Buckinghams, in 1964. At Christmas, as for some years now, he would go and stay at Rockingham Castle with his friend Lady Faith Culme-Seymour (a daughter of Lord Sandwich) and her husband, being amused at the mixture of grandeur and servantless domesticity. (He was by now less prejudiced against the aristocracy and had other aristocratic friends, among them Lord Harewood.)

There were the usual losses through age. His sight was weakening; he had gone deaf in one ear, which disturbed his enjoyment of music; and he could no longer play the piano. The process of decay interested him, and he analysed it frequently in his Commonplace Book and diary, telling himself in future entries to try avoiding the pronoun 'I'. There were, he noted (22 January 1962), some positive gains from age:

> What pleases and is new: visual interests, today the sunlight swayed over the vase of flowers and made them dance, and appear to open and shut; in the flat the relation, as I lay in bed, between the spire of St Utrillo's[1] and the slab of the lighted gas-fire. Connected with my failing, faded, and therefore yearning eyesight?

More and more he was conscious of living in scraps and from moment to moment. 'In a short walk,' he noted in his Commonplace Book in 1962, 'visual delicacies and splendours rush at me as frequently as, perhaps more frequently than, ever, but the power to retain them has gone.'

With age, his passion for giving grew. He was continually finding occasions to help friends and protégés, and made several large public benefactions. He gave several thousand pounds to the Fitzwilliam Museum in Cambridge towards the buying of a Greek sculpture, and

---

[1] William Plomer's nickname for the church on Turnham Green, visible from his flat windows.

when the London Library, in need of funds, asked for gifts from
members and well-wishers, to be auctioned at Christie's, he donated
the manuscript of *A Passage to India*. (It fetched £6,500, then a
record price for a manuscript by a living author.) He was rich,
anyhow by his own modest standards, and, true to his principles, he
was troubled by the money and did not wish for more. He said as
much to a fellow-don, Maurice Hill,[1] in the Combination Room at
King's, in the April of 1964 – with odd consequences. Hill had asked
him how much he earned by his writings; Forster had told him, and
let slip that he had £20,000 or so lying idle in his current account.
This for some reason enraged Hill, who called Forster an 'ass' and
strode out of the room. Forster, equally incensed, wrote Hill a letter
the same evening, saying: 'Don't stride from the room with the air of
having hurled a devastating bolt when you have done nothing of the
sort. Your trouble is that you have not read my books properly.'
Hill apologized. But a week later, Forster astonished the Buckinghams by making them a present of £10,000.

He counted himself happy: loved, cared for, sought after, and still,
after so many deaths,[2] surrounded by friends. From time to time he
was plagued with sexual longings, but not too painfully. 'I am rather
prone to senile lechery just now – want to touch the right person in
the right place, in order to shake off bodily loneliness,' he wrote to
Joe Ackerley (16 October 1961). 'I think it would and suppose it could
easily be fixed in Japan. I shan't go there, and the loneliness is not
total or tragic. Licentious scribblings help and though they are
probably fatuous I am never ashamed of them.'

There was one acute grief in his life, the tragedy of his godchild,
Rob Buckingham. Rob had grown a young man of much character:
gentle, intelligent, and strong-minded. He had resisted all attempts
to uproot him from the working class and had become a plumber.
He had got married in 1953 and possessed two sons, and he and his
wife Sylvia had become greatly attached to Forster, and he to them.
In 1961, however, Rob had fallen mysteriously ill; and after many
false diagnoses, he had been discovered to be dying from Hodgkin's
disease. There had followed a year of misery – recoveries, relapses,

---

[1] Maurice Hill (1909–66), a distinguished geophysicist. He was at this
time already suffering from a fatal disease.
[2] John Simpson died in 1955; Frank Vicary in 1956; H. O. Meredith in 1964.

and a last despairing visit to a Weymouth sanatorium – and in September 1962 he had died. Forster grieved bitterly. Two days after Rob's death, as he was hunting for some papers in his bureau, he felt a scratching at his trouser-leg and, turning, perceived a kitten; it tempted him for a moment to superstition. 'What a time some mourners would have had with her as a Kar,[1] or a messenger from the corpse,' he reflected. He wondered if Rob's death would disturb the 'symbiosis' of his and the Buckinghams' life. He longed to talk with May about Rob, when she could bear it. 'I like what she says. I *think* life may run smooth again, but we all have shattered nerves.'

*   *   *

In November 1964 Forster had a mild stroke in Cambridge, being left for a week or two afterwards with slurred speech and difficulty in writing. Another stroke followed in April of the next year, while he was with the Buckinghams in Coventry, and its effects lasted longer. For a month or two, Bob Buckingham had to write his letters for him; and his speech was slightly but permanently impaired – he would from now on momentarily grope for words or have difficulty in articulation. His memory also worsened, and he began to make muddles – forgetting faces and appointments.

It was clear to him that his remaining days must be a preparation for death. He had once said that he would like to die 'in an odour of sanctity', and the wish made itself felt. He was beginning, quietly, to strip himself of possessions, pressing friends to accept books and pieces of his furniture. A habit was growing on him, also, of expressing gratitude – of exclaiming, during a meal perhaps, how lucky he was, how many things he had to be thankful for. Gratitude interested him as a sentiment. He wrote in his diary for 16 May 1964: 'How odd is this feeling of gratitude when one isn't being grateful to anyone. Pleasanter than if there was someone e.g. God – which would entail a feeling of obligation.' In June 1964 he went to stay with William Golding in Wiltshire, and they visited Figsbury Rings, the inspiration of *The Longest Journey*. It was his first visit for sixty years. As they walked the downs, they discussed the near-extinction of Chalk Blue butterflies, through pesticides, when one flew between them and settled on a tall grass stem, in the very entrance to the Rings.

---

[1] A 'fetch' or wraith. In the antechamber of Tutenkhamun's tomb there are inscribed the words 'May thy Ka live!'

Forster, in a pantomime of the world's ruthlessness, danced after it, brandishing his walking-stick, with a cry of 'Kill! Kill!'[1] His private thoughts were all of gratitude:

> I exclaimed several times that the area was marvellous, and large
> – larger than I recalled. I was filled with thankfulness and security
> and glad that I had given myself so much back. The butterfly was
> a moving glint, and I shall lie in Stephen's arms instead of his
> child.[2]

As time went on the decay of his memory became a problem. He still kept up his business correspondence in his own hands, not being willing to use an agent, but he was not really coping with it, or even keeping up with his private correspondence. Joe Ackerley would come up to Cambridge to help him and to write letters for him, but there were bothers and confusions, mislaid cheques and broken appointments. I went up to see him in King's on 12 October 1965, and his first words were, 'I get worse, you know' – meaning he was losing his memory. There followed a tiny comedy, recorded in my diary:

> I said I was reading Tolstoy, and asked him if he agreed that one
> *forgot* Tolstoy, more so than with other novelists, and if so why?
> He smirked fleetingly at the tactless allusion to forgetting, saying
> that he agreed to the fact but 'disowned' drawing any conclusion.
> He told me an American friend of his had been reading 'The Death
> of Ivan Ilych' to him and it had made him (the American) so ill,
> that they had to leave the end till another day. 'So – obviously –
> he hadn't read it before?' I said. 'He had,' said M., 'and, *relevantly*,
> he had forgotten it.'

It vexed Forster that his forgetfulness was annoying people, otherwise it did not depress him unduly. A different trouble had arisen for him – to him more serious. At the time of his first stroke, when it seemed he might be dying, he had spoken very freely to Bob Buckingham about his own love for him, and this had had a strange consequence. Bob, on his return to Coventry, had spoken of it to May, in tones of consternation. He told her he had never known of these feelings of Forster's. Indeed he said, somewhat implausibly, that he had never even known that Forster was homosexual. It had shocked and upset him, he told her, and he would never be able to feel quite

---

[1] Related to the author by William Golding.
[2] At the close of *The Longest Journey* Stephen Wonham sleeps out on the hillside with his baby daughter in his arms.

the same towards Forster. Soon, in fact, there began to be trouble between them. Bob would be impatient with Forster. He would shout him down in conversation, would complain to May and to other friends about Forster's muddling and obstinacy, and would fret at his long stays in Coventry. Forster was upset by the change, though he did not fathom the cause, and so was May on his behalf. It was, she knew, partly that Bob hated old age; he had been as impatient with his own mother when she was 'failing'. Also, she guessed, he was jealous over herself. She made a great fuss of Forster when he stayed in Coventry, and did so more than ever as he grew frailer, and Bob would feel neglected – sometimes developing ailments himself out of unconscious rivalry. And it was true, as even May found, that Forster was a demanding guest. He was used to maids and would leave his clothes where they fell in his bedroom, expecting others to tidy them. He disliked the television and would shut his eyes before it, or put his fingers in his ears. He needed conversation, and would think it odd that May should busy herself with housework instead of talking to him.

As for the 'revelation' about Forster, May did not know what to think. She had known of course that he was homosexual, but had never thought of the friendship with Bob as a sexual one. It only now dawned on her why Joe Ackerley, and others, kept insisting how 'marvellous' she had been about the friendship. But whatever the facts, they did not perturb her. A curious reversal of earlier rôles took place among the three of them, and it was now May who saved the relationship. She fought passionately in Forster's cause. She told Bob that he was their dear friend and benefactor and that so long as he lived, their house should be his home.

As for Forster, though puzzled, he took the change in Bob calmly, being helped in this by his attitude towards death. For him, it was just one more episode in their friendship, no more significant because it happened near the end. He watched Bob's moods nervously but loved him no less fondly, and there were long periods when Bob was his old affectionate self.

*   *   *

There were other strains and fallings-away among Forster's friendships. The tie between him and Ackerley remained strong. Ackerley's letters to friends were still full of Forster, reporting his jokes and his state of health and bemoaning his muddles. Nevertheless there was a change. Ackerley sometimes felt that he had 'fallen from grace' in Forster's eyes, and he, for his part, would take issue with Forster over animals. He wrote to Plomer (6 November 1966):

> There is a rowan tree in Bob's front garden in Coventry, and when I was last there I was watching, with interest and pleasure, the blackbirds and thrushes eating the berries. They would pluck one, hold it visibly for a moment, like a coral bead, in their beaks, then swallow it at a gulp. I mentioned this to Morgan. He said: 'Yes, aren't they a nuisance.' Astonished I said: 'Why a nuisance?' He said: 'I like to see the berries on the tree.' I still think that selfishness could hardly go further; the birds are in trouble enough for eating *our* food without being reproached for eating their own.

There was, too, a soreness over money in Ackerley's mind. On his aunt's death, his sister Nancy had come to live with him, and he was worried about Nancy's future as well as his own. He thought Forster ought to give him some permanent provision, as he had done with the Buckinghams, whereas Forster only gave him occasional bounties. Eventually, in November 1966, on a friend's advice, he wrote to Forster, frankly asking him to settle some money on him, and Forster sent him a cheque for £1,000, saying it was 'both easy and pleasant' for him to do so. It was generous, but not what Ackerley had hoped. He was piqued, not so much because of the money as because he guessed Forster's motive in not giving more, which was that he would drink it away. In April of the next year, under the influence of this disappointment, he sold Forster's letters to Texas University, for £6,000. It was arranged that the letters should be under seal till Forster's death and for some years afterwards, but it left him uneasy, and he prayed Forster might never find out.[1]

At about the same time, Forster began to wonder about Plomer's projected book on himself, which seemed not to have made much progress. (It may have been Ackerley who brought the subject up, for Ackerley had rather turned against Plomer, considering him too 'slippery' and establishment-minded.) Ackerley drafted a letter to Plomer, for Forster to sign, designed to make Plomer 'put his cards on the table'. And meanwhile a letter from Forster, in Ackerley's handwriting, was also sent to me, asking me if I would like to write a book about him, and I agreed – not knowing of the arrangement

---

[1] It is not certain whether he ever did.

with Plomer. Ackerley had thought his letter to Plomer 'admirable' and one that could give no offence, but Plomer was upset and angry. He did not remonstrate with Forster himself, but told Ackerley that why he had not discussed his book with Forster was that he did not want to remind him of his death. In a second letter (8 May 1967) he said aggrievedly: 'When I first knew Morgan, I was struck by his fondness for the word 'muddle'. In his old age he seems to have made one. As he does not seem to know what he is doing, I don't suppose anybody else does!' Against me he bore no grudge. Indeed before long we became friends and he gave me the few notes he had made on Forster.

I began, on my visits to Forster, to ply him with questions about himself and his life. He answered my questions tersely but indulgently, with – as always – odd, very charming *nuances* of phrasing. His memory for past events was still fairly good; sometimes, though not often, he would get confused over facts, and occasionally he became deliberately vague. At my request, he lent me his locked diary, grew anxious and asked for it back, and then gave it to me again. He told me he did not intend to read what I wrote about him – an announcement that took me aback for a moment, till I saw how considerate it was. Later on, King's elected me to a research fellowship, and from then on we were often in each other's company.

* * *

On 4 June 1967, Joe Ackerley died in his sleep. Forster was with the Buckinghams at Aldeburgh when the news arrived. They did not tell him till last thing at night, knowing he had a way of sleeping bad news off, and he seemed not to take it in, but next day at breakfast he said quietly that it was a sad day for all Joe's friends. When Ackerley's ruthless and remarkable autobiography, *My Father and Myself*, came out the next year, he got May Buckingham to read it to him but was depressed by it. He wrote in confusion to Duncan Grant, thanking him for his letter – though in fact Grant had not written to him – and saying how much he agreed with Grant about Joe's book, 'though no one else will':

> It seems so ill-tempered, and such a reproach to all his friends. Did any of his friends (except of course Queenie) love him or appear to love him?[1] I wish I could give him a good smack!

[1] Evidently meaning to say that no one would have guessed from the book how much love he had received from his friends.

Ackerley, a few months before his death, had written an obituary article on Forster,[1] depositing it with the *Observer* for future use. It was a brilliantly written and moving portrait, expressing unstinted admiration and love for Forster. Its climactic sentence ran:

> I would say that in so far as it is possible for any human being to be both wise and worldly wise, to be selfless in any material sense, to have no envy, jealousy, vanity, conceit, to contain no malice, no hatred (though he had anger), to be always reliable, considerate, generous, never cheap, Morgan came as close to that as can be got.

*   *   *

In the New Year's honours list of 1 January 1969 Forster was awarded an O.M., and the College organized a luncheon during the same month in honour of this and of his ninetieth birthday. It was quite a small and private affair as compared with the birthday party of ten years before. At his own choice, he sat between two cousins – Philip Whichelo, an artist and stage-designer, from his mother's family, and Meyrick Owen, a schoolmaster, from his father's.[2] He looked intensely old – sitting rather silent and slumped, though in command of proceedings. The College servants had made him a birthday cake, in the form of a book bearing the titles of his novels, and he sawed away at a corner of it, murmuring 'I'd better do this now, in case I do something more important later.' The Vice-Provost, Edward Shire, then presented him with a copy, bound in green leather, of the symposium *Aspects of E. M. Forster*, just published by Edward Arnold & Co. under the editorship of Oliver Stallybrass. He looked at it suspiciously and asked who he was to thank for it. 'I suppose, Messrs. Arnold and Stallybrass,' said Shire. Forster beamed vaguely, and Tom Coley called across the table, 'You might think of thanking yourself,' which pleased him. Opening the book, he encountered his own photo. 'Well, that's all right,' he said; and then, feeling attention on him still, 'How intelligent I look!'

He was now burdened with age. He was deaf, was not able to read much or to write more than the briefest of letters. In conversation with friends, and on his own terms, he was still much as he had always been, but with strangers he could be jaw-dropped and blank.

---

[1] The article appeared in the *Observer* in abbreviated form on 14 June 1970, and the full version was published later the same year in pamphlet form by Ian McKelvie.

[2] See the family trees on pp. xxii–xxiii.

Even in the case of friends, he would sometimes muddle their identities, becoming expert at concealing the fact. In March 1970 Christopher Isherwood came to see him at King's, and they met by chance on the staircase. Forster exclaimed: 'That's most extraordinary!', apparently not recognizing Isherwood, or having thought him dead. 'What's wrong Morgan, have I changed so much?' asked Isherwood. 'Thicker!' replied Forster, now quite in command of the situation; and when they reached his rooms he examined Isherwood, all round for signs of thickness. 'Don't look at the back of my neck that's my weakest point,' said Isherwood; so Forster made a particular study of it.[1]

*   *   *

My rooms in King's were on the same staircase as Forster's, and at about 6 p.m. on Friday 22 May 1970 I heard a loud shout, and then another. I realized it was Forster and went down, finding him lying on the floor just inside his door -- he had fallen in his bedroom and had crawled from there. I went to find a porter; together we lifted him onto the sofa, and I summoned a doctor. The doctor, who was a friend of Forster's, was non-committal; nevertheless, Forster guessed at once that he had had a final stroke. I was expecting guests at 9 p.m. and by that time he was outwardly perfectly calm. He insisted on my bringing my guests down to his room, and for a few minutes he was quite gay; he said of one of his legs, which was paralysed, that it was all right but 'did rather dominate'.

By next day he was helpless, having lost the use of both his legs, and was no longer in any doubt that he was dying. What he wanted above all was to be taken to Coventry, but the Buckinghams were unable to come for a few days. It was a blow, and for a moment he was despairing, murmuring 'I wonder what will become of me'; then quite quickly he rallied. Some friends and I took charge of him, with the College matron's aid, getting him up and dressing him and putting him to bed. He was stoical and gay. Only at night was he miserable, groaning 'Oh dear, oh dear.' His formula for this was that he was 'cross'. One morning he told me he had groaned so much in the night that a neighbour had come in to him; 'and I only did it because I was cross.' Once an eccentric King's don, John Saltmarsh, came to see him in his bedroom, discoursing lengthily upon steam-ploughs and

---

[1] Related by the painter Mark Lancaster, who was present.

the mission field. Forster looked dead to the world, but as his visitor left murmured, 'He's really very nice, that old bore.'

On Wednesday 2 June Bob Buckingham came and took Forster back to Coventry, and once there, and having been put to bed, he became perfectly serene. On the following Saturday Eric Fletcher and his wife arrived. The whole party gathered at Forster's bedside before dinner and again after dinner, and, breaking a lifelong habit of abstemiousness, he drank a great deal, talking very charmingly and with great cheerfulness. After this, day by day, he steadily grew weaker. On 6 June, for most of the morning, he held May Buckingham's hand in silence, opening his eyes when she tried to take it away – till at last he fell asleep or unconscious. He died, without recovering consciousness, early the next morning.

He had left instructions that he was to be 'disposed of' wherever he happened to be at the time of his death, and without religious observances. The responsibility fell on the Buckinghams, and they decided that he should be cremated. Bob Buckingham felt diffident about giving a funeral address. He felt, none the less, that there ought to be some ceremony, so he arranged for music to be played on a record-player in the chapel; remembering *Howards End*, he chose the *scherzo* from Beethoven's Fifth Symphony. Despite this, it was for the mourners a slightly depressing experience, as all such non-religious rituals are; but as we filed back towards the cars there was a diversion. The undertakers' men were peering inside the bonnet of the leading Rolls, evidently unable to make it start. The chief undertaker approached, pressing his black gloves to his forehead in a theatrical gesture, protesting that never, never in twenty years, had such an unfortunate thing . . . And at this Sprott, who had been gloomy, brightened greatly, remarking that Forster's spirit was clearly at work.

Notes

VOLUME ONE

Page 32 *A friend of the Whichelos wrote a *Hiawatha*-style poem about these sprees aboard the *Doris* and it is from this that I have been quoting. The verses end:

> Could I tell you of the laughter,
> Of the stories told at midnight
> Of the Cuckoo and the Dunn-bird,
> Of the teasing tumbling schoolboys,
> Tiresome, mischievous young schoolboys,
> Of the chatter of the gals, gals,
> Giggling, whinnying their fingers . . .
> Of the bathing in the morning
> When the girls with blinds tight-fastened
> Wondered at the shrieks of laughter,
> Wished that they might join the bathers,
> Like the girls across the Channel;
> Of the merry, sunny Sundays,
> Nineteen men and three small maidens,
> Talking, laughing, flirting, drinking,
> Punting, rowing on the river,
> Fishing, doing everything they ought not,
> Could I tell in language fitting
> All the fun upon a houseboat,
> You would say, 'O Pucky Ruby,
> When you next go down to Datchet,
> Take me with you Pucky darling,
> Let me too be there beside you,
> There beside you on the houseboat,
> In the Moon of falling leaves.'

Datchet. August/September, 1886.

Notes

Page 32   †His obituary in *The Man of the World (With Which is Incorporated 'The Bird O'Freedom')* cast no light on it:

> *Wednesday* 23 August 1893. Much shocked to read in this morning's paper the notice of poor Percy Whichelo's death, which took place at Dinard on the 12th. It is only a few weeks that I noted his marriage. His was a most gentle and lovable nature, and although perhaps a trifle weak of purpose, I do not think he ever made an enemy, whereas his many kind actions should have procured him hosts of friends. I remember two kind deeds of his which he never referred to himself, but which, now that he is no more, deserve recording. Two well-known men about town, Ian Macintosh and 'the Major', Bob Hope-Johnstone, were not many years back stricken unto death within a very few months of each other, and Percy Whichelo, when other friends of the sick men held aloof, found them medical attendance, skilled nurses, and, best of all, eased their last moments with his cheery presence . . .

Page 44   *It begins with the words: 'At dinner Margaret . . .' However, Forster's profoundest portrait of his young self is Ralph Moore in *A Passage to India* – Ralph, whose brief apparition at the end of the novel is so moving and central to the book's design. Aziz gets the impression, at first, that the timid, strange-looking Ralph is 'almost an imbecile'. But there is 'one thing he always knows' – he knows when people are being unkind; and with his sureness over spiritual and human matters he is the agent of such reconciliation as there is in the book.

Page 77   *Sir Charles Tennyson in *Cambridge from Within* (1913) gives a description of Ainsworth, under the guise of 'a philosopher from King's', addressing a meeting of another Cambridge discussion society: '. . . we are forestalled by a philosopher from King's, who makes a dash for the fireplace, climbs on the curb, puts his back against the mantelpiece, and launches into a long harangue . . . He has a singularly involved style of gesture and exegesis. He writhes against the overmantel, shrugging and twisting his shoulders, like an intellectual Atlas upbearing a world of argument. He is incessantly climbing on and off the curb, twisting his forelock between his forefinger and thumb, taking his pipe out of his mouth and stroking his forehead, chin, or the bridge of his nose, with the stem of it. Meanwhile his periods get more and more involved, his manner more and more provocative . . .'

Page 116   *A liberal intellectual at this period was almost by definition a pedestrian. Bertrand Russell tells in his Autobiography how he once arrived at an inn at the Lizard, and when he asked for a bed the landlord enquired if his name were G. M. Trevelyan. ' "No," I said, "you are expecting him?" "Yes," they said, "and his wife is here already." This surprised me, as I knew that it was his wedding day. I found her languishing alone, as he had left her at Truro, saying that he could not face the whole day without a little walk. He arrived about ten o'clock at night, completely exhausted, having accomplished the forty miles in record time . . .'

Page 143   *The story is a curious one. Sir Syed's son Syed Mahmud, the father of Masood, was a distinguished jurist, but, in his early fifties, partly through chagrin at not being appointed Sir Syed's successor at Aligarh, he became an alcoholic and had some kind of mental breakdown. One night Morison was woken by a frightened message from Syed Mahmud's wife, to say that he had taken their son out into the garden, in the dark and freezing cold, and was teaching him to plough the lawn with a wooden plough. Morison hurried over, wrapped up the shivering and terrified boy in his greatcoat and sent him to his own home, and then stayed to keep the boy's father company, while the latter, with great lucidity, discoursed for the rest of the night on the history of agriculture. He explained to Morison that he had been trying to teach Masood a political lesson – that the only thing India needed from the West was improved techniques of agriculture. Masood thereafter remained in the Morison household.

The government of India helped to finance Masood's studies at Oxford, which indicates the importance they attached to the goodwill of Aligarh.

Page 149   *In the original draft there was a chapter of pure phantasmagoria, in which Stephen, parted from his clothes while bathing and then knocked on the head by a flying soda-water bottle, wanders naked in the woods, like the first man, worshipping trees and the sun. 'It fitted in well,' said Forster later, 'but it became too odd for him [Stephen].'

Earlier versions of Stephen's Christian name were 'Harold' and 'Siegfried', and the suppressed chapter is very reminiscent of the forest scene in Wagner's *Siegfried*.

Page 215   *Masood had gone back to India and Anglo-Indians very reluctantly, writing plaintively to his friend Sherwani from shipboard: 'Dans ce bateau-ci il y a de vrais Anglo-Indiens qui nous détestent. J'ai déjà gouté la vie qui m'attend aux Indes et pour vous dire la vérité elle n'était pas bonne . . . Hélas! j'ai dit adieu au charmant pays qui s'appelle l'Europe, et où demeure mon bien aimé. Quand j'y pense le désir de me tuer devient bien fort mais les pensées de ma chère mère viennent à mon secours . . . Brulez cette lettre car elle vient de mon coeur.'

Page 217   *In *Sowing* (1960) Woolf quotes a letter from Forster written at the time of his own departure for Ceylon and beginning with a characteristic touch of 'truth-telling'. 'Dear Woolf, I nearly was in Cambridge yesterday, but it didn't come off. I don't think, though, that I really wanted to see you again.

Notes

'This letter is only to wish you godspeed in our language, and to say that if you ever want anything done in England will you let me know? It's worth making this vague offer because I'm likely always to have more time on my hands than anybody else.

'I shall write at the end of the year. I knew you much less than I like you which makes your going the worse for me.'

Page 227 *When George V visited Aligarh as Prince of Wales, he was astonished to find portraits of the Sultan and the German Emperor on the walls of students' rooms. He asked them anxiously, 'Do you really admire such people?' and made a full report to the Cabinet.

Witnesses at the Commission of Enquiry accused one of the English teachers of constantly baiting students for their pro-Turkish sympathies and declaring that if he had his way, he would make the Sultan Abdul Hamid his *punkah-wallah*. It was also said that students were offended at being addressed as 'You rogue', 'rascal', 'idiot', or 'scoundrel' – not realizing that in England these were 'endearments'.

Page 227 †In 1906 it conveyed a confidential message to the College's Secretary, Moshin-ul-Mulk, that the Viceroy would welcome it if he were to organize a deputation to him, demanding reserved seats for Muslims in the Legislative Councils. The deputation was sent and duly welcomed, and as a sequel there came into being the Muslim League, the direct progenitor of Pakistan. (See S. K. Bhatnagar, *History of the M.A.O. College, Aligarh* [Aligarh, 1969], p. 233.)

Page 228 *There is an account of him in Halide Edib's *Inside India* (1937). Describing him as he was in 1935, she writes: 'Externally he had not changed much. The same small moustache, the brooding mouth with that delicate design which one associated with the Hindu, very black and energetic eyebrows stretched over his deep-set eyes. They were purposeful eyes, very kind in spite of the unwavering determination in their depths. His clothes had that masculine elegance which one associated with London. He talked very little, but always to the point.'

Page 238 *And not without reason. At the time of the *Swadeshi* movement he wrote to Darling (8 December 1908): 'No local worries at present, excepting that little Swadeshi is begun in J.B. [Junior Branch] in the shape of shops and I am watching it carefully and simply waiting to crush it when it starts in S.B. Because I think now that Swadeshi is the beginning and signal for disloyalty and anarchism . . . Regarding Bengal we are reading a lot to convey the idea of the movement. O the whole thing to me is ghastly and believe me that I am determined to serve your nation if for nothing else at least for the sake that it possesses the noblest man like you and that is my pride.'

VOLUME TWO

Page 62 *He had a more personal encounter with Shaw a few years later, in 1926, which he found disappointing. 'You can imagine how excited I was to be invited [to lunch],' he wrote to G. H. Ludolf (11 July 1926), 'and how disappointed to find an old old gentleman and a cushiony wife. Shaw was pleasant and amusing, but I felt all the time that he'd forgotten what people are like (can it be that he never knew and that this accounts for something that's lacking in his plays?). She [Mrs Shaw] wanted to talk mysticism, and denounced "atheists" with the accents of a rural dean. I came away with the hump for, surely, two of the best things in life are human beings and beauty, and both seemed to get ruled out.'

Page 119 *For instance, Masood quoted the couplet from the Urdu of Ghalib (1797–1869), poet laureate to the last of the Moguls:

> Not all, alas! only a few, have come back to us in the
>   form of tulips and roses.
> How beautiful, O God! must have been some of the faces
>   that lie hidden in the dust!

This is echoed by Forster in Chapter 9 of *A Passage to India*, when Aziz recites poetry to his friends: 'Whatever Ghalib had felt, he had anyhow lived in India, and this consolidated it for them: he had gone with his own tulips and roses, but tulips and roses do not go.'

In his article, Masood remarked: '. . . with us in the East, poetry is still a living force, and we are not ashamed of giving vent to the emotions it evokes'.

Page 164 *In similar manner, writing to James Kirkup (6 May 1942) about some remarks of Eliot's on Virginia Woolf, Forster complained: 'I lose all patience with him when he starts guarding himself.' He also disapproved of Eliot's reverence for pain. In 1963, after reading Eliot's 'Little Gidding' aloud to himself, he wrote in his Commonplace Book:

331

I feel now to be as far ahead of him [Eliot] as I was once behind. Always a distance – and a respectful one. How I dislike his homage to pain! What animal except the human could have excogitated it? Of course there's pain on and off through each individual life, and pain at the end of most lives. You can't shirk it and so on. But why should it be endorsed by the school-master and sanctified by the priest until

the fire and the rose are one

when so much of it is caused by disease or by bullies? It is here that Eliot becomes unsatisfactory as a seer, as Coventry does as a shrine. That misfire-cathedral has given Christ a green face and the Angel of the Agony matches for legs.

Despite this, he thought 'Little Gidding' a 'wonderful' poem.

Eliot admired Forster's 1929 essay on himself ('T. S. Eliot and his Difficulties') and wrote Forster a very interesting letter in acknowledging it (10 August 1929). He congratulated Forster on detecting the 'bluff' in his prose-style, but told him he exaggerated the relevance of the War to 'The Waste Land', which might have been just the same had there been no war.

Page 186 *Kidd read an article by A. P. Herbert in the *Week End Review* (5 August 1933), about the activities of police *agents provocateurs* against after-hours' drinking in night-clubs. Herbert's sanctimonious tone annoyed him, and he challenged Herbert, as the 'champion' of freedom', to protest at – what he thought an infinitely more serious evil – the use of *agents provocateurs* against the Hunger Marchers. Herbert rose to the challenge. There were various published exchanges between them in the *Week End Review*, and eventually A. P. Herbert offered, if Kidd would swear an affidavit against the police, to go with Gerald Barry (the editor of the *Week End Review*) to the Commissioner of Metropolitan Police, Lord Trenchard, to demand a public inquiry into the use of *agents provocateurs*. The deputation duly took place; Trenchard responded with a written statement denying the need for an enquiry; and in the October 28 number of the *Week End Review* A. P. Herbert wrote pointing out inconsistencies in Trenchard's statement and warmly praising Kidd for his public spirit in raising the whole issue. It was out of these events that the N.C.C.L. took shape.

Page 187 *It was a bitterly cold day, and, according to Claud Cockburn, H. G. Wells, who had been ill, suddenly dug his umbrella into the mud of Hyde Park, exclaiming: 'I refuse to go any further. I detect your plan. At any moment now, as a result of some prearranged signal on your part, the situation will get out of hand, the police will charge, a dozen prominent authors and legislators will be borne to the ground, and you will have the incident you desire.' It struck Cockburn, who had not previously thought of it, as quite a good idea. (See C. Cockburn, *In Time of Trouble* (1956), pp. 241–2.)

Page 187 *Robert Skidelsky, in his *Oswald Mosley* (1975) p. 357, quotes a report from the police Special Branch asserting that in 1934 (when Kidd was writing to the *New Statesman* that his Council 'expressed no opinion' as to the desirability of anti-fascist demonstrations) 'the activities of the N.C.C.L. were directed, via Kidd, from Communist Party headquarters'. Sylvia Scaffardi, Kidd's close associate at this period, denied this strongly in conversation with the present author in 1977. She said that Kidd was never a Communist or a member of any political party. There was, she said, some contact between the Council and the Communist Party head-quarters on the matter of providing observers to cover meetings and demonstrations. She herself had twice visited their headquarters for this purpose. (Mrs Scaffardi has given a long and interesting account of the early days of the N.C.C.L. in her – so far unpublished – autobiography.)

Page 190 *It was, however, invoked in a major trial in December 1975, when fourteen members of the British Withdrawal From Northern Ireland movement were accused of conspiring to incite soldiers to desert and of being in possession of seditious leaflets. Their acquittal was hailed by the N.C.C.L. as a vindication of their long campaign against the Act.

Page 226 *As Samuel Hynes puts it in *The Auden Generation* (1976): '. . . Auden and Isherwood recognized that the war in China was different – that in its scale, its confusion, its huge destruction of cities and people, it was the war that was coming. And so the two young men travelled half-way round the world, not to report a war, and certainly not to participate in it, but to testify how they felt in the presence of war, and what meaning the experience had for them.

Page 237 *They met once more, in 1960, at a party at the Savoy Hotel, when Joe Ackerley was receiving the W. H. Smith Literary Award for his novel *We Think the World of You*. Daley told Forster that he was writing his memoirs, but that Forster was not to worry: he (Harry) had become discreet in his old age, to which Forster replied, amicably, that he could say what he liked: he (Forster) had become indiscreet in his old age. Daley's memoirs, 'This Small Cloud' – a remarkable book, so far unpublished – were, as he had promised, entirely discreet and made hardly any mention of his literary friends.

Page 238 *See *Hansard* 13 June 1940: '*Major Sir Jocelyn Lucas* asked the Parliamentary Secretary to the Ministry of Labour whether British citizens of military age, such as Mr. W. H. Auden and Mr. Christopher Isherwood, who have gone to the United States and expressed their

Notes

determination not to return to this country until war is over, will be summoned back for registration and calling up, in view of the fact that they are seeking refuge abroad?

Mr. Assheton: I have no information with regard to Mr. Isherwood. Mr. Austin gave an undertaking before leaving the country that he would return if called upon to do so; he is outside the age groups so far required to register under the National Service (armed Forces) Act.

Mr. Mathers: On a point of Order. There is no mention of Mr. Austin in this Question.

Sir J. Lucas: Is my hon. Friend aware of the indignation caused by young men leaving the country and saying that they will not fight? If they are not registered as conscientious objectors will he see that they lose their citizenship?'

Page 280 *Harry Daley, who was still friendly with Ackerley, was caustic on the subject of Queenie. He wrote to the author (24 November 1968): 'In no time Joe turned the Dog into a noisy, dangerous creature that rushed about barking and made conversation impossible, and was too hysterical to stand still for even the 100th of a second for me to take the photograph Joe so much wanted. Although Joe, shouting at the bloody thing to be quiet, made almost as much noise as the Dog, and had endless abusive exchanges with bus conductors (some of whom got bit on the bum) who refused to carry the Dog, to say nothing of neighbours complaining and police calling with warnings, he was convinced that he and his dog were the envy and admiration of the whole of Putney . . . Joe put up this act, any dog would have served, and he squeezed every ounce of pleasure from it. It was a good exhibition with in my opinion, about as little to do with sex or love as Joe's previous "love affairs" with human beings.'

Page 291 *There were George Richmond drawings of Marianne Thornton, of Forster's aunts Ella and Edith Forster and of his grandfather Charles Forster. Elsewhere in the room were a painting of his great-great-aunt Marianne Sykes in Turkish costume, by Sir George Chalmers; an engraving of Gainsborough's portrait said to be of Henry Thornton but actually of Henry's father John; an engraving of Richmond's portrait of Wilberforce; a drawing by his great-aunt Lucy Thornton of 'Interior of Holy Trinity Church, Clapham Common' (c. 1825); etc.

Page 300 *In October 1953 a Police Court magistrate was reported (inaccurately) as saying that in his court alone more than 600 cases of homosexual importuning were tried every year. Reacting to this, the Liberal statesman Viscount Samuel, in a speech in the Lords (4 November 1953) on 'the moral state of the nation', said that, in addition to increased juvenile crime and growing laxity over adultery, 'the vices of Sodom and Gomorrah, of the Cities of the Plain, appear to be rife among us.' He blamed the weakening of the moral law on the two world wars and on 'strange new doctrines in physiology and psychology' and foresaw retribution, 'not in earthquake or conflagration but in something much more deadly, an insidious poisoning of the moral sense.'

Forster had commented on the same report in an article 'Society and the Homosexual: a Magistrate's Figures' in the *New Statesman* for 31 October 1953, asking, if not for change in the law for homosexuals (which he thought unlikely for many years), at least for 'less social stigma under the existing law'. He sent a copy of his article to Lord Samuel, who replied (29 November 1953) that he was 'far from quarrelling with its general tendency' but concluded: 'If homosexuality between adults is legalized, is it not likely that it may become very widespread, possibly catered for by brothels of a special type? Incomprehensible and utterly disgusting as it appears to all normal people, it seems to have the capacity to form a habit as potent as alcohol or narcotics.'

Page 305 *For the occasion Siegfried Sassoon sent him a poem, written on the back of a photograph of King's chapel with a collage of Forster's head in the west window. It ran:

> In bygone days I sometimes sauced a
> Confederate crony – Morgan Forster.
> Query: do I now dare accost a
> Figure as famed as E. M. Forster?
> I do. In bed with glum lumbago
> Watch I my words upon their way go.
> And wafted by affectionate wings,
> Join the glad 'goings on' at King's.
>
> With Morgan I can still be 'matey'
> Though grown so eminent at eighty.
> I, ever most unintellectual,
> And as a thinker, ineffectual,
> I, a believer in believing,
> Can hail his genius for perceiving
> Reasoned humanities which led
> Where angels have not feared to tread,
> And thus, forbearing further fuss,
> Award my friend an Alpha Plus.

Forster, in copying it into his Commonplace Book, wrote: 'Lovely skilful sincere stuff and illustrating that "I love you though I never trouble to see you" attitude which is also characteristic of Ben and Peter, and which I do not share.'

Appendix:
The Maharaja of Dewas (Sir Tukoji Rao III)

His marriage-troubles

The early marital troubles of the Maharaja of Dewas were obscure and complicated, involving political rivalries between him and his fellow Mahratta princes, the Maharaja of Kolhapur and the Gaekwar of Baroda, and manoeuvres on the part of all of them *vis-à-vis* the British. Soon after the marriage-alliance with Kolhapur had been arranged in 1907, the Gaekwar of Baroda, a relative of Tukoji's and one of the most powerful princes in India, had tried to persuade Tukoji to marry his own daughter instead, or even (for it was embarrassing for her still to be unmarried at 16) to take her as a supplementary wife. Tukoji had refused, and he and his bride-elect were married in Kolhapur in March 1908, the ceremony being performed with great pomp, though among quarrels and sinister rumours – such as that the bride would be put to death five days after the ceremony, as a sacrifice to avert plague and famine, and the bridegroom would go out of his mind. (Malcolm Darling, who attended the wedding with his sisters, gives a lengthy account of it in *Apprentice to Power* [1966].) The ceremony performed, however, Tukoji discovered to his chagrin that for another two years he was not to be allowed to live with his bride (who was then 14) or even to see her. He protested, but a committee of ladies of the Palace upheld the ruling; and, by now thoroughly overwrought, he fell into a dangerous fever, being nursed through it devotedly by Malcolm Darling.

In a way the marriage never went right after this. The bride and bridegroom managed to meet unofficially (the ban on their doing so seems to have been a sort of ritual prohibition, intended to be flouted), and in October 1908, in a further ceremony, the consummation of the marriage was proclaimed and Tukoji brought the Rani back to Dewas. Within a few months, however, there was a quarrel. The Rani suspected an affair between him and one of her maids-of-honour and returned in dudgeon to Kolhapur for a stay of many months. She was by now pregnant, and in May 1909 she gave birth to a son (Vikramsinha), but when Tukoji went to see them, she still appeared implacably – and by now rather mysteriously – indifferent and hostile. The affair was prejudicing Tukoji's whole standing at Kolhapur, and he retaliated by refusing to see the child.

Eventually, after his return to Dewas, a letter arrived from the Rani which partly explained the mystery. According to her, her aunt, a Baroda woman, had told her that Tukoji was plotting with Baroda to have her poisoned and to marry the Gaekwar's daughter in her place. The Rani had asked why, even if he intended the marriage, he should need to murder her, to which her aunt had replied that he was afraid of the Maharaja of Kolhapur – not on the latter's own account but because of his influence with the British. The Rani, in her letter, asked Tukoji how much of the story was true, saying that even if it were all true she would rather die than 'be protected by this bad woman', and Tukoji (so he reported to Malcolm Darling) replied swearing total innocence, 'on all oaths and in a most vivid manner', and threatening to kill himself unless she believed him.

Matters were now patched up between them, and the Rani returned to Dewas; but before long there were further disputes, leading, in 1915, to a permanent separation. Meanwhile, in March 1912, on a visit to Kolhapur, Tukoji had met and fallen in love with Bai Saheba, a family dependant of the Maharaja of Kolhapur, then 14 years of age and about to be trained as a dancing-girl. He brought her back to Dewas and (according to his later account to Darling) married her in April by the so-called 'Third form of marriage'.

The young prince's flight and later scandals.

The events of 1927–28, when the young prince Vikramsinha took flight from Dewas, evidently had their origins in the troubles just described. The story of the flight, and what led up to it, is intensely confused, quite different versions emerging from Josie Darling's letters,[1] the A.G.G.'s correspondence with the Political Department[2] and the Maharaja of Kolhapur's letter to Government House, Bombay.[2] (For instance, it was part of the story that reached official ears that Tukoji had sent armed men to ambush the escaping prince and that they had opened fire on the prince's car. Josie Darling, however (in a letter to her son, 11 January 1928) explained the matter thus:

> Vikram one day motored over the border, at the Sipra river, and informed the loyal Sirdar, who was sitting beside him, that he was going to leave Dewas for ever. The Sirdar had a revolver. Sharman, from the back seat, cried 'Give me the pistol, quick! I will fire at the tyres and prevent his going.' Silly old Sirdar gave him it. Sharman rapidly fired 4 shots at the mudguard on Vikky's side. Then they sped to the Residency, said Uncle Tukki [i.e. Tukoji] had posted men in ambush to kill Vikky – behold the bullet marks!)

One thing is clear, it was at this moment that Tukoji lost the confidence of the British, with results fatal to himself. It so happened that the two British officials most closely concerned with Tukoji's later history were brothers, Sir Reginald and Sir Bertram Glancy. Sir Reginald, a personal friend of Tukoji's, was A.G.G. at Indore at the time of the young prince's flight and acted with great good will, doing everything he could to reconcile the father and son and to minimize the public scandal. He was, however, finally alienated by Tukoji's behaviour: by his vacillation and tortuousness, his insistence that there should be no inquiry, and his unforgiveness towards his son. He began to doubt Tukoji's good faith, and probably passed on his doubts to his younger brother Sir Bertram, who was Political Secretary and 'right-hand man' to the Viceroy.

In the later stages of the Dewas drama – the British attempt to impose officials and advisers on Tukoji, Tukoji's fantastic flight to Pondicherry, and his eventual deposition in favour of his son – Sir Bertram had the deciding voice, and his attitude to Tukoji was throughout cold and hostile. In 1932 Tukoji, who was ill, called in an old friend of his, a retired army surgeon named Sir James Roberts, to help him with the State's affairs. A colleague of Sir Bertram

---

[1] Now in the possession of Malcolm Darling's daughter, Mme April van Biervliet.

[2] In the India Office Library.

Glancy's in the Political Department – though urging Sir James to accept the help of a government adviser – reported that Sir James must be allowed to stay for some time, otherwise the Maharaja would 'certainly crash'. Glancy, on the other hand, did his best to get Sir James removed ('His activities in India states have never been of benefit to anyone but himself'), and he blocked the appointment of any successor – pronouncing Malcolm Darling, whose name was suggested, undesirable and to be 'as gullible as Sir James Roberts'.

Early in 1935, a year or more after Tukoji's removal to Pondicherry, Malcolm Darling was still making heroic efforts to help him, offering to act as his plenipotentiary in negotiations with the *Raj* and at the same time pleading with him, for the sake of his own peace of mind, to accept his fate and to return to his country as a private citizen. While in Delhi, Darling asked Sir Bertram Glancy for an interview about Tukoji's affairs, but Sir Bertram refused to see him, granting him no more than a lengthy telephone conversation. It was his attitude that caused Forster, in *The Hill of Devi*, to speak of the British handling of Tukoji as 'impeccably right and absolutely wrong'.

Index

Forster's writings are indexed under the entry for Forster himself

VOLUME ONE

'A Adolphe Gaiffe' (Banville), 159n
Abinger, 45–7. *See also* 'West Hackhurst'
Abinger Hall, 5–6
Abu, Mount, 251
Ackerley, J. R., 234, 235
Acland, Francis Dyke, 176
Acton, Lord, 55
Aeschylus, 70
'Ages of Man, The' (Meredith), 61n
Agra, 233
Ahmed Khan, Sir Syed, 143, 144n
Ainsworth, A. R., 63, 69, 262; and 'Apostles', 76, 77, 105; partial model for Ansell in *Longest Journey*, 77
Albany Review, 163
Alford, Robert, 142n
Ali, Mohammed, 227, 228–9
Ali, Shaukat, 227, 228–9
Aligarh, 142–3, 226–8, 264; Muslim Anglo-Oriental College, 142–3, 227, 264
Allahabad, 245, 247, 248–9
Ansari, M. A., 228, 264
Ansell (garden-boy), Forster's idyllic friendship with, 30–31
'Apostles, The' (Cambridge Conversazione Society), 75–9, 104–7, 150
Aristides (Italian chauffeur), 169–70
Aristophanes, 70
Aristotle, 70
Armour, W. S., 245
Arnim, Beatrix (Trix) von, 127, 128, 134, 154
Arnim, Evi von, 127, 134, 154
Arnim, Count Henning August von, 124, 125, 129, 130
Arnim, Liebet von, 127, 129, 134, 154
Arnim, Mary Beauchamp, Countess von – *see* 'Elizabeth'
Arnold, Edward, 153, 166n, 171, 172, 185
Arnold, Matthew, 70, 149, 181
Asiatic Studies (Lyall), 184n
Aurangabad, 252–3
Austin, Alfred, 155

Awakening of India, The (MacDonald), 184n
Aylward (formerly Synnot), Maimie, 15, 16, 132, 143, 187; lifelong friendship with Lily Forster, 10, 11; devotion to Forster, 10, 11, 40; second marriage, 27–8, 109; Forster's holidays with, 116, 177; on *Howards End*, 190

Backe, Fräulein (governess at Nassenheide), 127, 128
Baldeo (Hindu servant), 225, 230, 241, 251
Bankipore, 246–7
Banville, Théodore de, 159n
Barabar Hills, 247–8
Barger, Florence, 63n, 152n, 179, 186, 206, 207, 228, 258, 259; 'my only woman friend', 204; close friendship, 219
Barger, George, 63, 152, 219; and religious controversy at King's, 99, 100, 101
Barwell, N. F., 104, 106
Basileona, 72
'Battersea Rise', Clapham, 3, 4, 46
Baveno, 168
Beddoes, Thomas, 159
Belfast, 211–14
Bell, Vanessa, 163, 192
Belloc, Hilaire, 109
Benares, 245–6
Bennett, E. K., 176
Berlin, 125–6
Beveridge, Sir William, 38
Bhagavad Gita, 216
Birrell, Francis, 172
Blackwood, William & Sons Ltd, 123
Blake, William, 7n
Blomfield, Sir Arthur, 7
Bookman, 135
Bookseller, 135
Bournemouth, 11, 19, 36
Bracknells, The (Reid), 210
Bridget, St, 178
British Dominion in India (Lyall), 184n

Index

Brooke, Rupert, 177
Brookfield, Charles, 205
Browning, Oscar, 53–4, 59, 61, 68, 72, 79–80
Browning, Robert, 55, 70, 115
Buckingham, Bob, 110n
Bulmer, E. F., 55n, 58n
Butler, Samuel, 159n, 203, 258, 259

Cacciola, Salvatore, 109n
Cadenabbia, 81–2, 84
Cambridge, 49–80, 97, 98, 104–7; King's, 49, 51–60, 72–3, 75, 97, 99–101, 104–7, 199; Trinity, 104–7; Conversazione Society ('The Apostles'), 75–9, 104–7, 150; 'truth' of, 49; and role of professions, 50; scepticism at, 62; religious controversy, 99–100
Cambridge Local Lectures Board, Forster's extension lectures for, 110, 121, 122, 138
Cambridge Review, 72n, 73
Candler, Edmund, 249
Cantab, The (Leslie), 62n
Caravanners, The ('Elizabeth'), 156
Carpenter, Edward, 159n, 256–7, 258
Chamberlain, Sir Austen, 122
Chesterton, G. K., 108
Chevalier, Albert, 51
Chhatarpur, 234–7; Maharaja of, 215, 234–7, 240, 243
Chilham, 155
Chipman, Leo, 64, 65, 66
Chirol, Valentine, 230n
Church Times, 113
Churchill, Winston, 213–14
Cicero, 70
Clapham, 3–4, 8, 10
Clapham Sect, 3–4
Cnidus, 101, 102–3
Cohen, Lord, 66n
Collingham, David Horace, 71
Comrade, The, 227, 229
Conrad, Joseph, 159, 189
Coode, B. H., 202
Cooke, A. H., 53n
Cortina d'Ampezzo, 95–6, 104
Cortona, 86, 87
Costogno, 168
Curle, Richard, 115
Cust, R. H., 84–5

Daily Mail, 170
Daily Telegraph, 188
Dante Alighieri, 159, 170
Darling, Josie, 184, 203, 205, 213, 230, 244, 245
Darling, Malcolm Lyall, 138, 160, 179, 216, 245; and Room With a View, 171; and Raja of Dewas State Senior, 184–5, 238, 239, 240, 241, 243, 244; as magistrate in Lahore, 229–30
Dartmoor, 116
Darwin, Frank, 50, 54
Darwin, Horace, 50
Davies, J. Llewellyn, 174n
Davies, Theodore Llewellyn, 141n
Deceased Wife's Sister Bill (1907), 157–8
Delhi, 228–9, 249–51
Dent, Edward Joseph, 80, 82, 94, 95, 97, 98, 104, 160, 164, 173; Forster's letters to, from Italy, 83–4, 91, 93; in Italy, 103, 169; on Room With a View, 170
Dent, J. M. & Co., 94n, 110
Dew-Smith, Alice, 163

Dewas State Senior, 184, 238, 239–45
Dewas State Senior, Tukoji Rao III, Raja of, 184–5, 238–45, 249–51
Dicey, A. V., 174
Dickinson, Cato Lowes, 174
Dickinson, Goldsworthy Lowes, 61, 72, 80, 110, 148, 176, 184, 187, 191, 198, 202, 203, 256; Forster's entry into circle of, 59–60; and 'Apostles', 77, 79; developing friendship with Forster, 79, 204; Forster's letters to, from Italy, 86, 89, 90, 91; and Independent Review, 107, 108; influence on Howards End, 173; emotional conflict, 186; in India, 215, 216, 219, 220–1, 225, 230–1, 232, 233–7, 246; first seen by Forster as 'solid figure', 232; shocked by Forster's erotic stories, 258
Dickinson, H. N., 159
Dickinson, Hester, 172–3, 174, 203
Dickinson, Janet, 172–3, 174, 203
Dickinson, May, 172–3, 174, 203
Dowland, Agnes, 119–20
Doyle, A. Conan, 70
Duncan, Sara Jeanette, 232

'East Side', Clapham, 4, 10, 12–13, 23
Eastbourne, Kent House School at, 33–8
Eckhard, Oscar, 186
Edib, Halide, 264
'Elizabeth' (Countess von Arnim, later Countess Russell), 122, 128, 134; engages Forster as tutor, 123, 125–6; background and character, 124–5, 131–2, 151–2; revised opinion of Forster, 130; Forster's less eulogistic opinion of her, 130–2; admires Longest Journey, 151; caravanning tour, 154–6
Ellem, Elizabeth, 207n
Ellora, cave-temples of, 254
Emma (maid at 'Rooksnest'), 22
English Review, 204n
Epipsychidion (Shelley), 107
Euripides, 70
Ex Voto (Butler), 203n

Fagu, 233
Fanny's First Play (Shaw), 200
Farman, Henri, 161n
Farrer, Effie (Katherine Euphemia Wedgwood), 5, 6, 8, 9, 115n
Farrer (later Darwin), Ida, 6, 11, 50n
Farrer, T. H. (later Lord), 5, 46
Felton (Northumberland), 64; Acton House, 63–6, 111
Ferrer, Francesco, 178
Figsbury Rings, 116–17, 119
FitzGerald, Edward, 159n
Flecker, James Elroy, 205
Florence, 83–6, 101, 103
Following Darkness (Reid), 212, 237
Forster, Alice Clara ('Lily') (mother), 19, 20–21, 23, 28, 32, 36, 51, 65, 73, 97, 123, 128, 138, 143, 162, 163, 256, 258, 259; character, 2–3, 5–6, 13, 14, 103, 120; as Marianne Thornton's protégée, 3, 4–6, 8–9, 11–13; as governess, 5–6; marriage to Edward Forster, 6, 7–8; birth of sons, 9; widowed, 10–11; 'duel' over possession of Forster, 11–12; independence, 14; house-hunting, 14; moves to 'Rooksnest', 15–18; love-affair with Forster, 21–2, 44; legacy from Marianne, 24; and local society, 25;

Forster's letters to, from school, 33, 34, 39–40; and 'facts of life', 37–8; problems of Forster's school and of new home, 39–40; move to Tonbridge, 40; rejects proposals of marriage, 44; tour of Normandy churches, 44–5; Forster's letters to, from Cambridge, 51, 56–7, 68; move to Tunbridge Wells, 57; and Forster's loss of faith, 62; Forster's 'little girl' role with, 67; in Cambridge, 71; tour of Italy, 80, 81, 82 *et seq.*; her letters from, 83, 84, 86–8, 89, 92, 93, 94–5; in Italy again, 101, 103–4; move to South Kensington flat, 109; move to Weybridge, 119–20; on *Where Angels Fear to Tread*, 136; Forster's letters to, from Italy, 168, 169–70; shocked by *Howards End*, 187; unhappiness, 192, 196, 197, 204, 215, 217–18; affected by mother's death, 195, 197, 204; changed relationship with Forster, 197, 204, 217–18, 219; Forster's letters to, from India, 225–6, 230, 234, 240–3; happy reunion, 255

Forster, Rev. Charles (grandfather), 6–7

Forster, Charles (great-grandfather), 6

FORSTER, EDWARD MORGAN: ancestry, 1–9; birth, 9; christening, 10; childhood among women, 11–25, 28–9; molly-coddling, 19, 24, 44; dolls, 20–21; love-affair with mother, 21–2, 44; other relatives, 25–9; friendships with garden-boys, 30–31; schooldays, 33–48; home-sickness, 34, 39–40; unpopularity, 34–5; romantic friendships, 35–6; mystified by 'smut', 36–7, 39; sexual drama, 37–8; at Tonbridge School, 40–44; miseries, 41, 42–3; tour of Normandy churches, 44–5; academic success, 47–8; at Cambridge, 49–80; quiet first year, 50–57; maintains school friendships, 51, 52, 57; reading-list, 55, 70; quarrel with landlady, 56–7; new friends and influences, 57–64, 69–70, 79; loses religious faith, 62, 98, 156; College prize essay, 64, 70–71; 'hunting, shooting and fishing' holidays, 64, 65–6, 111, 136; undergraduate writings, 72, 73; begins novel, 73–5; second class degree, 72, 73, 80; elected to 'Apostles', 75, 77; recognizes his homosexuality, 78; question of career, 79–80, 93–4, 97, 101; travels in Italy, 80, 81–96; initial disappointment, 82; begins to appreciate Italy, 90, 96; writes 'senti-mental articles', 90, 91; plans 'Lucy' novel, 91, 95; discovers power of imagination, 92–3, 103; lecturing, 97, 110, 122, 138, 147, 174–6; affair with Meredith as second 'grand discovery', 98; resumes Cambridge life, 98, 104; and religious controversy, 99–101; Greek cruise, 101–3; and *Indepen-dent Review*, 107, 108–9, 113–14; begins *Where Angels Fear to Tread*, 109; his diary, 114, 121–2, 130–1, 132–3, 141, 145, 152–3, 155, 159, 161, 171, 178, 179, 185–6, 187, 191, 204–5, 218, 219, 224, 227, 231, 233, 237, 247, 251, 256, 258, 259; nostalgia for Italy and Greece, 115–16; solitary journeys and walking-tours, 116–19, 152–3; move to Weybridge, 119; dispirited, 120–1; eight good resolutions, 122; first novel accepted, 123; in Germany, 123, 125–34; first novel published, 135–6; meets Masood, 143; falls in love with him, 146; speech on 'Pessimism in Literature',

147–8; admits to being a sentimentalist, 148; success of *Longest Journey*, 149–52; Shropshire walking-tour, 152–3; caravan-tour, 154–6; attracted to conformism, 160–1; reflects on modern civilization, 161–2; discontent with own work, 165; finds himself sought after, 166–8; Italian holidays, 168–70, 202–3; *Room With a View* published, 170–1; begins *Howards End*, 171–3; enters into literary life, 176–7; playwriting efforts, 178, 199, 200–201, 214–15; prepares for visit to India, 183, 184, 190–1, 215–16; prepares for (and fears) fame, 185, 190–1, 198; difficulties with mother, 187, 192, 197, 204, 217–19; 'arrival' with *Howards End*, 188–91, 199; fears breakdown and sterility as writer, 191, 192, 199, 249; enters into 'Bloomsbury', 192–3; 'speaks out' to Masood, 194–5, 202; publishes short stories, 199; writes erotic short stories, 200, 258; has portrait painted by Fry, 205, 206; in-complete novel, 207–10; his mental ap-proach to India, 222 3; voyage, 223–5; in India, 225–54; journey to Aligarh, 225–6; met by Masood, 226; country expedition, 226; and Indian politics, 227; at 'orgy' in Delhi, 228–9; with Darlings in Lahore, 229–32; at Muslim wedding, 233; in Chhatarpur, 234–7; meets Maharaja of Dewas, 238, 239; in Dewas, 240–5; rejoins Masood at Bankipore, 246; visits 'Marabar Caves' originals, 247–8; in Hyderabad, 251–4; return to England, 255; sense of futility, 255; writes homosexual novel, 257–8, 259; confusion in family life, 258–9; inability to create, 259; and coming of war, 259 60

PERSONAL TRAITS AND INTERESTS: adult education, 110, 138, 147, 174, 175; appearance, 19, 43, 66, 111; attachment to inanimate objects, 15, 20; awkwardness, 44, 94; church architecture, 43, 44, 48, 82–3; demureness, 43, 44, 66; ear for tone of voice, 74; facetiousness, 113, 138–9, 158, 200; friendships, 35–6, 38, 47, 51, 55, 59–60, 79, 155, 166–8, 180–1, 193–5, 202–3, 219; girlishness, 19, 23, 43, 67; health, 19, 42, 81, 84, 185, 196; helpless-ness, 44, 84; homosexuality, 78–9, 98, 110, 111, 141, 146, 153, 160, 181, 182–3, 193–5, 219, 255; imagination, 19–20, 92–3; landscape, 116, 119, 168, 226, 237; literary sterility, fear of, 192, 199, 204, 249, 258; misogyny, 98, 104, 180; music, 43; pas-sionate nature, 14–15; precocity, 19; reading, 19, 43, 55, 70, 159, 216; schoolboy friendships, 35–6; self-appraisal, 114, 121–2, 130, 159, 171, 191, 196–7, 204–5, 258; sentimentality, 110–11, 148, 152, 156; sexual experience, 37–8, 78; sexual frustra-tion, 98, 110, 146, 182–3, 255; spirit of place, 92, 116, 119, 177–8; sport, 52, 66, 136, 216; whimsicality, 67

VIEWS ON: aestheticism, 58, 85; argu-ment, 77; art, 206, 207; bad behaviour, 104, 105; business, 50; class attitudes, 74; convention, 160–1; coteries, 58; culture-snobbery, 173–4, 199; death, 132, 179, 185, 195, 198; fame, 190–1, 198; friendship, 52, 90–91, 166–8; homosexuality, 98n, 111, 257–60; human value in art, 82; humour,

175–6; left-hand writing, 89–90; literary professionalism, 185–6, 198; money, 159, 172, 185, 191, 198; nature, 137; optimism and pessimism, 132–3, 147–8, 159; painting, 85; physical pain, 43; politics, 108, 180, 222, 227, 247; religion, 35, 52, 62, 98, 99–100, 112, 156, 162–3, 199; schooldays, 48; scientific invention, 161–2; sex, 36–8, 78, 183; sport, 66, 111; suburban life, 57, 74, 133, 160–1; suicide, 141; war, 259; women's suffrage, 180

WRITINGS:

Abinger Harvest, 101n, 237n, 246n, 258n

'Adrift in India' articles, 246n, 258n

Aeneid translation, 110, 115, 120, 132

Arctic Summer (unfinished), 170, 199, 204, 207–10

'Between The Butts and Figsbury' (poem), 177–8

'Breaking Up', 48n

'Celestial Omnibus, The', 163n, 173, 199

Celestial Omnibus, The (volume), 199, 211

'Cnidus', 102–3

Deceased Wife's Husband, The (extravaganza), 158

'Eternal Moment, The', 109, 112, 113

'Feminine Note in Literature, The', 192–3, 208

'Gino' novel – see *Where Angels Fear to Tread*

Heart of Bosnia, The (play), 199, 200–201, 204

Hill of Devi, The, 248

Howards End, 11, 50, 160, 162, 175, 187, 215; 'Rooksnest' evoked in, 16; model for Wilcox family, 25; germ of, 142, 165; 'breaths' of Housman in, 153n; scheme for, 165, 172–4; Schlegel sisters' originals, 172–3; culture-snobbery in, 173–4; writing of, 177, 185; success of, 188–91; turning-point in Forster's career, 190, 198; his mood of reaction against, 210

'I saw you or I thought of you' (poem), 165

'Influence of climate and physical conditions upon national character' (school essay), 47–8

'Literature or Life?', 42n

'Long Day, A', 72

Longest Journey, The, 41, 74, 103, 104, 137, 148, 211, 263; Jackson original, 43; source of 'secluded dell', 56; Mrs Failing original, 64, 125n; 'Cadover' original, 64; 'Apostles' portrayed in, 77, 150; King's v. Trinity antithesis in, 107; spirit of place in, 116, 177; effects of Figsbury Rings incident, 116–19; original plot of, 118; critical reception, 149–52

'Lucy' novel – see *Room With a View*

'Machine Stops, The', 162

'Macolnia Shops', 90, 109

Maurice, 98, 257–60

'Nine Gems of Ujjain, The', 237n

'Opinions of Mistress Louisa Whichelo, the Chastiser of her Sex' (poem), 29

'Other Boat, The', 224

'Pack of Anchises, The', 72

Passage to India, A, 38, 201, 216n, 220, 231n; opening *motif*, 103; models for 'Chandrapore' and 'Marabar Caves', 247; Forster's young self as Ralph Moore, 262

'Point of It, The', 196, 204

'Purple Envelope, The', 121

'Road from Colonus, The', 103

'Rock, The', 139–40

Room With a View, A (also referred to as 'Lucy' novel), 74, 97, 109, 119, 160, 165; Mrs Honeychurch original, 2; Charlotte original, 65; early versions, 82n, 84–5, 95, 96n; foreshadowings of, 86–8; early note on, 91; opening *motif*, 103; writing of, 120, 153–4; suburban setting, 161; critical acclaim, 170–1, 176

St Bridget (play), 178, 202

'Story of a Panic', 92, 103, 113–14

'Suppliant, The', 246

'Ten shadows flecked the sunlit road' (poem), 156

'They are Nottingham lace!' (fragment), 73–5, 91, 97

'Thousand putties twinkled, A' (poem), 183

'Tragic Interior, A', 72, 73

'Via Nomentana', 90–91

'We were not good enough for Heaven', 168

Where Angels Fear to Tread (also referred to as 'Gino' novel), 1n, 11, 27, 104, 114, 118, 120, 131, 137; suburban life in, 57; 'Monteriano' original, 94n; origin of plot, 109; choice of title, 123; reception of, 135–6

Forster, Edward Morgan Llewellyn (father), 6–11, 14n, 45, 62, 218

Forster, Emily (aunt), 64–5, 66; model for Charlotte in *Room With a View*, 65

Forster, Henry Thornton (uncle), 9

Forster, Archdeacon James, 46

Forster, Laura (grandmother), 6

Forster, Laura Mary (aunt), 7, 8, 11, 14, 27, 69, 112, 161, 187, 195, 215, 218, 255; furthers Forster's career, 45, 47, 50, 59, 80, 97; her life at Abinger, 45–7; Henry James's remark to, 164; and Working Men's College, 175

Forster, May (great-grandmother), 6

Forster, William Howley (uncle), 64–6, 67, 111, 136; model for Mrs Failing in *Longest Journey*, 64, 125n

Fowler, Eliza (great-aunt), 71, 195, 196

Fowler, Frank (great-uncle), 71

Fowler, W. Warde, 70

Franklyn family, 18, 25, 141

Franklyn, Frankie, 18, 30, 142

Frazer, Sir James G., 62

Freud, Sigmund, 191

Friday Club, 192–3

Fry, Roger, 56, 86n, 108, 173, 193; cover-design for *Celestial Omnibus*, 199; portrait of Forster, 205–7; art theories, 206; influence on *Arctic Summer*, 207

Fulford, Francis Woodbury, 47, 52, 57–8

Furness, J. M., 219

Furnivall, F. J., 174 and n

Galsworthy, John, 189, 210

Garden God, The (Reid), 212

Gardner, Arthur, 69, 101

Gardner, Professor E. A., 101

Gaselee, Stephen, 104

Gaunt (ex-tutor at Nassenheide), 155, 156, 160, 166, 179

George III, 24

George V, 220, 247n, 264
Ghālib, Asadullah Khān, 144
Glehn, Mrs von, 164
Godbole, Mr, 249
Gokhale, G. K., 230n
Golden Bough, The (Frazer), 62n, 175
Goldsmith, Ruth, 119
Gollancz, Israel, 212
Gooch, G. P., 174
Goodall, Charles, 239, 240, 241, 243
Gosse, Sir Edmund, 186n; on *Howards End*, 189–90
Graham, Catherine (great-great-aunt), 2
Graham, Lieut-General Sir Gerald, 2
Grant family, 50
Grant, Alister, 100–101
Grant, Duncan, 150
Graphic, 150
Graveson, Caroline C., 140
Greenwood, L. H. G., 77, 98
Greifswald University, 133–4
Grey, Sir Edward, 176, 227
Grove, Sir George, 174
Guildford, 121, 122
Gurnard's Head, 139
Gwalior, 234

Hālī, Altaf Husain, 144
Hardinge of Penshurst, Lord, 239, 247
Hardy, Godfrey Harold, 76
Harris, Frank, 177, 188
Harrison, Frederic, 174
Harrogate, 256
Hasluck, F. W., 69
Haward, Lawrence, 69, 98
Haworth (Kent House schoolfriend), 36
Hawtrey, Ralph George, 76, 193
Headlam, Walter George, 59
Henson (Kent House schoolfriend), 35
Hepburn, Alexander, 175, 176
Herringham, Sir Wilmot Parker and Lady, 215, 216
Hervey, Mr (tutor), 29–30, 31, 34, 39
'Highfield' (Stevenage), 25
Hill, Agnes, 45
Hindoo Holiday (Ackerley), 234
Hirst, Francis, 107
History of the Popes (Pastor), 178
Hobhouse, A. L., 76
Holmbury St Mary, 112n, 161n
Holroyd, Sir Charles, 260
Homer, 70
Hope-Johnstone, Bob, 262
Housman, A. E., 152–3, 159n, 205
Housman, Laurence, 199
Howells, William Dean, 55
Hughes, Tom, 174n
Hutchinson, C. P., 33, 37–8
Hyderabad, 251–4

Ibsen, Henrik, 70
In the Days of the Comet (Wells), 162n
Independent Review, 102n, 107–9, 113, 121, 130, 173, 205n
Indore, 238, 239
Innsbruck, 95
Inside India (Edib), 264

James, Henry, 212; Forster meets, 163–5
James, M. R., 53, 59, 69
Jebb, John, Bishop of Limerick, 7
Jenks, Edward, 107, 109, 113

John Bull, 150
Jowitt, Rev. William, 25, 39, 141
Jowitt, Mrs, 37, 39, 141

Kalidasa, 216
Keats, John, 133
Kent House School (Eastbourne), 33–8
Keynes, John Maynard, 76, 99, 113, 114; and 'Apostles', 76, 78, 105; homosexuality, 78; on *Longest Journey*, 150
Khyber Pass, 231
Kipling, Rudyard, 55
Kitchener, Lord, 68
Knowles, James, 5
Kynsey, Dr Bert, 32

Lahore, 229–32, 249
Lamb, Walter, 106
Leslie, Shane, 62n
Life and Habit (Butler), 258
Litchfield, Henrietta, 10–11, 136, 175
Litchfield, R. B., 174n, 175
London, University of, extension lectures, 110n
Loti, Pierre, 192n
Luard, Major, 238, 239
Lubbock, Sir John, 114n
Lubbock, Percy, 59n, 69
Lucan, 70
Lucca, 94
Luce, Gordon, 215, 219
Lucretius, 70
Ludlow, J. M. F., 174n
Ludlow, 152
Lyall, Sir Alfred, 184n
Lyttelton, Alfred, 164
Lyttelton, Edith, 164

Macaulay, W. H., 215
MacCarthy, Desmond, on *Longest Journey*, 150
MacDonald, Ramsay, 184n, 230n
Macintosh, Ian, 262
Mackintosh, Sir James, 115
MacMunn, Howard, 47, 51, 52, 69, 157
McTaggart, J. M. E., 105, 106
Maeterlinck, Maurice, 70
Man Shakespeare, The (Harris), 177
Man of the World, The, 262
Manchester, 140, 141
Mantua, 169
Maradick at Forty (Walpole), 185
Marathon, 102
Marius the Epicurean (Pater), 132
Marlowe, Christopher, 159n
Marsh, Sir Edward, 177, 179, 185, 189, 190, 213–14
Marshall, Archibald, 188
Masefield, John, 177
Masood, Syed Ross, 214, 215, 216, 217, 263; arrival in Forster's life, 143; personality, 143–6, 202; passion for friendship, 145, 167–8, 193–4; Forster in love with, 146, 171, 180–1, 182, 183, 191, 193–5, 196, 202–3, 233; at Oxford, 167; praises Forster's insight into Indian soul, 194; accepts Forster's avowals coolly, 194, 195, 202–3; shares Italian holiday, 202–3; in India, 226, 227, 228–9, 246–7
Masterman, C. F. G., 107, 108; on *Where Angels Fear to Tread*, 135; on *Longest Journey*, 149

Index

Mathews, Charles Myles, 69, 140
Maurice, F. D., 174 and n.
Mawe, Cecilia, 101, 219
Mayor, J. E. B., 70
Memoir Club, Bloomsbury, 119, 132n
Meredith, Christabel, 141, 152, 186, 208n
Meredith, Edith, 69n
Meredith, George, 46, 70, 115
Meredith, Hugh, 60, 68, 69, 72, 73, 150, 152, 205; atheism, 60, 62; influence on Forster, 61–3, 97–8; arrogance, 63; and 'Apostles', 75, 76, 77, 97; love-affair with Forster, 98, 110, 140, 146, 182, 183; and religious controversy at King's, 99, 100, 101; impressed by *Where Angels Fear to Tread*, 123, 135–6; problems of career and private life, 140–1, 186; marriage, 141; makes love to Forster, 183; in Belfast, 211, 212, 213; Forster's reappraisal of, 258
Merrill, George, 256, 257
Merz, Ernest, 179
Milan, 82, 84
Millthorpe, 256, 257
Milton Bryan, 8
Mirza, Abu Saeed, 202, 252–4
Mirza, Ahmed, 202, 245, 248, 252
Mr Burden (Belloc), 109
Mollison, William Mayhew, 51, 52, 57, 69, 71, 152
Mon Frère Yves (Loti), 192
Mont St Michel, 44, 45
Moore, G. E., 49, 62, 164n, 217n; and 'Apostles', 76, 77
Moore, T. Sturge, 159n
Moral Idea, The (Wedgwood), 115, 168
Morison, Sir Theodore, 142–3, 215, 235, 246, 263
Morley, A. M., 43
Morning Post, 149
Morrell, Lady Ottoline, 176
Mounsey, J. E., 69
Much Wenlock, 152

Napier, Sir Lennox, 111n
Napier, Lady (Mabel Forster), 111n
Napier, Joseph, 111n
Napier, Marjorie, 111n
Naples, 91, 92
Nassenheide, 124–34
Nature and Effects of the Paper Credit of Great Britain, The (Thornton), 3
New Weekly, 258
Newbolt, Henry, 176
Nijinsky, Vaslav, 255
Nixon, J. E., 54–5, 68
'Noise that You Pay For' (Dickinson), 173

Orta, 203
Outlook, 150, 170
Oxford, 167

Pankhurst, Christabel, 180
Paris, 145, 180–1
Pastor, L. von, 178
Pater, Walter, 132, 159n
Patiala, 249
Pavia, 83
Period Piece (Raverat), 136n
Perugia, 86–8
Peshawar, 231–2
Phillimore, John Swinnerton, 153
Phillips, General Guy, 31

Phillips, Lisle March, 206
Pindar, 70, 101
Pinero, A. W., 70
Pisa, 94
Plato, 70
Plautus, 70
Plomer, William, 153n
Plymouth, 195
Port Said, 223
Poston family, 25, 142; model for Wilcoxes in *Howards End*, 25, 165
Poston, May, 142
Preston, Kate, 28, 161, 255
Preston, Maggie, 28, 255
Preston, Rev. William, 27, 28
Public School Magazine, 51
Punch, 188
Pym, Ruthven, 8, 16
Pym, Mrs Ruthven (Harti Thornton), 24n

Rahim, Mr Justice Abdur, 230n
Raschid, M. A., 202
Ravello, 92
Ravenna, 169–70
Raverat, Gwen, 10, 50n, 136n
Reid, Forrest, 177n, 210–12, 237, 249
Rome, 88–91
Ronaldshay, Lord, 230n
'Rooksnest' (Stevenage), 15–19, 28–31, 40
Rossetti, Christina, 55
Rothenstein, Sir William, 216, 245, 246
Ruskin, John, 174
Russell, Bertrand, 108, 112, 140, 198, 262; praises *Longest Journey*, 151
Russell, Countess – see 'Elizabeth'
Rye, 163–4

Saintsbury, George, 70
Sakuntala (Kalidasa), 216
Salt, Henry, 257
San Gimignano, 94
Sanger, Charles P., 193, 198
Sanger, Dora, 193, 198
Saturday Review, 188
Sayle, Charles, 113–14
Scholar Gipsy, The (Arnold), 149
Scott, Peter, 52n
Scott-James, R. A., on *Howards End*, 188–9
Seager, Mr (private school), 39, 60
Searight, Kenneth, 224, 231–2
Shakespeare, 159n, 177
Sharma, Nrusinh, 245–6
Shaw, Bernard, 70, 200
Shelley, Percy Bysshe, 107
Sheppard, John Tresidder, 99, 100, 104; his paper on 'King's or Trinity?', 104–7
Sherwani, M. K., 167, 202
Shorter, Clement, 176
Shrewsbury, 153
Shropshire Lad, A (Housman), 152, 153
Sidgwick, Frank, 199
Sidgwick, Henry, 75
Sidgwick & Jackson, 199
Simla, 232–3
Smedley, Isaac, 43
Smith, Rupert, 102, 158, 160, 166, 225, 247, 248–9
Smollett, Tobias, 70
Songs of Innocence (Blake), 7n
Sophocles, 70
Spectator, 149, 170
Spencer, B. A., 69, 89

Spender, Emily, 87
Stanmore, Lord, 186n
Steinweg, Herr (tutor at Nassenheide), 128, 133–4
Stephen, Adrian, 106
Stephen, Caroline, 50, 69
Stephen, Sir Leslie, 45
Stephen, Julia Jackson, Lady, 11
Stevenage, 15, 25, 141–2; 'Rooksnest', 15–19, 28–31, 40; 'Highfield', 25, 142; 'The Grange' school, 39–40, 60
Stokoe, F. W., 126, 166n
Strachey, Lytton, 66, 70, 104, 108; and 'Apostles', 77, 105, 106, 107; homosexuality, 78, 98n; on *Longest Journey*, 150
Swain, Edmund Gill, 69
Swinburne, A. C., 70
Swinford Manor, 155
Swiss Family Robinson (Wyss), 19, 23, 30, 31
Sykes, Major Cam, 5, 31
Sykes, Emmy, 5, 15
Symonds, J. A., 86, 159n
Synnot, Henrietta, 4, 5, 9, 10, 13, 15, 23
Synnot, Inglis, 8, 10
Synnot, Maimie – *see* Aylward
Syracuse, 91

Tayloe, Dr, 4, 5
Taylor, William, 30
Tennyson, Alfred, Lord, 191
Tennyson, Sir Charles, 262
Tennyson, Frederick, 191n
Tennyson, Hallam, 191n
'Teppi' (governess-housekeeper, Nassenheide), 129, 154
Tesserete, 202–3
Tetrazzini, Luisa, 103
Thompson, E. V., 138, 139, 182
Thornton, Henry, 3–4
Thornton, Henry Sykes, 157n
Thornton, Marianne ('Monie') (great-aunt), 1, 27–8, 46n, 64; benefactress of Lily Whichelo, 4–6, 8–9, 11–13; possessiveness, 8, 12; concern for Forster, 12, 14–15, 19, 23–4; death, 24; leaves money in trust for Forster, 24
Thucydides, 70
Times, The, 149
Tomlinson, Henry, 75
Tonbridge, 40, 41, 57
Tonbridge School, 41–4, 47–8, 51, 55
Tonbridgian, The, 51
Towards Democracy (Carpenter), 256
Tragedy of Nan (Masefield), 177
Trench, Herbert, 178
Trevelyan, Elizabeth ('Bessie'), 113, 190
Trevelyan (later Cacciola), Florence, 109n
Trevelyan, G. M., 78, 97n, 105, 109n, 190, 233, 263; Forster's introduction to, 69–70; advice on career, 93–4, 97, 160; and *Independent Review*, 107, 108
Trevelyan, Sir G. O., 46
Trevelyan, Julian, 112
Trevelyan, R. C., 112–13, 120, 154, 199; on *Longest Journey*, 150; on *Howards End*, 190; in India, 215, 216, 219, 223, 224–5, 230, 231, 232, 233–7, 246
Troy, 102
Tunbridge Wells, 57
Turner, George Douglas, 232
Turner, Saxon Sydney, 106

Ujjain, 237

Valla, Lorenzo, 192
Varallo, 203
Vaughan Williams, Ralph, 136
Venice, 168
Venice by Night exhibition (1904), 116
Verrall, A. W., 70
Virgil, 110
Volterra, 94

Waldron (Kent House schoolfriend), 35–6
Waldstein, Professor, 56
Walpole, Hugh, 125, 185–6
Ward, Mrs Humphry, 233
Waterlow, Alice, 163
Waterlow, Margery, 154
Waterlow, Sydney, 122–3, 163, 186–7, 204
Watson, William, 70, 176
Webb, Sydney, 174
Wedd, Nathaniel, 53n, 54, 55, 63, 80, 165 influence on Forster, 58–9, 73; on Greek cruise, 101; and *Independent Review*, 107–8
Wedgwood, Fanny Mackintosh, 115
Wedgwood, Hensleigh, 115
Wedgwood, Hope Elizabeth, 46, 115n
Wedgwood, Julia ('Snow'), 115, 136, 168; on *Howards End*, 190
Wells, H. G., 162
Wenlock Edge, 152
'West Hackhurst' (Abinger), 8, 45, 46–7, 122, 161, 195, 218
Westlake, J., 174n
Westminster Gazette, 149
Weybridge, 142, 143, 157, 160, 165, 166, 181, 200, 204, 255; 'Harnham', 119–20, 183, 206
Whichelo (later Kynsey), 'Fair' (aunt), 32, 121
Whichelo, Georgiana Louisa (aunt), 25–6, 32, 259
Whichelo, Gerald (cousin), 196
Whichelo, Harry (uncle), 27, 31, 32
Whichelo, Henry Harcourt Robert (uncle), 30
Whichelo, Henry Mayle (maternal grandfather), 1, 2
Whichelo, Horace Winder (uncle), 8, 26–7, 32, 44
Whichelo, John (great-great-uncle), 1
Whichelo, John Graham (uncle), 26, 27, 32
Whichelo, Louisa (grandmother), 2, 4, 8, 15, 40, 97, 109, 120; model for Mrs Honeychurch, 2; Forster's affection for, 28–9; on *Where Angels Fear to Tread*, 136; death, 195–6, 197
Whichelo, Mary Eleanor (Nellie) (aunt), 25, 26, 32, 258
Whichelo, Percy James (uncle), 31–2, 262
Whichelo, Percy (cousin), 30, 258
Whichelo, Philip Mayle (uncle), 26, 27, 32, 165
Whichelo, Raymond (cousin), 196
Whichelo, Richard (great-great-uncle), 1
Whichelo (later Alford), Rosalie (aunt), 25, 26, 136, 142, 195, 258
Whiteing, Richard, 70
Whitman, Walt, 159n
Wilberforce, William, 3
Wilde, Oscar, 115
Wilson, Mona, 205
Wood, Rev. 'Joey', 41–2, 55

Index

Woolf, Leonard, 76, 105, 216–17
Woolf, Virginia, 193, 205, 216–17
Woolley, Victor, 137, 168–9
Working Men's College, 94, 97, 147, 173–6, 204

Worters, Sydney, 47, 51–2, 56
Wray (garden-boy), 30
Wylde, May, 251–2

Young, Hilton, 97n

VOLUME TWO

Abinger, 197–204, 234–5, 246, 250–2, 254; pageants, 197–9, 226; Piney Copse, 199–200, 202–3; Forster leaves, 264–8; nostalgic visits to, 289. *See also* West Hackhurst.
Abinger Chronicle, 251
Achille (French sailor), 161, 186
Ackerley, J. R., 119, 134, 143, 157, 165, 166, 170, 178, 180, 183, 184, 185, 213, 259, 265, 283, 303, 307, 319; beginning of friendship with, 116–17; homosexuality, 117, 136–7, 140–1, 158–9, 162, 212, 226, 249–50, 280; as private secretary to Maharaja of Chhatarpur, 117; growing friendship with Forster, 135–7; dramatic success, 139; correspondence with Forster, 139, 160, 161–2, 174, 177, 217, 234, 255, 284, 304, 312, 317; discovery of father's double life, 161–2; literary success, 180, 248, 329; and Lily Forster, 217; as *Listener* editor, 248, 301; obsession with dog Queenie, 280, 313, 330; on Forster's intent listening, 293n; refusal to surrender Forster's letters, 304–5; misanthropy and changed relationship with Forster, 313–15, 321; soreness over money, 321; death, 322–3; his obituary article on Forster, 323
Ackerley, Nancy, 314, 321
Ackerley, Roger, 116, 141, 161
Adl, Gamila el, 51, 103
Adl, Mohammed el, 52, 57, 67, 109, 110, 133; meetings and growing friendship with Forster, 36–41, 45, 49–50; nights together, 40–41, 50; his marriage, 50–51; depression and illness, 50–51; arrest during Egyptian disorders, 59–60, 62–3; meets Forster at Port Said, 70; on Forster's philanderings, 85–6; last illness, 103–4, 105, 107–8; death,

108; Forster's 'letter' to, 113–14, 115; Forster's dream of, 114
Agra, 92, 99
Ajanta, 262
Akbar, Ali, 101, 102n
Albert Herring (Britten), 283n
Aldeburgh, 281–4, 285, 286, 297, 303, 322
Alexandria, 19, 22–51; Red Cross 'searching', 22–4, 33–5, 41–2, 50; social life, 24–5; Forster's study of history and topography, 44; his book on, 57, 74, 104, 109, 113
Alford, Robert, 300
Alford, Rosalie (aunt), 105, 217, 256, 289, 298, 300, 305n
Ali, Ahmed, 260, 261
Ali, Asaf, 275
Ali, Hashim, 261
Aligarh, 156, 218
All-India P.E.N., 259–61
All the Conspirators (Isherwood), 177
Altounyan, Ernest, 206
Amritsar massacre (1919), 58, 60–62, 122
Amsterdam, 209
Anastassiades, Pericles, 24, 43
Andersen, Hedli, 223
Anjuman-e-Taraqqi-e-Urdu, 219
Annan, Noël, 305
Annie Get Your Gun (Berlin), 270
Antonius, George, 24, 26, 119n
'Apostles, The' (Cambridge Conversazione Society), 224n, 268, 291
Appelbe, Ambrose, 187n
Apprentice to Power (Darling), 220n, 333
Aragon, Louis, 192
Areopagitica (Milton), 254–5
Arnold, Edward, 4
Arnold, Edward and Co., 53, 210, 323

Arvin, Newton, 246n
Ascent of F.6, The (Auden and Isherwood), 207, 213–14
Ashbee, C. R., 46n
Aspects of E. M. Forster (ed. Stallybrass), 323
Assheton, Ralph, 330
At the War (Northcliffe), 23
Athenaeum, 54, 119, 210n
Auden, W. H., 180, 207, 212, 224; collaboration with Isherwood, 213–14, 227; visits China, 223, 227; changed political attitude, 227; sonnet to Forster, 227–8; migration to America, 229, 232, 237–8, 281; press and parliamentary attacks on, 237–8, 329–30
Aylward, Mr, 117
Aylward (formerly Synnot), Maimie, 49, 117

Babel, Isaac, 192
Bai Saheba (Maharani of Dewas), 75–6, 80–1, 152, 219, 334
Baldeo (Hindu servant), 74, 78, 84, 85
Barbusse, Henri, 192
Barger, Florence, 9, 52, 97, 130, 134, 167, 216, 226, 256, 302; Forster's letters to, from Egypt, 35, 39, 40, 44, 49, 50, 51, 104; South African cruise, 159–60; Forster bored by, 160; joins Forster and Lily at Abinger, 234, 251
Barger, George, 52, 130, 159–60
Barnes, Rt Rev. Ernest, Bishop of Birmingham, 188
Barnes, George, 239, 240, 250
Baroda, Gaekwar of, 333, 334
Barry, Gerald, 328
Bartholomew, A. T., 118n
B.B.C., 170–3, 180, 239–42, 250
Beerbohm, Max, 251
Beethoven, Ludwig van, 252–3
Behrman, S. N., 55n
Belfast, 52, 269
Bell, Clive, 56, 66, 164, 223n
Bell, Gertrude, 19, 20
Bell, Julian, 1n, 223–4
Bell, Quentin, 224
Bell, Vanessa, 135, 223n
Benda, Julien, 192
Bengal, 261–2
Bennett, Arnold, 153, 154
Bennett, E. K. ('Francis'), 45, 268, 283, 298, 302–3, 306
Bergson, Henri, 221
Berkeley (California), 273–4
Beveridge, Annette, 19
Beveridge, William, Lord, 307
Bhau Sabib (brother of Maharaja of Dewas), 71
Bidar, 101
Biervliet, April van, 335n
Billy Budd (Britten), 283–6, 287
Bing, Geoffrey, 187n
Birrell, Francis, 63n
Blake, William, 312
Bombay, 70, 97, 263

Bone, Charles, 201, 202
Bone, Henry, 201, 264, 265, 267, 289
Boot, Sir Jesse, 9
Borchgrevink, Aïda, 24–5, 41
Bosanquet, O. V. B., 28–9
Boulder Dam, 274
Boy (Hanley), 191
Brecht, Bertolt, 192
Brentford, Sir William Joynson-Hicks, Viscount ('Jix'), 153, 154
Breton, André, 192
Bridges, Katherine Dianthe Farrer, Lady, 263, 264, 265
Bridges, Robert, 55, 111
British Association, 159
British Council, 259, 307
Brittain, Vera, 187
Britten, Benjamin, 213, 223, 281–2; friendship and collaboration with Forster, 283–6, 287; minor frictions, 285–6
Brooke, Jocelyn, 287
Brooke, Mary ('the Ranee'), 3
Brooke, Rupert, 3, 18–19, 173
Brown, E. K., 246
Browning, Oscar, 43n
Broyd family (Abinger), 197
Brunswick Square, Bloomsbury: *No. 26*, 165n, 184; *No. 27*, 135, 165n
Bucharest, 174
Buckingham, Bob, 204, 209, 213, 217, 221, 223, 234, 236, 256, 257, 263, 273n, 279, 280, 283, 298, 306, 315; beginning of friendship with Forster, 165–6; their relationship, 166–9, 182–5, 319–20; effect of marriage to May Hockey, 169, 182–3; broadcast dialogue with Forster, 172–3; as object of rivalry between wife and Forster, 182–3, 185, 205; happy married life, 183, 205–6; and N.C.C.L., 186, 188; Forster's letters to, 210, 215, 226, 229, 249, 260, 270, 272, 273, 275, 314; during London blitz, 239, 246, 248; urges Forster to write another novel, 253; hitch in friendship, 282; American visit, 284; move to Coventry, 287–8; considered as literary executor, 304, 315; Forster's gift of £10,000, 317; and Forster's last days, 318, 319–20, 324, 325; changed attitude to Forster, 319–20; and Forster's death and cremation, 325
Buckingham, May, 169, 184, 212n, 217, 256, 265, 283n, 286, 288, 306, 315, 317, 318, 322; rivalry with Forster over Bob, 182–3, 205; in sanatorium, 205–6, 209; improved relationship with Forster, 206, 285, 320; Forster's letters to, 210, 268; nurses Forster after operation, 285; at his death-bed, 325
Buckingham, Robin Morgan, 205, 256, 306; Forster's godson, 184; tragic death, 317–18
Buckingham, Sylvia, 306, 317
Built in Jerusalem's Wall (Bennett), 45n
Bunyan, John, 312
Burrell, Bill, 285, 303

Bush, Alan, 241, 242
Butler, Samuel, 3–4
Butts, Anthony, 178
By Sea and Land (Young), 65
Cadmus, Paul, 246, 254, 255, 270, 275, 276
Caian, The, 306
Cairo, 48, 103
Calcutta, 261
Cambridge, 124, 143–4, 158, 314, 318; 'Apostles', 224n, 268, 291; Forster's life and friendships in, 268, 277–9, 288, 291–300, 302; his generosity to, 316. *See also* King's College.
Campbell, Roy, 178
Candler, Edmund, 125
Cape, Jonathan, Limited, 153
Capek, Karel, 192
Carpenter, Edward, 12, 40, 125, 159; Forster's letters to, from Alexandria, 30, 34, 35
Carrington, Dora, 122, 138, 167–8
Catlin, Professor George, 187n
Cavafy, Constantine, 24, 31–3, 54, 115, 138, 161
Cavafy, Paul, 32
Cecil, Lord Robert, 19
Chalmers, Sir George, 330
Chamberlain, Neville, 228, 229
Charlton (Charlton), 212n
Charlton, Leo, 136, 158, 161, 180, 212, 213
Chelmsford, Frederic Thesiger, Viscount, 68n
Chertsey Meads, 115
Chesterton, G. K., 172
Chhatarpur, 93–4
Chhatarpur, Maharaja of, 93–4, 117
Chicago, 274
Chiswick, 234, 279, 305
Christopher and his Kind (Isherwood), 179n, 227n
Churchill, Winston, 113, 206n, 242
Clark, Professor W. E. Le Gros, 187n
Clark Lectures (1927), 143–4
Clemenceau, Georges, 210
Clouds Hill, 121, 207, 276
Cockburn, Claud, 187, 328
Coley, Tom, 269, 299, 305, 323
Collard, Dudley, 187n
Collier, John, 167n
Colquhoun, Archibald, 310
Connolly, Cyril, 237
Conrad, Joseph, 303
Cooper, Alfred Duff, 241, 242
Coventry, 288, 318, 320, 321, 325
Crabbe, George, 281–2
Cracow, 174
Craft of Fiction, The (Lubbock), 146–7
Crevel, René, 192
Cromer, Evelyn Baring, Earl, 21
Crook, Arthur, 294n
Crown Film Unit, 256n
Crowther-Smith (later Scaffardi), Sylvia, 187n, 329
Crozier, Eric, 283–4, 285, 286, 287
Culme-Seymour, Lady Faith, 316

Da Silva's Widow, and Other Stories (Malet), 107
Daily Herald, 53, 59; Forster as literary editor, 63–4
Daily News, 53, 112
Daily Worker, 243, 298
Daley, Harry, 166, 180, 183, 313, 330; friendship with Ackerley, 139–41; affair with Forster, 141–3, 157; broadcasts, 157; ending of affair, 236–7; his memoirs, 329
Darling, Josie, 2, 18, 60, 61, 151–2, 335
Darling, Malcolm, 18, 71, 79, 240, 279, 286, 333, 334; anti-Germanism, 1–2; and Amritsar affair, 60–2; and Leslie affair, 95, 96, 97–8; Forster's letters to, 123, 124, 176; and Dewas scandal, 152, 220, 336
Das, Dr G. K., 70n
Davies, Margaret Llewelyn, 17
Day Lewis, C., 222, 224, 230
Death of Ivan Ilych, The (Tolstoy), 319
Delhi, 260
Dent, Edward Joseph, 12, 13–14, 118n
Deolekr, Major, 72, 73, 79, 86
Desani, G. V., 277n
Dessera festival, 96–7
Devi, hill of, 75
Dewas State Senior, 71–91, 94–8, 286
Dewas State Senior, Tukoji Rao III, Maharaja of, 71, 72, 73, 124n, 286; invites Forster to be private secretary, 27–9, 65, 67; and Masood's visit, 74–5; domestic and political disorders, 75–7, 96; and former secretary Leslie, 79–80; festivities at birth of daughter, 80–81; and Forster's confession of homosexuality, 83–6; and A.G.G.'s supposed slight to Forster, 86–7; and *Gokul Ashtami* festival, 87, 89; on tour, 91–2; and Leslie affair, 95, 96, 97, 98; and Forster's departure, 98; scandal and ruined reputation, 151–3, 334–6; tragic last years and death, 219–21; early marital troubles, 333–4
Diary for Timothy (M.o.I. film), 256
Dickinson, Goldsworthy Lowes, 17, 29n, 40, 106, 124, 126, 137, 170, 210, 269; closer intimacy with Forster, 4; Forster's letters to, from Egypt, 34, 41, 45–6, 103; pacifism, 46; Forster's holidays with, 52, 66; Forster's letters to, from India, 72, 76, 91, 92, 93–4; death, 175–6; his biography written by Forster, 176–7
Dickinson, Hester, 176n
Dickinson, Janet, 176n
Dickinson, May, 176n
Dr Zhivago (Pasternak), 303
Donaldson, Canon, 241n
Doone, Rupert, 213, 223
Dorking and Leith Hill Preservation Society, 226
Dorking Refugee Committee, 250
Dover, 212–13, 226

'Dover' (Auden), 212, 213
Down There on a Visit (Isherwood), 228n, 229n
Du Côté de Chez Swann (Proust), 107
Dyer, General Reginald, 122–3

East Molesey, 264
Eddington, Sir Arthur, 158
Edward VIII (as Prince of Wales), 100
Egyptian Labour Corps, 57, 62
Egyptian Mail, 43, 109
Ehrenburg, Ilya, 192
Eliot, T. S., 48, 115, 143, 164, 272, 327–8
Elizabeth II, 288
Encounter, 302
Englefield Green, 52
Erdman, Charles, 312
Erewhon (Butler), 3
Ethan Frome (Wharton), 270
Eversden (airman), 43

Fabian Society, 62
Fadiman, Clifton, 246n
Farrer, Thomas Cecil, 2nd Baron, 198, 199, 201, 226; clashes with Forster and Lily, 202–4
Farrer, Euphemia Wedgwood, Lady, 200
Farrer, Evangeline Knox, Lady, 201–2
Farrer, Cecil, 203, 254
Farrer, Mrs Cecil, 203, 254
Farrer, Frances, 265, 267
Faux-monnayeurs, Les (Gide), 144, 178
Fay, Eliza, 138
Ferney, 233
Fielden, Lionel, 170n
Figsbury Rings, 318
Finlay, Professor (Harvard), 272
Fisher, H. A. L., 241
Fletcher, Eric, 275n, 278, 306, 325
Forbach, 186
Forester, C. S., 275
Forster, Alice Clara ('Lily') (mother), 19, 49, 70, 72, 110, 121–2, 133, 144, 157, 210, 212, 292n, 306; attitude to Forster's friends, 4, 134, 167, 175, 217; Forster's letters to, from Alexandria, 22, 24, 27, 42; and his home-coming, 52; difficult relationship, 52, 105, 135; letter to Forster on his departure for India, 67; Forster's letters to, from India, 73–4, 76–7, 80–1, 88–90, 91, 97n, 98, 100, 102; life at Abinger, 197, 201, 234–5, 250, 251–2, 254; later years, 216–17, 234–5; Forster's appreciation of, 217; during Second World War, 274–5, 250, 251–2, 254; death, 255–7, 259
Forster, Charles (grandfather), 292n, 330
Forster, Edith (aunt), 330
FORSTER, EDWARD MORGAN: aligned with Bloomsbury friends on war, 1; diary, 2, 4, 52, 54, 108, 115, 130, 134, 135, 137, 239, 256, 258, 260, 262, 263, 274, 275, 276, 282, 285, 318; gives up creative work, 3; more open in expressing feelings, 13;

shows *Maurice* to friends, 13; considers non-combatant service, 19; in Alexandria as Red Cross 'searcher', 19–20, 22–4, 33–5, 41, 50; social life, 24–5; refusal to 'attest', 26–7; dislikes Egypt and Egyptians, 29; visits hashish 'den', 29–30; change in sexual fortunes, 35–41; meets Mohammed el Adl, 36; given general control of 'searchers', 41; writes for local press, 42; flies for first time, 42; studies history and topography of Alexandria, 44; pessimism over post-war world, 45–6, 48; return to England, 52; still in mother's power, 52, 105; difficult moment in career, 53; literary journalism and reviewing, 53–4, 63–4; membership of clubs, 56, 66, 109, 134n; and Egyptian politics, 57–8, 62, 103; and Indian affairs, 58, 60–62, 70, 106, 122 3, 125–30; laments his literary sterility, 64; seeks other posts, 64–5; accepts post as secretary to Maharaja of Dewas, 67; in India, 70–102; his duties and routine, 71–2, 74; distress at waste and disorder, 76–8; sexual desire, and satisfaction with palace servants, 81–6, 91; position at court enhanced after diplomatic incident, 86–7; at religious festivals, 87–90, 96–7; cynicism over changed Anglo-Indian relations, 92–3; visit to Chhatarpur, 93–4; leaves Dewas, 98; in Hyderabad with Masood, 98–102; birthday celebration, 102; few days in Egypt with ailing Mohammed, 103–4; crippling depression on return to England, 105–6; burns his indecent stories and resumes *Passage to India*, 106–7, 119–20; and Mohammed's death, 108, 113–15; constructs second Alexandrian book, 109, 115; his Commonplace Book, 111n, 165, 167n, 169, 175, 183–4, 214–15, 216, 246–7, 252, 253n, 278n, 310, 315, 316, 327–8, 331; concern over Empire misdeeds, 111–13, 115; dreams of Mohammed, 114; begins friendships with Ackerley and Sprott, 116–18; meets T. E. Lawrence, 121; inherits West Hackhurst, 122, 133, 201; success of *Passage to India*, 123–30; increasing prosperity, 130; reasons for giving up novel-writing, 131–3; difficulties with mother, 135; finds flat in London, 135; new circle of friends, 136, 165; various small literary tasks, 138; resumes indecent story-writing, 138, 148–50; experiences working-class life, 142–3, 157, 158–9; gives Clark Lectures, 143–4; accepts three-year fellow-ship from King's College, 144; condemns suppression of *Well of Loneliness*, 153–5; first president of 'Young P.E.N.', 155; feels 'off' literature and Cambridge, 157–8; visits South Africa and Egypt, 159–61; controversy over D. H. Lawrence, 163–4; forms lasting relationship with Bob Buckingham, 166–9; as broadcaster, 170–3; break with P.E.N., 173–4; in Rumania and

Index

Poland, 174; rejects Polish lady's marriage proposal, 175; writes Dickinson's biography, 176–7; considers own future biographer, 176–7; as influence on young writers, 177–80; bitterness over Bob's marriage, 182–3; holiday with him, 184–5; involved in public activities, 186–96, 221–2, 231–2, 242–5, 254–5; first president of N.C.C.L., 186, 187; as non-party political and social polemicist, 190–2; at Paris International Congress of Writers, 192, 193–6; writes book for village pageants, 198, 226; clashes with Farrer family, 201–4, 226, 253–4, 265; invited to edit T. E. Lawrence's letters, 207–8; selects articles for *Abinger Harvest*, 210; prostate operation, 210; sued for libel, 211; resigns editorship of Lawrence letters, 211, 232; concern over European crisis, 214–15, 221–2, 225–6, 230–1, 233; nocturnal dream-life, 215–16; better relations with mother, 216–17; loss of two closest Indian friends, 217–20; loses trust in political gestures, 222–3; defines his faith and philosophy, 223, 225; as symbol and hero, 229; valedictory visit to Switzerland, 233; pessimism on outbreak of war, 233; tours blitzed areas of London, 239; clashes with B.B.C., 240, 241–2; broadcasts to India, 240, 247, 254, 256; increased reputation in America, 246; American friends, 246, 254, 269–71, 273, 276; 'war work' in Abinger, 250; and mother's death, 255–7, 262; involved in M.o.I. film, 256; erotic fantasies, 257; revisits Alexandria, 257; has to leave West Hackhurst, 263–8; Hon. Fellow of King's, 264; resident in College, 265, 268–9, 277–9, 288, 291–300, 305, 317, 319, 323–4; in America, 269–76, 284; at Harvard Symposium, 272; as object of pilgrimage, 277–8; active London existence, 279–80; resigns from N.C.C.L., 281; collaboration on opera, 283–6, 287; seventieth birthday, 283; second operation, 285; breaks ankle, 286; assembles *Hill of Devi*, 286; success of *Two Cheers for Democracy*, 287; renounces 'homes' and 'roots in the land', 288, 289; made C.H., 288; writes biography of Marianne Thornton, 290, 300; Furbank's meetings with, 297–300, 302–3, 305–8, 322; writes tragic short story based on earlier fragment, 301–3; interest in own career and reputation, 304; eightieth birthday, 305; idolization, 309; last major reviews, 310; invites Plomer to write his *Life*, 311, 312, 321–2; strains and falling apart of friendships, 312–15, 320–1; failing powers, 314–16, 318, 319, 323–4; foreign holidays, 316; public benefactions, 316–17; suffers strokes, 318, 319; preparation for death, 318; invites Furbank to write *Life*, 321–2;

awarded O.M., 323; ninetieth birthday, 323; death and cremation, 324–5
PERSONAL TRAITS AND INTERESTS: abstemiousness, 325; agnosticism, 227n, 306; ancestral pride, 289; appearance, 25, 134, 229, 271, 292; conversation, 292, 293–4, 320; courtesy, 294; cultural organizations, 194–6, 221–2, 254, 259; depression, 65, 105, 256–7, 282; dreams, 114, 215–16; erotic fantasies, 257; forgetfulness in old age, 319; friendships, 2, 4–13, 17–18, 24–5, 34–41, 44–5, 49–51, 52, 54–7, 113–15, 116–21, 133–8, 141–3, 147–51, 157, 159, 165–9, 178–86, 208–9, 213, 246, 249–50, 275, 278–9, 285–6, 312–14, 319–20; fussiness, 313; generosity, 50, 53, 74, 103, 118, 130, 141–2, 143, 159, 277, 288, 314, 316–17, 321; gestures, 293; gossip, 293; governessy manner, 296; gratitude, 318, 319; health, 18, 26, 210, 221, 285, 286, 305, 314, 315–16, 318, 319, 323, 324; helpfulness to authors, 116, 120, 147–8, 150–1, 260, 275, 277, 302n; helplessness, 306–7; 'homelessness', 264, 266, 282, 288, 289; homosexuality, 14, 18, 35, 38–41, 71, 81–6, 91, 102, 132, 134, 137, 141, 167–8, 185–6, 319–20; human relationships, tiredness of, 282; humility, reputed, 295; hysterical rages, 135, 182; imaginative life, 297; judgement, 296; landscape, 22, 260, 273, 274, 276; lecture style, 144; liberalism, 224–5, 245; listening faculty, 293; literary sterility, 64–6, 102, 105, 131–3, 282; madness, fear of, 229; misogyny, 56, 175, 182; 'modernity', 177–8; modesty, 295; moral realism, 245–6; music, 34, 80, 252–3, 281, 285, 316; mystical self-forgetfulness, 216; old-maidishness, 17, 309n; pacifism, 1–2, 26–7; pageant-writing, 197, 226; plain speaking, 294; quarrels, 9–12, 41, 250, 285, 288, 296; reading, 44, 48, 143, 210, 215, 246, 298, 302, 303, 310; *recueillement* discipline, 252; restrictive remarks, 297; self-knowledge, 108, 114–15, 132; sensitivity, 295–6; sexual experience, 35, 36n, 40, 85–6, 91, 137, 141, 161, 185, 286; sexual frustration, 35, 81–5, 317; shyness, 25, 295; sightseeing, 101, 160, 174, 260, 262, 269–71, 272–4; solitude and meditation, 260, 262; strangers, treatment of, 294–5; superstition, 131, 318; 'tea-tabling' fictional method, 177; teasing, dislike of, 296; timidity, 17, 149, 295; trees 199–200; village activities, 197–9, 226
VIEWS ON: anti-semitism, 236; apologies and explanations, 143; 'aristocracy', 225; *avant-garde* in fiction, 143–4, 177; betrayal of friends or country, 225; broadcasting freedom, 241–2, 255; censorship, 153–5, 241–2, 255; Christ, 306; civil liberties, 186–91, 231–2, 241–5; 280–1; civilization, collapse of, 214, 222; class attitudes, 41, 52, 162, 203–4, 266; 'commitment', 222; communism, 190, 191, 193, 222, 230–1,

236, 244, 280–1; criticism, 54, 65, 124–130, 145–6, 150, 236, 272; death, 310, 315, 318; decaying powers, 314, 316; devotion, 298; 'fair-mindedness', 125–6, 129–30; fascism, 193; fictional concept of 'life', 146; fictional form, 106; 'fluid' and 'granular' writing, 120; flying, 43; flying-bombs, 254; freedom, 193–4; friendship, 2, 159, 162, 214, 295–6; ghost stories, 298; happiness, 169; homosexuality, 14, 18, 55, 154–5, 162; honours, 288; human nature in war conditions, 45–6; human relationships, 46, 124; idolatry, 90; imperialist misdeeds, 57–60, 62–3, 111–13, 115; intellectuals, 55; kindness, 300; landowning, 122, 204; lesbianism, 155; libel laws, 232; literary fame, 53, 131–2, 260, 263, 268, 269, 277–8, 279; literary biography, 298; literary speculation, 158; literature in wartime, 2–3; 'lost leaders', 238; memory, 116; middle age, 54, 160; ministerial snub technique, 231; money, 183–4, 236, 317; old age, 300, 305, 316; 'old-fashionedness', 176; orgies, 298; pain, 328; politics, 222–3; quarrels, 296; revolution, 303; silence, 252; slang, 300; social progress, 46; stealing, 300; story-telling devices, 303; totalitarianism, 230–1; tradition, 289; war, 1–3, 18, 45–6, 48; wisdom, 278; women, 175, 217; writer's double duty, 221

WRITINGS:

Abinger Harvest, 48n, 112n, 174n; selection and choice of title, 210; libel action, 211

Alexandria: a History and a Guide, 44, 57, 74, 104, 109, 113

Aspects of the Novel, 132, 178; origin as Clark Lectures, 143–4; V. Woolf on, 146–7

Celestial Omnibus, The (volume), 6, 7, 107

'Chess at Cracow', 174n

'Comment and Dream: On a Deputation', 231n

'Conversations in the Train' (radio dialogue), 172–3

'Cotton from the Outside', 43

'Dr Woolacott', 148, 149–50

'Entrance to an Unwritten Novel', 301n

'Eyes of Sibiu, The', 174

'Ferney', 233n

'Flood in the Office, A', 211

'Freedom of the B.B.C., The', 171

Goldsworthy Lowes Dickinson, 176n

'Happy Ending' (later 'Ferney'), 233n

'Higher Aspects', 43

Hill of Devi, The, 88–90, 220n, 286, 290, 313, 336

Howards End, 3, 10, 14, 53, 107, 124, 131, 166, 177, 228n, 313, 325; Frieda Lawrence on, 8–9; reissued, 53; Mrs Wilcox re-created as Mrs Moore (*Passage to India*), 133; 'revolutionary' opening sentence, 177; Beerbohm on, 251

'In My Library', 292n

'India After Twenty-five Years' (radio talk), 261n

'Jew-consciousness', 236n

'Last of Abinger, The', 197n

'Last Parade, The', 221–2

'Liberty in England' (speech), 193–4

'Life to Come, The', 114–15, 121, 302n

'Literature and the War', 2–3

Longest Journey, The, 279n, 294, 318–19

'Luncheon at Pretoria', 160n

Marianne Thornton, 290, 300, 313

Maurice, 4, 18, 35, 39, 56, 145, 306; friends' reactions to, 13–17, 208, 304; wish-fulfilment element, 17, 132; T. E. Lawrence's reluctance to read, 148–9; revision of ending, 304

'Mrs Miniver', 235n

'My Wood', 199–200

'New Censorship, The', 154

'1939 State, The' (later called 'Post-Munich'), 230

'Notes on Human Nature Under War Conditions', 45–6

'Other Boat, The', 302, 303

'Our Graves in Gallipoli', 112–13

Passage to India, A, 92, 122, 163, 282, 327; Egyptian and Indian experience recalled in, 22, 70; resumed writing of, 106–7, 119; 'out of time', 106; Proustian influence, 107, 119–20; *Seven Pillars* influence, 119–20; critical acclaim, 123–6; 'going away from each other' theme, 124; mystery of caves scene, 124; 'fairness' of treatment of Indian problems, 125–6; attacks on treatment of Anglo-Indians, 126–30; success of, 130, 131; Mrs Moore a reworking of Mrs Wilcox (*Howards End*), 133; translations, 138–9, 175n; dramatization, 307–8; manuscript sold, 317

Pharos and Pharillon, 32n, 43n, 115, 163

'Poetry of C. P. Cavafy, The', 32

'Post-Munich', 230n

'Prince's Progress, The', 161

'Raison D'Etre of Criticism in the Arts', 272

'Reflections in India, I: Too Late?', 92–3

Room With a View, A, 3n; reissued, 53

'Society and the Homosexual: a Magistrate's Figures,' 331

'Story of a Panic', 8

'T. S. Eliot and his Difficulties', 328

'Tercentenary of the "Areopagitica", The', 255n

'They Hold Their Tongues', 231n

'Top Drawer But One, The' (later 'Mrs Miniver'), 235n

Two Cheers for Democracy, 160n, 197n, 219n, 230n, 233n, 235n, 236n, 255n, 261n, 272n, 292n; critical acclaim, 287

'West Hackhurst: a Surrey Ramble', 204n, 254

'What I Believe', 225

Index

Where Angels Fear to Tread, 7, 131; first American edition, 53
'Woodlanders on Devi', 79n
Forster, Edward Morgan Llewellyn (father), 266, 267, 291
Forster, Ella (aunt), 330
Forster, Laura Mary (aunt), 99, 140n, 200, 256; death, 121–2
Fowler, Eliza (great-aunt), 50n
Fox, Ralph, 192
Freeman, David, 187n
French, Jared, 270
Frere, Sir Bartle, 24
Freud, Sigmund, 131
Fry, Margery, 288
Fry, Roger, 18, 66, 138, 210, 224
Furness, Sir Robert Allason, 24, 30, 37, 40, 41, 48, 103
Futehally, Zeenuth, 277n

Galsworthy, John, 53, 155, 173
Gandhi, Mahatma, 69, 77
Gandhi and Anarchy (Nair), 122–3
Gangavati, 101
Garnett, David, 63n, 135n
Garnett, Edward, 150
Garnett, Ray, 135n
Garsington, 109–10
Geneva, 233
Gertler, Mark, 110
Ghalib, Asadullah Khan, 327
'Ghosts' (Ackerley), 116
Gide, André, 144, 178, 192, 195
Giehse, Therese, 213
Gillott, Ted, 275n
Glancy, Sir Bertram, 335, 336
Glancy, Sir Reginald, 335
Gokul Ashtami festival, 87–90
Golding, William, 318
Goldring, Douglas, 187n
Goodall, Charles, 70
Gorki, Maxim, 192
Gosh, Gopal, 261
Gosse, Sir Edmund, 55
Gould, Gerald, 63n
Grand Canyon, 272–3
Grant, Duncan, 5, 66, 109, 140, 322
Grant Duff, Virginia, 22, 23, 25, 27; Forster's quarrel with, 41–2
Graves, Robert, 206
Greatham (Sussex), 5, 9–10
Greene, Graham, 309n
Grieve, Mackenzie, 59n
Growing (Woolf), 310n
Guest, L. Haden, 57
Guest, Mrs Haden, 187n

Haggard, Sir Henry Rider, 93
Hague, The, 209
Hali (Desani), 277n
Hall, Radclyffe, 153–4, 155
Ham Spray House (Berks), 138
Hamilton, Gerald, 209, 214

Hamilton College (Upper New York State), 246, 272, 284
Hammersmith, 140–2, 158, 165, 180, 223
Hampi, 101
'Hampson, John' – *see* Simpson, John
Hanley, James, 191, 192, 193
Hardy, Thomas, 55, 110–11, 307, 314
Harewood, George Lascelles, seventh Earl of, 316
Harrison, Kenneth, 278
Harrison, Mary St Leger ('Lucas Malet'), 107
Harrison, Tom, 198
Harvard University, 267, 272
Haskell, Francis, 298, 300
Hawker, Harry G., 59
Heard, Gerald, 136, 140, 141n, 232, 237
Helouan, 103
Hemlock and After (Wilson), 298
Her Privates We (Manning), 206
Herbert, A. P., 328
Hermes, 109
Heytesbury House (Wilts), 180, 181
Hill, Agnes, 234, 256, 259, 264, 265, 267, 289
Hill, Maurice, 317
Hindoo Holiday (Ackerley), 180, 313
Hoare, Sir Samuel, 231
Hogarth, D. G., 206n
Hogarth Press, 109, 138
Hoggart, Richard, 311
Holi festival, 72–3
Horizon, 237, 248
Horne, E. A., 128–30
Howard, Brian, 209
Hutchinson, Jeremy, 311–12
Huxley, Aldous, 56, 63n, 172, 192, 195, 237
Huxley, Julian, 187
Hydari, Sir Akbar, 99–100, 102
Hydari, Amina Bibi, 99–100
Hyderabad, 28, 99–102, 262
Hyndman, Tony, 215
Hynes, Samuel, 329

I Saw in my Dream (Sargeson), 302
Ibsen, Henrik, 145, 159
Information, Ministry of, 256
International Congress of Writers (Paris, 1935), 192–6
Iqbal, Sir Mohammed, 218
Isherwood, Christopher, 33n, 177–8, 184, 207, 212, 215, 216, 324; influenced by Forster, 177, 179; first meeting and correspondence, 179; firm friendship, 208–9; and production of *Ascent of F.6*, 213–14; visits China, 223, 227, 329; loss of political faith, 227, 228–9, 232; regards Forster as symbol and hero, 229; in America, 232, 237–8, 246' 330; pacifism, 232, 237; Forster's letters to, 233, 234, 259; criticized for 'desertion', 237–8, 329–30

Jaipur, 259, 260–1
Jennings, Humphrey, 256n
Jones, Henry Festing, 3, 292n

Journey to a War (Auden and Isherwood), 227–8
Jung, Sir Amin, 262
Jung, Nawab Nizameth, 100

Kew Gardens (Woolf), 56
Keynes, John Maynard, 24, 66, 118, 265
Khajuraho, 94
Khilafat campaign, 69
Kidd, Robert, and National Council for Civil Liberties, 186–9, 191, 244, 281, 328, 329
Kidwai, Jalil A., 218n
Kilham Roberts, Denys, 232
Kimberley, 160
King, William, 197, 267
King, Mrs William, 250, 267
King's College, Cambridge, 124, 322; offers Forster three-year fellowship, 144; Forster's 'residence' as Hon. Fellow, 264–5, 268, 278–9, 288, 291–300, 305, 317, 319, 323–4
Kipling, Rudyard, 307
Kirkup, James, 327
Knollys, Eardley, 293n
Knopf, Alfred, 53
Knowles, Pat, 207
Kolhapur, Maharaja of, 219, 333, 334
Kylsant, Lord, 235n

Lacket, The (Wilts), 18
Lady Chatterley's Lover (Lawrence), 311–12
Lally, Gwen, 198
Lampedusa, Prince of, 310
Lancaster, Mark, 324n
Laski, Harold, 122–3
Lawrence, A. W., 207
Lawrence, D. H., 132, 163, 311–12; first meeting with Forster, 5; his Rananim Utopia, 5, 6–7; attack on Forster's life-aims, 7–8, 9–10; Forster's visit to, and quarrel with, 9–13; on importance of human relations, 124; death of, and hostile obituaries, 163–4
Lawrence, Frieda, 5, 7, 8–9, 12, 164–5
Lawrence, T. E., 119–21, 132, 144, 179, 183, 191n; Forster's letter of criticism on *Seven Pillars*, 120–1; growing friendship and correspondence, 147–51; and Forster's homosexual writings, 148–50, 302; later life and death, 206–7; Forster asked to edit his letters, 207–8; editorship resigned by Forster, 211
League of Nations Committee for Intellectual Co-operation, 196, 221
Leavis, F. R., 144n
Leggatt, Tim, 316
Lehmann, Beatrice, 241n
Lehmann, John, 192, 196, 221
Lehmann, Rosamund, 222
Leopard, The (Lampedusa), 310
Leslie, Colonel W. (secretary to Maharaja of Dewas), 71, 77, 78, 79–80; quarrel with Forster, 94–8

Leveaux (lawyer and theosophist), 44
Levin, Harry, 272
Lewis, Wyndham, 110
Liddell, Robert, 32n, 115
Lingsagur, 101
Lions and Shadows (Isherwood), 177, 223n
Listener, 180, 213, 248, 281, 301, 314
'Little Gidding' (Eliot), 327–8
Lloyd of Dolobran, Lord, 207
Lloyd George, David, 111, 113
London Library, 317
Lovett, Charles, 283n
Low, Barbara, 10
Luard, Lt-Col. C. E., 29
Lubbock, Percy, 20, 42, 146–7, 309
Lucas, Sir Jocelyn, 329–30
Ludolf, G. H., 44, 45n, 103, 109; Forster's letters to, 88, 101, 105, 107, 133n, 327
Lugard, Major, 125
Lyme Regis, 52, 66

Macaulay, Rose, 283n, 286, 289; praises *Passage to India*, 123–4 .
McCardie, Mr Justice, 122–3
MacCarthy, Desmond, 66, 170n, 208
MacDonald, Sir Murdoch, 210
MacDonald, Ramsay, 56, 189
McKelvie, Ian, 323n
Malarao Sahib, 72, 73, 85
'Malet, Lucas', 107
Malraux, André, 192, 194, 195
Manchester Guardian, 57
Mandu, 95
Mann, Erika, 213
Mann, Heinrich, 192
Mann, Klaus, 209
Manning, Frederic, 206
Mansfield Park (Austen), 210
Mansourah, 49–50, 103
Mark on the Wall, The (Woolf), 56
Marshall (later Partridge), Frances, 135n
Marshall (later Garnett), Ray, 135n
Marshall, Mrs M. A., 135, 165n
Martin, George, 272
Martin, Kingsley, 187, 189, 244n
Masood, Akbar, 156, 157, 218–19
Masood, Anwar, 156, 157, 283n
Masood, Syed Ross, 70, 72, 86; marriage, 4; Forster's letters to, from Alexandria, 22, 27–8; visits Forster in Dewas, 74–5; cynicism over 'liberal reform', 92; Forster visits in Hyderabad, 99–103; and Forster's sex-life, 102; Forster's letters to, 106, 144; and *Passage to India*, 119, 130, 327; divorce, European travels and financial ruin, 156; Vice-Chancellor of M.A.O. University at Aligarh, 156, 218; death, 218–19
Masood, Zorah, 99, 156
Massingham, H. J., 63n, 110
Matheson, Hilda, 170, 171, 172
Mathew, Sir Theobald, 311n

Index

Matthews, Very Rev. W. R., 238n
Mau, 94
Maugham, Somerset, 179, 309
Maura (Singh), 277n
Mauron, Charles, 138–9, 192, 193, 194, 233, 252, 255, 305, 316
Mauron, Marie, 138–9, 255
Mawe, Cecilia, 234, 251
Mawe, Elaine, 234
Max Gate, 55, 110–11
'Maximilian Society', 251
Meade family (Abinger), 267
Medley, Robert, 213
Melville, Herman, 283–4
Memoir Club, 66, 109, 254
Memorial, The (Isherwood), 179, 209
Meredith, Christabel, 52
Meredith, Hugh, 13, 52, 283n, 317n
Mermen, Ethel, 270
Meynell, Viola, 5
Michelangelo Sonnets (Britten), 281
'Micheldever' (Ackerley), 248
Millay, Edna St Vincent, 55n
Millis, Captain, 242
Milne, A. A., 112
Milton, John, 255
Mint, The (Lawrence), 150–1
Mirza, Abu Saeed, 99
Mirza, Ahmed, 99
Mirza, Sajjad, 262
Mr Norris Changes Trains (Isherwood), 208–9
Mrs Miniver (Struther), 235
Montagu, Edwin Samuel, 61, 68n, 100n
Montagu-Chelmsford Report (1918), 68
Moore, G. E., 224n
More Charlton (Charlton), 212n
Morel, E. D., 1
Morison, Cotter, 297
Morison, Sir Theodore, 93, 156, 157
Morrell, Lady Ottoline, 5, 11–12, 18, 109–10, 118, 164, 291n
Mortimer, Raymond, 140
Mount Lebanon Shaker colony, 271
Munich crisis (1938), 228–9, 230
Murray, Gilbert, 221
Murry, J. Middleton, 54
Musil, Robert, 192
My Dog Tulip (Ackerley), 314
My Father and Myself (Ackerley), 322
Myslakowska, Mrs, 175

Nagpur, 91
Naidu, Mrs Sarojini, 261
Nair, Sir Sankaran, 122–3
Nation, 53, 58, 115
Nation (New York), 225
Nation and Athenaeum, 92, 101, 138, 146, 153, 163
National Council for Civil Liberties, 186–90, 191, 221, 231, 242–5, 280–1, 329
National Council of Labour, 243
National Union of Journalists, 231

National Union of Railwaymen, 155
Natural Bent, The (Fielden), 170n
Nature of the Physical World, The (Eddington), 158
Neighbour, O. W., 226n, 304
Nevinson, H. W., 187, 243, 245
New Leader, 112, 138, 199
New Statesman, 128, 130, 171, 195, 230, 231, 331
New Writing, 221
New York, 269–70, 273–4, 276
New Yorker, 271
Newby, P. H., 287
Nicolson, Harold, 171, 172, 237
Night and Day (Woolf), 56
1917 Club, 56
Northcliffe, Lord, 23
Nottingham, 313
Novel Club, 66

O'Dwyer, Sir Michael, 122–3
Obscene Publications Act (1959), 311
Observer, 310n, 323
Official Secrets Act (1920), 231
Ogilvie, Sir Frederick, 241n
Oliver, Edith, 246, 269, 305
Ould, Hermon, 173, 255n, 259
Overtures to Death (Day Lewis), 222, 230
Owen, Meyrick (cousin), 323
Owen, Wilfred, 112
Oxford, 307
Oxford Times, 119n
Oxford University, 288n

Paris, 192, 193–5, 221–2; Exhibition (1937), 221–2
Paris Review, 309
Parker, Dorothy, 309
Partridge, Frances, 135n
Partridge, Ralph, 135n, 138n
Passion Before Death, A (Hanley), 191n
Pasternak, Boris, 192, 303
Pears, Peter, 281
P.E.N. Club, 155, 173–4, 232, 254
Penguin Books, 311–12
People's Convention, 241
Perkin, Bernard, 276
Peter Grimes (Britten), 281, 282
Petre, Diana, 161n
Philo, 44
Pickthall, Marmaduke, 125
Playfair, Sir Nigel, 139
Plomer, William, 180, 210, 212, 217, 257–8, 283, 302n, 316n; Forster's letters to, 124n, 181, 225, 246, 249, 251, 254, 266, 278, 282, 284, 288, 305; beginning of friendship, 178–9; invited to write *Life*, 311, 312, 321–2; falling apart of friendship, 312, 322
Plumed Serpent, The (Lawrence), 163
Plunkett, Sir Horace, 125
Pollitt, Harry, 215
Polycrates, 132
Port Said, 70, 103

Porter, Katherine Anne, 194
Porter, Samuel Lowry, Lord, 232
Poston, Elizabeth, 283n
Potter, Stephen, 299
Powell, Sir Alan, 242
Preston, Kate, 144
Preston, Maggie, 144
Pretoria, 161
Priestley, J. B., 156, 188, 192
Principles of Social Reconstruction (Russell), 46
Prisoners of War (Ackerley), 139
Pritchett, V. S., 287
Proust, Marcel, influence on Forster, 107, 109, 116, 119
Prufrock and Other Observations (Eliot), 48
Prussian Officer, The (Lawrence), 9

Quilley, Jules, 4

Ramsey, I. E. St Clair, 300
Randall, Sir Alec, 174
Rathbone, Eleanor, 188
Rau, Santha Rama, 308n
Raven, Simon, 279
Raymond, Ernest, 232
Read family (Abinger), 267
Read, Ernest, 197
Read, Herbert, 179, 304
Red Cross, 19–20, 22–3, 26, 42, 50
Redgrave, Michael, 241n, 256
Rees, Morgan Goronwy, 222
Reform Club, 134, 300, 302, 303, 306, 307
Reid, Forrest, 3, 5, 44, 62, 63, 66, 67, 130, 142; attitude to *Maurice*, 14; and Forster's literary sterility, 64; Forster's letters to, 252, 254; death, 269
Reith, Sir John, 170, 171–2
Rhondda, Lady, 243
Richmond, Sir George, 122, 330
Roberts, Sir James, 219, 335–6
Rockingham Castle, 316
Roerick, William, 246, 269–71, 276, 299
Root, Mr and Mrs Edward, 246, 272
Rowe, Robert, 31n
Rowlatt, Sir Sydney, 68n
Roy, Jamini, 261
Russell, Bertrand, 1, 10, 46, 63n, 93–4, 172

St Helena, 160
St Rémy, 316
Salmon, C. V., 240
Salt Lake City, 274
Saltmarsh, John, 324
Samuel, Herbert, Viscount, 300, 330–1
Sandys, Duncan, 231
Santiniketan, 262
Sargeson, Frank, 302
Sassoon, Hester, 181, 207
Sassoon, Siegfried, 53, 63, 110, 119, 134n, 157, 183, 207, 299; correspondence with Forster, 47–8, 120, 121, 122; first meeting and growing friendship, 54–6; homo-

sexuality, 55; renewed friendship with Forster, 180–1, 184; marriage, 181; his poem on Forster's eightieth birthday, 331
Saturday Night at the Greyhound (Hampson), 179
Savile Club, 56n
Schiff, Sydney, 251
Schiff, Violet, 251
Scaffardi, Sylvia, 187n, 329
Scott, C. K., 63n
'Sedition Bill' (1934), 188–90, 329
Sencourt, Robert, 45
Serge, Victor, 195
Seven Pillars of Wisdom (Lawrence), 121, 147, 148, 151, 179; influence on *Passage to India*, 119–20
Shaw, Bernard, 62, 155, 196, 221, 241, 327
Sheppard, John Tresidder, 24, 264, 279, 300
Sherwani, M. K., 99, 218
Shipley, H. H., 126–7
Shire, Edward, 323
Shuttleworth, Lawrence, 2, 4, 13, 41
Si le grain ne meurt (Gide), 195
Sibiu, 174
Sidgwick, Frank, 107
Sidgwick, Henry, 176
Simpson, John ('John Hampson'), 179, 188, 213, 214, 234, 239, 252, 283n, 317n
Singh, Huthi, 277n
Sitwell, Sir Osbert, 266
Skidelsky, Robert, 329
Smith, Rupert, 74, 92, 125
Snowden, Philip, 55
Society of Authors, 232, 240
'Some Aspects of Urdu Poetry' (Masood), 119, 327
Sons and Lovers (Lawrence), 312
South Wales Miners' Federation, 155
Spectator, 237, 238, 310
Spender, Stephen, 117n, 180, 209, 210, 215, 224, 225
Sprigge, Sylvia, 251
Sprott, Velda, 198
Sprott, W. J. H. ('Sebastian'), 137, 159, 178, 213, 217, 259, 263, 283n, 291n, 311, 325; beginning of friendship, 118–19; homo-sexuality, 118, 137, 185; correspondence with Forster, 119, 156, 167, 168, 169, 182, 185, 198, 226, 243, 251, 260, 261, 262, 270, 280, 315; considered as literary executor, 304, 313, 315; awkwardness with, 313, 314–15
Stallybrass, Oliver, 144n, 323
Stevenage, 264
Stopes, Marie, 250
Strachey, James, 18
Strachey, John, 192
Strachey, Lytton, 18, 40, 138, 153, 167; praises *Maurice*, 15–17
Strongest, The (Clemenceau), 210n
Struther, Jan, 235
Summerskill, Edith, 187n
Sunday Times, 153

Index

Swaffer, Hannen, 188
Swinnerton, Frank, 63n
Sykes, Marianne (great-great-aunt), 330
Synnot, Henrietta, 117n

Tablet, 298
Tales of Sarras (Bennett), 306
Tennant, Stephen, 184
Tennyson, Sir Charles, 306
Terni, E., 44
Third Man, The (Greene), 309n
Thomas, Alan, 249n
Thomas, Alun, 187n
Thompson, E. V., 125
Thompson, W. H., 187
Thomson, Sir Courtauld, 26, 27
Thornton, Sir Hugh and Lady, 289
Thornton, John, 330
Thornton, Lucy (great-aunt), 330
Thornton, Marianne (great-aunt), 330;
    Forster's biography of, 289–90, 300
Time and Tide, 243–5; Forster as columnist
    on, 189, 190–1, 313n
Times, The, 58, 198n, 220, 308; praise of
    Forster, 107; hostile obituary of D. H.
    Lawrence, 163n
To the Lighthouse (Woolf), 144
Toller, Ernest, 192
Tolstoy, Leo, 120, 303, 319
Toulon, 161
Toynbee, Arnold, 115
Toynbee, Philip, 225
Trenchard, Lord, 328
Trevelyan, Elizabeth ('Bessie'), 125, 210
Trevelyan, G. M., 19
Trevelyan, Julian, 223
Trevelyan, R. C., 31, 43, 125, 223n, 251
Trilling, Diana, 274–5, 296n
Trilling, Lionel, 245, 274–5, 296n
Turbott Wolfe (Plomer), 178
Twilight in Delhi (Ali), 260
Two Stories and a Memory (Lampedusa),
    310n
Tyringham (Mass.), 270–1, 276

Ujjain, 75
Ulysses (Joyce), 143, 171
Union of Democratic Control, 1
Upward, Edward, 177

Valassopoulos, George, 33, 115, 138
Valéry, Paul, 221
Vaughan Williams, Ralph, 198, 226, 242
Vicary, Frank, 34–5, 52, 130, 159, 317n
Vidler, Canon Alexander, 306
Vikramsinha (son of Maharaja of Dewas), 71,
    75, 151–3, 334–5
Voges, Marietta, 273
Voges, Noel, 273–4
Voltaire, 233
Voyage Out, The (Woolf), 17

Wadia, Mrs, 263

Wall, A. M., 243
Walpole, Hugh, 53
Walton Regatta, 257
Wanderer's Necklace, The (Haggard), 93
War and Peace (Tolstoy), 215
Warm Country, The (Windham), 275
Warner, Rex, 225
Washington, 275–6
Waterlow, Sydney, 64
Waugh, Alec, 232
Waugh, Evelyn, 180
We Think the World of You (Ackerley), 307n,
    329
Webb, Beatrice, 125, 186
Wedd, Nathaniel, 268
Week End Review, 328
Well of Loneliness, The (Hall), 153–5
Wells, H. G., 155, 170n; and N.C.C.L., 187,
    188, 189, 328
West, Rebecca, 63n, 245
West Hackhurst (Abinger), 121, 140n, 156,
    157, 167, 175, 188, 197, 223, 234–5, 250–2,
    254, 256, 257; inherited by Forster, 122,
    133; his loss of, 200–202, 263–8, 289
Weybridge, 49, 52, 105; Harnham, 4, 133,
    134, 137
Weybridge Literary Society, 2
Whichelo, John (great-great-uncle), 292n
Whichelo, Mary Eleanor (Nellie) (aunt), 217,
    289, 298, 300, 305, 306
Whichelo, Horace Winder (uncle), 27
Whichelo, Percy (cousin), 234
Whichelo, Mrs Percy (Dutchie), 234
Whichelo, Philip (cousin), 216, 323
Whichelo, Philip Mayle (uncle), 234, 252
Wichelo, Tom, 136, 180, 212
White Peacock, The (Lawrence), 12
Why Do I Write? (Greene), 309n
Wilkinson, Patrick, 268, 283n, 288
Willcocks, Sir William, 210
Williams-Ellis, Amabel, 187n, 192
Wilsford Manor, 184
Wilson, Angus, 298, 302
Windham, Donald, 275
Winstanley, D. A., 22
Women in Love (Lawrence), 12n
Wood, J. B., 28–9
Woolf, Leonard, 17, 18, 57, 63n, 146, 153,
    155, 192, 280; Forster's letter to, from
    Alexandria, 25; invites Forster to write on
    Egyptian question, 62; urges him to con-
    tinue Indian novel, 105–6; as publisher,
    109, 138, 178; advises Forster to write
    autobiography, 300; his *Growing* the
    subject of Forster's last review, 310n
Woolf, Virginia, 17–18, 20, 66n, 148, 178,
    180, 181, 192; growing intimacy with
    Forster, 56–7, 109, 143–4; on his departure
    for India, 67; on his return, 105; Forster's
    letters to, 143, 144, 145, 193; clash with,
    145–7, 153; on *Aspects of the Novel*, 146;
    and *Well of Loneliness* case, 153–5
Working Men's College, 2

Wright, Ralph, 123
Writers in Defence of Culture, 192, 221

Young, Hilton (later Lord Kennet), 12n,
   64–5, 235–6

'Young P.E.N.' Club, 155, 173

Zabel, Professor Morton Dauwen, 246n, 274n
Zagloul Pasha, Saad, 57
Zohra (Futehally), 277n